Viêt Nam Exposé

Viêt Nam Exposé

French Scholarship on Twentieth-Century Vietnamese Society

EDITED BY
Gisele Bousquet and Pierre Brocheux

THE UNIVERSITY OF MICHIGAN PRESS
ANN ARBOR

Copyright © by the University of Michigan 2002
All rights reserved
Published in the United States of America by
The University of Michigan Press
Manufactured in the United States of America
⊗ Printed on acid-free paper

2005 2004 2003 2002   4 3 2 1

No part of this publication may be reproduced,
stored in a retrieval system, or transmitted in any form
or by any means, electronic, mechanical, or otherwise,
without the written permission of the publisher.

A CIP catalog record for this book is available from the British Library.

Library of Congress Cataloging-in-Publication Data

Viêt Nam exposé : French scholarship on twentieth-century Vietnamese society / edited by Gisele Bousquet and Pierre Brocheux.
    p. cm.
  Includes index.
  ISBN 0-472-09805-5 (cloth : alk. paper) — ISBN 0-472-06805-9 (pbk. : alk. paper)
  1. Vietnam—Social conditions—20th century.   2. Vietnam—Economic conditions—20th century.   I. Bousquet, Gisèle L. (Gisèle Luce), 1952– II. Brocheux, Pierre.

HN700.55.A8 V54 2002
306'.09597'0904—dc21   2002020294

Contents

Foreword   *John K. Whitmore*   vii

Introduction   *Gisele Bousquet*   1

PART I
Vietnamese Society in the Early Twentieth Century

1 Who Has Power in the Village? Political Process and Social Reality in Vietnam
   Philippe Papin   21

2 Village Rebellions in the Tonkin Delta, 1900–1905
   Philippe Le Failler   61

3 Rethinking the Status of Vietnamese Women in Folklore and Oral History
   Nguyên Van Ky   87

4 Administrative Practices: An Essential Aspect of Mandarinal Training (Nineteenth–Early Twentieth Century)
   Emmanuel Poisson   108

5 In the Shadow of the Colonial Hospital: Developing Health Care in Indochina, 1860–1939
   Laurence Monnais-Rousselot   140

PART II
Vietnamese Intellectuals: Contesting Colonial Power

6 Prince Cuong Dê and the Franco-Vietnamese Competition for the Heritage of Gia Long
   Agathe Larcher-Goscha   187

7   A Vietnamese Scholar with a Different Path: Huynh Thuc Khang, Publisher of the First Vietnamese Newspaper in *Quôc Ngu* in Central Vietnam, *Tieng Dan* (People's Voice)
    Phan Thi Minh Le   216

8   The 1925 Generation of Vietnamese Intellectuals and Their Role in the Struggle for Independence
    Trinh Van Thao   251

9   Henriette Bui: The Narrative of Vietnam's First Woman Doctor
    Tran Thi Liên   278

PART III
Postcolonial Vietnam: From a Welfare State to a Market-Oriented Economy

10 The Economy of War as a Prelude to a "Socialist Economy": The Case of the Vietnamese Resistance against the French, 1945–1954
    Pierre Brocheux   313

11 The Chronicle of a Failure: Collectivization in Northern Vietnam, 1958–1988
    Florence Yvon-Tran   331

12 Labor Restructuring in Vietnam
    Xavier Oudin   356

13 Agro-Commodity Chains in Northern Vietnam: New Mechanisms for Old Stakeholders
    Pascal Bergeret   373

14 Commuting from the Village to the City: Analyzing the Patterns of Migration of the People of the Northern Village of Hay to Hanoi
    Olivier Tessier   387

15 Facing Globalization: Vietnam and the Francophone Community
    Gisele Bousquet   421

    Contributors   457

    Index   459

John K. Whitmore

Foreword

Let us consider Vietnam over the entire twentieth century. Not just the wars, Doi Moi, revolution, refugees, or colonialism but the Vietnamese people should be our focal point as they have survived these varied traumas and continued the flow of their own lives through the years as best they could. How were social and economic, as well as political, decisions made? What structures continued despite ongoing change? How did Vietnamese society in 2000 differ from that in 1900 and how did it get that way?

This francophone collection, by both French and Vietnamese scholars, forms a very nice chain of essays covering the past century from beginning to end and Vietnamese society from bottom to top. We have views of villages, the urban elite, and the links between them as they were in both colonial and socialist times. Therein we receive insights into the major transformations that occurred throughout the century.

The collection of essays included here is an admirable and valuable effort, bringing as it does the variegated interests and results of this scholarship into our own language. The editors are to be commended for their belief in the necessity of this effort as well as for the difficult work it took to accomplish it. By doing so, they have opened up to the anglophone world a breadth and depth in the study of modern Vietnam heretofore often ignored as classes have pursued political topics.

To be found in these essays are both scintillating detail and very interesting interpretations. The authors show us good use of archival materials, interviews, firsthand observation, and quantitative data. They have utilized their access to the archives, the countryside, and Vietnamese communities to great effect. By following their own interests, they have plumbed these resources and done much to fill in the missing context of political events. They add excellent detail and deepen our interpretations of these events, pursuing as they do aspects not yet examined by anglophone scholars.

We get to see the progressive impact of village-state relations from the beginning of the century to its end. We see Vietnamese-foreign relations go from the colonial era to that of globalization, involving political, economic, and cultural aspects. We also see individual Vietnamese, male and female, heretofore little known, as they struggled on their own terms to confront the changing scene. We see nineteenth-century elements continue to have significance in the twentieth and wonder what twentieth-century elements will emerge to influence our new century. The tendency will be to pick and choose among these excellent pieces according to the readers' (and their classes') interests. Instead I challenge those concerned with Vietnam to sit down and read this insightful work straight through—the readers will considerably deepen their understanding of this fascinating land and its people.

Gisele Bousquet

Introduction

This collection of essays, written by French and French-Vietnamese scholars at French institutions, provides a unique opportunity for the English-speaking audience. For decades, French and francophone scholars have contributed to contemporary scholarship in Vietnamese studies. However, few of their works have been published in English, as cultural and political differences have for many years maintained a boundary between French and American scholars. This project is intended both to introduce new scholarship in Vietnamese studies and to initiate a forum of exchange between anglophones and francophones that will bridge that gap.

Writing beyond Politics, Wars, and Violence

The essays in *Viêt Nam Exposé* are part of a new trend in the field of Vietnamese studies, writing that goes beyond politics, wars, and violence.[1] The contributors to this volume are not ignorant of the magnitude of the bloody conflict that engulfed Vietnam during the twentieth century in endless wars that killed millions of people. Neither do we deny the impact and consequences of these wars on Vietnamese society. But many books, articles, and reports in various languages are still devoted to Vietnam and its wars.[2] In American libraries, the largest book collection on Vietnam is essentially about the Vietnam War and its aftermath. Like our Vietnamese colleagues, who have themselves moved beyond the conflict, we Western scholars of Vietnam are investigating historical issues that have been neglected in the past. We are engaging in research that addresses the current social and economic situation in Vietnam and the challenges ahead as the country becomes more and more integrated into a global economy.

Unlike many books on Vietnam written in the twentieth century, this collection of essays does not embrace a political agenda. Most of the contributors to this book, in particular scholars who are resident in Hanoi and others who are currently pursuing research in Vietnam, want to distance themselves from matters related to current Vietnamese politics.

Such political disengagement, in both the United States and France, is doubtless possible only now because, unlike other generations before them, today's new generation of French and American scholars is not confronted with either war or colonialism about which they cannot remain silent. It does not mean, however, that foreign scholars carrying on research in Vietnam today are not confronted with political problems. In fact Vietnamese authorities may disapprove topics that might threaten the new and still somewhat fragile cooperation between Vietnam and French scholars. Unfortunately, when the Vietnamese authorities suspect the researcher, the visa is not always granted, studies in villages may be circumscribed, the researcher may be given limited access, and access to archive materials may not be forthcoming.

In the early twentieth century, French scholars often worked within the boundaries of the colonial bureaucracy and were engaged in research that furthered the interest of colonialism in Vietnam. With the rise of Vietnamese anticolonialism, French scholars challenged this colonial discourse in Vietnamese studies and embraced instead an anticolonial position supportive of Vietnamese nationalism. The work of Paul Mus[3] represents the post–World War II continuity of this trend in French scholarship on Indochina and simultaneously introduces this politically engaged scholarship. Another historian of the same generation, Jean Chesneaux,[4] recaptured the focus on contemporary history and analyzed the internal dynamism of Vietnamese history.

As the Indochinese conflict intensified with the American military intervention in Vietnam, many French and French-Vietnamese scholars of Southeast Asia not only condemned the hostilities but strengthened their anticolonialist positions and rallied in support of the Vietnamese cause. Examples of this scholarship include the work of French writers Pierre Brocheux, Daniel Hémery, Georges Boudarel, Philippe Langlet, Philippe Devillers, Alain Ruscio, Charles Fourniau, and Georges Condominas; French-Vietnamese scholars Trinh Van Thao and Le Thanh Khoi; and the Vietnamese scholar Nguyên Khac

Vien.[5] A quote from Hémery illustrates best the sociopolitical context at that time.

> Since its development in the 1960s, French modern and contemporary history in Southeast Asia, like its American counterpart, indirectly contributed to the construction of a national gaze, leveled on societies' and postcolonial states' past, just as these societies were themselves in search of their self-historical definition; this, paradoxically, contributed to the invention of [those societies'] traditions and a homogeneous representation of their past, silencing their internal factionalism and divisiveness.[6]

After 1975, during Vietnam's postwar economic transformation and political reforms, which forced thousands of Vietnamese refugees from central and southern Vietnam to flee into exile, French scholars once again assumed a role of political advocacy, but this time it was to criticize the Vietnamese government in its practice of socialism. Two important publications illustrate the political stand of such work. The first is an article by Pierre Brocheux and Daniel Hémery, "Le Vietnam exsangue: Echec economique mais determination politique," published in *Le Monde Diplomatique* in 1980. This was a criticism of a system that failed to fulfill its socialist expectations. Both authors had seen Vietnamese socialism firsthand when they visited Vietnam in the fall of 1979, although at that time foreigners who went to Vietnam were on official visits supervised by the Vietnamese authorities and were not allowed to have personal contact or nonofficial exchanges with Vietnamese people. The second influential publication, *La bureaucratie au Vietnam*, a collection of essays edited by Georges Boudarel in 1983, was also critical of the economic and political situation in Vietnam.

In 1986, the Vietnamese government began reforming its economy by abandoning its former "Soviet"-style economy in order to adopt a market economy. Under these economic reforms, Doi Moi (New Change), attitudes toward Western foreigners changed and communications between Vietnamese and foreigners were no longer prohibited. The opening up of the Vietnamese market to foreign investors also marked a new trend in academic exchanges between Vietnamese and foreign research institutions. And it is in this context that over the last decade a new scholarship in Vietnamese studies has emerged in both France and the United States.

Viêt Nam Exposé is a contribution to this new scholarship that attempts to understand Vietnamese society from within its own social reality rather than through the gaze of a colonial administrator or political activist. We do not intend to cover all aspects of Vietnamese society in this single volume, nor to cover all regions of Vietnam equally. We present here an *"esquisse"* of twentieth-century Vietnamese society. The reader will find that some topics, such as religion, ethnic minorities, and politics, are not included in this collection and that many of the essays focus on northern rather than southern Vietnam. The current Franco-Vietnamese research cooperation programs, most of them based in Hanoi, have tended to favor research projects in northern Vietnam. Moreover, this book is intended to supplement American scholarship on Vietnam rather than reiterate the ground American scholars and their graduate students have covered and are currently researching in southern Vietnam.

An Overview of the French-Vietnamese Academic Collaborative Project

Even when Vietnam was closed to most Western scholars, some French scholars were able to maintain a presence there. In 1970, even before the end of the American war, Vietnamese and French scholars and academics began to collaborate on scientific research projects. And, despite the 1975 American economic embargo, France cooperated with the Socialist Republic of Vietnam, providing a measure of technical assistance and humanitarian aid throughout Vietnam's postwar reconstruction. In France, a group of French scientists and prominent French scholars created the Collectif Interuniversitaire d'Aide au Vietnam, a collective university aid program to Vietnam that was in 1975 renamed Le Comite de Cooperation Scientifique et Technique avec le Vietnam (Committee for Scientific and Technical Cooperation with Vietnam). According to the French historian Pierre Brocheux,[7] this committee exerted an important influence over French governmental policies toward Vietnam, which was then isolated from other European countries by the American embargo.

After the implementation of the economic reforms, Doi Moi, in

1986, France increased its bilateral exchange with Vietnam to include, among other things, the current framework for cooperation in scientific research. During the late 1980s, the Franco-Vietnamese scientific cooperation and education exchange programs started to fully develop and expand. For instance, in the field of education Vietnamese students are being given French scholarships to study at French universities and French students receive French scholarships to study Vietnamese language and culture at Vietnamese universities. In addition, arrangements are made for Vietnamese scholars to go to France for short-term visits at French research institutions, while French scholars and technical experts reside in Vietnam to work on joint projects at Vietnamese institutions or inside Vietnamese ministries. This current framework of cultural exchange among French and Vietnamese institutions has contributed to the current level of expertise of a new generation of French scholars, who are for the most part fluent in Vietnamese and over the years have gained considerable research experience in Vietnam. Some studies presented in this book, in particular the ones with data based on Vietnamese field and archival research, are the products of this collaboration.

Contested Academic Boundaries

When I first went to Vietnam in the summer of 1991, and in the following years, I was quite intrigued by the fact that the French community was and still is the largest Western community in Vietnam despite the acrimony of Vietnam's French colonial past. In the spring of 1997, I decided to investigate the French community during the preparation year for the Seventh Francophone Summit in Hanoi, which was to be held in the fall of that year. In the course of my research in Hanoi, I came in contact with French scholars and students at French academic institutions who were doing research at Vietnamese and French research institutions. Many of them I met at the École Française d'Extrême Orient (EFEO). The EFEO tended to be the headquarters for French academics and intellectuals in transit. It was there that I found out who was doing what and where in Vietnam. While American universities were slowly setting up programs in Vietnam, their French counterparts already had an operating research program. Although French scholars participate in international conferences on Vietnam, particularly in Europe (for example, Euro-Viet), their work is often unknown in the United States. At the same time, francophone American scholars are more interested in French colonial archival materials than are contemporary French scholars of Vietnam. As we develop Vietnamese studies at American universities, I believe that contemporary French scholarship must and will make a valuable contribution to our knowledge of Vietnam and our understanding of social transformation in Vietnamese society.

After reading the reviews of the manuscript and engaging in the revisions, it became apparent that this project challenges some fundamental assumptions located at contested academic and national boundaries and raises issues of exclusion and legitimization. On one hand, French scholars wondered if the project was not another form of hegemony, an attempt by American academic institutions to appropriate foreign scholarship. On the other hand, American scholars questioned the project's legitimacy. They suspected that French scholars were staking an ultimate claim over Vietnamese studies, and they were deeply suspicious of the francophone project. But the originality and merit of this book lies in its very location at these contested boundaries and in its attempt to open a new dialogue between French and American academics despite suspicions on each side.

A Multidisciplinary Approach to the Study of Vietnamese Society

Viêt Nam Exposé presents in chronological order the complexities of power relationships in Vietnamese society in the twentieth century. One of these relationships is that between the French and the Vietnamese, defined at the beginning of the century by colonial power and transformed after decades of power struggles into a bilateral economic partnership. Another important relationship is the one between members of the Vietnamese elite and intellectuals as they competed during colonial rule for power in villages and at court and during the anticolonial war when they defended antithetical political ideologies. Then there is the gender relationship, embedded in patriarchal Vietnamese society and contested in the colonial context. Finally, the period from the Vietnamese declaration of independence in 1945 to the present has been one in which power relationships in Vietnamese society have come to be defined mainly in terms of the economy.

Part I, "Vietnamese Society in the Early Twentieth Century," takes a microapproach to the study of aspects of Vietnamese society on the eve of the irreversible social transformation that occurred as the colonial infrastructure took root in Indochina. Part II, "Vietnamese Intellectuals: Contesting Colonial Power," contains biographical accounts of Vietnamese intellectuals who tried to reform their society under colonial domination. Part III, "Postcolonial Vietnam: From a Welfare State to a Market-Oriented Economy," traces Vietnam's search for a viable economic model while maintaining itself as a socialist state. In "Vietnamese Society in the Early Twentieth Century," the first three chapters focus on power relationships at the village level. Chapter 1 analyzes the village's internal political processes, chapter 2 deals with the power relationship between villagers (colonized) and French administrators (colonizers) induced by the colonial context, and chapter 3 shows the articulation of power in gender relations in village culture. Using Vietnamese sources ranging from the National Vietnamese Archives in Hanoi to folklore and oral tradition, these authors analyze the power relationships within particular strata of Vietnamese society, giving an emic perspective of the issues. Using village archives in "Who Has Power in the Village? Political Process and Social Reality in Vietnam," Philippe Papin reexamines the roles and statuses of the *ly truong* (village mayor) and other village notables who played central political roles in the village. Papin argues that political processes at the local level were based on relationships among powerful families who competed for power in the village rather than on the prescribed roles and functions of officials. The social backgrounds and careers of the *ly truong* are important clues for understanding village political intrigues. Papin shows how the village political system altered over time under French colonial rule, resulting in changes in the role of the *ly truong*.

Chapter 2 addresses the complex relationship between the French authority and the Vietnamese villagers over tax reforms. In "Village Rebellions in the Tonkin Delta, 1900–1905," Philippe Le Failler studies the relationship between French tax administrators and the Vietnamese peasants. For the peasants, colonial tax collection provoked violent incidents throughout northern Vietnam, sometimes leading to revolts against the French customs officers. For their part, the French colonial administrators interpreted such resistance movements as rebellions against colonial power. Le Failler argues that French political labeling of such revolts as rebellions may have been premature in the early part of the century. He suggests instead that we must understand the social context in which the taxation took place. For instance, in addition to direct taxes, peasants were subject to many indirect taxes, which raised the price of goods such as alcohol and salt, forcing the peasants to reduce their consumption.

In chapter 3, "Rethinking the Status of Vietnamese Women in Folklore and Oral History," Nguyen Van Ky confronts the question of gender. He compares the official texts of the elite, the interpretations of which follow the Confucian rules of conduct, to the ordinary language of Vietnamese peasants, which suggests other considerations. Like Papin, Nguyen Van Ky offers a new interpretation of Vietnamese village life, in this case based on the analysis of proverbs, sayings, and folk songs (*ca dao*) in the work of Nguyên Van Ngoc and Vu Ngoc Phan. Nguyên Van Ky argues that the oral and popular traditions demonstrate evidence for a higher status of women in Vietnam before the Chinese conquest. And, he argues, the remainder of a former matrilineal Vietnamese society has been kept alive in the collective memory through folklore and oral history in spite of the adoption of Confucianism.

The following two chapters, "Administrative Practices: An Essential Aspect of Mandarinal Training (Nineteenth–Early Twentieth Century)," by Emmanuel Poisson, and "In the Shadow of the Colonial Hospital: Developing Health Care in Indochina, 1860–1939," by Laurence Monnais-Rousselot, examine the power structures in Vietnamese and French elitist institutions, the Vietnamese mandarinal education, and the French colonial health care institution. Chapter 4, "Administrative Practices," offers a new and different interpretation of the power relations within the Vietnamese mandarinal administration. By studying their curricula vitae, Poisson concludes that the Vietnamese mandarins' training at the beginning of the twentieth century was not simply based on the study of the Confucian classics: in fact an apprenticeship was the key to success in a mandarinal career. Under the Nguyên, this apprenticeship was slowly abandoned over the years, but Poisson argues that the French colonial authority reintroduced the concept when it created the *hâu bô*, a school for training Vietnamese civil servants. This, according to Poisson, strongly resembled the training of the mandarins. Poisson discusses at length the political implications of the school and the extent to which French authority used it to court the Vietnamese mandarinal elite.

Chapter 5 discusses the ambitious colonial project that established a network of health care facilities all over Indochina. Laurence Monnais-Rousselot, in "In the Shadow of the Colonial Hospital," studies the patterns of development of the health care system throughout Indochina. She argues that the policy of the system was not only to care for all people regardless of ethnicity but also to adapt itself to local needs. Thus, colonial medical institutions in Vietnam were far ahead of their time. They offered Western medicine while simultaneously integrating local medical practices into their programs. The network extended from hospitals in cities to rural medical clinics, taking regional diversity into consideration. The success of this health care network in Vietnam, which still exists today, was due, Monnais-Rousselot suggests, to both its local adaptation and its ability to change to meet different needs at different times and reflects the extent of the penetration of the French system among the Vietnamese.

Part II, "Vietnamese Intellectuals: Contesting Colonial Power," reexamines the role of members of the educated Vietnamese elite in the nationalist movements and their contributions to Vietnamese society in the mid–twentieth century. The more visible political figures of this period of conflict and turmoil have caught the attention of historians, while many other intellectuals, whose contributions to the struggle for independence and to Vietnamese society, equally important, have been forgotten. Using biographical materials, chapters 6–9 trace the lives of exceptional individuals who actively participated in Vietnam's struggle for independence. In chapter 6, "Prince Cuong Dê and the Franco-Vietnamese Competition for the Heritage of Gia Long," Agathe Larcher-Goscha presents a new interpretation of the political activities of Prince Cuong Dê and his place in Vietnamese history. As the direct descent of Gia Long, the prince was the legitimate and recognized heir to the Vietnamese throne. But the French colonial administration, though recognizing his claims, accused him of being a nationalist and condemned him to exile. While in Japan, the prince joined the nationalist movement of Phan Bôi Châu for a short time, but he was considered a traitor by the nationalists because he allied himself with the Japanese. Larcher-Goscha argues that the prince had his own political agenda, which was to regain the throne of Gia Long. The Vietnamese intellectual and publisher Huynh Thuc Khang was a nationalist, not a controversial political figure like Prince Cuong Dê. In chapter 7, "A Vietnamese Scholar with a Different Path: Huynh Thuc Khang, Publisher of the First Vietnamese Newspaper in *Quôc Ngu* in Central Vietnam, *Tieng Dan* (People's Voice)," Phan Thi Minh Le presents the life of this man, whose contribution to the national cause, she argues, has been forgotten. Huynh Thuc Khang was a scholar who had been jailed early in his life by the French for political activities. In 1927 in Hue, he created the newspaper *Tieng Dan*, written in *quôc ngu*[8] (colloquial Vietnamese). Huynh Thuc Khang was both an educator and a political activist who took a modernist Confucian approach and used his newspaper to educate his fellow countrymen in history, literature, and politics. But Huynh Thuc Khang chose to play by the French rules in order to publish his newspaper. For example, he submitted a French translation of every Vietnamese article published in *Tieng Dan* to the French authority. He refused to ally himself with either the Vietnamese political party supported by the French governor or the Communist Party of Ho Chi Minh. Phan Thi Minh Le argues that, nonetheless, Huynh Thuc Khang, for sixteen years the publisher of *Tieng Dan*, contributed by educating and preparing its readers for the Vietnamese revolution. Unlike Cuong Dê and Huynh Thuc Khang, who participated in the anti-French colonial struggle but never joined the Vietnamese communist party, the generation of Vietnamese intellectuals of 1925, who were educated at French schools in Vietnam, rallied to Ho Chi Minh during the anticolonial war of 1945–54. In chapter 8, "The 1925 Generation of Vietnamese Intellectuals and Their Role in the Struggle for Independence," Trinh Van Thao wants to understand why these Vietnamese petit bourgeois intellectuals adhered to Marx's ideology of class struggle and participated in the Vietnamese socialist revolution. Examining their social backgrounds and curricula vitae, Trinh Van Thao argues that although francophone, these intellectuals were not alienated from their own culture. On the contrary, Trinh claims, they rallied to the anticolonial struggle because it gave them the opportunity to fulfill their filial piety and sense of responsibility toward their ancestors and their native land, duties that lie at the heart of Confucian political culture.

The last biographical essay on a Vietnamese intellectual of the mid–twentieth century focuses on the life of the woman intellectual Henriette Bui. As the first Vietnamese woman doctor ever graduated from a French medical school, Henriette Bui experienced and transcended the gender and racial inequality of Vietnamese society under colonialism. As Tran Thi Liên points out, there are very few materials on women in the archives. For chapter 9, "Henriette Bui: The Narrative of Vietnam's First Woman Doctor," Tran collected data from newspapers, archival materials, and personal interviews with Dr. Bui. Born in the early twentieth century, Henriette Bui belongs to what Trinh Van Thao calls the generation of the intellectuals of 1925. Tran Thi Liên traces Henriette Bui's professional and personal struggle during her work in Vietnamese hospitals under French colonial rule. Thus, the biography of Henriette Bui is a personal account of social injustice embedded in the relationship between colonizers and colonized people. Henriette Bui's life history also complements Monnais-Rousselot's study on the Indochinese health care system. Tran's essay gives us a better understanding of how the hospitals of that network functioned and how the "native" personnel were treated in a French colonial medical establishment. In addition, this essay presents a view of life in Saigon under the Vietnamese Republic.

Part III of the book, "Postcolonial Vietnam: From a Welfare State to a Market-Oriented Economy," focuses on Vietnam's biggest challenge at the present time, the building of a strong and healthy economy. The quest for an economic model started at the time of Ho Chi Minh's declaration of independence in 1945 and continued during the resistance war against the French until 1954. From 1959 to 1988, the Democratic Republic of Vietnam (DRV) adopted Soviet-style collectivization, which was later abandoned because it failed to meet its economic objectives. After introducing the economic reforms of Doi Moi in 1986, Vietnamese leaders launched the country on a new path of economic transformation. No longer a welfare state, Vietnam under a market-oriented economy is facing new problems related to labor relations. These include an increase in unemployment and rural-urban migration. In the countryside, the new reforms brought a drastic increase in agricultural production, particularly in rice. But the lack of crop diversity in the region of the Red River delta resulted in the stagnation of agricultural industry, which threatened the income of farmers. Rural migration, not always permanent, brings its own set of social and economic problems. There have been changes in international relations as well. Vietnam has joined the global economy. Since 1986, Vietnam has joined a variety of nonsocialist international organizations, among them the Francophone Community. Membership in that community raises far more important issues than linguistic concerns, and it entails complex political and economic issues as well.

In chapter 10, "The Economy of War as a Prelude to a 'Socialist Economy': The Case of the Vietnamese Resistance against the French, 1945–1954," Pierre Brocheux investigates the various means on which the Democratic Republic of Vietnam at the end of 1945 had to rely in order to create an economy. As a young state trying to overcome the destruction of World War II, a famine that killed over one million people, and a war of resistance against the French, Vietnam and its newly formed government, the DRV, faced many challenges. Brocheux asks how the leadership was able to cope. How did it come up with a model of a sustainable economy that people would willingly follow, and how was the government able to force its policies on people who had so little? Brocheux argues that the leaders implemented a local sustainable economy that was inserted into the village economy, thus saving agriculture, handicrafts, and local trade from French destruction. Furthermore, Vietnam's close relationship with Asian countries such as China and Thailand was vital to its military success. These countries were used as military bases to recruit soldiers and serve as "safe havens" for Vietnamese troops. After 1954, the DRV in northern Vietnam depended on rural collectivization and industrialization. But Brocheux argues that, although the state-owned enterprises and rural cooperatives were the pillars of the economy, the government continued to allow family production, setting the scene for the present economic program, Doi Moi. Other economic measures such as the centralized policy of collectivization, which lasted almost thirty years, failed to lead Vietnam to economic prosperity and was eventually abandoned. In chapter 11, "The Chronicle of a Failure: Collectivization in Northern Vietnam, 1958–1988," Florence Yvon-Tran deconstructs the socialist political discourse on collectivization in Vietnam and shows how the Vietnamese communist party, which had envisioned a socialist transformation in the rural areas, never achieved its goal of increasing productivity. Yvon-Tran traces the chronology of the collectivization policy and demonstrates how it failed to gain the support of the Vietnamese farmers. She shows how in late 1958, because a few rural households had voluntarily joined the cooperatives, the Vietnamese government changed its policies and forced the farmers to participate in the collectivization program. But Yvon-Tran argues that the state's inability to control and manage the rural cooperatives, as well as the development of a black market in rural areas, forced the government to abandon the program. Like other French scholars in this volume, Florence Yvon-Tran lived in Hanoi for over two years in the early 1990s, not only collecting data in Vietnamese archives but conducting interviews with peasants in the Red River delta.

In chapter 12, "Labor Restructuring in Vietnam," Xavier Oudin, using quantitative data, presents an overview of the shift in labor practices since the economic transformation under the 1986 policy, Doi Moi. Comparing the Vietnamese labor situation to that of other Southeast Asian countries, Oudin argues that Vietnamese labor laws no longer apply to current labor relations in Vietnamese society. In fact, in the past Vietnam's labor laws were some of the most advanced in the region in terms of social protection of the work force. Tracing the changes in labor practices and the economy that led to the economic reforms, Oudin suggests that in 1965 the labor force was employed in state enterprises and collective units. By 1986, nonwage labor had drastically increased and wage workers represented no more than 15 percent of the Vietnamese labor force. With inflation, the state enterprises laid off their workers, who then became increasingly self-employed. Many became petty traders. In the rural sector, Oudin describes similar patterns, with the labor force shifting from collective to family units. According to Pascal Bergeret, the current stagnating agricultural incomes threaten not only the agricultural industry but the economy of rural households because farmers are forced to migrate to the cities to maintain their standard of living. In chapter 13, "Agro-Commodity Chains in Northern Vietnam: New Mechanisms for Old Stakeholders," Bergeret shows how agricultural production in Vietnam has drastically increased since the end of collectivization in 1988 under the political reforms. But in the Red River delta the production of food crops such as rice and pork was already increasing before the reforms. Unlike other countries, Vietnam was able to increase production without diversifying its agricultural output or modernizing the industry. But Bergeret argues that without diversification the rice-based economy in the Red River delta has resulted in low growth in agricultural income. Bergeret also analyzes patterns in agro-commodity chains in order to show how and why producers are reluctant to diversify their agricultural enterprises. Comparing the three agro-commodity chains of rice, pork, and garlic, he argues that producers prefer trading commodities such as rice, which represents a lower risk to them. But he also argues that eventually this lack of diversity in the Red River delta will jeopardize the income of farmers and destabilize already fragile rural-urban boundaries. The study of the village of Hay presented by Olivier Tessier in chapter 14, "Commuting from the Village to the City: Analyzing the Patterns of Migration of the People of the Northern Village of Hay to Hanoi," presents a case study illustrating the economic transformation that Oudin documents and the current problem of income that Bergeret presents. Based on his fieldwork in the northern village of Hay, Tessier analyzes the patterns of migration from Hay to Hanoi. He traces the networks, the migrants' motivations, and the length of time spent in Hanoi by the people of Hay. He suggests that unemployment, the lack of financial resources, and the little land available after the 1993 land distribution are the main push factor in the current rural migration in Vietnam. Job opportunities in the city for unskilled labor in construction has attracted rural migrants to search for employment in cities. Unlike other scholars in the Vietnamese academy, Tessier argues that this rural migration is, at least in the case of Hay, not permanent. In fact, he suggests that 70 percent of the people of Hay who have worked in Hanoi tend to return to the village on a regular basis, and sometimes they settle back permanently.

The last essay, chapter 15, "Facing Globalization: Vietnam and the Francophone Community," by Gisele Bousquet, unravels two major issues underlying the Francophone Summit in Hanoi in 1997. The first one concerns Vietnam's entering the global economy as a new player, and the second reveals Vietnam's new relationship with France at the beginning of the twenty-first century. Vietnam's new strategy as it enters the international market has been to gain membership in many international organizations in order to protect its markets and increase its international trade. It joined the Francophone Community in 1986 at a time when the United States still maintained its economic embargo against the country. And nine years later Vietnam joined the Association of Southeast Asian Nations (ASEAN), in 1995, the same year in which the economic embargo was lifted. Vietnam is one of the poorest countries in the world, and Vietnamese leaders know that it needs partnerships in order to survive. On 11 February 2000, Vietnam with 190 other developing nations participated in the Tenth United Nations Conference on Trade and Development (UNCTAD). In a recent interview, the secretary general of UNCTAD, Rubens Ricopero, illustrated the mood of the conference by suggesting that since 1998 poor countries have been getting poorer and have not benefited from the economic growth experienced by developing countries. The other aspect of the Francophone Summit in Hanoi in 1997 was the building of a new Franco-Vietnamese relationship. Although Vietnam is no longer a francophone country, the purpose of the summit was not simply to promote the French language. The organization's agenda had a lot more to do with politics and economic matters than linguistics. With the election of a new general secretary, the Francophone Community wants to challenge the leadership of the United States as a superpower and compete in the new global economy. Vietnam's membership in the Francophone Community and Vietnam's close relationship with France has facilitated Vietnam's access to the European Union market. And France has also gained from the new partnership, since Vietnam represents an anchor for French business expansion in Asia.

Acknowledgments

I would like to thank my coeditor, Pierre Brocheux, of the University of Denis-Diderot in Paris. His academic rigor and his long, active career as a historian of Vietnam were critical in identifying the French scholars living in France who contributed to this volume. He also insisted that none of the essays in this edited volume should have been previously published in French, Vietnamese, or English. This gives originality and uniqueness to the volume. I would like to thank John K. Whitmore at the University of Michigan for his early interest in this cross-cultural project, his great support during the whole process, and his guidance and editorial work in the revision of the manuscript.

It is just as important to recognize the contribution of the French and French-Vietnamese scholars who participated in this project. It was a particularly difficult task for scholars whose second language is Vietnamese rather than English and for French-Vietnamese scholars whose mother tongue is Vietnamese while English is their third language. They were asked to adapt their writing to an American style in order to ease the reading of those not familiar with French writing and had to finance the translation of their own papers.

I would like to thank the people who translated various chapters and made this cross-cultural and bilingual project possible: Claire Beliard, Robert Carradice, Claire Duiker, Christopher Goscha, Andrew Hardy, Evelyne Lagaune, and Duy Tâm. In addition, I want to extend my great appreciation to my dear friends and colleagues Elizabeth Colson, Lyn Lowry, and Claire Beliard for helping me edit this manuscript. Their suggestions and comments were crucial for its revision; to Nancy Elliott for her support and patience throughout this endeavor; and to Ingrid Erickson at the University of Michigan Press for her support in pursuing this project, which began with an idea and only slowly developed into a coherent manuscript.

NOTES

Center for Southeast Asian Studies, University of Hawaii.

1. Adam Fforde, *From Plan to Market: The Economic Transition in Vietnam*. Boulder: Westview, 1996; John Kleinen, *Facing the Future, Reviving the Past: A Study of Social Change in a Northern Vietnamese Village*, Singapore: ISEAS, 1999. Among some recent Ph.D. dissertations, see Bernard Henry Henin, "Transformation of Vietnam's Upland Farming Societies under Market Reform," Ph.D. diss., University of Victoria, 1999; Chuenchanok Kovin, "The Role of Universities in the Development of Greater Mekong Subregional Economic Cooperation," Ph.D. diss., University of Illinois, Urbana-Champaign, 1999; Christine Le, "On Different Ground: A Contextualized Understanding of the Concept of Self of Women in Vietnam," Ph.D. diss., New York University, 1999; Leslie Marie Lipper, "The Logic of Swidden: Poverty and Environmental Determinants of Household Farming System Choice," Ph.D. diss., University of California, Berkeley, 1999; Nguyên Trian, "Ninh Phuc Temple: A Study of Seventeenth-Century Buddhist Sculpture in Vietnam," Ph.D. diss., University of California, Berkeley, 1999; Dara James O'Rourke, "Community-Driven Regulation: The Political Economy of Pollution in Vietnam," Ph.D. diss., University of California, Berkeley, 1999; Thomas Otto Sikor, "The Political Economy of Decollectivization: A Study of Differentiation in and among Black Thai Villages of Northern Vietnam," Ph.D. diss., University of California, Berkeley, 1999; A. Nora Taylor, "The Artist and the State: The Politics of Painting and National Identity in Hanoi, Vietnam, 1925–1995," Ph.D. diss., Cornell University, 1997; and Trân Hoa Phuong, "Vietnamese Higher Education at the Intersection of French and Soviet Influences," Ph.D. diss., State University of New York, Buffalo, 1998.

2. Among the most recently published books on the Vietnam War are Kenneth J. Conboy and Dale Andradé, *Spies and Commandos: How America Lost the Secret War in North Vietnam* (Lawrence, KS: University of Kansas, 2000);

Andrew E. Hunt, *The Turning: A History of Vietnam Veterans against the War* (New York: New York University Press, 1999); Fredrik Logevall, *Choosing War: The Lost Chance for Peace and the Escalation of War in Vietnam* (Berkeley: University of California Press, 1999); Richard H. Shultz, *The Secret War against Hanoi: Kennedy's and Johnson's Use of Spies, Saboteurs, and Covert Warriors in North Vietnam* (New York: HarperCollins, 1999); Lewis Sorley, *A Better War: The Unexamined Victories and Final Tragedy of America's Last Years in Vietnam* (New York: Harcourt Brace, 1999); and Robert R. Tomes, *Apocalypse Then: American Intellectuals and the Vietnam War, 1954–1975* (New York: New York University Press, 1998).

    3. Paul Mus, *Hô Chi Minh, le Vietnam, l'Asie* (Paris: Éditions du Seuil, 1971); *L'angle de l'Asie* (Paris: Hermann, 1977).

    4. Jean Chesneaux, *Le Vietnam: Études de politique et d'histoire* (Paris: F. Maspero, 1968); Jean Chesneaux, *Contribution à l'histoire de la nation vietnamienne* (Paris: Éditions sociales, 1955); Jean Chesneaux, Georges Boudarel, Daniel Hémery, and Nguyên Khac Viên, eds., *Tradition et révolution au Vietnam* (Paris: Anthropos, 1971).

    5. Pierre Brocheux and Daniel Hémery, *Indochine: La Colonisation ambiguë, 1858–1954* (Paris: Découverte, 1995); Pierre Brocheux, *The Mekong Delta: Ecology, Economy, and Revolution, 1860–1960* (Madison: Center for Southeast Asian Studies, University of Wisconsin, Madison, 1995); Daniel Hémery, *Ho Chi Minh: De l'Indochine au Vietnam* (Paris: Gallimard, 1990); Daniel Hémery, *Révolutionnaires vietnamiens et pouvoir colonial en Indochine: Communistes, trotskystes, nationalistes à Saigon de 1932 à 1937* (Paris: F. Maspero, 1975); Georges Boudarel and Nguyên Van Ky, *Hanoi, 1936–1996: Du drapeau rouge au billet vert* (Paris: Autrement, 1997); Georges Boudarel, *La Bureaucratie au Vietnam* (Paris: L'Harmattan, 1983); Georges Boudarel, *Giap* (Paris: Éditions Atlas, 1977); Philippe Langlet, *Khâm-dinh Viêt-su thông-giám cuong-muc (L'Ancienne historiographie d'État au Vietnam)* (Paris: École Française d'Extrême-Orient, 1985); Philippe Devillers, *Guerre ou paix: Une interprétation de la politique extérieure soviétique depuis 1944* (Paris: Balland, 1985); Philippe Devillers, *Histoire du Viêt-Nam de 1940 à 1952* (Paris: Éditions du Seuil, 1952); Jean Lacouture and Philippe Devillers, *La fin d'une guerre; Indochine, 1954* (Paris: Éditions du Sueil, 1960); Alain Ruscio, *Le credo de l'homme blanc: Regards coloniaux français, XIXe–XXe siècles* (Brussels: Editions Complexe, 1995); Alain Ruscio, *La décolonisation tragique: Une histoire de la décolonisation française, 1945–1962* (Paris: Essidor/Editions sociales, 1987); Alain Ruscio, *Les communistes français et la guerre d'Indochine, 1944–1954* (Paris: Harmattan, 1985); Charles Fourniau, *Annam-Tonkin, 1885–1896: Lettrés et paysans vietnamiens face à la conquête coloniale* (Paris: L'Harmattan, 1989); Charles Fourniau, *Le Vietnam face à la guerre* (Paris: Éditions sociales, 1966); Georges Condominas, *L'espace social à propos de l'Asie du Sud-Est* (Paris: Flammarion, 1980); Georges Condominas, *Nous avons mangé la forêt de la pierre-génie Goô (Hii saa brii mau-yaang Goô), chronique de Sar Luk, village mnong gar (tribu proto-indochinoise des Hauts-Plateaux du Viet-Nam central)* (Paris: Mercure de France, 1957); Trinh Van Thao, *L'école française en Indochine* (Paris: Karthala, 1995); Trinh Van Thao, *Vietnam: Du confucianisme au communisme, un essai itinéraire intellectuel*

(Paris: L'Harmattan, 1990); Lê Thành Khôi, *Histoire du Viêt Nam: Des origines à 1858* (Paris: Sudestasie, 1981); Lê Thành Khôi, *Socialisme et développement au Viêt Nam* (Paris: Presses universitaires de France, 1978); Lê Thành Khôi, *Le Viêt-nam: Histoire et civilisation* (Paris: Éditions de Minuit, 1955); Nguyên Khac Vien and Huu Ngoc, *From Saigon to Ho Chi Minh City: A Path of 300 Years* (Hanoi: Thê Gioi Publishers, 1998); Nguyên Khac Vien, *Contemporary Vietnam, 1858–1980* (Hanoi: Foreign Languages Publishing House, 1981); Nguyên Khac Vien, *The Long Resistance, 1858–1975* (Hanoi: Foreign Languages Publishing House, 1978); Nguyên Khac Vien, *Histoire du Vietnam* (Paris: Éditions Sociales, 1974).

6. "Tout au long de ses développements, depuis les années soixante, a l'instar de son homologue américaine, l'historiographie moderniste et contemporaneiste française de l'Asie du sud-est participe indirectement a—et aussi procède de—la construction d'un regard national sur le passe des sociétés et des etats post-coloniaux, a la recherche de leur auto-definition historique, assez paradoxalement a l'invention de leur tradition et des représentations homogenéisantes de ce passe, volontiers silencieuse par contre sur leurs clivages et leur heterogeneites internes." Quoted from Daniel Hémery, "Les recherches française en histoire moderne et contemporaine de l'Asie du Sud-Est depuis les annees 1960: Un etat des lieux," in *Liber Amicorum: Melanges offerts au Professeur Phan Huy Le* (Hanoi: Publications de l'École Française d'Extrême Orient, 1999).

7. Discussion with Pierre Brocheux, March 2000, Paris.

8. *Quôc ngu* is the roman alphabetization of the Vietnamese language.

Part I

Vietnamese Society in the
Early Twentieth Century

1 Philippe Papin

Who Has Power in the Village? Political Process and Social Reality in Vietnam

Introduction

The study of villages and Vietnamese rural society is tributary to a long historiographical tradition that, without interruption, has been pursued since the colonial era and the socialist period up to the present time. Let us state at the outset that this study fits into a general framework of ideas, which, though broad and highly diverse, has nonetheless benefited from the work of several generations of Vietnamese and foreign researchers, to whom we must pay tribute. But this short study enters also into a relationship of opposition to a certain historiographical legacy, which, across the ideological spectrum, has made the village into an immobile structure, naturally balanced and endowed with a political apparatus that has been described and explained in a way that seems to us entirely questionable. This last issue, namely, the distribution of power and the mode of government, is the subject of our inquiry in the present essay.

The system of village power is traditionally presented as a three-tiered structure: the Council of Notables on top, the officials of the commune in the middle, and an undifferentiated peasant mass at the base. According to this vision, it is precisely the access to public office that is supposed to give the villager the opportunity to pass from one tier to the next, in the context of a life that proceeds by *stages:* peasant, registered taxpayer, official of the commune (and perhaps the canton), notable, and, finally, with the elevation "from honorable mat to honorable mat," up to the highest point in the council.[1] In this perspective, power is defined not by the officeholder's social group but by his *position* within the community, although the origin of this position is never specified. If the position gives power, we may wonder what gives the position. In fact, what is described here is a village without history, a village without a past, without an "engine"—an inert mechanism that permanently aims at balance and the sharing of tasks, with the subtext that penury necessitates solidarity, cooperation, and redistribution (forms of the famous "moral economy of the village").

When power in the village is mentioned, it is in reality a normative definition which is sought, a definition capable of encompassing all the systems and all the people. But village books of customary law, texts issued by the court, and even colonial legislative documents provide this encompassing definition: the system of power appears in these contexts to lie in the hands of "notables," former mandarins and literati, wise old men or young candidates for the examinations. It is rare indeed to see the evocation of regional differences. The figure of the notable is often mobilized as the keystone to this edifice. But never is there an explanation of the notable's function, nor any definition of what a notable is, where he came from, what he did, how he gained his post, and the nature of his post. The notable functions a little like the deus ex machina of ancient tragedies: he does not explain himself, does not vary, possesses neither origin nor future, but intervenes abruptly to reply to the embarrassing question: who runs Vietnamese villages?

But the exercise of power is not the *representation* of power by those who hold it, and the forms of its exercise are not local *variations* from a normative text. This may seem evident, but it conceals an important methodological approach, which can be summed up by means of the following question: who to believe: those who talk about "the village" or those who live in villages, those who wield power (and define it) or those who live under it? At present, only the former have expressed themselves, not because they enjoy any particular legitimacy but quite simply because the latter's voice has not been heard. The powerholders' vision dominated.

The recent discovery in Hanoi of communal archives has given rise to a veritable "Copernican revolution" that has allowed us, for the first time, to hear what the villagers had to say. Great piles of documents (approximately four thousand dossiers) are now available to us, and they now constitute a new and exciting point of departure for our interrogations. In the following pages, we aim less at a sketch of the chronological evolution of village life than at a definition of the *real* functioning of power in the village. New sources call for new methodologies, and in this essay I have deliberately opted to keep clear of the grand theoretical frameworks and normative documents produced by the upper echelons of Vietnamese society. My objective is, in contrast, to plunge deeply into the very heart of village social life at the end of the nineteenth century and attempt a detailed examination of the "microaffairs" of the time, of local life. These are packed full of information that, reorganized and synthesized, provides a clear definition of the nature and functioning of power in the village, which is a good deal more convincing than that which has dominated our thinking to date. What I am attempting to achieve here is, in the end, very simple. It is an analysis of the fragments, not of any discourse but of a social reality itself, understood through the documents generated by the village itself. The village lives, moves, and is subject to constant challenges, and this rather obvious observation allows me to pose the key question of this study: faced with documents from village archives, with trials, denunciations, riots, murders, clan struggles, spoliation, fiscal manipulations, and landless peasants—what remains of the ideal and homogeneous "village community"?

1. The Crucial Role of the *Ly Truong:* An Introductory Analysis

In the political structure of all Vietnamese villages, one man held a primordial position. His decisions had daily consequences for all families in the community. This was the *ly truong,* or "village mayor," on whose conduct the smooth—or not so smooth—functioning of village life depended. An analysis of the political role of this official is the necessary point of departure for our study of power in the village.

The Council of Notables (*hôi dông ky muc*) was headed by the first notable (*tiên chi,* "the first on the paper"), seconded by the second notable (*thu chi*), and included all those men who had occupied communal office in the past as well as currently serving agents (*ly dich*), former mandarins, old people (*lao*) or "rich and honorable people" (*phu quy*), literati, and so on. Among them, themselves part of the group of currently serving agents, were to be found those essential characters, omnipresent in the documents: the *ly truong* and his principal assistants, the *pho ly* (responsible for the execution of the *ly truong*'s orders) and the *huong truong* (responsible for public works).

Using information taken from normative texts (especially village customary law books) and from well-known models drawn from large villages of literati (which were often the only ones studied), our traditional understanding of the organization of power in the village has rested on a hierarchical conception of the Council of Notables, presented in the following terms. First came the old men (*lao nhiêu* and *lao hang*), then dignitaries holding an imperial title (*chuc sac*), then "Confucian" literati (*tu van*), then candidates at the examinations (*huong thân* and *thi sinh*) and former communal and canton officials (*chuc dich*), and finally the soldiers and the *ly truong* in office.[2] In fact, the whole society of the time found its place in this outline. But this model—for mere model it is—is far too broad for most villages.

In this hierarchical analysis—in which the *ly truong* was evidently at the bottom of the ladder—the quantitative factor was quite simply ignored. But there were of course, and this point is crucial to our understanding of power in the village, many more former *ly truong* in the Council of Notables than there were former mandarins or literati.

A quantitative analysis of sociological reality leads us to the following question. Mandarins and literati were indeed classified according to rank, but whom did this concern? Or rather, how many people did it concern? The typological hierarchy of the council was pertinent only for villages with strong traditions of learning (like Dông-Ngac or Yên-So, always used as examples),[3] but in reality the majority of villages had no literati, no mandarins, no graduates, no candidates. Or they had them in very low proportions. In other words, the customary books set down plenty of places for these people, but that does not mean that those places were occupied. With at most one or two former petty mandarins per village, the classification was completed rapidly indeed.[4]

Let us take a close look at a single district, for purposes of illustration. The *Register of the Communal Authorities in the District of Hoàn-Long*[5] (near Hanoi) allows us to count exactly 533 notables (*ky muc*) of whom 117 were in 1905 currently serving (*ly dich*). As a whole, the group of notables was not huge, especially if we add that it was spread evenly throughout the whole district (on average, they made up exactly 13 inhabitants in every 1,000).[6] This view from 1905 allows us to obtain a sort of snapshot of the situation at a particular date: in the ranks of the Council of Notables was assembled the entire administration of the previous years (here 1882–1905), with a few "gaps" (here 1888–90 for the *ly truong* of Nam-Dông, for example), which may be put down to deaths. As in all these cases, the date of entry to a place among the *ky muc* corresponded exactly to that of leaving the position among the currently serving agents (*ly dich*). This is the crucial dividing line, which we can identify within the Council of Notables: on one side those who had held communal office in the past, on the other those still in office.

Our example raises a simple question: who were the notables? And to answer this we need to examine what those men serving in 1905 were doing *prior* to that date. Where in fact did they come from? The results are quite clear: eight out of ten notables were simply very modest former officials of the commune (*ly truong, pho ly,* and *huong truong*). The former *ly truong* alone comprised precisely one-third of the Council of Notables, due to the rapid turnover in this post (three years). After them came the former canton officials (5 percent) and the old men and soldiers (2.5 percent). By contrast, the mandarinate and its officials (*tho lai, thông lai, lai muc*) were virtually absent (less than 1 percent). The Council of Notables was thus, above all else, an assembly of former and modest commune officials, and village power thus remained well and truly in the hands of men who had come up through the ranks, who were born and had worked in the commune itself. Its members came from the local peasantry, and the Council grouped competent, experienced men, men who were familiar with the machinery of power and the subtleties of village social life.

The Council of Notables was not a sort of council of savants. It was not made up of former mandarins, graduates, and men of letters. It was not an abstraction, the pure and angelic reflection of the "village community" and its "traditional hierarchy," but it was in fact a site of power and conflict. More than this, it was a site of conflict *for* power.

If the council was not made up of savants, its members were mainly the "little people" who had exercised modest authority in the village. The typical notable was a former *ly truong* or *pho ly* who had worked for several years before joining the council to play another role, a role henceforth more important for the fact that his past experience had given him a clear understanding not only of the functioning of communal administration but also of the networks and alliances in action within the village. The former communal official knew everybody, all the families and their little secrets, all the polemics and past conflicts; he had dispensed enough favors to build up a clientele, but, as a result of his role as arbitrator, he had also alienated a good number of villagers. His authority as a notable was thus indissolubly linked to the power he had previously wielded as an employee of the commune. It was thus on two counts (serving official, then notable) that the communal officials, especially the *ly truong*, appear to us to have played a central role in the distribution of village power. It is to them that we must now turn our attention.

The serving officials, or *ly dich*, ranked below members of the Council of Notables. They were responsible for the day to day running of the village. The *ly truong* was the head of the communal officials, a sort of village mayor, backed up by his assistants, the *pho ly* and the *huong truong* (these last were responsible for public works in the village and the maintenance of roads and dikes). The communal officials were few: in a third of all cases, there was just a single *ly truong*, and, in another third, this *ly truong* was seconded by a *pho ly*. The executive body of the Vietnamese village was thus a light structure composed of a maximum of one or two people.[7] In the village, "executive power" well and truly belonged to the *ly truong*.

Who were these *ly truong*, the men in charge of the village? Given the extremely long process of working out dates of birth, I have limited myself to a small sample of five large and representative villages.[8] For officials entering office between 1865 and 1905, the average age was thirty-one for the first communal post occupied. In these five villages, as everywhere else, the age hierarchy was as follows: the *ly truong* was always the oldest (on average thirty-one to forty-two years old), then came the *huong truong* (twenty to thirty-six), and finally the youngest of all was the *pho ly* (twenty-eight to thirty-two). Communal officials entering office were thus young men in their twenties, just starting out in their careers.[9]

How long did officials remain in office? Was there any confiscation of power by local potentates? For almost one-third of the *ly truong* in our 1905 sample, the average period of service was 3.16 years, thus conforming to the 3-year rule governing the *ly truong*'s period of office.[10] It was quite surprising to discover that there was no powerholder who remained in place for a long period of time. The maximum period was only 13 years at Vinh-Phuc (1891–1904), and there are only six cases of *ly truong* who kept their posts for longer than 6 years.[11]

What was the situation thirty years later? Our only source is a list, drawn up in 1938, of *ly truong* currently in office, which means that we remain ignorant of the dates on which they left their posts. But certain corrections in this unique and precious document can help us. In 1942, some names on the 1938 list were crossed out, owing to the recent dismissal or resignation of serving *ly truong:* these corrections note the date of retirement for some of these people, exactly eight cases out of 57 villages. These eight cases represent the sole data upon which we can rely for our knowledge of the exact length of service during the 1930s.[12]

Examination of these eight cases indicates a radical change from the situation in 1905. All eight cases were of men whose service lasted longer than 6 years. The average length of service, moreover, is very high: no less than 13 years at the head of the commune's administration against 3.16 years in 1905. By its nature and extent, the change is vast. It deserves closer and more exhaustive statistical analysis, an approach that takes into account not only the eight cases noted here but all the other currently serving officials. If, by way of hypothesis, we retire all the *ly truong* at the date of December 1942—the last date to figure in pencil on the registers—we will find *ly truong* who had occupied their positions for a very long time, which confirms our conclusions from the eight established cases.[13] At this point in time, when they had not yet finished their periods of service, some cases already appear remarkable, quite beyond comparison with the situation in 1905. Eleven cases in particular stand out, each of them exceeding 9 years of service (three mandates). And, while the majority of those eleven had not completed their fourth mandates in 1942, three of those men had completed the fourth mandate, three had already served five terms of office, and one was a few months short of a staggering eight terms. In all, in nineteen villages (eight established cases and eleven minimum cases) the *ly truong* remained in office for surprisingly long periods, between 6 and 25 consecutive years (at Nam-Dông, for example, Nguyên Van Tu stayed in office for 24 years).[14]

This phenomenon is important: while the age of accession to office was similar at both dates, *ly truong* in the 1920s and 1930s kept their posts much longer, at the head therefore of groups of veritable local potentates.[15] Given these data, we propose the following conclusion. From a springboard toward the Council of Notables, the office of *ly truong* had become a career in itself. This radical change in power, this pronounced tendency toward patrimonialization, will be the guiding line in our reflections on the power of the *ly truong*.

2. The Career and Qualifications of the *Ly Truong*

At the head of its administration, the *ly truong* was at the center of all village affairs. He played a double role, both as the leader of the commune in the eyes of higher authorities and as someone actively involved in these affairs.[16] He is omnipresent in the archives. Although his rank was most modest, his complicity, his silence, his power, and his seal made him the strongman of the village. His position within the structures of power in the village was, however, far from static, and it had undergone numerous transformations over the centuries previous to our sample. Let us stop for a moment, then, before going into the detailed analysis of the *ly truong*'s career path in the late nineteenth century and take a brief look at the origins and evolution of this most peculiar village institution.

The term (and office) of *ly truong* first appeared at the beginning of the fifteenth century during a period of Chinese domination: it referred then to the head of a *ly*, that is, a village, which, according to the texts, was made up of 110 families. Some dozen years later, in 1428, King Lê Loi undertook a vast administrative reform of the kingdom: communes were classified into three categories, by the number of their registered taxpayers, with at the head of each one, two, or three *xa quan*.[17] In 1466, King Lê Thanh Tông replaced the term *xa quan* with *xa truong*,[18] and in 1483 he defined the rules by which they were recruited: former employees of the mandarinate or candidates at the examinations were to be chosen, aged over thirty, with a knowledge of characters and conduct beyond reproach.[19] Later various decrees further specified the conditions of recruitment, notably the ban on members of the same family exercising the functions of *xa truong* together (1488 and 1496).[20] In the seventeenth century, King Lê Du Tông reiterated these general principles and, in what seems to have been a new policy, gave the *xa truong* responsibility for collecting taxes, imposing at the same time the rule limiting the period of service to three years. Until then, and although little is clear, it appears that the *xa truong* had been recruited at examinations organized at the district level. In 1735, this recruitment system, which made small mandarins of the *xa truong*, was definitely abandoned in favor of election by the village community. From this moment, wrote Phan Huy Chu, "the abandonment of recruitment by examination ensured that the office of xa truong was no longer a respected one."[21] The sparse indications that we possess all point in the same direction—that of the progressively venal and "villagized" nature of the job.

With the great administrative reforms of Minh-Mang—and a certain sinicization of institutions that accompanied them—we return to the former term *ly truong*, but it was then limited to a single man per commune, whatever its population. Villagers could also elect a *pho ly*, for villages with more than 50 registered taxpayers and a second for those with more than 150.[22] The responsibilities of the *ly truong*, which were vast, were defined and at the same time it was reiterated that they did not belong to the body of the mandarinate, and that by consequence they could not sit at the Council of Notables with the officers and graduates (*chuc sac*): this was the departure point for the ascent of the Council, which took over essential power, at the expense of the *ly truong* who was after all just a very small notable.[23]

As we have seen, by the late nineteenth century, the *ly truong* was a young man beginning his career. He was generally from the upper echelons of the registered taxpayers, and his difficult functions, thankless but often lucrative, constituted until the beginning of the twentieth century an "examination of passage" toward true notability (*ky muc*). Strictly speaking, he belonged in the Council of Notables but he sat at the lowest level—in the right-hand row of the communal house.[24]

This lowly status had—in the vision from outside the village—consequences for the *ly truong*'s image. In particular, he was associated in good-natured mockery with the figure of the good peasant half-wit, of which the character Ly Toét quickly became the archetype. Born in 1930 or 1931, Ly Toét emerged as the hero of plays in the renovated popular theater (*chèo cai luong*) and most notably of a play entitled *Ly Dinh Du* (The Ly Truong of Dinh Du Village), which definitively fixed the traits of this *ly truong* caricature: the very symbol of the peasant idiot, dazed by the progress of mechanical civilization, always rather ridiculous with his eternal black umbrella symbolizing both his status and the ultimate in elegant propriety. When he "goes up to town," it is to throw surprised glances all around him, which hurts his eyes, with the nickname Toét, which makes reference to an eye infection. The newspapers immediately seized upon this figure, who, from the beginning of the 1930s, became the object of innumerable caricatures: the good Ly Toét trying to stop a municipal sprinkler in Hanoi, which he thinks is losing its essence; the good Ly Toét climbing an electric pylon to light a cigarette; the good Ly Toét sententiously affirming that Europeans have no saliva but a sort of glue that allows them to seal an envelope by licking it, and so on.

His status, from an administrative point of view, situated him between the villagers and the mandarins, and he was as a result designed to be the scapegoat for both parties. A Vietnamese expression designated him as "the man with the head like a pestle and an arse like a chopping board" (anh dâu chây may dit thot). From above as from below, between the devil and the deep blue sea, he was the intended victim in any situation of difficulty.

One did not seek the office of *ly truong* to make a career. This was quite simply impossible. The professional horizon of the *ly truong*, or rather of a few of them, was limited to the posts of deputy head or head of a canton. These men were chosen from among the currently serving *ly truong* by an electoral college composed as follows: on the one hand, former and current canton heads and deputy heads; and, on the other, representatives of each village in the canton. Among these village representatives, and although the system varied at times, currently serving *ly truong* were always to be found along with the first and second notables and a soldier.[25] Canton officials were thus always former *ly truong* and were always elected by a college essentially composed of former *ly truong*. The vast majority of serving canton officials in Hanoi (Hoàn-Long) between 1894 and 1911 made their careers in a similar way. Nguyên Van Doàn offers a pertinent example. Born in 1866 in the village of Yên-Lang, son of the *ly truong*, he had started out as the *pho ly* of his village (1888), then served as *ly truong* (1898) before being elected as deputy head of the canton (1904), then as head of the canton (1908), which allowed him to obtain the minimal mandarin grade of 9–2. In twenty years, Nguyên Van Doàn passed from village auxiliary to canton head, and as such he was representative of the whole personnel of the canton administration: in 1905, the eight canton heads of which the origin is known were all former *ly truong*.[26] The leadership of the canton represented the pinnacle of the village career, but it was not easy to attain: with six or seven communes in each canton, competition was strong, and it was often necessary to resign oneself to seeing one's turn pass.

Cases of such promotions were consequently quite rare. Out of 416 "major notables" in our sample, we find only 29 people (7 percent) who occupied several different offices in the course of their existence. In reality, the majority of employees occupied only a single office during their lives: out of 138 *ly truong*, only 6 became deputy heads of cantons and only 5 heads of cantons. Further, only 7 out of 19 *pho ly* and 6 out of 76 *huong truong* managed to become *ly truong*.[27] In truth, fine careers were rare. In total, only 29 people attained superior office after their first post, and the majority of them moved up no more than a single rank in the communal hierarchy; only 2 people moved up two ranks (or three posts) and just 1 moved up three ranks (four posts), going from *huong truong* to head of canton, in the village of Lac-Trung. To sum up, out of 416 people, just 1 followed a true career path that allowed him to rise in the hierarchy. To put it bluntly, the exercise of communal office, with the post of *ly truong* at the forefront, represented little and led nowhere. The career of the *ly truong* was slow, hardly brilliant and closed.

It was, as such, representative of all the communal offices. Before the 1920s, one did not become an official of the commune to make a career in the administration—what could one expect, if not the post of canton head? The point was to get into the Council of Notables.

In this sense, in the late nineteenth century the office of *ly truong* was both cul-de-sac and springboard. It was, however, a springboard of use *only within the village*. To exercise communal office for three years did not allow one to achieve a fine and prestigious career, but it did offer the possibility of rising above one's social origins, and that was in itself a great deal. The office of *ly truong* was, for this reason, in extreme demand and, as the archives prove, easily abandoned. Only dismissal definitively prevented accession to the Council of Notables, which explains why, in cases of scandal, the serving *ly truong* maneuvered to transform his potential dismissal into a (voluntary) resignation. The *ly truong* of Khuong-Thuong, on the point of being dismissed after his implication in a 1902 tax fraud, obtained the signal favor of resignation in exchange for the return of the 40.5 piasters he had stolen. He was thus able to remain within the body of notables.[28]

It was undoubtedly the impossibility of building a career that explains the short average duration of the period in office of the 133 *ly truong* in our 1905 sample: the social objective was not to remain in the cul-de-sac but rather to get in and out as quickly as possible, so as to join the council in the best possible place. But how do we explain the changes that, from the 1920s on, led *ly truong* to keep their posts for between six and eight years and sometimes a good deal longer? How do we account for the tendency toward the constitution of power blocs?

The first reason is institutional: the famous communal reform of 1921 had dispossessed the existing notables of their main powers to the benefit of the lineages and clans represented by the *tôc biêu*. From the *ly truong*'s point of view, it was no longer necessary to quickly get into the council, which had lost most of its authority. In contrast, the second motivation—the prospect of material gain—became an even more powerful impulse given that the economic development of the suburbs of Hanoi brought with it infinite resources for a smart *ly truong*. There was no longer any reason for him to leave office quickly; on the contrary, it was in his interest to keep it as long as possible to maximize his profits. In all evidence, this evolution was due to the erosion of the role of the notables, or rather to the erosion of the latter's political power. Divested of their prestige and dispossessed of their responsibility for distributing communal land, a place among the notables did not exercise the same attraction as in the past: the council was no longer the site nor a unique form of power.

It was noted above that the *ly truong* came from the upper echelons of the registered taxpayers. In Yên-Lang in 1913, the two candidates for the post of *ly truong* possessed 600 and 1,100 piasters' worth of property.[29] When he was elected *ly truong* of Yên-Lang in 1917, Nguyên Bach enjoyed a patrimony estimated at 2,000 piasters.[30] In the 1920s, all *ly truong* possessed as much as 1,500 to 2,000 piasters.[31] At Quynh-Lôi, three candidates presented themselves at the election of 14 April 1914 to replace an outgoing *ly truong* who had judged it preferable to resign after a scandal. Trân Xuân Chung, thirty-two years of age, was elected by fifty-nine votes (out of fifty-nine bulletins and ninety registered taxpayers), defeating Nguyên Van Kiêm (twenty-five years of age) and Nguyên Van Châu, who was disqualified because he was "exempt" (he was in fact the *pho ly*). Chung and Kiêm had property estimated at 500 piasters and Châu at 1,000. This was no mean sum: 500 piasters was worth six tons of second-grade rice, enough to feed a family of five people for four years. It represented five years' salary for a street head, the counterpart of the *ly truong* in the city of Hanoi.[32] These candidates were no simple peasants: they had a little money. Having some money has always been a requirement for the *ly truong*'s position, which Minh-Mang had reiterated emphatically when he noted its primacy among the two qualities deemed necessary to the exercise of the *ly truong*'s functions: "to have property and be competent" (*vât luc cân can*). As district head, Nguyên Duy Thiên wrote in March 1910, without beating about the bush, that "the absence of education is no major obstacle to the job of *ly truong,* but the lack of money, indeed, could cause considerable difficulties." Certainly, it was better to have capital than an education, and very often in cases of conflict or electoral dispute the district head chose, by default, the richer candidate.

The *ly truong* was not, however, a "village cock" or large landowner. At Nhuoc-Công, a poor man like Nguyên Van Chi was elected only on his fourth attempt and possessed in all the sum of fifty piasters, enough to feed himself for four months (1906).[33] At Hoàng-Mai in 1902, the *ly truong* Nguyên San was in exactly the same situation. As far as land was concerned, it was rare that a *ly truong* owned a great deal. Like the land registers of the beginning of the nineteenth century, the numerous dossiers I have consulted make only a single mention of a *ly truong* who was a large landowner or a rich man. Nguyên Duc Nghinh has made an exhaustive study of the 254 notables and *chuc dich* of the forty-one communes of the district of Tu-Liêm (situated to the west of Hanoi); of these, one-third owned no land and a quarter had between one and three *mâu*. Of the sixty-five *xa truong* in his sample, based on data from the late eighteenth century, more than half owned less than three *mâu* (of which a quarter were landless) but none possessed more than twenty *mâu*. There was just one *xa truong* who was slightly better off than average (sixteen *mâu,* eight *sào* at Miêu-Nha).[34] Historically speaking, the *xa truong* belonged to the intermediate class of small landowners and were as such fully representative of the society for which they had the responsibility of leadership.

The *ly truong* of the late nineteenth century were also poorly paid. Available customary law books reveal figures that vary between eight to ten and thirty to fifty piasters, with the extreme examples of Vong-Thi village, whose *ly truong* received nothing at all, and Phuc Xa, offering the unusually high sum of ninety-six piasters.[35] Salaries were highly variable, both in terms of amount and in the manner of their payment (in cash or in communal land for three villages). Communal archives indicate that in 1908 the *ly truong* of Khuong-Thuong was paid nearly one *mâu* and five *sào* of land; thirty years later, in 1942, the customary law allocated to him a salary of fifty piasters.

There had evidently been a shift from payment in paddy to a fiduciary remuneration.[36] This shift was of economic significance but was first and foremost *political* in its ramifications: at the end of the period, the power of the *ly truong* tended to free itself from the land, including its symbolic dimension. The ritual of the land *granted* by the village, on an insecure basis and which had to be farmed by hand, the plot prettily named "the paddy field of the writing brush"—this piece of land had given way to a regime of salaries and an undeniable bureaucratization. This is perfectly in line with what I noted concerning the progressive lengthening of terms of office, which indicated a de facto emancipation of the *ly truong* with respect to notables who were becoming less powerful. To pinpoint a small but significant step in this direction, by the mid-1920s most villages paid "assignment expenses" when the *ly truong* had to travel more than five kilometers from the village, although this allowance was extremely modest (generally 0.4 piasters per day).[37] If we turn now to the village budgets, we note the existence of a category "salary expenses for commune officials," which corresponded to 5 percent of total expenditures.[38]

In general, *ly truong* salaries were low and unattractive: on average, they received from the village a payment of perhaps 30 piasters a year, that is to say, five times less than their counterparts, the street heads in Hanoi. This salary could not provide a living, as a rapid calculation demonstrates: 30 piasters a year makes on average a maximum of 3 piasters a month. In 1933, second-grade rice was worth 6.3 piasters per hundred kilograms; the salary of a *ly truong* allowed him to buy fifty kilograms of rice a month, enough for a family of five to live on for a fortnight.[39]

The *ly truong* was now in reality *neither truly rich nor truly poor*. He started off with a patrimony of perhaps 1,500 piasters but was paid a miserable salary and given access to a tiny patch of land. To be a *ly truong*, you had in fact to have some small sum of *initial capital*. This allowed one to carry out a veritable "electoral campaign" (with the purchase of votes) and reassure the notables but also, once elected, to cope with the different *risks* inherent to the profession: a *ly truong* who failed to collect all the taxes paid out of his own pocket if he did not want to be dismissed. Some villages even wrote this clause into the customary law books (as at Nam-Dông); in 1898, the *ly truong* of Quynh-Lôi had to borrow money to pay, himself, the 77.5 piasters that were short after tax collection, out of a total of 258.34. The responsibility (financial, certainly, but not exclusively, as we shall see) of the *ly truong* was no empty concept, and we should bear in mind this positive compensation for the hundreds of small exactions of which he was frequently guilty. To put it in trivial terms, the *ly truong* needed to build up a "war treasury" in case of ill fortune, if the taxes did not come in due to poor harvests or, just as frequently, due to the obstruction of a hostile family who refused to pay up to put him in difficulty. The fact that the *ly truong* had some money was in the interests both of the district mandarin (who could be sure of receiving the amount of tax due from the village) and the villagers (who could try, with limited risk, to avoid paying). By consequence, the possession or not of a "small capital sum" was often a determining criterion in the choice of a *ly truong*.

3. Becoming a *Ly Truong:* Election, Ploy, or Lineage Intrigue?

In theory the *ly truong* was elected at the communal house (*dinh*) by the *dân hàng xa,* who included all the registered taxpayers, men, in other words, between eighteen and fifty (or sixty) years of age, who had joined the village at least three generations previously and paid taxes.[40] All the registered taxpayers took part in the vote, except those in the category "exempt" (from paying tax, *dinh miên sai*), in other words, the officers and literati (*chuc sac*), soldiers, serving officials of the canton and commune (*ly dich*), and old people: in short, almost all the members of the Council of Notables. In theory, then, the *ly truong* was not chosen by the council but by the common citizens (*bach dinh*) of the commune, the healthy adult males (*trang dinh*), aged from twenty to fifty, who paid tax and were liable for corvée. There was, therefore, still in theory, potential renewal of the elite, as the *ly truong*, once elected, would join the council: nonnotables elected those who would become notables. But infringements of the rules were numerous, and "election lawsuits" (*don bâu*) that have reached us prove this quite clearly.

- *The first infringement* affected the electoral body. In a good number of cases, all the *ky muc* took part in the vote, without distinction of age or links in the village. At Quynh-Lôi, for example, old people (*lao nhiêu*) were allowed to vote at the election of Nguyên Van Oanh on 5 April 1920. There were thus 118 voters for 102 registered taxpayers, 16 too many. This irregularity having been denounced by Oanh's rival and brought to the attention of the French resident, the district head had to offer an explanation. And the explanation is significant because it allows us to see that the 16 extra voters were "honorable" people, previously registered taxpayers whose votes had little influence on the final result. This was both a wise and prudent observation.[41]
- *The second infringement* permitted the election of a *ly truong* who was not yet registered on the village tax roll (this was, let us note, a condition of eligibility). Several weeks before the poll, an older taxpayer was recategorized as an old person (exempt, therefore, and ineligible to vote), which made room on the tax roll for the future *ly truong*, who had been chosen in advance. This took place without modification of the total number of registered taxpayers and thus the total amount of the tax. From the outside, the operation appeared quite invisible. In August 1914, at Quynh-Lôi, Trân Xuân Dinh was thus moved up into the ranks of the old people, although he was only fifty-one years old (instead of the required sixty): here again, the district head ratified the fact, claiming that Dinh had already paid the banquet of honor (*khao vong*).[42] Manipulations sometimes went even further: at Hô-Khâu beside the West Lake, after denunciation of the *pho ly* who wished to replace his superior, it was discovered that the *ly truong* elected in April 1909 had assumed office under a false name. Under the name Tuât, he had in fact bought (under contract) the name of his cousin, who was at that time absent from the village, one Nguyên Van Nghênh. It was under this borrowed name that he was elected in April 1909. The inquiry proved, in addition, that the *pho ly* who had made the complaint was himself not registered on the tax roll.[43] At Yên-Lang, Nguyên Van Si was elected in February 1913 with a comfortable majority over his rival Nguyên Duy Hàn (sixty-one votes to forty-nine), but the latter pointed out, with reason, that Si was not registered in the commune. The district head made a decision, nominating Ngu-

yên Duy Hàn to the post of *ly truong* without further trial.[44] For the few affairs of this sort that have come to light, how many took place without the knowledge of the mandarins?

- *The third infringement,* a more expected one, affected the functioning of the poll. At the election of the *ly truong* of Thinh-Hào in 1914, fifty-five voting papers were received for fifty-one voters. The district mandarin did not burden himself with further procedures and had the vote taken again, by count of hands. This vote was subsequently annulled by the resident, but it is no less indicative of the real administration of the commune for that.[45] At Mai-Dông, in 1912, seven people voted using registered taxpayers' cards borrowed from a neighboring village, and one voter who had two cards presented himself twice to vote. What was less expected, and has never been noted until now, was the way in which the vote was conducted. Each voter filled out a voting paper, on which he wrote the name of his chosen candidate. In the archives, I had the good fortune to come across a unique series of such voting papers relating to the 25 January 1912 election of the *ly truong* of the village of Mai-Dông.[46] At the bottom of these small handwritten papers, which to my knowledge are the first to have been used in historical analysis of the structures of power in the village, large Chinese characters indicated the name of the chosen candidate. But what should most particularly be noted was the number, in characters, that figured at the head of each paper: this indicates nothing less than the voter number on the electoral roll. In other words, the vote was not anonymous: at the result of the election, it was easy to find out who had voted for whom, as the numbers corresponded to known registered taxpayers in the village. The election was thus considerably distorted by this procedure, in which all secrets were abolished.

All these infringements of the principle of the free election may be explained by the maneuvers of families which, in underhanded ways, tried to impose their own candidates: a *double* investment, in the event of success, as not only was immediate control over the village executive assured but also, in time, a further place at the council was gained. Clan struggles for the election of the *ly truong* have left impressive traces in the communal archives, which allow us to observe cases in which someone overstepped the mark, causing scandal, on which occasions the district head would intervene.⁴⁷ We will not speak here of all the ways in which family ties interfered in the process of electing the *ly truong*. A few cases will suffice, such as that of Duong Dinh Huy, who was *ly truong* of Vinh-Thuy from 1913 to 1923 because his family held all the important posts in the village: his father, Duong Van Viên, was the first notable (*tiên chi*); his paternal uncle, Duong Van Tao, was head of canton; and members of his lineage were also *pho ly* and second notable. Rightly convicted in 1921 for illegal sales of places of honor, Duong Dinh Huy was so well protected by his family that he was sentenced very lightly: a four-month suspension from office from January to April 1922.⁴⁸ One might mention the case of Nguyên Bach, *ly truong* of Yên-Lang, who owed all to his uncle Vu Liên, former district head of Hoàn-Long, who had become first notable of the commune and wielded enormous influence. Often it is family networks that explain the curious unanimity of elections: at Quynh-Lôi, the *ly truong* finally elected—Trân Xuân Chung—was not the richest of the three candidates but was credited with all the votes. This suspicious unanimity was explained in an anonymous complaint that shows the underside of the affair: Trân Xuân Chung, who had already briefly held the post in 1910, was in fact the nephew of Trân Xuân Tich, first notable since 1909, former *ly dich*, and brother-in-law of the former *ly truong*, Sai Van Vu.⁴⁹ Evidently, the support of a clan was preferable in the eyes of the voters to the possession of a fortune. More than money, family interests and the complex functioning of lineage strategies played a primordial role in the constitution of village oligarchies, oligarchies of which the *ly truong* was the official representative. Voter behavior was governed by political and not economic considerations.

But lines of family relationships are less interesting to us than the movements made by different families in their attempts to obtain a monopoly over communal office. In this respect, the case of Quynh-Lôi is once again particularly instructive: on 27 July 1909, Trân Xuân Tich was elected first notable of the village of Quynh-Lôi over Nguyên Van Duc. He was, however, the brother-in-law of the *ly truong* Sai Van Vu, elected the previous year over Nguyên Van Vinh, son-in-law of Nguyên Van Duc. Several months later the *pho ly* Nguyên Van Lac was replaced by Trân Xuân Truoc, a further relative of the new first notable Trân Xuân Tich and of the new *ly truong*. In two years, under the onslaught of intrigues and vote buying, the three principal posts in the commune's administration fell from one clan to another, from the Nguyên Van to the Trân Xuân.

In 1911, the wind changed again, when Nguyên Van Chinh became *ly truong* and favored the election of his brother Nguyên Van Thuc to the post of *pho ly:* this time the *ly truong*'s father was the first notable and his father-in-law was the second notable. The Nguyên Van had once again taken charge. This example allows us to appreciate just how relative was our traditional fine theoretical ordering of the Council of Notables. At Quynh-Lôi, the pursuit of communal power gave rise to an unquenchable hatred between the Nguyên Van and Trân Xuân lineages: it came up every year, in all the documents, and sometimes in extreme forms, such as in 1909 when, having gained office, Trân Xuân Tich managed to arrange for the demotion and sentencing to three years at hard labor of his old enemy Nguyên Van Duc, who had secretly attempted to place in his house a series of false documents aimed at implicating him in rebel conspiracies.[50] This clan struggle was terrible and brought with it a crowd of details that are impossible to reproduce here, but all bore a close relation to the question of power and, more and more, to the money that power generated. Murder, indeed, was committed to get rid of an irritating *pho ly*.[51] It is not easy now to describe the tense atmosphere of the village of Quynh-Lôi, to write this history made of "human flesh" (Marc Bloch), to relate the series of traps, ruses, schemes, intrigues, and low maneuvering that constituted the backdrop to the relations between the Nguyên Van and the Trân Xuân. Elsewhere, and later on, we may find their echo in the implacable struggle to which the Vu Dinh and the Trinh Ba gave themselves in the semi-imaginary novel by Nguyên Khac Truong charmingly entitled *Of Men and as Many Ghosts and Witches*.[52]

From the point of view of the upper levels of the administration, that is, the mandarin in charge of the district (*tri huyên*), the real conditions of the election were of little importance. Infringements on the polls and the troubled jostling of the lineages were not exceptions to the rule: they made the rule. Seen from above, from the mandarin's

Office	Nguyên Van Family	Year	Trân Family
First Notable	Nguyên Van Duc	in 1909 was replaced by	Trân Xuân Tich
Ly truong	Nguyên Van Vinh	in 1908 was replaced by	Sai Van Vu
Pho ly	Nguyên Van Lac	in 1909 was replaced by	Trân Xuân Truoc

offices from which the sixty-odd villages of the district were simultaneously run, indulgence was a sensible option for a *district head,* for whom the important thing was to deal with matters as quickly as possible. The basic rules of the mandarin administration required that "small matters" be dealt with in five days, "matters of average importance" in ten days, and "large matters" in twenty days. To settle things quickly, the mandarin had to delegate and was less interested in formal legitimacy than in the docility and competence of his village subordinates. In 1890, the deputy head of the canton (*pho tông*) of Thuong (the eastern part of the West Lake) was the object of numerous complaints. In a rare move, the *district head* decided to dismiss him but explained clearly that this decision was not at all motivated by the exactions of this official but, more pragmatically, because no one in the district obeyed him anymore.[53] How could he administer under such conditions?

4. From the *Dinh* to the Paddy Field: The Role and Powers of the *Ly Truong*

The hidden powers of the notables were real, but they must not lead us into thinking that the *ly truong*'s role was simply that of an executive of the council. As, moreover, most notables were never other than former *ly truong* or communal officials themselves, there is a certain audacity in imagining that they could have had enough prestige or credit to control a person of the social and administrative importance of the *ly truong*. Second, the *ly truong* certainly owed his position to one village clan or another, but did this mean that he was "a simple puppet agitated by the commune between herself and the mandarin"?[54] Nothing is less sure, and the concrete examples cited below demonstrate this clearly. In reality, the idea of a *ly truong* as a simple factotum of the Council of Notables has its origin in the academic distinction, too rigid and too Western, between "those who deliberate" and "those who execute," with the presupposition that the former control the latter. This distinction has no basis in any precise Vietnamese reality, except perhaps the regard brought by French jurists into villages said to be "traditional." The concept of a separation of tasks and, a fortiori, of powers was foreign to the political processes of the village. Moreover, the inclusion of the *ly truong* in the family networks and the jostling of lineages is sufficient evidence of the fact: it is not the separation of powers we can see but on the contrary the will to achieve a *unity of command.* Power in the village tended toward concentration, not distribution. Thus, there is a level of contradiction in the assertion, on the one hand, that the *ly truong* was a simple executive of the council (with, understood, the idea of a separation of tasks) and, on the other hand, that the council made every effort to place, as *ly truong,* a man loyal to the dominant clan. If he was really a simple executive, what need would one have to bring the *ly truong* into one's camp? What need would one have to push forward a brother, a cousin, or a son-in-law? The horizon of a family clan was in reality the whole range of village powers and a unity of direction. Let us not underestimate, therefore, the role and authority of the *ly truong.* It was he, and not the notables, who ran the village on a day-to-day basis. It was he, further, who had at his disposition essential nonmaterial goods: information, local intelligence, and a variety of small services that were as decisive when they could be offered as when they had already been so.

To define the role of the *ly truong* presents the difficulties of variety, variability, and multiformity and must often be seen in terms of context or occasion. An affair that had never before arisen in a village would be dealt with by the *ly truong,* and the case became "jurisprudence": this type of affair was henceforth the *ly truong*'s business alone. Let us first try to give some order to the diversity by defining three essential spaces in which the *ly truong*'s power was deployed.

Unexpectedly, it was above all the *police role* of the *ly truong* to which most matters that arose in Hanoi's villages between 1884 and 1930 related. Along with the *tuân truong,* when there was one, the *ly truong* was responsible for the organization of the village guard (*tuân*), for the incidental organization of the harvest, and almost always for the recruitment of the watchmen.[55] At Nhât-Tân in 1908, he presided over the assembly of the *giap,* which decided to nominate twenty-eight watchmen (seven per *giap*) to be divided between the village and the canton.[56] The night watchmen were nominated for a year and paid with "the rice dew" (*lua-suong* or *suong-tuc*), that is, a sheaf or swath (*luom*) of rice taken from the first harvest of each *sào* of privately owned paddy fields, except those of notables, who were exempt.[57] If certain villages, like Nghi-Tàm, authorized payments either in rice or in money (customary law book of 1938, article 63), most of them had substituted "money dew" for rice dew, and villagers paid their due not in kind but in ringing, cursing cash. From the 1920s on, the price seemed to stabilize around 0.6 piasters per *mâu,* to which a further piaster per brick house and half a piaster per thatched house should be added.[58] In some cases, the watchmen received only this sum, in others they received additional salaries,[59] and sometimes they received only half (0.3 piasters per *mâu*), while the rest filled up the communal cash box (at Ngoc-Xuyên, for example). In all, the cost of the village guard represented, in 1924, 6 percent of expenditures, with the highest rates in the extensive villages of the periphery: 14 percent at Yên Lang Ha and 15 percent at Phuc-Xa. It could happen—as at Thanh-Nhàn in 1904—that the *ly truong* did not call upon one or two of the watchmen and appropriated for himself their allotted rice dew. This maneuver was nonetheless risky, as the service provided by the watchmen implied the responsibility of those who organized it, as much the serving officials as the watchmen themselves; in case of theft, they had to compensate the victim.

> One night in April 1893, about ten thieves entered the house of one Ngoan of the village of Hoàng-Mai and stole from him, according to the district head's report: *"three female buffalo, one cooking pot, and six copper plates, two basins, some clothes and some religious articles"*; the guard arrived very late on the scene of the crime and, the next day, the district head immediately sent to prison the canton head and his assistant, the *ly truong* and the *pho ly*; they were freed several days later, having paid to Ngoan the sum of ninety-eight piasters, corresponding to the value of the objects stolen from his house.[60]

This power to nominate watchmen and organize the guard was more important than one might believe, as the security of the village was at stake. Regular checks were made, and fines rained down on the *ly truong*'s head if the guard was incomplete or if, as often happened, the watchmen were asleep (Yên-Lang in 1910). In case of attempted pillage, the guard raised the alarm, and the *ly truong* had to run there straightaway. Some enjoyed real success, like the *ly truong* of Thinh-Hào, who managed, with the watchmen, to arrest seven bandits who were subsequently sentenced to three to nine years of hard labor.[61] The question of the protection of property, private and collective, gave the *ly truong* a degree of power that we must not underestimate. From there to the role of police assistant there was but a single step, and this step was often taken. In 1919, we are witness to a veritable "*ly truong* commando," who carried out an inquiry and finally apprehended a clandestine Mont de Piété situated in the village of Thai-Hà.[62]

The second function of the *ly truong* was *fiscal.* It was the *ly truong* in person who had to maintain the tax register, call the villagers, and very often lay siege to this household or that to get the occupant to pay his dues. The theme of the grasping *ly truong* who defrauds the tax system and keeps the money for himself, who taxes the exempt and raises the amount owed by the others, who steals and robs, is a classic one in village literature and certainly contains a good deal of truth. But it does not exhaust the issue and above all does not explain the *reason* for these exactions. To point to greed for gain is a little short, especially as we know that the *ly truong* was not the most needy in the village and, moreover, risked a great deal by deceiving his world. Here, again, we find in the classical description a real contradiction: it is asserted that the *ly truong* was a simple and modest executive, but at the same time it is noted that he enjoyed sufficient authority to commit thousands of exactions (as the complaints testify). If the *ly truong* was a minor figure, why was he left to do this? Things were more complicated, but before looking at them let us measure the risk taken by the *ly truong,* given that, in the event that the taxes were not paid, his punishment was immediate.

- The first risk was his removal from office pure and simple, which, let us recall, annulled his hopes of joining the ranks of the notables. In 1899, the district head succeeded after numerous difficulties in collecting the whole tax payment due from the district of Vinh-Thuân, apart from the two hundred piasters corresponding to the village of Khuong-Thuong. He had the village buffaloes seized, but, as he started to sell them, the village inhabitants interrupted and freed all the animals. The following day, the *ly truong* lost his post and the village was fined.[63]
- The second risk for the *ly truong* was to pay the tax from his own pocket, from the small initial capital that had favored his election. Unfortunately for one *ly truong*—one Bai, *ly truong* of Khuong-Thuong between 1908 and 1912—this happened three times. To

pay the tax, he had on several occasions to borrow money at interest, notably from an Indian in Hanoi, who, like many of his compatriots, specialized in this lucrative activity. Crippled with debt, the *ly truong* Bai handed over his stamps and the tax roll to his old mother before taking flight in November 1912. No one knows what happened to him, as his name does not reappear in later archives. He had taken the risk of managing the village's fiscal affairs but had lost: this failure condemned him not only to the loss of all hope of social promotion but, worse still, to exile and all the reprobation that entailed.[64]

To have capital and to substitute it—provisionally—for that of poor payers was the only way of avoiding this sort of unpleasant situation. The tax owed by Khuong-Thuong amounted to 200 piasters, and Bai could not have had property amounting to a great deal more than this: if, hypothetically, we imagine that one-third of the inhabitants did not pay, three years would suffice to ruin him. All in all, Bai was not rich enough to remain in office. At the same time as he borrowed, he had sought to fill his "war treasury" by means of a number of classic exactions. From 1908 to 1912, the archives clearly show three testified spoliations: defrauding of a testament (1.5 *mâu* of good paddy land), encroachment onto communal land (2 *mâu*), and confiscation of the salary of the teacher (*huong su*).[65] If to that we add the daily quota of small services sold here and there and other business about which the archives are silent, we may see that he was visibly on course for self-enrichment. Or, rather, he was attempting to escape from the terrible spiral of debt and usury. His case was not isolated: in 1903, the *ly truong* of Yên-Lang had, for the same reasons, to borrow 150 piasters from a trader in Bamboo Street in Hanoi.[66] As we have seen, it was often by necessity—to make good the tax collection—that the *ly truong* had to use ill-recommended methods. He was constantly chasing after money. If, indeed, he only had to worry about state taxes, his situation would have been tolerable; but we must not forget—although we lack the sources—that the whole internal fiscal and financial situation of the village depended on him. This included the sale of places, symbolic banquets and the "entry fee" payable on the taking of an office or the receipt of a title (*khao*), fines, land rents, transfer fees, the payment of the rice dew, occasional levies in case of dike rupture or flood, the sale of exemptions from watch-mens' duties, and so on. In contrast to the idealized description that has too often dominated, we must affirm that much money circulated within the village and it was, again, the *ly truong* who found himself right in the middle of this financial network, with for him the permanent risk of having to substitute his own fortune for that of people who did not pay or who paid late. We may understand that the initial capital was rarely sufficient.

The best way of avoiding these troubles was thus to increase the amount of the tax collected so as to *anticipate* nonpayment and preserve a margin of security. This was the method used by most *ly truong*, notably the predecessor of Bai. He collected taxes on all the private paddy land in the village at the higher rate (first class), even on those fields that, because of their yields or the quality of their rice, should have been categorized as second or third class and taxed accordingly. He pocketed the difference between the sum collected and the real fiscal burden, as it was registered on the roll. Denounced by a villager (this was a further, supplementary risk) and interrogated by the *tri huyên*, the *ly truong* made the following simple and, all things considered, logical reply. The day before tax collection, the tax had been paid on only 64 *mâu* out of 230 of paddy land in the village; by taxing each *mâu* without distinction at the higher rate (1.5 piasters), it was possible to make good the losses incurred by the 166 *mâu* that remained unpaid. The rate was less important than the amount, and this point of view was shared by both the district head and the French fiscal authorities. In this affair, the *ly truong* was simply and quite gently reprimanded but not punished. Of the money pocketed by the *ly truong*, we will never really know how much he used for tax purposes and how much he kept for himself (for the following fiscal season, the payment of fines, the compensation of watchmen, or the repair of a fence, a well, or a canal).

We should stress here that fiscal manipulations, known to all, represented a sort of "risk salary." In other words, the exactions were not due to the situation of the *ly truong* but to his *responsibility*, a quite different state of affairs. To take onto oneself the risk of punishment, of dismissal, of being beaten to death,[67] exiled, or quite simply of losing one's fortune, and to do all that for a miserable salary, that is what justified, in everyone's eyes, the little indelicacies of the *ly truong*. After all, had one ever seen an equitable allocation of tax in a village? Was fiscal overcharging so strange or so scandalous? It is unlikely because, in general, the *ly truong* made the fiscal assessment by means of a very simple and unique calculation: he added the land taxes, the corvées, and the head taxes together and divided the total by the number of registered taxpayers, whatever their status or fortune. At Nam-Dông, Trân Van Chuc thus divided among the registered taxpayers of the village the 317.02 piasters required by the district head, which amounted to 2.05 piasters per inhabitant; he paid the tax to the district head and asked him to pressure those who were slow to pay up, as he had advanced the money and was not sure he would be able to cover his costs.[68] At Co-Xa, on a sandbank in the Red River, Nguyên Viêt Tuân went even further. According to a complaint from the inhabitants, confirmed by the district head's inquiry, he started by confiscating the register of taxpayers and land (normally kept at the communal house), and then he refused to post the list of registered taxpaying and nonregistered inhabitants. The paupers of the village (*cung dinh*) saw themselves wronged by the allocation of tax, as apparently Nguyên Viêt Tuân made use of the confusion, knowingly created and maintained by himself, to oblige the nonregistered inhabitants (*ngoai tich*) to pay more than the registered taxpayers (*nôi tich*). The land tax was no better distributed because he had simply divided the taxable land area by the number of inhabitants (registered or not).[69] In short, iniquity was the rule, and the little attentions of the *ly truong* were of no great importance, especially if they allowed the village to avoid problems with the district mandarin.

I do not wish to imply that these exactions were passively accepted by the population. On the contrary, the documentary basis of this study is largely composed of the very numerous *complaints* written by the villagers themselves. But it was not so much the nature of power in the village that engendered the anger of the inhabitants but rather the *abuse* of that power. Payable services, trivial arrangements, and financial and fiscal deals were accepted but within a certain limit. Beyond that limit, complaints, scandals, and denunciations provoked an inquiry by the mandarin and finally reached the archive. Before this limit, it was quite simply the daily life of the village and the normal distribution of power in rural Vietnamese society.[70]

The third essential function of the *ly truong* was evidently *administrative*. He was, by definition, the man elected to represent the village to the mandarin, and the following formula was always to be found at the head of the chapter on the *ly truong* in village customary law books: "the ly truong is the representative of the village community for the execution of administrative affairs at mandarin level."[71] Symbolically, the district head (*tri huyên*) was always present at the ceremony during which a newly elected *ly truong* would receive his warrant and his stamp or chop (*triên*). This was the mark of his power and his position, halfway between the village and the district. Curiously, for reasons unknown (perhaps bad luck, quite simply) I was unable to find a single *ly truong*'s warrant. By contrast, the trace of his chop appears on all official documents of the commune, which were written in roman letters and, in the center, in "ancient-style" Chinese characters. To possess chops was so important that, according to the Governor Hoàng Trong Phu, the protracted shortage of *deputy* heads of canton and commune (*pho tông* and *pho ly*, 205 vacant posts in 1925 in the single province of Hà-Dông) can be explained first and foremost by the fact that these assistants held no chop. People were less willing to present themselves for election because these two posts were quite unattractive: no chops, no power.[72]

To possess a chop was important, and we recall that the *ly truong* Bai entrusted his chop to his mother before taking flight. We touch here upon the crucial question of certification but also on that of taxes, as, in theory, after payment the *ly truong* had to give the taxpayer a receipt decorated with the mark of his chop. It is superfluous to dwell on the multiple occasions on which their receipts were not stamped in order to enforce a second tax payment. In the course of their *daily* lives, villagers had continually to call upon the *ly truong* and obtain from him the famous "stamp" from which he drew one of his powers. For example, a registration of births, marriages, and deaths (*état civil*) required a payment to the *ly truong*: one *ly truong* even received two piasters to certify the good health of a woman suspected by the *tri huyên*, after denunciation and quite correctly, of being a victim of the plague (Thai-Hà, 1908).[73]

But the main thing was, of course, the certification of land transactions. Here the power of the *ly truong* was vast, as in reality the status of this or that plot of land depended only on him. The street heads (*phô truong*, the urban equivalent of the *ly truong*) in Hanoi had lost this power when in May 1903 all the communal land was handed over to the municipality, and this was the departure point for their irreparable decline. In the countryside, in contrast, this function remained entirely in the hands of the *ly truong*. Acts of transfer were certainly registered by a receiver, but he did this on the faith . . . in the *ly truong*'s chop. No one controlled him because it was specifically the *ly truong*'s role to do this. If he certified a plot of land as private, it was henceforth perfectly alienable and the owner (or self-confessed owner) could rent it or sell it. One Dinh, an inhabitant of Rice Street, in April 1904 bought a plot of land in the village of Thai-Hà, a plot that the *ly truong* had certified as *private* but a subsequent inquiry showed to be *communal,* thus inalienable.[74] The power to certify was one of the essential foundations of the system of land encroachment: it was by this means that Lê Ba Ngu, cousin of the *ly truong* and son of First Notable Lê Ba Doàn, had usurped 1.5 *mâu* of communal land at Thinh-Hào.[75] At Thai-Hà, the *ly truong* permitted the sale to Nguyên Van Huy of a house situated on a plot of communal land (for sixty piasters): once the transaction was signed and registered, it was impossible to go back. The *ly truong* was berated by the *tri huyên,* but he set, as usual, to his game of pleading ignorance and avoiding blame by asserting that he had been deceived by the vendor.[76]

In all of these cases, affairs such as these have reached us because they touched upon communal land, theoretically inalienable, but we should realize that all transactions—above all, private transactions—followed the same procedural rules. This was the case, for example, for acts of land mortgage. Rather than multiplying our examples, let us content ourselves with explaining the principle upon which they worked.[77] When person A borrowed money from person B, this loan was secured by some property or goods, the ownership title of which was handed over to the creditor. Recognition of the debt was signed by both parties and countersigned by the *ly truong,* who placed on it his chop. Clearly it was the *ly truong*'s chop that gave this document its value, and all documents recognizing debts that have been unearthed in the archives bear this mark. In case of nonpayment, the *ly truong* passed a copy on to the *tri huyên,* who enforced the law, having the mortgaged property seized. Here the *ly truong* played a role similar to that of a notary, and, seen from the village, this role was extremely important because it touched upon a part of the law of which the *ly truong* was, all in all, the *guarantor.*

The question this immediately raises is the following: were "notables," as in China, moneylenders? Was this one of the sources of their power and strength? In truth, no document allows us to respond categorically to the question: of all the communal archives I have been through (more than 210 large dossiers), none contained a single recognition of debts by a villager to a notable nor indeed any process of *local* indebtedness. Evidently, this is quite curious, and we should be extremely wary, given that the absence of documentation in no way signifies the absence of fact: these papers were private, and they may well not have been archived (but why then were certain other papers archived?). It is not easy to decide one way or another. My opinion, in this uncertain situation, is that the evidence we have does not point in the direction of a thesis affirming the existence of "moneylending notables." First, we are certain that, in Red River delta villages, notables were not large landowners (which distances us from our Chinese reference, it should be noted in passing). Nor did they necessarily possess sizable sums of capital or land rent incomes—surpluses to lend. Furthermore, nothing proves that they were richer than anyone else, that they had grabbed, for example, resources linked to nonagricultural activities (commercial or artisanal). Finally, we should remember that these notables had simply come from the local middle peasantry and it is difficult to see how these former commune officials could suddenly have come across enough money to lend out at interest. Evidently, none of this is certain, but in the absence of tangible proof let us suspend judgment and remain with the idea of a village financial network that engaged everyone, was fluid, and left the village at least as often as it entered it.

Conclusions

It is not easy to draw conclusions about this question of "power in the village." The real form of the *ly truong*'s designation, the cul-de-sac nature of his office, his fortune, the sale of places of honor, illegal registrations on the roll, all of this shows that there existed in the village a certain mobility, administrative and social, limited, or rather *complicated,* by the play of lineages and precedence rules. The little-known stratum of the middle classes, which were neither poor nor honored, played a capital role in the process of elite formation, and we urgently await monographic studies that will help us to understand these people better. In conclusion, I would like to widen the scope of this study and place its results in their historiographical context. The documents themselves point in this direction, allowing us understandings not only of the details of village life but, much more importantly, of the workings of an entire political system, not only in the colonial period but for centuries before that. Why should we not imagine, on the basis of the very flimsy documentation available for the preceding periods, that this system (with the inevitable ebb and flow of structural detail) worked on the same principle? We should not proceed from the assumption that there is any fundamental difference between grassroots history and the grand history of nations. On the contrary, the first should inform us, in a very profound sense, of the second. It is, then, not for the troubling pleasure of a rather vain exercise in criticism that I wish to open this study to the historical debates that have defined our understanding of Vietnamese rural society. It is simply to demonstrate the dangers of a globalizing vision, "seen from above," and the advantages of this approach, which attempts to situate our vision "below," at the level of the document, the event, and individual lives. In an attempt to synthesize, let us regain a little height.

If we wish to reach a meaningful understanding of the nature of power in the village, we should have a clear idea from where we speak. As I suggested earlier, our documents in no sense allow us to posit a separation between "those who decide" and "those who execute." To affirm this is to return to the idea of a communal equilibrium, a "moral economy," a conception of village political life of which the inadequacy is most clearly demonstrated in the person and office of the *ly truong*. This idea was founded on the assumption of a certain coherence of political structure whereby a homogeneous and hierarchically organized group of notables managed village affairs, in the interests of all, through the person of their straw man, the *ly truong*. This last was not the notables' man but only a fraction of that: he was the man of a clan, of a family, of a lineage.

This observation, as we take a little distance from the nitty-gritty of village politics and seek to understand the workings of this system of power, leads us to a new and rather surprising issue, which has the advantage of summing up our argument: why was the *ly truong* elected and not appointed by the Council of Notables? If he really was the council's executive agent, why was there any need in the eighteenth century (1735) to move from appointment by the mandarin to election by the registered taxpayers of the village? After all, one could just as well have kept the appointment system, removing it from the hands of the *tri huyên* and placing it in those of the notables themselves. This did not happen because, as we now know, the council was never a unified body. In view of this reality, which I hope has been sufficiently demonstrated in this short essay, I would like to risk two hypotheses.

The first hypothesis is the following: it is possible that since its institution the election of the *ly truong* always functioned as a "political test," like a revelation in the public arena of the relations of strength among the clans of the village. The election had the incomparable advantage of allowing the village, every three years, to take stock of the situation. Reading the archives, it is not always possible to see how the alliances came together, but for contemporaries the election of such and such a *ly truong* signified the victory of such and such a faction. It was not a trivial village head denuded of authority who was elected; it was not a subordinate thirsty for social ascension; it was the representative of the clan who, for the moment, had won. We should immediately add that it would be wrong to understand these clans or lineages as constituted groups, members of the same family, or subgroups of brothers-in-law, cousins, sons-in-law, and nephews. Detailed studies are unavailable, but it would be interesting to carry out research so as to discover whether, as I think, these clans corresponded to what were called, not so long ago, "social classes." Let us be clear: if at Quynh-Lôi we were able to establish the importance of family clans, it was above all because the members of a family all had the same name (Trân Xuân versus Nguyên Van) and also because the archives note in black and white, here and there, lines of relationship among the obscure individuals who tore each other apart over power between 1905 and 1925. Without the coherence of family names and the exceptional volubility of the archives, we would doubtless have seen and understood nothing of this struggle between persons. But we should beware of this documentary "divine surprise." Certainly it has allowed us to establish a perfect coincidence between family and clan, but it should not cut off other avenues of research: coincidence of fortune, interests, landholding, and, in general, social standing. The clan that took power was certainly also a defined social group, and *we should not forget that sometimes the poorest classes managed to take power.*

In fact, as the council was basically made up of members of the intermediate classes, not the elite, and as all the registered taxpayers voted (thus, simple peasants, too), the poorest had a chance. It was not all played out in advance in favor of the rich; power was never acquired, and—this is the second hypothesis—the election of the *ly truong* was thus not only a "political test" (at that date, what was the favor of this clan or that) but also a "social test" (at that date, what were the relations of social strength in the village). The situation of the *ly truong* was thus a sort of litmus test of the political and social state of the commune. Here the dividing lines were not *horizontal*, separating administrative levels or "rungs of power" (*peasant → official → notable*), which would be as many stages in the lives of sociologically undifferentiated individuals. They were, on the contrary, *vertical*. From top to bottom, from the notable to the peasant, dividing lines determined the nature and functioning of power in the village. These were the different social groups that spread out in strips—from the paddies to the Dinh—across the whole political space of the village.

NOTES

École Française d'Extrême-Orient, Hanoi. I would like to thank Andrew Hardy for translating this essay.

1. Jan Breman, *The Shattered Image: Construction and Deconstruction of the Village in Colonial Asia* (Dordrecht: Foris Publications, 1988), 5, CASA Comparative Asian Studies, no. 2.

2. A normative classification, by no means false but purely theoretical, may be found, for example, in P. Souvignet, *Variétés tonkinoises* (Hà-Nôi: Schneider, 1903), 188–93; or in Phan Huy Lê and Vu Minh Giang, *Cac gia tri truyên thông và con nguoi Viêt-Nam hiên nay* (Hanoi: Nha Xuat Ban The Gioi, 1996), 164 n. 1, 309–10. For colonial era authors, consult Nguyên Van Phong, *La société vietnamienne de 1882 à 1902* (Paris: PUF, 1971), 96–109.

3. For example see Nguyen Van Huyên in *De l'institution des castes dans commune annamite* (Hanoi: Taupin, 1938), 59–64, Institut Indochinois pour l'Etude de l'Homme, compte-rendus des séances de l'année, 1938. The author distinguished ten different classes, but what was true for the exceptional case of Yên-So was not so elsewhere.

4. An attentive reading of the customary books should instill a sense of prudence. Let us take a random example, that of the village of Yên-Lang. Article 4 of the customary book of 1917 indicates that "the village possesses few educated people but is inhabited above all by masons (*thô môc*) who work here or leave to join up as soldiers; under King Minh-Mang, a person of the Pham family exercised the functions of commander in Son-Nam (Son-Nam *tông trân hiêp trân*); under Duy-Tân, another was vice preceptor at the court (*thai tu thiêu*

bao); and, finally, under Thành-Thai, a person from our village became district head (*tri huyên*) and then prefect (*tri phu*). At present, we have no graduates of the great examinations but only a bachelor (*tu tai*) from the Pham lineage." Thus, in one century we find at Yên-Lang only three people who occupied important offices. A single villager possessed a diploma, and even this was only a modest one. As we may imagine, the Council of Notables of this typical Hanoi village was hardly overcrowded with dignitaries and officers. See "Customary Book of the Village of Yên-Lang," drawn up by Vu Liên Luoc in the second year of Khai-Dinh (1917), manuscript in characters kept at the Han-Nôm Institute under the reference A.2901, article 4.

5. National Archives Center (NAC), Résidence de Hà-Dông, E6, 758, *Relevé des autorités communales de la zone suburbaine, 1905*. This document takes the form of handwritten pages indicating, village by village, the authorities in place, their previous posts, and the number of notables, registered taxpayers (villagers resident in the village for three generations who paid tax and, by so doing, had access to communal charges and communal land), and non-registered taxpayers. This document is precious in that it is both unique and precise: for each village, the name and date of accession of each member of the Council of Notables is indicated. Furthermore, as the date of birth is often mentioned, allowing us to calculate the age of each of these people, we have before us in fact a detailed statement, almost a spontaneous snapshot of the official village elite group. These figures are not of course perfect, particularly with regard to registered taxpayers, which the village had an interest in hiding so as to pay less tax. They nevertheless correspond perfectly to data from the land tax registers which, near the city, were carefully checked. One may further imagine that the dissimulations, if they are confirmed, affected different villages in the same way, which would thus permit comparisons expressed in terms of proportions. See NAC, Résidence de Hà-Dông, 4053, *Rôle d'impôts fonciers, 1902*.

6. The correlation between the two series (inhabitants and notables) is remarkable: 0.804. A perfect correlation would have been 1, a noncorrelation 0, an inverse correlation −1.

7. If we set aside the 13 canton heads and deputy heads among the 117 officials in our sample, 104 serving officials remain: half were *ly truong*, 31 percent were *pho ly*, and 19 percent were *huong truong*. There were of course exceptional cases, like the village of Vinh-Thuy, which in 1913 had only one *ly truong* but four *pho ly*. The notables put pressure on the *tri huyên* to keep them on, but the latter asked them to return to a single *pho ly*; finally, as always, a compromise was reached and Vinh-Thuy kept two *pho ly*. NAC, Résidence de Hà-Dông, 1728, *Elections des pho-ly et ly-truong de Vinh-Thuy, 1902–1927*.

8. These embraced nonetheless 126 cases out of a total of 416 (one-third).

9. Unfortunately, documents concerning later periods are few and far between. We have been able to find only a single global summary for the *ly truong*; this document indicates that the *ly truong* in office in 1938 entered at an average age of 34.6, a similar age, therefore, to that established for the year 1905 (34.4). This stability is all the more remarkable for the fact that it was

maintained over time for positions that themselves underwent very profound modification. NAC, Résidence de Hà-Dông 764: *Contrôle des autorités communales du huyên de Hoàn-Long, 1938–1942*. This average was calculated by myself on the basis of fifty-seven villages.

10. The margin of error (*écart type*) (2.04) is, on average, very low, indicating the existence of very few exceptions. The dates of start and end of office are most often noted in the archives, which means that we do not have to have recourse, once again, to the five-village sample. The data are calculated from the list of "major notables" who exercised, in the past, communal functions. We could not use the list of "serving officials" in 1905 because by definition this list could not give the end of the period in office, which was current. Let us specify, too, that we have counted here all the communal officials, even in cases in which an individual occupied two or three successive posts—a canton head is only counted in circumstances where he was a former commune official.

11. Quan-La (1885–94), Xuân-Tao (1875–83), Hô-Khâu (1889–97), Liêu-Giai (1885–92), Luong-Yên (1886–96), and Vinh-Phuc (1891–1904).

12. Vu Dinh Binh (Yen Thai, September 1920–August 1940), 19.9 years in office; Hoang Van Thai (Dai Yen, November 1923–December 1942), 19.1 years; Dô Dinh Phâm (An-Hoà, July 1927–May 1942), 14.8 years; Duong Van Thân (Vinh-Thuy, January 1928–July 1942), 14.5 years; Nguyên Van Vân (Giang-Vo, November 1931–September 1942), 10.8 years; Nguyên Dinh Khanh (Vong-Thi, June 1931–December 1939, 8.5 years); Nguyên Van Biêu (Công-Vi, February 1934–January 1941), 6.9 years.

13. The average obtained from this December 1942 hypothesis is 4.6 years (3.16 in 1905), but of course it has no meaning, as it takes into account absurd cases such as that of a *ly truong* who, elected in October 1942, had only three months' service to his name, while he evidently remained in office a great deal longer.

14. Nguyên Van Tu (Nam-Dông, since April 1919), 23.7 years; Phuong Van Quan (Xuân-Tao, since June 1925), 17.5 years; Nguyên Duy Sinh (Thinh-Quang, since November 1926), 16.1 years; Nguyên Viêt Hoi (Thai-Hà, since December 1927), 15 years; Bui Van Kê (Ngoai-Châu, since September 1930), 12.2 years; Dinh Van Thuoc (Hô-Khâu, since January 1931), 11.9 years; Lê Ba Du (Thinh-Hào, since January 1931), 11.9 years; Dao Van Hê (Thu-Lê, since May 1931), 11.6 years; Luu Van Chi (Xuân-Biêu, since July 1931), 11.4 years; Ngô Quang Kim (Ngoc-Hà, since February 1932), 10.8 years; Nguyên Khac Hôi (Linh-Quang, since August 1932), 10.3 years.

15. This situation is highly reminiscent of that of street heads (*phô truong*) in the same period. See Philippe Papin, "Hanoi et ses territoires: Espace colonial et espaces sociaux," *Bulletin de l'École Française d'Extrême-Orient* 82 (1995): 201–30.

16. On the evolution of the role of the *ly truong* and communal affairs in relation to the central authorities, see Vu Quôc Thông, *Phap chê su Viêt Nam* (Saigon: Tu Sach Dai Hoc Sài Gon, 1973), 158–254.

17. *Dai-Viêt Su Ky Toàn Thu*, 2:297: Rule of the twenty-seventh day of the

eleventh month of the *Thuân-Thiên* year (1428), and Viêt Su Thông Giam Cuong Muc Chinh Biên, 20 vols, vol. ix (volume 13 of the original); Hanoi: NXB Su Hoc, p. 13 of this volume and p. 873 of entire collection.

18. *Dai-Viêt Su Ky Toàn Thu*, 2:411.

19. Cited in Phan Dai Doan and Nguyên Quang Ngoc, eds., *Kinh nghiêm tô chuc quan ly nông thôn Viêt-Nam trong lich su* (Hà Nôi: Chinh Tri Quôc Gia, 1994), 16.

20. *Dai-Viêt Su Ky Toàn Thu*, 2:503, 515.

21. *Lich Triêu Hiên Chuong Loai Chi*, 3 vols. (Hanoi: NXB khoa hoc xa hoi, 1992), 1: 480.

22. *Dai Nam Thuc Luc-chinh biên* (Hanoi: NXB Su Hoc, 1963), 2:84. For the sinicization of Vietnam in the nineteenth century, there are evidently numerous sources. We will restrict ourselves here to noting the decree of 1825, by which the court ordered that all names of villages and cantons should be written in Chinese (*han*), banning all Sino-Vietnamese characters (*nôm*).

23. For precise examples, see Nguyên Minh Tuong, *Cai cach hành chinh duoi triêu Minh-Mênh* (Hanoi: NXB khoa hoc xa hoi, 1995), 161.

24. This is according to the edict of the fourteenth year of the reign of Tu-Duc. See Nguyên Tu Chi, "Le Lang traditionnel au Bac Bô, sa structure organisationnelle, ses problèmes," in *Le village traditionnel* (Hanoi: Thê Gioi, 1993), 109. Less well known but just as important, by the same author, see "Dân chu làng xa," in *Gop phân nghiên cuu van hoa và tôc nguoi* (Hanoi: Nha xuat ban Van Hoa Thong Tin, 1996), 273–99.

25. NAC, Résidence de Hà-Dông, 1243, *Canton de An-Ha, affaires diverses et élections des chefs et sous-chefs de canton, 1893–1929*.

26. In 1905, out of ten serving *ly truong*, five were former *pho ly*, three were former *huong truong*, one was a former *khan thu* (head of the watchmen), and one was a former head of canton. NAC, Résidence de Hà-Dông, E6, 758, *Relevé des autorités communales de la zone suburbaine, 1905*. Note that the interval of time between the post of *ly truong* and that of canton head was highly variable. Out of eight cases, we can determine seven intervals: 2, 5, 5, 9, 17, 18, and 23 years of difference between the two posts. See also NAC, Résidence de Hà-Dông, 756, *Notices individuelles des chefs et sous-chefs de cantons, 1900–1911*.

27. To this one might legitimately object that the sample chosen is unsatisfactory, given that, among the major notables the youngest had not reached the pinnacle of their careers in 1905. If we get around the difficulty by looking at the sample in relation to the conventional date of 1885—leaving a margin of twenty years for those careers to take their course—we can see that out of eleven promotions of *ly truong* only two took place before 1885 and out of eight promotions of *pho ly* only two took place after that date. Thus, quite surprisingly, mobility was greater after 1885 than before, despite the number of younger people in the latter period.

28. NAC, Résidence de Hà-Dông, 1217: *Archives communales du village de Khuong-Thuong, 1899–1903*.

29. NAC, Résidence de Hà-Dông, 1239, *Archives communales du village de Yên-Lang, 1910–1913*. Procès-verbal du 3/2/1913.

30. NAC, Résidence de Hà-Dông, 1242, *Canton de An-Ha, élections des pho-ly et ly-truong, réformes communales, village de Yên-Lang, 1917–1927*.

31. For example, one of Hoàng Dinh Mao, *ly truong* de Khuong-Thuong en 1921. NAC, Résidence de Hà-Dông, 1220, *archives du village de* Khuong-Thuong, *1914–1918*. Document 114.

32. NAC, Résidence Supérieur du Tonkin (RST), 72698, *Rapports et statistiques commerciales des provinces du Tonkin, 1911*. The salary of the street heads in Hanoi had been eight piasters per month since the decree of 7 July 1914.

33. NAC, Résidence de Hà-Dông, 1224, *Archives communales de Nhuoc-Công, 1897–1928*. *Tri huyên*'s report number 186 dated 14 June 1906. In 1906, second-quality rice was worth an average of five piasters per picul, according to bulletins in NAC, Résidence de Hà-Dông, 3430, *Statistiques rizicoles de la zone suburbaine, 1906–1908*.

34. Nguyên Duc Nghinh, "Vê tài san ruông dât cua môt sô chuc dich trong làng xa thuôc huyên Tu Liêm vào cuôi thê ky XVIII dâu thê ky XIX," *Nghiên Cuu Lich Su* 165 (November-December 1975): 49–57.

35. Reference details at the Social Science Library in Hanoi: Thinh-Quang Huong Uoc (HU) 572, Phuc-Xa HU 509, Yên-Thai HU 577, Tam-Lac HU 570, Vinh-Phuc HU 573, Ngoc-Xuyên HU 565, Ngoc-Hà HU 564, Ngoai-Châu HU 563, My-Duc HU 567, Luong-Yên HU 560, Nghi-Tàm HU 62, Nam-Dông HU 561, Vong-Thi HU 574, Khuong-Thuong HU 558, Tây-Hô HU 571. References at the National Archives: Yên-Phu and Quan-La (in characters) in Résidence de Hà-Dông.

36. NAC, Résidence de Hà-Dông, 1218, *Archives communales de Khuong-Thuong, 1904–1909*. *Tri huyên*'s report dated 27 July 1908.

37. In 1923, the notables of Yên-Lang informed the *tri huyên* of the fact that the sum set aside for the travel expenses of the officials (*tiên phi tôn câp cho ky ly di viêc quan*) had been spent. They requested permission to use money allocated for repairs to the pagoda and *dinh*, which was granted. NAC, Résidence de Hà-Dông, 1241, *Archives du village de Yên-Lang, 1923–1928*. Letter of 15 October 1923.

38. Salary expenses for the *ly truong* and *pho ly* were a maximum of seventy piasters (5 percent of total expenditures) at Nhât-Tân and a minimum of five piasters at Yên-Lang Thuong (1 percent). Travel expenses (clause 1: *Tiên phi tôn câp cho ky ly di viêc quan*) occupied 4 percent of these budgets. Data from NAC, Résidence de Hà-Dông, *Affaires indigènes, communes indigènes réformées*, dossiers 2397, 2398, 2399, 2400, 2401, 2403, 2404, 2407, 2408, 2409, 2410, 2415, 2417, 2418, 2419, 2420, 2421. See also NAC, Résidence de Hà-Dông, 1345, *Affaires indigènes, communes non réformées*.

39. Bulletin contained in the dossier NAC, Mairie de Hà-Nôi, 4537, *Renseignements relatifs aux prix de divers denrées sur les marchés de Hanoi, 1932–1936*. The price of second-grade white rice fluctuated in 1933, a year chosen at random, between 7.3 (25 September) and 5.35 piasters (25 November). The figure of 6.3 is that of 31 October, which corresponds to the average for the year according to my calculation.

40. This was reiterated in black and white by the decree of 20 December 1913, by the *résident supérieur* of Tonkin.

41. NAC, Résidence de Hà-Dông, 1299, *Archives communales du village de Quynh Lôi, 1924–1928.* Folder: *Dossiers des ly-truong,* 221.

42. NAC, Résidence de Hà-Dông, 1298, *Archives communales du village de Quynh Lôi, 1914–1923. Tri-Huyên's* report dated 25 August 1914.

43. NAC, Résidence de Hà-Dông, 1396, *Archives communales du village de Hô Khâu, 1900–1913. Tri-Huyên* report number 18 to the resident and annex of interrogations, notes from the resident, 14 April 1909.

44. NAC, Résidence de Hà-Dông, 1233, *Archives communales du village de Yên-Lang, 1910–1913.* Election fine dated 3 February 1913 and some annexes.

45. NAC, Résidence de Hà-Dông, 1233, *Archives communales du village de Thinh Hào, 1914–1929.* Election fine of the *Ly truong,* 16 May 1914.

46. NAC, Résidence de Hà-Dông, 1263, *Elections des pho-ly et ly-truong de Mai-Dông, 1906–1926.* Voting printing materials are in *tri huyên* report number 58, dated 25 January 1912.

47. This is what the *tri huyên* Bui Trac wrote to the *tông-dôc* in 1924: "Tôi phung xet làng Quynh Lôi này làng to dân dông, cai luong da lâu mà luong chanh rât nat, chi vi nhung nguoi dàn anh chia ra be dang, ta su nhung nhiêu, kiên cao khich bac nhau luôn." (I see that Quynh Lôi, a large and populous village, reformed a long time ago, is totally divided and disorganised by factions that commit thousands of exactions and accuse each other constantly.) In NAC, Résidence de Hà-Dông, 2400, *Affaires indigènes, communes indigènes réformées, Quynh Lôi, 1918–1924.* Letter dated 10 March 1924, p. 1 v°.

48. NAC, Résidence de Hà-Dông, *Canton de Hoàng-Mai, élections des pho-ly et ly-truong de Vinh-Thuy, 1902–1927.*

49. NAC, Résidence de Hà-Dông, 1299, *Archives communales du village de Quynh Lôi, 1924–1928.* Chemise, *Dossiers des ly-truong,* 229. I have reconstituted the genealogy from information in dossier 1298 (1914–23). Although it is impossible to verify, the complaint asserted that even the *tri huyên* helped the *tiên chi* to put pressure on the voters, using threats.

50. NAC, Résidence de Hà-Dông, 1297, *Archives communales du village de Quynh Lôi, 1911–1913.* Judgment and materials from the trial at the fourth chamber of the court of appeal of Hanoi, 10 November 1909.

51. In fact, the *pho ly* Tân was mysteriously assassinated in October 1904; his body had been dragged as far as the neighboring village of Hoàng-Mai. The *tri huyên's* inquiry failed to establish any certain guilt, but strong suspicion fell on the currently serving *ly truong* (Nguyên Van Vinh) and his father-in-law, the first notable Nguyên Van Duc. The report notes clearly that these two characters were certainly the perpetrators of the crime—or at least commissioned it—but no concrete charge could be made against them. See NAC, Résidence de Hà-Dông, 1295, *Archives communales du village de Quynh Lôi, 1904–1907. Tri huyen's* report number 594, dated 11 November 1904.

52. Nguyên Khac Truong, *Des hommes et autant de fantômes et de sorcières* (Hanoi: NXB Thê Gioi, 1996).

53. NAC, Résidence de Hà-Dông, 1365, *Archives communales du village de Nhât Tân, 1889–1899*. Report of 12 February 1890.

54. P. Souvignet, *Variétés tonkinoises* (Hanoi: Schneider, 1903), 192.

55. This was "incidental" because generally the peasants themselves watched their fields from small cabins set up on the edges. At Vinh-Thuy, however, a small path alongside a stream was significantly named the *duong vê nông* (crop protection path) because it was on the route of the night watchmen. See NAC, Résidence de Hà-Dông, 1246.

56. NAC, Résidence de Hà-Dông, 1367, *Archives communales du village de Nhât Tân, 1905–1909*. Letter of the *ly truong* and the notables to the resident, 21 July 1908.

57. At Khuong-Thuong in 1906, two watchmen were punished with three days in prison because they protested against the exemption from payment of *suong tuc*, from which the notables benefited. NAC, Résidence de Hà-Dông, 1218, *Archives communales du village de Khuong-Thuong, 1904–1909*. Piece 277, August 1906.

58. Social Sciences Library: customary law book of the village of Luong-Yên, HU 560, article 26; Ngoai-Châu HU 563, article 59; Tam-Lac HU 570, article 61; and so on.

59. Salaries could be symbolic (five piasters per year at Ngoai-Châu in 1937) or, on the contrary, substantial (twenty-four piasters at Luong-Yên in 1938). See the customary law books of Ngoai-Châu HU 563; and Luong-Yên HU 560, article 27.

60. NAC, Résidence de Hà-Dông, 1218, *Archives communales du village de Hoàng-Mai. 1887–1894*. Tri huyên's report ("*l'affaire bufflesse*") dated 11 April 1893. Same crime and same punishment at Yên-Lang in 1891 (NAC, Résidence de Hà-Dông, 1236).

61. This punishment had replaced the one hundred strokes of the cane set down in the decree of the tenth year of the reign of Tu-Duc (1857). NAC, Résidence de Hà-Dông, 1232, *Archives communales du village de Thinh-Hào, 1909–1913*. August 1909.

62. This operation was carried out by the respective *ly truong* of the villages of Thinh-Hao, Van-Chuong, and Thai-Hà. The *tri huyên*'s report relates in detail this whole *rocambolesque* affair, which implicated an energetic group of singing girls from Thai-Hà. ANV, Résidence de Hà-Dông, 1367, *Archives communales du village de Thai-Hà, 1914–1922*. Tri huyên's report dated 15 July 1919.

63. NAC, Résidence de Hà-Dông, 1217, *Archives communales du village de Khuong-Thuong, 1889–1903*. Tri huyên's report dated 7 July 1899.

64. As no one knew where the *ly truong* had fled, the affair was closed. NAC, Résidence de Hà-Dông, 1219, *Archives communales du village de Khuong-Thuong, 1910–1913*. Tri huyên's report dated 10 December 1912.

65. NAC, Résidence de Hà-Dông, 1218, *Archives communales du village de Khuong-Thuong, 1904–1909*. Tri huyên's report dated 27 August 1908.

66. The debt note, duly drawn up, is in NAC, Résidence de Hà-Dông, 1238, *Archives communales du village de Yên-Lang, 1909–1919*.

67. This is what happened to the *ly truong* Lai of Nam-Dông in February 1905. For a sad story of stolen taxes, he and his father were beaten by the three brothers Trân Van Tô, Trân Van Nhu, and Trân Van Vân. Trân Van Tô took flight, but for the *ly truong* Lai the damage was already done: as he himself admitted, he had totally lost face in the village and the prestige of the commune was reduced. The *tri huyên*'s inquiry showed that his accounts were in order and that the three brothers were in contempt. He was declared innocent but preferred to resign in October 1905. NAC, Résidence de Hà-Dông, 1221, *Archives communales du village de Nam-Dông, 1883–1906*. Plainte du 27/02/1905, lettres du 1/04/1905, 4/04/1905 et 8/04/1905, démission du 12/10/1905.

68. NAC, Résidence de Hà-Dông, 1222, *Archives communales du village de Nam-Dông, 1907–1913*. Lettre du *ly-truong* au *tri-huyên* en date du 19/10/1911 et the response of *tri huyên* and *ly-truong* dated 15 December 1911.

69. NAC, Résidence de Hà-Dông, 1342, *Archives communales du village de Co-Xa, 1897–1910*. Written in characters dated the fifth day of the fifth month of the fourth year of Duy-Tân (1910). This document was translated into Vietnamese by Vu Van Sach, vice director of the Vietnam National Archives, to whom I would like to express my thanks.

70. Alongside these cases, which are explained by a certain logic internal to the village, it is nevertheless undeniable that there existed some activities that aimed at personal enrichment. At Quynh-Lôi, the *ly truong* Nguyên Van Chinh managed to pocket more than two hundred piasters at one time (in the 1914 tax season). In NAC, Résidence de Hà-Dông, 1298, report 167 of the *tri huyên*, July 1914. I am unable to confirm this statistically, but it seems that this type of radical, systematic, and personal corruption most affected villages where clans were strongest, as at Quynh-Lôi. In such places, there was no barrier to the exactions of the *ly truong*, who, all in all, was acting this way for the enrichment of the entire clan.

71. "Ly truong là nguoi thay mat dân mà thua hành viêc quan."

72. NAC, Résidence de Hà-Dông, 2388, *Pénurie prolongée dans le personnel des pho-tông et pho-ly des diverses circonscriptions de la province de Hà-Dông faute de postulants aux emplois vacants, 1925*. Lettre de Hoàng Trong Phu au Résident en date du 8/09/1925.

73. NAC, Résidence de Hà-Dông, 1227, *Archives communales du village de Thai-Hà, 1908–1913*. Plainte de Nguyên Van Bach, 22/06/1908.

74. NAC, Résidence de Hà-Dông, 1223, *Archives communales du village de Thai-Hà, 1904–1907*. Document 48, April 1904.

75. NAC, Résidence de Hà-Dông, *Archives communales du village de Thinh-Hào, 1905–1908*. The dossier extends from October 1907 to July 1908.

76. NAC, Résidence de Hà-Dông, 1226, *Archives communales du village de Thai-Hà, 1904–1907*. Acte de vente du 3/02/1904 et pièces annexes. The case of Dinh is described in the same dossier, document 48, 9 April 1904.

77. See, for example, Résidence de Hà-Dông, 1234, *Archives communales au village de Thinh-Quang, 1891–1913*. Pièce n° 40.

GLOSSARY

chuc dich	former communal and canton officials
chuc sac	title holder or holder of a court function
dân hàng xa	all the registered taxpayers, men between eighteen and fifty (or sixty)
dinh	the communal house
dinh miên sai	"exempt" from paying tax
don bâu	election lawsuits
hôi dông ky muc	Council of Notables
huong su	salary of the teacher
huong truong	one of the *ly truong*'s principal assistants, responsible for public works
khao vong	the banquet of honor
ky muc	notables
lao nhiêu and *lao hang*	old men
lua suong or *suong tuc*	the rice dew, that is, a sheaf or swath (*luom*)
ly dich	serving agents former mandarins, or village officials currently serving
ly truong	village mayor
ngoai tich	nonregistered inhabitants
nôi tich	registered taxpayers
pho ly	one of the *ly truong*'s principal assistants, responsible for the execution of the *ly truong*'s orders
phu quy	rich and honorable people, literati, and so on
thi sinh or *huong thân*	candidates at the examinations
tho lai, thông lai, lai muc	assistant of district mandarins
thu chi	second notable
tiên chi	first notable
trang dinh	healthy adult males
triên	stamp or chop received by the *ly truong* as a warrant
tuân	the organization of the village guard
tu van	Confucian literati

2

Philippe Le Failler

Village Rebellions in the Tonkin Delta, 1900–1905

Introduction

Rebels, pirates, revolutionaries, and nationalists—confusion reigns in the sources over the question of the nature of opposition to French colonial power in Tonkin at the beginning of the twentieth century.[1] The period under consideration is that of the establishment of state tax monopolies, a relative pacification of the countryside, and the end of a certain type of resistance, the surrender in fact of the last Black Flags. All the sources agree, nevertheless, that opposition persisted, a real opposition albeit a dispersed one. Its effects are clear: occasional violence, expressed in ways that were more or less directly aimed at the colonizing power and its representatives. This violence was, en bloc, described as "rebellion." But the reality and the nature of the violence, or of these phenomena of resistance, are yet to be established.

The archives of the *résident supérieur* of Tonkin contain, among other treasures, a sizable number of files concerning village rebellions at the beginning of the century. The authors of the different reports were generally colonial functionaries but could also be members of the Vietnamese administration. Evidently the term *rebellion,* for the French, embraced a whole series of different attitudes according to whether it described an isolated or a collectively organized incident. In essence, people were considered to be rebelling if they refused a demonstration of authority, whatever its form. This refusal ranged well beyond simple defiance, implying a recourse to action—often more spontaneous than reasoned—in the form of resistance to power.

It would be tempting to reject the term *rebellion* for its excessively imprecise character. Used in such undifferentiated ways, it led to an amalgamation of situations, which, if they presented similarities in their mode of action, drew on motivations that were quite different. To establish degrees of revolt is as hazardous as defining its nature, and it would be dangerous to attempt a typology of the hostile actions of Tonkin delta villages toward colonial functionaries. However, the term *rebellion*, employed without discernment and leading to a series of typological responses by the colonial authorities, created a certain unity of treatment with regard to the different forms of opposition. It is for this reason that I maintain it for the present, with the abovementioned reservations.

The rural population, and thus the majority of people, often had a rather diffuse understanding of authority when the latter did not impinge on its immediate environment: people recognized the role of notables and mandarins, less clearly that of more distant authorities, and had—with a limited number of exceptions—no direct relationship with the colonizer. This situation is less surprising for the fact that the occupier, though present in their minds, was conspicuously absent from the immediate environment of most of the population.

If we leave out the border areas, where a military presence made itself felt in the form of patrols, as well as the agricultural and forestry concessions, direct contact between French people and the rural population was rare. However, limited though these contacts were, we do find a number of accounts—relatively few—that allow us to consider such zones of direct contact as particularly important in the generation of revolts.

It was, paradoxically, in the densely populated Red River delta region that we find a significant number of rebellions, and the vast majority of these were closely associated with the problematic implementation of a fiscal regime relying basically on indirect taxation. Though invisible, the enemy was above all a mechanism—that of the tax authorities. Here we come up against a crucial aspect of the colonial relationship, which deals with both economic and political domains and allows us to determine, if not the nature of the exploitative relationship, at least some of its modalities. We may do so through a study of the sources tracing incidents that took place in villages.

The appearance of the foreigner, in the person of the customs official, allowed the incarnation of resentment, giving body and reality to the foreign presence. Indeed, in many villages these "tax soldiers" were very often the only whites with whom people had to deal: they embodied the "occupation." Their appearance represented a sudden transition from the reported fact of the country's domination by a foreign power to the actual experience of that unpleasant fact, in itself a significant step. This allowed the formation of a site—between contraband, tax collection, rebellion, and repression—where movements of resistance against taxation could take shape, oriented of course by preoccupations with food and daily living but nonetheless the breeding ground for a veritable process of rejection.

Direct Administration—The Colonial Choice

The low number of French in Indochina at the beginning of the century (20,000 people, soldiers included, in 1900 for a population of about 13 million) was equaled only by the British representation in India, where a regime was set up to ensure the delegation to local authorities of all or part of the responsibilities of empire. But this sort of political regime, systematically implemented in India, did not correspond—far from it—to the principles of centralization and direct administration that prevailed in France and consequently in French dependent territories and even protectorates. Instead, the principle of a double administration was established. On the one hand, there was an omnipotent authority that was almost absent outside of urban centers and district towns; on the other, there was an administration that possessed a real presence throughout the territory but few powers, an authority limited to the role of passive agent, passing on decisions that were quite foreign to it. These agents who played the role of intermediaries between the desiderata of the colonial administration and rural people did not have a clear mandate and authority to implement changes at the local level.

Fiscal Exploitation

The principles of taxation were extremely simple: provincial authorities were responsible for the land tax, the head tax (direct taxes in general), and the management of water control systems, rice reserves, and so on; the government general was responsible for customs revenue and, above all, indirect taxes.

Direct taxation was implemented through the mandarin administration, usually on the basis of land cultivation. This basis was never examined or challenged, and the system was in effect adapted to preexisting structures and customs. Problems were rare and resolved locally, creating a certain flexibility in the system's implementation. The French did no more than reproduce, in their own terms, the previous administration. The amount of tax due from a given community was fixed by the state, and the village was left to collect it. In case of a shortfall, the responsibility was collective. This was a tax collected in terms of quantity, not quotas. But the same was not true for indirect taxes, decided upon in Hanoi and Haiphong by the Department of Customs and affecting the consumer, the individual. For the Vietnamese system, this was an innovation.

Among the multiple taxes and duties levied on the Vietnamese population, those linked to the monopolies had a particularly strong impact. The three state tax monopolies of salt, alcohol, and opium[2] were the pillars on which rested the public coffers and guaranteed fixed returns of money independent of the economic situation. Whether the harvest was good or bad, the population did not reduce its consumption of salt or alcohol, and, as for the consumer of opium, his or her addiction was the best guarantee of increasing consumption.

Revenues from the monopolies came into the sphere of government general finances and were collected by the Indochina Department of Customs and Monopolies. Almost all the resources of the general budget were drawn from the monopolies and went toward the reimbursement of large sums of borrowed money (200 million gold francs),[3] used for the construction of railways, roads, and ports—in short, an infrastructure intended to promote the colony's development. One-fifth of receipts went toward the servicing of this debt. The officials responsible for collecting these taxes were thus accountable only to the governor-general and the policies decided by him—distant indeed from the economic realities of the different provinces. We may comprehend, given the considerable financial stakes, the desire of the government general to keep its hands on the administration of indirect taxation. The centerpiece of this situation was the salt and alcohol monopolies. They were levied on products of daily consumption: salt was an indispensable condiment (sold at prices up to seven times its production value) used for food preservation and in the production of *nuoc mam*; locally produced rice alcohol was used in a number of ways, notably in the celebration of cult rituals.

Contraband alcohol gave rise to the majority of problems. The establishment of an alcohol monopoly outlawed all production of traditional rice alcohol, with its burnt, bitter flavor. Substituted for this was a clear spirit, manufactured by the French monopoly according to French tastes, little appreciated by the people, who were nonetheless made to consume it. Whatever else it may have been, the substituted alcohol was too expensive. Large-scale contraband was the result, and it existed in every village. The French administration replied by sending in its customs officials.

The high duties levied on products previously subject to low taxes (salt),[4] or no taxes at all, were thus notoriously unpopular. Designed as taxes on consumption, with the levy included in the sale price, they were presumed to be invisible and painless because they were indistinguishable within the total product price. However, they fell upon the whole population without regard for wealth, and did so in a mechanistic way by taxing an essentially incompressible form of consumption that was not in proportion to the fluctuations of economic activity and the individual's taxpaying capacity. It was precisely this stability of consumption, and thus of tax revenue, that was the main advantage of the monopolies. But it was a theoretical advantage only, which assumed the existence of an absolute monopoly, without alternative forms of supply along clandestine networks, at least in a marginal proportion. Contraband is the natural gauge of indirect taxation, its volume being proportional to the value added collected by the monopoly, which of course merits this name only if it effectively dominates the market. Although the system's inappropriateness was understood very early on, its persistence was irremediable, unless the system established in 1897 were to be entirely re-created.

The unpopularity of indirect taxes was reinforced by their collection, within the framework of a direct monopoly, by French functionaries. This direct contact between the local taxpayer and the French administration was accompanied by constant inspections, involving tax investigations, visits to people's homes, and other repressive measures, which came up against a population entirely unused to this type of taxation, as the traditional state never entered the village. Taxpayers thus expressed their discontent with regard to the colonizer, while direct taxes were still collected by the mandarins and village authorities, who managed to avoid causing ostensible damage to the image of the French authorities. This choice of direct inspection made the colonial power run the risk of tax revolt, a risk that was all the more dangerous for the fact that the high surplus collected on these cheaply produced items of daily necessity rendered them expensive, to the point of making them appear to be luxuries.

The Juridical Context: French Justice or Mandarins' Justice

It would have been possible to leave the collection of these indirect taxes to the administrators—provincial heads—who would have paid them into the coffers of the general budget. They could, in this way, have marked out a certain autonomy, concentrating under their authority the whole financial and fiscal organization of the province. Moreover, their knowledge of the districts' taxpayers and their authority would have permitted the avoidance of certain frictions. But this option was regarded with skepticism, given the permanent conflicts between the French and native administrations, on the one hand, and between the administrations of different French government departments on the other. The main danger was the opposition between local and general interests for which the general budget, dependent on provincial administrators, would have paid a high price. The province head, under the influence of local imperatives, would have had a legitimate tendency to sacrifice the general budget's revenue to the advantage of his own budget. Should village authorities have been left full rein to deal with the repression of fiscal fraud? Frézouls, director of the Customs Department, replied to this question in unmistakably plain terms: "The fiscal legislation decreed by the French authorities can only be implemented by a French administration."[5] The Customs and Monopolies Department did not consider giving up its prerogatives. But, outside of juridical action, Frézouls felt that in this matter local authorities possessed a police authority independent of French correctional jurisdiction. If native authorities took it upon themselves to wish to second the administration in affairs of contraband repression, he wondered if it was wise to ban them from enforcing the law. By virtue of the principle *non bis in idem*, it was impossible to superimpose French over native jurisdiction for the repression of the same activities. But, without there being actual superimposition, there could be simultaneity, the sphere of native law being preventative, or effective only in the case of offenders caught in the act.

However, the law considered that reports written by inspectors of customs and monopolies concerning a contravention reported by native officials were of no juridical value (problems of translation leading to procedural annulment and discharge). The whole project of contraband repression by local authorities, initiated by the *résident* of Son Tay Province, David, was thus emptied of meaning, as local authorities who, having reported a contravention, saw no punishment follow lost their enthusiasm and certainly their prestige as well.

The general prosecutor of Indochina took refuge in a categorical decision: only the Department of Customs and Monopolies had the juridical right to carry out investigations and visit people's houses, and only the officials of this department could handle inquiries into denounced activities: "As far as Mr. David's proposition that native tribunals judge all contraventions reported by the Phu and the Huyen with regard to indirect taxation, it is inadmissible."[6] This held—unless a new treaty were agreed upon—as French jurisdiction was, in taxation matters, the only applicable one in Annam and Tonkin in all cases (notably if one of the parties was not a Vietnamese subject).

To sum up, native authorities were limited to the surveillance of contraband and its denunciation to the Department of Customs and Monopolies, which was alone authorized to act, in strict execution of the decisions of law regarding indirect taxation.

The remarks made by the director of the customs and the general prosecutor illustrate clearly the main contradiction within the political and fiscal system imposed by the colonizer: the application of the texts of law took place without the least explanation offered to the populations concerned, from whom was expected, in the absence of any understanding of the spirit of the law, total obedience to the letter. But the law, which was as it happened French in its principles and foreign to Vietnamese customs, implied in fiscal matters the notion of individual responsibility. The colonizer was thus going to attempt to give itself the power of inspection and punishment *à la française* within Vietnamese society.

On the Modalities of Investigation in the Villages

To go inside a Vietnamese village,[7] today as yesterday, is not a banal event for an outsider. This closed world constituted a real entity, strong, obeying its own rules, which one could not attempt to abrogate without a violent collision with the sentiment of local solidarity. The law bowed more often to village customs than vice versa; certain forms of custom were owed respect, of which French customs officials were unaware, when they did not deliberately choose to pass over them. The point of discord between the provincial *résidents* and the Department of Customs and Monopolies existed in the practice of having customs officials accompanied by an escort of the Native Guard. For the *résidents*, the lack of an escort reduced the village's responsibility, the soldiers having an "appeasing" presence, but the customs and monopolies officials, who wished to count as much on the element of surprise as on the absence of French witnesses, opposed the principle of a systematic escort.

> I do not think this can be admitted. The escort is not and cannot be obligatory; this would represent a displacement in the attributions of each service and would in addition impose too heavy a responsibility on the *résidents*. I think that for investigations, apart from reported cases [of persons] caught in the act and on-the-spot lawsuits during inspection rounds, . . . the head of the relevant district, military post, or brigade must remain the only judge of the need to request an escort.[8]

However, in a good number of cases customs officials had to call upon the Native Guard when difficulties arose. Then, as a result, the *résident*'s office shouldered, in the eyes of the population, part of the responsibility for the incidents that occurred, staining its prestige thereby. From this emerged strong opposition from the *résidents*, the vast majority of whom preferred to make escorts obligatory.

> I have been at the head of the province of Cau Do for three years and have a perfect knowledge of its spirit, and my insistence has no other goal than to avoid a return to the inevitably violent and sometimes bloody incidents of which the province was the theater before my arrival.[9]

A regime of systematic escorts had been established before the arrival of René Crayssac at the head of the Department of Customs and Monopolies, and it yielded conclusive results. As an immediate consequence, the number of compromises and seizures increased. But often when monopoly officials operated alone or with a few *linh co* (soldiers of the Native Guard) there resulted the very worst sort of difficulties, riots, and often the lack of convictable evidence. The opinion of *résidents* in such cases was plain: "when one goes to a dangerous place, one requests an escort."

> I know that many of them still prefer this mode of operation, despite its risks, because the principal guard, *who is often an embarrassing witness*, participates in the profit of the seizure, reducing thereby the profit accruing to the customs officials, but it presents all sorts of dangers of which I have the duty to inform you. Having done so, I consider that today my responsibility is fulfilled and I will not insist any further.[10]

Between security and efficiency, the positions of the different departments were irreconcilable. Crayssac, director of the customs, did not find this inconvenient. On the occasion of an investigation followed by a rebellion in a village in Gia Lam, which came to blows and insults, he noted that quite probably such incidents could have been avoided with an escort provided by the province head. But "it is unfortunately admitted that the requisition of an escort is most often incompatible with the speed and discretion that ensure the success of this sort of enterprise. Besides, nothing allowed us to foresee that the whole population would rise up against an investigation that was aimed against just one of its members."[11]

In certain cases, the operation was carried out in the absence of a French official. An informer, accompanied by a sailor or several *linh*, sufficed, quite illegally. By consequence, the question of the investment of principal guards with the functions of a judicial police officer was raised: should Native Guard officers be accorded a right of initiative for investigations and seizures? In such a case, numerous accidents were to be feared, as these officers were unaware of monopoly regulations, given that no one had gone to the trouble of instructing them. Finally, and especially, the *linh* were soldiers. The amalgamation of the civil and the military, for operations relating to tax, shows the gap that could arise between the principle of daily administration of a country in peacetime and the implementation of a system that was imported and imposed. To send soldiers to accompany customs officials was to give villages the signal that "pacification" was not yet completed. The aberrations, as much juridical as functional, that the French encountered were inscribed in the very fiber of the protectorate system's structure.

Denunciation

The majority of operations undertaken by the fiscal authorities responded to denunciations. They were of all sorts, sometimes anonymous, and it is easy to lose one's way among the motives that could lead such and such an element of a community to denounce its peers. The whole range of human emotions may be recognized—*jealousy, vengeance,* and *interest* are the key words, and there is no reason to promote the idea of any sort of civic spirit or community loyalty. Neighbors, relatives, competitors wrote to the mandarins and customs officials to inform about this jar of fermenting rice or those grams of opium forgotten under a pallet bed.

This habit of denunciation, strongly rooted in custom and traditionally carried out by means of a letter to the mandarin or to the superior of a contested administrator, had apparently always received mitigated reactions from the authorities. They feared that too many denunciations would engender an atmosphere of destructive suspicion. There was a constant need to regulate this domain, which has existed up to the present time, in order to prevent the accumulation of groundless or slanderous allegations. This explains, in counterpoint, the use of letters signed in the name of another person.[12] Any maneuver was justified, whether it was to find the identity of the informer or to resolve the basic issue in question, as long as it got the inquiry under way.

Although denunciations were an ancient and very widespread norm in Vietnam (as indeed in China), the fact that they got as far as the colonial authorities without significantly changing customs and traditions tended to introduce an exterior factor that was difficult to situate in the administrative equation. The involvement of French people in the internal life of the village community was generally regarded as unacceptable interference by an authority whose validity was not recognized and was thus illegitimate. But, to qualify our reflection on the village conceived as a homogeneous unit, we should note that the intervention of foreigners could, on occasion, feed into internal quarrels within the village community and overwhelm the balance of power.

The suspicion of partiality was thus systematic and extended well beyond the reality of customs law implementation. It was perceived in fact as an attempt by the French authorities to break the links of mutual aid within the village, even when it was on the basis of informants that the French officials acted, as if, respecting the forms, people refused to believe that, faced with the foreigner, anyone could have failed to observe the elementary rules of solidarity—and appearance—and could have gone so far as to address themselves to them. We should, as a corollary, underline the fact that mention was rarely made of what happened *after* the investigation, of how accounts were settled within families or the village.

The sources give a strong impression of close links of complicity between informers and large-scale smugglers, and of the latter with the authorities, in a complex of criss-crossed interests capable of putting the best disposed of inquiry officials off the trail. A small affair might be denounced to conceal the turning of a guilty blind eye. A minor conspirator might be compromised to facilitate the success of a large operation, to see a mandarin praised and promoted, and so on. French customs officials were not always duped over the real motives in the cases, but, under orders, they seem to have limited themselves to the facts of the contraband without seeking to go further and understand the real power plays involved and above all the impact of their own intervention on the struggles between clans and factions. The population observed the extent to which these officials were manipulated and remained the eternal losers, mixed up in a world that was quite foreign to them; their unpopularity increased accordingly.

Investigation Followed by Rebellion

Investigation generally took place at the first light of dawn. The customs officials, generally one or two Frenchmen, accompanied by two or three *linh* and/or sailors, came into a village house along with an informer. They only rarely warned the authorities before the investigation but demanded their presence for the preparation of the different reports.

The search took place with or without the presence of the presumed guilty party and led to the discovery of jars of fermenting rice and contraband alcohol. In a scenario repeated numerous times, members of the family who were present would rise up and lead their neighbors in revolt. A more or less hostile crowd would surround the tax officials. In a reflex of solidarity, without necessarily understanding the reason for the foreigners' presence, the population would shower them with blows, for failing to have been invited to enter, to force them to leave. The acknowledged goal was the destruction of the evidence. The customs officials, faced with this threat, had to beat a retreat. The main targets of village anger were the Vietnamese guards, informers, and sailors. It was they who were insulted, and more rarely beaten, as people sought to confiscate their weapons.

In most cases, things went no further than this, although such incidents were still characterized as rebellion by the colonial authorities. More unusually, giving in to the panic brought on by such threats, the guards made use of their weapons to get away, firing into the air for warning and, rarely, wounding one or two villagers whose only arms were bamboo sticks and yokes. As for the seizure itself, it was generally limited to a few jars of alcohol, some distilling tools, some pots for fermentation, and sometimes a bit of opium, but all in all not a great deal. There were, however, some cases of particularly fruitful collections when whole villages were involved in contraband distillation.

The Case of the Contraband Village

A characteristic example is that of the village of Yên Phu (canton of Xuan Lai, district of Da Phuc, province of Phu Lo), which was a repeat offender as much in terms of contraband as rebellion.[13] On 23 September 1903, an official and two guards breached the main gate of the village at five in the morning; a *"tam tam"* alarm was raised, the inhabitants fled to the east of the village, and a din of pots clanging together and jars breaking could be heard. The *ly truong* and notables were called, but all had fled, no doubt with their stills in hand.

It seems that everyone in Yên Phu was involved in distillation. In a search of the pond, customs officials discovered a vast quantity of jars, broken and not, containing fermented rice. The customs officials alone destroyed more than one hundred jars, and at least as many more were broken by the smugglers, a total of about three thousand kilograms of fermented rice. As for the alcohol, given the smell, a large quantity had been destroyed and a pond there showed a faintly oily layer on its surface, evidence of the hundreds of liters that had been poured away. In view of its quantity, the evidence was destroyed on the spot.

Meanwhile, the men of the village, armed with pointed bamboo sticks, harassed the militia, one of whom was struck in the face and fired into the air. Another had his cartridge pouch torn from him and fired in the same way. As he called for retreat, the customs official saw that his way was barred by a group of six or seven people, including one woman, armed with bamboo sticks. He fired three blanks.

> At the entrance to the village where I arrived, another group of natives threatened the guards and *linhs* who were regrouping for departure. I placed myself before this group and informed them, in Vietnamese, that the first of them to strike either a militiaman or myself laid himself open to immediate death by revolver. This threat seems to have cooled the ardor of these fanatics, who went to join the majority of the population at the main gate of the village. After getting the militiamen to fix bayonets, we passed through the main gate of the village, where we were welcomed with a broadside of ignoble insults. It was above all myself upon whom converged these pearls from the crowd, a vulgar and obscene repertoire indeed. I gathered on my way a few truncated phrases: "The French are thieves . . . wait till we come and make you chet in your house in Phu Lo . . . we will cook you like a pig, etc.," and others that I will pass over in silence. A woman who seemed the most inveterate of all pulled up her skirts and showed me her . . . forms while proffering insults that I could not very easily understand.[14]

The village, considered a vast clandestine distillery, had only twelve registered taxpayers but seemed to be very rich, with every inhabitant there owning buffalo and cows. Gariod, the *résident* at Phu Lo, in correspondence with the *résident supérieur* of Tonkin,[15] tended to play down these events. The village of Yên Phu was certainly culpable, but he estimated that if a rifle sling and cartridge pouch had been damaged it was due mainly to wear and tear on the material. As for the shots in the air, they were due to the guards' lack of composure. He proposed a fine of one hundred piasters payable to the provincial budget. The *résident supérieur* found this insufficient. Finally it was decided, on the *résident*'s suggestion, to carry out a partial destruction of the bamboo hedge surrounding the village.[16]

From these facts, we can see that the destruction of evidence was commonplace—the disappearance of the body of the crime amounted to its annulment, given that no member of the community ever dared to bear witness against another. This attitude might appear naive from the perspective of French notions of justice, notions that led in some instances to the kidnapping by villages of customs officials, who were made to sign a certificate of "nonseizure." These documents were certainly of no juridical value but indicated the complete ignorance of a population faced with a new way of doing things.

The Second Investigation

In all cases of rebellion, particularly when the village population succeeded in getting the customs officials to leave without evidence, an expedition was organized, which seems to have aimed more at punishment than inquiry. The customs officials returned the following day, accompanied by a sizable escort capable of discouraging any hostile demonstration from the population. The latter often had taken flight, leaving the old people and children in the village. The women fled, too, having played a preponderant role in the opposition to the customs officials. It was they, preserved by their status as women and strong with their prerogatives in the home, who had insulted the officials, hitting them and destroying evidence. The customs officials did not dare lay a finger on them.

The notables stayed behind to confront the anger of the ridiculed functionaries and to attempt, at their request, to convince the people to return so as to determine the role of each of them. All of this explains the difficulty of bringing to justice those guilty of acts of rebellion or outrage and, by the same logic, the high proportion of collective punishments.

False Rebellion

The question of the characterization of events is fundamental. The only testimony taken into account was that of the French officials, a situation that led to a strong temptation to exaggerate trivial events, giving them a significance likely to attract the attention of the superior authorities in the Department of Customs and Monopolies. The corporatist reflex did the rest.

But rebellion was sometimes no more than a fantasy, resulting from contempt or a partial or abusive interpretation of events. A typical case[17] was that of a French official who had only been in the protectorate a short while (and was thus excusable in the eyes of his superiors). The day of the investigation in question happened to fall on the same day as the market, where people were selling great loads of housing thatch. Numerous coolies, on their way to harvest, were going to the paddy fields along the road, carrying pointed bamboo sticks. Alerted by the recriminations of the old mother and wife of the guilty party, who were protesting his innocence, all these people stopped and gathered round to witness the scene. The official then panicked and characterized the affair as a rebellion, although no violence had manifested itself on the part of the population. As for the notables, when they arrived the customs officials had already left. There was, moreover, contempt of individuals, by which a Vietnamese man, characterized as *"inconnu"* by the customs officials, was the same who had brought the evidence to the officials. The *résident supérieur* concluded that it was impossible to impose a fine for that, but the Department of Customs and Monopolies axiomatically never repudiated its officials, however serious the blunder. Thus, a number of innocent people moldered away in jail in the name of the infallibility of public officials.

Cases of Real Violence by or against Customs Officials

It happened that events took a truly violent turn. A village could, at the height of its anger, seize the officials, strip them of their weapons, beat them, and put them in the stocks. In the same way, a customs official could use his weapons and wound or kill an inhabitant of the village. The first case resulted in a judgment at the Assizes for the main perpetrators and the destruction of the village bamboo hedge, the second in an informal arrangement between the administration and the victim's family.

The Establishment of Responsibility in Case of Rebellion: Individual or Collective

The rule seems, from the archival texts, to have been quite simple: the individual responsibility of those producing contraband was accentuated in the case of rebellion and aggravated their juridical situation. Then came the individual responsibility of the perpetrators of rebellion: family, neighbors, and villagers, according to the importance of events. Then, systematically, came that of the notables, and finally that of the community as a whole, if individual responsibilities could not be determined. It was necessary, to begin with, to check the respective complaints, which invariably accused such and such a guard of having made use of the investigation to steal an object here, a sum of money there, when it was not of having himself planted the evidence. These accusations, which were frequent, were not without foundation and show the extent to which the customs officials felt themselves all powerful. There was a strong temptation to perpetuate a tradition of pillage that in the past had made for the officials of the alcohol and opium monopolies a reputation as half functionaries and half brigands.

 The administration's principle was that coercive measures should only affect the tiniest proportion of the population so as to "spare the peaceful and honest section of the population these constant and oppressive investigations to which the customs administration is obliged to have recourse, to stop contraband."

 However, with the help of confusion, the tendency was toward summary justice, the punishment of the collective *"pour encourager les autres."* The system of individual responsibility came up, from the inquiry onward, against a wall of solidarity. French justice was in no position to proceed to the conviction of such and such an individual and could only resort to the incrimination of the village, according to Vietnamese rules, with punishments that were themselves drawn from the penal code of Gia Long. Tribunals rarely put themselves to the trouble of demonstrating the responsibility of this person or that, or even of simply reading the reports presented by the customs officials. The system ended up in frequent abuses of justice, which led to the intervention of the provincial *résident*, who was preoccupied above all with the maintenance of order: such and such a notable was convicted, despite the fact that at the time of the events he was far from the scene, or so and so was convicted while in fact it was he who had served as informer to the customs officials.

The Responsibility of Mandarins and Notables

As a general rule, it was considered that village authorities responsible for order were at fault in any case of rebellion, as they had not acted to prevent the aggression. They were by the same token blamed for not aiding customs officials during investigations and for refusing to bear witness, in short, for not having appeared to cover with their authority the intrigues of the customs officials.

In affairs of contraband, the Department of Customs and Monopolies found it incredible that, in almost every case, the village authorities were unable, immediately after the seizure, to come up with the identity of the guilty parties. They ignored thereby the possibility that the contraband activity might have been carried out by individuals from outside the village. We may appreciate here the gulf that separated the customs administration, with its mechanistic conception of authority, from the *résidents*, who were in much closer touch with the reality of the notables' power. Thinking simplistically, the customs officials, and even more so the higher levels of the department's administration, systematically judged the village authorities responsible for hindrances to their action or quite simply their lack of success.

The notables were regarded as particularly well placed to know about cases of fraud, given the proven solidarity of the communal system in Vietnam. It was easier for them than for Europeans to seize proof of contraband and catch fraudulent people; thus, according to this logic, in any case of fraud they were either accomplices or inefficient. To safeguard their prestige, the notables refused, in the vast majority of cases, to help customs officials when it came to making a report about a crime. They arranged to be absent or inaccessible. Complaints were hurled at the "culpable indifference of the notables." But the notables, whatever they did, had to bear a sizable proportion of the fines, penalties, and sentences. In affairs of rebellion, after the establishment of individual court cases, the dismissal of the *ly truong* and the *pho ly* was called for because "by their attitude it was they who in general excited the people under their administration."[18]

Nonetheless, when an affair came before the tribunals the liberation of incarcerated notables was demanded, the collective responsibility disappearing before that of the individual when the latter was identified. This shows up the absurdity of the system, in the light of examples of villages where the notables did everything to prevent the crime from being committed and helped the customs officials. They could not identify the guilty parties but were convicted nonetheless.[19] The range of punishments was as follows.

- For the mandarins, disciplinary transfer and relocation. A post in the highlands, or at least far from the delta, was an extreme form of sanction. It was necessary nonetheless to take into account which posts were vacant, and it remained difficult for the French to get fully involved in mandarin nomination systems.
- For notables, deprival of their stamps of office and for mandarins of their letter of appointment. This was a temporary measure, except for mandarins at the lowest degree of the mandarinate, whose letters were not returned. Other mandarins were demoted by a degree or class. This measure could be used separately or in conjunction with the two other forms of punishment.
- For the *pho ly* or *ly truong*, dismissal and imprisonment by administrative order. This led to his replacement and consequently to upheaval in the administrative equilibrium of the village.

The demotion and dismissal of mandarins and the fining of notables was a result of the manifest interference of one authority over another. While the French considered themselves to be the real upholders of the law, at the same time they obliged the mandarins and village authorities to implement a variety of double law. In punishing them for the incoherence of this situation, in certain cases they deprived the local administration of excellent officials. The whole thing led to a destabilization of the mandarinal system of justice due to the destruction of the mandarin's prestige. There were also cases in which it was the mandarins, notables, or village leaders, often the *pho ly* or *ly truong*, who engaged in contraband activities and were pursued as traffickers, troublemakers, and calumniators, with the aggravating circumstance of holding office.

The Collective Responsibility of the Village

Whatever happened, the colonizer needed to reinforce the habit, the system even, of the collective fine, of communal responsibility. This went along with the incrimination of the notables and goes far beyond the isolated example. While doing this, the *résidents* were aware of the risk of acting without discernment and increasing the anti-French feeling among members of the population.

Collective punishment took place in the form of either a common fine, to be collected by the notables, or a measure of oppression, like the destruction of all or part of the bamboo fence surrounding the village. We should, however, note an important fact, that the fines and other punishments were fixed by the tribunals and escaped, due to that fact, the fines of the government general. This led to a natural tendency on the part of the customs officials to give preference to compromises before judgments.

Compromises Before Judgment

In most cases, with the exception of rebellions involving the Native Guard, the Department of Customs and Monopolies preferred to compromise. Simple affairs of contraband rarely ended up before the judges; fines, damages, and interest were decided upon in a discretionary manner by the customs department.

Although the administration of the province did not have to get involved in such compromises, which properly belonged to the customs service, it considered that they were the surest way of reaching an arrangement, given that the fines handed down by tribunals were often too high (five hundred francs) and could not usually be collected in their entirety. Auctions usually offered a derisory yield. But the amount of the compromise was fixed by the receipts department in Haiphong, which had little knowledge of local wealth and the mechanism of supply and demand. A margin of latitude left to local receivers would have been more effective.

Administrative Fines

Paid in equal parts into the local and provincial budgets, fines could be inflicted upon part or all of a village. In theory, only the incriminated hamlet was affected, as it was sometimes isolated from the others. But generally collective fines were levied on the whole administrative unit concerned; for a fraudulent hamlet, the whole village was incriminated, with all the risks inherent in such a situation. The fine was calculated, in part, on the basis of the village's land area.

Increases in the Number of Registered Taxpayers in the Village

This type of financial punishment made its appearance in 1903. The number of registered taxpayers was increased by the number of individuals convicted for contraband. This represented a permanent financial sanction levied on the whole community.

Partial Destruction of the Bamboo Hedge

This last measure, the use of an old imperial punishment, was extreme and relatively rare. It was above all intended to set an example. The process of intimidation was accompanied by the publicizing of the punishment throughout the district or province. It was necessary to act with great circumspection:

> This punishment, though no longer as important as in the past—due to the pacification of the country—nevertheless presents the advantage, beyond the financial loss it entails, of striking the spirit of the natives, who know that we resort to it only in cases of exceptional gravity.[20]

As for the total destruction of the bamboo hedge, while it was possible in theory this punishment was never implemented.

Corvée

Financial punishments (introduced by the colonizer) coexisted with punishments drawn from the Vietnamese juridical system. Thus, we see French language texts that mention people sentenced to floggings, corvée, and so on. All corvée sentences, however, were redeemable according to codified scales.

Collection of the Fines

The sale of an offender's goods was the only means by which the administration could oblige the payment of fines and penalties. But these sales were carried out by village authorities who had every latitude to estimate the value of the goods. This turned out to be, with great regularity, inferior to the sum to be collected. It remains to be discovered whether this was due to fraudulent appropriation[21] or if it was common to underestimate the value of goods sold, to keep them from the French and afterward return them to the offender, in a certain sense staging his bankruptcy. Furthermore, the amount of the fines seems out of proportion to the wealth of the convicted people. An individual fine of fifty piasters required the liquidation of all the criminal's possessions, movable and fixed. The whole thing took place under conditions that remained quite foreign to the French administration.[22] As noted by Scalla, inspector of the Hanoi area, in a communication to his vice director on 19 April 1903:

> I am making the most of this occasion to inform you that the sale of the property of the debtors in the province of Cau Do never gives satisfactory results. I have been told time and time again that the native authorities paid into my coffers only a small proportion of the profit from the sale, or even sold only a part of the debtor's property. . . . The execution of judgments in the province of Cau Do exists only in name. The sale of debtors' goods is no more than a source of illicit gain for the native authorities. An effective inspection would return the situation to that laid down by regulation of law.

This gave rise to a legitimate tendency to apply financial punishment to the community, even when individual responsibilities were clearly established. The case was simplified by the recognition of collective responsibility.

> When the village's responsibility is involved and if the individual guilty of contraband activity is unable to pay the fine or compromise penalty, I do not hesitate to give the same advice to the authorities: the sale of property by the authorities, which they must carry out regularly, or the distribution of the cost among the inhabitants, causes, in my opinion, even more serious abuses than the contraband itself.

Financial punishments inflicted on villages ranged from 30 to 300 piasters, as shown on receipts recording administrative fines handed down to villages for alcohol contraband and rebellion. The average penalty per village in 1901–2, however, was around 150 piasters.[23] It was frequently stipulated, moreover, what proportion the notables should pay (around one-third) and what proportion was owed by the population. The *ly truong* and *pho ly* were responsible for collecting the sum. Sometimes the prolonged presence of the antifraud brigade in a province represented, by the multiplication of its fines, a veritable leeching process capable of altering the population's "normal" ability to pay taxes. This was noted by the *résident* of Hà Nam.[24]

> But the tax rolls are now being prepared, and the payment of land and head tax must take place next July. I would not be surprised if the heavy contribution demanded of the inhabitants through the payment of fines for the contravention of indirect tax laws will create temporary problems among [the population] at the time of tax collection, which will make it even more difficult.

From contraband, which affected the individual, to related effects, which squeezed the whole community, fiscal pressure in Vietnam under colonial domination had repercussions that went beyond the initial framework of administrative implementation. A failure of will to collect the tax collectively, using the village as the fiscal unit, combined with the inability to establish individual responsibilities in case of problems meant that the issue was automatically politicized. In this context, the use of collective punishment by French justice, which thought it was following established custom, alienated village political authorities and seriously discredited them.

Conclusion: Tax Rebellion Represented as a Form of Anticolonial Resistance

The word *rebellion* virtually changed its meaning according to whether it was the expression of individual or collective will. In fact, this idea, which was characterized by acts ranging from symbolic to violent manifestations of rejection of authority, seems, in common parlance, contrary to the collective interest. The rebel, particularly in an Asian context, seems to be more or less an outlaw. Thus, when the term *rebellion* is applied to a collective unit it gains legitimacy.

The use of the term *rebellion*, which was not neutral,[25] having been applied several years earlier to Vietnamese resistance fighters, implied an assimilation—by wordplay that came close to nominalism[26]—of the discontented peasant by the armed partisan. The amalgamation of political agitation and tax revolt took place without discernment; it was a temptation to which certain French administrators, especially directors of the Department of Customs and Monopolies, had recourse for reasons of facility. They were prisoners of a conception of the centralized and dominating state, whose prerogatives in matters of taxation could brook no contradiction; this feeling was exaggerated in Vietnam by its situation as a colony. The French saw politics where it did not yet exist, in the village, which protested against the penetration of customs officials; they did so without seeing it where it did exist, in the establishment of indirect taxation on everyday items of consumption.

Abstraction is not the strong point of country people, and nationalist discourses, however well supported and despite a national history marked by resistance against the Chinese, were still lacking in substance. Numerous stories about the French invaders were making the rounds, but the threat was not immediate: the enemy remained, at the beginning of the century, predominantly invisible and thus inconceivable and impossible to stigmatize except to a few men of letters. Antitax rebellion created a favorable basis for the development of a better-argued resistance, which would pick up the opposition of the majority at a later date and in a nationalist perspective. For reasons of legitimacy, it would be considered later on that the resistance movement was initiated in the countryside, although it was others who subsequently provided the theoretical substratum that was lacking there. It is true that we have for long periods ascribed the paternity of movements rejecting foreign invasion to intellectual elites, who theorized and left written traces of their actions and reflections. In so doing, we have logically obscured the fact that the majority of people also had opinions, reflexes of opposition, and that these took shape in disturbances brought to their daily lives.

NOTES

Institut de Recherche sur le Sud-Est Asiatique (IRSEA), Aix-en-Provence, and l'École Française d'Extrême-Orient, Hanoi. My thanks to Andrew Hardy, who has kindly translated this essay.

1. The abundance of terms not only marks the point of view of observers and their positions but by means of a mirror effect perpetuates the idea of a single reality deformed by the prism of national and political options, which history confirmed by making a choice, heavy with meaning, between the different concepts.

2. The opium monopoly was peculiar in that, by taxing an "optional" product, it was conceived as a disguised levy on the Chinese, who represented proportionally the mass of consumers.

3. Indochina had to bear the weight of two loan reimbursements: an 80 million franc loan (1896), of which 43 million were intended to pay the protectorate's debts (including the purchase of the opium franchise in Tonkin); and a 200 million franc loan (1898), which was absorbed by the infrastructure program.

4. The tax on salt was introduced in 1720 in the form of a 20 percent levy on production; this "state salt" was then resold at a higher priority but a higher price than private salt.

5. *Frézouls, Directeur des Douanes et Régies à RST,* 4/8/1901, National Archives Center (NAC), Résidence supérieure du Tonkin, RST 74659.

6. *Le procureur général, chef du service judiciaire de l'Indo-Chine à RST,* 31/7/1901, RST 74659.

7. The sources make no distinction among communes (*xã*), villages (*làng*), hamlets (*xóm, thôn*), and so on. This inevitably poses a problem for the historian and may be understood in the following manner: the French customs authorities, who had little concern for the subtleties of Vietnamese administrative geography (nonetheless established on solid foundations), were more interested in handing down punishments that would set examples than in precisely determined incrimination. In my rendering of administrative units at the local level, I have unfortunately been obliged to follow the practices on which the French sources were based. In most cases, the ambiguous term *village* has thus been retained.

8. *Frézouls, Directeur des Douanes et Régies à RST,* 1/4/1902, NAC, RST 74659.

9. *de la Noe, Résident à Cau Do, à RST*, 12/2/1902, NAC, RST 74659, underlined in the original text.
10. Ibid.
11. *Village de Kim Son, huyên de Gia Lâm, province de Bac Ninh, à RST*, 8/5/1905, NAC, RST 74659.
12. In fact, the Gia Long code decreed that any anonymous letter or poster of denunciation should be burned immediately and not be acted upon. Its author, if discovered, risked strangulation. If the letter was signed with a false name, it, too, could not be acted upon. Thus arose the practice of signing it with the name of another inhabitant of the village (*Code annamite*, translated by Philastre PLF [Paris: Ernest Leroux, 1876], 2:395–96).
13. Village of Yen Phu, canton of Xuan Lai, district of Da Phuc, province of Phu Lo, 23/11/1901. This was an investigation (alcohol) provoked by a denunciation; the inhabitants rushed to a village pond and threw into it the jars and other receptacles containing rice alcohol, which could not be seized as a result of the population's hostility. The village was sentenced on 25 November 1901 to a fine of forty piasters, payable to the local budget (NAC RST 74659).
14. *Rapport de Bellamoix, chef de poste à chef de circonscription des Douanes et Régies, Hanoi*, 28/9/1903, NAC, RST 74659.
15. *Gariod, Résident à Phu Lo, à Résident Supérieur du Tonkin*, 16/10/1903, NAC, RST 74659.
16. *Village de Yen Phu, canton de Xuan Lai, Phu de Da Phuc, Province de Phu Lo*, 5/11/1903, NAC, RST 74659.
17. *Résident de Sontay à RST*, 18/11/1904, NAC, RST 74659.
18. Annotation of the receiver at Bac Hat, 29/9/1903. In this village, where a large quantity of opium was seized, the customs department wished to make an example of the village, handing down an administrative fine and dismissing and imprisoning the notables. In a telegram received by the *résident supérieur*, sentences were requested of three months of detention and thirty strokes of the cane (redeemable) and for the *pho ly* fifty strokes of the cane (redeemable).
19. Case of the hamlet of Man Dich, village of Thuong Cam, canton of Hoi Khe, district of Vu Tien, province of Thai Binh, 8/10/1904, NAC, RST 74659. Two jars were placed in a paddy field, and two coolies ran away. In this case, the *résident supérieur* of Tonkin himself was incapable of recognizing that only a compromise could put an end to the imbroglio.
20. *Résident à Nam Dinh à RST*, 26/8/1903, NAC, RST 74659.
21. There were cases in which the *ly truong*, guilty of numerous acts of corruption, kept for himself the money yielded by a sale. This practice should be blamed on the system whereby the *ly truong*, a clan's representative, exempted the clan from taxation and, to keep to the quota, generally overtaxed those who were not of the same family.
22. A judgment was handed down, sentencing an offender convicted of alcohol contraband to the sale of his goods (he was, besides, in prison); the sale yielded the sum of $20.42, but the notables confirmed that its actual yield

was in fact $100.00, the difference having been pocketed by the *ly truong* and his assistant. After the inquiry, the sum of $49.23 was added, reaching $69.65, and not $100.00. The inquiry concluded that a wrong initial estimate of the goods' value had been made. *Noe, Résident à Cau Do, à RST,* 14/4/1903, NAC, RST 74659.

23. This sum is equivalent in value to four tons of paddy, enough to feed a family for more than three years.

24. *Résident à Ha Nam à RST,* 15/3/1905, NAC, RST 74659. In two months and nineteen days, the roving customs brigade drew up 113 reports: "If we suppose that each offender in these reports was sentenced to the minimum fine for alcohol manufacture laid down in the decree of 20 December 1902, in other words, 500 francs, the result would be financial penalties borne by the inhabitants of the province amounting to a total of 56,500 francs." The *résident* admitted that compromise sentences would come into play, as well as acquittals, which would reduce the sum to around 20,000 francs.

25. Borrowed from the Latin *rebellare,* from *bellum* (war), *rebellion* is thus a "return to war."

26. Rebellions that were not really rebellions, monopolies that were not really monopolies—we note here that the excessively swift collage of European terms on different cultures leads to an interesting slipping of meaning. French terms did not adhere to Vietnamese reality, and the discrepancy highlights the singular lack of understanding between the two cultures, which remained fundamentally estranged.

3

Nguyên Van Ky

Rethinking the Status of Vietnamese Women in Folklore and Oral History

Introduction

When one takes a close look at Vietnamese society, one may be startled by the paradoxical status of women: their low social representation, or absence thereof, and their actual place in society, testified to by history and confirmed by legends, or even their preeminence in some oral traditions and symbolic representations. Does one not say in Vietnamese: "When the enemy is at the gate, the woman goes out fighting" (Giac den nha dan ba phai danh)? And, indeed, they were made to contribute to the war effort against the Americans. Drawn into the Thanh Nien Xung Phong (Committed Youth), hundreds of thousands of Vietnamese females sacrificed their youth by answering "aye" to the call of "the country needs you," enrolling and going to the front in order to accomplish the hardest tasks. A good many of them had not yet had time to savor the taste of love before falling into the oblivion of history. Those who survived and are still alive today live in such a state of moral and material abandonment that they often have had to form a community within the community (a village) to cope with the general indifference.[1] The history of these women and this movement is yet to be written.

Apart from a few isolated cases, the existing studies that deal with women's issues do not allow a global vision, nor do they trace back the course of time in order to find out whether their position has always been the same. Those who hope to address this question will inevitably encounter source-related problems, at least insofar as ancient history is concerned. As for the colonial period, there is sufficient material to form a relatively truthful idea of reality.[2] It is, for instance, acknowledged that during the 1930s Vietnamese women, that is, those of the more educated or progressive classes, began to liberate themselves from the social yoke or family ties, forcing other social actors to place the issue at the forefront of the national debate. But the movement was not to be pursued after 1945. The urgency of the national war of independence set the question aside and relegated it to a hypothetical agenda. Because of the paucity of classical sources (be they archives, annals, miscellanies, or memoranda), which do not dwell much on the subject when they exist, the historian needs to find other ways and means. Consequently, oral sources as well as cultural traditions may be of use to fill the gap. A new way was thus paved in the 1950s by Phan Khôi, who took the initiative in considering language as a historical source.[3] It is on this most promising path that I shall endeavor to follow suit, dedicating myself to the roles and representations of women in Vietnamese society.

In this respect, the riches of proverbs, sayings, and folk songs (*ca dao*) constitute an unequaled and immeasurable stock of information. I refer in particular to two collected volumes: one by Nguyên Van Ngoc, many times reedited, whose first edition dates back to 1926; and the other by Vu Ngoc Phan, which may now be regarded as a classic of its kind.[4] As shrewd observers, the Vietnamese describe what they see and feel through compositions that, albeit succinct, are endowed with rhyming qualities and much common sense. Every domain of human activity is represented in this treasury of the Vietnamese language: therein, love takes a nonnegligible place, humor finds good terrain, bawdiness flourishes, morality wages its authority, psychology has its fair share, social relations are reflected with clarity, and peasant life is detailed in full. If every period produces its own linguistic sequence so as to translate a multifaceted reality, borrowing foreign words seems to be an essential part of that process.

Gender Relations in Legends and Vietnamese History

Since the dawn of the Christian era, the Vietnamese woman has shown both determination and combativeness. These qualities have been demonstrated in the persons of the Trung sisters. Let us just remind ourselves that they are the first historical figures—as opposed to mythical ones—to have assumed rebellion against Chinese domination. According to Nguyên Trai, a scholar whose literary talent was coupled with a military career, they renamed the country Hùng Lac, Hùng being undoubtedly the name of the clan, and Lac that of the ethnic group wherefrom the Vietnamese people are descended. Another text reveals a no less puzzling detail: the two siblings' surname was Hùng.[5] How, then, not to be tempted to speculate on a relation between this term, *Hùng*, and the homonymous first dynasty of Vietnam? Having had a close look at it, what does one see: a name, Hùng, borne by two different families, separated by an interval of three centuries, that is, if one refers to the official historiography, dating from the beginning of the Hùng dynasty at around 2600 B.C. and its fall at the end of the third century B.C.? This would simply mean that each of the eighteen Hùng sovereigns, *all males,* should have reigned for an average period of one hundred years if one is to agree with the date of the Trung sisters' rebellion in 43 A.D. Indeed, all common sense prevents us from considering something so ludicrous. Through the grace of what miracle could all Hùng sovereigns have enjoyed a longevity as surprising as supernatural? Moreover, one knows that the legend of the Hùng dynasty appeared for the first time as late as the fifteenth century, during the Lê dynasty, after the Ming had been ousted. This precision ought to be underlined, for, as noted by Ta Chi Dai Truong, no document prior to that date has ever mentioned the existence of such a legend.[6] How did it suddenly come into existence in the fifteenth-century official history, namely, Ngô Si Lien's *Dai Viet su ky toan thu* (The Complete History of Dai Viet)? Is it a mythification or the will of the new ruling dynasty to rewrite history and in so doing erase those parts of history that would not conform with the official line?[7]

Be that as it may, the history of Vietnam and its monarchs has always been strewn with legends, which, in the absence of written sources, can prove, within their own limits, to be useful material. If the founding myth of the Viet people may now be read in textbooks, the mystery of its true origin remains whole. Ethnologist Nguyên Tu Chi is the only one to have attempted to fathom it. Let us, in turn, briefly recall this legend and read it to the letter.

Vietnam's national history in its legendary part relates that the

Viet people descend from a mythical couple, Lac Long, an offspring of the dragons, and Au Co, a fairy. They gave birth to a hundred eggs, out of which a hundred sons were hatched. Notwithstanding this happy progeniture, the couple had to part because of astrological incompatibilities—one belonging to the water element and the other to the fire element. But before each went his or her own way, Lac Long and Au Co divided up the children: half followed their father back into the waters, the territory of the dragons, while the other half went with their mother to the mountains. Comparing this legend with a similar Muong version, Nguyên Tu Chi sees in this separation a symbol of the divorce, at a date undetermined, between the two cousin peoples, the Viet and the Muong.[8] This hypothesis is yet to be confirmed. For the time being, let us limit ourselves to the narration of this most astounding legend.

What has become of the fifty sons who followed in the footsteps of their dragon-father and returned to the waters? Nobody knows. For if the Viet people have been able to develop and prosper they could only have done so on firm ground, where the fifty others remained with their mother, Au Co. (Despite the fact that they live on a long coast, the Vietnamese have always preferred the mainland.) At this stage of the inquiry, one may ask oneself how fifty males—those who stayed with the mother—were able to reproduce without the aid of any other female, except their own mother. Did they marry among neighboring tribes, and in this case which ones? And how is it, then, that the legend should not have retained the female factor in the national reproductive process? Did Au Co resume her role of genetrix? In the latter case, incest would have been the original mode of reproduction in those pristine times—we are in 2000 B.C., remember! In other words, the Vietnamese people would be the descendants of the fifty sons who remained with their mother. So here, it goes without saying, the maternal element becomes essential. Must one conclude that this legend, which appeared in the fifteenth century, the golden age of Confucianism in Vietnam, should have left such a patent trace of a matrilineal society? Another detail ought to be noted: the "hundred sons" produced by this mythical couple may be an unambiguous indicator of the Confucian predominance of men over women. But how could the forebears of the Vietnamese people in 2000 B.C. have conceived a theory that had not yet been born? Was Confucius not Buddha's and Socrates' contemporary in the sixth century B.C.? The legend proves utterly anachronistic in the face of historical evidence. However, in the share of their progeniture, Au Co appears to have been the strict equal of Lac Long, since she was entitled to half of the children. Is this proof of the legend's feeble construction, if one accepts it as the work of the Confucianists—who considered males to be superior to females—or must one just see a deliberate emphasizing of a difficult transitory period during which two antagonistic systems were at loggerheads? Or is it just an indication that the practices evoked had not quite disappeared at the moment of the legend's fabrication?

This legendary story is testified to in the common phrase, known to every Vietnamese, *Con rong, chau tien,* "Children of the dragon, granchildren of the fairy," a proud epithet that the Vietnamese have bestowed upon themselves to legitimize their origin. Here again one notices that *dragon* and *fairy* are not on the same hierarchical level. The former is placed just above the ego level, whereas the latter is once removed from there (grandmother or great-grandmother, since the term *chau* is used both by grandchildren and great-grandchildren). The dissymmetry, both parental and temporal, situates the female element prior to the male. From this expression, at least two assumptions may be made: First, relations between parent (the father) and child are closer; consequently, the male takes precedence over the female. The second hypothesis is the grandparents' position, in this case that the grandmother is more important than the parents, represented here in the person of the father, because the elder comes before the younger. This temporal indicator, which recalls the respect of ancient rituals, forces one to acknowledge a prevalence of women over men. In short, the male-female opposition remains, although the male is no longer, as has often been the case, represented as the omnipotent figure.

In another respect, if one looks at the literary form of the phrase *Con rong, chau tien,* what comes to mind is the scholarly style of parallel sentences (*câu dôi*), very much in fashion in the Chinese classical culture. In the phrase, *con* (child) is opposed to, or rather finds, its parallel (*doi*) in *chau* (grandchild), likewise for *rong* (dragon) and *tien* (fairy). Conceived by a Confucianist scholar, this expression could only have come into being during the sinicization period. It is highly probable that it should have appeared at the same time as the aforementioned founding myth in the fifteenth century.

A last remark: the dragon is one of the four wonder animals, embodying imperial power in Chinese symbolism, introduced in Vietnam at the very earliest in the beginning of the Christian era. This remark also applies to the Lac Long and Au Co episode and specifically to Lac Long. The adoption of this honorific symbol could only have been the work of the sinicized ruling classes. *Long* is, besides, a Chinese term for "dragon," the Vietnamese vernacular being *rông*. In the same perspective, one may also read in textbooks a variant in which *Lac Long* becomes *Lac Long Quan* (Lord/His Worship Lac Long) and *Au Co* becomes *Bà Au Co* (Mistress Au Co). *Lac Long* is here qualified with the title *Quan*, used for a person of high rank. The nominal group "Lac Long + Quan" follows the Chinese syntax; conversely, it is the Vietnamese syntax that is applied to the feminine element "Ba + Au Co." Two rationales therefore cohabit in the same tale: the male element imbued with Chinese thought and the female reflecting Vietnamese usage, syntactical and otherwise.

As for the term *tien*, it is a Chinese-based word that may be translated as "fairy," "immortal," or "being that has attained immortality through wisdom and detachment" (*tu* in Vietnamese). One observes that *tien* in Chinese is formed by two characters: "mountain," preceded by the radical "man." In other words, *tien* ought merely to designate "the man in the mountain." Would it be pushing it too far to assume that the feminine ancestor of the Vietnamese—the fairy Au Co—was a Montagnard? Did the population of today's Vietnam not correspond with a slow emigration from the south of China and through the mountains to the plains? One could, of course, carry on speculating endlessly, but with the true intention of finding new paths, and without prejudice or partiality, to prepare the ground for further fields of investigation is no vain endeavor. Even though this last interpretation may seem far-fetched, the term *tien* nevertheless conveys a Chinese notion that could not have been introduced into Vietnamese society before its sinicization. One falls once more into an absolute anachronism.

Challenging Confucian Values on Women's Status

Let us concentrate for a moment on the Confucian component of Vietnamese morals. As a child, every Vietnamese had to learn at school the following poem by heart.

Cong cha nhu nui Thai Son[9]
Nghia me nhu nuoc trong nguon chay ra
Mot long tho me kinh cha
Cho tron chu hieu moi la dao con.

(The good deeds of Father are as great as Mount Thai Son
The virtue of Mother is as bountiful as springwater
  gushing from its source
Wholeheartedly is Mother to be revered and Father
  respected
So that the child's way may be accomplished.)

This proverb, epitomizing the gist of Confucian morals, was probably diffused during the sinicization period, which roughly corresponds to the beginning of the Christian era up to the fifteenth century, perhaps a little later. Here one is not so much faced with a problem of dating as of meaning. The third line tells us that Mother is "to be revered and Father respected." However, *revere* and *respect* are not synonymous: one generally reveres gods, deities, supernatural beings, or humans transformed into divinities. But in this precise case it is the mother one reveres and not the father. How blasphemous for a society that gives a dominant, let alone omnipotent, position to the father! How contradictory with Confucian values! Ought one not to see, through this anodine formulation, the survival of some archaic social model wherein the mother is more important than the father? In other words, this reading of Confucianism—which apparently gives precedence to the father in the family structure—has been unable to eradicate all traces of a more ancient (or perhaps at the time still extant) society of a matrilineal type that revered the motherly figure. Great is the temptation to locate this cult of a mother goddess in a more universal pattern, ubiquitous in the history of mankind. Here, one deals not only with linguistics but with semantics. The permutation of the verbs *revere* and *respect* could have been done without altering the rhymes; besides, such contraventions of the versifying rules are often encountered in the oral tradition. And when one knows the rigor with which the classical scholars made their choice of words to express their ideas, one can only assume that the terminology used in this moralistic proverb did not merely answer the requirements of poetics but surely expressed another consideration, that is, that of recalling ancient practices in order to keep them alive. In that way, one could say that the author, despite his Confucian background, did not wish entirely to deny his deep social and cultural origins. Another instance may be found that makes us lean toward this interpretation. The following folk song brings further evidence thereof.

Lay cha ba lay mot quy
Lay me bon lay con di lay chong

(Before Father, I bow my head to the ground three times
  and kneel
Before Mother, I bow my head to the ground four times
[When leaving home] to take a spouse.)

Lay, the act of touching one's forehead to the ground, is in Asia a sign of submission, respect, or veneration. Why does the daughter bow only three times before her father and four before her mother? Why this asymmetry in favor of the mother? Contrary to the Confucian reading, this folk song (*ca dao*) is no deed of a scholar; it just mirrors those customs common to the nonsinicized Vietnamese society, or at least widespread among the social classes ignorant of the Confucian morals. This presumption is reinforced by the fact that here the daughter tells her parents that she is to take a spouse; she does not submit passively to the parental will. This ought to be stressed: the normally "done thing" for girls of Confucian education was to leave one's decision to marry to the discretion of the parents.

In the spoken language, the married couple is phrased *vo chong* (wife-husband). If one refers to social precedence—and one knows how much importance the Vietnamese give to such matters—the order of the words puts the woman before the man. How ironic! These two words (*vo chong*) belong to the vernacular and not to the Chinese-based vocabulary used in the more literary, philosophical, or scientific domains. The phrase may have been constructed when the Vietnamese still lived under Chinese influence, and their language, being less rich, sufficed to express their vision of the world. It is most likely that in distant times Vietnamese women had a more important role than men. It explains why one used to and still continues to say *vo chong* and not the converse. Does the saying not go thus: *Nhat vo nhi troi*

(First comes one's wife, then comes heaven)? This is absolute blasphemy, for who places heaven above everything else, so much so that it has been deified and a cult to it rendered! This proverb contains two Chinese words—*nhat*, "first," and *nhi*, "second"—and could only have found its origin during the sinicization period. Nonetheless, the state of affairs seems to have been in total contradiction to the established order. One finds oneself again on the matrilineal side.

In Vietnam's traditional society, in a wedding it is the man who asks the woman's hand and all costs are incurred by him; it is the very meaning of *cuoi* in the expression *cuoi vo*, "take a wife." However, the reading of *ca dao* (folk songs) teaches us otherwise, and in many cases quite the contrary. For instance:

> *Rap renh nuoc chay qua cau*
> *Ba gia tap tenh mua heo cuoi chong*

> (Troubled runs the water 'neath the bridge.
> The old woman prepares herself to buy a pig and take a spouse.)

or even:

> *Gia bao nhieu mot ong chong*
> *Thi em cung bo du dong ra mua*

> (However much it costs to get a man,
> I'll have saved enough to purchase one.)

If one may be reticent in the case of the first *ca dao*, owing to the woman's old age, the phrase *cuoi chong* is unambiguous and probably gives an insight into what used to be common practice. As for the second folk song, there is little doubt as to who is speaking: it is a young girl, to wit, the personal pronoun *em*, which is used by a girl/woman when modestly speaking of herself. In the second verse, the verb *mua*, "purchase/buy," is explicit enough: the woman buys her husband and not the converse.

So it seems that in the olden days, when Vietnamese society did not yet conform to the Chinese moral and social organizational model, it was the woman who made the choice; moreover, she could marry more than one man. The existence of polyandry is testified by various folk songs.

> *Nguoi ta thich lay nhieu chong*
> *Toi day chi thich mot ong that ben*
>
> (Others would fain have many a husband.
> I'd rather have only one but ever close at hand.)
>
> *Tram nam tram tuoi tram chong*
> *Phai duyen thi lay chong ong to hong nao xe*
>
> (In a hundred years' time, you're a hundred years old and can wed a hundred husbands.
> Finding a man is not the doing of some genie of matrimony.)

The first folk song needs no further commentary; as for the second, "a hundred husbands" is not, of course, to be taken literally, but it means that a woman may marry as many husbands as she will. Here is an interesting point: according to the woman, if she weds as many times as she wishes, it is not due to the goodwill of some genie. The Chinese notion of a genie (*ong to hong*, the oldster who weaves the red threads of marriage) capable of sealing happy unions is being rejected. Two practices and two moral codes are clearly in contradiction; one is local, while the other has been borrowed and grafted upon the former.

If the folk songs allude to ancient customs contradicting the moral code of conduct of the ruling classes, one finds other instances that reflect the conflict between these two social models as well as the difficult transitional period during which both coexisted. Take, for example, the following.

> *Ngay sau con te ba bo*
> *Sao bang luc song con cho lay chong*
>
> (Though when I die you will make an offering of three cattle,
> I'd much rather you granted me permission to marry while I am still alive.)

In Vietnamese, this *ca dao* is without ambivalence. The mother speaks to her son. Confucian morality forbade a widow to remarry and obliged her to submit to her eldest son's will in virtue of the three precepts of obedience (*tam tong*). *Marry* here means "remarry," for one is concerned with a widow, that which is not explicit in the folk song. Doubtless, this was a time when Confucianism triumphed in Vietnamese society: note the importance of the son's position, from which the mother expresses her desire to subtract herself. As the woman is the depository of traditions and the conveyor of collective memory, her wish—as illustrated in this folk song—must refer to some prior social practice. This *ca dao* not only gives an example of a conflict of generations but also that of two antagonistic sets of values that succeeded one another or became intricately intertwined. In other words, it could be roughly dated from the beginning of the sinicization period.

With regard to the term *tê*, one ought to dwell on it a little longer. *Tê* is a ritual that consists of a sacrifice made to a revered person (say, Heaven, Confucius, or a tutelary genie). Only males are allowed to officiate, pronouncing out loud codified formulas of Chinese origin, which, albeit short, are incomprehensible to the mortal coil. Since this ceremony is borrowed from the Chinese tradition, the spectacle has an exotic semblance: precise and solemn gestures, pomp and circumstance, ornate vestments, and so on. In the colloquial sense, *tê* carries an altogether different meaning when used by an angry woman in the expression *ba tê cho mot tran*, which could be translated as "[This] old woman/grandmother [standing before you] is going to teach [you]." So here the woman assumes a superior status (that of grandmother) in order to express her wrath and scorn, and *tê* means "to abuse and ridicule somebody with insults." Could this change of significance be a deliberate act on behalf of women meant to mock and mimic the original male ritual? The ritualistic formulas have become in their mouths terms of abuse and foul language. When the Vietnamese woman is ready to fight her enemy, *any* enemy, one can grant that it will be a show worth any spectacle of a man sacrificing before the altar. She shakes and gestures toward the despised individual, blatantly abusing him; she might even lift her skirts before an assembly of witnesses to show her parts and shame the person. The scene lasts as long as she deems necessary. Facing such a situation, the "victim" has no choice but to clear off as quickly as possible so as not to be exposed any longer to public ridicule. Could this be interpreted as the response of a gender, excluded from certain rituals, expressing its rebellion? If this be the case, it would take us back to the times when Chinese morals were the rule but women kept affirming their social position and wanted to repossess the relics of a remote past when they were still the chiefs.

The Representation of Incest in Oral Tradition

Let us go back to the notion of incest. If many societies repress incestuous acts, others seem either indifferent or consenting, and one is not lacking in such examples. In the Vietnamese oral tradition, there is this instance.

> *Con gai muoi bay cho ngu voi cha,*
> *Con trai muoi ba cho nam voi me.*

> (A girl of seventeen, let her not sleep with her father.
> A lad of thirteen, let him not lie with his mother.)

This proverb is to be construed as a recommendation or a prohibition. If society needs to make certain rules of a prohibitive nature in order to preserve social harmony and morality, it may be that it is faced with a situation that it deems alarming. In other words, if certain things need be so expressly spelled out one can assume, with more or less certainty, that such things found their cause in reality. Be that as it may, prohibition in any society responds to a reality, whether social, human, moral, cultural, political, or economic. It concerns those practices that constitute a menace to the community or are in contradiction with it; one does not forbid a thing or a concept that does not exist. Which government would forbid, say, people to look at themselves in a mirror? Vietnamese society has given cause to many a telling proverb.

> *Chau cau mà lay chau co*
> *Thoc lua day bo giong ma nha ta*

> (If the maternal uncle's nephew marries the paternal aunt's
>   niece,
> our house will have its stores full of rice.)

Vua chua cam doan lam chi
De doi con di chang lay duoc nhau

(Wherefore do kings and lords forbid
two sisters' children to marry each other?)

The first proverb gives clear indications as to degree of kinship between the spouses. The union in this case is judged auspicious and will bring prosperity. In fact, the nephew/niece (*chau*) of the maternal uncle (*cau*) and the niece/nephew of the paternal aunt (*co*) are, in an indirect manner, termed as "siblings." Their union is assimilated to an incest that, far from being disapproved, seems highly commended. As for the second proverb, it not only tells that the prohibition was decreed by kings and lords[10] but that the common people, on the contrary, did not mind intermarriages, namely, in the case of first cousins. In the religious tradition, the couple *"Ong Dung Ba Da,"* which, according to the legend, contains a brother and sister, is worshiped as tutelary genies in the Red River delta.[11] Without attempting to go through all the world's traditions, one notes the presence, as in most founding myths, of an original couple, either a brother and a sister, or a mother and a son. In Greek mythology, it is Gaia who, at the beginning of the universe, mates with her son Uranus in order to beget the Titans. With the Baruyas of New Guinea, the founding myth traces the origin of mankind back to the primordial union of a brother and a sister.[12] Could one not regard these tales as some crystallization of the human collective memory, bequeathed from generation to generation under the form of myths? In other words, could these not be some sort of archetype whose authors have been lost in the limbo of immemorial time? In spite of this original incest—which may shock more sensitive souls—Greek myths have never ceased to occupy one of the most highly regarded chapters in the history of human civilization. If Confucianism, however, considered such incestuous acts as a menace to law and order, the common people saw no cause for reprimand in unions involving kinsmen, at least to a certain degree of relationship.

On the linguistic level, the Vietnamese word for incest is *loan luan*, a Chinese-based word, which means literally: "anarchical morals, inverted or drifting morality." If the Vietnamese had to borrow the word from the Chinese, it is because the idea of "incest" probably did not exist in their body of conceptual representations. Had such a state of affairs posed, in their eyes, any problem, they surely would have created a word for it. Is a foreign word not clear evidence that the object or concept that is described in the language borrowed from did not exist in one's own? Examples abound.

However, one needs to be circumspect when dealing with this kind of question—fascinating as it may be, in fact, one of the anthropologist's most studied subjects—for its emotional load is most explosive. The past, whether it be historical or mythical, cannot be gauged with today's eyes, since every period has its own raison d'être and its proper representational system. Nevertheless, it would be as absurd to defend a custom on the sole merit of its finding its cause in the past. The quest for meaning is paramount and prior to any other consideration, be it ideological or philosophical, affective or moral. Unless and until the hidden meaning has been cleansed of its parasites, one cannot hope to see a glimmer of comprehension.

Modernity and Women's Quest for Equal Rights

Decades later, under French colonial power, Vietnamese women embraced modernity with their already historical gains and cultural practices. At the beginning of the twentieth century, the Franco-Vietnamese education, and the media, contributed to major changes in Vietnamese society. These two agents of modernity, although limited in Vietnam[13] and under the control of French colonial authority, did provide Vietnamese women with social and political spaces, which were traditionally dominated by men.

By 1920, many Vietnamese women held university degrees and eleven of them were granted fellowships to study in France. In Paris in 1935, Hoang Thi Nga, of Hanoi, was the first Vietnamese to receive a Ph.D. in science[14] from a French university. In the past, under ancient dynasties, women were not even allowed to participate in the mandarinal examinations. These examinations gave men status and social recognition, granting the brightest graduates the privilege of having a stone stele in the literature temple in Hanoi.

In 1936, after the election in France of the Popular Front party, and during the period of high expectations for social change, Vietnamese women activists created a committee to write a "guest book" in each city, Hanoi, Saigon, and Hue, during the months of August and September. This new form of activism among Vietnamese women was praised in the newspaper *Dan Ba Moi,* in an editorial written by Nguyên Thi Kiem, a journalist well known by her readers. The title of the article shows a great deal of cynicism, "The Building of the Indochinese Congress: For the First Time Women of Three Regions Have Found Ways to Meet in Order to Engage in Politics."[15] But Nguyên Thi Kiem had no illusions when she wrote:

> To engage in politics is to work in the highest spheres of power in order to claim equal rights for a group of people that one is representing or hopes to represent. In a way, its true meaning is to be able to "engage in politics" in any country in the world. But in our country, which is under colonial power, its meaning is very limited. What do we have to defend and claim as rights? In our country, to engage in politics is to accumulate testimonies, take pictures to document our misery so we can beg for a little bit more from French authority. And we don't even get much opportunity to do that. This is why there is no difference between Vietnamese men and women when they engage in politics.

But of course, these opinions could not have been expressed if there were no newspapers to support women's rights. In Vietnam during the period 1929–36, there were three feminist newspapers or at least newspapers that supported women's rights: *Phu nu tân van,* published in Saigon from 1929 to 1934; *Phu nu thoi dam,* published in Hanoi from 1930 to 1934; and *Dan Ba Moi* published in Saigon from 1934 to 1936.

The number of copies of each of these publications was quite astonishing at the time: 2,000 copies for *Dan Ba Moi,* 6,000 for *Phu nu thoi dam,* and 8,500 for *Phu nu tan van.*[16] As a comparison, in 1936 there were 111,000 people living in Saigon and 149,000 in Hanoi.[17] These weekly newspapers were written for both men and women readers. All the topics were of general social interest to both genders and included articles on premarital virginity and early marriage, polygamy and widows' remarriage, and romantic love and free choice of a spouse. In other words, Vietnamese women were claiming their equal rights in a male society. The interest of these newspapers is that they challenge a male society in which men were not only at the center but had supreme power. And at the same time these newspapers initiated dialogues by publishing special columns in which readers could express themselves. In other words, they created a platform for open discussion, which in turn contributed to the intellectual endowment.[18] In addition, male writers were supporting women's rights as was the case in the publication of *Tô Tâm*, a romantic novel by Hoang Ngoc Phach, former student of the École Normal Supérieure of Hanoi. Ten years later, in his novel *Doan Tuyet* (The Break), the writer Nhat Linh, alias Nguyên Tuong Tam, saved a woman from an abusive family. The Vietnamese family, a representation of Confucian society, was contested by the women's movement.

In any event, the participation of Vietnamese women in the political arena was not simply a product of Vietnamese history. Vietnamese women at the time were also supported and encouraged by other women's movements around the world, in particular in China and the Western countries. On the other hand, one could have argued that this new frenzy of liberation had a downside. In 1930, weekly newspapers in Hanoi constantly noted the rising number of suicides by Vietnamese women. A small lake was renamed as "grave of beauty," Mo Hong Nhan.[19] But in reality these tragedies, which provoked high emotions among the readers, were not as abnormal as the media presented them. In fact, the level of suicide in Hanoi for both men and women was relatively low in comparison with that in Europe during the same period. There were 2.7 suicides per 100,000 people in Vietnam, while in France there were 20.2. Thus, public opinion was very much influenced by the media's dramatization of current events.

By 1930, women who were placing women's issues on the Vietnamese national political agenda included Dam Phuong, Nguyên Thi Kiem, Thuy An, and Nguyên Thi Khang.[20] It is also important to note that this Vietnamese feminist movement was limited to the urban boundaries of the cities of Hanoi and Saigon. The life of the majority of Vietnamese peasants was far removed from urban concerns and political debates and was still dictated by the cultural patterns of previous generations. This does not mean, however, that Vietnamese women in the countryside were totally submissive to men's authority. On the contrary, only a few privileged people who wanted to imitate the urban cultural lifestyle followed Confucian cultural practices. On the other hand, the majority of peasant women worked side by side with men in the fields and enjoyed some level of equality. Such equality was derived from their rural mode of subsistence. In villages, religious practices were respected and had a significant impact on gender relations. For instance, during religious holidays women often went for a two- to three-day trip to visit a distant pagoda. Men stayed home and had no problem with their wives traveling with other woman friends or relatives. This is another example of how Vietnamese women gained and claimed some rights and independence throughout history.

Conclusion

This work of clearance is still at its locating stage; from now on we may start to form some ideas. We must agree with Phan Khoi, who argues that Vietnamese society in effect went through a matrilineal system, lasting at least till the era of the Trung sisters, before adopting the patriarchy. Relying on variegated material as well as implacable demonstrations, he rightly objects to his antagonists, "Where were the men, then—if one assumes that Vietnam was patriarchal—since it had fallen to women to conduct the rebellion?"[21] Thus, this hypothesis calls into question the myth of the Hùng kings who, according to official historiography, succeeded to the throne from father to son during eighteen generations and over a period of two millennia. This father-to-son dynastic rule is in utter contradiction to a matrilineal succession, and in that respect the existence of the Hùng kings is indefensible. This does not entail the nonexistence of the Vietnamese people as such but means that their rulers were not those whom they pretend to have had. But in the cases of both the legendary couple of the dragon and the fairy and the Hùng dynasty, both instances seem to have appeared for the first time in the fifteenth century with the compilation and revision of the *Dai Viet su ky toan thu* by Ngô Si Lien. It is most likely that after independence was snatched at the hands of the Ming, the author, with the court's encouragement, inserted those episodes in order to forge and instill a stronger sense of national identity. The fact that the Trung sisters should have borne the same patronym, Hùng, and that their kingdom was named Hung Lac responds to a similar nationalistic rationale. A strong desire to assimilate both clans, the Trung sisters' and the Hùng kings', the founding dynasty, and efface every matrilineal aspect underlay this new edition of national history. All the clues had been confused from the start, giving a semblance of coherence with this two-thousand-year succession of Hùng sovereigns uninterrupted until the Trung sisters' rebellion. What was built is a construction with an impressionist facade, resting on improbable foundations that easily fall in pieces with the first breeze of historical criticism.

This long list of puzzling facts would not be complete were one not to add those elements furnished by the oral tradition and popular practice. To that extent, *quan ho* gives us interesting material regarding the relations between men and women. Based on alternate songs inspired by love, this local tradition places males and females on an equal footing.[22] As for ritualistic traditions, take the case of the goddess Lieu Hanh, who, hunted down by the authorities under her last avatar, had to take vengeance by wreaking havoc before seeking the Buddha's protection. Does she ultimately symbolize in the popular psyche what the Vietnamese woman used to be? The cult of Lieu Hanh finds an echo among the people, and seeing the autonomy of her disciples, all females but for a few exceptions, it shows how relative the position of men may be. An insight into the primeval times when the woman was the head of the family? At any rate, all these elements make us think that, despite the adoption of Confucianism as a basis for social organization and in view of superseding the matrilineal system, the collective memory has preserved relics of the old system through the oral and popular traditions. If the assumption of the existence of a matrilineal system in Vietnam is accepted, the case is far from being unique in Southeast Asia. Today on Vietnamese territory there are still ethnic minorities that have such a societal model of organization. Lai Cua's recent research has revealed the existence of a small community, called Na, living between Yunnan and Tibet, whose peculiarity is to have neither fathers nor husbands.[23]

The elements furnished in this essay constitute the pieces of a jigsaw puzzle, the reconstitution of which requires, of course, many more pieces. Will the feminine figure appear on the face of this restored palimpsest? In the affirmative, it will provide us with very useful information on a world where the woman used to rule as mistresses. Besides, the mystery remains intact as to when and why Vietnamese society switched to the patriarchal model. Was it an effect of Chinese colonization or a deliberate choice on the part of the natives? What did the new system bring compared to the old one? Did this shift, probably decided by the ruling classes, have the sole consequence of removing women from power? Could women have reacted to this power taking or did they just have to accept it? This mutation may also be construed as a logical sequence in a societal organization based on obsolete oral traditions incapable of fighting a formalistic culture based on literacy. So the founding myth of the dragon and the fairy, and, incidentally, the Hùng dynasty episode, could have been wholly fabricated for the cause. But, on the other hand, why not interpret these legends as the adaptation of more ancient myths whose original meaning has been betrayed? Finally, a myth does not come out of nothing, for all myths plunge their roots deep into the terrain of human reality and the further one penetrates into the maze of history the more questions one meets. Here, again, one can only state facts and raise questions, but before finding the adequate solutions might one not try to set the record straight?

NOTES

Independent scholar, Paris. This essay was first presented as a paper at Euro-Viet III, Hanoi, 14–17 July 1998. I would like to thank Duy Tâm for the translation of this essay and Gisele Bousquet for her comments in its revision.

1. See the documentary entitled *Mot thoi dang nho* (A Period Worth Remembering) produced in 1995 by the Liberation Society of Cinematographic Productions, which was dedicated to women, dead or alive, on the twentieth anniversary of the liberation of Saigon.

2. See Nguyên Van Ky, *La société vietnamienne face à la modernité: Le Tonkin de la fin du XIXe siècle à la Seconde guerre mondiale* (Vietnamese society confronting modernity: Tonkin from the end of the nineteenth century to the Second World War) (Paris: L'Harmattan, 1995).

3. Phan Khoi, "Thu tim su lieu Viet Nam trong ngon ngu" (In search of the historic sources of Vietnam through the language), *Van Su Dia*, nos. 1–3 (1954). Nguyên Van Ngoc, *Tuc ngu phong dao* (Sayings and folk songs), 2 vols. (Saigon: Mac Lam, 1967).

4. Nguyên Van Ngoc, *Tuc ngu phong dao* (Sayings and folk songs) (Saigon: Mac Lam, 1967). Vu Ngoc Phan, *Tuc ngu, ca dao, dan ca Viet Nam* (Sayings, folk songs, and airs in Vietnam) (Hanoi: Social Science Editions, 1978).

5. *Tan dính Linh Nam chich quai, Vu Quynh*; Buí Van Nguyên dich thuât, chú thích, dân nhâp (Fantastic tales of Linh Nam). Hà Nôi: Khoa hoc xã hôi, 1993.

6. Ta Chi Dai Truong, *Than nguoi va dat Viet* (Genies, man, and Vietnamese land) (Westminster, CA: Van Nghe, 1989).

7. This work is known to have been composed from more ancient scripts

and compilations of tales collected throughout the country. Its author says in the preface that he chose to leave aside those parts that he deemed did not conform with reality and were in his opinion too bizarre. At the end of the day, the writing of such a work, which has become a classic, answered a pressing call: to make up for the losses incurred during the war against the Ming.

8. Nguyên Tu Chi, *La cosmologie muong* (Muong cosmology), with a preface by Georges Condominas (Paris: L'Harmattan, 1997), 23.

9. Mount Thai Son is located in China.

10. Dating Vietnamese proverbs is a complex subject. If one succeeds in solving the problem, it could open up new perspectives. As far as this particular proverb is concerned, one may deduce from the terms *vua* (king) and *chua* (lord) that the prohibition might have been enacted in a period when the power was shared by the Lê dynasty and the Trinh clan (i.e., the sixteenth to the eighteenth centuries). At any rate, the prohibition of incest among certain members of the family is stated in the fifteenth-century Code of the Lê.

11. See Nguyên Van Ky, *La société vietnamienne*.

12. Maurice Godelier, *La production des grands hommes* (The making of great men), (Paris: Fayard, 1985).

13. As an example for the academic years 1938–39, there were 740 girls and 4,512 boys registered in the public high schools of the three regions (Tonkin, Annam, and Cochinchina).

14. G. Boudarel and Nguyên Van Ky, *Hanoi, 1936–1966: Du drapeau rouge au billet vert* (Hanoi 1936–1966: from the red flag to the green bill) (Paris: Autrement, 1997).

15. *Dan Ba Moi*, 26 October 1936.

16. David G. Marr, *Vietnamese Tradition on Trial* (Berkeley: University of California Press, 1981), 220.

17. *l'Annuaire statistique de l'Indochine* (the Annual statistics of Indochina) (Hanoi: Imprimerie d'Extrême-Orient Editeurs, 1937).

18. Nguyên Van Ky, *La société vietnamienne*, 261–82.

19. Ibid., 337–55.

20. Dam Phuong was the first to encourage Vietnamese women to be aware of women's issues in society, to be educated, and to be organized. She was an activist and a writer. Many of her articles were published in the newspaper *Nam Phong*. Nguyen Thi Kiem, a poet known as Manh Manh, was one of the first publishers of the newspaper *Phu Nu Tan Van*. Thuy An, the pen name of Luy Thi Yen, was the publisher for the weekly newspaper *Dan Ba Moi*. During the uprising of Nhan Van Giai Pham (1956–58), she was accused of counterrevolutionary activities and sentenced to jail for having supported and participated in the Vietnamese Hundred Flowers Movement. See G. Boudarel, *Cents fleurs ecloses dans la nuit du Vietnam* (Paris: Bertoin, 1991). Nguyen Thi Khang was the publisher of the newspapers *Phu Nu Thoi Dam* and *Monde*.

21. Phan Khoi, "Thu tim su lieu Viet Nam."

22. See Dang Van Lung, Hong Thao, and Trân Linh Quy, *Quan ho: Nguon goc va qua trinh phat trien* (Quan ho: Its origins and evolution) (Hanoi: Social Science Editions, 1978).

23. Lai Cua, *Une société sans père ni mari: Les Na en Chine* (A society with neither father nor husband: The Na of China), (Paris: PUF, 1997).

GLOSSARY

ca dao	popular song
cau	uncle (mother's younger brother)
cau doi	parallel sentences
cha	father
chau	nephew, niece, or small child
co	aunt (father's younger sister)
con	child
cong	from Confucian ideology (could be translated as "merit, kindness")
cuoi	to take a wife (or husband)
dan ba	woman
dan ong	man
dao	way, direction
duyen	destiny, charm, and grace
giac	an individual or a group that is threatening to take power regardless of its geographical or ethnic origins
hieu	from Confucian ideology (could be translated as "filial piety")
Hùng	legendary Vietnamese dynasty
kinh	to respect someone
lay	to prostrate oneself, bow down to the ground
loan luan	incest
long	Sino-Vietnamese term for *dragon*
me	mother
nghia	from Confucian ideology (could be translated as "faithfulness, charity, devotion")
rong	dragon
tam tong	from Confucian ideology, a woman's three duties: as a child, to obey her father; as a wife, to obey her husband; and as a widow to obey her son
tê	ritual ceremony reserved for special occasions, for example, when the king pays his respects to Heaven or villagers pay their respects to the village deities or Confucius
tho	venerate
tien	immortal
vo chong	married couple, literally "wife-husband"

4 Emmanuel Poisson

Administrative Practices: An Essential Aspect of Mandarinal Training (Nineteenth–Early Twentieth Century)

Introduction

Were the Vietnamese mandarins who received a literary education based on abstract knowledge, once in positions of power in the Vietnamese administration, ready to fulfill their responsibilities or was it in fact their subordinates who made decisions? And was the training of these mandarins dissociated from reality and incompatible with their expected leadership, as has often been written?

In this essay, I argue that before graduation candidates of the civil service examinations and some sons of mandarins received a well-rounded apprenticeship in practical matters. These candidates were, in fact, very knowledgeable about current events. The first Nguyên emperors, like the emperors of the Lê dynasty,[1] attached great importance to this apprenticeship, whereby future civil servants would familiarize themselves with administrative practices, both in ministry offices and in the field, in prefectures (*phu*) and districts (*huyên*).

French authorities of the Protectorate of Tonkin wisely took note of this apprenticeship period at the end of the "pacification." At the beginning of the 1890s, the mandarinate underwent a transformation—from a mandarinate "of conquest" to a more "administrative" one—compelling the French to reestablish this training as it was practiced in the first half of the nineteenth century. The mandarinate career was then restructured according to the former rules of a precolonial Vietnam. However, with this apprenticeship at the core of their education, the mandarins faced slower promotions in the administration and restricted access to some mandarinal positions.

The data for this essay were drawn from two major sources: the curricula vitae collected in 1897 in each province for the imperial inspector (*kinh luoc*), and the individual career files established under the protectorate. The study of these documents demonstrates that a large number of mandarins posted to the provinces of North Vietnam at the beginning of the protectorate had completed an apprenticeship under the reign of Tu Duc (1848–83). Once this training was accomplished, they were officially appointed to a position in the Ministry or in the local government as district magistrate (*tri huyên*). Over the years, this apprenticeship was virtually never put into question. What, then, were the motivations for building the school for *hâu bô*?[2] Its later transformation into the School for Mandarins (Si Hoan Truong) resembled to some extent the former mandarinal training provided under the Nguyên.

1. Recruitment of the District Magistrates and Prefects (1884–92)

The curricula vitae of the mandarins of the provinces of Hà Nam, Thai Binh, Hai Phong, Hung Yên, Son Tây, and Hung Hoa, found in the registers of the imperial inspector, show the diverse backgrounds of the candidates for prefect (*tri phu*) and district magistrate. Some were graduates of regional examinations, others were former military mandarins at the end of the reign of Tu Duc, and still others were individuals who had raised troops to join the military ranks.[3] According to the registers of 1897, nearly 50 percent (seventeen of thirty-five) of the district magistrates currently in office did not have university degrees.[4] In 65 percent of the cases, their entry into the administration was a result of their having joined the ranks of the conquest and the pacification.[5] Only three out of thirty-two prefects and district magistrates in office in 1897 were titled, that is, holding the rank of 5b (prefects) or 6b (district magistrates). In other words, the majority were composed of lower ranking mandarins, those holding a rank of 7b and below.

Most of these administrative positions required a great deal of interprovincial mobility, as new officials were frequently transferred from one province to another. This practice, once an exception, soon became the rule. As a result, many prefectures were run by a succession of interim officials. The district of Kim Anh, for example, changed district magistrates six times in less than two years (between 10 June 1896 and 21 April 1898).[6] Furthermore, as interim officials they had little authority, especially in areas where there were many graduates of the examinations and retired mandarins. The district magistrate of Phu Xuyên in 1898 is a good example;[7] as is the case of Dinh Ky Than, district magistrate of Thach Thât. The latter is described by the governor-general (*tông dôc*) of Son Tây in 1891.

> Thach Thât district is known as the region of scholars. . . . It must be governed by someone who has a university degree. But the appointee, Dinh Ky Than, began his career as a simple secretary without any university diploma, and his mandarinal status is still quite low (so far he has only obtained the level of *dê lai*: ninth degree). His current nomination was only provisional and temporary. If he remains in office for a long time, it could be feared that the local population will no longer submit to his authority.[8]

The interim position within a district or prefecture could no longer be considered a simple apprenticeship. The large number of acting deputies with low rank is a result of the "scarcity of civil servants"[9] and the "scarcity of capable people"[10] mentioned by the authorities of the protectorate. Other remarks of the time indicate that this was due to a recruitment policy based on loyalty to the protectorate, not on competence.[11] Local Vietnamese and French administrators were aware of the need to appoint educated men to administrative positions in the delta. The imperial inspector in 1892, for example, refused to support a proposal by the provincial officials of Hung Yên who wanted to appoint Trân Nhu Niên as district magistrate of Tiên Lu. A simple *lai muc* (secretary) intern with no rank at all, he commanded no respect with the local district heads, nor with the many scholars and notables in his prefecture.[12]

These various problems were further complicated by the instability of certain regions. One district, for example, might require an entirely new type of administration following a political upheaval. In this way, the more unstable districts would have to be governed by an official whose "repressive techniques" were stressed during the recruitment process. But as the "pacification" progressed, this type of civil servant often turned out to be poorly adapted to the job, like Pham Huu Uyên, the district magistrate of Câm Khê.[13] Another example is Pham Huy Bich, an official without a diploma who was later transferred from the district of Phu Yên to that of Trân Yên (Yên Bay Province),[14] where his military experience was better appreciated.[15]

2. The Reestablishment of the Apprenticeship

The First Step: Reducing the Number of Supernumerary Civil Servants

The reestablishment of the use of *hâu bô* in 1892 was soon coupled with a decree by the imperial inspector in 1897[16] prohibiting the appointment of supernumerary civil servants. Provincial mandarins were no longer allowed to hire their own underlings, an act that had allowed them to bypass official approval by the authorities of the protectorate. These "unofficial" mandarins, moreover, were not remunerated for their services. A similar decree in 1889[17] prohibited the employment of other officials: *hâu phai* (expectant delegate), *sai phai* (entrusted with a mission), *tung phai* (attaché under orders), *tuy phai* (sent under orders), and *si bô* (waiting for an appointment). This decree, however, was given little respect, judging by the preponderance of these officials in 1895. They were particularly numerous in the provinces of the Red River delta, compared to the number of *hâu bô:*[18] eight officials versus seven *hâu bô* in the province of Hà Nôi, and fourteen versus seven *hâu bô* in Hai Duong Province.[19]

It is difficult to make a distinction among these four official positions since the career files of these civil servants rarely contained detailed information about the nature of their work. The few more concrete examples show that these officials were appointed to accomplish ad hoc missions, which could take on a military character, as was the case with Phan Huu Tri[20] and Lê Ngu. The latter "had obtained the title of *tu tai* [lesser regional graduate] in the third year of Dông Khanh; in the fourth year, fifth month, he was sent to Hung Hoa Province on an informational mission regarding the activities of an outlaw; in the fifth year, second month, he was promoted to the grade of *hàn lâm viên dai chieu* (9b) to carry out his duties as district educational officer (*huân dao*) of Tam Nông."[21]

These missions could also be administrative in nature. This was the case with Nguyên Van Binh, who was removed from his post as acting district magistrate in February 1891 and then named "expectant delegate" (*hâu phai*) in the provinces of Hung Yên (September 1891–June 1894), Bac Ninh (June 1894–April 1895), and Hà Nôi. In the latter two provinces, he was given the task of overseeing the maintenance work on the dikes.[22] Phan Kê Tiên, who was a top regional graduate (*cu nhân*) in the thirty-second year of Tu Duc (1879), was first sent to the province of Hà Nôi as *hâu phai*. It was in this capacity that he was appointed acting district magistrate of Dan Phuong from the fifth to the seventh month of the first year of Kiên Phuc (1884), then of the prefecture of Tung Thiên from the seventh to the eleventh month.[23] In this sense, these officials played a role that strongly resembled that of the *hâu bô*. This explains the frequent confusion, up until 1897, in the same career file among the titles of *hâu phai*, *sai phai*, and *hâu bô*.

This surfeit of officials sparked two kinds of criticism. First, their placement completely escaped the control of the central authorities. Second, they were reproached for being corrupt because of the lack of remuneration. The imperial decree to prohibit further use of these unofficial civil servants was thus quite understandable. And to further remedy the situation the *hâu bô* were accorded a monthly salary of thirty ligatures.[24]

Objectives of the Apprenticeship

The transformation from a mandarinate "of conquest" to one "of administration" thus began with the reestablishment of the use of *hâu bô* in 1892. This change took place by means of a change in recruitment policy, which aimed at better controlling the qualifications of future mandarins and familiarizing them with administration practices.

The first task was to verify the proper qualifications of the candidates for the post of district magistrate. Each mandarin received an annual evaluation, detailing his employment record and activities. Often, however, the information provided therein was terribly incomplete. Sometimes the only document provided by provincial mandarins as proof of their training was the curriculum vitae prepared by the candidate himself. In 1891, one *résident* de France stressed "the need for reestablishing the *hâu bô*, five or six per province." Provincial authorities often recognized the fact that they knew nothing about the past or previous service record of the officials being proposed to them. The reestablishment of the use of *hâu bô* took care of this problem since it was henceforth possible to eliminate candidates whose nomination was not justified and to promote those who would distinguish themselves through good work.[25]

The second step toward transforming the mandarinate into a more administrative one was to familiarize the graduates of the examinations with administrative practices. This was achieved by reestablishing the apprenticeship—an institution that had been in use since the beginning of the Nguyên dynasty. This tradition was expressly demanded by the initiators of the 1892 decision regarding *hâu bô*, like the *résident supérieur*, Mr. Brière. The emperors, in fact, had attached great importance to the apprenticeship completed by the young *hâu bô*. The latter were to be familiarized "with the ensemble of administrative activities,"[26] as indicated in a law of 1837. The language used in these imperial rulings brought out the truly probationary nature of this training period: "thi chinh lâm dân."[27]

The Vietnamese monarchs put much emphasis on this mandarinal training and were disappointed to see, in 1826 and 1836, that many *hâu bô* remained without work in the provincial capitals. This is because the provincial mandarins tended to entrust the duties of the acting district magistrate to their administrative assistants (*thông phan*) and registrars (*kinh lich*.)[28] The emperor deemed the latter unqualified and would have preferred the work be assigned to the young *hâu bô* graduates.[29] Emperor Minh Mang (reigned 1820–41) particularly stressed the risks of appointing inexperienced graduates to an official post as prefect or district magistrate. He presented the risks in realistic terms: "Do we ever ask a debutante to sew or work a precious brocade?"[30] He then cited as an example the case of Truong Suong, who, "under the Han dynasty, had served as *kinh triêu*[31] for only five days. How could he then have governed the people in the name of the emperor?"[32] But the emperor then noted harshly that the majority of *hâu bô*, who would later "have a responsibility to the people" when appointed to civil service posts, were not being initiated into the administrative practices of the prefectures and districts. In other words, they remained idle since provincial mandarins did not send them out on missions.

This problem remained in effect for a long time, for in the sixth year of the reign of Thiêu Tri a ruling stated that a civil servant should be transferred to another province if he had waited for three years and still found no vacancies that could provide him with a job.³³ This same reasoning explains certain measures that required the students of the Imperial Academy (Quôc Tu Giam)³⁴ and "older" *cu nhân* to find work in the ministries as apprentices (*hành tâu*) and to renounce their preparation for the examinations in the capital.³⁵ Under the reign of Tu Duc, Nguyên Truong Tô, in a petition called *Tê câp bat diêu* (Eight urgent matters), dated 15 November 1867, pointed out that the court had similar difficulties in implementing the internship for this apprenticeship. For instance, he condemned the discrepancy between knowledge and the lack of practice in the apprenticeship of the future mandarins and he advocated the necessity of a required internship for the *tu tài* and *cu nhân* as public servants in the Six Boards.³⁶ An ordinance of the first year of Thành Thai (1889)³⁷ repeated the fact that all graduates had to complete an apprenticeship, but it apparently had little effect. Then, in 1892, the authorities of the protectorate reiterated this demand for a mandatory training period and redefined its terms and conditions.

Young apprentices and prefects were also given instruction manuals for administrative practices, like the *Si hoan châm quy* and the *Si hoan tu tri*. The latter was written by Nguyên Công Tiêp in the third year of Minh Mang (1822). They contained very precise information regarding fiscal matters, weights and measures, and hydraulics—issues of use to the young mandarin. These manuals showed some obvious similarities with the Chinese manuals of the eighteenth century, which have been praised by the sinologist Etienne Balazs.³⁸

Terms and Conditions of the Training Period

Now that we have established the importance of the training period, we must specify the terms and conditions and show the permanence of the institution. Until 1884, the apprenticeship could take three forms: an apprenticeship in the provinces as *hâu bô*, in the provinces as mandarin-teacher, and in the ministries.

Provincial Apprenticeships
It is first of all surprising that, in 1892, the use of *hâu bô* was reestablished by a law issued by the *résident supérieur*. In fact, the term ap-

pears very frequently in the career files of mandarins between 1884 and 1892. In the registers of 1897, for example, most *hâu bô* were older mandarins who had already been assigned permanent positions in the bureaucracy. Only a few of the young students were named *hâu bô* shortly after passing their examinations. This dichotomy reveals the true nature of the term *hâu bô*, which does not mean "apprentice" but literally "expectant appointee." Until 1892, it designated two types of situations: mandarins already assigned a post in the bureaucracy who took a leave of absence, and the graduates of the palace examinations waiting to be placed as apprentices.[39]

A mandarin already engaged in an administrative career was required to undergo a certain waiting period after taking a leave of absence from his post. This was the case with Dao Trong Tê, who was appointed *hâu bô* to the office of the imperial inspector after a bereavement leave in the second month of the eighth year of Thành Thai (1896).[40] Another example is Trân Xuân Son, who was appointed *hâu bô* in Nam Dinh Province in the first year of Kiên Phuc (1884) after a convalescent leave.[41] Nguyên Huu Tô, as acting district educational officer in Quang Nam, was named *hâu bô* after a parental care leave.[42] A mandarin who had been suspended from his functions could also be named *hâu bô*, as was the case with Nguyên Liêm. He was called back as *hâu bô* of Thai Binh Province after having been dismissed from his post as district magistrate of Tiên Hung for grave negligence in overseeing the construction of the dikes in the eighth month of the sixth year of Thành Thai (September 1894).[43]

The second type of *hâu bô* referred to those students who had passed one of the examinations at the palace (*hach khiêu*). Those eligible to take the examination were either graduates of the regional examinations or "shade students" (*âm sinh*),[44] who could then be named *hâu bô* as apprentices in the provinces.[45] These palace examinations had been established in an ordinance of the seventh year of Minh Mang (1826) for the top regional graduates (*cu nhân*) and students of the Imperial Academy.[46] In this way, Phan Huu Tu, originally from the prefecture of Dông Thành in Nghê An, graduated *cu nhân* from the regional examination of Nghê An in the third year of Thiêu Tri (1843) and was appointed "expectant appointee" of Hung Yên Province after having passed the palace examination in the first year of Tu Duc (1848). Bui Dam had also been admitted as a student at the Imperial Academy in the eighteenth year of Tu Duc (1865). He passed the palace examination in the sixth month of the thirty-second year (1879) and was then named an expectant appointee.[47]

The apprenticeship could take two forms: the *hâu bô* would either be sent on an ad hoc mission to resolve a hydraulic, fiscal, or judicial problem, or he would take on the duties of an interim position. Thus, in 1836 Emperor Minh Mang called upon provincial mandarins to appoint *hâu bô* to take care of legal matters. They were sent to the closest prefecture and district seats in the province to form an investigative commission with the prefects and district magistrates.[48] This type of mission was obviously based on the imperial system, as the language of the 1892 law reveals: "They [the *hâu bô*] could also be sent into the interior of the province, either to supervise the construction of the dikes or to initiate administrative investigations, etc."[49]

By providing examples from as late as the 1920s, we shall show that this apprenticeship, whereby *hâu bô* and acting district magistrates familiarized themselves with local administrative practices, had achieved permanence in the bureaucratic landscape of the protectorate. Trân Van Ky, a former free student of the school for *hâu bô*, passed the school's exams in 1903 and was appointed to the province of Phu Lô. He was evaluated with high recommendations: he "knows *quôc ngu* and some words of French, . . . [was] assigned to the construction of roads and dikes,[50] [and] accompanied land surveyors in their work."[51] The *hâu bô* could also be sent as assistants (*tro biên*) to the busier regions to help the acting prefects or district magistrates, as in the case of Trân Van Ky: he "proved his knowledge in administrative affairs as assistant during the one-month leave of the *dông tri phu* of Yên Lang, during which time he provided much help to the district educational officer in the expedition of his affairs. He also taught some of the classes given to the communal teachers."[52] In February 1909, he received his appointment as *hâu bô* in Thai Nguyên, to serve as acting district magistrate of Phô Yên. He died in December 1910, just before being assigned a permanent post. Yet another example is that of Doan Quan, graduate of the School for Mandarins, who was appointed apprentice district magistrate in September 1917 and then sent to the office of the governor-general of Hà Dông. He was sent to work at the Commission for Demarcation of Villages in the province in November 1917.[53]

The apprenticeship could also take the form of an interim position as district magistrate, as stipulated by a decree of the seventh year of Minh Mang.⁵⁴ This training period was intended to test the administrative capacities of future mandarins. The language of the 1892 law, then, clearly harkens back to this imperial regulation: "These civil servants [the *hâu bô*] could be employed as interns in the prefectures and districts or in the offices of the regional capital, or designated to temporarily carry out the duties of *huân dao, giao thu, tri huyên,* [or] *tri phu,* in the case of vacancies."⁵⁵

The following examples illustrate this kind of activity: Ngô Kim Liên entered the Imperial Academy in the seventh year of Minh Mang (1826). Two years later, he was named "expectant appointee" of Bac Thành, where he served successively as acting district magistrate of Son Duong, Tam Duong, and Thuy Anh.⁵⁶ Phan Trong Dich graduated as *cu nhân* from Hanoi in the twenty-seventh year of Tu Duc (1874). In the fourth month of the thirty-second year (1879), he had been given the rank of *diên tich* (8a), and was posted to the province of Nam Dinh as *hâu bô*. He served as district magistrate of Vu Ban and of Thu Tri, then as prefect of Vinh Tuong and Thai Binh.⁵⁷ Nguyên Huu Tuong, the son of Nguyên Huu Dô,⁵⁸ graduated as *cu nhân* from Thua Thiên in the third year of Dông Khanh (1888), the session of Mâu Ty. In the fourth month of the fourth year of Thành Thai (1892), he earned the rank of *diên tich* (8a), and was sent to the office of the imperial inspector as an expectant appointee employed as district magistrate of Nam Truc.⁵⁹ Another example is Trân Van Ky, who had also been sent on many ad hoc missions: he "taught *quôc ngu* as acting *huân dao,* and his candidacy was proposed for the position of *huân dao.*"⁶⁰ Pham Chu Trinh, who graduated as *cu nhân* of Hà Nam in 1908 and graduated from the school for *hâu bô* in July 1913, was first posted as acting district magistrate in Vinh Yên Province. He was then sent to the district of Hoàn Long at the request of Hoàng Trong Phu, governor-general of Hà Dông. The latter justified this request by citing the shortage of personnel ever since the district of Hoàn Long had been attached to the province. The governor-general needed a civil servant who would be "sent upon rounds in villages to assure the proper maintenance of civil records and also to see that the 'customary of the village' (*huong chinh*) was established in a number of villages, followed-up, and executed with the desired punctuality." The success of communal reforms depended on it, according to Hoàng Trong Phu. Trinh remained an intern for two and a half years (December 1913–June 1916).⁶¹ These various examples illustrate the diversity of the work practiced by the *hâu bô* during their apprenticeships.

Apprenticeships as Mandarin-Teacher

Some graduates of the examinations underwent an apprenticeship under different conditions. While not officially *hâu bô,* they familiarized themselves with the management of public affairs as district educational officers (*huân dao*) or prefecture educational officers (*giao thu*). Sometimes they were called upon to serve as prefects or district magistrates in the absence of the latter. This type of activity was established by Minh Mang in an ordinance of the sixteenth year of his reign,[62] later under Tu Duc in 1848,[63] and then under Dông Khanh in 1887.[64]

Trân Xuân Son is a good example. He graduated as a lesser regional graduate in the twenty-first year of Tu Duc (1868), was appointed that same year as *huân dao* of Nam Xang, and then served concurrently as acting district magistrate of the same region in the thirty-first year of Tu Duc (1878).[65] It was the same with Pham Huu Thanh, who graduated as a lesser regional graduate in 1884, then as a top regional graduate in 1891. He served as *huân dao* of Yên Dung (Bac Giang Province) from October of 1891 to April 1896, was on leave from April 1896 to March 1899, and was entrusted with the functions of district magistrate of Dan Phuong and then of acting district educational officer of Gia Lâm District in July 1899. In 1905, on top of his duties as district educational officer, he was "put in charge of current affairs during the absence of the *tri huyên,* detained for two months in Tu Son for the repair of the dikes,"[66] and described in 1906 as "conscientious and active, provides much help to the *tri huyên* of Gia Lâm, seems to have the desired qualities to enter into active administration."[67]

Dang Van Hoa is another example. He graduated as *cu nhân* of Hà Nam in 1897, was appointed auxiliary district educational officer of Thanh Ba (Hung Hoa Province) in August 1898, and was made permanent district educational officer (with a rank of 8a) in February 1902. In that same year, he was named district magistrate of Thanh Ba, concurrently with his functions as *huân dao.* He was later appointed examiner (*so khao*) at the examinations of Nam Dinh in 1903; *huân dao* of Kim Bang (Hà Nam Province) in May 1907; and district magistrate second class (7a) of Luc Ngan (Bac Giang Province) in July 1908.[68] He then distinguished himself "in the overseeing and management of the reconstruction works of the dikes" in 1906.[69] He was nominated in 1903 for inscription in the "list of promotion" and officially inscribed on Têt in 1907.[70]

Apprenticeship in the Ministries
Finally, an apprenticeship in the provinces was not the only way to become familiar with public administration. Some graduates, or *âm sinh*, were appointed as apprentices (*hành tâu*) in one of the Six Boards (Luc Bô) or in other offices of the central government.[71] An ordinance of the first year of Thành Thai (1889) reiterated the need for graduates to complete an apprenticeship if they wanted to embark upon an administrative career.[72] Thus, Dao Trong Ky, after having graduated as *cu nhân* from Nam Dinh in the seventeenth year of Tu Duc (1864), was assigned in the twenty-second year (1869) as an apprentice in the Silk Threads Office (Ty Luân So).[73] This office was subordinate to the Grand Secretariat (Nôi Cac) and was in charge of drafting the emperor's ordinances, receiving petitions, and storing the manuscripts of these decrees and ordinances.[74] As a last example, Vu Khac Hiêu graduated from the examinations of Nam Dinh in the thirty-second year of Tu Duc and then began as an apprentice in the Ministry of Public Function.[75] This type of apprenticeship disappeared after the separation of the two administrations of Annam and Tonkin.

3. From the School for *Hâu Bô* to the School for Mandarins

The simple restoration of the apprenticeship could only achieve so much, however, and in the early 1890s it seemed that something else would have to be done to train future civil servants. Thus, in November 1896 the imperial inspector Hoàng Cao Khai proposed that a school be created to teach French and *quôc ngu*. It was to be created in his own offices and destined for the use of thirty *hâu bô*.[76] His proposal was accepted, and the school was officially opened on 2 February 1897. The school was for the use of top and lesser regional graduates, *âm sinh*, appointed as *hâu bô* in the provinces, as well as for "free students" who had never been *hâu bô*. At the end of six months, all students had to take an examination. The hardest working were immediately assigned to posts in the administration by order of merit. The weakest continued to take courses.

Hoàng Cao Khai's plan to establish classes in French and *quôc ngu* had three objectives: to improve the functioning of the administration, to train the children of mandarins, and to eradicate the idleness of the *hâu bô*. The classes involved the reading and writing of *quôc ngu* and French and easy conversations in French using administrative terms regarding the collection of taxes, the construction of dikes, and the justice system. The pedagogical ambitions of the imperial inspector seemed, in fact, rather modest. But the practical and concrete orientation he gave to the school was never questioned, not even during the reforms of 1906 and 1912. Of course, the curriculum was diversified and the length of the course of study was prolonged,[77] but practical subjects like agronomy, practical geometry, and hygiene always remained central.[78] This teaching thus prepared the students for an apprenticeship in the provinces.

Providing education for the children of mandarins was the second concern of Hoàng Cao Khai. At that time there were no schools for these children, and Khai had remarked that the provincial schools could not fulfill this function. These provincial schools had been established under the protectorate to teach French in preparation for administrative duties. Khai explained why most mandarinal families were not keen on these schools. Most of the students were "from poor families . . . , [so] the best job they could hope for was that of interpreter. . . . The latter position would never be considered as prestigious as a mandarin. This is why the families of high rank prefer that their children learn Chinese characters and take the literary examinations, so that they may later enter into the mandarinate."[79] Also, to attract the children of mandarins to his school, the imperial inspector did not put any lower age limit on the admission of *âm sinh*. Nevertheless, the age of the first students to pass through the school was relatively high: the average age was thirty-seven for the *hâu bô* and thirty-one for the free students,[80] which was considered an obstacle to the success of the apprenticeship.[81]

The third objective of the school was to eradicate the idleness of the *hâu bô*. The following remarks of Hoàng Cao Khai reveal the limits of the law of 1892 and echo those of the emperors, Minh Mang in particular. It seems that the *résidents* de France and the provincial mandarins didn't always give the *hâu bô* a chance to learn about public affairs: "When there is a vacant post it is not always the *hâu bô* who are appointed, and often the appointees are people who were never *hâu bô*. Often the *hâu bô* have to wait three or four years before they find a job. We are creating this school so that they can find work and be appointed immediately."[82] According to a government circular of 9 January 1897, students who had passed an examination, completed a sufficient apprenticeship as a *hâu bô,* or already worked in an administrative position could, at the end of six months, be provided with a job as vacancies opened, as long as they did not prefer to resume their studies. As for top and lesser regional graduates, *âm sinh,* who had not yet worked in the administration and were following courses as free students, following this first exam (at the end of six months), they could be appointed as *hâu bô* in the provinces to fill positions left vacant by the appointment of previous *hâu bô,* to a job in the active administration, or to teaching.

Between 1906 and 1911, French authorities in the protectorate were obliged to profoundly reform the system of mandarinal apprenticeships as well as the school for *hâu bô* itself. These reforms came about as a result of problems within the institution of the *hâu bô,* on the one hand, and of changes within the mandarinate on the other. The separation of the mandarinate into two bodies—for teaching and administration—was projected in 1908 and brought about the disappearance of the apprenticeship as mandarin-teacher.[83] Pedagogical training no longer served to further administrative functioning. Furthermore, the apprenticeship in the ministries was discontinued upon the division of the administration of Annam and Tonkin, coupled with the split of the mandarinate of the north into two separate bodies. This left the school of the *hâu bô* as the only remaining practical training establishment for public administration. But even this institution was going through a crisis, sparked by overpoliticization and the general lack of employment among *hâu bô.*

Criticism was primarily aimed at the insufficient preparation of some students enrolled in the school of *hâu bô* and more particularly of the *âm sinh.* Despite the strict rules relating to the responsibilities of the *âm sinh* at the end of the nineteenth century,[84] it seems that obtaining that title was much less rigorously controlled. The title was sometimes awarded even when the candidate had not taken an examination, since the protectorate wanted to "create a number of partisans for itself."[85] The case of Lê Ky, the uncle of Governor-General Lê Hoan, is a good example of this. As district magistrate of Tiên Du, Ky wrote to the *résident* de France to ask that his son, Lê Manh Trinh, be admitted to the school for *hâu bô.* He made no allusion to any examination required for the title of *âm sinh,* and proof of his son's competence was rather thin.[86]

There was also a problem of cheating on the examinations, which was denounced in particular by a "group of provincial advisers" in 1909.[87] The latter also criticized the excessive generosity of the protectorate, which led to the appointing of *ấm sinh* who were inexperienced and ignorant of the Chinese characters necessary for the functions of district magistrate.[88] This criticism is corroborated by other sources as well.[89] In 1906, radical measures were adopted to halt these abuses, whereby: "No one [could] take on administrative functions if he [did] not have a university degree."[90] According to this principle, then, the *ấm sinh* could no longer become prefects or district magistrates. In reality, however, this new regulation had little effect.[91]

Beyond the problem of the *ấm sinh*, the lax recruitment of the free students came under fire. We find proof of this in a handwritten note printed in the margin of the decree appointing Trân Van Ky, former free student of the school for *hâu bô*, as *hâu bô* of Phu Lô Province: "The free students were admitted with the provision that no position or job would be guaranteed to them upon their graduation. The recruitment process then became a bit more lenient, and they were even permitted to follow courses that had begun a long time before."[92] As an example, Dao Quang Tich, the son of a mandarin, who was admitted to the school as a free student,[93] only stayed one year (1902–3)—versus three years for the scholarship students. In practice, it was decided that free students should be named to tenured positions more slowly than the scholarship students as district magistrates or district educational commissioners.[94] A quota was also established for the admission of the *ấm sinh*.[95] Moreover, a variety of measures were adopted to improve the quality of their selection. First, starting in 1910, the examinations for *ấm sinh* in Hanoi were to take place at the *résidence supérieure*, in the presence of a special commission.[96] Second, from 1907 onward all students wishing to enter the school for *hâu bô* would have to pass a test in the Chinese language. This would permit "the elimination of those young *ấm sinh* who are very weak in Chinese."[97]

The apprenticeship, however, was eventually deemed ineffectual. Most *hâu bô* remained without work, the *résidents* and the provincial mandarins leaving them idle in the regional capitals—despite the fact that the authorities at the *résidence supérieure* had frequently reminded provincial leaders to supervise and take over the training of these apprentices.[98] The lack of work had two causes: the low salaries of the *hâu bô* and the ambiguity of their status.

In 1906, the salary of a *hâu bô* was roughly ten to twelve piasters, which led to a higher incidence of abuses and corruption during their missions in the prefectures and districts. Table 1 shows how long it took for these salaries to rise. The gap between the monthly salary of a student at the school for *hâu bô* and a district magistrate got slightly narrower between January 1898 and April 1906, but it widened again in May 1906. A new gap appeared, however, between the salaries of graduates of the school and those who had not passed through its doors, favoring the former. This financial incentive given to graduates of the school, accorded in January 1908, was clearly destined to encourage *hâu bô* to enroll in courses in the school. Then, in 1911, the Reform Commission doubled the salaries of mandarin-apprentices, solidifying their renewed status.

The idleness of the *hâu bô* was also a result of a problem faced by provincial mandarins, who were reluctant to hire these young civil servants with no experience in administrative affairs. They hesitated to assign the *hâu bô* tasks in the provincial bureaucracy, for it gave them an advantage over prefects and district magistrates. Such tasks could be anything from confidential missions and investigations to helping out a provincial administration commissioner (*bô chinh*) or judicial commissioner (*an sat*) who was too busy with work, replacing a district magistrate with legal problems, and settling an affair that was not important enough to require the presence of a provincial mandarin. This reluctance to hire *hâu bô* was a result of the ambiguity of their status. The term itself designated either a young graduate of the school for *hâu bô* who had been sent to the provinces upon graduation or an "occasional aide" to provincial mandarins. The latter, for example, might be a career civil servant who was sent to the provinces after a leave of absence to work in the offices of the governor-general. Here he could take over the duties of interim positions or fill vacancies caused by illness, death, or the suspension of a prefect or district magistrate in the region.

It was clear that the first type of *hâu bô*, the student, had great problems commanding the respect of prefects and district magistrates while he was on a mission. This is why the *résidents* and provincial mandarins hesitated to entrust him with investigations or work in the

TABLE 1

	hậu bổ (still in school)	hậu bổ (already working in province)	tri huyện (district magistrate)	Income of the tri huyện (district magistrate) in relation to that of the hậu bổ (still in school).[1]	Income of the tri huyện (district magistrate) in relation to that of the hậu bổ (already working in province)
1892 (January)[2]	30 lig. (= 4 piasters)	30 lig. (= 4 piasters)	160 lig. (=25 piasters)	5.3 times more	5.3 times more
1897 (September)[3]	30 lig. (= 4 piasters)	30 lig. (= 4 piasters)	160 lig. (=25 piasters)	5.3 times more	5.3 times more
1898 (January)[4]	50 lig. (= 7 piasters)	30 lig. (= 4 piasters)	160 lig. (=25 piasters)	3.2 times more	5.3 times more
1899[5]	8.3 piasters	5 piasters	26.67 piasters	3.2 times more	5.3 times more
1906 (May)[6]	12 piasters	10 piasters	46.66 piasters[7]	3.8 times more	4.6 times more
1912 (February)[8]	31.6 piasters (apprentice district magistrate)		46.66 piasters[9]	1.5 times more	

[1] The salary of the district magistrate (*tri huyện*) was divided by that of the *hậu bổ* (still in school) and in the next column by that of the *hậu bổ* (already working in province).

[2] Arrêté (4/01/1892) of Lanessan, Gouverneur-Général de l'Indochine in NAC, RST 57395: *Augmentation de solde du personnel de l'administration indigène* (1887–1931).

[3] Circular 928 (9/17/1897) of the Résident Supérieur: "Report of the salaries of the local administrative personnel, in ligatures, with the conversion in piasters at a rate of 7 ligatures," in the *Bulletin Officiel de l'Indochine Française*, in the section Annam-Tonkin, 1381. The new scale of salaries took effect from 1 January 1898.

[4] Arrêté (12/31/1897) of the Résident Supérieur in the *Bulletin Officiel de l'Indochine Française*, part of Annam-Tonkin, 9.

[5] DNDLTY, 240–43.

[6] Arrêté 1581 (5/26/1906) of the Résident Supérieur establishing the tariff in piasters of the local administrative personnel in NAC, RST 46464. Also see DNDLTY, 252–53.

[7] This figure corresponds to the salary of a tenured district magistrate (rank of 6b).

[8] Chart of the salaries annexed to the royal ordinance of 2/3/1912 in NAC, RST 57395.

[9] This number corresponds to the salary of a district magistrate first class (6b). It does not take into account the indemnity of duties.

interior and ended up by generally losing interest in him. This left the *hâu bô* in his regional capital with no work. To remedy this situation, graduates of the school for *hâu bô* were no longer required to complete an apprenticeship.[99] Instead, they were immediately appointed to the post of district magistrate as vacancies opened up, given priority over all other candidates. Only the worst students still had to complete an apprenticeship of at least two years upon graduation. This measure was criticized, however, because it appointed candidates who were too young, or who lacked experience, to the head of certain regions.[100] Because of this problem, the measure was not strictly applied.

The issue of age was the most difficult to settle: how could they reconcile a change in the mandarinate based on the recruitment of young students with the need to have apprentices who were old enough to be able to command respect?[101] To lessen the ambiguity of the status of *hâu bô* and give a better impression of this apprenticeship, the *hâu bô* were given a new title: apprentice district magistrate (*hâu tuyên tri huyên*). This new "denomination would indicate more clearly the nature of the training imposed."[102] Moreover, in 1912 the school for *hâu bô* was transformed into the School of Mandarins (Si Hoan Truong). The terms and conditions of the apprenticeship were then redefined and made more rigid.

Inexperience was not necessarily linked to age,[103] but also to the level of difficulty of the *hâu bô*'s first appointment. An apprentice who had undergone his training period in a relatively trouble free region would find himself poorly prepared for the functions of a prefect. This is made clear in the example of Pham Van Triêu, an *âm sinh* graduate of the school for *hâu bô* in 1913. He received very good marks as acting district magistrate in Son Tây, where he was twice appointed acting district magistrate of Tung Thiên (in 1914 and 1915). During this time, he distinguished himself through his zeal in working on the dikes.[104] He was then named district magistrate of the difficult region of Kim Son, a job for which he was ill prepared by his three years of "not very absorbing work as acting *tri huyên* in Son Tây," according to the *résident* de France at Ninh Binh.[105] Kim Son was in fact the region of Ninh Binh that was the hardest to administer because of its dense population (there were sixty-six villages). This situation was made even more difficult, however, "because its regional seat was very close to the bishopric, so interference by the mission was felt, either openly or more subtly, in all matters of business." Triêu, in fact, did experience difficulties later in trying to "move between the Catholics and the Buddhists."[106]

A similar example is Pham Van Thiêu, a graduate of the School for Mandarins and a very good student (fourth in the final exam). In September 1914, he was appointed acting district magistrate of Hà Nam, representing the local provincial authorities to the Commission of Regional Boundary Demarcation. He was given very good marks, as expressed by the following report: "Thanks to his spirit of conciliation, he was able to avoid a number of legal battles between communities."[107] After a three-year apprenticeship as acting district magistrate of Hà Nam, he was named district magistrate of Gia Lâm in July 1917. But the *résident* de France deemed him too young and lacking in experience: "[He] does not currently have sufficient authority over the communal and local authorities [during the reconstructing of the dikes at Giang Hô]."[108] The *résident* also stated that it would have been better if Thiêu had begun his career in a less important district than Gia Lâm.[109]

In order to compensate for the inexperience of these apprentices, the administration often assigned them to tenured posts, where they could work with experienced prefects and district magistrates, and placed them at the head of the busier regions.[110] Some examples, like that of Nguyên Nhu Duy, show that this solution was sometimes still practiced at the end of the nineteenth century. In 1893, Nguyên Nhu Duy was a young mandarin who had recently arrived in the province of Hung Hoa. Governor-General Lê Hoàn had put forth the proposal that he be named district magistrate of Tam Nông, which was very close to the regional seat.[111] This solution became more widespread in the years 1908–10. Thus, apprentices often received permanent appointments to prefectures that were close to the provincial capitals, where they would learn more regarding the practical application of theoretical studies and where control was easier to exercise.[112] Another example is that of Nguyên Duc Chiêu.

> A former student of the school for Si Hoan [School for Mandarins], he took part in the permanent mission created under the government of Paul Beau and spent several months in France. If you agree to designate him for [the district of] My Lôc, I will be able to advise him and guide him as need arises, to follow him closely in any case, and more accurately

judge his true worth. The head of the district is less than one kilometer from the center of the city [of Nam Dinh].

From then on, the appointment of an apprentice was made dependent upon his ability to carry out the duties of district magistrate or prefect. In reality, this evaluation of a candidate's abilities was not new. In the first half of the nineteenth century, it could not be assumed that a *hâu bô* would be assigned a tenured position in the administration. It was dependent upon provincial mandarins, who decided whether the candidate would be able to carry out his duties as prefect or district magistrate. This was the case for Nguyên Duc Tu, who had to undergo such an examination in the thirtieth year of Tu Duc (1877). The provincial mandarins of Hai Duong proposed Tu's nomination, "having found him diligent, educated, and able to serve as prefect in a difficult jurisdiction."[113]

This sort of evaluation had not completely fallen out of use in the first years of the protectorate, as may be seen in some rare examples like that of Lê Huy Phan. In 1887, the latter had been deemed "diligent and ready for his appointment as prefect" by the provincial mandarins of Nam Dinh.[114] This evaluation was officially reconfirmed in 1912.[115] The probationary character of the apprenticeship is illustrated by the example of Pham Quang Khiêt. He was an *âm sinh*, son of a former governor-general, Pham Van Toàn. He was named *hâu bô* of Nam Dinh in February 1911 and then assistant (*tro biên*) to the district of Truc Ninh in October and November 1915. He was proposed for the job of registrar, for he seemed "especially capable of working in the administration." He had at the time five years seniority as *hâu bô*.[116]

Conclusion

In this essay, I have shown the importance of the mandarinal recruitment process and the apprenticeship's practice in Vietnam, aspects often neglected in other historical research. For instance, the question of the practice, that is, internship of the apprentices, during both the colonial period and under the Nguyên dynasties, didn't used to be discussed in the literature because many studies were often based on either secondary sources (books, reports) or official texts (decrees, laws). In contrast, this detailed study of careers and curricula vitae gives us a better understanding of all aspects of this apprenticeship. And, as this chapter demonstrates, such an apprenticeship cannot simply be reduced to a theoretical education. Finally, I have argued that the reestablishment of the mandarinal apprenticeship and the creation of the school for *hâu bô,* two essential aspects of the rehabilitation of the mandarinate at the end of the French pacification, also greatly contributed to the revitalization of the mandarinate and reconciliation with the mandarinal elite. In fact, both the practice of internship and the school for *hâu bô* had been integrated into the mandarinal curriculum as early as the fifteenth century.

The colonial authorities in Tonkin adopted this ancient practice but did not simply reproduce it. The French, however, integrated into this traditional administrative practice new knowledge in order to improve the efficiency of mandarinal training. The mandarins who received an apprenticeship were not simply bureaucrats but also practitioners. They were administrators able to deal by themselves with matters such as repairing dikes, raising taxes, and issues relating to laws. In schools, this apprenticeship was to complement the existing training. Thus, it trained mandarins to become cultural brokers for the colonial rural reforms. For instance, the success of this hybrid apprenticeship relied essentially on the mandarin's abilities to negotiate with villagers. The mandarins played an important role, allowing the French colonial administration to finance its new infrastructure, introduce reforms, create registry offices, implement new laws, and promote new crops and handicrafts. But in this colonial context the position of the mandarins was ambiguous, being the agents of "modernity" and change but at the same time local tax collectors representing the colonial authorities.

NOTES

École Française d'Extrême-Orient, Hanoi. I would like to thank Claire Duiker for the translation of this essay.

1. Since the reign of Lê Thanh Tông (1460–97), a candidate for a mandarinal position had to be an intern for three years and then be evaluated (*so khao*) before he could graduate. If the intern (*thi quan*) received a negative evaluation, he was excluded from the bureaucracy. Lê Kim Ngân, *Tô chuc chinh quyên trung uong duoi triêu Lê Thanh Tông (1460–1497)* (Saigon: Tu sach

vien khao ca hoc [TSVKCH], 1963), 159. Phan Dai Doan et al., *Môt sô vân dê vê quan chê triêu Nguyên* (Hue: Nha Xuat Ban [NXB] Thuân Hoa, 1998), 45.

2. The term *hâu bô* literally means "a civil servant waiting for an appointment." But it can also mean, as in the present case, an "intern in the administration as a civil servant."

3. National Archives Center (NAC), *Kinh luoc* Collection, Thanh Thai 9 (1897): *To trinh cua cac tinh Son Hung Tuyên giu nha kinh luoc vê viêc lai* [Report on the staff by the provincial mandarins of Son Tây, Hung Hoa, and Tuyên Quang to the attention of the imperial inspector's office] (register 2521); *Ly lich cua quan viên van vo thuôc cac tinh Thai Binh—Hai Ninh—Hà Nam và Hai Phong* [Curricula vitae of the civil and military mandarins of the provinces of Thai Binh, Hai Ninh, Hà Nam, and Hai Phong] (register 2520); *Danh sach quan chuc và ly lich quan chuc van vo cua cac tinh Lang Son, Cao Bang, Hung Yên* [Lists and curricula vitae of the civil and military mandarins of the provinces of Lang Son, Cao Bang, and Hung Yên] (register 2515).

4. Among prefects, the figure is 36 percent.

5. Among prefects, the figure is 75 percent.

6. Letter (4/21/1898) from the Résident Supérieur to the Résident de France of Bac Ninh, in the career file of Nguyên Hoàng Oanh, district magistrate, 1887–1899 (NAC, Résidence Supérieure du Tonkin, RST, 18318). The dates given refer to the official's entry into the administration, not to his taking over as district magistrate.

7. The district of Phu Xuyên had a large number of graduates of the civil service examinations. The people of this district, in fact, did refuse to submit to the authority of the district magistrate, who did not have a diploma. Pierre Pasquier, *L'Annam d'autrefois: Essai sur la constitution de l'Annam avant l'intervention française* (Paris: Société d'éditions géographiques, maritimes, et coloniales, [1907] 1929), 110–11.

8. Letter (1/16/1891) from the Governor-General of Son Tây to the Résident de France in the career file of Dinh Ky Than, district magistrate, 1878–1892 (NAC, RST 15434).

9. This phrase was employed by the *chef du service des affaires indigènes* in 1892 to justify a proposal by the imperial inspector, who wanted to reintegrate an official, Nguyên Thê Dông, into the administration—even though he had received very poor marks. Career report (4/22/1892) from the Chef du Service des Affaires Indigènes to the Résident Supérieur in the career file of Nguyên Thê Dông, district magistrate, 1886–1895 (NAC, RST 18370).

10. Résident de France of Cao Bang, in a letter (3/12/1891) to the Résident Supérieur, proposing the nomination of Pham Van Tiêm to the post of acting district magistrate of Thach An, in the career file of Pham Van Tiêm, district magistrate, 1893–1912 (NAC, RST 31444).

11. Report (10/27/1891) of Résident Supérieur Brière to the governor-general of Indochina, regarding the recruitment practices of civil servants to the local administration (NAC, RST 46376). The analyses of Luro, de Lanessan, and Pasquier lead to the same conclusion as that of Brière: that recruitment was based above all on loyalty, without concern for education or authority. E. Luro,

Cours d'administration annamite, S.l.n.d; 355/220, 510p., polygraphié, p.80. J. B. de Lanessan, *La colonisation française en Indochine* (Paris: Félix Alcan, 1895), 11–12; Pasquier, *L'Annam d'autrefois,* 110.

12. Letter (twenty-third day, fifth month, fourth year of Thanh Thai [6/17/1892]) from Hoàng Cao Khai to the Résident Supérieur in the career file of Trân Nhu Niên, district magistrate, 1892–1910 (NAC, RST 31528).

13. Letter (2/21/1893) from Vice Résident de France Goy of Hung Hoa to the Résident Supérieur of Tonkin in the career file of Pham Huu Uyên, district magistrate, 1876–1893 (NAC, RST 16294). The career of Pham Van Ky, a defector from the military mandarinate, also illustrates this difficult change: "Was a good partisan leader and, as such, rendered a great service. They made a real mistake by making him a *tri huyên,* for he now stands out in his duties not only through total incompetence but with a rapacity that makes him hate the locals. I am obliged to bar him from almost all work." Statement by the Résident de France of Thai Nguyên in the career file of Pham Van Ky, district magistrate, 1894–1909 (NAC, RST 31425).

14. Brevet 90 (3/6/1903). Résident Supérieur of Tonkin in the career file of Pham Huy Bich.

15. Personal evaluation (12/1899) in the career file of Pham Huy Bich.

16. Decision 230 (6/21/1897) by the imperial inspector, approved and disseminated by the Résident Supérieur in a circular of 7/3/1897.

17. *Dai Nam diên lê toat yêu, Nguyên Si Giác phiên âm và dich nghia. Thanh pho.* [A summary of the statutes of imperial Vietnam (hereafter DNDLTY)], translated into Vietnamese by Nguyên Si Giac (Ho Chi Minh City: Nhà xuât ban Thành phô Hô Chí Minh, 1993), 55.

18. In the *arrêté* of 4 January 1892, the number of *hâu bô* was established at eight for the office of the imperial inspector; seven for each of the provinces of Hanoi, Bac Ninh, Nam Dinh, Hai Duong, and Son Tây; and four for each of the other provinces. NAC, RST 72003: *Code civil annamite en caractères avec traduction en français (Extraits d'ordonnances royales),* 1907.

19. Responses of the provincial leaders of Tonkin to circular 274 (7/5/1895) from the Secretary General of Indochina in NAC, RST 73541: *Liste des lettrés non pourvus d'emplois officiels* (1894–1895).

20. Curiculum vitae of Phan Huu Tri in NAC *Kinh luoc* Collection, register 2521, p. 25. Cf. also the career file of Phan Huu Tri (1893–1899), NAC, RST 17335.

21. From the curriculum vitae of Lê Ngu, prefect of Doan Hung (Hung Hoa Province) in 1897, in NAC *Kinh luoc* Collection, 2521, p. 42. (The pagination was done after the editing of the records. This excerpt and those following have been translated from the Chinese by the author.)

22. Letter (seventeenth day, fifth intercalary month, seventh year of Thanh Thai) from Nguyên Van Binh to the Secretary General of Indochina in the career file of Nguyên Van Binh, district magistrate, 1882–1891 (NAC, RST 18361).

23. From the curriculum vitae of Phan Kê Tiên, acting prefect of Quôc Oai (Son Tây Province) in 1897, in NAC *Kinh luoc* Collection, 2521, p. 17.

24. Hoang Cao Khai proposed establishing the monthly salary of the *hâu bô* at thirty ligatures, since that of the *huân dao* [mandarins of a rank immediately higher than the *hâu bô*] was forty ligatures. Brière supported this proposition, which was then included in article 4 of the *arrêté* of 4 January 1892. NAC, RST 46376: *Rapport (27/10/1891) de Brière, Résident Supérieur, au Gouverneur Général de l'Indochine, au sujet du mode de recrutement des fonctionnaires de l'administration indigène*. Arrêté (4/1/1892) Lanessan, Gouverneur Général de l'Indochine in NAC, RST 57395: *Augmentation de solde du personnel de l'administration indigène* (1887–1931).

25. Letter (11/18/1891) from Mr. Auvergne, Résident de France of Bac Ninh, to the Résident Supérieur of Tonkin, in the career file of Dao Nguyên Phô, district magistrate, 1890–1892 (NAC, RST 31093).

26. Ordinance of the eighteenth year of Minh Mang. DNDLTY, 54–55. *Khâm Dinh Dai Nam Hôi Diên Su Lê* [Official compendium of institutions and usages of imperial Vietnam (hereafter HDSL)] (Hue: 1993), 2:274–75.

27. *Thi*: "to test, experiment, try out"; *chinh*: "to administer, govern"; *lâm*: "to run, govern"; *dân*: "people." Expression used by Minh Mang during the seventh year of his rule (1826). *Minh Mênh Chinh Yêu ban dich cua Hoàng Du-Dông* [Book on the essentials of the rule of Minh Mang (hereafter, MMCY)], Saigon: Uy ban dich thuât, phu quôc-vu-khanh dac-trách van-hóa, 1972–74 (citation from the original text written in Chinese characters).

28. MMCY, 1:219.

29. Ibid., 191–92, 219.

30. Ibid., 219.

31. Mandarin at the court with important functions.

32. MMCY, 1:191–92.

33. DNDLTY, 54–55; HDSL, 2:275.

34. Literally, the "College of the Sons of the State," the Imperial Academy was Vietnam's first university, established in 1076 to educate the sons of mandarins in government administration and the Confucian classics. Originally in the Temple of Literature in Hanoi, it was transferred to Hue in 1802.

35. Thus, from 1847 onward only students of the Imperial Academy and top regional graduates younger than twenty-five were allowed to resume their studies between two sessions of the metropolitan examinations. HDSL, 2:271.

36. Truong Ba Can, *Nguyên Truong To: Con nguoi va di thao* (NXBTPHCM, 1988), 241. Regarding this petition, see Mark W. McLeod, "Nguyen Truong To: A Catholic Reformer at Emperor Tu-Duc's Court," *Journal of Southeast Asian Studies* [JSAS] 25, no. 2 (September 1994): 313–30.

37. DNDLTY, 55–56.

38. Etienne Balazs, *La bureaucratie céleste* (Paris: Gallimard-Tel, 1968), 267–89.

39. Regarding the Chinese origin of the institution (*hou bu*), see Charles O. Hucker, *A Dictionary of Official Titles in Imperial China* (Stanford: Stanford University Press, 1985), 226; and *Yu Lu Nian, Zhong Guo guan zhi da ci dian* (great dictionary of the mandarin in China) (Hei Lung Jiang ren min chu ban she, 1992), 2:1209.

40. From the curriculum vitae of Dao Trong Tê, acting district magistrate of Vu Tien (Thai Binh Province) in 1897, in NAC *Kinh luoc* Collection, 2520, p. 12.

41. From the curriculum vitae of Trân Xuân Son, provincial educational commissioner (*dôc hoc*) of Hà Nam in 1897, in NAC *Kinh luoc* Collection, 2520, p. 49. In 1845, Nguyên Khoa Quyên, former district magistrate of Duy Tiên, was in a similar situation. *Dai Nam Thuc Luc chinh biên* [Primary compilation of the Veritable Records of Imperial Vietnam (hereafter DNTL)], translated into Vietnamese (Hanoi: Nha Xuat Ban Khoa Hoc, 1971), 25:372–73.

42. DNTL, 13:170.

43. From the curriculum vitae of Nguyên Liêm, prefect of Vinh Tuong (Son Tây Province) in 1897 in NAC *Kinh luoc* Collection, 2521, pp. 18–19.

44. "Shade students" (*âm sinh*) were so called because they benefited from the special merits of their fathers to bypass the regional examinations. They were, however, trained at either the provincial schools or the Imperial Academy of Hue.

45. The oldest text we know from the Nguyên period dates back to the seventh year of the reign of Minh Mang (1826). The emperor approved of sending *cu nhân* and students of the Imperial Academy into the provinces as *hâu bô*. t.5, p.170. MMCY, t.1, 1972, p. 191. The same recommendation was recalled in 1835 (Minh Mang 16). The text pointed out that the *âm sinh* who passed their examinations, like the students of the Imperial Academy, could be nominated as *hâu bô*. MMCY, 1:182. See also HDSL, 2:330.

46. An ordinance of the first year of Tu Duc (1848) specified the conditions of age and the nature and frequency of the examination, which was given to the *tôn sinh*, sons of the imperial family who were students of the Imperial Academy, and *âm sinh*. The sessions of the examination were organized by the Ministry of Rites in the years Thin, Tuât, Suu, and Mui and covered three areas: a commentary on the classics (*kinh nghia*), a poem in prose (*phu*) of two rhymes, and an essay (*van sach*) on two or three short questions. DNDLTY, 65.

47. From the curriculum vitae of Bui Dam, acting prefect of Khoai Châu (Hung Yên Province) in 1897, in NAC *Kinh luoc* Collection, 2515, p. 50. The biography of Phan Huu Tu can be found in the *Dai Nam Liêt Truyên chinh biên* [Primary compilation of biographies of Imperial Vietnam] (Hue: 1993), 4:270.

48. MMCY, 1:219.

49. Arrêté (1/4/1892) of J.-M. de Lanessan, Gouverneur-Général de l'Indochine (art. 2) in NAC, RST 57395. A circular of 1904 defined the terms and conditions of the apprenticeship in very similar terms. Circular 140 (9/29/1904) by Mr. Fourès, Résident Supérieur, in Bulletin Administratif du Tonkin (hereafter BAT), 1904, 881.

50. Annual evaluation by the Résident de France of Phuc Yên (11/14/1904). Career file of Trân Van Ky, district magistrate, 1903–1911 (NAC, RST 31521).

51. Annual evaluation by the Résident de France of Phu Lô (12/15/1903), career file of Trân Van Ky.

52. Annual evaluation by the Résident de France of Phuc Yên (11/1/1907), career file of Trân Van Ky.

53. Annual evaluation by the Résident de France of Hà Dông (11/25/1917), career file of Doan Quan, 1919–1922 (NAC, RST 31162).
54. Decree of the seventh year of Minh Mang (1826). HDSL, 2:272.
55. Arrêté (1/4/1892) of J.-M. de Lanessan, Gouverneur-Général de l'Indochine (art. 2) in NAC, RST 57395.
56. *Dai Nam Liêt Truyên chinh biên*, 4:53.
57. From the curriculum vitae of Phan Trong Dich, provincial administration commissioner (*bô chinh*) of Son Tây in 1897, in NAC *Kinh luoc* Collection, 2521, p. 4.
58. Cao Xuân Duc, *Quôc Triêu huong khoa luc* [A list of successful provincial examination candidates of this dynasty, 1807–1918] (Ho Chi Minh City: Nha xuat ban thanh pho Ho Chi Minh, 1993), 495.
59. From the curriculum vitae of Nguyên Huu Tuong, judicial commissioner (*an sat*) of Hà Nam Province in 1897, in NAC *Kinh luoc* Collection, 2520, pp. 48–49.
60. Annual evaluation by the Résident de France of Phuc Yên (10/30/1905), career file of Trân Van Ky, 1903–1911 (NAC, RST 31521).
61. Letter (14/04/1915) from Hoàng Trong Phu, Governor-General of Hà Dông Province, to the Résident de France in the career file of Pham Chu Trinh (NAC, RST 31453).
62. Ordinance of the seventeenth year of Minh Mang. MMCY, 1:219. The text is also cited in DNTL, 18:171.
63. "When there are vacancies for the position of district magistrate (*tri huyên*) or district magistrate in the highlands (*tri châu*), provincial mandarins will give priority to *hâu bô* who will be named as these positions open up. If there are no more *hâu bô* in the province, the minister of public functions will appoint top regional graduates who have not yet been named educational officers." DNTL, 27:153–54. The last part of the quote implies that fulfilling the duties of an educational position could also serve as an apprenticeship.
64. "The metropolitan graduates and *cu nhân* will be appointed as apprentices in the ministries, in mandarinal offices, or will carry out the duties of mandarin-teachers. At the end of the apprenticeship—one year for the metropolitan graduates and three years for the top regional graduates—they will be named as prefects, district magistrates, or *tri châu*." Ordinance of the second year of Dông Khanh (1887). DNDLTY, 78–79.
65. From the curriculum vitae of Trân Xuân Son, provincial educational officer of Hà Nam in 1897, in NAC *Kinh luoc* Collection, 2520, p. 49.
66. Résident de France of Bac Ninh (10/16/1905) in the career file of Pham Huu Thanh, 1894–1924 (NAC, RST 31447).
67. Résident de France of Bac Ninh (11/13/1906) in the career file of Pham Huu Thanh.
68. Annual Evaluation (1898–1908) in the career file of Dang Van Hoa, 1898–1916 (NAC, RST 31123).
69. Résident de France of Hung Hoa (15/11/1906) in the career file of Dang Van Hoa.

70. Résident de France of Hung Hoa (12/30/1903), and Résident de France of Bac Giang (11/12/1907), in the career file of Dang Van Hoa.

71. Ordinance of the first year of Minh Mang (1820). HDSL, 2:270–71. Nguyên Si Hai, "Tô chuc chinh quyên trung uong thoi Nguyên so (1802–1847)" [The organization of the central authority under the first emperors of the dynasty of the Nguyên], Ph.D. diss., Truong luat khoa dai hoc, 1962, 174; Nguyên Minh Tuong, *Cai cach hành chinh duoi triêu Minh Mênh* [The administrative reform under the rule of Minh Mang] (Hanoi: 1996), 267. Alexander B. Woodside also mentioned this type of internship in *Vietnam and the Chinese Model: A Comparative Study of the Nguyen and Ch'ing Civil Government in the First Half of the Nineteenth Century* (Cambridge: Harvard University Press, 1971), 86. Regarding the Chinese origin of the institution (*xing zou*), see Hucker, *A Dictionary of Official Titles in Imperial China*, 247; and *Zhong Guo guan zhi da ci dian* (Hei Lung Jiang ren min chu ban she, 1992), 2:1217.

72. DNDLTY, 54–55.

73. From the curriculum vitae of Dao Trong Ky, Governor-General of Son Hung Tuyên in 1897, in NAC *Kinh luoc* Collection, 2521, p. 2.

74. Nguyên Si Hai, *To chuc chinh quyen trung uong thoi Nguyen so (1802–1847)* Hue: Nha xuat ban Thuan Hoa, 130–31; Dô Bang, Nguyên Danh Phiêt, Nguyên Quang Ngoc, and Vu Van Quân, *Tô chuc bô may nhà nuoc triêu Nguyên—giai doan, 1802–1884* [The organization of the state apparatus under the Nguyên between 1802 and 1884] (Hue: 1997), 52.

75. In the career file of Vu Khac Hiêu, 1891–1895 (NAC, RST 31597).

76. Report 36 (11/23/1896) from imperial inspector Hoàng Cao Khai to the Directeur des Affaires Civiles in *Création de l'Ecole des hâu bô* (NAC, RST 46352).

77. The length of study at the school for *hâu bô* was set at six months in 1897, then three years in 1903. Arrêté (6/07/1903) of Luce, Résident Supérieur par interim (art. 6) in BAT, 1903, 509.

78. The detailed exposé of the program established in 1906 is included in the annex of the Arrêté of 9/10/1906, BAT, 1906, 874–78.

79. Report 36 (11/23/1896) from the imperial inspector Hoàng Cao Khai to the Directeur des Affaires Civiles in *Création de l'Ecole des hâu bô* (NAC, RST 46352).

80. I have established these averages based on the age distribution provided by Salles. Report (10/2/1898) by Salles, inspector of the colony during his assignment time in NAC, RST 46352, *Création de l'Ecole des hâu bô*.

81. Salles, who made a study of the school's functioning one year after its creation, wished to go farther than the imperial inspector. He proposed establishing the age requirement at no older than thirty years. This proposal was adopted and included in an *arrêté* of 1903, which reorganized the establishment. Report (10/2/1898) by Salles, inspector of the colony during his assignment time in NAC, RST 46352; Arrêté (6/07/1903) of Luce, Résident Supérieur par interim (art. 1) in BAT, 1903, 508.

82. Report 36 (11/23/1896) from the imperial inspector Hoàng Cao Khai to the Directeur des Affaires Civiles in NAC, RST 46352.

83. The first step toward this separation was the creation of a pedagogical section in the heart of the school for *hâu bô* in 1909. Arrêté (4/14/1909) of Morel, Résident Supérieur in BAT, 1909, 490–91.

84. An ordinance of the first year of Thanh Thai (1889) restated the ordinance from the first year of Tu Duc (1848) regarding the examination of the *âm sinh*. An ordinance of the second year of Thanh Thai (1890) restated the ordinance of the fourth year of Tu Duc (1851) on the courses taken by the *âm sinh*. DNDLTY, 68–69.

85. Letter (4/25/1908) of the Résident de France Sestier to the Résident Supérieur of Tonkin on the recruitment of indigenous personnel (response to Letter 152 [4/14/1908] of the Résident Supérieur) in NAC, RST 46464: *Travaux de la commission chargée d'élaborer les règlements relatifs au personnel de l'administration indigène, 1907–1911*.

86. He put forth several arguments: "He knows Chinese characters well enough, and a little French. . . . Almost all the *âm sinh* are allowed to take courses at the school for *hâu bô*." To reinforce his claim, he cited the royal ordinance of the first year of Hàm Nghi: "The title of *âm sinh* is awarded to the eldest sons of civil mandarins of the fifth rank, both first and second class." He then brought up the fact that he held the rank of 5a and had entered into the administration of the protectorate nearly twenty-three years before and that he had "always worked with enthusiasm and devotion." Letter (6/1/1910) from Lê Ky to the Résident de France of Bac Ninh in the career file of Lê Ky, NAC, RST 31292. Sestier had a similar discourse: "Today, in the minds of many . . . it seems that just being the son of a mandarin means having the right to become a civil servant." Letter (4/1908) from Résident de France Sestier to the Résident Supérieur of Tonkin on the recruitment of indigenous personnel (response to Letter 152 [4/14/1908] of the Résident Supérieur) in NAC, RST 46464.

87. Letter (10/15/1909) from a "group of provincial councilors" to the Résident Supérieur of Tonkin, in NAC, RST 73577: *Choix des âm sinh pour les emplois de l'administration indigène* (1909). In 1910, Tissot and Buffel du Vaure, members of the Conseil de Perfectionnement de l'Ecole des Hâu Bô, also recognized that the instruction given to the *âm sinh* of Tonkin left much to be desired. Official report of the meeting of the Conseil de Perfectionnement de l'Ecole des Hâu Bô (7/11/1910) in NAC, RST 46464.

88. Provincial advisers cite the case of *âm sinh* at the school for *hâu bô* in 1909, who were only sixteen or seventeen years old.

89. "The free students . . . received very bad grades on the written exam, [so] the commission had believed they were not to make them take the oral part." Official report of the commission that had to classify the examination results at the end of the first year of the school for *hâo bô* (June 1902) in the career file of Dào Quang Tich, *tri châu*, 1902–1930, (NAC, RST 31097).

90. This principle had been advocated by the Conseil de Perfectionnement de l'Enseignement Indigène during the first meeting and included in the Arrêté of 11/16/1906, which reorganized the educational system for the local residents of Tonkin (article 58). Note (9/14/1909) from Bouzat, Chef du

Deuxième Bureau [Sûreté], to the Résident Supérieur on the subject of a letter (10/15/1909) from a "group of provincial advisers" to the Résident Supérieur du Tonkin in NAC, RST 73577.

91. This is according to Bouzat. Note (9/14/1909) from Bouzat, Chef du Deuxième Bureau, to the Résident Supérieur regarding the letter (10/15/1909) from "a group of provincial advisers" to the Résident Supérieur du Tonkin in NAC, RST 73577.

92. Handwritten note in the margin of Arrêté 353 (8/27/1903) of the Résident Supérieur, appointing Trân Van Ky, *hâu bô*, to the province of Phu Lô, in the career file of Trân Van Ky, district magistrate, 1903–1911 (NAC, RST 31521).

93. Letter (5/13/1902) from the Résident Supérieur to the Commander-in-Chief of the troops in Indochina; list of the graduates of the school for *hâu bô* (05/13/1903) in the career file of Dào Quang Tich, *tri châu*, 1902–1930 (NAC, RST 31097).

94. "*Huân dao* and district magistrates should not be appointed to a tenured post until after they have completed an apprenticeship of at least two years, or at least not before any scholarship students." Handwritten note in the margin of Arrêté 353 (8/27/1903) from the Résident Supérieur appointing Trân Van Ky *hâu bô* of Phu Lô Province, in the career file of Trân Van Ky, district magistrate, 1903–1911 (NAC, RST 31521).

95. In 1908, Bouzat was the first to propose to limit the number of scholarships to the *âm sinh* by one-third. It was taken up again in 1910 by the Conseil de Perfectionnement de l'Ecole des Hâu Bô (7/11/1910), then included in article 4 of an Arrêté of 1912. Note (April 1908) from Bouzat to the Chef du Deuxième Bureau of the Résidence Supérieure: synthesis of the advice of the provincial heads on the recruitment of the local administrative personnel in NAC, RST 46464; Letter (10/15/1909) from a "group of provincial advisers" to the Résident Supérieur of Tonkin in NAC, RST 73577; Official report of the meeting of the Conseil de Perfectionnement de l'Ecole des Hâu Bô (7/11/1910) in NAC, RST 46464. Arrêté 365 (4/18/1912), dealing with the reorganization of the school for *hâu bô* in BAT, 1912, 723.

96. This proposal was formulated in 1908 by Bouzat and Sestier and then by provincial advisers in 1909. It was adopted and included in the royal ordinance of the fourteenth day of the third month of the fourth year of Duy Tân (4/23/1910), reforming the conditions of the *âm sinh* examination. On the other hand, two proposals by provincial councilors were not adopted by the protectorate: the extension of the period of study of the *âm sinh* and *hâu bô* (from three years to five), on the one hand, and the requirement for *âm sinh* to complete an apprenticeship of eight to ten years upon their graduating from the school, either as a clerk in the French administration or as a scholar in the local administration. Note (April 1908) from Bouzat to the Chef du Deuxième Bureau of the Résidence Supérieure: synthesis of the advice of the provincial heads on the recruitment of the local administrative personnel in NAC, RST 46464; Letter (10/15/1909) from a "group of provincial advisers" to the Résident Supérieur on Tonkin in NAC, RST 73577; NAC, RST 73575: *Examen des*

âm sinh et octroi du titre de viên tu aux fils de mandarins: Pièces de principe (ordinances royales; brevets de âm sinh), 1885–1930.

97. Bouzat took this initiative. Note (9/14/1909) from Bouzat, Chef du Deuxième Bureau, to the Résident Supérieur; Letter (10/15/1909) from a "group of provincial advisers" to the Résident Supérieur of Tonkin in NAC, RST 73577. Thus, Pham Chi Trach, elder son of Governor-General Pham Van Toàn, was not admitted to the preparatory classes of the school for *hâu bô* "because of the low marks he received on the examination given to *âm sinh* who had signed up." Letter (10/7/1910) from Mr. Simoni, Résident Supérieur, to the Résident de France of Nam Dinh in the career file of Pham Quang Khiêt, *hâu bô* (NAC, RST 14540).

98. "Called upon to make up almost exclusively the higher cadres of the local administration, they were the object of attention and surveillance that was most particular/very special on your part, and not to be immobilized, without serious motives, in the employ of *hâu bô*." Circular 140 (9/29/1904) of the Résident Supérieur to the Résidents Chefs de Province in NAC, RST 46322: *Stage d'un an dans les bureaux des mandarins provinciaux que doivent faire les hâu bô à leur sortie de l'école* (1904).

99. Article 9 of the Arrêté of 9/1/1906.

100. In 1911, two members of the Reforms Commission, the *résidents* of Bac Giang (Lacombe) and Hà Dông (Le Gallen), stressed that the problem of having a district magistrate who is too young was all too real. Official report (2/7/1911) of the Reform Commission in NAC, RST 46464.

101. One year after the creation of the school for *hâu bô*, Salles advocated the recruitment of *hâu bô* among the *cu nhân* and *tu tai* who were at least thirty years old. Hoang Trong Phu, like Salles, especially believed that the level of French among the students was not sufficient because they were too old. NAC, RST 46352: *Création de l'Ecole des Hâu Bô*, reports from Hoang Trong Phu (2/14/1898) and Salles, Inspecteur des Colonies (10/2/1898).

102. The Council for the Improvement of Indigenous Education had proposed, in 1906, to completely replace the use of *hâu bô* with the hiring of apprentice district magistrates and prefects that would be exclusively limited to the graduates of the school for *hâu bô* following their university schooling. These proposals were taken up again by the Reform Commission of 1911. Report of 2/7/1911 from the Reform Commission in NAC, RST 46464.

103. Pham Gia Thu, graduated as *cu nhân* in 1903 and then graduated from the school for *hâu bô* in 1910. He was appointed to Kiên Xuong (Thai Binh Province) as apprentice prefect (adjunct to the prefect) in October 1910. At the end of the first year of the apprenticeship, the *résident* de France who evaluated him wished him to be named district magistrate in his own province of Quynh Côi, "a place that is both unimportant and easy to govern." This proposal was rejected because he was deemed too inexperienced. Annual evaluation of November 1911 and Note (10/19/1911), Chef du Deuxième Bureau of the Résident Supérieur in the career file of Pham Gia Thu, district magistrate, 1911–1913 (NAC, RST 31450).

104. Annual evaluation by the Résident de France of Son Tây (11/15/1915).

Career file of Pham Van Triêu, district magistrate, 1908–1926 (NAC, RST 31454).

105. Annual evaluation by the Résident de France of Ninh Binh (11/20/1918). Career file of Pham Van Triêu.

106. Ibid.

107. Annual evaluation by the Delegate of Phu Ly (10/25/1915). Career file of Pham Van Thiêu, district magistrate, 1914–1920 (NAC, RST 31446).

108. Ibid.

109. Annual evaluation by the Résident de France of Bac Ninh (11/1917). Career file of Pham Van Thiêu.

110. Mr. Sestier, Résident de France at Bac Ninh, made this proposal in 1908. Letter (April 22, 1908) from Sestier, Résident de France of Bac Ninh, to the Résident Supérieur du Tonkin (Deuxième Bureau) on the recruitment of local personnel (response to Letter 152 [4/14/1908] of the Résident Supérieur) in NAC, RST 46464.

111. Letter (8/5/1893) from Lê Hoàn, Governor-General, to the Résident de France of Hung Hoa in the career file of Pham Ba Quyên, district magistrate, 1891–1893 (NAC, RST 31431).

112. Letter (1/14/1914) from Mr. Tissot, Résident de France of Nam Dinh, to the Résident Supérieur in the career file of Lê Van Thuy, district magistrate, 1893–1917 (NAC, RST 31319).

113. From the curriculum vitae of Nguyên Duc Tu, Governor of Hai Phong in 1897, in NAC *Kinh luoc* Collection, 2520, p. 61.

114. From the curriculum vitae of Lê Huy Phan, judicial commissioner of Son Tây in 1897, in NAC *Kinh luoc* Collection, 2521, p. 4.

115. Article 10 of Arrêté 365 (4/18/1912) stipulated that "At the end of this apprenticeship, they will be appointed, before all other candidates, to positions as prefects or district magistrates as they open up, with the condition that they be recognized as being able to take on these duties." Arrêté 365 (4/18/1912) regarding the organization of the school for *hâu bô* in the BAT, 1912, 724.

116. Annual evaluation of the Résident de France of Nam Dinh (11/1915). Career File of Pham Quang Khiêt, *hâu bô* (NAC, RST 14540).

GLOSSARY

an sat	judicial commissioner
bô chinh	provincial administration commissioner
cu nhân	top regional graduate
giao thu	prefecture educational officer
hành tâu	apprentices in the ministries
hâu bô	(1) civil servant waiting for an appointment; (2) intern in the administration as a civil servant

hâu phai	expectant delegate
huân dao	district educational officer
huyên	district
kinh lich	provincial registrar
kinh luoc	imperial inspector
lai muc (dê lai)	district or prefecture secretary
phu	prefecture
Quôc Tu Giam	Imperial Academy
sai phai	entrusted with a mission
si bô	waiting for an appointment
Si Hoan Truong	School for Mandarins
thông phan	provincial administrative assistant
tông dôc	provincial governor-general
tri huyên	district magistrate
tri phu	prefect
tro biên (tro ta)	district assistant
tu tai	lesser regional graduate
tung phai	attaché under orders
tuy phai	sent under orders

5   Laurence Monnais-Rousselot

In the Shadow of the Colonial Hospital: Developing Health Care in Indochina, 1860–1939

Introduction

Historiography has been particularly unfair to colonial medicine and colonial medical policies. A few studies in the field of "science and empire" have shown the relationship between colonialism and the establishment of health care in the colonies.[1] There are almost no studies on the issue in Indochina.[2]

In this chapter, I present the history of French colonial health care in Indochina by studying medical institutions such as hospitals, clinics, maternity wards, and dispensaries and by showing how these institutions were built and run during 1860 and 1930. I would argue that such an approach allows us to better understand the overall colonial health care project as well as the main stages of development of its policy. This chapter examines the premises for the implementation of public health care in Indochina, the controversy over the unequal access to health care in urban and rural areas, and the development of a colonial-indigenous care system able to bring health care to all Indochinese people and to train its local medical personnel. The data are mostly drawn from archival materials containing both administrative and medical records.

1. The Building of a Health Care Plan in Indochina as an Integrated Part of the French Colonial Project

The analysis must first take into account the context within which the project arose. First, the health care plan in Indochina was established as a direct result of French colonial domination. This link is undeniable and alone should be sufficient to temper much of the criticism leveled at colonial medical policy. Second, it took place within a tropical environment that was rife with disease, thus creating a health risk for both the native inhabitants and the colonizers. Finally, these developments occurred during a time of great scientific change in both theory and practice. Against the backdrop of these various circumstances and the emergence of "modern" medicine, the history of the Indochinese hospital system can be broken into three distinct chapters: a primary phase of establishing the first health care facilities; a second period of active construction; and, finally, a time of reflection, which led to a reorganization of the hospital network. This last phase was based on an increasing urban-rural split and the need to adapt to local demands. The general history of health care in the Indochinese Union follows this progression: a first phase of trial and error (1860–1905), followed by a period of organization (1905–18), which led to an adaptation to local conditions (1918–39).

The AMI: A General Overview

In 1860, Cochinchina was coming under colonial rule. This was but a prelude to the definitive takeover of the region—Saigon fell to the French in 1861, and Cambodia became a protectorate in 1863. The French victory in the area led to the first antismallpox vaccinations of the local populations[3] and the creation of the first civilian hospitals. Further progress, such as that of defining a policy of health care and the subsequent taking over of these first activities by the governor-general (*gouverneur général*), would have to wait for the advent of the Third Republic in France and the pacification of the countryside. In fact, officials of the new Republic soon tried to concretize their ambitions regarding health care in the colonies, ambitions that were motivated by political as well as economic and "humanitarian" factors (Monnais-Rousselot 1999: 59–63).

The French health care mission came under the general order of its "civilizing mandate" (*mandat civilisateur*). "Vaccinate, Record, Disinfect" (*Vaccination, déclaration, désaffection*) became the motto of this new plan, which had been inspired by the French model (Gouvernement Général de l'Indochine 1907; Clavel 1908). Colonial medical policy was enacted through a variety of legislative and regulatory decisions, which were, for the most part, transplanted directly from France into the colonies without the least concern about how they would work overseas. On 7 January 1890, a decree issued by the Office of the State Secretary of the Colonies translated this concern into reality. The decree included plans for the establishment of a Colonial Health Advisory Council, a Colonial Health Corps (Corps de Santé Colonial, a unit of "colonial doctors," *médecins coloniaux*), and provisions for hospital service in the colonies and protectorates. In 1895, these colonial hospitals were made available to all segments of the population, civilian, military, or indigenous. For the time being, however, all hospitalization costs had to be paid by the patient. Two years later, the minister of colonies, André Lebon, drew up a preliminary organizational outline of health care institutions and entrusted this hospital network to the newly formed Colonial Health Corps.[4] The French health care plan was therefore clearly based at the outset on the treatment of disease well before individual health care systems were proposed for each territory.

A health care plan for Indochina was drawn up between 1897 and 1902. Under the orders of Governor-General Paul Doumer, much attention was paid to this "rich and exploitable colony." In 1897, a general budget for Indochina and the first "medical assistance" program were created. The latter included the creation of a health care director for each territory and the application of the French law of 1892 (making it mandatory to have a medical degree in order to practice) in Cochinchina. In 1902, the French public health law was put into practice throughout Indochina, and the Hanoi School of Medicine was opened for the creation of local "auxiliary doctors" (*médecins auxiliaires,* a term that had been created in the French colonial context to designate local physicians who remained subordinate to their French counterparts, the colonial doctors). Meanwhile a law passed in January 1898 established a preliminary outline for a plan regarding the classification of hospitals, the conditions of admittance, and their general functioning. The French authorities essentially wanted to do everything possible to "strengthen and increase the work force."

With the establishment of the Indigenous Medical Assistance Program (Assistance Médicale Indigène), or AMI, in 1905, these decisions became a concrete reality (Gouvernement Général de l'Indochine 1911). The program was a prototype, the first of its kind in a French territory along with that of the AOF (Afrique Occidentale Française—French West Africa). It already had the use of a variety of different medical facilities and stores of medicine. It rested on the dual principles of consultation and making rounds, as well as stressing a vaccination program.[5] The AMI, in fact, was a vast health care program unto itself, involving both preventive and treatment programs. The basic hospital network was but one part of it, as is shown in the following report.

> The AMI . . . is mostly aimed at the indigenous population: its essential goal is to combat the frightening mortality rate, caused by ignorance and prejudice, by means of a campaign of basic hygiene, an ongoing battle against disease, and the improvement of sanitation in the region. . . . In order to carry out such a widespread program, we need more than just a few hospitals in urban centers and a few offices for consultations. We need constant action within the population itself: through conferences, informal discussions, having doctors make rounds through the villages; we must educate the natives, and teach them how to protect themselves against smallpox, leprosy, and typhoid fever, how to defend themselves against the plague, cholera, malaria; in a word, how a nation can preserve its health and get strong.[6]

Be this as it may, the preventive program of the AMI would remain dependent on the smooth functioning of a medical treatment program.

In May and June of 1905, Governor-General Paul Beau, supported by the enlightened counsel of the director of health, Charles Grall, decided to proceed with the application of this vast health care project. The "duty to help" (*devoir d'assistance*) normally involved free health care in facilities which were funded by various budgets (especially local, provincial, and municipal).[7] In keeping with this "colonial duty," the French administration issued an entry ticket to each patient, guaranteeing the reimbursement of hospitalization costs.[8] Doctors of the AMI Corps would not demand payment from "poor natives" (*indigents indigenes*) for consultations, but could ask the more affluent local citizens to pay for services, or else could create their own private clientele.

The appointment of governors-general Antony Klobukowski in

1908 and then Albert Sarraut coincided with the severing of the umbilical cord between France and its Far Eastern territory. While remaining true to the principles set forth by the Ministry of Colonies, all health care decisions hereafter occurred in and for Indochina. Although Klobukowski did not advocate the expansion of the health care system, which in his opinion would have been too costly, he supported a secular medical assistance program "for the benefit of individuals suffering from acute or chronic illness."[9] Albert Sarraut, who succeeded Klobukowski in 1911, was more generous than his predecessor. He considered AMI to be "an indispensable part of colonial development" (1923). This issue was at the crux of an Indochinese health care program that Sarraut deemed fundamental during his famous speech at the Temple of Literature [Van Mieu] in Hanoi in April 1919.

These two successive mandates led to the creation of a managed health care plan and a battle against infectious diseases. This new effort was promptly placed under the direction of the inspector general of health and sanitation services (*inspection générale de l'hygiène et de la santé publique,* formerly the *direction de la santé*) in 1909. In theory, the new health care policy was based on the following principles: a balance between administrative and technical support (i.e., between administrators and physicians), an equal dose of both prevention and treatment, and especially an increased awareness of general hygiene, both public and private (education of the local populations, provisions for clean drinking water, and better sanitation in urban centers). In practice, every outbreak of a new epidemic became an added incentive to speed up measures. Specialized campaigns against epidemics soon began to yield encouraging results (in the case of plague and cholera),[10] and the treatment of syphilis and leprosy took on a more "humanized" approach.

Once Sarraut came to power, the entire "sanitation" process was placed under the framework of a five-year plan (1911–15). Specialized facilities were on the rise, and the health care system found itself endowed with new functions: providing care for lepers, the internment of the mentally ill, and the care of pregnant women. The Indochinese Union was then divided into zones, each one composed of one or two provinces in order to facilitate access to health care in the five territories. Added to this physical expansion was a qualitative diversification, which rested on specialization, the development of small, rural facilities, and the increase of services in urban institutions (construction of isolation wards, maternity hospitals, and paying consultations).[11] But before turning to this period of widespread construction let me first return to its foundations, that is, to the first public hospitals.

The First Hospitals and Their Activities: The Establishment of a Public Network

Among the three physicians present during the conquest of Tourane [Da Nang] in 1859–60, Dr. Duteuil tried to relieve his compatriots of the *fièvre des bois* ("jungle fever," i.e., malaria) since he could not offer them evacuation to a nearby hospital (Duteuil 1864). Another physician, Dr. Laure, went to Saigon in 1861 with an expeditionary corps of three thousand sailors, five other physicians, and the director of the first health service and the first military hospital, Dr. Lalhuyeaux d'Ormay. Laure explained that the opening of the first two stationary military field hospitals in the region had been a blessing for him and his colleagues, who had all been weakened not only by malaria but by dysentery, cholera, diarrhea, and all sorts of "gastric and bilious fevers" (1864). Far beyond what the French had expected, the conquest of Indochina soon became synonymous with dying for the cause. Penetration into the Annam-Tonkin region was literally obstructed by the inescapable presence of polymorphous and aggressive diseases.[12]

Colonial doctors and medical authorities of the time were frustrated by the lack of medical facilities for the civilian population. The first facilities were logically located near military garrisons. In 1871, for example, there was talk of establishing a sanatorium in Tonkin to take care of the medical needs of on-site personnel.[13] The invention of mobile field hospitals (*infirmeries-ambulances*) began to relieve an emaciated medical corps, which lacked the means to care for its itinerant patients. It seems that nothing official had yet been proposed for the native population; at least the military correspondence of the time says nothing about the issue. Even in the greater Saigon area, the hospital situation was military in nature, consisting of the navy hospital, with two hundred beds; the maritime field hospital of Choquan; the so-called Fort du Sud field hospital; the field hospital of Bien Hoa; and, for army units that had come to support the naval effort, the hospital at Choquan and the field hospital of My Tho (Laure 1864). Outside of another dispensary in Choquan and a few scattered field hospitals, civilian health care remained the domain of the religious communities, where they were present, that is, in the south.[14]

In reality, two health care policies were superimposed. In the 1880s, there already were a number of medical stations in Cochinchina, mostly in the garrison towns. Each physician on duty was obligated to offer vaccinations once a week and treat the troops and government workers (both European and Indochinese). This practice then spread to the protectorates. At the same time, health care establishments sprang up here and there to form a barrier against the spread of disease. They were usually constructed on high ground and in the cleanest part of an urban center, usually outside the city limits. Originally intended for the use of colonists, these health care facilities progressively began to serve the local populations as pacification progressed (Monnais-Rousselot 1999).

The first infirmary in Cambodia was built in Kompong Long in 1863 by Doudart de Lagrée (sent by the French administration on a "scouting mission"). Dr. Hennecart offered his services to the troops and the royal family. In 1866, a military medical unit was created in Phnom Penh while civilian care was left in the good hands of the Church. The construction of a hospital-hospice for the civilian population would not begin until 1881.[15] In the rest of the protectorate, the number and form of health care institutions would depend on the nature of the pacification. In 1885, a field hospital was built on the banks of the Tonlé Sap; in 1886, there already were medical posts in Kratié, Kampot, and Takéo. The first organized medical care for the Khmer population had its origins, in fact, in an insurrectional movement of 1885. That year the dispatch of additional troops led to the need for new medical facilities, which would then be used for the benefit of the civilian population.

In Tonkin as well, more or less stationary facilities answered to the needs of pacification. In 1883, the military barracks in Hanoi and Haiphong were transformed into hospitals. At the same time, other posts were created in the provincial capitals of Hai Duong and Quang Yen. Elsewhere pagodas were requisitioned. The invention of the mobile field hospital, however, was the most important innovation in the region. The "oil spot" technique (a strategy adopted by the French to pacify a particular region by first taking a relatively secure area and then gradually moving outward) obliged colonial forces to go deeper into rural areas. Thus, they needed to establish medical facilities in their wake, as they were told by the colonial authorities in France. The codified principles of such a plan rested on the flexibility of adapting to the medico-surgical needs of the area, reducing the administrative work and minimizing costs. The resulting facilities, consisting of twenty to fifty beds, immediately won the approval of the few physicians on site and led to their proliferation between 1885 and 1888, when they were turned over to wider civilian use.[16]

It was also a military need that led to the embryonic development of civilian health care in Annam. The first infirmary, set up in the outbuildings of the *résidence générale*, would serve as a starting point for the antismallpox campaign of 1887. In 1889, a second building came into existence "in the middle of the rice paddies" (Gaide 1921, 203) before the first hospital worthy of that name took over seven years later. As for Laos, it was its entry into the union in 1893 that finally sparked the establishment of the first medical services for its inhabitants. The field hospital in Khong (1896), created at the same time as the hospital of Luang Prabang, received its first indigenous patients while awaiting the opening of the hospital of Paksé.[17]

It was thus during the years of military progression that the first Indochinese hospital network was established and the concept of medical assistance to the local population finally matured. After the French conquest was completed, the mobile field hospitals were transformed into stationary field hospitals, some dispensaries were improved, and the few existing hospitals prepared to receive a civilian clientele. It was not enough, however, to simply recuperate preexisting structures.[18] The colonial government had to dedicate part of its first efforts to the hospital infrastructure. It should be recalled that this priority fit into a much larger political strategy: to treat someone and see him or her get well constituted one of the surest ways, it was held, to earn the good graces of the Indochinese. Within this logic of domination, emphasis was again placed on Saigon, Hanoi, and the principal urban centers. When the AMI was finally made official in 1905, it already had seventy-two institutions operating within Cochinchina. The first "indigenous hospital" (*hôpital indigène*, i.e., constructed to treat the native populations), that of Choquan, remains the symbol of this effort.

The Choquan Hospital: Exemplary Initiative and Colonial Showpiece

The Indigenous Hospital of Choquan fulfilled perfectly the role that had been outlined for it, that is, as a shining example of a new urban medical assistance program. The director of the hospital at the time, Sister Benjamine, described the way in which it was built. Before the seizure of Saigon in February of 1859, the land on which the hospital now stands had been occupied by a market and the residences of rich Vietnamese. It was in May of 1860 that the nuns of St. Paul de Chartres set up three consultation rooms there. After the battle of Ky Hoa (Chi Hoa) in 1861, the French took control of much of Cochinchina. This allowed them to construct a summary field hospital in Choquan, since the military hospital, "situated in a more healthy area . . . in the very heart of Saigon . . . in one of the highest spots in the city and the farthest from the swamps," was not enough to satisfy the growing demand. The dispensary on the banks of the river in Saigon, run by the military as well, had been invaded by prostitutes in need of care. The governor of the colony at that point asked the nuns to take over.[19]

The dispensary was transferred to Choquan in 1864, immediately after the evacuation of the field hospital, whose patients had been moved to the military hospital. For two years, the bishop of Saigon, Monsignor Lefèvre, had been supervising medical care in a "great straw hut," which received up to thirty patients a day. Unfortunately, he did not have the financial means to assure its functioning. Once more, the colonial government intervened, underscoring France's interest in the health care issue. The government organized the transport of those under the bishop's care "to the empty rooms of the field hospital." In a few years, the hospital network in the Saigon area began to take shape, with a large-scale indigenous hospital as its most important project.

The Choquan hospital officially opened its doors on 1 September 1864 and met with unhoped-for success.[20] In 1869, the *Rapport du Président de la Commission de l'Assistance Publique de la ville de Saigon sur les établissements hospitaliers* praised its activities as the surest indication of the warm welcome given to colonial and Western medicine by the local population.[21] The report also praised the hospital's system of using separate wings, its pleasant and well-adapted buildings, and its low mortality rate. But this smoothly run operation did not last long. The patients often showed up without their entry tickets, and the buildings quickly became dilapidated as a result of flooding and the stifling heat. The hospital had in a sense become the victim of a passing fad. Constructed in haste to accommodate the wave of public enthusiasm, it now needed real organization. Its makeshift construction and lack of funds could no longer assure its smooth functioning, and no official health care project at that point supported its activity.

The hospital underwent a complete reform, instigated by the French navy, which ran the hospital at the time. An administrator from the Department of the Interior was put at the hospital's head in 1874 and ran the institution with an iron hand. According to Sister Benjamine, who consequently saw herself pushed out of the way, the number of patients (400 to 500 per day) fell by 50 percent. By 1875, only 978 patients checked into the hospital during the entire year. But with some later readjustments the hospital possessed two main buildings and received a few psychiatric cases (1886). Its staff consisted of two military physicians on loan from the navy, two French civilian nurses, and a group of Indochinese nurses.[22] Nevertheless, the staff, defending the independence of their practice, had trouble accepting this naval control. As part of the first official health care plan (1897), an executive entrusted the management of the hospital to a medical doctor—a decision that could only strengthen the hospital's success. In 1905, the hospital director, Dr. Angier, wrote a report that stressed above all the constant rise in the number of paying patients (well-to-do Indochinese coming in for operations).[23] The price of a single day of hospitalization had already increased to .5 piasters since 1904 for common patients and to 1 piaster for paying patients and administrative personnel.

In 1905, two new wings for the treatment of contagious diseases were completed, making the separation of the sectors of activity a reality. In his report, Angier praised the ingenious idea, which had led to the construction of these isolation wards, describing them as "permanent structures, with a metal framework supporting a roof, and mobile partitions made of straw, which one can simply burn after an epidemic." This principle would prevail hereafter in the construction of most isolation wards. Furthermore, the hospital had two operating rooms: one for bandaging, the other for "sterile operations" in keeping with the rules of "modern" surgical art, benefiting from the new operating techniques used in France.

In 1909, the staff of Choquan hospital was reorganized. The numbers were especially strengthened to meet the hospital's needs in treating both French civilians and locals. Four European nurses, a pharmacist, two secretaries, and fourteen local nurses, as well as fifteen orderlies, helped the two doctor-directors in their daily activities.[24] The hospital then became a training hospital for the School of Practical Medicine of Choquan, which had opened its doors in 1904, making the first indigenous hospital in the union a model for others to follow. Its organization and expansion would soon serve as a model for new hospitals in all the "cities" of Indochina. The latter, however, would be spared the vicissitudes of development encountered by Choquan, which had come some fifty years before the establishment of the AMI.

2. The Development and Expansion of Medical Facilities

Meanwhile, major cities had already begun to establish "indigenous hospitals." Between 1860 and 1883, new facilities sprang up throughout Cochinchina, and then in neighboring Cambodia (1866–90), before reaching Tonkin (1883–92) and Annam (1892–98). It is thus very clear that the process of pacification played a role that was not only primordial but positive in the expansion of this civilian health care network.[25] The general hospital in Hue opened its doors in 1896, two years after the inauguration of the hospital in Hanoi and the same year as those in Chau Doc (Cochinchina) and Luang Prabang (Central Laos). The hospital in Vinh received its first patients in 1898. Between 1890 and 1911, the main facility in Phnom Penh (mentioned earlier) was constructed and enlarged according to a well-thought-out plan. In the more recently pacified regions, new medical posts were created and staffed by the military physicians who still remained.

The creation of the AMI would finalize this new trend. Most importantly, it provided the means by which these local hospitals could staff themselves with medical personnel recruited ad hoc (doctors from the AMI corps were soon reinforced by "auxiliary doctors" and a mostly local subaltern staff) and by which the indigenous populations could take advantage of these care facilities.

Nomenclatures and Norms (of Construction)

The public hospital sector, which took definitive shape in 1905, divided the new institutions into two categories according to their vocation: the hospitals of the General Service, for military and colonial personnel, and the hospitals of the AMI for French civilians and locals. This division would soon lose all meaning, given the disproportionate growth in the two groups. By the end of the 1920s, there were only four hospitals left for the General Service (the Grall hospital in Saigon, the Lanessan in Hanoi, one in Haiphong, and the field hospital of Fort Bayard in the Chinese concession of Koung Tchéou Wan) (Ferrer 1972). Mixed hospitals (*hôpitaux mixtes*), which were open to both Europeans and Indochinese, acquired increasing importance, even if it was often difficult to physically segregate the two categories of patients, not to mention those who were paying for their stay. However, let us return to this division of hospitals and its meaning.

This division of hospitals, which predated the AMI (1898), was reinforced in 1904 when the Direction du Service de Santé established two administrative health care zones. The first zone included Annam-Tonkin and the Koung Tchéou Wan, with twenty-three consultation rooms, four hospitals, seven infirmaries, nine infirmary-field hospitals, and thirteen medical posts. The second zone spanned Cochinchina, Cambodia, and Laos, which had one general hospital, seven infirmaries, one infirmary-field hospital, and fifteen medical posts. This amounted to a total of 1,262 beds available for Europeans, compared to 679 for the locals.[26] Under the AMI, the terminology was based on more precise criteria. It included all hospital institutions, properly speaking, including general hospitals (mixed and indigenous), specialized facilities, medical centers (which mostly received transfer patients), and dispensaries for outpatient care. Legislative measures in 1914–15 took into account this internal hierarchy. At the top of the list were hospitals and maternity wards, further down were the clinics, while at the bottom level the dispensaries and consultation rooms were systematically dependent on the larger facilities. The last category included the "first-aid posts" (*postes d'assistance*). Last, under the title "specialized facilities" were the treatment facilities for leprosy, tuberculosis, ophthalmology, and venereal diseases.[27]

The building of these facilities usually remained linked not only to the constraints of the site and to the intended purpose but also to the financial means of the region and its climate. There were, however, several general constraints that had to be respected: (1) the separation of European and Indochinese patients (by providing either separate buildings or rooms for the more wealthy hospitals or simple partitions within the communal rooms for more modest ones); (2) the complete isolation of those with contagious diseases (who were confined to quarantine in a lazaret outside of the urban perimeter or in a "disposable" hut several hundred meters from the main building); (3) all facilities would ideally be built in a clean and healthy environment, safe from flooding and crosswinds. To optimize the possibility of good health outside of the metropolitan areas, most facilities were constructed upon pilings. In this way, they could avoid both the chance of an unwelcome encounter with local wildlife and the humidity of the ground. They should be built of wood, thatch, or sometimes tile to protect against any climatic or pathologic eventuality. Quite often, though, dispensaries had to make do with a makeshift framework and clay.

Most of the facilities had a common room-kitchen and lodging for its staff. Less frequently there was a room designed for daily washing and general disinfecting and even less often a room for bandaging and surgical operations. These little architectural luxuries, which had become the norm in France, remained subject to the availability of local funds, as were the stocks of medicine, equipment, and medical instruments. Most important was that the main facility of each regional center be able to respond to the local demand for medical care. This was the case with the field hospital of Pak Hin Boun, one of the first health care facilities in Laos, constructed in 1900.

> Located at the extreme point of confluence of the Nam Hin Boun and the Mekong, on slightly elevated ground, the field hospital was far from any human habitation. Its three buildings were built parallel to each other and oriented along a NE-SW line . . . , a very well chosen layout and one that is very hygienic because the breeze blows almost always from the SE. The three buildings are constructed of wood (flooring, beams, columns, pilings), thatch (partitions, walls), and in straw (roofing); the windows are of full wood paneling except in the large building A, which has blinds but no glass

panes. Building A is raised up on pilings, to about 2.8 meters [about 9 feet] above the ground. It is made up of three rooms . . . : 1. two lateral wings, rooms designated for Europeans . . . ; 2. a central room lit by two full-length windows, which serves as consultation room, pharmacy, operating room, and doctor's office at the same time. . . . Building B is built on a brick foundation and has five rooms: 1. a kitchen; 2. an isolation room; 3. a store; 4. a bathroom; 5. the lodging of the native nurse. . . . Building C has only one big room, which is for the native patients and has six beds, which was later increased to ten. It is also equipped with medicine and surgical instruments; the medicine is ordered twice a year by a pharmacist from Saigon and a pharmacist from Paris; the instruments come from a large surgical house in Paris; they are as complete as possible and allow the performing of almost any operation.[28]

This idyllic portrait obviously reflects a specific case. In other cases, the passing of time necessitated frequent reconstruction, from whatever basic materials could be found, since the climate inexorably led to rapid dilapidation. The Lao field hospital was going through what the hospitals in Saigon and Phnom Penh had, sadly, already experienced, to the distress of those in charge of the public finances. In fact, rural huts—which had an average life span of about three years—were the first facilities to tax the health care budget. The need was so great that it is impossible to even count the many demands made by physicians for medicine, instruments, and even beds to receive a greater number of patients. The government's response, when it did intervene, usually took several months and sometimes even several years. Further proof of internal problems can be seen in the mass of health reports, which repeatedly deplored dilapidated conditions and the flouting of basic rules of hygiene. Two years after the violent typhoon of 1912, the doctor-in-chief of Nha Trang reported that the main medical facility had still not received replacement windows. In 1914, the hospital of Vinh did not have running water, and the offices, whose construction had started two years before, were still not finished.[29] Harsh criticism came from medical agents and government employees alike, with common complaints about working conditions: huts hot as furnaces and tiny and overpopulated rooms.[30]

In any event, the vast hospital network stretching across Indochina in 1910 was still striking from a quantitative point of view. It is easy to understand, then, just what a financial burden this great infrastructure must have been. In fact, most of the funds allotted to health care each year went toward this massive project. In 1931, a special budget was created as an annex to the general budget, allotting 3 million piasters, which would once again be divided among the health services of the large colonial construction projects (like the railway, 260,000), the establishment of a clean water system (760,000), and especially new medical facilities (1,650,000).[31] The conditions of access to medical care remained another difficult question (who would pay, how much, etc.). Outside of these problems, the range of health care options broadened. The most obvious signs of this growth were the regulated construction of isolation and maternity wards, a range of subfacilities, and the availability of an increasingly more complete set of medical instruments. The fact remains, however, that among the variety of medical care facilities available in Indochina disparities regarding quantity as well as quality were widening.

Some Quantitative Landmarks

The years 1906–8 saw the first wave of construction under the normative framework of the AMI. This activity was mostly seen in the increase in medical posts outside of the principal urban centers (excluding Laos). In 1904, Tonkin had three hospitals and thirteen field hospitals; in 1908, its total size (infrastructural potential) had increased 2.5 times. During this same period in Annam, the smaller figure of three AMI facilities increased nearly sixfold. However, even before the second wave of building could get started (1911–18), it became clear that this widespread construction, in large part dictated by colonial priorities, was also beginning to run into a number of obstacles. While in 1908 Cochinchina was graced with a network of sixty medico-social institutions, neighboring Cambodia had to content itself with only one-sixth as many health care institutions and still did not have any specialized facilities.

Of course, the *résidents supérieurs* (the chief French administrators in each protectorate) and the provincial administrators did not always follow the priorities defined by the government general. The case of Annam illustrates this point. In 1920, this recently pacified territory had nearly fifty health care establishments. This growth can be explained by the fact that after 1911 the *résident supérieur* had taken a personal interest in the health care question (Gaide 1921). Once again, the situation in Annam attests to the fact that it was in the nerve centers (both politically and economically) that the qualitative and quantitative expansion could most realistically take place. The *résident* had focused his efforts on the reconstruction of the provincial hospital in Hue. Moreover, centralization was considered the key to the success of a provincial health care program. Until the 1930s, a number of regulations reiterated the obligation of each regional capital to possess its own hospital and maternity ward, without otherwise making the distinction among the geographic, economic, or human situations of these populated regions and their surroundings.

The years 1906–8 did not leave much room, either, for cautious initiatives to extend medical care to certain regions.[32] The local authorities had been called upon to help out, in theory in order to persuade the populations of the pertinence of these health care measures and to get them involved in the construction projects. On the (strong) advice of the administration, village notables promised to promote generous donors to the rank of mandarin.[33] The creation of the Associations d'Assistance Médicale et d'Hygiène Publique had apparently been another alternative. Depending on subscriptions and donations from their members, these associations took on the role of creating and running regional medical facilities. However, for lack of reliable and disinterested donors, both initiatives were soon called into question.[34]

Table 1 shows that at the beginning of World War I the bulk of the medical infrastructure of Indochina was in Vietnam and in an urban environment.[35] In Tonkin, hospitals of every type were concentrated around Hanoi. There were eighty-two establishments within the city limits in 1920. But the farther one moved from the city the more health care options dwindled. In Annam, the distribution seemed more balanced, with institutions in both coastal and regional centers. It was nonetheless rare to find any kind of medical services in the interior of the country. The majority of these facilities were medical posts and dispensaries. Out of the 1,787 beds available to the Indochinese in 1920, 537 were in Hue, 222 in Thanh Hoa Province, and 140 in Vinh. Cochinchina, for its part, had more than sixty medical institutions to its name, thanks to the important road and river traffic along the axis linking Saigon, Ben Tre, My Tho, Sa Dec, Long Xuyen, and Chau Doc.

TABLE 1. Distribution of Facilities within the Hospital Landscape in Indochina (1908–15)

	Hospitals and Field Hospitals					Infirmaries and Dispensaries					Total				
	Cochin-china	Annam	Tonkin	Cambodia	Laos	Cochin-china	Annam	Tonkin	Cambodia	Laos	Cochin-china	Annam	Tonkin	Cambodia	Laos
1908	22	11	23	2	4	20	6	16	6	—	42	17	39	8	4
1910	19	5	?	?	4	?	9	?	?	—	?	14	?	?	4
1913	22	14	24	14	4	11	6	16	7	1	33	20	40	21	5
1915	22	?	?	?	4	12	?	?	?	—	34	18	42	39	4

Once again, however, the concentration thinned out as one moved closer to Cambodia and further from the banks of the Mekong River. The twenty or so establishments in Cambodia, in fact, were all located within the capital except for those in the provincial capitals of Battambang and Kampot. As for Laos, ten medical facilities were counted—about one per major town but still nothing that could really be called a hospital.

Yet it is paradoxical, if one takes into account the distinction between the results of the first and second wave of construction, that this distribution of medical facilities reveals the rise of a new phase: that of the dissemination of small-scale facilities. But before turning to this change in direction let us return to a few of the qualitative aspects of the health care picture at the time of World War I.

Qualitative Viewpoint

The fervor for hospital construction came later to the north. In the first years of the twentieth century, however, the Indigenous Hospital of Hanoi experienced a remarkable evolution. It was a place of both treatment and of cutting-edge research, and it seemed to be much appreciated by the local population. It was a hospital with a mission: it had to put up a good show in front of its rival in the south as well as representing the capital of the union. In 1902, it also became a training hospital for the local "auxiliary doctors." In 1908, Governor Klobukowski took note of these positive results, even if he stopped short of supporting them—given his position on the health care question. After visiting the hospital grounds, he deplored the fact that there were more often one hundred patients per room instead of ten (its theoretical capacity).[36]

In 1909, a law acknowledged this exponential growth by redefining the parameters of the hospital's operations, which had been established only five years before. The hospital services properly speaking (its maternity ward, its leper clinic, the asylum of Te Truong, and its outbuildings), were all rethought to optimize results while reducing costs. In 1912, a medical inspection of the city of Hanoi run by the General Inspection of Health Services concluded that more needed to be done: to "construct a morgue in the Indochinese hospital, replace the older wings, increase the enrollment of the School of Hanoi, replace the leper clinic of Bach Mai with a hospital for contagious diseases, develop the Chinese hospital . . . , [and] create two new consultation rooms in populated neighborhoods."[37] The report was explicit: they would have to build, rebuild, and specialize: to build to respond to a growing demand (a leitmotiv that illustrates a growing acceptance of Western methods of treatment), to rebuild to combat the weather damage that caused a tremendous strain on limited budgets, and to specialize to make the capital a recognized center of French medicine and a showcase for its scientific expansion.

During this period, new projects began to take shape throughout the union that were more concerned with the quality than the quantity of the buildings and services proposed. There was greater interest in the diversity and "adaptability" of new facilities to local needs. The fact that the AMI's budget doubled between 1912 (1,527,000 piasters) and 1914 (3,120,000 piasters) was not an accident. The General Inspection of Health Services wanted to have the most uniform and positive effect on all five territories of the union. In the wake of legislation approved by Sarraut, a special service for leprosy was established in Tonkin, confirming this trend toward specialization. "Assistance for the mentally ill," which had been declared the order of the day in 1910, finally took shape in 1918.[38] Of particular importance in terms of my present study is the fact that the maternity wards turned out to be an indispensable part of each hospital. Whether annexed or simply attached, they always had their own staff, buildings, and administrative autonomy. They spread throughout the major cities and regional capitals and became a sort of avant-garde of medical care. They were the facilities that penetrated deepest into the Indochinese countryside, oftentimes being the only contact between the local people and Western medicine. As we shall see, time would prove them right.

To complete this spectrum of health care facilities, I must mention the importance of training hospitals. Following Hanoi's example, the Indigenous Hospital of Choquan began to accept nurses and midwives from the School of Practical Medicine of the city upon its opening in 1904. While the need for more staff was cruelly felt, many of these hospital complexes appeared to the administration to be a perfect training ground since they didn't cost much and could be operational immediately. The new policies of the 1920s encouraged even rural establishments to educate local subalterns by offering two- to three-month internships or periodic refresher courses given by permanent staff members.

By 1918, of course, there were still many regions, primarily in Cambodia and Laos, that had to make do with a loose network of makeshift hospitals that were poorly supported. The colonial administration in Hanoi had a variety of means at its disposal to combat these inequalities, but there was another idea that came to the fore in the days following World War I: the necessity of bringing health care to the patient. It was at this point that the Indochinese patient began to be seen as an individual. Several new approaches to medical care were born of this trend. More attention was now paid to "social diseases" (*maladies sociales*; i.e., those dependent on social factors like poverty and promiscuity as well as those controllable within a social context like public health and hygiene) as well as to the necessity of adapting to the geographic and ethnic diversity of Indochina (Monnais-Rousselot 2000). Moreover, medical activity was becoming resolutely more mobile. In 1929, the creation of an independent Bureau of Social Assistance, under the General Inspection of Health Services, solidified this change in approach.

3. Unequal Access to Health Care in Urban and Rural Areas

Upon the founding of the AMI, the five countries of the Indochinese Union were divided into medical zones, all of which functioned in the same way. In the regional capitals, there was one principal institution under the direction of a doctor-in-chief, each equipped with a maternity ward run by a midwife. In accordance with AMI regulations, provincial infirmaries, other maternity wards, and rural dispensaries were created within each region. The establishments in the provincial capitals clearly dominated this vertical distribution, which was strongly defended by Sarraut (1912–14). Furthermore, the law stipulated that the type of hospital care would vary the farther one moved from the urban centers, adapting to needs and availability. In reality, however, the disparities were more complex (Gaide 1931). The policy regarding construction was in fact orchestrated in successive waves, depending on the region, the means available, and the administrators. Furthermore, the postwar effort to adapt medical care to local circumstances had started to generate certain regional contrasts. Finally, it was in this period that a second health care policy arose, one based on the needs of a rural population.

Maturity and Adaptation: A More Subtle Approach

The official report on the functioning of health care services in the years 1914–18 details Governor Sarraut's initiatives on health care issues.[39] The report encouraged an effort to realize these initiatives, but it also advocated a return to a theory of construction, which in many respects was inappropriate. Then World War I brought its share of problems, such as budget and staff cutbacks, and delayed the application of an ambitious five-year plan; but these same obstacles led to greater efficiency in hospital services (Monnais-Rousselot 1999: 117–18). Medical education for Indochinese was restructured in order to make use of local personnel, and free access to health care was finally ratified.

After the war, official efforts turned not only toward improving the competence of medical personnel but to their mobility and the expansion of assistance to rural areas. In fact, these developments did not occur ex nihilo but depended upon a variety of factors, only one of which was the four years of war. As a result of this long learning period—and with the help of medical personnel—much was learned about the Indochinese milieu, its diseases, what was expected, and the popular reaction to health care. More than a *caesura*, the 1920s marked a transition in which the "time factor" played a large role. In 1911, Dr. Rangé, the inspector general of health services, announced new health care measures better adapted to the needs of rural Indochina.

> The provincial hospital must be reserved for exceptional cases, for surgical procedures that should not in any circumstance be performed at home. However, we can still increase the number of dispensaries or consultation offices; there should be one in every relatively important village. Every week, or even more often, a mobile doctor would make the rounds of these areas, make contact with the locals, give them their medication, teach them little by little the basic principles of hygiene, and thus give to the mass of peasants

more services than the hospital doctor ever could. . . . It is not a question of systematically increasing the number of hospitals; on the contrary, it would be more useful to the mass of peasants to increase the number of dispensaries and maternity hospitals and to augment the number of mobile doctors and midwives.[40]

In 1914, his successor, Albert Clarac, acquiesced: the mobility of medical personnel would have to make up for the absence of actual facilities. This effort would allow the early diagnosis of the "truly sick."[41]

In 1918, a decree issued by the Ministry of Colonies proposed a new classification of colonial health establishments based on both importance and function. To alleviate the cost and difficulty of transporting hospital materials, a project was begun to create central AMI pharmacies. In 1924, the French stepped in again and organized specialized care in hospitals overseas. At the same time, the third five-year plan was inaugurated and called for the organization of a rural assistance plan (finally enacted into law in 1927). Two of its instigators, Governor Merlin and Inspector-General Audibert, coined a simple phrase that would become a guiding principle: "The doctor should go to the patient and not the patient to the doctor." The second innovation called for more protection against "social diseases" (with respect to tuberculosis, venereal and eye diseases, and malnutrition) and, more importantly, child welfare. The application of this project, of which medical assistance was but one aspect, obviously required a new organization of the entire health care establishment. These reforms were then completed by means of a separation of civilian and military sectors and a redefinition of the fields of prevention and treatment (1918–31).

The coming to power of the Popular Front in 1936 only strengthened these new principles as well as the urgency of putting them into action, given the more delicate political context. It was in this period that the director of Civilian Health Services, Dr. Hermant, instituted the most successful program dedicated to the peninsula.[42] He was probably influenced by the "list of grievances" (*cahiers de voeux*) written up by the inhabitants, which had reached the administration some weeks earlier (1937). Drawing upon thirty years of experience, Hermant insisted on the protection of the Indochinese from all forms of contagion. He especially promised medical assistance to everyone

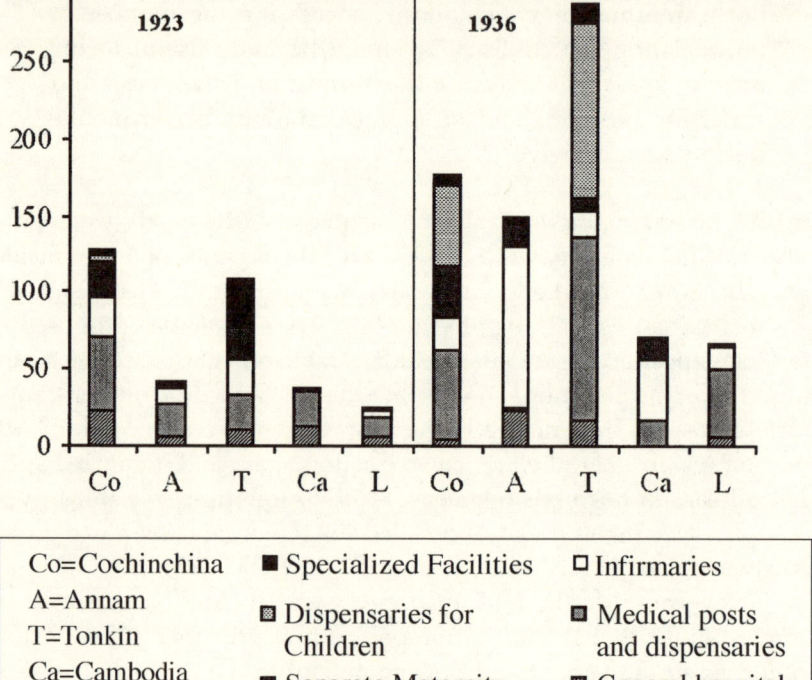

Graph 1. Qualitative and quantitative distribution of health care establishments in Indochina in 1923 and 1936

when traditional medicine would not work. Unfortunately, there was neither the time nor the means to implement this law, but it confirms an unwavering desire to systematize health care and adapt it to local needs.

The increased number of infirmaries and first-aid stations, each equipped with a bandaging and consultation room, was made possible by means of a reshuffling of personnel. In 1937, 121 medical doctors were employed by the AMI, five of whom were Indochinese—a title that the latter could claim after 1921. But it was above all a local staff of 109 auxiliary doctors, 35 pharmacists, 418 midwives, and 3,133 nurses and *ba mu* (the Vietnamese term of a rural midwife) that took over operations. Furthermore, the construction of access roads to isolated regions improved the means of transport, which aided the implementation of these new measures.

At the same time, the health care plan of 1918 focused on the construction of medical facilities, as the growth curve in the hospital volume attests. Thereafter, the doctor posted to the region in question would have an important voice in the decision-making process. And by the end of the 1920s a "zone of operations" was evaluated for each project.[43] The watchword, "always more facilities," had evolved over the years. What is striking about the physiognomy of the hospital system in the 1930s is the number of rural infirmaries (432 out of 594 AMI establishments) and maternity hospitals. In 1930, Dr. Francière, director of health services in Laos, spoke frankly of a "veritable growth crisis" (which the budget could not support).[44] In that same year, Cambodia and Laos each had more than 60 health care facilities, of which two-thirds of the former and three-quarters of the latter were but humble infirmaries. However, it was in the capital cities and deltas of Tonkin and Cochinchina that one found the most impressive hospital network.

Large Cities and Populated Provinces: The Same Infrastructural Checkerboard?

In Hanoi or Saigon, the hospital network was integrated into an urban landscape that had progressively improved sanitary conditions and was close to essential services. Of course, all of this new construction had to follow a strict plan of hygiene—since the first law regarding public health had been established in 1867 in Saigon. The municipal health policies of Saigon and later Hanoi (both of which were aware of being the centers of colonial attention) rested on three main objectives: to establish hospitals for Indochinese people, to teach hygiene and control infant mortality rates, and to develop large sanitation projects.[45] In the 1930s, the Cochinchinese capital aimed at creating massive hospitals with a tenfold increase in services, research laboratories, private clinics, and consultation rooms. All of these facilities would be based on an urban plan developed by both physicians and architects. The buildings were soon completed, erected side by side; the hospitals grew, the streets optimizing the passage from one to another. The vestiges that remain of this vast operation (in the current neighborhood of the former Grall hospital and the Pasteur Institute) are convincing proof of the emphasis put on hospital development by the colonial authorities. The hospital system thereby reflected the benefits of a medical assistance program, which, in its turn, reflected the benefits of the mother country.

Another key area of development was the Saigon-Cholon region, which saw new facilities spring up in just a few years: a tuberculosis institute, cancer prevention services, an ophthalmological clinic, and an ear, nose, and throat clinic. These local institutions were soon joined by a mental asylum (Bien Hoa, 1919), an institute of pediatrics (1927), and an institute for the prevention of venereal diseases (1929). They also acquired the cooperation of the Hospital Association of Cochinchina, an active complex supported by essentially private financing since 1919. In 1930, it brought together the core of the general health care facilities in the territory (the Indigenous Hospital of Cochinchina, the Drouhet Hospital, and the Choquan Hospital, which together employed sixteen physicians and fifty-six nurses), as well as its medical training establishments (the training school for nurses and native midwives).

The goals stated in the health report of 1912 concerning the city of Hanoi had been realized at the price of incredible sacrifices and financial expense. In spite of this, the Indigenous Hospital of the Protectorate was heralded as the most important AMI medical facility in Tonkin in 1930. The management of the hospital, as well as that of its maternity ward, had been under the direction of the head of the School of Medicine since 1923. Its medical staff was large (there were 106 nurses alone) in order to ensure the proper functioning of medical, surgical, and specialized services. This sprawling infrastructure was joined by a hospital for contagious diseases, the Ophthalmological Teaching Center of Indochina (1917), the Central Pharmacy of Tonkin, and laboratories for hygiene and the repression of fraud. Added to this were strictly municipal services like the Radium Institute (1928) and private clinics and maternity hospitals, all of which formed a particularly extensive hospital network. In the 1930s, when Governor-General René Robin erected the hospital complex of Bach Mai, the Hanoi metropolitan area became the indisputable health care capital of the union.[46]

In the 1920s, French authorities implemented an ambitious plan offering both preventive and treatment services in Saigon and Hanoi. In the 1930s, the major cities of Indochina contained a hospital complex that was significant for its size, its polyvalence, and its specialization. As such, it provided a veritable conglomerate of medical and paramedical personnel that could only benefit the remainder of the territory. It is more difficult, however, to evaluate the development of health care services in the secondary hubs of Indochina (such as Phnom Penh, Vientiane, Hue, and Haiphong) or in the more populated provinces. At most, I can set forth a few hypotheses regarding the characteristics of this development.

In some areas, development took place as the consequence of a former missionary presence. This was the case in Phnom Penh. Like the imperial capital of Hue, Phnom Penh obtained the title of municipality as a consequence of relatively rapid urbanization: the city had nearly 100,000 inhabitants in 1920. More importantly, municipal status was required to obtain a charter regarding hygiene. Thus, in 1930 the Khmer capital boasted a mixed hospital equipped with special services dedicated to the treatment of children as well as state of the art services (such as an ophthalmological institute and an ear, nose, and throat clinic). Dispensaries at Ang Duong (1919) and Lanelongue (1926) were funded by the municipal budget, as was an infirmary in the Chrui Changar palace. Certain private projects associated with the AMI completed this organizational picture. In 1937, the French envoy from the Popular Front, Justin Godart, claimed to be satisfied with the situation (Godart 1994, 47): "Municipal dispensary of Ang Duong. Municipal Hygiene Department: good organization, mobile sterilizers, kennel for dogs, which catch three hundred rats every morning. Dispensary Lanelongue (small) St. Lazare, which is interesting for its preventative treatments. . . . Dispensary for prenatal consultations run by the Society for the Protection of Mothers and Children. . . . Mixed hospital (very good)."

In the case of Haiphong, the city's proximity to Hanoi and its status as a commercial port simultaneously favored the establishment of its health care system.[47] It was endowed with modern facilities, a Bureau of Hygiene that was in constant communication with that of the capital, and an independent service of maritime health police. Haiphong was then established as an annex to the health care program of the greater Hanoi area in 1930. Hue, on the other hand, did not enjoy the same kinds of advantages. The imperial capital did not have an important geographical location. Municipal authorities were then forced to take private initiatives to provide the necessary impetus.

Indeed, until the 1930s Hue would remain the only health base in the entire protectorate. Its principal hospital contained as many specialized services as that of Hanoi. Its bacterial laboratory guaranteed the same services as those of the Pasteur Institute in Hanoi and Saigon. The only sign of decentralization was the Central Pharmacy, which was located in Tourane until 1930.

As for Vientiane, the researcher must rely more on guesswork since historical sources are ambiguous at best. Vientiane was neither a municipality, nor the site of a preponderant colonial population, nor very populous. Yet the city was endowed with an extensive hospital network (mixed hospital equipped with a wing for contagious diseases and with a school for nurses and midwives, a central pharmacy, and a bacterial laboratory). Perhaps as a sign of its relatively low colonial importance, however, hygiene and sanitation projects were nonexistent. Moreover, the concentration of hospital facilities inside the city was not well suited to a scattered and sparse population.[48]

It is clear from these diverse examples that there was no standard form of development and no uniformity in the history of health care in these Indochinese cities. There was, however, a common denominator: as centers of the decision-making process, these cities also became home to much new construction and the presence of a great number of medical personnel. This convergence of labor illustrates some of the limits of an urban health care model.

The concentration of health care facilities in Indochina reveals a logical pattern: the capitals of the richest and most populous provinces—for the most part in Cochinchina and Tonkin—also became important medical and health care centers. For some of these cities, adaptation came early and worked effectively from the start. In 1917, for example, the provincial medical service in the provincial capital of Gia Dinh (Cochinchina) was run by a doctor who went to the principal infirmary three times a week. Every Wednesday he made the rounds to inspect the medical stations staffed by nurses and the maternity hospitals, which were in the hands of midwives. In short, even though there were no large facilities in the region—the hospital was still under construction—the activities of mobile, subordinate personnel often made up for the insufficient stationary facilities and apparently generated good results.[49]

Often, though, a gulf opened between these microcapitals and the villages and regions that depended upon them for health care. In

1926, the Indochinese doctor Henri Marcel conducted a survey on health care in 818 Tonkin villages in the populous province of Ha Dong (615 inhabitants per square kilometer on average). He denounced the poor sanitary conditions, as well as the flagrant contrast between the well-stocked provincial capital and the three isolated maternity clinics, and sparse provisions, which would have to satisfy the needs of the rural population (1926, 40–57). In 1930, each province in Laos possessed at least one rural infirmary, which monitored the spread of epidemics, distributed the usual medicines, and dispensed urgent medical care. Short of being able to guarantee equal access to medical care, however, the authorities needed to improve the support given to these small posts. Annam would undertake such a project in the second half of the decade.

Rural Assistance and Mobile Medicine: The Example of Annam

In the 1920s, those areas that relied most on a policy of mobile and rural assistance were broken down into definable geographic entities: regions that were sparsely populated, isolated, difficult to access, or populated by mountain people or other ethnic minorities. Until the years following World War I, the majority of these regions (such as Cambodia, Laos, and the Annam hinterland) only occasionally felt the benefits of the AMI plan. In 1908, the local director of the Health Services in Cambodia, Dr. Menaut, devised a plan to bring medical care to the region of Kompong Cham. In 1912, his system was still attempting to make up for the absence of staff and facilities.

> In each of the 150 *khums* in the area of Kompong Cham, in the home of the village chief or *mekhum*, there is a stock of medicine. This medicine is kept locked in a small chest to preserve it and is accompanied by a medical guide. [The chest] contains quinine, lactic acid, soda sulfate, boric acid, picric acid, permanganate of potassium, and cotton bandages. . . . The doctor makes the rounds, which put him in contact with the local people; but, as each village can scarcely be seen but once a year, and since it is always good that the doctor knows what is going on, an information service was established by way of mandatory monthly reports by the *mekhums*. Created in 1908,

this operation is still functioning. Special pieces of paper are distributed to each village chief, who records the number of births, deaths, and epidemics with the number of cases and death toll, the demand for the next rounds of the doctor in his village, or new medicine for his chest. These papers are collected and filed at the *résidence*, which then transmits the information to the doctor.[50]

From the data presented in the graph 1, one might see this kind of localized initiative in Cambodia and Laos as part of a real movement for the spread of medical services.[51] Their delay in matters of health care organization continued, however, to accentuate the inequalities. Phnom Penh and especially Vientiane were not in a position to uphold their roles as centers of prevention and treatment. The functioning of their health care mechanisms remained crippled by lack of funds and staff. In 1930, despite its 52 infirmaries and 13 provincial hospitals, the Protectorate of Laos could put only 529 beds at the disposition of Lao patients, only as many as the hospital of the Protectorate of Hanoi alone. In 1936, 82.4 percent of the hospital facilities of the peninsula (737 structures counted) were in Vietnamese territory, of which 38 percent were in Tonkin. Of course, the Vietnamese population was five times greater (at about 20 million) than that of Cambodia and Laos combined. But, despite the progress made in these rural areas, the health care network was still not well adapted to the scattered and sparse population of the two protectorates.

In 1937, many physicians called for greater access to health care in rural Indochina during the Conference of Oriental Countries on Rural Hygiene in Bandung. Meanwhile, Annam continued to thrive under its new health care plan (SDN 1937).[52] In March of 1936, for example, the doctor-in-chief of Quang Tri Province asked for the creation of another medical post in Lam Ho (an extremely malaria infested region twenty-five kilometers from the provincial center). In May, not only was the request accepted but the establishment was under construction.[53] Even more importantly, the three health care missions of Dr. Lieurade allowed him to visit some 100,000 patients and above all led to the construction of ten infirmaries in Kontum between 1936 and 1938 (Lieurade 1941). Annam owed this efficiency in part—at least this is what the archives of the *résidence supérieure* reveal—to the fact that certain villages agreed to take measures into their own hands. Credit must also be given to both the colonial and Indochinese authorities of 1935. The Local Health Bureau called for all health care expenses to be returned to local budgets for later reimbursement by the provinces. This decision led to a better use of funds and a more efficient decision-making process. This budgetary independence and the greater authority of the health administration were the keys to "health care success" in Annam.[54]

In 1935, under the direction of a Dr. Terrisse, the process got under way in Annam with the creation of the first communal infirmaries, which were initially dedicated to the treatment of ocular infections. Each infirmary served a group of villages and was set up at minimal cost in spare office space or communal buildings (hence the name). The administration of the region also called for the building of infirmaries in the most isolated villages, with a native teacher serving as nurse. The latter soon acquired a simple pharmacy, composed essentially of tincture of iodine and quinine. In 1936, a system of road signs was finally placed along the Mandarin Route to indicate the existence of a medical facility. Basic first-aid stations (*dépôts de pansements*) were then erected along the main roads. Finally, the regional administration began to display a growing concern for minority groups, a trend that was sparked by a proposal by the *résident* of Phan Rang to train nurses of "Moï" nationality and send them to their villages of origin.[55]

The provision of health care in Annam developed along three principal lines: the area of traditional pharmacology, the training of a native nursing staff, and the formation of a corps of Ba Mu. In Thanh Hoa Province, a veritable "model of health care organization" (Godart 1994, 38) achieved gratifying results after two trial years. As a result, the mid-1930s saw an increase in small rural posts and medical rounds throughout the protectorate, and in 1938 the region was divided into sectors of rural assistance. The project soon ran into obstacles, however. By 1939, only three sectors out of the twenty-two were working effectively due to a lack of staff, medicine, and enthusiasm on the part of the local population. Still, Governor-General Jules Brévié recognized the potential merits of Annam's program and encouraged its expansion.[56]

The experience of Annam represents a successful implementation of the rural medical assistance plan, as it had been defined at the end of the century's first decade. Under this plan, a division still existed between a small urban network and an immense rural one, but it was of a lesser magnitude than before. Two systems thereafter coexisted and sometimes were even complementary. The first was a vast system of specialized hospitals that served patients within its zone of operations as well as the most serious "rural cases." The second often consisted of just a dispensary equipped with a bare minimum of supplies but run by a local staff. The dispensary attracted patients, familiarized them with the principles of consultation and Western therapies, offered primary care, and prevented illnesses that would otherwise have necessitated a journey into the city for hospitalization. The differences between the Indigenous Hospital of the Protectorate of Hanoi and the medical post at Lam Ho were less a sign of inequality than a reflection of the different medical needs of the two worlds. Further analysis of the rate of development between urban and rural areas will show whether this conclusion is justified.

4. The Indochinese Hospital: A Colonial Institution

Throughout Indochina, medical treatment was always provided through the prism of three alternatives. The first, consultation, offered the most advantages, both in the hospital and in the dispensary. By nature optional, it was a time of advice, prevention, and rapid care. Hospitalization, for its part, was more random and costly and was dependent upon the success of persuading the patient to take advantage of this service—an issue to which I shall return. Finally, the prescribing of medication was accepted from the beginning, perhaps because in traditional medical practices the use of medication in conjunction with therapy was already common. In addition, the use of medication often obviated the need for a stay in the hospital, thus making it a much more pleasant alternative. But before evoking the complexity of the link between the native populations and Western medicine let us first examine the range of health care and hospitalization options offered to the Indochinese patient.

Hospital Care Options Widen

Hospitals can do little in the face of epidemics, since they are poorly adapted to fight disease when the primary struggle must be preventive. On the other hand, the hospital can still find solutions for—or at least provide relief from—endemic and "social diseases." This is the official framework within which the hospital functions; but this limited view needs to be rectified. In many cases, the hospital had to make up for the absence of prophylactic measures or the impossibility of their systematic application. Thus, in the absence of being able to prevent intestinal parasites, each case had to be detected in the hospital environment to limit its development.[57] Discovered in the course of clinical tests, intestinal parasites thus became the third most important ailment treated in the hospitals. The hospital, in turn, became the best weapon against it. An even clearer example was the struggle against the (presupposed) leading cause of death in Indochina, malaria. In 1915, malaria represented 12.8 percent of hospitalizations and 12.9 percent of hospital deaths. In 1929, these numbers had decreased to 10.1 and 10.2 percent, respectively (Gaide 1931)—and this is without taking into account the cases detected during the course of a hospital visit. Throughout the period of colonization, malaria would remain the leading cause of hospitalization.

These statistics should not, however, minimize the importance of preventive activity. The distribution of quinine (begun in 1909), combined with surveillance of workers' groups and the destruction of the anopheles mosquito, and especially the creation of a Pastorian plan in 1930, all assuredly played a significant role in the struggle against malaria (Monnais-Rousselot 1999, 160–64). Furthermore, the statistics concerning the incidence of malaria are not the only evidence of the evolution of hospital activity in Indochina between 1860 and 1939. To be convinced of this fact, the reasons why people sought hospital care and the results obtained have to be examined.

Given the mediocre results obtained by the leprosy clinics in 1918, in 1923 Albert Sarraut stressed that therapy be made a priority: "There is, in effect, no prophylactic weapon more powerful than a truly active therapy because it can strike directly into the minds of the natives. . . . Leprosy will cease to be considered a defect, and lepers will no longer refuse outpatient treatment when they realize that even if they are not completely cured of their affliction they will almost certainly receive at least a fairly clear and lasting improvement."[58] Results achieved in succeeding years showed this to be true. The use of chaulmoogra oil advocated by the Pastorian Louis Boëz became general practice. In a few years, the use of chaulmoogric ethers led to the healing, in only eight weeks, of hundreds of patients from Annam, Tonkin, and Cambodia.[59] But this therapeutic invention for curing Indochinese lepers was not only a precursor for the treatment of disease; it also had profound social consequences. It introduced the concept of the individual, the colonized citizen, as an individualized patient. Physicians no longer just attacked the disease; they now also treated the patient (Monnais-Rousselot 2000). The struggle against leprosy in the 1930s could of course not yet do without physical segregation. It did, nevertheless, bring to the fore the important role played by the hospital in the adaptation of medico-social policy.

The assault on infant mortality was also launched well before the establishment of the Bureau of Social Assistance (1929). Umbilical tetanus was the first childhood disease to catch the attention of several hospital practitioners. In the first years of the twentieth century, a Dr. Montel in Saigon undertook a large-scale operation against it.[60] Following his example, a variety of new methods were developed to encourage women to give birth in maternity hospitals. More important still was the development of an internal system to educate native midwives (to teach them how to cut the umbilical cord and the subsequent bandaging). Progress made in obstetrics and nutrition, and evolution in the fight against infectious diseases, put the priority on child health care. Children were vaccinated against smallpox, then against tuberculosis (from 1925). They received personalized attention in children's hospitals and maternity wards outfitted with outpatient services and specialized consultations, child care, and nurseries equipped with milk for infants (*gouttes de lait*, services that guaranteed healthy milk for children, as well as providing health statistics and the detection of a number of diseases like tuberculosis) (Monnais-Rousselot, forthcoming). Pregnant women were also monitored: they were treated for malaria and syphilis and educated about the risks of abortion and the importance of following the basic rules of hygiene.

Maternity hospitals thus quickly found themselves at the center of the children's health care project. In the cities, as in the countryside throughout Indochina, they were much more than a simple place to give birth, whether annexed to a hospital, located in an isolated environment, or in private institutions. They became a site for consultations of all sorts: prenatal, questions of sterility, and postnatal. These 1935 health statistics already show very encouraging results in terms of hospital attendance on several levels.

It would be important, of course, to evaluate these statistics in the context of the total number of births for that year, of the number of children under five years old, and of the infant mortality rate in order to evaluate the full significance of the effort. I would also have to be able to calculate the regionalized rates of the use of maternity hospitals. If I take the number of official births for the year as 618,221, this means that 1.65 percent of women made postnatal consultations in medical facilities. This would seem to be a fairly low rate, but it amounts to an important number, considering the number of births. This number went from 2,604 in 1904 to 84,384 in 1939, an increase of more than thirty-two times over thirty years.[61]

It was once again within the hospital system that important work was done on a variety of other ailments. It was again Dr. Angier who was the first to study the manifestations of tuberculosis, mental illness, and ocular diseases in the patients of Choquan in 1905.[62] In 1922, "social diseases" accounted for 11 percent of hospitalizations and 13 percent in 1936 (and 16 and 17 percent of deaths, respectively). According to the reports of the Inspection Générale des Services Sanitaires, these diseases affected three times as many people in 1936 as in 1922 (338,953 versus 133,412). And these statistics only include hospitalizations for tuberculosis, venereal or skin diseases, bronchitis, and cancer.[63] In the absence of corroborating statistics, which would provide a more realistic figure, those of 1936 already testify to a larger medical mobilization with regard to social diseases. At the turn of the century, the hospitalization of Indochinese prostitutes—a process that had been monitored by nuns—was more like a jail sentence. Thenceforth, however, as a phenomenon of modern city life, venereal diseases were treated in specialized facilities: at the Indigenous Hospital of the

TABLE 2. The Role of the Health Care Facility in the Protection of Indochinese Child Welfare in 1935

Nature of the Consultation	Number of Patients	Number of Consultations
Prenatal	13,558	31,026
Postnatal	10,202	25,004
Children from 0 to 2 years	27,974	43,786
Children from 2 to 5 years	80,030	207,702

Source: Data from Beudiment, Pierre, "Protection de la maternité et de l'enfance indigène dans les colonies françaises en 1935," *Annales de Médecine et de Pharmacie Coloniales* 33 (1935): 504–64.

Protectorate of Hanoi (1925), at the Brieux dispensary in Hue (1928), and then in those of Haiphong and Phnom Penh. At the same time, new research facilities were built to better control these outbreaks.

Dr. Angier also organized an outpatient service for the blind in 1905. In January 1921, an ophthalmological institute (the Sarraut Institute) opened its doors in Hue. It was very clear that this costly and remarkably well equipped building was not the product of chance but answered a definite and acknowledged need within the community. In fact, the ophthalmological clinic in Hanoi had for several years made major advances in the fight against trachoma. In its wake, a similar institute opened in Phnom Penh (1924), before the mobile ophthalmology brigades were sent out into the protectorates, but this goes beyond the scope of this study. It was the fight against tuberculosis, in fact, that was the keystone of the medico-social project of the postwar period. However, if hospitals were the chief instrument for disease research in the 1920s they would soon play only a passive role in a mainly preventive fight (with the use of the Bacillus Calmette Guerin [BCG] vaccine).

In the important battle against tuberculosis, I should not forget to evoke another essential function of the health care system. Hospitals, especially the city complexes, had from the first years of colonization served as centers of medical research, which could be rapidly applied; some even considered them a place of ideal experimentation. The case of beriberi, for example, is very telling in this respect. Its symptoms were studied in the Choquan Hospital at the beginning of the twentieth century.[64] Examples like this, which go beyond the scope of my current study, still merit attention because of their importance, a fact that will become clear in the next section.

Indochinese Responses: Primary Sketch of the Rate
of Health Care Development

Statistics concerning the establishment of a health care system in Indochina reveal the importance of the hospital presence as well as an increasingly more favorable public opinion in Indochina toward Western medical practices. As I demonstrated in my doctoral dissertation, there was a constant and steady evolution in the demand for hospital care. Moreover, the characteristics of this demand changed over time. From the end of the nineteenth century, there was a veritable explosion in the number of people seeking hospital care in the principal metropolitan areas of Vietnam. Surgery became a perfect "advertisement" for the system, given its almost faddish popularity, as many rich Vietnamese called upon its services. Many colonial physicians made their reputations and secured their clienteles based on one successful operation. At the same time, the consumption of medication bore witness to the growth in the number of places and methods of distribution.

My research then emphasized the close relationship that existed from the 1920s onward between the increased offers of treatment and the change in the demand for hospital care (Monnais-Rousselot 1999, 387–97). Involvement in the development and management of a local hospital network within Annam, which I have discussed, illustrates this relationship and its implications. In 1937, the Guernut Commission surveyed the Indochinese regarding health care and found a surprisingly unanimous demand for better medical assistance through the creation of health care facilities in each community, or at least in each district. They also wanted the free distribution of medication to make up for the lack of hospital service in isolated areas.[65]

From a more quantitative perspective, the evolution of the mortality and pathology rate of hospitals is most revealing. The colonial archives are full of data on hospital attendance (a statistic that physicians had to include in an annual report starting in 1907). Of course, it is harder to find data regarding makeshift or very isolated posts. The aforementioned data nevertheless underscore the essential role of the health care system in the fight against the most widespread ailments, from the most serious to the most benign.

First of all, these statistics allow us to assess the reasons why Indochinese patients sought hospital services. In fact, statistical studies since 1905 all followed similar rules of classification, since the patients were immediately diagnosed and classified upon check-in. In 1922, out of the 133,412 hospitalizations in the union, there were 44,860 cases of "general disease" (half of which were for malaria) and 23,777 for childbirth—which shows that the hospital had become the most popular site for giving birth. There were 14,279 cases of hospitalization for venereal and skin diseases (syphilis excepted). Syphilis alone accounted for 5,024 cases. Then came digestive and respiratory ailments, including dysentery, tuberculosis, and beriberi. Cancer was more rare, and cases of smallpox, cholera, or plague were sporadic. In

1936, the 338,953 hospitalizations were categorized as follows: 66,684 for surgical procedures, 52,196 for malaria, and 45,248 for social diseases (of which 11,920 were for tuberculosis and 11,031 for syphilis), 18,915 for skin diseases, and 11,727 for parasitism. These numbers again reveal a growing acceptance of hospital care among the local population. This acceptance is shown in graph 2.[66]

It is easy to see that the total number of hospitalizations was 7.5 times higher in 1937 than in 1907. Of course, for a variety of reasons one cannot apply this percentage of increase to all five territories—among which the absence of reliable data and the disparity in the hospital concentration led to less exponential growth in the territories that received the first health care establishments. In spite of this, however, these figures tell much about those regions that were traditionally considered resistant to the offer of colonial medical care and were poorly served by medical facilities: the number of hospitalizations is 30 times higher in Cambodia in 1937 than in 1907 and 20 times higher in Laos.

Statistics regarding the number of "consulting patients" versus the number of consultations confirm that the number of patients seeking hospital care increased everywhere. For the most part, this implies a voluntary action on the part of the patient, be it through daily visits to a large clinic in Hanoi or a weekly visit to a Lao dispensary. In other words, these statistics do not tell us why the patient went to the hospital—something for which I have little information—but they do give information on the number of visits, their frequency, and their recurrence, all of which are indicators of a more global trend. Between 1907 and 1937, the number of patients increased almost twenty-five times, and the number of consultations by more than twenty. Moreover, the annual average number of consultations per patient went from 2.7 to 2.3, a stable ratio that also bears witness to the fact that the patient not only called upon the doctor but repeated this action. Or, again, to return to the example evoked earlier, pregnant women paid the doctor a prenatal visit before giving birth in the maternity hospital, thus accepting the validity of the need to monitor this natural act.

I have tried to discover the reason why an Indochinese would go to the hospital and whether this individual trip then became a mass phenomenon. I have given some partial answers to the first question, and responded briefly, but in the affirmative, to the second. It remains

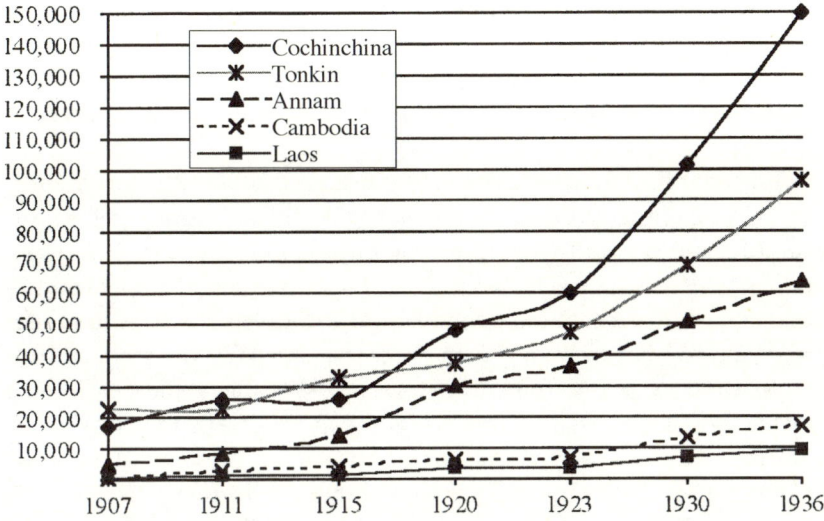

Graph 2. Hospitalizations in French Indochina: Evolution of the recourse to health care (1906–36)
Note: Most of the statistics in this chart are taken from the annual Health Services reports, which explains the absence of reliable and concordant data for the years prior to the creation of the AMI in 1905 (CAOM, Gougal, dossiers 65 324–65 332).

to be determined what were the results of these visits and particularly the results of the hospitalization. In 1885, the mortality rate in the hospitals of Saigon increased to 5.54 percent. Roughly the same statistics were found in Phnom Penh in 1889 (6 percent).[67] A 1922 study in Cochinchina revealed a hospital mortality rate of 4.7 percent. In 1936, this rate was estimated at 4.35 percent for the whole of the union—reasonable in a hospital context. In order to discover the reasons for

TABLE 3. The Health Care Structure: Reflection of the Indochinese AMI (1907–37)

	Hospitalizations	Consulting Patients	Consultations
1907	46,441	249,128	678,494
1913	69,474	599,236	1,688,390
1919	121,842	1,245,336	2,918,255
1925	203,275	2,328,552	5,071,000
1931	241,518	3,846,000	7,748,000
1937	346,000	6,060,000	13,974,000

this drop in the mortality rate, the conditions of the investigation have to be refined again.

Even if the statistics concerning the mortality rate from malaria, tuberculosis (10 percent in 1936), digestive tract diseases (10 percent), and respiratory diseases (8 percent) are clear signs of a general poor state of health, they give a distorted interpretation of the situation.[68] Certain percentages turn out in reality to be encouraging: beriberi, for example, killed four times fewer people in 1936 than in 1922 (4.45 percent). Moreover, the great increase in the number of surgical operations (nearly 20 percent of hospitalizations in 1936) and cases of cancer are testimony not only of a firm acceptance of Western medical care among the local population but to the success of the medical care solicited (1.8 percent mortality rate). As for the incredible rise in the number of births and the disappearance of infantile tetanus (no cases reported in 1936), they again give a precise idea of both a desire for health care, which was becoming commonplace, and the efficiency of the newly organized (post–World War I) system.

The hospital, the dispensary, and the simple consultation answered the increased demand for Western medicine under the AMI. In the space of thirty years, hospitalizations, consultations, and consulting patients increased by a factor of fifteen, even twenty, everywhere in the union. It can even be supposed that physicians now recognized the symptoms of disease and began to convince their patients of the necessity of a preventive stay in the hospital. The positive results obtained in these new medical facilities could only continue to convince patients to return, not just at the last moment but in anticipation of being cured. In the 1930s, the indigenous hospital was not a hospice or a home for the aged where patients would simply wait to die—and it was certainly not considered to be such.

Conclusion

The building of a health care system in Indochina was probably one of the most ambitious projects of the French colonial empire. Every governor-general in the colonies strongly supported the idea of a universal health care system for all Indochinese people by encouraging the building of many "modern" medical facilities. Between 1930 and 1936, the number of facilities continued to grow, and the diversification of their functions became standard practice. Hospital care was no longer limited to urban centers and no longer concentrated in specific areas. A parallel movement in rural areas had sprung up, consisting of primary care clinics, which spread throughout the health care landscape with a regularity suited to its needs. However, its implementation was unequal in each Indochinese country.

As mentioned earlier, this chapter presents the history of the French colonial health care system by studying its medical institutions and analyzing the various colonial policies and their political contradictions within the colonial system. It has not, however, taken into consideration health practices and the relationship between Vietnamese physicians, Vietnamese patients, and those institutions. The essay by Dr. Tran (chapter 9, "Henriette Bui") complements this study by presenting the Vietnamese perspective in the context of the colonizer-colonized paradigm. Nevertheless, in spite of its downfall, this colossal colonial health care institution in Indochina, representing one of the pillars of the French colonial *mission civilisatrice*, was not dismantled after decolonization. I would argue that because of the developing hospital network at its earlier phase of implementation, which was more and more adapted to local need and based on tropical more than colonial concerns, it survived in an ambiguous political context.

NOTES

Department of History and Centre d'Etudes de l'Asie du Sud Est, University of Montreal, Canada. I would like to thank Claire Duiker for the translation of this essay.

1. Michael Worboys, "Science and British Colonial Imperialism, 1895–1940," University of Sussex, Ph.D. diss., 1979; Norman G. Owen, ed., *Death and Disease in South East Asia: Explorations in Social, Medical, and Demographic History* (Singapore: Oxford University Press, 1987); David Arnold, *Imperial Medicine and Indigeneous Societies* (Manchester: Manchester University Press, 1988); David Arnold, *Colonizing the Body: State Medicine and Epidemic Disease in Nineteenth Century India* (Berkeley: University of California Press, 1993); Roy McLeod, *Disease, Medicine, and Empire* (London: Routledge, 1988); Megan Vaughan, *Curing Their Ills: Colonial Power and African Illness* (Cambridge: Polity Press, 1991); Mark Harrison, *Public Health in British India: Anglo-Indian Preventive Medicine, 1859–1914* (Cambridge: Cambridge University Press, 1994); G. M. Van Heteren, A. Knecht van Eekelen, and M. J. D. Poulissen, *Dutch Medicine in the Malay Archipelago, 1816–1942* (Amsterdam: Rodopi, 1989);

Daniel Headrick, *Tools of Empire: Technology and European Imperialism in the Nineteenth Century* (New York: Oxford University Press, 1981); *The Tentacles of Progress: Technology Transfer in the Age of Imperialism, 1850–1940* (New York: Oxford University Press, 1988); Deepak Kumar, *Science and Empire: Essays in the Indian Context (1700–1947)* (New Delhi: Anamik Prakashan, 1991); Patrick Petitjean, Catherine Jami, and Anne-Marie Moulin, *Science and Empires* (Boston and London: Kluwer Academic Publishers, 1992).

2. In addition to some studies on doctors and colonial medicine in France and in general (Lapeyssonnie 1988; Pluchon 1985; Clappier-Valladon 1982) and some academic work (medical dissertations such as Puidupin 1990; Ferrer 1972; and Mianet 1962), only one study takes into account the whole spectrum of issues related to the implementation of a health care system in Indochina (Monnais-Rousselot 1999).

3. The first widespread campaign against smallpox in Cochinchina (the innoculation of nearly 13,000 children) would not take place until 1878. In 1936, 6,297,000 Indochinese would have been vaccinated (Monnais-Rousselot 1995).

4. Centre des Archives d'Outre-Mer (CAOM), Fonds [Collection] du Gouvernement Général (Gougal), dossier 6688.

5. CAOM, Gougal, dossier 15 262.

6. CAOM, Gougal, dossier 6 719.

7. CAOM, Gougal, dossier 6 719.

8. In 1905, reimbursement was set at 2.75 francs for Indochinese, 11.00 francs for officers, and 5.50 francs for other Europeans—a very low rate that would soon cause serious problems for the tightest budgets.

9. Speech by Governor-General Klobukowski at the Conseil Supérieur des Colonies, October 29, 1910 (reprinted in Gouvernement Général de l'Indochine, *Rapport au Conseil du Gouvernement* (Hanoi: Imprimerie Nationale, 1913).

10. CAOM, Ancien Fonds Indochine, dossier Y21 (3); Gougal, dossiers 6 738–6 and 739.

11. The legislation of June 1914 was largely devoted to these reorientations (CAOM, Gougal, dossier 15 279).

12. Service Historique de l'Armée de Terre (SHAT), 10 H 72, dossier 3.

13. Service Historique de la Marine (SHM), BB3 836.

14. It is not my intention here to reexamine the characteristics of the private and religious health care systems. It is my aim, rather, to focus on medical activity in the colonial sense of the term. Let me simply remark here that the first indigenous hospitals in Cochinchina were former religious structures that had been annexed by the administration in the 1860s.

15. CAOM, Fonds des Amiraux, dossier 1 225.

16. CAOM, Ancien Fonds Indochine, carton 322, Y 01 (1); SHAT, 10 H 71, dossier 2.

17. CAOM, Gougal, dossiers 6694, 16 323, 16 329.

18. CAOM, Ancien Fonds Indochine, carton 323, Y 01 (6).

19. Archives Nationales du Viet Nam (ANVN), Center 2, Ho Chi Minh

City (HCMCity), Fonds du Gouvernement de la Cochinchine (Goucoch). Their holdings are inexhaustable on the subject, particularly regarding the first decades of the Choquan hospital's existence. Of particular interest are the hospital report of 1874 (IA.8/157 [18]) and that of Sister Benjamine in 1880 (dossier 3490). The report of the administrator, André, in 1885 can also be found at the CAOM (Amiraux, dossier 10542).

20. ANVN, HCMCity, Goucoch, IA.8/157 (18).
21. ANVN, HCMCity, Goucoch, dossier 3 500.
22. This staff profile shows that they were ahead of their time in deciding to employ a local subordinate staff, well before any official rulings or educational structures existed for this purpose (ANVN, HCMCity, Goucoch, IA.8/091 (2)).
23. ANVN, HCMCity, Goucoch, IA.7/251 (2).
24. ANVN, HCMCity, Goucoch, IA.7/286 (1).
25. CAOM, Fonds de la Direction du Contrôle, carton 649.
26. CAOM, Fonds de la Direction du Contrôle, carton 654.
27. This general organization was completed by the creation of central pharmacies, lazarets, laboratories, and mental asylums (CAOM, Gougal, dossier 1 5279).
28. CAOM, Ancien Fonds Indochine, carton 323.
29. ANVN, HCMCity, Fonds de la Résidence Supérieure d'Annam (RSA), dossier 778.
30. The holdings of the Direction du Contrôle (CAOM), which include reports from the *inspecteurs des colonies,* are very telling on this subject.
31. The funds allocated to health care institutions would double in 1932 to reach three million piasters (Gouvernement Général de l'Indochine, *Budget spécial des grands travaux et dépenses sanitaires sur fonds d'emprunt* [Hanoi: Imprimerie d'Extrême-Orient, 1931]).
32. Ministère des Colonies, *Rapport sur la situation générale de la colonie* (Hanoi: Imprimerie d'Extrême-Orient, 1913).
33. ANVN, Hanoi, Fonds de la Résidence de Nam Dinh, dossier 5 504.
34. ANVN, HCMCity, Goucoch, IA.8/ 191 (1); CAOM, Gougal, dossier 16 461.
35. A map in the Health Services report of 1919 illustrates this (CAOM, Gougal, dossier 65 328).
36. Archives départementales françaises de l'Yonne, Fonds Klobukowski, dossier 20J 18.
37. ANVN, Hanoi, Fonds de la direction locale de la santé du Tonkin, dossier 442.
38. These decisions reveal that the development of mental health care in Indochina was more of a social action than a medical one and show that the hospital was used more for internment and segregation than for treatment.
39. CAOM, Gougal, dossiers 65 324–65 331.
40. Archives départementales françaises de l'Yonne, Fonds Klobukowski, dossier 20J 18.
41. Like his predecessor, Albert Clarac felt that the AMI should not make

hospitals into centers for social assistance (ANVN, HCMCity, RSA, dossier 778).

42. CAOM, Guernut Commission, carton 22, Bb.

43. At the end of the 1920s, Dr. Lavau introduced the notion of a "zone of operations" into the Indochinese health care system ("La zone d'action d'un hôpital de l'Assistance," *Bulletin de la Société Médicochirurgicale de l'Indochine* 6 [1928]: 235–37). For the Cochinchinese province of Sadec, he established this zone at five kilometers. Dr. Chesneau studied this same phenomenon in Laos and then in South Annam in 1932 ("Le rayonnement des dispensaires d'une province du Moyen Laos," *Annales de Médecine et de Pharmacie Coloniales* 29 [1931]; "Le rayonnement des infirmeries d'une province du Sud-Annam," *Annales de Médecine et de Pharmacie Coloniales* 31 [1933]: 538–42). His calculations are more precise, taking into account the specific climatic, geographic, and cultural conditions of each region. His conclusions are, however, redundant.

44. CAOM, Fonds de la Résidence Supérieure du Laos (RSL), S 4.

45. CAOM, Amiraux, dossier 12 237.

46. In this context, I should also mention the importance of the city's Bureau of Hygiene. Since 1902, it was under the direction of Dr. Le Roy des Barres, also founder of the Radium Institute (ANVN, Hanoi, RST, dossier 78 701).

47. CAOM, Gougal, dossier 26 370.

48. CAOM, Fonds de la Direction du Contrôle, carton 680.

49. ANVN, HCMCity, Goucoch, IA.8/234 (1).

50. CAOM, Fonds de la Résidence Supérieure du Cambodge (RSC), carton 280.

51. The reason I found almost no separate maternity hospitals in these countries is because most of them were attached to rural clinics.

52. An account of Annam's exemplary health care policy in the 1930s is available thanks to the abundant documentation of the Fonds de la Résidence archived in the ANVN (Center 2, Ho Chi Minh City).

53. ANVN, HCMCity, RSA, dossier 3 704.

54. CAOM, Guernut Commission, carton 22, Bb.

55. ANVN, HCMCity, RSA, dossier 3 362.

56. ANVN, HCMCity, RSA, dossier 3 878.

57. The preventive measures were, in fact, both costly and poorly received. The project involved the building of latrines in each village and metropolitan area in Indochina.

58. Circular from the Ministère des Colonies, March 1923 (Gaide, L., 1931).

59. Drs. Gaide and Bodet, "La prévention et la traitement de la lèpre," *Exposition coloniale internationale* (Paris: Imprimerie d'Extrême-Orient, 1931).

60. Dr. Montel, "La surveillance de la natalité indigène: *De la prophylaxie du tétanos ombilical à Saigon*, 1905–07," *Annales d'Hygiène et de Médecine coloniale* 9 [1908]: 72–85.

61. Excerpted from "Protection de la maternité et de l'enfance indigène

dans les colonies françaises en 1935," *Annales de Médecine et de Pharmacie Coloniales* 33 [1935].
  62. ANVN, HCMCity, Goucoch, IA.7/251 (2).
  63. I also have no data on the treatment of eye diseases.
  64. ANVN, HCMCity, Goucoch, IA.2/251 (2).
  65. CAOM, Guernut Commission, carton 107, dossier 18.
  66. Most of the statistics in this chart are taken from the annual Health Services reports, which explains the absence of reliable and concordant data for the years prior to the creation of the AMI in 1905 (CAOM, Gougal, dossiers 65 324–65 332).
  67. ANVN, HCMCity, Goucoch, IA.8/091 (2); CAOM, Amiraux, dossier 23 855.
  68. These percentages were calculated based on hospital statistics from the report of the General Inspection of Health Services for 1936 (CAOM, Agence de la France d'Outre-Mer, carton 237, dossier 296).

REFERENCES

Clappier-Valladon, Simone. 1982. *Les médecins français d'outre-mer.* Paris: Anthropos.
Duteuil, Charles. 1864. "Quelques notes médicales recueillies pendant un séjour de cinq ans en Chine, Cochinchine, et Japon." Medical dissertation, Paris.
Ferrer, Michel. 1972. "Essai sur la présence médicale française en Indochine de 1858 à nos jours." Medical dissertation, Marseille.
Gaide, Laurent. 1921. "La médecine européenne en Annam, autrefois et de nos jours." *Bulletin des Amis du Vieux Hué* 4: 189–214.
———. 1931. *L'Assistance Médicale et la protection de la santé publique.* Hanoi: Imprimerie d'Extrême-Orient.
Godart, Justin. 1994. *Rapport de mission en Indochine, 1er janvier–14 mars 1937.* Paris: L'Harmattan.
Gouvernement Général de l'Indochine. 1908. *L'Assistance Médicale Indigène en Indochine française.* Paris: Challamel.
———. 1911. *Fonctionnement du service de l'Assistance Médicale en Indochine.* Paris: Larose.
Grall, Charles. 1907. *L'Assistance Médicale en Indochine.* Marseille: Moullot.
Lapeyssonnie, Léon. 1988. *La médecine coloniale: Mythes et réalités.* Paris: Seghers.
Laure, François. 1864. "Histoire médicale de la Marine française pendant les expéditions de Chine et de Cochinchine." Medical dissertation, Paris.
Lieurade, L. 1941. "Trois campagnes d'assistance mobile dans les pays moïs du centre Annam, Kontum, 1935–1938." *Médecine Tropicale* 1: 77–91.
Marcel, Henri. 1926. "L'hygiène publique dans une province du Tonkin (Ha Dong)." *Bulletin de la Société Médicochirurgicale de l'Indochine* 2: 40–57.

Mianet, Henri. 1962. "Un siècle d'évolution hospitalière: Histoire de l'hôpital Grall de Saigon (1861–1961)." Medical dissertation, Rennes.

Monnais-Rousselot, Laurence. 1995. "Autopsie d'un mal exotique à part: Variole et vaccine en Indochine (1860–1939)." *Revue française d'histoire d'Outre-mer* 82 (309): 505–27.

———. 1999. *Médecine et colonisation: L'aventure indochinoise, 1860–1939*. Paris: CNRS Editions.

———. 2000. "Du pluriel au singulier, du singulier au pluriel: Regards médicaux sur le corps malade en Indochine française, 1860–1939." In G. Boëtsch & D. Chevé, eds., *Corps sains, corps malades, corps exotiques: Le Corps dans tous ses états*. Paris: CNRS Editions.

———. Forthcoming. "La médicalisation de la mère et de son enfant: L'exemple du Vietnam sous domination française, 1860–1939." *Bulletin Canadien d'Histoire de la Médecine*.

Pluchon, Pierre. 1985. *Histoire des médecins et pharmaciens de la Marine et des Colonies*. Toulouse: Privat.

Puidupin, André. 1990. "L'hôpital Grall dans l'histoire franco-vietnamienne." Medical dissertation, Lyon.

Sarraut, Albert. 1923. *La mise en valeur des colonies*. Paris: Payot.

Société des Nations. 1937. *Conférence intergouvernementale des pays d'Orient sur l'Hygiène rurale, Rapport de l'Indochine*. Geneva: Société des Nations.

Part II

Vietnamese Intellectuals:
Contesting Colonial Power

6 Agathe Larcher-Goscha

Prince Cuong Dê and the Franco-Vietnamese Competition for the Heritage of Gia Long

> Ky Ngoai Hau, heir of Prince Canh to the Vietnamese People: . . . "Remember that it was only after great pain that the Vietnamese dynasties succeeded in building the kingdom that we have lost. We must take it back."
> —Cuong Dê, "Manifest to the Country," 1906

> Pigneau de Béhaine, the bishop of Adran, allowed the Annamese emperor, Gia Long, to reunite the pieces of his broken empire. The bishop inspired so much confidence in the great monarch that when he left the palace with the king their two horses walked side-by-side.
> —Albert Sarraut, *L'Indochine Française*, 1930

Introduction

The appearance of Cuong Dê on the Asian political scene has been little studied by contemporary historians interested in the multiform beginnings of Vietnamese nationalist movements. If his presence next to better-known revolutionaries on the eve of World War I is acknowledged, the portrait we have of him is often dull. This is doubtless because he walked for years in the shadow of Phan Bôi Châu, one of the greatest heroes of Vietnam today. In forgetting Cuong Dê in this way, though, contemporary historiography has unwittingly reproduced a colonial vision of this prince. Between 1906 and 1945, this colonial representation continually stressed the endemic mediocrity of his personality, underscoring his weak character and harping on that something or other of amateurism present in everything he did.

This chapter seeks to underscore two less studied aspects of Cuong Dê's activities. First of all, it is necessary to reevaluate his commitment to and his position within the nationalist movement organized by revolutionaries between China and Japan before World War I. In this way, we will see that Cuong Dê was not content merely to follow his allies into exile, nor was he simply going to heed blindly all their political projects. On the contrary, he obstinately and gradually went about achieving his own objectives, often against their wishes. This unsuspected determination on his part would effectively modify the orientations of his partners, sometimes even forcing them to revise their strategies in unexpected ways that have not yet been fully appreciated.

Second, we try to cast some new light on French perceptions of Cuong Dê's activities and to show that the insignificance colonial writers attributed to him hid the concern they demonstrated when it came to dealing with him. For, as an exile, this Vietnamese prince embodied a very tangible threat to a colonial power that understood his historical claims to the Vietnamese past in very challenging terms. On the one hand, by raising the banner of his ancestor, Gia Long, in the name of the Vietnamese nationalist cause, Cuong Dê mobilized a familial memory whose legitimizing heritage had been officially claimed by the colonial administration itself since the end of the nineteenth century. On the other hand, the presence of a direct pretender to Gia Long's throne on the outskirts of Indochina—whose legitimacy was recognized by the French themselves—was much more worrisome than either the governor general of Indochina or the court of Hue was willing to admit in public.

1. Phan Bôi Châu and Cuong Dê: The Disturbing Success of a Strategy of Alliance

When Cuong Dê made his decision to go into exile in January 1906, he was an elegant young man of twenty-four who seemed to have enjoyed his simple and quiet life at Hue.[1] Born in 1882, he was the son of Prince Anh Nhu, well known at the court for having seen his candidacy for the throne repeatedly rejected. Anh Nhu taught his son the traditional duties of respecting his ancestors and ensured that the preservation of the memory of their lineage would have a special meaning. Early on, Cuong Dê developed a remarkable sense of responsibility toward the cult of his ancestors, all the more so upon the death of his father in 1896, when he became the last direct representative of the senior branch of the descendants of Gia Long. Gia Long, of course, was the founder of the Nguyên dynasty, who unified Vietnam after a long civil war against the Tây Son (1773–1801). He had thirteen male offspring, of whom Prince Canh was the firstborn son. Canh became the originator of the dynastic branch known by the title of Anh Duê, of which Cuong Dê represented the fifth generation.[2] Cuong Dê inherited the rank of a noble, but one that indicated that he did not belong to the reigning branch. His title, Ky Ngoai Hau, meant literally that he existed "outside of the imperial capital."

Cuong Dê lived in the capital of Hue, not far from the Imperial College (Quôc Tu Giam). His overall behavior had never attracted any particular attention from the colonial authorities nor generated any great interest in the court. Only his filial devotion seemed noteworthy. Certain students, mainly laureates passing through the capital, had been struck by the devotion he showed to his lineage. This was especially the case during Cuong Dê's guided visits into the private world of his family's mementos. These tours, according to one student, "attracted many among the curious."[3] In one of the rooms of his ancestor's house, the guide would enthusiastically show them the exotic objects that Prince Canh had brought back from his trip to France (1787) with a famous missionary and good friend to his father.

No one could have predicted Cuong Dê's sudden decision to take up the life of an exile. His desire to abandon Hue was never apparent in the affection he showed toward the cults of his ancestors, the care with which he tended the temple of the Eastern Palace (Dông Cung), constructed by Gia Long just to the south of Hue to honor his eldest son, or the pride he took in being photographed before the tomb of his eminent ancestor with his eldest sister and her sons.[4] Notified belatedly by the Council of the Royal Family, the colonial authorities were caught completely off guard by his departure. That something was amiss was clear, however, when, on returning from a trip to Hue, Léon Sogny, then secretary at the *résidence* in Annam, stumbled upon the palanquin of Cuong Dê being carried across the Col des Nuages on its way to Tourane.[5] Sogny, the future head of the police for central Vietnam, must have understood the importance of keeping this prince in view, a personality who had obviously been too hastily written off as weak and harmless.

Phan Bôi Châu was also going to learn this the hard way. Like the French, he would emphasize Cuong Dê's mediocrity, somewhat naively until he understood Cuong Dê's real nature and much more bitterly when he figured out that his disciple had duped him. As Phan Bôi Châu declared peremptorily in 1925: "Cuong Dê had an absolutely average intelligence and education, and I found him too inferior to have any influence over me."[6] In pronouncing these words, he could not have hidden from his French listeners the opportunistic nature of his collaboration with Cuong Dê—nor the rivalry that had been growing between them. Indeed, since 1903–4, a group of scholars from central Vietnam associated with Phan Bôi Châu were keen on locating among the members of the royal family an individual of "high rank whose quality would capture the imagination" of the mandarinate.[7] It was also hoped that if a clever propaganda campaign were well orchestrated this character would be able to rally new support to the cause. In his memoirs, Phan Bôi Châu recalled the advice that had been proffered to him by the scholar Nguyên Ham, a former partisan of the Cân Vuong movement.[8] Aware that the resistance not only needed a standard-bearer but also money in order to grow, he proposed to use the presence within the group of a symbolic name that would inspire confidence among the rich royalists of the south and for whom they would be ready to invest morally and financially. Nguyên Ham elaborated his plan along these lines.

> Cochinchina is a gold mine and a rice granary. It's there that the Nguyên were able to found their dynasty. When Gia Long rebuilt the country, he took all his resources from there. If today we put on the throne one of his descendants, it will be easy for us to appeal to the people down there.[9]

With these words of encouragement, Phan Bôi Châu began prospecting carefully among the members of the royal family in order to find a prince capable of "winning hearts"[10] and stimulating donations in Cochinchina. Following several failed attempts, he was reminded of the existence of Cuong Dê. His genealogy made him a veritable godsend, the right man if ever there were one. Cuong Dê quickly accepted the offers of collaboration that Phan Bôi Châu and Nguyên Ham made to him during a series of meetings. For their part, his interlocutors were sufficiently satisfied to find in him the right nationalist credentials needed to take him onboard as the standard-bearer of the Reformation Society (Duy Tân Hôi), recently formed in Canton in January 1906. Cuong Dê became president of this association, which sought to liberate Vietnam from the French and undertake a dynastic revision in his favor. However, they had badly misjudged the real reasons why this prince had been able to leave his country so easily to follow them into a tortuous life of exile and secrecy. Indeed, the profound malaise that Prince Cuong Dê had escaped upon leaving the imperial capital would only dawn on his companions gradually. They would soon be disappointed to have chosen their man only too well.

It was in Japan that Phan Bôi Châu discovered the depth of the personal motivations of his protégé and began to suspect the unfortunate consequences of this on the group's inner cohesion. Cuong Dê left Hue in January 1906. After a short visit to China, he arrived in Tokyo in March of that year. For his first stay in Japan, he remained with Phan Bôi Châu until 1909. Together these two men were the principal instigators of the Voyage to the East movement (Dông Du), organizing the patriotic trips of several hundred Vietnamese students and assuring the political and military training of what was to be the future revolutionary elite.[11] If this patriotic emigration has been the object of remarkable historical works, clarifying in particular the Asian context of Vietnamese nationalism, the deterioration of relations between the two leaders remains largely unexplored. This is in part due to the lack of attention as to how Cuong Dê's political beliefs could provoke increasing irritation in those around him.

Colonial sources attest to a change in Cuong Dê's attitude shortly after his arrival in Tokyo. In the freedom of his clandestine life, and with ample financial support, Cuong Dê was determined to claim the Vietnamese throne for himself by affirming his historical legitimacy in an open competition with the reigning branch and the monarch ruling under French "protection." This evolution, predictable in a way, was the logical outcome of his recruitment. After all, Am Vo, Nguyên Ham, Dang Tu Kinh, and Phan Bôi Châu, among others, had come looking for a prince of royal blood capable of mobilizing a Nguyên legitimacy in politically and financially profitable ways. Their mistake was to have underestimated the impact of Cuong Dê's humiliation at the hands of the court of Thanh Thai. It should be recalled that this king had been named following the death of Dông Khanh (1889) and over the candidacy of Cuong Dê's father, Anh Nhu, in particular, who was only supported by a few French administrators and a minority of mandarins.¹² Besides the pain of seeing his father pushed aside, a series of incidents had made life even more difficult, if not precarious, for Cuong Dê in Hue. As he would repeat it later, he felt "threatened" by the mandarins who were silently hostile to him.¹³ He affirmed also that he had been torn between the desire to criticize the conduct of the king and the feeling that to transgress the law of silence "would have been [his] ruin."¹⁴

In the end, Thanh Thai inflicted the decisive blow, one that had a profound effect on the sensitivity of the young man. One day in 1905, during a visit to the temple of Dông Cung, where Cuong Dê had just arrived to honor Prince Canh, the king ripped from the altar a portrait of the deceased and proceeded to burn it before the young prince's eyes.¹⁵ This act captured well the strong rivalry between the reigning (Chanh he) and nonreigning (Phiên hê) dynastic branches. The Duy Tân Hôi recruiters had perhaps not quite grasped the implications of all this. What is sure is that they had in no way foreseen that Cuong Dê would be able to free himself of his minor and purely symbolic role in their group in order to pursue his own personal destiny.

In order to avoid the tight police surveillance working through French consular services in Asia and to respect Japanese instructions calling for caution, the arrival of Prince Cuong Dê in Tokyo had been handled with great discretion. However, the rigors of the military institutions he attended, as well as the limitations placed on his movements by his mentor Phan Bôi Châu, annoyed Cuong Dê, who had increasing difficulty in checking his ambitions and his impatience. And this was only a year after his installation in Japan. Although we do not know the exact date, in 1907 Cuong Dê introduced ritual practices to further his main goal of ensuring his dynastic restoration. He did this "against the wishes of Phan Bôi Châu."¹⁶ Nonetheless, if his principle had been acknowledged by the founding members of the Duy Tân Hôi, getting it truly implemented, Cuong Dê quickly realized, was quite another matter. Cuong Dê took the initiative by requiring all the newly arriving Vietnamese students to Japan to present themselves before him dressed in ceremonial garb and performing the traditional *lays*, the deferential bows that a subject owed his sovereign.¹⁷ In addition, the prince bestowed on himself a reign title while awaiting his return to rule in Vietnam. He quickly accustomed himself to signing letters, handing out calling cards, and issuing requests under the name of Gia Thanh. The first character of this signature was an allusion to the reign title of Gia Long.[18] For anyone reading it, the similarity would have immediately situated Cuong Dê as a direct descendant of Gia Long and would have reinforced the idea that he was the heir and the modern-day continuator.

Photographs of Cuong Dê in royal costume were soon in circulation. Nominations to various functions were issued within this "parallel Court" circulating on the outside. Signed by him, some of these documents were even picked up in Cochinchina, where the prince obtained the best fund-raising results for the cause. Following a raid on one of the hotels founded by Gilbert Chieu in My Tho (named Minh Tân), donation records were discovered in the name of the pretender listing his Cochinchinese contributors. Also of help were the statements of Vo Van Thien. He had attended meetings in this hotel, during which the emissary of the prince for Cochinchina, Bui Chi Nhuan,[19] bestowed certificates stamped with Prince Cuong Dê's seal to several members. All of these facts underscored to the colonial authorities the fullness of southern Vietnamese support for the prince.[20] The texts Cuong Dê prepared and dispatched in various ways to Vietnam embodied the aspect of the solemn call for the restoration of the sovereign to his rightful throne. He sent at least three directly to the court in Hue to support his arguments, one in 1906, another in 1917, and yet a third in 1919. One letter addressed to the Council of Regents made its way into the hands of the new king, Khai Dinh, who had just recently ascended the throne. In this letter, Cuong Dê stipulated: "The nation of the ancestors is under foreign domination. . . . Concerning the restoration of the country, we have assigned ourselves the mission to recover it."[21] There could be no ambiguity in Vietnam as to what Cuong Dê was saying.

In short, Cuong Dê had established the symbolic attributes of sovereignty in exile. He had also rapidly broken the rules of a minimum of discretion that Phan Bôi Châu had hoped to impose on him for his own security. But there were other reasons for Phan Bôi Châu to worry. In particular, the prince's successful propaganda was eschewing the geography of the Dông Du's recruiting to his disadvantage. There are reasons to think that Phan Bôi Châu did not look favorably on the growing number of new students arriving in Japan from Cochinchina in the prince's name to the detriment of those heralding from Annam and Tonkin, Phan Bôi Châu's traditional recruiting ground. Following an investigation, Léon Sogny underlined the following reasons for a growing rivalry in the back rooms of the Duy Tân Hôi in Japan.

> Luck has quickly favored Cuong Dê in Japan thanks to the infatuation the Cochinchinese showed for him. Indeed, the latter constituted the majority of the overseas students and they brought with them or received a lot of money [from home]. Compared to them, the Tonkinese and the Annamese looked like poor relations. Very skillfully, Cuong Dê knew how to flatter the Cochinchinese, and they all declared themselves devout royalists. Phan Bôi Châu understood that he had been swindled (*roulé*) by the young prince and that the latter would be the main beneficiary of the conspiracy. Nonetheless, Phan Bôi Châu could not solve the problem by dropping Cuong Dê because he realized that he would need him increasingly to fill the party's coffers. In any case, he probably harbored the secret intention that, over the long term, he would succeed in damaging the credibility of the prince and rally all the students to his cause. . . . Yet his efforts were systematically undermined by the recalcitrance of the Cochinchinese, who only wanted to obey Cuong Dê.[22]

It is thus hardly surprising that Phan Bôi Châu urged Cuong Dê to write an appeal to the Cochinchinese with the admitted intention that the money collected would thereafter be redistributed to "provide for the needs of the émigrés from the center and north, which would be good policy."[23] And, indeed, this appeal obtained very good results.

Phan Bôi Châu was not the only one to suffer from these paradoxically disturbing victories being scored by Cuong Dê. If Phan Chau Trinh had decided to make a brief trip to Japan, it was not just to see for himself the new strength of this country that had so fascinated Vietnamese elites since Japan's victories over the Russians and the Chinese. Profoundly upset by the success of Cuong Dê's legitimizing propaganda, Trinh attempted to get his antiroyalist views accepted among the overseas students. It appears that the control of the prince's mentor, Phan Bôi Châu, did little to reassure Trinh's fears that Cuong Dê was getting out of hand. That there was a problem became clear when Trinh's attempt to bring back with him to Vietnam a small group of students "belonging" to the prince was a last-minute failure.²⁴ Cuong Dê reacquired his flock just before its departure.²⁵ Future events would show that Phan Châu Trinh was not about to forgive Cuong Dê for the challenge he posed the former in the fight for the nationalist high ground. If Trinh hoped to get beyond the well-trodden path of the royalist tradition, it appears that the monarchy remained a viable nationalist rallying point for a majority of (southern?) Vietnamese before World War I.

2. The Impossible Maintenance of "Sacred Unity"

When the decision was made to expel the Vietnamese émigré network in Japan, Phan Bôi Châu was already sure about one thing: Cuong Dê had but one consistent political program, his own.²⁶ And he would do everything in his power to achieve it. Even if his most determined adversaries—whether Vietnamese or French—would later have a vested interest in blackening his record by stressing his obsessive quest for power, it does not seem excessive to think that his quest was most determined on the eve of World War I. Three elements give credence to this idea: (1) the state of mind with which Cuong Dê envisioned a new set of alliances in Siam, (2) the difficulty he had in reconciling his position within the newly baptized Vietnamese Restoration Association (Viet Nam Quang Phuc Hôi), and (3) the motives for his trip to Europe. It is not my aim to analyze these points in detail here but to consider them as signposts that can help us to better track the autonomous road Cuong Dê chose to take. In this essay, I can only suggest their consequences for the independent line defended by Cuong Dê on the eve of World War I.²⁷

Following the Franco-Japanese diplomatic accords and the expulsion from Japan of the Dông Du movement, many students had to take refuge in other host countries—in China and Siam in particular. The voyage of Phan Bôi Châu and fifty or so Vietnamese students to the village of Ban Tham near Bangkok is well known, as is the fact that their trip was officially facilitated by Siamese authorities. The steps taken by Cuong Dê are perhaps a little less so. After his expulsion from Kobe in October 1909, Cuong Dê moved from one place to another, spending time in Hong Kong, Macao, and Canton and traveling to Siam in 1910, 1911, and 1912. From Siam, he organized fund drives and propaganda networks in Cochinchina, with the aid of his trusted ally Bui Chi Nhuan. He expanded his contacts with agents of the Japanese and German consulates in Bangkok.

He also tried to develop, based on the example of Phan Bôi Châu, links to the Siamese Chakri court. It was in this way that Cuong Dê met a prince of royal blood, a former governor of Siemreap Province, and a paternal uncle of the king named Chao Trom Pa Chat. Cuong Dê hoped to gain his help for a Vietnamese insurrection.[28] That these Siamese did not take Cuong Dê seriously, judging the organization of his partisans too weak, is not the point here. What interests us is to understand through which historical, traditional, and even familial looking glass Cuong Dê envisioned his forays into Siam. Like Phan Bôi Châu, he hoped to find some support among the Vietnamese communities located in the Bangkok area; but he may well have focused on the descendants of the companions of Gia Long who had themselves immigrated to Bangkok at the end of the eighteenth century.[29] During the wars against the Tây Son, the fugitive pretender had twice taken refuge in Siam (1784, 1785–87). Some of his troops would never return to live in Vietnam, preferring to make their homes in Siam. Later another influx of emigrants would arrive, consisting this time of Vietnamese Catholics fleeing religious persecution under the reign of Minh Mang.[30]

As a direct descendant of Gia Long, Cuong Dê wanted to march in the footsteps of his ancestor, renew his links with the Vietnamese communities, however Siamized, and induce the court of Chulalongkorn, and later Wachirawut, to rally to a cause that he considered to be already successfully written in the past. These were not necessarily all word games on Cuong Dê's part. The prince's action must be situated firmly within the ancient system of dynastic alliances that the colonial intervention had certainly sent into decline but had not yet completely neutralized. That history did not repeat itself and his projects did not succeed as he would have liked did not necessarily discourage Cuong Dê. After all, as he would confide to one of his correspondents in June 1916, the example of his ancestor, ever present in his spirit, taught him the importance of perseverance and patience.[31] Had not Gia Long taken twenty-two years to come to the throne, Cuong Dê asked rhetorically, with his own plight obviously in mind? Whether the ways of the past would be sufficient or not, no one knew, but he was ready to test all the possible solutions, even the newest ones, if it meant achieving his own restoration.

If the reasons for Cuong Dê and Phan Bôi Châu's actions differed in Siam as early as 1910, the political upheavals in China would divide the two men's paths even more a year later. Upon learning of the Chinese revolution, Phan Bôi Châu left Siam in 1911 for Shanghai and Canton, hoping that the Chinese would offer new possibilities for financial and military aid to the Vietnamese émigrés. The successes of the Kuomintang, the coming to power of Sun Yat Sen, the formation of the Provisional Government of the Republic of China (January 1912), and the crumbling of the Manchu dynasty (February 1912) provided an incredible revolutionary groundswell right on the periphery of French Indochina. Bearers of hope, these events prompted the Vietnamese émigrés in southern China to create a new league more in line with the times than the Duy Tân Hôi. Once again, it was in Canton that the Vietnamese Restoration Association took form in 1912. By means of a network of agents and secret societies inside Vietnam, this new party was able to activate a virulent propaganda campaign and stimulate considerable political unrest, notably a number of attacks that would put the colonial authorities on alert in 1913. For his part, Cuong Dê felt he was being tracked by the agents of the French police and thus did the same by going to Hong Kong at the beginning of the year. He stayed there for the most part until his departure for Europe in 1913.

For the first time ever, one could see the outlines of a Vietnamese national government taking form in exile. Indeed, during the founding meeting of the Quang Phuc Hôi the political roles in the future government of the Vietnamese Republic were divided up among the participants (Phan Bôi Châu, foreign affairs; Tan Thuat, first secretary; Nguyên Thuong Hien, finance; Hoang Trong Mau, military affairs; Nguyên Cam Giang [Nguyên Hai Than], internal affairs).[32] Cuong Dê does not recall in his memoirs having attended this inaugural session, during which he was apparently elected president (*tong dai bieu*) of the directing committee.[33] And perhaps not without reason. If we can believe colonial intelligence reports, his nomination to this post was very contested. The prince received the votes of Nguyên Thuong Hien, a committed royalist, and of Phan Bôi Châu for financial reasons and because maintaining an essential cohesion was key to the group's survival.³⁴ Yet the prince had some powerful detractors, Hoang Trong Mau in particular. The latter was worried that the traditionalism of Cuong Dê would give rise to hesitation among Chinese republican revolutionaries who were ready to back the Vietnamese and some of whom had even begun to provide proof of it.³⁵ That the prince lugged around everywhere his ivory plaques engraved with the characters *hoang tôc than vuong* (prince of the royal family) annoyed Mau immensely. By flaunting his conservative attachments to the kingdom of Annam, the pretender to the Nguyên throne had become a definite handicap at this juncture. Hoang Trong Mau enjoined him violently to bend to the new imperatives of the group, going so far in a moment of anger to strike him in the face with his cane. The French police gained a clearer picture of the scene thanks to the statements of Hong Luc (alias Tu Dich), who was interrogated in Hue in October 1918 concerning his activities in Phan Bôi Châu's group. According to his version, if Cuong Dê had bent to the collective will it was only for a fleeting moment.

> Trân Huu Luc, Phan Ba Ngoc, [Nguyên] Hai Than, and Hoang Trong Mau took the floor and, addressing themselves to Cuong Dê, made him understand that Chinese aid could only be obtained on the sole condition that they renounce the idea of [installing] a monarchical regime by replacing it with a republican one. . . . The morning after . . . Hoang Trong Mau and Phan Ba Ngoc took up the conversation of the preceding evening, saying to Cuong Dê that the group decision was very reasonable. They asked the prince if he had decided to follow them along this new path. *Cuong Dê, taken by a violent anger, pointed out that until now the group had used his name and his influence to lead the revolutionary campaign* and that today they had abandoned him without taking into account the favors he had provided; under these conditions, the group was free to act as it thought best, and he, Cuong Dê, reserved the right to do the same. With that said, Cuong Dê left the table and departed.³⁶

The founding meetings of the Quang Phuc Hôi confirmed the rupture of the contract with Cuong Dê, ever more weary of serving as a mere sponsor. Cuong Dê was determined to act on his own now.

Aware that he had been manipulated, it was now his turn to use the alliance that Phan Bôi Châu had offered him almost ten years ago. In the last months of 1912, the prince distributed in Hong Kong his own currency in competition with the resistance money produced under the direction of Hoang Trong Mau for the Quang Phuc Hôi, whose value depreciated as a result of Cuong De's actions.[37] In addition to the sums collected by Cuong Dê's currency-issuing scheme were the profits gained from a fund-raising drive he had personally and audaciously led himself in Cochinchina from March to June 1913. As Phan Ba Ngoc noted bitterly,[38] thanks to the twenty or thirty-thousand piasters he pocketed, Cuong Dê was able to leave for Europe in September 1913. Phan Bôi Châu made a final attempt to dissuade him from going but to no avail.[39] Cuong Dê was marching to a different revolutionary drummer.

Cuong Dê's trip to the West (August 1913–April 1914) culminated the break with his former partner and marked a new tack in the prince's program toward a possible reform-minded alliance with the French. If the chronology and the sequence of events of his trip to Germany and England remain nebulous for historians,[40] at least Cuong Dê's motives are better known to us today. This is particularly the case because the colonial authorities were closely following his every move and reflecting on its meaning. Moreover, the French carefully collected the explanatory letters written by the pretender to the governor-general, Albert Sarraut; the colonial minister, Albert Lebrun; Phan Châu Trinh; and his traveling companions. The colonial understanding of Cuong Dê's European projects was right on one matter: he had not come "to submit himself pure and simple" to the French, as Louis Marty would put it. Marty described the motives of his voyage in terms of bargaining (*marchandage*) and compromise.[41] Judging from what his letters reveal, Cuong Dê was clearly in favor of colonial reforms in a certain number of political and social areas. And let us note in passing that Cuong Dê's openness to reformism provides another angle for studying the complexity of this revolutionary's political ideas, which were not limited exclusively to the realm of his restoration. Indeed, his ideas must be placed within the larger context of a Franco-Vietnamese reflection on the politics of reform. Admittedly, this is not the place to analyze this vast subject but rather to note that the prince was not an isolated case.[42] Like others, he presented a list of national and personal claims as to the direction these colonial reforms should take. Among them was a call for a return to a strict policy of a protectorate for Indochina as well as a dynastic restoration in his favor as part of a state that would enjoy internal autonomy.

Cuong Dê's determination to make himself heard in the Colonial Ministry and to negotiate the rights of the Vietnamese within his version of the redefined colonial context was a failure. The reasons are diverse and complex, extending far beyond the aim of this article. We need only note here that the intermediaries he had chosen to contact the Colonial Ministry were not up to the task or else they displayed an outright unwillingness to collaborate with him. This was certainly the case with Phan Châu Trinh, who did not want to deal with Cuong Dê again. Moreover, the main interlocutor whom Cuong Dê wanted to meet, Albert Sarraut, was absent during most of this time. (He had been embarked on a mission to China at the end of 1913, thereby postponing an eventual contact with the prince in Europe.)[43] In any case, it does not seem that the French ever intended to open a dialogue with the prince.

But why did the French fail to rally this famous "rebel" prince to their colonial cause at such an opportune reformist moment? In my view, the difficult historical dilemma posed by Cuong Dê for the colonial authorities goes a long way toward explaining why in 1913 they missed what was undoubtedly their last chance to neutralize him before he resolicited France's colonial competitors, especially the Japanese. The rest of this chapter will show how the colonial powers were paralyzed in dealing with his case and why, unlike their earlier actions toward other "rebel princes," they hesitated to arrest him or even to "park" (*garer*) him somewhere out of the way.[44] I suggest that part of the answer lies in understanding that it was impossible for the French to recuperate Cuong Dê in that such an operation would have run counter to a collection of long-standing colonial myths, ones that Cuong Dê's very presence could call into question if he returned to Vietnam. At the time, no amount of distance would have allowed colonial authorities to get beyond these myths, which *were* the subjective reality they experienced. These myths imposed a certain mindset through which they understood events. To arrest Cuong Dê would also be dangerous, for his image could be transformed into one of a martyr. And this the colonial authorities wanted to avoid at all costs.

3. Cuong Dê's Challenge to the Colonial Myth of Legitimization

When French authorities learned belatedly of Cuong Dê's flight from Vietnam in 1906, the government general lost no time in opening an investigation to establish the reasons for his defection and the nature of his legitimacy. The opening of this investigation was all the more important given that the planned deposition of King Thanh Thai in Hue could leave the existing royal power in a vulnerable position. This deposition had been actively prepared by the *résident supérieur* of Annam, Fernand Lévecque, since 1906 and was officially accepted by the metropolis in July 1907. It was finally adopted at the end of August 1907 by Governor-General Paul Beau.[45] When he named, without any preconceived ideas, the young son of Thanh Thai to succeed his father to the throne, Beau was well aware of the demands of Cuong Dê. He knew of his quality as the "direct descendant of the emperor of Annam" and even recognized his position as the "legitimate heir to Gia Long."[46] Worried, for another two years, from 1908 to 1909, the government general conducted a large number of studies in order to sort out Cuong Dê's genealogy very carefully and establish the beginnings of his career as the pretender to the throne. Except for a few details, the conclusions and structural explanations of these studies were identical.

An exploration of Cuong Dê's family history quickly led to the submission of Anh Nhu's 1889 failed candidacy to the throne upon Dông Khanh's death, a key episode that seemed to have been forgotten even though it was not so far removed from the present. The support given to Anh Nhu by the general resident of Annam-Tonkin, Pierre Rheinart, and Governor-General Etienne Richaud constituted a major obstacle to those who wanted to deny Cuong Dê his legal arguments.[47] Why would the son's cause not be legitimate if that of his father had seemed to be so in the eyes of these colonial authorities? Moreover, Cuong Dê's main argument for getting his rights recognized was his membership in the *senior* dynastic branch, which, in his view, would have prevailed had Minh Mang not usurped the throne.[48] It turns out that French authorities, not to mention an entire colonial way of thinking, shared this point of view. Both were convinced that Minh Mang had "usurped" the throne destined for Prince Canh and, after his death, for his children.

This concordance of views becomes apparent in a reading of the vast summary of all available information on Cuong Dê established by Léon Sogny in 1923. Although Sogny was a remarkable connoisseur of Vietnamese history, he would continue, erroneously, to give substance to Cuong Dê's thesis by accusing Minh Mang of having falsified Gia Long's succession in order to brush aside the legitimate branch of the throne. It was not until 1946 that Sogny would radically call into question this version of the story, one that he had himself supported.[49] I provide this example to show that the French and Cuong Dê shared for a long time the same view of the dynastic history of the Nguyên. It was for this reason above all that the colonial authorities could not easily accuse Cuong Dê of misrepresenting the truth, for they decrypted the past much as he did.

Several French notes backed up Cuong Dê's version, stressing the misfortune that had unfairly descended upon his family and often relating the facts as if they had been felt from the inside.[50] Sometimes these notes evoked the cruel provocation of Thanh Thai against Cuong Dê; at other times they recalled in detail Gia Long's change of mind about his successor, a decision that was at the heart of all the misfortunes of the Anh Duê branch and his last representative. The resident superior's following remarks serve as a good example of the widespread mind-set about Cuong Dê, which few colonial insiders could transcend at the time.

> Cuong Dê is the direct descendant of the fifth generation of Gia Long. He belongs to the *senior branch.* Upon Gia Long's death, the crown should have been passed to Mi Duong [sic], whom he had designated as prince heir, *but Minh Mang would usurp the throne.* Anh Nhu, the son of Duc Tho, grandson of Mi Duong, and father of Cuong Dê, was the candidate to the throne in 1889. Upon his [father's] death in 1896, Cuong Dê was the only *representative of the legitimate branch.*[51]

There were more cautious judgments as to the legitimate rights of the pretender, noting how a group of clever revolutionaries were manipulating the symbolic value of his name to resurrect his legitimacy for their anticolonial needs. In 1909, the resident of Annam, Elie Groleau, was convinced that Phan Bôi Châu was plotting opportunistically by intelligently reviving, thanks to certain personalities in his entourage, Vietnamese national and historical memories so as to "wear down" (*user*)⁵² the protectorate's right to rule in the eyes of the public. If Phan Ba Ngoc and Cao Dat helped Phan Bôi Châu resurrect the aura of Phan Dinh Phung, Cuong Dê did the same for the memory of Gia Long.

Whatever the case, in the chambers of the *résidence supérieure,* one had nevertheless to be practical about the succession of Thanh Thai. It was thought that the defendants of the pretender's cause could not blame the French authorities for having "given the deposed king one of his own sons for a successor, the direct descendant of an effectively reigning family for almost a century."⁵³ In opposition to the natural right to the throne claimed by Cuong Dê, Groleau opposed the legitimacy born of a long exercise of power. In the end, Groleau's analysis did not directly criticize Cuong Dê's claims but sought merely to lower the level of danger posed by Cuong De's challenges in showing that they were much more opportunistic and manipulative than sincere. Yet such a judgment could be easily demolished if Cuong Dê firmly held his own over a long period of time. That is exactly what happened.

For obvious reasons, Cuong Dê argued that the order of succession by male primogeniture had not been respected upon the death of Gia Long. And to my knowledge no colonial report covering this period contests this affirmation. If it was, in fact, partially wrong, it was accepted by the French for other reasons that had little to do with historical accuracy. Indeed, further research would have easily allowed the colonial authorities to demonstrate the patchiness of Cuong Dê's argument and save themselves from the inextricable embarrassment into which the prince had thrown them. The problem was that by recognizing Cuong Dê as the sole representative of the "legitimate monarchy"⁵⁴—as Louis Marty had done—the French could deliver a harsh blow to the current reigning king. Duy Tân and Khai Dinh would then appear "less" legitimate than this pretender in exile.

The question, then, is to ask why the colonial powers were resigned to recognize, reluctantly, the "legitimacy of the claims"⁵⁵ of Cuong Dê. If his argument was manifestly dangerous, why did they not attempt to call his claims into doubt? It was certainly not because of a lack of counterarguments. The simple events of the past would have provided them. The rules of succession of the ancient seigniors (*chua*) of Cochinchina (Dang Trong) held that the inheritor of the throne would be the firstborn of the empress, herself a legitimate wife and wife of the first rank.[56] In accordance with this law, Gia Long had thus named Prince Canh as his presumptive heir.[57] When the latter died of smallpox in 1801 at the age of twenty-one, Gia Long transferred his choice to his grandson, My Duong (eldest son of Prince Canh). However, near the end of his life, Gia Long retracted his choice. Though the fourth son of a concubine, Prince Nguyên Phuc Dam was called upon to reign under the name of Minh Mang. However, this unusual designation at the core of Cuong Dê's objections was regularized thanks to a reform imposed by Gia Long establishing testamental measures (*gia thien ha*), in all likelihood aimed to head off all challenges to his successor. Moreover, Prince Dam had been adopted at a young age by the principal wife of Gia Long, Princess Thua-Thien Cao. This rendered his nomination doubly legal.[58] It is striking to note that the administrators in the *résidence supérieure* or the government general failed to exploit these key facts. Were they unaware of them? It is hard to believe so, given the erudition of such men as Sogny. Did they have other reasons not to deploy them?

In my view, the colonial perception of Cuong Dê was largely linked to how Gia Long had been represented in administrative and intellectual minds in Indochina since the late nineteenth century. It was a myth, and a remarkably well structured one, which the French had erected in Gia Long's memory. For this reason, it needs to be considered here, if only briefly, in order to understand how this myth would influence the colonial judgment of Cuong Dê.[59] The struggle of Nguyên Phuc Anh (Gia Long) against the Tây Son, a fight to put his ancestral lineage "back on the throne," fascinated countless French missionaries, admirals, and governors as well as historians, journalists, novelists, and various other artists. This exceptional French interest in a Vietnamese figure of the past had a lot to do with the presence at his side of a French missionary from Picardy named Bishop Pigneau de Béhaine. With courage and devotion, this famous missionary aided and counseled his Vietnamese friend in these hard years of fighting.[60] Today we can see how the shifts in successive memories over time tended to recast the objective reality of their friendship and their mutual aid into a subjective one, reconstructed and invented in France as well as Indochina for essentially political needs.

According to the logic of colonial legitimization, the assistance provided by Pigneau to the Nguyên fugitive assumed three new, if misleading, qualities. First, colonial historiography held that this French aid had been requested (*sollicitée*) by Nguyên Phuc Anh, with the latter usually depicted as the one doing the asking. It was important to show that the initiative had been consciously taken by the pretender to introduce the French into the solution to the problem of the country's internal affairs—even at the risk of forgetting that Pigneau's aid to Nguyên Phuc Anh had not been so clearly solicited in the first place. Moreover, the fact that Nguyên Phuc Anh had no problems accepting the nonratification of the Treaty of Versailles (1787)[61] was generally passed over in colonial studies. Interestingly, even though the Treaty of Versailles was actually declared null and void and deliberately not applied at the time, and this to the relief of Gia Long, it was nonetheless presented in "origin-seeking" colonial quarters as the "key charter of the Franco-Vietnamese community" (*la charte fondamentale de la communauté franco-vietnamienne*).[62] Although the end of colonial historiography is very recent, we can already see the degree to which it brushed over those events in the historical canvas that did not please it.[63]

The second supposed characteristic of this French aid to Gia Long is that it was *exclusive*. Dutch and English offers of assistance to Nguyên Phuc Anh, not to mention the aid the Portuguese, Chinese, and Siamese actually provided to Gia Long, were singularly underestimated, even blackened out, in French works of the colonial period.[64] Gia Long had entered *de force* into a privileged Franco-Vietnamese universe devoid of a more complex regional context. Finally, many were those who held that French aid had been *vital* to Nguyên Phuc Anh, both literally and figuratively. The future king owed his life to Bishop Pigneau, who had housed and nourished him several times during periods of difficulty and great pain. Without the aid organized by Pigneau, the Nguyên would never have known how to use their army and navy, the fortifications à la Vauban could never have been replaced, his command would have withered, and even the will of Gia Long would have faltered. It was not long before Gia Long owed this bishop his restoration to the throne. Given that these ideas were widely accepted at the time, it is not hard to see why the leap from there to the conclusion that "the" French ("*la*" France) had saved "the" Vietnam from a self-destructive civil war was almost natural.[65]

By underscoring the shortcomings of this commemorative and edifying historiography, it is not my aim to minimize in any way the contributions of Bishop Pigneau or those who followed him; rather it is to analyze why and how these men became pretexts later on for a number of administrators and intellectuals who needed to legitimize colonial power and their special relations with Vietnam. By way of a double game of exaggerations and forgetting, *another* history of the Nguyên conquest and the French origins in Indochina was officially created. This history had become a myth by the eve of World War I, when the story line was accepted as truth. Pigneau acquired a place as the precursor of the protectorate and "founder of modern Indochina" (*fondateur de l'Indochine moderne*).[66] Pigneau's friendship with Gia Long would later allow governors like Albert Sarraut and Pierre Pasquier to affirm, and no doubt believe themselves, that the Franco-Vietnamese collaboration they were pushing in the present had deep roots in the past.[67] The founder of the Nguyên dynasty, restored in the colonial memory (*dans l'imaginaire colonial*) by France, incarnated loyalty. One wanted to believe that he had remained grateful to his death to the French for their assistance. The proof seemed to be his relative clemency toward the Catholic communities in his kingdom as well as the encouraging proclivity of Prince Canh toward this religion as Bishop Pigneau's loyal pupil. In short, these historical simplifications were enough to satisfy the colonial believers.

The historian must sometimes take into consideration less that which is "real" than that which people could believe as real in order to shed some new light on certain stubborn questions that might otherwise remain unanswered. I have found such an approach essential to interpreting the paradoxical colonial perceptions of Cuong Dê. In a way, the new testamental measures established by Gia Long in favor of Minh Mang fall among those events that resemble boulders standing in the middle of a river. Huge, they sometimes perturb the flow of the course of the water. When André Salles, a former colonial inspector, explained to Khai Dinh during the latter's trip to France in 1922 that it was not out of fear of Western designs on Vietnam that Gia Long had changed his mind about his successor, Salles was sidestepping some of these big myth-breaking boulders. After all, how could one admit the king's suspicions of French intentions and still proclaim that he "had remained loyal to [French] friendship to his last day"?[68] Later, given the undeniably "anti-French" and certainly anti-Catholic policies of Minh Mang's reign, it was inconceivable to colonial France that Gia Long could have freely chosen him. It was easier to believe in the thesis of a "usurpation" of power than to call into question their teleological version, a very truncated one, of Vietnamese history. When Cuong Dê demanded his right to the heritage of his great ancestor, he was reinforcing in a way the colonial arguments concerning Minh Mang's illegitimacy. This helps explain the vague sympathy of early governmental views of Cuong Dê's perspective.

But in having fled with Phan Bôi Châu and having conceived his dynastic projects in nationalist terms Cuong Dê had become an unspeakable "rebel" for the colonial power and its memory. This heretical misfit of the Nguyên lineage, one that the French never questioned and that they believed attached Vietnam to France, was going to create a chronic malaise for colonial propaganda. Indeed, Cuong Dê had successfully nationalized the memory of Gia Long, at least between 1906 and the outbreak of World War I. In his appeals to the nation, he invoked the past greatness of the Nguyên as conquerors and civilizers (most notably in the "barbarian" territories of Cambodia) as well as the amazing efforts of the founder of the dynasty, "sleeping one day in Siam, another in Cambodia, traversing the mountains here and crossing the seas there to reconstitute his empire."[69] To develop his propaganda, he relied on the historically mixed feelings of the Cochinchinese for the northerners as well as an ancient hostility of Cochinchina for Minh Mang, which Cuong Dê's cause reignited.[70] His blame fell upon Minh Mang's successors (Thieu Tri and above all Tu Duc), all incapable of protecting Gia Long's heritage, resisting the invaders, and avoiding the loss of the kingdom.

He demanded from the protectorate that it respect its promises and learn from World War I, which had shown that all great powers could decline and, inversely, the weak could become strong. To turn the tide in its favor, three conditions had to be met, ones that he presented to Khai Dinh and Sarraut: (1) France had to recognize the people's right of self-government, (2) the Vietnamese monarchy had to be reformed profoundly and its mandarinate modernized, and (3) the powers that be had to accept the alternative solution that his restoration to the throne would represent. The Hue court, directly threatened by Cuong Dê's plans, reacted with the greatest firmness from the outset. The Council of Regents condemned his flight from Vietnam in 1909 by asking the protectorate to implement a repressive diplomacy against his activities abroad. In 1914, a new decision of the council pronounced this time the removal of the prince from the List of the Royal Family. Cuong Dê officially lost his title, his name, and even the right to leave a trace of his royal membership. The adoption of his patronymic name, Nguyên Van (not Phuc) De, as well as his removal from the royal genealogical book were sanctioned. This measure was presented as a pure formality. Removal from the Ton Nhan Phu (Council of the Royal Family) was legally required when one of its members had been condemned to death. This was the case with Cuong Dê, condemned to death in absentia the previous year by a decision of the criminal commission of 5 September 1913. The exclusion he felt was proportional to the fear he would provoke. An outlaw in the eyes of the colonial government, banished for high treason by the court of Hue, Cuong Dê was condemned to the life of an exile. His life would be one of expectation. The example of Gia Long would be his hope, his consolation . . . and his illusion, too.

Conclusion

In spite of the surprises he created and the controversies born in his entourage about his positions, Prince Cuong Dê would remain for a long time absent in studies of Vietnamese nationalism for the reasons suggested in this essay. He first suffered as a result of a colonial historiography that continue to describe him as mediocre and manipulated by bigger revolutionary fish. Challenged in its own realm of legitimization, the colonial power recognized his just right to rule but finished by condemning him to death, failing that lifetime exclusion, for turning the nationalist past against them in a rebellion that echoed strangely of Gia Long's struggle against the Tây Son. He would suffer a second time because of contemporary Vietnamese historiography, which, like the state historiography of the Nguyên in olden days, had the primary task of legitimizing the powers that be. His long-lasting recourse to the Japanese after World War I would put him on the "bad side" of official history. And yet the hope he had placed in Japanese support was not unfounded when one thinks of how his cause was integrated into a vast political, Pan-Asian project that could have made him the Pu Yi of Annam. After all, the Japanese certainly knew how to manipulate Asian kings against their European-backed competitors, as Sogny and Marty would learn only too well.[71] There is much more to say about the activities of the prince from the 1920s on, but after World War I the double problematic that he wanted to follow before the war no longer had its raison d'être. This essay seeks essentially to elucidate the success of Cuong Dê's animation of a southern Nguyên legitimacy[72] "throughout the sprawling territory of the ancient empire of Gia Long,"[73] one that paradoxically destroyed his early alliance with Nguyên Ham and Phan Bôi Châu and ensured his sidelining by the French themselves. This essay has also tried to show why Cuong Dê was at the origin of one of the first attempts to decolonize the memory of Gia Long, a tendency not without some faint echoes today.

NOTES

Membre du Groupe d'Etudes sur le Viet Nam Contemporain a Sciences Politiques et membre Associe du laboratoire Peninsule Indochinoise, EPHE-EFEO Paris. I would like to thank Christopher Goscha for the translation and Professor Vinh Sinh for his helpful comments on this essay.

1. An official *Dictionary of Historical Figures of Vietnam* gives 11 January 1882 as Prince Cuong Dê's date of birth. See Nguyên Q. Thang and Nguyên Ba Thê, *Tu Diên Nhân Vât Lich su Viet Nam* (*A Dictionary of Historical Figures of Vietnam*) (Hô Chi Minh City: Nha Xuât Ban Khoa Hoc Xa Hôi, 1992), 596–97. Colonial sources give the date as 6 May 1882. See, for example, "Note secrète au sujet du prince Cuong Dê," Hanoi, no date, in box 357, grouping: Service de Protection du Corps Expéditionnaire (hereafter SPCE), Centre des Archives d'Outre-Mer, Aix-en-Provence (hereafter CAOM).

2. For more on Cuong Dê's genealogy, see Van Raveschot, "Histoire de Hoang Tu Canh et de Cuong Dê," Hanoi, 15 November 1909, 4 p., box 357, SPCE, CAOM; and Léon Sogny, Rapport de la Sûreté Générale de l'Indochine, "Cuong Dê," Huê, 20 November 1923, box 359, SPCE, CAOM.

3. Phan Bôi Châu recounted this version of his first meeting with Cuong Dê during the preliminary interrogations he underwent for his trial in 1925. He recalled that Cuong Dê had taken him and other colleagues on a visit to the house of the prince's ancestor, Anh Duê. At this time, Cuong Dê was in charge of tending to the cult of his ancestor, thereby locating this episode after 1896, the date of Anh Nhu's death. See Gouvernement général de l'Indochine, "Interrogatoires, Affaires Phan Bôi Châu, Commission criminelle, Année 1925," pp. 13–14, box 352, SPCE, CAOM.

4. Cuong Dê's flight was not known to the French authorities in Hue until March 1906. By this time, he had already reached Japan. Sogny, "Cuong Dê," 2.

5. As recalled by Sogny in "Note sur Cuong Dê et sa famille," Saigon, 30 September 1946, p. 2, box 359, SPCE, CAOM.

6. Gouvernement général de l'Indochine, "Commission criminelle, *Affaire Phan Bôi Châu,*" 1925, [no date given for the interrogation], p. 2, box 354, SPCE, CAOM.

7. Nguyên Ham's words as cited by Phan Bôi Châu in ibid.

8. From the province of Quang Nam, Nguyên Ham (1863–1911), alias Tiêu La, had come to Hue in 1885 to take the bureaucratic exams. Shortly after his arrival, Ham Nghi took to the *maquis.* Ham became an active member of the "royalist movement." In contact with Phan Bôi Châu after 1903, he would be arrested following the political unrest of 1908 in Annam. After having aided the Duy Tân Hôi with his commercial activities, he would die in 1910. See Nguyên Q. Thang and Nguyên Ba Thê, *Tu diên nhân vât lich su Viêt nam,* 633.

9. Phan Bôi Châu, *Mémoires,* translated and annotated by Georges Boudarel, *France Asie/Asia* 194–95 (1968): 31.

10. Phan Bôi Châu, *Mémoires,* 31.

11. On the *Dông Du,* see Vinh Sinh, ed., *Phan Bôi Châu and the Dông-du,* Lac-Viêt series, no. 4.8 (New Haven: Yale University Southeast Asia Council, 1986), in particular the article by Vinh Sinh, "Japan and Vietnam: Some Preliminary Thoughts about Their Interaction," 151–72.

12. Nguyên Thê Anh, "La Monarchie des Nguyên de la mort de Tu-Duc à 1925," Ph.D. thesis, Université Paris IV, 1987, 2:497; *Monarchie et fait colonial au Viêt-Nam (1875–1925): Le crépuscule d'un ordre traditionnel* (Paris: L'Harmattan, 1992).

13. Cuong Dê, "Proclamation à la Cour d'Annam," 20e jour du 1er mois de la 4e année de Khai Dinh (20 February 1919), pp. 2–3, box 357, SPCE, CAOM. This is a French translation of the text, already translated, in Vietnamese.

14. Ibid., 3.

15. This incident is related in the following notes: Anonymous, "Note sur le prince Cuong Dê," no. 39, pièce 304, Hanoi, 29 July 1919, p. 2, box 357, SPCE, CAOM; and Van Raveschot, "Histoire de Hoang Tu Canh et de Cuong Dê," 4.

16. Sogny, "Cuong Dê," 2.

17. Relying on the files constituted by the Criminal Commission in charge of the trials of 1913, Sogny recorded Cuong Dê's change of opinion in Japan in his report on the activities of the prince, completed in 1923 (Sogny, "Cuong Dê"), 3–4.

18. This information was obtained under the judicial directive of 1913, including various documents signed by Cuong Dê both under his (eventual) ruling name, Gia Thanh, and his patronym, Nguyên Phuc Dân. Note that here the use of the character *phuc* is the same as the one used by the *chua* (seigneurs) of Cochinchina. See the contents of these files in box 357, SPCE, CAOM.

19. Bui Chi Nhuan was born in the province of Long An. He first went to Japan. After the Franco-Japanese accords, his expulsion from Japan led him to

Siam. From his hideout in a Bangkok pagoda, he would serve as the main fund-raiser in southern Vietnam for Prince Cuong Dê in collaboration with Nguyên Thanh Hien. Extradited from Siam in 1913 to the French, he was condemned by the Criminal Commission to hard labor at Poulo Condor. See Nguyên Q. Thang and Nguyên Ba Thê, *Tu diên nhân vât lich su Viêt nam*, 31.

20. For more details on the prince's propaganda campaign in Cochinchina, see Gabriel Michel, Procureur général en Indochine, "Rapport au Gouverneur général d'Indochine," Saigon, 28 April 1909, pp. 16–18, file 28 (2), box 8, grouping: Nouveau Fonds (hereafter NF), CAOM; and Louis Marty, "Note sur l'agitation anti-française en Indochine," 28 February 1916, pp. 49–51, file 28 (2), box 8, NF, CAOM. Pierre Brocheux has also written on the contacts between Gilbert Chiêu and Cuong Dê in "Note sur Gilbert Chiêu (1867–1919), citoyen Français et patriote vietnamien," *Approches Asie* (1992), vol. 1: 72–81.

21. "Lettre de Cuong Dê au Conseil de Régence," March 1917, pp. 1–2, French translation of the Vietnamese and Chinese text, both in box 357, SPCE, CAOM.

22. Ibid.

23. Phan Bôi Châu, *Mémoires*, 67.

24. Sogny, "Cuong Dê," 4.

25. Direction de la Police et de la Sûreté fédérales, "Phan Chu Trinh," secret, Saigon, 16 September 1949, pp. 1–2, box 372, SPCE, CAOM.

26. For a reflection on the dynastic restoration of the Nguyên, see Nola Cook, "The Myth of the Restoration: Dang Trong Influences in the Spiritual Life of the Early Nguyên Dynasty (1802–1847)," in Anthony Reid, ed., *The Last Stand of Asian Autonomies: Responses to Modernity in the Diverse States of Southeast Asia and Korea, 1750–1900* (Melbourne: Macmillan, 1997).

27. I treat these matters in much greater detail in two chapters of my Ph.D. thesis, "La légitimation française en Indochine: Mythes et réalités de la collaboration franco-vietnamienne et du réformisme colonial, 1905–1945," Université Paris VII, 2000.

28. "Interrogatoire de Hong Luc dit Tu Dich, arrêté et interrogé en 1918 à Huê," in Sogny, "Cuong Dê," 41–42.

29. See the annotated comments of Georges Boudarel in Phan Bôi Châu, *Mémoires*, 117, n. 120.

30. The history of these Vietnamese emigrations to Siam has been recently examined by Christopher E. Goscha in "La présence vietnamienne au royaume du Siam du XVIIème au XIXème siècle: Vers une perspective péninsulaire," in Nguyên Thê Anh and Alain Forest, eds., *Guerre et paix en Asie du Sud-Est* (Paris: L'Harmattan, 1998), 211–43.

31. Gouvernement général de l'Indochine, "Lettre de Cuong Dê adressée à Lê Gia Than, expédiée du Japon en date du 20 juin 1916," French translation signed by Yang, p. 2, box 357, SPCE, CAOM.

32. According to Marty, "Note sur l'agitation anti-française en Indochine," 40, in comparison with the roles noted by Phan Bôi Châu in his *Mémoires*, 135.

33. In late 1943, Cuong Dê dictated his memoirs to a Japanese journalist, later published in Vietnamese in Saigon in 1957 by Tùng Lâm as *Cuôc Doi Cach Mang Cuong Dê* [The revolutionary life of Cuong Dê] (Saigon: Tôn Thât Lê, 1957).

34. Sogny, "Cuong Dê," 13.

35. For example, the discussions under way with the governor of Shanghai to obtain a deposit of thousands of piasters for the realization of Vietnamese revolutionary projects risked compromise if the royalist position of the prince did not change. See "Interrogatoire de Hong Luc," 44–45. Hong Luc's real name was Nguyên Duc Cong. Hoang Trong Mau headed the Quang Phuc Hôi section in China, where he took care of monetary matters in particular. See Marty, "Note sur l'agitation anti-française en Indochine," 45. He would be arrested and then executed in Hanoi in 1916.

36. "Interrogatoire de Hong Luc dit Tu Dich," 44–45; my emphasis.

37. The prince had himself played a part in the printing of these revolutionary notes for the Quang Phuc Hôi before having his own notes printed in Hong Kong in 1913. See Marty, "Note sur l'agitation anti-française en Indochine," 41–46.

38. "Interrogatoire de Phan Ba Ngoc," April 1918, in Sogny, "Cuong Dê," 36–37. According to Marty, with this money Cuong Dê was able to travel first class, frequent the best hotels, and lead a life of the *grand seigneur* during his time in Europe (ibid., 42).

39. A letter sent by Phan Bôi Châu to Cuong Dê on 26 March 1913 shows that the former tried to resume his association with the prince by placing the national interest ahead of personal quarrels and "past problems." The original letter and its French translation are in box 357, SPCE, CAOM.

40. The dates of this trip remain unclear. Contradictory dates are provided by the governor-general in Hanoi, consular services in Hong Kong, and the Parisian ministries of foreign affairs, colonies, and war. See Patrice Morlat, *Les affaires politiques de l'Indochine (1895–1923), Les grands commis: Du savoir au pouvoir* (Paris: L'Harmattan, 1995), 148–50. A critical comparison of the sources, however, allows us to establish that the date of his trip to Europe had to occur between August 1913 and April 1914. See Larcher-Goscha, "La légitimation française en Indochine."

41. "Note manuscrite de Louis Marty," 15 October 1916, p. 2, box 358, SPCE, CAOM.

42. Agathe Larcher, "La voie étroite des réformes coloniales et la 'collaboration franco-annamite' (1917–1928)," *La Revue Française d'Histoire d'Outre-Mer* 82, no. 303 (1995): 387–420.

43. According to Thai Van Kiêm, Cuong Dê met Albert Sarraut, who had gone to London to meet the prince. Thai Van Kiem states that Sarraut explained to Cuong Dê "the desire of the French government to offer him the throne of Vietnam on the condition that he agreed to cooperate with the French." Thai Van Kiem says that the prince refused. See Thai Van Kiêm, "Un grand patriote: Le prince Cuong Dê," *France-Asie*, 6 no. 106 (March 1955): 484–88. I have not been able to verify these interesting facts.

44. Sogny, "Note sur Cuong Dê et la sa famille," Saigon, 30 September 1946, p. 1, box 359, SPCE, CAOM.

45. On this dynastic rule, see Nguyên Thê Anh, *Monarchie et fait colonial au Viêt-Nam;* and Nguyên Thê Anh, "L'abdication de Thanh Thai," *Bulletin de l'Ecole Française d'Extrême-Orient,* vol. IXIV (1977): 257–64.

46. "Lettre du gouverneur général de l'Indochine au ministre de France à Tokyo," 10 May 1906, Hanoi, box 356, SPCE, CAOM.

47. For an argumented explanation of the motives for French aid to Anh Nhu, see the revealing report of Governor Richaud to the Ministry of the Navy, 11 February 1889, p. 107, volume 74, *Mémoires et Documents,* Asie, Archives of the Ministère des Affaires Etrangères (hereafter MAE).

48. See, for example, Cuong Dê, "Proclamation à la cour d'Annam," 20 February 1919, original and French translation in box 357, SPCE, CAOM; and Cuong Dê, "Lettre adressée au ministre des colonies, Albert Sarraut," 1 September 1923, box 356, SPCE, CAOM.

49. Compare the two reports on Cuong Dê written by Sogny, covering the period between 1923 and 1946: "Cuong Dê," 1; and "Note sur Cuong Dê et sa famille," 1.

50. Anonymous, "Note manuscrite sur Cuong Dê," Hanoi, 29 July 1909, box 357, SPCE, CAOM; Van Raveschot, "Histoire de Hoang Tu Canh et de Cuong Dê"; "Note du résident supérieur d'Annam au gouverneur général," Huê, 5 November 1909, box 357, SPCE, CAOM.

51. "Extrait d'une note du résident supérieur d'Annam de 1909, pièce 230 au dossier B" (of the Criminal Commission of 1913), box 357, SPCE, CAOM.

52. "Rapport de Elie Groleau, au Gouverneur général," Huê, 14 October 1909, p. 9, vol. 35, PA95, MAE. See also the anonymous report (of the *résident* of Annam?) to the governor-general, undated, on the unrest of 1908, vol. 6, PA44, MAE.

53. "Rapport de Groleau, au Gouverneur général," 14 October 1909, 3.

54. Marty, "Extrait de la note sur l'agitation anti-française en Indochine"; "biographie du prince Cuong Dê, note dactylographiée," box 359, SPCE, CAOM.

55. "Rapport du résident supérieur d'Annam Groleau au gouverneur général," Huê, 14 October 1909, p. 2, vol. 35, PA95, MAE.

56. Nguyên Van Huyên, *La civilisation ancienne du Vietnam* (Hanoi: Editions Thê Gioi, 1994), 113–16.

57. On Gia Long's installation of a system to legitimize his own power, see Philippe Langlet, *L'ancienne historiographie d'etat au Viêt Nam (raisons d'être, conditions d'élaboration, et caractère au siècle des Nguyên)* (Paris: École Française d'Extrême-Orient), 1990, vol. 1.

58. This is noted in Léopold Cadière, "Le tombeau de Gia Long: Renseignements touristiques," *Bulletin des amis du Vieux Huê,* special issue, no. 3 (1923): 325–27.

59. For more on the creation of a French myth based on Pigneau de Béhaine, see the first part of my thesis on this subject, Larcher-Goscha, "La légitimation française en Indochine."

60. For a recent, detailed, and critical analysis of the bishop's action, see Frédéric Mantienne, "Les relations entre la France et la péninsule indochinoise aux XVIIe et XVIIIe siècles," Ph.D. thesis, École Pratique des Hautes Études, IVeme section, Paris, 1998, 2:292–371.

61. In the name of Gia Long, this treaty was written by Pigneau who had come to the court of Louis XVI to seek military reinforcements in exchange for commercial and religious rights in Cochinchina.

62. Georges Taboulet, *La geste française en Indochine* (Paris: Adrien-Maisonneuve, 1955), 1:161.

63. See Mantienne, *Les relations entre la France et la péninsule indochinoise.*

64. Long before its time, the work of Pierre-Yves Manguin had already pointed up the dangers of this colonial historiography. See Manguin, *Les Nguyên, Macau, et le Portugal: Aspects politiques et commerciaux d'une relation privilégiée en Mer de Chine, 1773–1802* (Paris: École Française d'Extrême-Orient, 1984). For refreshing studies of the Nguyên period, see Li Tana, *Nguyên Cochinchina: Southern Vietnam in the Seventeenth and Eighteenth Centuries* (Ithaca: Cornell University, Southeast Asia Program, 1998); the articles by Frédéric Mantienne, Keith W. Taylor, Alain Forest, and Nguyên Thê Anh in Nguyên Thê Anh and Alain Forest, eds., *Guerre et paix en Asie du Sud-Est;* and Huynh Lua, ed., *Nhung van dê van hoa Xa Hoi, thoi Nguyên* (Cultural and Social Problems in the Time of the Nguyên) (Ho Chi Minh City: Nha Xuât Ban Khoa Hoc Xa Hoi, 1995).

65. To cite but three titles among many others entangled in this historiography, see Claude Maître, "Pierre Pigneau, évêque d'Adran, initiateur de la politique française en Indochine," *La Géographie*, no. 2 (1914): 68–76; Marcel Gaultier, *Gia Long* (Saigon: Imp. Ardin, 1932); and Georges Taboulet, "La vie tourmentée de l'évêque d'Adran," *Bulletin de la Société des Etudes indochinoises* 15, nos. 3–4 (1940): 9–41.

66. Taboulet, *La geste française en Indochine*, 237.

67. For example, see the preface penned by Pierre Pasquier for Gaultier's biography of Gia Long (Gaultier, *Gia Long*).

68. André Salles, "Visite de S. M. l'Empereur à la Société de Géographie le 10 juillet 1922," *Bulletin des Amis du Vieux Huê* (1922): 321–34.

69. "Adresse de Cuong Dê du 27 octobre 1906," translated by Deloustal, p. 1, box 357, SPCE, CAOM.

70. We are thinking of the events of Le Van Duyet's revolt in particular. See Lê Thanh Khôi, *Historie du Vietnam des origines à 1858* (Paris: Sudestasie, 1987), 369.

71. Cuong Dê was not unaware of the risks he was taking in trying to return to the throne on the Japanese bandwagon. He took considerable measures to hide the existence of a Japanese wife as well as a son born of this union.

72. According to Thai Van Kiêm, the surname that Cuong Dê chose in Japan (Ichio or Kazuo?), Minami, meant "hero of the south." See Thai Van Kiem, "Un grand patriote: Le Prince Cuong Dê," 487.

73. "Rapport du résident supérieur d'Annam au gouverneur général," Huê, 5 November 1909, p. 3, box 357, SPCE, CAOM.

SELECTED BIBLIOGRAPHY

Cook, Nola. "The Myth of the Restoration: Dang Trong Influences in the Spiritual Life of the Early Nguyên Dynasty (1802–1847)." In Anthony Reid, ed., *The Last Stand of Asian Autonomies: Responses to Modernity in the Diverse States of Southeast Asia and Korea, 1750–1900*. Melbourne: Macmillan, 1997.

Huynh Lau et al. *Nhung Van Dê Van Hoa Xa Hoi, Thoi Nguyên* (Cultural and Social Problems in the Time of the Nguyên). Hô Chi Minh City: Nha Xuât Ban Khoa Hoc Xa Hoi, 1995.

Langlet, Philippe. *L'ancienne historiographie d'Etat au Viêt Nam (raisons d'être, conditions d'élaboration, et caractère au siècle des Nguyên)*. Paris: École Française d'Extreme-Orient, 1990.

Mantienne, Frédéric. "Les relations entre la France et la péninsule indochinoise aux XVIIe et XVIIIe siècles." Ph.D. thesis, École Pratique des Hautes Etudes (IVeme section), 1998.

Nguyên Q. Thang and Nguyên Ba Thê. *Tu Diên Nhân Vât Lich Su Viet Nam* (A Dictionary of Historical Figures of Vietnam). Hô Chi Minh City: Nha Xuât Ban Khoa Hoc Xa Hôi, 1992.

Nguyên Thê Anh. *Monarchie et fait colonial au Viêt-Nam (1875–1925): Le crépuscule d'un ordre traditionnel*. Paris: L'Harmattan, 1992.

Phan Bôi Châu. *Mémoires*. Translated and annotated by Georges Boudarel. *France Asie/Asia*, 194–95 (1968): 263–470. See also the new translation of Vinh Sinh and Nicholas Wickenden, *Overturned Chariot: The Autobiography of Phan Bôi Châu*. Honolulu: University of Hawaii Press, 1999.

Tung Lam. *Cuôc Doi Cach Mang Cuong Dê* (The Revolutionary Life of Cuong Dê). Saigon: Tôn Thât Lê, 1957.

Vinh Sinh and Nicholas Wickenden, trans. *Overturned Chariot: The Autobiography of Phan Bôi Châu*. Honolulu: University of Hawaii Press, 1999.

7

Phan Thi Minh Le

A Vietnamese Scholar with a Different Path: Huynh Thuc Khang, Publisher of the First Vietnamese Newspaper in *Quôc Ngu* in Central Vietnam, *Tieng Dan* (People's Voice)

Introduction

After the French colonized Vietnam, the situation in Central Vietnam, Trong Ky, then called Annam, was not as developed as it was in Cochinchina and Tonkin. When in 1927 the first issue of *Tieng Dan* (People's Voice) was published, the people of Central Vietnam were eager to read it. They knew that its publisher was a former political prisoner known for his anti-French colonial politics and his disagreement with the court at Hue.

Despite many difficulties and political pressure, Huynh Thuc Khang managed to publish his newspaper until 1943 and wrote most of its articles himself. Most of his subscribers[1] were people living in the countryside. Khang lived during a transition period in Vietnam when three cultures (Vietnamese, Chinese, and French) coexisted. Khang also had the good fortune to experience, although for a short period (1945–46), Vietnamese independence. It was an experience that many of his companions in arms never had since they died before him.

Khang was a very important figure in twentieth-century Vietnamese history, but he has been often ignored by historians, who have devoted only a few lines to him. Khang said of himself "Dom tan chay nui" (a small ember, asleep under the ash, may set on fire a whole mountain). In this essay, I will present the life and contribution of Khang as the publisher of the first Vietnamese newspaper, *Tieng Dan* written in *quôc ngu*, in Central Vietnam, and as an activist during the anticolonial struggle in Vietnam.

1. Apprenticeship in Politics

Huynh Thuc Khang was born in 1876, in the province of Quang Nam, where his parents also originated, a province where people had already been in contact with foreigners (Faifoo)[2] in an earlier period. Vietnam was then still at war with French invaders, and part of the country[3] was already under French colonial control. But at that time Vietnamese society was not yet influenced by Western culture and its concept of "modernity." Vietnamese scholars still carried on their studies exclusively in Chinese, knowing nothing about Western science and commercial enterprises.[4] It seems that Vietnamese people were unaware of the Japanese Meiji Restoration (1868–1912) or at least they did not realize that it was the source of Japan's actual power. Khang was nine years old when his elder brother and cousin told of the fall of the stronghold at Hue and the sack of the imperial palace by the French soldiers of de Courcy in 1885.

In 1904, Khang obtained his doctorate, *tien si*, at the same time as his friend Trân Qui Cap. After devoting themselves to their studies and reading, thinking, and discussing with their peers, both Khang and Cap refused to attend the compulsory training course given by the ministry. Using his poor health and his filial duties toward his father as excuses, Khang returned to his native village. Following Khang's decision, Cap also returned to his own village. It was that same year, in 1905, when Phan Châu Trinh resigned as the minister of rites. Trinh then suggested to his two friends that they travel to South Vietnam in order to meet other scholars of their own generation with whom they could share their political ideas on reform. When the three of them arrived at Binh Dinh, they wanted to express their reformist ideas by presenting themselves under fake names[5] at a monthly examination.

The essays, which they all wrote in verse, are to this day very well known in Vietnam. Phan Châu Trinh wrote an essay entitled "Chi Thanh thong thanh" (To communicate with higher spirits, it is necessary to arrive at a level of study reaching perfection), and Trân Qui Cap and Khang wrote together an essay called "Danh Ngoc luong son" (To find the invaluable jade, it is necessary to climb the famous mountain). Near Nha Trang, the three of them even dared to visit a Russian ship, anchored in the bay of Cam Ranh. They thus proceeded on their journey to Phan Thiet. In his memoirs, Khang gave us an invaluable description of the province of Binh Thuan[6] at that time. But when Trinh became ill Khang and Cap, instead of pursuing their journey to the south, returned to Quang Nam where they became known as "the trio of Quang Nam" (bo ba Quang Nam). In Phan Thiet, they were not aware that Phan Boî Châu had already left for Japan on 23 February 1905. In 1906, Khang was teaching in the village of My An, which was part of the project to build schools in the whole province of Quang Nam. In his autobiography, he wrote that he never went to school to learn *quôc ngu* but instead learned it on his own. He was also the founder of a trade association, Hop Thuong Quang Nam in Faifoo, and an agricultural association, and he even built a cinnamon plantation. To show his "avant-garde attitude," which many scholars viewed with a certain contempt, he kept his hair short like European men. The king, Thanh Thai, before him had done the same and was the first Vietnamese monarch to give up the traditional chignon. The king even wore European boots.[7] A decree of the government had finally authorized the use of *quôc ngu* in Vietnamese schools. Khang started teaching in both *quôc ngu* and French at the school in My An. He also commented publicly on some Chinese classical books. These public meetings doubtless contributed to educating and introducing politics to the peasants—for instance, those of Dai Loc in Quang Nam.

The rebellion against income taxes broke out in February 1908. In his memoirs, Khang wrote that this peaceful revolt was led by young modernist scholars[8] who were unknown in the village. The earlier resistant movement, called Cân Vuong, "support to the king," was opposed to French authority in Vietnam. Although it was a national movement, it broke out locally in villages. Yet the elder generation of scholars, who supported the use of violence by the Cân Vuong movement, did not participate in the young scholar's political actions. In 1908, two other important events marked Vietnamese history: the attempt to poison the garrison in Tonkin and the violent rebellion of De Tham[9] in Yen The. These two latter events were as violent as the armed struggle of the Cân Vuong movement. In contrast, the tax movement that inspired young reformist scholars was peaceful and intended to defend people's rights.

2. Poulo Condore

Huynh Thuc Khang knew that the French crackdown would not spare him, and he returned to his own village, waiting for his arrest. He was seized on 24 February and escorted to the penal colony of Poulo Condore[10] where he arrived on 28 August.[11] In May, a court of justice sentenced him to life at hard labor for "antipatriotic activities, conspiracy with a foreign country, and misuse of the concept of people's rights."

But Khang never expressed any resentment nor showed any bitterness about his years in prison. On the contrary, he considered his imprisoned years as a "school of life" because they taught him to live with his fellow countrymen. On Poulo Condore, he appreciated the democratic spirit that governed its organization and internal rules, under the leadership of its two directors, Cudenet and O'Connell. There he also met three imprisoned Vietnamese priests[12] and came to realize how Christian Vietnamese were also unfairly treated. These priests shared with him the same patriotic sentiments and like himself cherished the idea of an independent Vietnam.

3. Phan Bôi Châu and Phan Châu Trinh, Khang's Two Mentors

After his release in 1921, Khang spent a few days in Saigon and Tourane and then went to Hue to present himself to Louis Sogny, chief of the French intelligence service in Indochina (Sécurité Nationale), and to several high-ranking mandarins of the Privy Council. In his autobiography, he wrote that at that time the mandarins of the court did not know that he had been released from Poulo Condore. And then he finally returned to his native village and worked as a craftsman carving tortoiseshell. In 1923, his former title, *tien si*, was restored to him. Nguyên Ba Trac, a former student of Trân Qui Cap, solicited Pierre Pasquier, the French *resident supérieur*, to let Khang enter the National Academy so that he could work on the new Han-Vietnamese (Chinese-Vietnamese) dictionary. Khang was asked to present himself at the office of the resident in Hue. The discussion with Pasquier was quite cordial, and they even agreed that French governors did know enough about Vietnam to control the country. However, Khang refused the offer with firmness and dignity: "I have lived among the people, whose problems I know very well. But, I must tell you the truth, the function of a mandarin does not suit me."[13]

Once again, he returned to his native village to work as a trader in traditional medicines but lived under French surveillance. Starvation and a cholera epidemic were spreading throughout his province. When he took a second wife in 1925, Phan Bôi Châu, the Vietnamese youth's national hero, was arrested in Shanghai and sentenced to death. Châu's death sentence was later changed to house arrest in Hue.

It was also the same year in which Phan Châu Trinh returned to Vietnam. Very ill, he wrote to Khang, asking him urgently to visit him in Saigon. Khang was unable to leave for Saigon soon enough because of administrative delays and arrived there only a few days before Trinh died. Khang attended his national funeral. Thereafter, Khang embarked on a long journey through all the provinces of Cochinchina. In 1926, he went to Hue, where he met with Phan Bôi Châu.

After Bao Dai became king, the power structure at the Vietnamese court changed. The former Privy Council became the new Chamber of the People's Representatives. Friends of Châu wanted Khang to join their political party, the Parti Progressiste Annamite.[14] On a small boat on the Perfumed River, Phan Bôi Châu and Khang discussed the latter's future. According to Dao Duy Anh, who attended the meeting, he recalled Châu trying to convince Khang to leave his rural retirement, lead a political party, or publish a political newspaper. Khang, still moved by Trinh's recent death and impressed with Châu's arguments, replied that he did not want to become a politician because he did not believe in its efficacy, but he agreed to publish a newspaper.[15] According to Vuong Dinh Quang, after the meeting Châu wrote a poem about Khang's success with his newspaper, which, Châu wrote, would grow like a bamboo to become a weapon and a tool to educate Vietnamese in democratic political processes. Then Khang returned to his native village and received an appointment by the French colonial authority as a mandarin at the French Institute of Classics and Ancient Civilizations. But once more Khang declined the position.

In December 1926, Khang applied to the French authorities for a permit to publish his newspaper and started a fund-raising campaign. By February 1927, he had already gathered thirty thousand piasters, and soon after the French colonial government published their approval of Khang's newspaper by publishing a decree[16] in the official French governmental newsletter. The French colonial government, in particular Pasquier, welcomed Khang's initiative because five years earlier, when they had met, Pasquier had complained to Khang that there were no Vietnamese newspapers in Central Vietnam.

From May to June, Khang went to Hanoi to buy the essential printing materials and recruit a team for his newspaper. The first issue of *Tieng Dan* was published on 10 August of that year. According to Dao Duy Anh, the complete team at the newspaper consisted of five people: Khang; Trân Hoanh, the technician; Trân Dinh Phien, from Phan Thiet; Nguyên Xuong Thai, from Tourane; and himself, from Tonkin. Before the first issue was published, the French colonial administration sent them a warning not to print any anticolonial propaganda. Khang's new career was inspired by both Châu and Trinh. And to pay tribute to his two friends and mentors every year Khang published articles about each of them in *Tieng Dan* to commemorate the days of their deaths. Over the years, his yearly publications on Châu and Trinh only reinforced the popularity and notoriety of these two Vietnamese political figures, who otherwise would have been forgotten.

4. President of the Chamber of the People's Representatives

The years 1925 and 1926 marked the beginning of Khang's new career and a time of political instability in Central Vietnam. By 1926, the situation was critical. The streets were in constant turmoil. There were daily demonstrations, which had begun a year earlier at Phan

Châu Trinh's funeral. Vietnamese were demanding the release of Phan Bôi Châu. On the French side, the protectorate system had just changed with the new consul, Alexandre Varenne, a well-known socialist. Facing new challenges, the French colonial authority was willing to compromise with the Vietnamese and allowed the Chamber of the People's Representatives to be established. Khang, who had refused to lead any political party in the past, saw these new political changes as an opportunity to serve his country. He presented his candidacy in three prefectures, describing himself as "a man of transition between the Annam of yesterday and the Annam of today." Elected with 614 votes, out of 644 electors, he was during the inaugural session chosen to be president of the chamber. The annual report of the Sécurité describes him in eulogistic terms; speaks about the dignity of his private life, his intelligence, and his personality; and concludes with these words: "There is no doubt that the administration will have to take him into account."

While all the representatives from Tonkin were landowners who collaborated with the French colonial administration, the representatives from Annam were young, liberal Vietnamese like Khang, who, elected by the people, were truly representing them. Sogny, chief of the French Sécurité, was not mistaken about it: One may affirm, without fear of being mistaken, that such propaganda is aimed against the influence of the French protectorate and corresponds to a wish for independence that is not even disguised.[17] During the first sessions, Khang told the *résident supérieur* what he thought about the critical situation in which Vietnamese people lived. He defended his ideas with great firmness but also much moderation. This moderation was all the more remarkable at a time when some French living in Vietnam were outspoken against French colonialism. They condemned:

> the abuses of power of all kinds by the administration of Indochina, which sacrifices the material and moral interests of the indigenous population, which is inhumanely handed over to the exploitation of a small number of industrial, commercial, or financial groups.

Their accusatory articles were published uncensored in French newspapers, but Vietnamese journalists who dared to write similar articles were arrested and jailed. Even Marius Moutet, the French minister of the colonies, at the Chambre des Députés, criticized the French colonial system as an "unworthy justice system of our country" and concluded his speech on a prophetic note: "Shall we understand at last that 25 million human beings cannot be reduced to slavery and live under a kind of feudal terror, which no European people would undergo without at once bursting into a revolution?"[18]

The personality of d'Elloy, the *résident supérieur*, a man of authority and rigidity, reinforced the representation of the French colonial administration, and Khang's liberalism and moderation also contributed to the representation of Vietnamese officials toward the colonial power. And it was Khang's moderation that his fellow-citizens did not always appreciate. They criticized him "for letting himself be trapped" and accused him of being blinded by the truly undemocratic policies of the French in Vietnam.

Khang's first confrontation with French authority was at the second session of the chamber. The representatives demanded reimbursement for their travel expenses. D'Elloy answered by sending them a note that was considered very rude. Khang responded with a letter of protest, signed by more than forty of the representatives. The letter, officially addressed to Pasquier, was published in Vietnamese newspapers of the north and the south. Then on 9 February 1927, Khang sent another letter of complaint, but this time personally addressed to Pasquier. Pasquier immediately went to Hue to discuss the matter and bring the situation under control, which he successfully did. As a result, d'Elloy was sent back to France and replaced by Jabouille. At that time, Khang had other of his requests met, such as the hiring of a new officer, receiving some funding, and obtaining new office supplies. Nevertheless, protectorate and security officers were worrying about Khang. Sogny wrote: "Phan Bôi Châu remains with Khang, a member of the People's Representatives, the prototype of undesirable and dangerous men."[19] For Fries, the *haut resident:* "Huynh Thuc Khang and the other convicts of 1908 should equally disappear from the stage."[20] On 23 August 1927, Khang opened the session by saying: "In Annam, absolutism continues to reign in spite of the proclamation of the Convention of 6 November (the Constitution, awaited vainly!) [and] the laws are still backward after several assertions of our liberal political institutions." Khang's speech was followed by one of Varenne, the general resident. Varenne's paternal discourse tried to stir up trouble among the Vietnamese by referring to a power struggle between the chamber and the king: "First, you have to take the existence of the Annamite government into account.... it will be necessary for you to be patient when Emperor Bao Dai is absent from the kingdom." And in his administrative report Fries singled Khang out: "he is taking advantage of not knowing French to make contemptuous remarks."[21]

Then Fries accused Khang of using French subsidies, recently granted to his newspaper.[22] Fries spoke of Khang as someone who skillfully took advantage of his position at the chamber to benefit his newspaper, *Tieng Dan*. And Fries argued that Khang's every request dealing with political power should be rejected. The relationship of mistrust between French and Vietnamese was increasing. Sogny wrote on 31 August: "The number of natives who subscribe to revolutionary ideologies has increased."

The second confrontation with the *résident supérieur* was at the opening of the following session. Because the agenda was given to the representatives too late, the meeting was canceled. In 1928, Khang made a speech asking the protectorate to respect the treaty of 1884. He argued that the Vietnamese's civil rights should be respected by opening schools, lowering taxes, and modernizing the archaic penal code. The response by Jabouille was a simple refusal.

> You think that the Chamber of the People's Representatives, here in Annam, is the same thing as the Chambre des Députés of France, where the deputies are freely elected by the will of the people; you believe that you've got the right not only to control the state but to take part in the administration of the protectorate; as for your own government, you are mistaken! If this is what you think, you are completely wrong.[23]

The cynicism of his answer removed Khang's last illusions about democratic processes in the chamber and any impact of his efforts to bring social change. Soon after, he submitted his resignation, followed by the resignation of four of his friends. As the president of the Chamber of the People's Representatives from 1926 until October 1928, Khang felt that he never resolved any issues because most of his requests were rejected. And instead of becoming a puppet of the French protectorate he resigned and devoted himself to his newspaper. Some people argued that his resignation precipitated the tragedy of the years 1930–31 in Tonkin and Annam and was a determining factor in the support of Vietnamese youth for Nguyên Ai Quoc's Movement for National Independence, organized from abroad.

5. Publisher of *Tieng Dan*

After his resignation, Khang resumed his work as the publisher of *Tieng Dan*. In addition to his team, of whom he spoke highly, he also recruited free-lance writers such as Vo Nguyên Giap and Nguyên Vy. The diversity of the political background of those writers, according to Khang, was a way to ensure the nonpartisanship of his newspaper. Their relationship with Khang was based on mutual trust. They respected and admired his honesty.

The noticeable longevity of *Tieng Dan*, sixteen years, amazed a lot of people. Some Vietnamese wondered if it was because Khang published anticommunist articles that he had gained the trust of French authority. But these unfounded accusations were from Vietnamese who collaborated with the French. In contrast, the people who worked on the newspaper credited Khang's personality for the longevity and success of *Tieng Dan*. Khang was a man of integrity and intellectual honesty, which earned him the respect of everyone. During the sixteen years of the publication of *Tieng Dan*, 1,766 issues were printed, although only 1,700 are currently accounted for. The rest have disappeared.

The following data give an idea of the number of printed copies: in 1929, there were 336,331 total copies[24] and from 1940 until 1943 between 1,200 and 1,300 copies per issue. From 1927 to 1936 *Tieng Dan* appeared three times a week but only twice a week between 1940 and 1943 because of World War II. Under censorship imposed by both the French protectorate and the court at Hue,[25] Khang had to give the French authorities a translation in French of every published article, which was an additional burden for the team. Mr. Dào Duy Anh (Ve Thach) was responsible for this task until his arrest in 1930. Although the censorship was lifted in January 1935, it was reinstalled in September 1939 under the Japanese occupation, which was even harder. Eventually all of these difficulties pushed Khang to temporarily cease publication of *Tieng Dan*.

Tieng Dan was presented in a format similar to that of newspapers published at that time in Cochinchina, Tonkin, and France (58 × 42 cm). However, the pagination of this newspaper was quite original, at least for Westerners, since it was to be read from right to left, like a Chinese newspaper, and the disposition of its 4 pages[26] would have diverted a modern reader. To the pages 1–2–3–4 of a modern newspaper there corresponded, respectively, 4–1–2–3 of *Tieng Dan*. Today, readers may be astonished by the lack of organization in *Tieng Dan*. Both the permanent staff and contributing writers never attended a school of journalism. Like Khang, they were scholars who went through rigorous Confucian training in Chinese classics, which characterized the quality of their writing. But it is remarkable that they managed to trick the French authority by using the "apparent lack of contents in their articles and the pompous wording of their titles to evade French censors."

One could argue that Khang was truthful to his earlier commitment, which he stated in an article in the first issue: "Justice leads the way of *Tieng Dan*, and the goal of the newspaper is to serve the people. It will not be used by any party, nor publish evasive propaganda material. . . . *Tieng Dan* will be, for our compatriots, a bitter drug, . . . and for the government an honest friend."[27]

Khang wanted his newspaper to be not only a source of information, dealing with national and international current events, but also a real "handbook of general teaching." The newspaper covered many subjects with only four general topics: "Tap Loai" (Variety) dealing with problems of health, advice to farmers, and so on; "Chuyen Doi" (Thus is Life), with anecdotes, moral thoughts, and so on; "Viêc trong nuoc" (Events in the Country) on the third page; and only in the 1930s subjects of domestic policy. On the first page, the heading was always "Viêc thé gioi" (Events of the World), with articles on topics ranging from the Sino-Japanese War to the war in Spain and World War II.

Tieng Dan was one of the first newspapers of that time to have advertisements. At the bottom of the second page, there was usually the serial number. There was also space for community matters. The newspaper was one of the first to serve the needs of its readers. For example, some articles were even written in French, and it reported on official court sentences, lottery drawings, and jobs. Some issues were historical and technical studies of, for example, the Indochinese railroad. Every year, to celebrate the first issue of the newspaper,

Khang dedicated many articles to commemorating important events such as the festival of Têt and the philosophical and political thought of Phan Châu Trinh. Khang usually wrote these articles himself.

Articles on Vietnamese contemporary literature and classics were often illustrated, with the original texts, Chinese or Nom, and an extensive translation into *quôc ngu*. These articles constitute an invaluable anthology of masterpieces, which, in many cases, would have been destroyed. Most remarkable were the articles about foreign literature and culture, such as the ones on China, France, and Japan as well as England, the United States, and Italy. Khang, who was an omniscient teacher, wanted to educate people about the geography of their own country. With the help of his colleagues, he published extensive descriptions of the various provinces of Vietnam, such as the mountainous area of Lam Vien, the high plateau, written by Trân Dinh Nam,[28] the different areas of Central Vietnam, and an economic and administrative survey of Haiphong. He also published on Vietnamese history, which he complained was not taught often enough. The history of Vietnam, he argued, was almost as old as that of China, but Vietnamese students knew more about ancient Chinese history than about contemporary Vietnamese history. Khang wrote many articles about events he had himself witnessed. He wrote about his experience in the Chamber of the People's Representatives and published personal accounts of other people who had participated or witnessed special historical events.

Khang had an extraordinary memory, which allowed him, for example, to reproduce very accurately the poetic works of some of his companions on Poulo Condore. He also started to write down memoirs of his life as a convict there. The memoirs were originally written in Chinese traditional verse. He translated them himself into *quôc ngu* when he published them in 1939, with the title of *Thi Tu Tung Thoai*.

Khang also published articles on the subjects of social justice and freedom such as freedom of thought, freedom of the press, freedom of movement, and justice for all. These articles generally denounced social injustices that people had reported to the newspaper. Most astonishing for a scholar of his renown was his liberal attitude. For instance, many articles were on women's issues.

Using his newspaper as an educational tool, Khang wanted to expose Vietnamese cultural mentalities and force his readers to think critically about their own behavior. Khang wanted them to question their cultural beliefs and improve themselves. In his articles, he denounced Vietnamese historical errors but kept his readers' patriotic enthusiasm by glorifying Vietnamese historical figures. Khang, however, did not want them to long for the past; instead he wanted them to work toward a better future.

In some of his writings, Khang discussed the basis for cultural conflict between Asian and European civilizations, East and West. He argued that Asian civilizations disregarded material goods and as a result did not encourage the development of inquisitive scientific minds, and he wrote that in contrast Western civilization was based on materialism, everyone's right to happiness, and the abolition of poverty and disease. Khang furthermore argued that Western civilization was not only materialistic but idealistic and spiritual. He claimed that democracy was a product of Western civilization; that it included ideas of freedom, tolerance, gender equality, and respect for human rights; and that it allowed the development of technology such as printing works, steam energy, railways, airplanes, electricity, and telegrams.

Khang did not want his readers to reject new ideas because of Vietnamese national pride. Thus, in *Tieng Dan* he encouraged them to understand Western philosophy. He believed that by understanding scientific and technological concepts they would themselves participate in modernizing Vietnam. He was inspired by the Meiji Restoration in Japan and the revolution of Sun Yat Sen in China.

Khang claimed that in order to modernize the fatherland everyone had to participate: "The rushes fall ready-roasted from the sky."[29] And he insisted that technology and science were the keys to the development of the Vietnamese economy. However, he warned that good moral values were also important. On the subject of political philosophy, Khang argued that it was essential in politics to have democracy, which respected everyone's political differences. In one of his articles, he used the example of the famous sentence of the despotic Louis XIV: "I am the State!" which was followed, a century later, by the bloody French Revolution of 1789. Khang concluded in his article that it was unfortunate that Confucian behavior permeated all relationships in Vietnamese society, for Vietnamese people did not question authority.

Khang also condemned colonial repression, which he argued sparked revolt. When he introduced new political ideologies in *Tieng Dan*, such as fascism, communism, and anticommunism, he tried to be nonpartisan. However, he always wrote about repression and injustice in totalitarian regimes. He also used moral concepts: "what remains longest in the life of human beings?"[30] In reference to capitalism, Khang discussed the role of material goods and money in modern society. He wrote a two-part article, one on a moral ("Does Money Provide Power?")[31] and the other on a philosophical question ("Avid for Money but Fearing Death").[32] Khang made clear his preference for a law-observing state, democracy, and human rights and his distrust of the autocratic: "Autocracy or State of Rights."[33] Khang's ideas on modernity and morality in Western societies were similar to those of Montesquieu, an advocate of a republic.

Khang used his newspaper to challenge the status quo in Vietnamese society. He questioned, for instance, the autonomy of Vietnam and the role of the Vietnamese parliament in a country under protectorate rule. He reiterated his ideas of a constitution for Annam. He believed in free schooling and an education adapted to the needs of Vietnamese people. He, for example, denounced "the horizontal teaching" of the French colonial school system, which efficiently trained the Vietnamese intellectual elite. Unlike his contemporaries, Khang respected women's intellect, and for twenty-seven years he encouraged Vietnamese women to discuss their problems.[34] In *Tieng Dan*, he encouraged them to write and express their opinions.

In the last years of the publication of *Tieng Dan*, Khang wrote a geopolitical analysis of coming events with remarkable accuracy. The topic of one of his articles was: "would there be a World War II?" and another was "the future world war."[35]

Khang for many years was able to work with French censors by agreeing at least officially with the protectorate's censorship guidelines. But in 1943 he no longer wanted to play the game. He refused to follow the guidelines, which had become for him unbearable. The temporary shutdown of *Tieng Dan* was not, however, because of politics but rather because of a literary quarrel. The quarrel had started many years earlier between the partisans of modern and traditional poetry. Inter alia, Pham Quynh defended "the modern ones" and Khang and Ngô Duc Ke "the old ones." For Khang and Ke, all literary work had to arise from moral principles. But Quynh wrote an article in which he claimed that Nguyên Du's book *Kim-Van-Kieu* was the very essence of the Vietnamese national identity. The quarrel continued for several years after the publication of the transcription in *quôc ngu* of

Nguyên Du's poem by Nguyên Van Vinh. Later Quynh claimed: "If Kieu exists, our language exists, our country exists." By using the word *language*, Quynh might have meant *quôc ngu*, and in this respect there would have been no quarrel. But Khang and his friends strongly disagreed with Quynh's association of Kieu and Vietnamese national identity. During World War II, when Governor Decoux wanted to mobilize Vietnamese youth after the Japanese victory, he organized public meetings to discuss the literary works of Du. Khang wrote a series of articles against the work of Du, but all were censored and never published. The French censors only allowed him to publish the first part of an article in which he praised the literary value of Du's work. He refused to partially publish his article. At the same time, Decoux published a decree in the French official newsletter—dated 23 April 1943—suspending the publication of *Tieng Dan*.

Today, the Vietnamese people realize the psychological, political, and cultural impact of *Tieng Dan* in Central Vietnam and other parts of the country. Most of the articles in *Tieng Dan* were written by Khang. In addition to current events, the philosophy of the newspaper included Confucian thoughts as well as those of the great political thinkers of eighteenth-century France. *Tieng Dan* introduced Vietnamese to gender equality, politics, economy, history, geography, humanities, and sciences. Although nowadays *Tieng Dan* appears a little austere and too sententious, for its time it was an "avant-garde" newspaper.

In 1943, when *Tieng Dan* closed down and Japanese troops controlled Vietnam, Khang received a message from Prince Cuong Dê. This message was brought to him by a Japanese emissary. Unfortunately, we do not know the content of the letter because there was no trace of it in the prince's documents. It is, however, possible that it was forged by the Japanese security office in an attempt to probe the position of Vietnamese scholars toward the Japanese forces. In response, Khang sent a letter to the prince, which was published posthumously in 1957 in Hue by Editions Anh Minh, entitled: "Buc Thu Bi mat cua Cu Huynh Thuc Khang Tra loi Cu Ky Ngoai Hau Cuong Dê" (Huynh Thuc Khang's Secret Letter to Cuong Dê). In this letter, Khang wrote, "until today, Vietnam had only one occupier, but now Vietnam has two of them!" He sent a similar letter to Sonoda, the Japanese officer. Sonoda had asked Khang to cooperate with the Japanese authority by encouraging his readers to join the final insurrection against the French.³⁶ In Southeast Asia, the Japanese represented themselves as the liberators of the "yellow race."

6. The Political Adviser

With the suspension of *Tieng Dan,* Khang, with a team of ten people, pursued the publication of books and translations. He did not, however, take advantage of the situation to publish his own works. Besides his essay of 1945, "Buc thu tra loi chung (y kien toi voi thoi cuoc)" (Open Letter to the People or My Opinion on the Current Situation),³⁷ Khang was never published while he was alive. All of his work was published posthumously. He was always writing articles and books for which he enjoyed tracing the characters before translating them into *quôc ngu.*

> In 1957, a secret letter in response to Cuong Dê
>
> In 1959, *Phan Tay Ho tien sinh lich su* (Biography of Phan Châu Trinh)
>
> In 1963, *Huynh Thuc Khang tu truyen* (Autobiography of Huynh Thuc Khang)
>
> In 1966, *Mot Vai Tien thoi nhan vat dong thoi voi Nguyên Truong To it ai biet: Nguyên Lo Trach* (A Contemporary of Nguyên Truong To, Known to Only a Few People), translation by Huynh Thuc Khang

Huynh Thuc Khang was writing at a time of extreme troubles for the country. Every month the Japanese asked the French colonial authority to collect taxes from the Vietnamese people. As a result, in March 1945, two million people died of starvation in northern Vietnam. The Vietnamese did not consider the Japanese as their "yellow brothers." They instead hated them more than the French, who during the Japanese occupation also suffered from hunger. On 10 March 1945, Yokohama, the Japanese ambassador, "offered" the emperor, Bao Dai, the independence of Vietnam, asking him to join "Great Asia." The next day, the emperor promulgated the end of the French protectorate by revoking all existing Franco-Vietnamese treaties and proclaiming the independence of Vietnam. He wanted to name Pham Quynh as spokesman for the new Vietnamese government to the Japanese, but his secretary, Pham Khac Hoe, dissuaded him. Instead he recommended that the emperor nominate either Huynh Thuc Khang or Ton Quang Phiet. Both were popular, and Hoe thought they would not compromise with the Japanese. Hoe went first to talk with Khang to sound him out and invite him to the palace at the request of the emperor. Khang, who mistrusted the Japanese because of their fascism and disliked the weak personality of the emperor, declined the invitation. Hostile to the monarchy, he let someone else tell Bao Dai to abdicate,[38] and he suggested to him that the current leadership should take more care for the people's welfare (*dan vi qui*). Khang also suggested that taxes be abolished for one year. But the emperor did not take Khang's advice into consideration.[39] The fourteen people chosen by Hoe to consult with the emperor gathered in April and unanimously advised Bao Dai to nominate Ngô Dinh Diem as the president. Ngô Dinh Diem was then considered to be favored by the Japanese. But Diem declined the invitation under the pretext of poor health. Trân Trong Kim, who had worked with the French and was then a "protégé" of the Japanese, presented to the emperor a list of fourteen potential ministers for his new government. Bao Dai retained only eight of them. With only eight ministers, the new Vietnamese government agreed to carry on the Japanese-Vietnamese policy of collaboration. Trân Trong Kim, still in Saigon,[40] discussed his role in this new government with the emperor. On 7 April, he agreed to preside over the new government.

    Waiting for the arrival of Kim at Hue, one of the new ministers, Hoang Xuan Han, a thirty-seven-year-old man, went to visit Khang to discuss the political situation.[41] The minister recalled finding Khang very distressed. Khang had fought all his life for the independence of Vietnam and thought that the opportunity had come. But because of the emperor's unwillingness to give up his throne, and under the current international circumstances, Khang refused to collaborate with the king and his new government. So when Hoang Xuan Han, who had already made up his mind about joining the new government, asked Khang for his advice, Khang became upset. The issue at stake was whether or not to help Bao Dai build an independent country. If Khang and other Vietnamese scholars refused to participate in this new government, they felt that it would only reinforce the French colonial assertion that the Vietnamese were unable to settle their differences and govern their country. Such an image would affect Vietnam's relationship with other countries, in particular the United States.

During the period of the Trân Trong Kim government, Khang was regularly kept informed by his two friends Trân Dinh Nam, the interior minister, and Ho Ta Khanh, the minister of the economy, who visited him. At the time, the situation in Vietnam was extremely complex. The Japanese could not control the major Vietnamese cities because of the resistance of the Viet Minh troops, who were receiving weapons and advice from military advisers of the American OSS.[42] The French provisional government of General de Gaulle sent Major Sainteny to Tonkin to serve as liaison with the Viet Minh leadership in China, which requested weapons and instructors to fight the Japanese. But in July Sainteny received from his liaison person in Tien Tsin (Tsing Tsi) not a request for more weapons but a memorandum with five points and a concluding remark: "Hoping that these conditions will be considered acceptable by the French government."[43]

7. Interim President of the New Republic

When Khang heard the news of the fighting, he thought that the Viet Minh were joining forces with the French. On 6 August, the first atomic bomb fell on Hiroshima and on 10 August Ho Chi Minh gave the order for a general insurrection. The Japanese capitulated, but in Vietnam they refused to surrender to the Allied forces so as to prevent the French from returning. After more fighting, the Viet Minh troops celebrated their victory on 2 September with a military parade in Hanoi. The same day Ho Chi Minh proclaimed the Democratic Republic of Vietnam. In Hue, Trân Trong Kim, aware of the fragility of the alliance among Vietnamese political parties and of his own weakness,[44] resigned. Emperor Bao Dai abdicated, and the flag of "Co quoc gia Viet Nam" replaced that of the emperor, "Co Chu Li."[45]

All of his life Khang had openly expressed his mistrust of the communists and did not hide his contempt for the Viet Minh troops, whom he considered to be the puppets of the communists. He approved of Ho Chi Minh's proclamation, but, as Nguyên Q. Thang wrote, he refused to credit any particular political party with the liberation. Khang wrote: "The proclamation of independence on 2 September was the result of the people's struggle." He even refused to print leaflets for the Viet Minh under the pretext that, as the publisher of a press, he had to remain neutral vis-à-vis his readership. On 29 October, on the occasion of the commemorative day of Phan Bôi Châu's death, in the grip of emotion, he pronounced this sentence, which seems sibylline only to those who are not Vietnamese scholars: "Yesterday's year of the cock does not resemble this year."[46]

At the beginning of January, Khang received two telegrams, one from Ho Chi Minh, the communist, and the other from Nguyên Hai Than, the nationalist. Both of the telegrams stated: "We invite Khang to join us in Hanoi and accept the position of interior minister. Please inform us of your decision."[47] The 29 August 1945 "Provisional Revolutionary Government" was formed by a coalition of different Vietnamese political parties, which included communists, nationalists, the Alliance Party, and those not affiliated with any political party. The position of leadership of the ministries of the interior and defense were to be given to Vietnamese with no political affiliation.[48]

There were four possible explanations for Khang's invitation to join Ho Chi Minh's government.

1. Ho Chi Minh certainly felt much respect for Khang, who was a contemporary of his father and his father's friend.
2. Pham Van Dong came from the same province as Khang.
3. Vo Nguyên Giap appreciated Khang's personality from the time when he wrote for *Tieng Dan*.
4. Khang was known as an upright patriot, though not bound to any party.

Khang hesitated to accept the invitation. But Ho Chi Minh's emissary, Nguyên Van Ngoc, police chief in Trung Bo, went to Hue and convinced Khang to go. In Quang Binh, the official car that took Khang to Hanoi was stopped by the police, and Khang was interrogated. It was all a mistake because of the lack of organization in the Vietnamese administration at the time. But Khang demanded to return to Hue. His request was refused, and he was taken to Hanoi. There Ho Chi Minh welcomed Khang to his home and kept him there overnight. Khang remained unmoved by Ho Chi Minh's offer. The following day, Nguyên Xuong Thai, Khang's traveling companion, handed him the last message from Ho,[49] which convinced Khang to accept the position of interior minister. On 1 March 1946, in his open remarks at the National Assembly, Ho Chi Minh presented Khang as "a virtuous, honored, and well-known man to the people."[50] By 3 March, the "Government of Union and of Resistance," Doan Ket Khang Chien, was officially installed.

Khang made his first speech as a minister in the large municipal theater of Hanoi while announcing the Government of Union and of Resistance on 7 March. This speech was published on 29 April 1947 in the newspaper *Su Thât* (The Truth). Those who attended were impressed by the powerful voice of a weak-looking old man.[51] The first taste of this new government was the announcement of a preliminary Franco-Vietnamese meeting, signed by Ho Chi Minh and Sainteny on 6 March. This meeting was to take place in Dalat between 20 April and 11 May. It was to finalize the bilateral agreement between France and Vietnam. A delegation of twenty-four Vietnamese was chosen to go to Dalat. Almost all of these relatively young delegates were aware of the importance of their mission for the future of Vietnam. Before leaving Hanoi for Dalat, both Ho Chi Minh and Khang met with them. While Ho gave them specific guidelines with eight points to follow, Khang gave them money for their traveling expenses and told them to be evasive if asked to comment on the Franco-Chinese treaty. When the young Vo Nguyên Giap wondered about his party's support, Khang told him: "When you need my assistance, I will be able, at any time, to obtain the support of all the people."[52]

Unfortunately, the talks in Dalat failed because the French were not willing to compromise. The meeting ended with no agreement, and Vo Nguyên Giap left, slamming the door.[53] In the meantime, Ho Chi Minh restructured his government and founded Mat Tran Hoi Lien Hiep Quoc Dan Viet Nam, the league of the Popular Resistance of Vietnamese National Front, led by Khang. Ho Chi Minh, the honorary president, appointed Nguyên Hai Than as vice president and during his trip to France nominated Khang as the interim president of the Republic. Ho Chi Minh left for France on 28 May to negotiate with the French government the independence of the three *ky* (parts of the country) and to discuss the terms of future Franco-Vietnamese economic cooperation.

Trân Trong Kim, last prime minister in the so-called Trân Trong

Kim government, recalled the time when he visited Khang as interior minister. Khang modestly told him that he had little to do. Khang said that he had only to sign the reports prepared and written by different committees. During his very short stay in the government and as the interior minister, Khang signed 106 decrees.[54] But after 29 May, as the interim president of the Republic, he signed from 92 to 202 decrees.

By June, the political situation in Vietnam had deteriorated. On the first of that month, the admiral d'Argenlieu urged Nguyên Van Thinh in Saigon to proclaim the "Autonomous Republic of Cochinchina." Giap was angry, but Ho told him that the conflict would be resolved at once at the Paris conference. In the meantime, the Vietnamese nationalist party leaders were dissatisfied with the talks in Dalat and with the fact that the Vietnamese delegation going to Paris was composed essentially of Viet Minh. They were also infuriated by the relationship between General Valluy[55] and Vo Nguyên Giap. They responded by publishing many accusatory articles in Vietnamese newspapers, calling a general strike for 27 May, and provoking violence.[56] In response, both Giap and Khang signed a decree on 5 June[57] asking people to unite and request government investigations in conflicting matters among different Vietnamese political parties.

It was at this critical time that the police investigated "the street On Nhu Hau." Around 8 P.M. on 12 July, at no. 7 of this street of Hanoi (Bonifacy Street),[58] headquarters of the Vietnamese Nationalist Party, was found a mass grave and torture rooms. Occupied in the past by the Chinese army, these villas were then given by the Chinese to the Vietnamese Nationalist Party. The police chief at that time,[59] who carried out the investigation,[60] said that when he reported the event to Khang and brought to his office the macabre exhibits (photographs and instruments of torture), Khang struck the parquet floor with his stick and said: "It is necessary to get rid of these traitors; they must be removed, as they are the traitors to their country. It's necessary to completely eliminate them."[61]

In the past, Khang, who claimed to be neutral in political matters, had showed some sympathy toward the nationalists. There was no evidence to incriminate the Nationalist Party, but after the discovery Khang's attitudes toward them changed. Hoang Xuan Han, in their defense, claimed that there might have been some Kuomintang Chinese disguised as nationalists who tortured and killed some rich Vietnamese. But the evidence of Viet Minh patriots among the corpses was enough to throw suspicion on the nationalist militants. Han had then argued that those Viet Minh, often disguised as itinerant Pho street vendors, were in fact spies. And finally Han accused the Vietnamese communists of having done the same by killing nationalists.[62] Until today, no one knows what really happened. Supported by General Valluy, Giap wanted exemplary punishment of the culprits.

Khang was disgusted not only by the massacre but by the Viet Minh's use of it as an excuse for revenge against Vietnamese nationalists.[63]

After his return from France, an empty-handed Ho Chi Minh wrote to the people:

> After four months abroad, now that I'm back home to find the people happy, I would like to thank Mr. Huynh, interim president, for his guidance, and I would like to thank the assembly for having worked together, in spite of difficulties, and for carrying on with its development.[64]

But a dramatic turn of events abruptly led to major changes. From 20 October to 28 November, French troops landed in Vietnam and attacked the port of Haiphong.[65] Forced into hiding, the Vietnamese government withdrew to the *maquis* in the countryside. Khang was appointed at the head of a new political party, Union and Resistance, and agreed to lead the organization of the Fifth Zone, the area including the districts of Nam (Quang Nam), Nghia (Quang Nghia), Binh (Binh Dinh), and Phu (Phu Yen). He went to Quang Binh to deliver his famous speech. There he, who had always been a moderate and a pacifist, was terribly upset by the arrival of French troops. He denounced the return of the French, as the "masters," as he called them, and accused the French of having made fools of Vietnamese people by letting them believe that they could live in an independent country. His speech was eloquent, but Khang for the first time gave a militant speech using violent language like the ones of Ho Chi Minh. He called for armed resistance against the French.

> Let us fight! Let us fight! Old, young, boys, girls, monks, workers, scholars! Let us gather and raise up to push back the enemies, to avenge the martyrdom of our ancestors! Let us fight on all fronts, military, political, economic, and cultural!

> Let us fight with weapons, sticks, knives, axes, and with all that we have in our hands! We fear neither their planes nor their submarines, which will fall before our unity.[66]

Thereafter, Khang returned to his native village, where he spent fifteen days, and then he made another speech calling for unity and resistance. Mr. Truong Phien, born in Khang's village and the son of one of Khang's friends, who is also a journalist for the *Giai Phong*, told me during an interview about the welcoming ceremony for Khang's return to the village: "A thousand years of life in Khang!" Khang would have sadly smiled and answered: "A thousand years is not possible, a few months perhaps."

A text of parallel sentences[67] from those days, which he composed for his old friend Nguyên Dinh Hien, is still at the prefecture of Que Son (Quang Nam). This text, both philosophical and nostalgic, is among the last writings of Huynh Thuc Khang.

> Dropped from heaven, he was worn out by twenty years on the dusty road of life. A laureate of examinations, he, in turn, meditated with disdain upon the universe, this theater where the provincial or court mandarin sometimes busied himself, or, on the contrary, did nothing, sometimes unconscious, another time awakened. Abruptly frightened on this sacred land, on ten occasions he went back to the village where he was born, its trees, hills, and mountains. He came back to the village of Tien. He burdened his soul with all the problems of the world.

8. The Death of Huynh Thuc Khang

Khang went to Quang Ngai but was very tired after the journey. He was forced to confine himself to bed. Knowing that his death was imminent, he wrote three telegrams, one addressed to Ho Chi Minh: "I am very sick, and I will not recover. During forty years I dreamt of independence and democracy; now, my dream has come true. I am dying in peace. . . ." ("Farewell," 14 April 1947).[68] The second telegram was addressed to Vietnamese soldiers: "You are the unknown heroes of this country! I wish you strength and courage. Never, on any account, never let our country fall again under the yoke of colonialism." ("Farewell," 19 April 1947).[69] And the third telegram, written as a philosophical testament, went as follows: "To friends of the parties and believers. . . . No political doctrine works if the people live in slavery. . . . No religion has the answer. They say that religion has no boundaries, and I believe it, too. I wanted everything without boundaries, but this day has not come." ("Farewell," 19 April 1947).[70]

Huynh Thuc Khang died on the first of March, probably of cancer of the prostate. He was buried in Quang Ngai. A monument was raised but later was damaged by the wars. In 1993, it was replaced by a modern building.

When he heard about the death of his old friend, Ho Chi Minh published a long letter[71] to all Vietnamese:

> Khang, the old fighter, . . . has just died. . . . Khang was an educated man, with a good mind and great morals. . . . he was deported for almost twelve years to Poulo Condore. . . . Confronted with cruelty, he never gave up. Khang was a man whom wealth could not divert; difficulties could not stop him; violence did not frighten him. During his life, Khang did not expect any honorific title; he never felt the desire to gain wealth nor to become a mandarin. He devoted his life to the fight for freedom and the independence of his people. . . . He used to say: "When it is time to rebuild our country, everybody will have to work together for the salvation of the nation. . . ." Here, he is gone before he could see what the revolution has accomplished. Khang is dead, but his spirit is still alive in the souls of twenty million of his fellow citizens.

From all over the country people paid respect to Khang. In Ho Chi Minh's words, "Born in a modest rural family, educated, Huynh Thuc Khang always lived in poverty." By filial devotion as much as by personal ambition, he obtained the highest distinctions in Chinese classical studies. He had an intellectual honesty, which guided everyone. He renounced the official honors of the mandarin to devote himself to promoting literacy in rural areas and bringing social and political justice to the people. During the first thirty years of his life, political events contributed to his own political awareness. His friendships and his studies led him to give up some of the too conservative and chauvinistic aspects of his Confucian education and to choose to be a patriot without being a modern reformist. As an intellectual, he undertook few journeys. He was generous and gifted and liked people. Even the long, painful, and unjust imprisonment on Poulo Condore was for him "a school of life" and left him with no resentment. But, when he realized that his dream for democracy in a country under the control of the French protectorate was possible, he devoted himself to journalism. He then continued to show intellectual honesty, patience, and prudence but also stubbornness in defending ideas he judged good for his country.

Conclusion

During the sixteen years of the publication of *Tieng Dan*, Khang prepared Vietnamese people for the liberation of the country, and I would argue that the success of Ho Chi Minh in 1945 was in part due to Khang's long publishing work at *Tieng Dan*. In addition to his political work, the numbers of Khang's articles devoted to his companions of captivity, Phan Bôi Châu, Phan Châu Trinh, and Trân Qui Cap, have contributed to our understanding of their poetical works. Without Khang's testimony, their work would have been lost. *Tieng Dan* is one of the few sources that contained a firsthand account of Vietnamese society in Annam at that time. Khang participated in Vietnamese politics, first as the president of the Chamber of the People's Representative and then as the interior minister of the newly established Ho Chi Minh government in 1945. Khang, a traditionally trained Vietnamese scholar, was a man of action, which led him to a path different from those of his contemporaries. Khang fought for social justice and dreamed of Vietnamese independence, and his life is in itself a testimony to change in Vietnam at a crossroads.

NOTES

Université Denis Diderot, Paris, France. I would like to thank both John K. Whitmore and Gisele Bousquet for their editorial work and guidance in the revision of this essay.

1. Most of the subscribers lived in Phan Thiet, and most were members of the Cong Ty Lien Thanh (Lien Thanh Society). See Dào Duy Anh, *Nho nghi chiêu hôm: hôi ký.* (Meditations at Twilight). Thanh Pho Hô Chí Minh (Saigon): Tre voi su hop tác cua Asia-Média, 1989.

2. *Faifoo (Hoi An)* or *do thi co*. See the descriptions given by Thich Dai San in *Hai Ngoai Su* (Diary of a Journey Abroad), translated by Nguyen Duy Bot (Hue: Hue University, 1960), 278.

3. Cochinchina.

4. The last triennal classical competitions took place in Hue in 1919.

5. Dao Mong Giac, a name that might have been the one of a known and respected family in Binh Dinh, Dao Phan Dua or Dao Tan.

6. Binh Thuan was a rich area in the southern part of central Vietnam.

7. As a matter of fact, it was Phan Châu Trinh (PCT) who first introduced the fashion of short hair and European clothes, which were woven in Quang Nam (people spoke of the "Tây Hô fashion," Tây Hô being a pseudonym for PCT).

8. It is true that scholars like Huynh Thuc Khang (HTK), Phan Châu Trinh (PCT), and Trân Qui Cap (TQC) had not taken part in the movement directly, but everybody knew how much they contributed to introducing democratic ideas to the Vietnamese people.

9. Truong Van Tham (1852–1913) was a patriot opposed to French colonialism who joined the Cân Vuong movement and led a resistance Vietnamese army from 1896 to 1913.

10. Phan Khôi, a witness to the events that took place then, wrote in his diary *"Sông Huong"* (The River of Perfumes) that after the repression against the tax movement in 1908 leaders of both clans "Am Xa" and "Minh Xa," were sent to prison. If it did not happen, many people would have died. Symposium 1995 "Euro-Viet II," *"Sources and Approaches"* in Aix-en Provence. See the article by Phan Thi Minh Lê.

11. The telegram (no. 1866 dated 18 September 1908, from "the Lieutenant governor of Saigon" to the director of the prison) was found in the Saigon Record Office (Record 2, I.A., 19/III/4). The author of the telegram asked for an urgent reply. Twenty-seven new prisoners were to be sent to the prison. He claimed that the prison was full and for security and health reasons he could not accept them under the circumstances. He requested new buildings and more guards.

12. Do Quang Linh, Nguyên Than Dong, and Nguyên Tuong arrived on Poulo Condore in 1911.

13. Minh Vien (HTK), *Tu Truyen (nien pho) (autobiography)*, ed. Anh Minh (Hue, 1963).

14. Chau had in fact written to Pasquier to collaborate with the French. But Pasquier had told him that no Vietnamese political party would be tolerated under a Vietnamese monarch.

15. Khang had always been a follower of PCT, subscribing to reformist ideas for the country.

16. CAOM (Centre Archives Outre-Mer of Aix-en-Provence), B.221, box 10, "Letter by Pierre Pasquier." No. 1856 A.I., on 23/5/1929. Authorization to be published no. 10546, 11/5/1929.

17. CAOM, P.I. (Indochinese politics) (annual report 26–27, signed by Sogny).

18. *L'Annam* (a newspaper edited in Saigon) of Monday 14 June 1926: "How to Prepare for a War in Indochina."

19. CAOM, G.G.I. 7 F 30 65504 A.I. no.: 492 E, Rapport de la Sûreté en Annam, May 23, 1927, from Higher Resident by interim in Annam to General Governor for Indochina (Fries).

20. CAOM R.S.I.D. 65504. no. 259/S.E. to M.G.G. of Indochina Hanoi (Fries).

21. CAOM P.I., D 2, session 1927 of the Chamber of the Representatives of the People, Report of the Higher Resident in Hue, 2 August 1927.

22. CAOM P.I., D 2, Session 1927 of the Chamber of the Representatives of the People, Report of the Higher Resident in Hue, 2 August 1927.

23. CAOM R.S., D 2, Speech of the Higher Resident Jabouille, 10 October 1928.

24. Alexander Woodside wrote that he had found this number on page 3 of the *Tieng Dan* of 1 March 1930, but omitted to note that the number was the number of subscribers not the number of sold copies. See Alexander Woodside, *Community and Revolution in Modern Vietnam* (Boston: Houghton Mifflin, 1976), 79.

25. Press censure was exerted only in Trung Ky.

26. Six pages for special editions on the occasion of death commemorations. It went up to six or eight pages on average but then down again to two pages during the recession of the 1940s, when there was a shortage of paper.

27. Anh Minh [Ngo Thanh Nhan], *Ngu Hanh Son Chi Si* (Patriots of the Ngu Hanh Mountains Area [of Quang Nam]), ed. Anh Minh (Hue: Nha Xuat Ban Anh Minh, 1961), 102. This work is of a great value since the first issue of the newspaper has been lost.

28. Interior minister under the government of Trân Trong Kim.

29. *Tieng Dan*, 10 March 1928, "Rat la cho cai tanh y lai cua nguoi minh."

30. *Tieng Dan*, 2 May and 5 May 1928, "Nguoi doi cai gi la song lau hon."

31. *Tieng Dan*, 21 March 1929, "Co qua la kim tien van nang khong?"

32. *Tieng Dan*, 11 December 1928, "Cai hai tham tien ma so chet."

33. *Tieng Dan*, 24 May 1933, "Nhan tri voi phap tri."

34. In the 1930s, the political situation in the world and in particular in Vietnam had changed. The style of other newspapers was influenced by politically active writers, young socialists or Marxists whose articles or pamphlets were of great interest to a young generation of provincial readers.

35. *Tieng Dan*, 14 April 1928.

36. Anh Minh, *Nha cach mang cong khai khong dang phai nao het cu HTK* (An Open-Minded Revolutionary, Member of No Party), ed. Anh Minh (Hue: Nha Xuat Ban Anh Minh, 1953), 148–49.

37. HTK clearly expressed his feelings about the presence of Japanese in *The Secret Letter of Cuong Dê:* "We used to have to undergo occupation by the French; now, in addition, we have to bear occupation by the Japanese."

38. Nam Son, *Minh Vien HTK tieu su va tho van* (Biography by HTK, Prose and Poetry), work not published yet, 41–42. Quoted in Nguyen Q. Thang, *Huynh Thuc Khang* (The Man and the Writer) *Con nguoi va tho van*, (Saigon: Nha Xuat Ban Phu Quoc Vu Khanh Dac Trach Van Hoa, 1972), 219.

39. Pham Khac Hoe, *Tu trieu dinh Hue den chien khu Viet Bac* (From the Court of Hue to Tonkinese Maquis) (Hue: Nha Xuat Ban Thuan Hoa, 1987), 24.

40. It seems that the Japanese tried to prevent him from reaching Hue (cf. Bao Dai, *The Dragon of Annam* [Paris: Plon, 1980]).

41. Testimony given by Mr. Hoang Xuan Han himself during an interview with the author in Paris.

42. Philippe Devillers, *History of Vietnam from 1940 to 1952* (Paris: Seuil, 1952), 133.

43. Ibid., 136.

44. Ibid., 138–39.

45. Names of the last two Vietnamese flags (one for TTK's government and another for the Democratic Republic of Vietnam as of 2 September 1945).

46. The name given to every other year is from matching the name of one of the twelve symbolic animals and the name of one of the ten numbered celestial symbols. Every particular match occurs again every sixty years. The "old year of the cock" means the year 1885, whereas the "present year of the cock" refers to 1945, which was the year of the proclamation of independence.

47. Anh Minh, *Nha cach mang cong khai khong dang phai nao het cu HTK*, 154.

48. Hoang Xuan Han, *Mot vai ki vang ve hoi nghi Da lat* (A Few Memories about the Meeting in Dalat) (Saigon: [s.n.], 1971).

49. "Please, do tell Khang. I know very well that he would sacrifice everything for his country. And now I am asking him to sacrifice his pride for his country." In Anh Minh, *An Open Revolutionist*, 155.

50. Ho Chi Minh, *H.C.M. Complete Works.* (Hanoi: Nha Xuat Ban Chinh tri quoc gia, 1995), 110–11.

51. Chuong Thau, *Tho Van HTK chon loc* (Selected Prose and Poetry by HTK) (Danang: Nha Xuat Ban Danang, 1989).

52. Hoang Xuan Han, *Mot vai ki vang*, 17–18.

53. Ibid., 68.

54. Trân Trong Kim, *Mot con gio bui*, (A Whirlwind) (Saigon: Vinh Son, 1969), 110.

55. A representative of the French Republic in Hanoi.

56. Hoang Van Dao, *Viet Nam Quoc Dan Dang, lich su dau tranh can dai 1927–1954* (The Vietnamese Nationalist Party, A History of the Modern Struggle, 1927–1954) (Saigon: Nguyen Hoa Hi, 1965), 319–24.

57. Decree (*sac lenh*) 96 *Van kien Dang* (Records of the Communist Party), Bo Quoc Phong (Ministry of Defense).

58. Nowadays Nguyên Gia Thieu Street, no. 7, Hanoi.

59. Le Gian, a former parachutist in the French Army, who was the police chief in Tonkin.

60. *Bao An Ninh Thu Do* (a newspaper) (Safety in the Main Town).

61. "Diet, diet, phai diet het bon phan nuoc hai dan nay moi duoc . . . diet, diet, phai diet het bon nay!"

62. These details were given during an interview in Paris on 19 June 1995 by Mr. Nguyên Van Su (who used to be a very young member of the Communist Party), and Mr. Nguyên Dinh Dau. Both witnessed the events that took place at that time.

63. Hoang Van Dao (324) wrote that HTK was told a few days before he died that Vietnamese nationalists had been slaughtered before the massacre of Nhu Hau took place. Khang was deeply saddened because he had never been informed but did not comment.

64. Ho Chi Minh, *Complete Works*, 170–71.

65. *Viet Nam nhung su kien 1945–1986* (A Problem of Vietnamese History) (Hanoi: Nha Xuat Ban Khoa Hoc Xa Hoi, 1990), 28.

66. Ho Chi Minh, *Complete Works*, 170–71.

67. This text had been kept by Khang's nephew, Dien Ban, in Quang Nam; later it was found by Nguyên Thanh.

68. Vuong Dinh Quang, *Tho van Huynh Thuc Khang* (HTK's Prose and Poetry) (Hanoi: Van Hoc, 1965), 192.

69. Ibid., 192.

70. Ibid., 192.

71. Ho Chi Minh, *Complete Works*, 352–53.

GLOSSARY

Anh Minh	Publishing house in Hue
Bo ba Quang Nam	The trio from Quang Nam
Buc thu bi mat cua cu Huynh Thuc Khang tra loi cu Ky Ngoai Hau Cuong De	Secret letter from Mr. H. T. K. to the Prince Cuong Dê
Buc thu tra loi chung (y kien toi voi thoi cuoc)	Open letter to the people, or my opinion on the current situation
Buoc dau tren con duong lich su tu tuong xa hoi	First steps on the way toward the history of socialist thought
Cân Vuong	Patriotic movement called "call for helping the king"
Chi thanh thong thanh	To communicate with higher spirits, it is necessary to arrive at a level of studies reaching perfection
Chuyen doi	Thus is life

Co chu li	Flag with Li character
Co Quoc gia Viet Nam	Flag of the Vietnamese state
Dan vi qui	The people's welfare
Danh ngoc luong son	To find the invaluable jade, it is necessary to climb the well-known mountain
Doan ket khang chien	Government of union and resistance
Dom tan chay nui	A small ember, sleeping under ashes, may set on fire a whole mountain
Han-Viet	Chinese-Vietnamese
Hop thuong Quang Nam	Trade Association in Quang Nam
Huynh Thuc Khang tu truyen	Autobiography of HTK
Kim Van Kieu	Renowned poem by Nguyên Du
ky	Territorial division of Vietnam under French occupation
Mot Vai tien thoi nhan vat dong thoi voi Nguyên Truong To it ai biet: Nguyên Lo Trach	A contemporary of Nguyên Truong To, known by just a few persons: Nguyên Lo Trach
Nom	System of transcription of the Vietnamese language derived from Chinese characters
Phan Tay Ho tien sinh lich su	Biography of Phan Tay Ho
quôc ngu	Transcription of the Vietnamese language in roman type
Su Thât	Newspaper: "The Truth"
Tap loai	Miscellaneous
Thi tu tung thoai	Poems written in the jail
tien si	Doctoral title
Tieng Dan	Newspaper: "People's Voice"
viec the gioi	Events in the world
viec trong nuoc	Events in the country
Viet Minh	Allied Vietnamese

BIBLIOGRAPHY

Ajalbert, Jean. *Les destinées de l'Indochine: Voyage, Histoire, Colonisation* (Destiny of Indochina: Travel, History, Colonization). Paris: Louis Michaud, 1909.

Anh Minh [Ngo Thanh Nhan]. *Dat Su Cu Phan Sao Nam* (Extraordinary Activities of Phan Boi Chau). Hue: Anh Minh XB, 1950.

———. *Ngu Hanh Son Chi Si* (Patriots of the Ngu Hanh Mountains Area). Hue: Nha Xuat Ban Anh Minh, 1961.

———. *Nha cach mang cong khai khong dang phai nao het cu Huynh Thuc Khang.* (An open minded revolutionist, member of no party: M. Huynh Thuc Khang.) Hue: Nha Xuat Ban Anh Minh, 1953.

Bao Dai. *La dragon d'Annam* (The Dragon of Annam). Paris: Plon, 1980.

Boudarel, Georges. 1969 "Memoires de Phan Boi Chau." In *France-Asie/Asia* 22: 264–468. (Translation and notation of Phan Boi Chau. Phan Boi Chau Nien Bieu).

Brocheux, Pierre. *Histoire de l'Asie du Sud Est: Révoltes, Réformes, Révolutions* (History of Southeast Asia: Rebellions, Reforms, Revolutions). Recueil: Presses université de Lille, 1981.

Cao Xuan Duc. *Quoc Trieu Dang Khoa Luc* (Triennial Examinations). Saigon: Bo Quoc Gia Giao Duc, 1962.

———. *Quoc Trieu Huong Khoa luc* (Regional Examinations). Thanh Pho Ho Chi Minh. (Saigon): Nha Xuat Ban Thanh Pho Ho Chi Minh, 1993.

Chesneau, Jean. *Contribution à l'histoire de la Nation Vietnamienne* (A Contribution to the History of the Vietnamese Nation). Paris: Editions Sociales, 1955.

———. "Stages in the Development of the Vietnam National Movement, 1862–1940." *Past and Present* 7:63–75.

Chuong Thau. *Tho Van Huynh Thuc Khang (chon loc)* (Selected Prose and Poetry by HTK). Danang: 1908.

Dai San [Thich]. *Hai ngoai ky su* (Diary of Travel Abroad). Translated from Chinese to Vietnamese by Nguyen Duy Bot. Hue: Université, 1960.

Dang Thai Mai. *Hoi Ky* (Autobiography). Hanoi: Nha Xuat Ban Hoi Nha Van Vi, 1985.

———. *Van Tho Cach Mang Viet Nam Dau The Ky XX* (Vietnam's Revolutionary Prose and Poetry in the Early Twentieth Century). Hanoi: NXB Van Hoc, 1964. An extremely valuable work, for both the author's historical essay and the many primary materials reprinted.

Dao Duy Anh. *Nho nghi chieu hom* (Meditations at Twilight). Thanh Pho Hô Chí Minh. (Saigon): Tre voi su hop tác cua Asia-Média, 1989.

Dao Trinh Nhat. *Dong Kinh Nghia Thuc* (Free School of Dong Kinh [Tonkin]). Hanoi: Mai Linh XB, 1938.

Dao Van Hoi. *Ba Nha Chi Si Ho Phan* (Three Patriots Named Phan). Saigon: N.p., 1957.

Hoang Xuan Han. *Mot vai ki vang ve hoi nghi Da lat* (A Few Memories of the Meeting of Dalat). Saigon: [s.n.], 1971.

Hoang Van Dao. *Viet Nam Quoc Dan Dang, lich su dau tranh can dai, 1927–1954.* (The Vietnamese Nationalist Party, a History of the Modern Struggle, 1927–1954). Saigon: Nguyen Hoa Hi, 1965.

Ho Chi Minh. *Works.* Hanoi: Nha Xuat Ban Chinh tri quoc gia, 1995.

Huynh Thuc Khang (Minh Vien). "Kinh cao dong bao phu lao khang chien thu." (An appeal to resistance addressed to the population, women, and elderly persons). In Nguyen Q. Thang, *Huynh Thuc Khang Con nguoi va tho van* (The Man and the Writer). Saigon: Nha Xuat Ban Phu Quoc Vu Khanh Dac Trach Van Hoa, 1972.

———. *Phan Tay Ho Tien Sinh Lich Su* (A Biography of Phan Chu Trinh). Hue: Anh Minh XB, 1959. Written in 1926. Perhaps the most reliable source available for data on Phan Chu Trinh, particularly for the period before 1911.

———. *Tu Truyen* (Autobiography). Hue: Anh Minh XB, 1963.

———. *Tap dien van cua ong Huynh Thuc Khang* (Speech by Huynh Thuc Khang). Hanoi: Chan Phuong, 1926.

———. *Cuoc khang thue o Trung Ky* (A Narrative of the Movement against Taxes in 1908 in Trung Ky). Hanoi: Ich Tri, 1946.

———. *Buc thu tra loi chung (Y kien toi doi voi thoi cuoc)* (An Open Letter to the People). Hue: Tieng Dan, 1945.

———. "Kinh cao dong bao phu lao khang chien thu" (An Appeal to Resistance Addressed to the population, women, and elderly persons). In Nguyen Q. Thang, ed., *Huynh Thuc Khang Con nguoi va tho van*. Saigon: 1972.

Isoart, Paul. *Le phénomène national viêtnamien de l'indépendance unitaire à l'indépendance fractionnée* (Vietnam's National Problem from United Indochina to Fragmented Indochina). Pref. de Michel-Henry Fabre. Paris: Librairie générale de droit et de jurisprudence, 1961.

Le Thanh Khoi. *Le Vietnam, histoire et civilisation* [Vietnam, History and Civilization). Paris: Les Éditions de Minuit, 1995.

Louis Hénard, Nicole. "Un épisode ignoré de l'histoire du protectorat de l'Annam en 1909" (An Obliviated Episode of the History of Annam under the Protectorate in 1909). *Bulletin de l'École Française d'Extrême-Orient*. LXXV. Paris: 1986.

Marr, David. *Vietnamese Anticolonialism (1885–1925)*. Berkeley: University of California Press, 1971.

Maybon, Charles. *Histoire moderne du pays d'Annam* (A Modern History of Annam). Paris: Plon, 1920. Deals with the period 1592–1820.

Mus, Paul. *Le Vietnam chez lui* (Vietnam at Home). Paris: Centre d'études de politique étrangère, 1946.

Ngo Thanh Nhan [Anh Minh]. *Cu Sao Nam 15 Nam Bi Giam Long o Hue* (Phan Boi Chau's Fifteen Years of Detention in Hue). Hue: Anh Minh XB, 1956.

Nguyên Hien Le. *Dong Kinh Nghia Thuc* (Free School of Dong Kinh [Tonkin]). Saigon: Published by the author, 1956.

Nguyên Q. Thang. *Huynh Thuc Khang Con nguoi va tho van*. (The Man and the Writer). Saigon: Nha Xuat Ban Phu Quoc Vu Khanh Dac Trach Van Hoa, 1972.

Nguyên The Anh. *Kinh Te va Xa Hoi Viet-Nam duoi cac Vua Trieu Nguyên* (Vietnam's Economy and Society under the Nguyên Dynasty Kings). Saigon: NXB Trinh Bay, 1968.

———. *Phong trao chong thue mien Trung nam 1908, qua cac Chau Ban trieu Duy*

Tan (The Movement against Taxes in 1908 as Seen through the Royal Chronicles of King Duy Tan's Reign). Saigon: Bo van hoa giao duc va Thanh nien, 1973.

———. *La Monarchie des Nguyen de la mort de Tu Duc à 1925* (The Nguyen Monarchy from the Death of Tu Duc to 1925). Paris: l'Harmattan, 1992.

Nguyên Trai. *Gia Huan Ca* (Songs of Family Exhortation). Saigon: Nha Xuat Ban Tan Vi, 1953. Prepared and edited by Dinh Gia Thieu.

Nguyên Van Ngoc. *Tu diep vien nhay du tro thanh Giam Doc Cong An Trung bo* (Carrier from a Parachutist and Spy up to the Director of Safety of Trung Bo). Hanoi: Cong An Nhan Dan, 1988.

Nguyên Van Trung. *Chu Nghia thuc dan o Viet Nam thuc chat va huyen thoai* (The Theory of Imperialism in Vietnam: Ideology and Mythology). Saigon: Nam Son, 1963.

Nguyên Van Xuân. *Phong Trao Duy Tan* (The Modernist Movement). Saigon: La Boi, 1970.

Nguyên Xuân Tho. *Histoire de la pénétration française au Vietnam (1958–1987)* (A History of French Penetration in Vietnam). Aiea, HI: Giao Hoi Phat Giao Linh Son The gioi trung tam van hoa linh son, Chua Linh Son, 1993.

Pasquier, Pierre. *L'Annam d'Autrefois* (Old Annam). Paris: Challamel, 1907.

Pham Cao Duong. "Mot vai chu truong cua Trieu Dinh Hue trong Hoa-Uoc Qui-Mui (25–8–1883)" (Some Assumptions of the Hue Court in the 1883 Peace Settlement). In *Su Dia* (history and geography) 2: 52–60 and 4: 104–10.

———. *Thuc Trang cua gioi nong dan Viet Nam duoi thoi Phap thuoc* (The State of Vietnamese Country Classes under the French Protectorate). Saigon: Khai Tri, 1967.

Pham Khac Hoe. *Tu trieu dinh Hue den chien khu Viet Bac* (From the Court of Hue to the Tonkinese *Maquis*). Hue: Nha Xuat Ban Thuan Hoa, 1987.

Pham The Ngu. *Viet Nam Van Hoc Su, Van hoc hien dai, 1862–1945* (A History of Vietnamese Literature: Contemporary Literature, 1862–1954). Saigon: Nha Xuat Ban Quoc Hoc Tung Thuc, 1965.

Pham Van Son. *Viet Su Tan Bien: Viet Nam Khang Phap Su* (A New Compilation of Vietnamese History: A History of Vietnam's Resistance to France). Saigon: Nha Xuat Ban Tran Huu Thoan, 1962.

———. "Thai-do va hanh-dong cua nhan-si Viet-Nam trong khoang dua the ky XX" (Attitudes and Activities of the Vietnamese Scholar-Gentry at the Opening of the Twentieth Century). In *Su Dia* (history and geography) 6: 37–62.

Phan Bôi Châu. *Khong Hoc Dang* (Clarifying Confucian Studies). 2 vols. Hue: NXB Anh Minh, 1957.

———. *Phan Bôi Châu Nien Bieu* (Year to Year Activities of Phan Bôi Châu). Hanoi: NXB Van Su Dia, 1957. One of the most valuable sources on the topic. French translation by Georges Boudarel, 1969.

———. "Viet-nam Vong Quoc Su" (History of the Loss of Vietnam). Saigon: Dai Hoc Van Khoa, 1961. Contains both the Chinese original and a Vietnamese translation by Ta Thuc Khai.

———. "Thu goi Toan Quyen Beau" (A Letter to Governor-General Beau). In *Nghien Cuu Lich Su* (Historical Studies) 66: 8–14. Also in the *Nguyen, Phan Chu Trinh:* 61–100. Original Chinese in Nam Phong 103: 25–34.

Phan Khoi. *Canh cao cac nha hoc phiet* (An Admonition against the Intelligentsia Cliques). Saigon: Phu nu Tan Van, 1930.

Phan Khoang. *Viet Nam Phap Thuoc su* (History of Vietnam under French Rule). Saigon: Khai Tri XB, 1960. The title is somewhat misleading, as more than half of the book deals with the period 1802–83.

Phan Thi Minh Le. "Huynh Thuc Khang (1876–1947) dans le courant des réformistes du Trung Ky, sous la domination coloniale française" (HTK in the Trend of the Reformists under French Domination). New system doctoral thesis, Université Paris VII.

Roubaud, Louis. *Vietnam la tragédie Indochinoise* (Vietnam, Indochinese Tragedy). Paris: Valois, 1931.

Thai Bach. *Thi Van Quoc Cam thoi Phap Thuoc* (Forbidden National Literature of the French Colonial Period). Saigon: Nha Xuat Ban Khai Tri, 1968.

Trân Huy Lieu. *Lich Su Tam Muoi Nam Chong Phap* (History of Eighty Years against the French). 2 vols. Hanoi: NXB Su Hoc, 1961.

Trân Huynh Sach. "Tran Qui Cap" (Biography by TQC). Unpublished document written in January 1958 by Tran Huynh Sach, TQC's pupil.

Trân Trong Kim. *Viet Nam Su Luoc*. (Outline History of Vietnam). Saigon: Tan Viet XB, 1958.

———. *Mot con gio bui* (A Whirlwind). Saigon: Vinh Son, 1969.

Trinh Van Thao. *Vietnam du Confucianisme au Communisme* (Vietnam from Confucianism to Communism). Paris: L'Harmattan, 1990.

Truong Ba Can. *Nguyen Truong To: L'Homme et ses écrits* (Nguyen Truong To: The Man and His Writings). Thanh Pho Ho Chi Minh: Nha Xuat Ban Thanh Pho Ho Chi Minh, 1988.

Tung Lam. *Cuoc Doi Cach Mang Cuong De* (The Revolutionary Life of Cuong Dê). Saigon: Ton That Le, 1957. Originally a 1943 interview in Japanese with Cuong Dê.

Viollis, Andrée. *Indochine SOS*. Paris: Gallimard, 1935.

Vong Dinh Quang. *Tho van Huynh Thuc Khang* (Huynh Thuc Khang's Prose and Poetry). Hanoi: Van Hoc, 1965.

———. *Hoi Ky ve cu Phan va cu Huynh* (Memories of the Honorable PBC and HTK). Hanoi: Van Hoc, 1992.

Woodside, Alexander B. *Community and Revolution in Modern Vietnam*. Boston: Houghton Mifflin, 1976.

Records

CAOM, Aix-en-Provence.
Personal files from the Service de protection du corps expeditionnaire, SPCE No.: 351, 352, 353, 354, 355, 364, 365, 366, 367, 368, 369, 370, 371, 372, 373, 374, 376.

General Safety: From Surete Generale Indochinoise: Series: 65455: (1) Sogny's Annual Report 26–27; 65463, 31/8/27. Sogny's Report.
Vietnam's Record Office: Antifrench Movements within Annamite Countries from 1905 to 1918, no. 124139.
Archives of the Vietnamese Communist Party. A collection of the decrees HTK signed as interior minister and temporary president during the year 1946.
French records:
A.F: C22, C.27.C.401, D.3433
N.F: 3: D.3433. C.50: D598, 968. C: 54: 633,
Residence superieure de l'Annam: Dossier 1, 2, 3, 4, 5.
Fonds Guernut: Government general de l'indochine: Carton: 53527.

Newspapers and Reviews:

Cochinchine Française. 1908.—*Courrier d'Haiphong.* 1980.—*Indochinoise.* 1908.
L'Avenir du Tonkin. 1908. L'Annam. 14 Juin 1926, no. 138.17/2/1927.—Huu Thanh. 1922–1924.—Song Huong (Hue). 1936–1937.
Tieng Dan. (1927–1943) [People's Voice]. Collection de Versailles. JO.94.195. Microfilm: D.996.—Trang An. (Hue). 1937–1943.—Trung Bac Tan Van. No. 5463. 4/7/35.
Bulletin de la Société des Etudes Indochinoises (B.S.E.I.). T.XXXVII. 1962. Texier Muriel. "Les origines du Mandarinat et des lettrés Mandarinat" [The Indochinese studies society's edition. Origins of Mandarinate and mandarin scholars]—Bulletin Des Amis du Vieux Hue (B.A.V.H.) (1914–1944).
Bulletin de l'Ecole Française d'Extrême-Orient (B.E.F.O.). T.LXXV. Paris. 1986.
Cahier de Voeux Annamites (Présenté à M. Alexandre Varenne). [A collection of Annamite wishes introduced to M.A.V.]. Saigon. 1925. Nghien Cuu Su Dia Ha Noi [Studies on history and geography] Hanoi. Nam Phong [South wind] (1925–26) no. 100–102, 104, 117, 112.
Phu Nu Tan Van. [The new woman]. (1929–1934) Su Dia Saigon [History and geography]. Ed. Saigon. (1975).

8

Trinh Van Thao

The 1925 Generation of Vietnamese Intellectuals and Their Role in the Struggle for Independence

Introduction

This research on intellectuals of the 1925 generation and on the fellow travelers of the Vietnamese Communist Party during the first war of resistance (1945–54) is part of a process of identification, description, and reconstitution of a total historical and social experience (revolution, conflicts of values, civil and foreign wars). The sole aim of this research is to understand the social meaning of the collective commitment of the intellectuals educated at the French School in Indochina (Vietnam) and to perceive the reality of the "cultures of each class" of these "new scholars." It develops by echoing and sometimes acting as a counterpoint to many works on contemporary Vietnam by historians and political scientists (Paul Mus, Jean Chesneaux, David Marr, Daniel Hémery, Pierre Brocheux). Beyond the simple sphere of Vietnam, the aim is to define the meaning of the social links between power and knowledge in the sinicized world. By scrutinizing intellectual postures identifiable in historical conjunctures that highlight intellectuals along with the other collective actors of the "society as a whole" and the state, this study plans to establish a dynamic sociology of the social classes in contemporary societies.

1. Asian Intellectuals: A Theoretical Background

Such was, in any case, the epistemological path taken in an earlier essay (*Viet Nam du confucianisme au communisme*, 1990) in order to understand the crisis of classic intellectuals, the *nho si* (scholars) stemming from the Confucian world, those of the 1862 and 1907 generations, destabilized by the sudden arrival of the colonial system. In order to study the social destiny of their "heirs" taken in the biological (filiation), social (class of the *nho si*), and cultural acceptance of the "1925 generation,"[1] the author intends to build up the notion of "scholar culture" from a combination of "biographical"[2] data accompanying the process of the scholar socialization, which can be broken down into three groups of indicators:

1. The patrimonial variables that define the "social being in his or her primo-socialization" (what one receives from birth to school): social origin of the family, geographical origin, symbolic capital of the family (titles and academic ranks of the parents, grandparents, and other ancestors of the lineage if necessary), sociability and proximity[3] network, religious[4] sociability, and last but not least the "geomancy" variable omnipresent in the collective imagination.[5]
2. Variables of consolidation: those that are a matter of "possession," the academic achievements (diploma, academic distinctions, recognized autodidact), professional career (professional status before, during, and after the revolution of August 1945) certifying maturity in scholarly, professional, artistic, and social skills.[6]
3. Variables of *enlargement* and *extension:* from symbolic capital to economic, political, or religious capital. Enter in this category all variables indicating social position changes except the sphere of professional specialization like the position within the Communist Party—and its "progressive" or "democratic allies"—or within the state and the instances of symbolic power (Front of the Homeland, Movement for Peace). The interest of this category is to show in the act how social appreciation is produced from symbolic capital and to bring up to date the new relational pattern between the state and the intellectuals.

Like Edward P. Thompson in his study of the English working class, the author considers "the class as a cultural and social forming, resulting from the process that one can study only if one examines the development during a relatively long historical period" (*The Formation of the English Working Class* [Paris: Gallimard-Threshold, 1988], 15). In this sense, this study is an integral part of the tradition of works that object to a priori constructions about relations between classes insofar as they ignore, or at least underestimate, the link stressed by the English historian between experiences of class and consciousness of class.

> The conscience of class is the way these experiences are translated in cultural terms and embodied in traditions, systems of value, ideas and institutional forms. Unlike the experience of class, the conscience of class does not appear as determined. One can indeed discern a logic in reactions of groups of people with similar professions facing similar experiences, but we can not formulate laws. The conscience of class arises in the same way in different places and periods (times), but never entirely in the same way. (13–14)

Thus, the objectification of class behaviors is effective and possible only by considering the "real context," which gives them meaning. The "staging" of historical conjunctures as "a sociological drama with multiple characters" (G. Balandier), as in each process coming from the sociology of action, requires here multiple "lightings" and recourse to the theories of socialization (Emile Durkheim, Maurice Halbwachs) and interaction (Erving Goffman) without objecting at all to the real effectiveness (i.e., relative) of notions derived from genetic structuralism. Or, in other words, the notion of "intellectual class" ceases to be an artifact only when it is put into perspective as a "collective actor" in a specific historical conjuncture.

Like Thompson, the author is convinced that the culture of class can only be perceived and expressed under categories of norms, values, and "collective subconsciousness" (P. Kaufman)[7] when it is in contact with the social experience with which it is intimately linked. In fact, it belongs to social philosophy[8] to speak about social classes independent of the real social movements in which they are involved. Such is the case for individualistic and credulous allotment peasants, for the inexperienced and swindled workers of June 1848, and for the shady politicians of the Eighteenth Brumaire . . . , for the new clerks and technicians of the state, for the gentlemen, for the administrators and writers . . . , for the Old Regime and the Revolution.

Conjuncturalistic intentionality was introduced twenty years ago through a modern reading of the journalistic and political writings of K. Marx and F. Engels (*Marx, Engels, et le journalisme revolutionnaire*, 3 vols. [Paris: Anthropos, 1978–80]). This reading was made, it is true, under the effects of the Althusserian categories of "theoretical practices" and ideological state machinery. Conjuncturalistic intentionality posed the postulate of the necessity to take into account both the structural trends (in the event, the variations of the European labor culture) and the singularity and opacity of the communist action in the 1940s (the real logic of the event). The author still thinks that what has saved the Marxist theory[9] of the history of speculative metaphysics are the masterpieces of the concrete analysis of concrete situations and of dramatic experiences undergone by nations and peoples throughout the last century and that, seen from this point of view, the line separating *Le 18 Brumaire de Louis Bonaparte* (the Eighteenth Brumaire of Louis Bonaparte, 1852) of Marx from *L'Ancient regime et la revolution* (The Ancient Regime and the Revolution) of De Tocqueville is faint.

In the perspective opened a few years ago by "*Viet Nam du confucianisme au communisme*" (1990), this research aims less to perceive the so-called laws of reproduction and intellectual socialization than to locate the founding paradigms of the Confucian ethic: adherence to community-family values, to the legitimacy of mandarin power (intellectual-communist) as guarantor of oriental monarchy (paternalistic total state), to asceticism and agrarian egalitarianism. This study aims also to reconstruct the mechanisms of transmission and reception of the ancestral inheritance by the "fellow travelers" of the 1925 generation who rallied more or less, totally or partially, to the political and social project of the VCP (Vietnamese Communist Party) in 1945, even if it entails unveiling—under the cover of a phraseology borrowed from the Bolshevist revolution and to a lesser extent from Maoism[10]— the remarkable continuity of the scholar culture of the fathers and their descendants and the weight of the mandarin habitus.[11] The issue of the study is to be found at the confrontation of the identitarian practices of the actors, with regard to the constraints of the event that they have undergone, with the social rationality reconstituted post festum by the observer. Here resides the ethical question of all anthropological research of this order, the social criticism of the intellectual itinerary of the Vietnamese radical Left in the 1920s.

2. Socialization and Intellectual Culture:
A Diachronic Approach to the Three Generations
of Conjuncture (1862–1945)

Faced with the polysemy of a sociologically indistinct category in modern societies that may allow ambivalent connotations, the only fellow travelers of the VCP evoked in this study are those who had access to the power of leadership, command, and notoriety, thanks to their own skills, whether general or specialized. In the sinicized cultural world, this concerns persons combining knowledge and power as Mencius defined it: "The intellectual governs men, the manual worker lets himself be governed by men" (lao tâm gia tri nhan, lao luc gia tri u nhan). Before the colonial irruption, the source of this intellectual power derives from a meritocratic-type educational system based on selection through competitive examinations. In Vietnam, the colonial authorities did, in fact, modernize the pedagogical content and rationalize the organization of the educational apparatus, in the spirit and on the lines of the French model, without modifying the social logic with which it was completely in tune.[12]

Like the Sino-Vietnamese linguistic (syntagmatic) structure that very often, in the final analysis, only determines the functional status of the syntagms according to their place in the sentence, this study adopts a deliberately pragmatic standpoint insofar as it only identifies the intellectual movement through its effective role objectified in and by historical conjunctures. The construction of the corpus proceeds from this double principle of unity (the revolutionary rupture) and plurality (the multiple situations undergone by the collective actor) via historical selection, that is, essentially coming from proper name indices in political, social, and literary history[13] reference books. The combination of sociological variables (age, sex, birthplace, social origin, diploma, career, intellectual works) and social practices, identified in the long term (1862–1945), of the individual biographies of 222 intellectuals and collective history highlights three "generations of conjuncture": that of the resistant scholars of the Cân Vuong movement (1862), that of the "modernists" of the Duy Tân movement (1907), and that of 1925 of the New Intellectuals formed in French schools. But, beyond the emergence of groups distinguished by their date of birth, their training framework, and their rites of socialization, the survey reveals all along the historical chain the reality of generational cultures, the affinities and/or incompatibilities.

Thus, the "minimal" combination of class variables (social scale), symbolic capital (the academic hierarchy), and the production order (literature) of the Cân Vuong[14] scholar generation opposes two groups of intellectuals clearly characterized, although unequally distributed.

> The majority group of mandarin resistant scholars of the Cân Vuong opposed to any compromises with the foreigner, mostly natives of the north and the center, graduates of the triennial competitive examinations, who produced a patriotic literature in verse and classic prose. Their symbolic figure is represented by the doctors (*tien si*) Phan Dinh Phung, Nguyên Quang Bich, and a southerner, the poet Do Chieu.[15]

> The group composed of intellectuals of the center and the south rallied to the colonial order and of extroverts by religious conversion (the Catholic Petrus Truong Vinh Ky),[16] opportunism (Hoang Cao Khai), or simple ambition (Tôn Tho Tuong),[17] producing on a mainly Confucian moral background works destined to facilitate the French-Vietnamese contacts in particular in the linguistic field (lexicography, translation, popularization).

The conjuncture of 1905 marked by the nationalistic awakening of the Far East (China and Japan) and the Duy Tân movement (modernization) prolonging through to Vietnam shows two different groups. The first is composed of the Duy Tân modernist scholars of the Tonkin Institute (Dong Kinh Nghia Thuc).[18] It brings together the graduates of the great classic competitive examinations who were opposed to the official mandarinate and the neophytes of an emerging "civil society" who prepared the economic, social, and cultural conditions of Vietnamese modernity following the example of the Chinese neo-Confucians. The second group, more heterodox, is composed of scholars and part-scholars of Nam Phong[19] (with mixed training, coming mainly from the school of interpreters). These were in quest of historical legitimacy and tormented by the underlying desire for syncretism between the Occident and the Orient. Although the modernists shone during the first decade, their decline began shortly after and was completed with the very symbolic disappearance of Vice Doctor Phan Châu Trinh and the arrest of Phan Bôi Châu. The cultural field passed from then on under the domination of the Nam Phong "syncretists." They were reinforced by the French victory at the end of World War I and by the colonial reformism of Albert Sarraut.

Finally, the conjuncture of 1925 heralded the irruption of a new intelligentsia protesting against the Western order with its own means and values learned and internalized at the French-Vietnamese school. This generation, whose history was inseparable from the contemporary process of the struggle for independence, saw the confrontation between two rival groups both challenging the colonial power increasingly weakened by the economic crisis, "the Popular Front," the French defeat in Europe, and the Japanese occupation in Asia. Opposed to the "petit bourgeois" and liberal intellectuals graduated from the French universities and *grand ecoles* and the heirs of the University of Hanoi, contributors to the Ngay Nay (1935–40) and the Thanh Nghi (1941–45) reviews, a new intelligentsia appeared. This radical and Marx-inspired intelligentsia came from high schools, the youth organizations, and the dynamic Vietnamese Student Association. They eagerly took up the radical slogans of nationalist leaders such as Nguyên An Ninh and Phan Van Truong. This new intelligentsia, which was largely infiltrated by the Communist Party and its allies, contributed to organs of opinion that became *virtual parties* (Antonio Gramsci).[20] However, the ideological antagonism between the different groups, from the radicalism and the voluntarism on one side to the apoliticism and the legalism on the other, often masked different social, geographical, generational, and cultural positions.[21] When replaced in the long process of struggle for national emancipation, the conjuncture of 1945 and the mechanisms of intellectual alignment bring out clearly a line of cleavage separating two different intellectual cultures. On the one hand, there was the "national-communist" culture of the leaders of the Viet Minh Front, derived from the Confucian scholars. This groups together the direct representatives or the descendants of the resistant scholars of the Cân Vuong, modernists of the Duy Tân, and the young radicals of 1925, who were still at the University of Hanoi in the 1940s. Most of them belong to the scholar culture of the north and the center. Like the essayist Dang Thai Mai, their vision of the world is in tune with the Sino-Soviet geopolitics of farming revolutions and messianic movements despite its industrial and scientific references.

On the other hand, there emerged the less clear-cut world vision of the leaders of the future Southern Republic (1954–75). It grouped together in a fluctuating entity of "rallied" scholars of former times, "syncretists" of the Nam Phong, and Westernizing intellectuals of *La Lutte* (The Struggle)[22] in the south and its equivalent *Tu Luc Van Doan* (Autonomous Literary Group)[23] in the north. They are the guardians of another, national-liberal, individualistic culture, which inclined them more toward a rather pro-Western[24] cosmopolitanism. Therefore, a double symmetrical equation can be established, which reveals the social rationality of the ideological and political scene of modern, contemporary Vietnam.

1. Cân Vuong (1885) + Duy Tân (1907) + radicals (1925) = national-communist culture (recurrent Confucianism + north/center + Sino-Soviet geopolitics)
2. The rallied (1885) + Nam Phong (1917) + Westernizing intellectuals (1930) = liberal-nationalist culture (individualism + north/south + pro-Western cosmopolitanism)

A gradual decolonization could have transformed this cultural duality into a political bipolarity indispensable for any form of democratic choice between a radical Marxist Left and a liberal, democratic Right. However like the other countries finding themselves in the sights of the superpowers that have fought for the world since 1945, decolonization became the stakes of an international "cold" war, which, transposed to the level of Vietnam, became a regional "hot" war. This disturbed the balance of power (nationalists-communists) without, however, modifying the balance of tendencies (Right-Left).[25]

This study plans to define the mechanisms and social logic of the intellectual commitment in the face of historical conjunctures as a determined collective action. This is determined, on the one hand, by the balance of tendencies—in this case the ethos of responsibility[26] as defined by M. Weber, or the mandarin habitus—and, on the other hand, by the circumstances of the balance of power at the time, as shown in the following diagram:

                    Ethos of social classes (scholarship and responsibility)
Political activism   *Socialization*
                    social networks (relations of power)
or

    intellectual political activism = relations of power + intellectual milieu and
                    socioeconomic environment

In other words, through the collective commitment of the Vietnamese intellectuals in 1945, the aim is to highlight the conjugated effects of the "consciousness of class" of the scholars opposed to the state and the peasants (to whom they were organically linked according to the Confucian tradition), and the sociability networks that are responsible for organizing them as a collective force. Consciousness of class (effects of structure) and sociability networks (effects of conjuncture) are simply the two faces of a same social logic, that of scholar socialization. The longitudinal approach to intergenerational relations from 1862 to 1945 reveals the existence of a sort of remarkable continuity from Confucianism to communism. Whereas the study of the fellow travelers of 1925 of the Communist Party brings out the diversity of the elements of the "intellectual culture," it also reveals the emergence of the Right-Left bipolarity of the heirs of 1862 and 1907 and of the coexistence of three subcultures: the liberal-progressive culture of the "back from France," the liberal-progressive culture of the "syncretists" of the University of Hanoi, and the communist culture of the French Communist Party (FCP) and the Comintern.

3. Intellectual Cultures: Synchronic Approaches to the Generation of 1925

In this section, representative intellectuals of the three cultural components will be treated. We will not return here to an earlier work devoted to the training of the leaders of the Vietnamese Communist Party from its historical chief to the most important members of the civil or military commandment apparatus.[27] Let us simply mention the fact that the various versions of the official history tend to pass over the scholarly, or even mandarin, social origin of most of the famous leaders, such as Ho Chi Minh, Truong Chinh, and Pham Van Dong, to name but a few.[28] In this corpus about the intellectual companions of

Uncle Ho, it suffices to read the autobiographical account of Trân Van Giau to grasp the substance of what is the social destiny of a communist leader in the first half of the twentieth century.

The Communist Culture

It would be more original to look more closely at the relation (cross-influence) between the communist socialization and the revolutionary conjuncture of the 1930s through the memoirs of a southern man, the former ambassador of the Democratic Republic of Vietnam to France, Mai Van Bô, who, without being the Saint Simon of Vietnam, has at least the outspokenness of a man of the land. It concerns a biography of his lifelong friend, the composer Luu Huu Phuoc, who wrote the hymn "Tieng goi thanh nien" (Call to the Youth), former minister of the provisional government of the National Liberation Front of the south.[29] The author describes how the intellectuals of the south (most of whom were from the well-off or middle classes of the Mekong Delta[30] and the Saigon area) came to Stalinism via the National Marxism (D. Hémery) of Nguyên An Ninh.[31] Thus can be observed the paths of people like Professor Phan Van Bach, the attorney Pham Ngoc Thuân, and Dr. Hô Dàc Di, uprooted from the scholar culture, who were French by education if not by conviction. They spoke out violently, in the language of Molière, against the colonial system in the name of the values of the French Revolution, of human rights and peoples' rights.[32] These southern communists took up the revolution with all the juvenile ardor of pure products of the university under the colonial system. They were in fact young people born in the 1920s who went to the University of Hanoi after the French defeat of 1940. They had the ideal profile of politically committed activists who were unreserved, unquestioning, and very often uncritical.

When recalling his adolescence spent at Can Tho College with his childhood friends, M. V. Bô particularly remembers the highly charged atmosphere of the late 1930s. The drivers of the buses linking the eastern capital (Saigon) to the western capital (Can Tho) brought news from Saigon: the preparation of the Indochinese Congress (aborted), the imminent arrival in Indochina of a Commission of Inquiry (Justin Godard mission). Far from the suspicious eyes of the supervisors, teenage pupils debated solemnly in the college courtyard about the national and international situation, as if they already belonged to some secret society. The arrival at the college of a young "back from France" intellectual, a graduate in literature and doctor in law, aroused the awakening national feeling (39–45).[33] Shortly afterward, they were to be boarders together at the great Lycée Pétrus Ky in Saigon. The D'Artagnan Luu Huu Phuoc then joined the "Three Musketeers" (Nguyên My Ca, Nguyên Thành Nguyên, and Mai Van Bô). They then realized that the conviviality between masters and pupils and between peers, which they had known and appreciated at Can Tho, was lost forever. Here everything was larger and more majestic; the school corridors seemed interminably long during their spare time. The sports ground appeared immense. Everything gave the impression of a quiet strength able to withstand the test of time. What remains is always the same unkind and unfriendly way the native pupils see the school authorities: the headmaster (Valençot), who used to stroke his long beard with delight, his fat belly hanging down to his knees despite an enormous belt, which he had to hitch up occasionally to be able to move;[34] the secretary general with his nose askew and his grayish face, as cold as ice; his Vietnamese assistant, who gesticulated and howled like an orator before the crowd each time he spoke to a pupil in his office. Almost twenty years after the description of the Lycée Buoi by Hoàng Ngoc Phach, the gallery of portraits of teachers is hardly better: "N. H. (a Vietnamese), still teaching despite pronounced marks of leprosy; his Alsatian colleague with the unbearable voice; the impressively stout old teacher with the cautious gait, his face ever red, who boasted to all around that only wine could quench his thirst and who had just completed a doctorate on religious sects in Indochina; the young female philosophy teacher with the face of a blonde doll, puffy cheeks, round eyes, a trumpetlike mouth . . . !" However, their ferocity is reserved for two or three really detested teachers. The teacher L. was a Vietnamese "back from France," with French nationality, and who despised the culture of his country of origin, about which he was completely ignorant. A teacher of literature, he dared to declare outright that "*Kim Vân Kiêu* is not a work of literature because Viet Nam has no literature"! The other target of the pupils was a French teacher of the final year, called J. "In class, he had the habit of stamping his heels on the desk and howling like a madman: 'This is the only way to get Annamites like you to start thinking!' . . . The boor disguised as a pedagogue, red in the face and his mouth poised to pour out obscene insults, or the witch G. with the owl-like eyes peering shortsightedly through glasses balancing on a pointed nose . . . their presence is a constant reminder of the reality of a humiliated and defeated country. . . . As for the Vietnamese teachers, they were conspicuous for their discretion as well as, for some of them, an immoderate taste for gambling" (47, 48, 49).[35]

However, in 1937 Petrus Ky is no longer the distant, silent ivory tower of the past. The social and political struggles on the outside never ceased to have repercussions in the very heart of the school despite elaborate precautions. Shortly after their arrival in Saigon, M. V. Bô and his friends witnessed the strike of the railworkers of the city and its suburbs (Di An), calling for pay raises. There followed rumors announcing the start of solidarity strikes in Gia Lâm and other parts of the country. Although the Indochinese Congress was finally suspended, the social movement continued to grow. On 1 January 1937, thousands of peasants from the suburbs and the surrounding provinces headed for the center to support the workers on strike by demonstrating behind banners demanding democratic liberties, social measures, and the release of political prisoners.

> Toward the end of 1937, other news announced the release of a thousand prisoners, most of whom were amnestied militant communists, and the agreement to the workers' claims for an eight-hour day. At that moment, we had particularly noted the fact that the militant communists had acted courageously against fascism and colonialism by demanding the creation of a front to struggle for peace, democracy, and rice for the workers. In our eyes, these are knights of modern times deserving admiration. We were happy to see that these fighters had regained their liberty. At the same time, some Trotskyists who claimed to be members of the Fourth International were considered by some to be revolutionaries. However, they attacked the communists and pretended to be revolutionaries, criticizing everything and everyone. What do they want? We were definitely unable either to understand or to befriend those people. (Mai Van Bô, Luu Huu Phuoc 1989: 50–51)[36]

The school year 1939–40 is marked by the beginning of the hostilities of World War II. Most of the pupils no longer had the heart to work. The French teachers whispered among themselves and looked stupefied. Only one thing was sure: they were about to embark on a ship out of control. The headmaster died in a plane accident when returning to France (Mai Van Bô, Luu Huu Phuoc 1989: 50–51).[37] A mathematics teacher taught them a totally new subject: passive resistance (60–61). During this episode the friends from Petrus Ky successfully created a pupils' association placed under the patronage of progressive personalities of Saigon like the pharmacist Trân Kim Quan and the engineers Hô Van Lai and Nguyên Van Duc.

After passing their baccalaureate exams in autumn 1940, M. V. Bô and his friends left for Hanoi to enter the university. Soon after witnessing the invasion of the Japanese army, they heard the news of the uprising of Bac Son. Shortly afterward arrived the news of the crushing of the communist movement of Nam Ky by the colonial authorities. The university was in a state of shock under the effects of the events: capitulation of France to Germany, capitulation of the colonial army in Indochina to the Japanese army, failure of the communist risings in the north and south. Public opinion is divided between partisans of the pro-Japanese "zone of co-prosperity" (Dai Dông'A), who demonstrated noisily, and the relatively discreet supporters of the colonial order. As for the "revolutionaries," they tried to get organized. In this context were launched the "back to the roots" movements (Hành Huong) Xêp But Nghiên (put away the inkpot and pen) and Thanh Nien Tiên Phong (avant-garde youth), all on the initiative of the VCP. These actions are in line with the will of the student leaders to focus on patriotic feeling, to make everyone aware of the historical and cultural unity of the country from north to south so as to neutralize the regional feelings still alive among young people from the three Vietnamese "countries."[38] During the period 1940–45, thanks to the IU (Indochinese Union) and its hostels, Hanoi was an ideal place for students from all over to mix and mingle. Under the pressure of events, the campus became a place for rival factions to struggle for influence. The VCP, VNQDD (Viet Nam Quoc Dan Dang), or the Kuo-Ming-Tang of Viet Nam, the Dai Viet, and others were already fighting among themselves to challenge the colonial power, which was still fierce albeit weakened. Student leaders stand out who made names for themselves in the conquest of the Student Association of Hanoi.[39] Until a clear majority appears, everyone accepts Pham Biêu Tâm (Hue), hospital intern, to head the Executive Committee of the Association of Vietnamese Students in 1941–42.[40] In 1942–43, with Duong Duc Hiên as president, the association will be superseded by the *tich cuc*, who will increase their hegemony in 1943–44 before failing by a small majority in 1945 against the tougher resistance of the partisans of the VNQDD.[41] However, for M. V. Bô, the dice were already cast, and there was no doubt that "in reality in 1944 the IU Hanoi had become a hotbed of revolution" (134).

On his return to the Viet Minh headquarters based in Viet Bat, Duong Duc Hiên argued for the creation of the Democratic party[42] (Dân Chu Dang), which was to become an "important" element of the Viet Minh.[43] By order of the leaders of the Viet Minh (or the party?) in Hanoi, M. V. Bô and his comrades were invited to return immediately to the south in order to prepare the general uprising. These statements reduce to very little the thesis of a spontaneous movement of the population! The reality is without any doubt more complex than our memorialist claims and than the vision given by history. However, the passage describing the inner conflict of Luu Huu Phuoc, torn between the pursuit of dental studies already advanced and revolutionary commitment, gives this impression (138, 139).[44]

On their return to the south (Nam Tiên), a bicycle journey of more than a thousand kilometers, M. V. Bô and his friends became closer to the intellectuals of Saigon and influenced them in depth in the framework of the local section of Hôi Truyên Ba Quoc Ngu.[45] This section grouped together bourgeois elements[46] that constituted the faithful core of the liberal intelligentsia of Saigon in all the radical movements known there from 1947 to the end of the war. However, in this race for power they came up against the local opposing groups: pro-Japanese of the *Viet Nam Phuc Quôc Dông Minh Hôi*; the Quôc Gia Dôc Lâp of Professor Hô Van Ngà; the Trotskyists, who took over the police and public safety departments abandoned by the Japanese; and the political-religious sects "Hoa Hao" and "Cao Dai," which were more or less militarized. M. V. Bô was faithful to the same version of history, attributing the southern intellectual movements to the initiative of the party (Xu Uy). He gave the communists all the credit for total control of the Thanh Niên Tiên Pong. This control was precisely assumed by the twenty or so students sheltering in the south, like one of their chiefs, Huynh Van Tieng (161).[47]

The final outcome of this socialization and politicization path of the student youth of the 1930s (1930–45) will be the takeover by the VCP on 25 August 1945 (despite a very divided leadership on the date of engagement), whose spearhead was constituted by paramilitary units of the Thanh Niên Tiên Phong.⁴⁸ The struggle for power ended, after a chaotic transition, with the elimination of the local opponent of the Xu Uy, putting, in fact, an end to the strategy of the united front advocated by Ho Chi Minh. The continuation of the long resistance and its extension to the North, after the failure of the diplomatic solution, provoked the moving of the focus of the French-Vietnamese war to the north and the absorption of the intellectuals of this tendency by the war machinery of triumphant Maoism. The uneasiness of this group of communists, since their withdrawal to the north of the 17th Parallel the day after the Geneva agreements, can be easily understood. So can the impatience shown by this group to start the struggle again to free the south in the 1960s.

The communist culture of which they are the guardians constitutes itself by severing links with the historical, cultural, and even linguistic roots of a country mutilated by colonization and at odds with a privileged social middle class, which most of them come from and which puts them in an awkward position vis-à-vis their collectivist ideals. Everything leads them to a strategy of escalation, refusal, and irreversibility and opposes them to the partisans of compromise represented by the intellectuals "back from France" and the "syncretists" of the University of Hanoi.

The Liberal-Progressive Culture of the "Back from France"

The Saigonese jurist Trinh Dinh Thao, with whom it is necessary to associate his colleague of Hanoi, Maître Nguyên Manh Tuong, has a typical profile of this specific culture of people who are educated in the mold of the French university. In an autobiography recently published in France (*Trinh Dinh Khai, Décolonisation du Viet Nam: Un avocat témoigne* (Trinh Dinh Khai, Decolonization of Vietnam: An Attorney Testifies), Maître Trinh Dinh Thao, Paris, 1944,⁴⁹ by his son, T. D. Thao presented himself as "son of Trinh Dinh Bao, first administrative secretary of the General Residency of Hanoi." This claim to the status of auxiliary (but nevertheless important) manager in the colonial administration is very surprising. In fact, usually children of this generation would prefer to conceal the duties held by their fathers under the colony as if they were shameful marks. Trinh Dinh Thao's father was proposed by Superior Resident Vayrac for a provincial mandarin position. He declined his superior's proposition but obtained as compensation the admission of his son, Trinh Dinh Thao, to the Paul Bert secondary school, whose headmaster was then Cyprien Mus.[50] This establishment, which will later be given the prestigious name of Lycée Albert Sarraut, offers to the few Vietnamese who are registered there an entirely European program. After the baccalaureat, Trinh Dinh Thao found a job as a tutor of the children of Governor Cognacq, whom he accompanied to Saigon when the latter was appointed lieutenant governor of Cochinchina. It was in the capital of the southern colony that he met and married the stepdaughter of the *dôc phu su* (colonial prefect) Tân Hàm Ninh. Thanks to the intervention of his parents-in-law, Trinh Dinh Thao was able to leave to continue higher studies in France. A law student in Aix-en-Provence, Thao obtained a law doctorate and began his career as an attorney at the Court of Appeals of Aix. This "royal" entry to the bar of Aix and later of Saigon suggests that Trinh Dinh Thao, like his northern compatriot Lê Van Kim, may have acquired French nationality (?).

Like Nguy Nhu Kontum, and in opposition to Hô Dàc Di, T. D. Thao emphasized the rather nice welcome of the metropolitans (17), the "cordial" atmosphere of postwar society, "the liberty and equality society" that he discovered when he arrived in France. He met the French schoolmates with whom he was to be especially linked, like the journalist Merry Bromberger and the future professor of economy Gaston Leduc. Having acquired a taste for democratic liberties in France, many of his compatriots chose to settle there. Only a minority envisaged returning to the homeland: Duong Bach Mai (law student and member of the FCP), Nguyên An Ninh, and Ta Thu Thâu, who will be found later on the editorial committee of the French-language newspaper *La Lutte* (The Struggle).

> During the 1920s, the majority of the Vietnamese students living in France were from Cochinchina, the rice granary of Indochina. They were sons of rich landowners, leading citizens and higher officials, and doctors who had the necessary political relationships and sufficient financial means to send them abroad and provide for their needs. They regrouped in universities in southern France such as Montpellier, Aix-en-Provence, Marseilles, Bordeaux, and Toulouse owing to the mildness of the climate and the amount of sunshine. In Aix-

en-Provence especially, a great number of Vietnamese had entered the various faculties of the city. They used to meet regularly every evening and during the weekend. The spirit of militancy was particularly driven by leaders such as Duong Bach Mai, Ho Huu Tuong, The Van Thu, and Nguyên Van Tao, who had already developed the themes of political claims that will be taken up later in the newspaper *La Lutte* (The Struggle). They rose up especially against the capitation tax imposed on all the natives between nineteen and sixty years old, according to their fortunes and their physical health. This form of taxation constituted a source of exaction by officials misappropriating public funds and was a source of humiliation. In fact, all persons liable for tax had to produce the receipt of payment at each police control, otherwise they would be arrested. They requested, also, the suppression of the omnipotence of low-ranking French officials in the colonial administration that discouraged Vietnamese graduates from serving in the public service in the interest of the population. (18–23)

Such was the context when the Congress of Aix-en-Provence of 1927 was organized by Trinh Dinh Thao, attorney at the Court of Appeals of Aix; the southern Duong Van Gia (attorney in Paris), former president of the Association of the Annamite Students of France; and Trân Van Thach, in charge of the Students Committee of Paris. It was the first time that nearly three hundred Vietnamese students of France and Belgium met in a political congress for three days from the nineteenth to the twenty-second of September within the law faculty. Three motions were made public after pungent debates, in front of a pit of brilliant local personalities at the same time amused, petrified, and incredulous. These texts demonstrate the iniquity of the colonial system imposed by the treaties of 1862 and 1874 and request their plain and simple abolition and the reunification of Viet Nam (23); they denounce injustices deriving from the administrative system governing the native population, its vexatious and repressive character. The last motion, more Marxist-inspired, analyzes and stresses in Marxist terms the parasitic role of the Chinese merchants in the appropriation of trade in the country, the keeping by the protectorate of a semifeudal agrarian system, and the policy of economic exploitation to which the colony was subjected. These texts, like other documents written shortly after by the university opposition in France, mark a clear difference from the thematic of the radical rejection that characterizes the process of Mai Van Bô and his friends. They derive from a political culture that could be qualified as liberal-progressive in the sense of the Enlightenment, indeed, also nationalistic but entering clearly into a problematic of the state-nation, of human rights and of self-determination of the people. Whether in Aix in 1927, in the House of Indochina in 1929, or during the Yên Bai repression in 1930, these are democratic ideals and formal rights[51] derived from the revolution of 1789 rather than the slogans of class struggle of the Bolshevist revolution that were proclaimed. And better than the president, Maître Nguyên Huu Tho (although a native of the south and liberal attorney in Saigon), Trinh Dinh Thao was a good representative of this democratic and liberal nationalism, formed at the Western school, and of the intellectual French by spirit and culture. It is not by chance that, in the twilight of his life as a "fellow traveler" of the Communist Party,[52] he expressed a certain disillusionment: "The heirs of Uncle Ho had accomplished his political testament by means of the reunification of Viet Nam but had forgotten his last recommendations. . . . I regretted especially that the concord and reconciliation policy has not been realized in South Vietnam in order to avoid exposing our nearest and dearest to the perils and sufferings of the 'boat people'" (170).

The Liberal-Progressive Culture of the "Syncretists" of the IU

Like the path of the writer Hoàng Ngoc Phach, this culture derives from three centers of syncretic socialization: the historical tradition of Thanh Nghe Tinh, the preservation of Confucian humanities, and the reception of French culture. In the preface to the work of Hoàng Ngoc Phach recently edited in Hanoi,[53] the writer Nguyên Huê Chi has rightly stressed the importance for the intelligentsia of the north and the center of geographical roots, in this case the village of Dông Thai, in the intellectual and political history of Vietnam. It is, by a strange coincidence, the home village of two great families of the center related to our writer, the families of Phan Dinh Phùng and Hoàng Cao Khai. The political history of the Cân Vuong has made of them two opposed archetypes. The first incarnates the virtues of the great patriotic chief of the Confucian resistance, while the second represents the figure of the scholar-collaborator, who had contributed by political ambition to the final victory of the occupation army. The intellectual biography, whether it stems from the north or the south, from the nationalist or communist sphere, amplifies this eternal duality of good and evil by depicting Phan Dinh Phùng (1847–95) as a Vietnamese Van Thiên Tuong.[54] Phan Dinh Phùng was a great laureate of the palace examination (1877), honest and inflexible. Censor at the court, he preferred to fall into disgrace rather than yield to the palace intrigues, a tragic and indomitable leader in the scholar resistance facing the French army. Hoàng Cao Khai (1850–1933), despite an indisputable literary talent and his university brilliance (successful *cu nhân* at the age of nineteen in 1868), would have to personify the sad figure of the social climber. The rapidity with which he reached the top of the mandarin hierarchy, from simple teaching official to the title of regent of King Thanh Thai and viceroy of Tonkin, proves to all that he collaborated with the enemy. Scholar by education and Confucian by conviction, he had not even the excuse of the rallied Christians like Nguyên Huu Bai, of a popular social extraction like the Tông Dôc Trân Ba Lôc, or a military origin like Nguyên Thân. Without rehabilitating the political role of Hoàng Cao Khai in the first phase of his career, the social family history of intellectuals of this region reveals, nevertheless, a more complex personality and especially a more tormented individual history.

In order to escape reprisals from Christians, pursued whenever the Cân Vuong movement became unsettled, the father of Phach, a scholar called Hoàng Mông Cân, had to leave Dong Thai with his family to put themselves under the protection of Hoàng Cao Khai at his property of Thai Hà'Âp on the outskirts of Hanoi. Under these circumstances, one learns that many resistance fighters of Hà Tinh were saved only thanks to a help system emanating in fact from the former viceroy.[55] Linked to the two famous families of Dong Thai, Hoàng Ngoc Phach's parents (like many of their native "compatriots") appealed to them for help in getting out of trouble. Family and village sociability clearly overrode here considerations of a political order. All the children from this background show a remarkable continuity in their intellectual itinerary as well as this geographical solidarity. The scholarly path of Hoàng Ngoc Phach illustrates the history of his peers, as he goes successively through the three ages of education in the first half of the twentieth century: classic Confucian studies via Chinese and Nom, French-indigenous studies resulting from reforms in classic teaching, and Western studies at the end of the curriculum (last year of secondary and higher studies). One finds in their writings and social practices the "common cultural core" fed on oriental humanities (especially Sino-Confucian) and Western humanities learned at the university. This characteristic cannot be found among the Westernizing iconoclasts, even the graduates of the "cream" of French universities and, to a lesser extent, among southern French-speaking students of the University of Hanoi. It is not by chance that Hoàng Ngoc Phach evokes in his memoirs, with just one stroke of the pen, both the "Tân thu" of the Chinese neo-Confucians and the French philosophers, in turn. He discovered them at the French School of Extrême-Orient and at the university library when he attended the High School of Pedagogy (of which he had pleasant memories, like Nguyên Lân and Dang Thai Mai). He also describes the "mal du siècle" (world weariness) he discovered in Chateaubriand, Victor Hugo, Alfred de Musset, Baudelaire . . . and the state of mind of a certain part of the Vietnamese youth during the years 1914–24, depicted in his novel *Tô Tâm*. Finally, he mentions the old dream of building the new Vietnamese literature on the basis of a synthesis of the West and the East.[56] It may be this lack of oriental culture that failed Trân Duc Thao in his later work *Phénoménologie et matérialisme didactique* (Phenomenology and Dialectic Materialism, 1950), especially compared to Cao Xuân Huy, whose philosophy lectures at the University of Hanoi have been published by the good offices of Nguyên Huê Chi (*Tu tuong phuong Dông goi nhung diêm nhin tham chiêu* [Oriental Philosophy and Perspective of Research] [Hanoi: NXB Vien Van Hoc, 1995]).

Conclusion

Apart from a tiny minority of "uprooted" persons cut off from the culture of origin, these men and women have never denied the historical heritage of their ancestors, their families, and the scholar class.[57] On the contrary, these "heirs" in the full sense of the term are the ones who are the best prepared to assimilate and integrate values learned in contact with Western culture. It is also in the name of this elitist culture on the whole, and not in the name of the rather simplistic dogmas of the Marxism-Leninism of the "back from Moscow" like Trân Phu, Le Hông Phong, or Hà Huy Tâp—or in the name of the peasant messianism of the Mao-inspired leaders "back from Beijing" like Hoàng Van Hoan and Hoàng Quôc Viêt—that they rallied massively to the cause of the resistance in 1945. In fact, this cause offers them (at least, the vast majority of them) the perfect opportunity to link up with the thread of history, to merge their scholarly history with that of the nation. An extraordinary self-affirmation and individualism or a tremendous combination of circumstances would be necessary to go against the tide. To defect from the country at that moment, when postwar France, whether Gaullist, socialist, or liberal, offered them no other collective alternative than to return to the empire, would mean to lose face, to cast oneself definitively out of one's group.[58] Pride in their class and reflexes conditioned by several centuries of socialization, the ethic of responsibility, and conviction leave them no other possibility than to fight[59] for independence. Marx felt it when he described in a passage often omitted from the "*Manifesto*" the movement of petit bourgeois intellectuals rallying to the communist cause. It is the interpretation of the meaning of this allegiance that is erroneous: neither by interest, nor by cowardice, but by excess of idealism. It was not under the sign of material lure and fear that the Vietnamese intellectuals supported the government of Ho Chi Minh but by attachment, in the physical sense, to the native country, in deference to the ancestors and to the moral code of responsibility, in a word, the basis of Confucian political culture.

NOTES

Université Aix-en-Provence, France. I would like to thank Evelyne Lagaune for translating this essay.

1. Here is taken up and developed the notion, already put to the test in Trinh Van Thao, *Viet Nam du confucianisme au communisme* (Viet Nam: From Confucianism to Communism) (Paris: l'Harmattan, 1990), which is basically close to the "social generation" defined in these terms by Gérard Noiriel, *Les ouvriers dans la société française; XIXe–XXe siècle* [Workers in French Society]) (Paris: Editions du Seuil, 1986): 317: "Besides just covering biological criteria of age the term of generation is particularly adapted when the research applies to a whole group of individuals *having gone through the same founding experiences and undergone the same initial forms of socialization*" (my emphasis).

2. On analysis of the biographical data, see Trinh Van Thao, *Les compagnons*

de route de Ho Chi Minh: Sociologie de la socialisation lettrée (The road companions of Ho Chi Minh: Sociology of the Scholars' Socialization), chap. 2.1: "Collective and Historical Memory" (manuscript). The present contribution is greatly indebted to this study.

3. About family socialization: if someone is abandoned by his or her biological mother, who did not accept frequent conflicts between women of first and second rank in polygamous families, someone else will be sheltered by the grandparents, uncles, aunts, or the elders. After the arrest of the father and the exile for political reasons, briefly some "details" of home life testify also that the colonial cataclysm has not spared family peace. On the other hand, the funding of educational costs by brothers, sisters, uncles, and aunts shows, on the contrary, the persistent solidity of family solidarity.

4. An example is the division between the father's Confucianist morality and the mother's Buddhist or Taoist worship, an ordinary situation in a syncretic culture between the "three religions."

5. This is the symbolic content of the ancestral fatherland, which is not always confused with birthplace, as, for example, Mount Hong, the Lam River, the expression "Nui Hong Sông Lam" for peoples of Nghê An, historical places for those of Ha Tinh, and the River of Perfumes for peoples of Hue. On the contrary, southerners seldom evoke the image of their native land, but who knows if later their children will evoke with equal emotion the provinces of Ben Tre, Cu Chi (Song Bé), Can Tho, or My Tho. These provinces have given a lot to the Vietnamese resistance, as the writer Nguyên Ngu notes (I have also mentioned this when I discussed the work of the southern writer Binh Nguyên Lôc): "The country where one has grown up partakes more or less of the constitution of one's character and aspirations. Your Tân Uyên [in the province of Biên Hoà-Dông Nai now], full of charms with its fresh waterways, its green forests, its hills, its small brooks, possesses a grandiose and picturesque beauty. . . . And the region extending along the right bank of the river Dông Nai has produced a Huynh Van Nghê, great war chief and poet, a Ly Van Sâm, a writer close to the Viet Minh and the National Liberation Front (NLF), a Binh Nguyên Lôc. . . . You say that my native country is full of charm, that's true; as for saying it is grandiose, I wouldn't know what to say. . . . Nevertheless, it is necessary to underline the fact that this earth has given birth to extreme figures. Some distinguished themselves by deeds of war; you know already who that concerns [the general Huynh Van Nghê, one of the best southern generals, who distinguished himself during the wars against the French and Americans]. There were graduates before '45 that you know also. Do not forget X, first-rate entrepreneur, and Y, the *Viet gian* [a bad Vietnamese, here a collaborator], unbeatable! So, from fine gold to pig mash, this country of mine will have known the complete range of the human condition." Nguyên Ngu-I, *Song và viet voi . . . (Vivre et Ecrire avec)*, California: Xuan Thu, undated: 235.

6. *All the rules of the game begin equal*, because one must not confuse those who remained in the country with those of the diaspora, the "naturalized" with the "natives," the status of "protectorate" with that of "colony."

7. *Le Monde,* 24 July 1998.

8. It is also what explains the general weakness of erudite works of Marxist inspiration in the 1960s, against which I wrote *Marx, Engels, et le journalisme révolutionnaire* (Marx, Engels, and Revolutionary Journalism) (Paris: Éditions Anthropos, 1978).

9. As, furthermore, the theories of its most consequent adversaries, M. Weber and V. Pareto. Insofar as no situation is reproduced identically without renouncing itself, putting collective actions back in their "context" means restoring the social and historical framework, this "sociological drama," its "mystery," its ever renewed and yet novel nature, and restoring to human action its ultimate "freedom," its final availability. It also means thinking interaction in terms not of certainties but of probabilities, of possibilities.

10. There is a "detail" that often escapes Western historians when they defend the thesis of the continuity of the Chinese revolution through to Vietnam: its chronology. The communism of Ho Chi Minh developed in Vietnam four years before the victory of Mao over the armies of Chiang Kai-shek and not the contrary.

11. Of all the notions derived from P. Bourdieu's theory of social reproduction, the notion of habitus (mandarin) appears to be the most relevant to designating a social code ritualized for centuries in China and Vietnam of the relationship between the scholar and the monarchical power and civil society: the ability to govern of individuals, "guardians of knowledge"; the monopoly of symbolic domination, whether in the form of political magistrature or moral magistrature; and the exclusion of women from the public sphere. After the short but difficult interlude of the Cultural Revolution in China, the mandarin habitus has been rushing back since de-Maoization, as testified by the race for diplomas of the Vietnamese and Chinese *nomenklatura* today. The egalitarian and iconoclastic utopia will have lived only as long as the "little red book"!

12. See Trinh Van Thao, *L'école française en Indochine* (The French School in Indochina) (Paris: Kartala, 1995).

13. See Trinh Van Thao, *Viet Nam du confucianisme au communisme* (Vietnam from Confucianism to Communism) (Paris: l'Harmattan, 1990).

14. This was a scholar resistance movement responding to the appeal of Emperor Ham Nghi. Led by the scholars of the north and center, it lasted no less than ten years (1885–96). See C. Fourniau, *Annam-Tonkin (1885–1896): Lettrés et paysans vietnamiens face à la conquête coloniale* (Annam-Tonkin (1885–1896): Vietnamese Scholars and Farmers Facing the Colonial Conquest) (Paris: l'Harmattan, 1989).

15. See Trinh Van Thao, *Viet Nam du confucianisme au communisme,* "Biographical and Bibliographical Forms."

16. It would be excessive to consider all Catholics as de facto rallied. The Catholic Nguyên Truong Tô (see ibid.) constitutes a famous example to the contrary but not an exception.

17. Tôn Tho Tuong (1825–77) is considered to be the southern equivalent of Hoàng Cao Khai. A fine scholar and good poet, he found in poetry the means

of justifying his rallying to the occupation army. The poet Phan Van Tri retorted curtly, condemning his disloyalty and opportunism.

18. It was created on the model of Keio University (Tokyo), which played an essential role in the training of new leaders in Meiji Japan.

19. This was the famous review edited by Pham Quynh from 1917 to 1934.

20. See Trinh Van Thao, *Marx, Engels, et le journalisme révolutionnaire.*

21. According to the former director of *Thanh Nghi,* age was important in the differences of perception and commitment between mature men, like the President Nguyên Van To of the association for spreading *quoc ngu,* and people of his age. Social positions have also been decisive in the differences between the editors of *Thanh Nghi* and the editors of its competitor, *Tri Tan.* See *Ky Niem Thanh Nghi* by Vu Dinh Hoè (Hanoi: nha xuat ban Van Hoc, 1997).

22. This was the newspaper in French that regrouped the radicals, communists, and Trotskyists of Saigon during the social and political struggle of the 1930s. See D. Hémery, *Révolutionnaires vietnamiens et pouvoir colonial en Indochine: Communistes, Trotskystes, nationalistes à Saigon de 1932 à 1937* (Revolutionary Vietnamese and Colonial Power in Indochina: Communists, Trotskyists, and Nationalists of Saigon from 1932 to 1937) (Paris: Francois Maspero, 1975). The declared alignment on international conflicts, the Marxist-Leninist overdetermination of the social and political language, must not hide the predominance of values derived especially from French Revolution Jacobinism.

23. A literary group gathered around the Nguyên Tuong brothers (Nhat Linh, Hoang Dao, and Thach Lam) and the writer Khai Hung, this editorial group dominated literary, cultural, and artistic life during the 1930s. In his autobiography, Nguyên Tuong Bach describes the dissolution process of this group between the Viet Quoc (Vu Hong Khan tendency) and the Viet Cach (Nguyên Hai Than tendency) when confronted with the frontist strategy of the Viet Minh (*Viet Nam, nhung ngay lich su [Vietnam, the Historical Days]* [Montreal: Nhom Nghien Cuu Su Dia Viet Nam, 1981], 76).

24. See the succinct but shrewd analysis of Maurice M. Durand and Nguyên Trân Huan in *Introduction à la Littérature Vietnamienne* (Introduction to Vietnamese Literature) (Paris: Maisonneuve and Larose, 1969).

25. The subsumption of confrontation between tradition and modernity and social conservatism and revolutionary radicalism under the effects of the cold war explains unnatural tendencies to rally (scholar heirs going over to communism and Marxists serving pro-Western regimes) without, however, perverting the rationality of collective motivations.

26. Transposed in the symbolic Sino-Vietnamese world, the ethos of responsibility depends on the public behavior of the Confucian scholar, obligations of commitment toward the king (*xuat*). Conversely, the ethos of conviction relies on the individual moral code and the intimate right of everyone to free himself (*xu*) from the social contract between the intellectual and the powers that govern.

27. See also Huynh Kim Khanh, *Vietnamese Communism, 1925–1945* (Ithaca: Cornell University Press, 1982); and Trinh Van Thao, *Viet Nam du confucianisme au communisme.*

28. On the latifundian origin of those from Nam Bo, see Nguyên Van Huong, *Hanh trinh một doi nguoi* (Itinerary of a life) (Ho Chi Minh City: Nha xuat ban Van Nghe, 1991).

29. Mai Van Bô, *Luu Huu Phuoc: Con nguoi su nghiep / L'homme et l'oeuvre* (The Man and the Work) (Ho Chi Minh City: NXB Tuoi tre, 1989).

30. Like Tran Van Giau, Duong Bach Mai, Huynh Tan Phat, and Huynh Van Tieng.

31. See Trinh Van Thao, *Viet Nam du confucianisme au communisme*.

32. One can oppose the francophiles of the beginning of the century, such as Phan Châu Trinh and Ngô Duc Kê, who discovered the republican and democratic values of the French Revolution . . . in Chinese!

33. This concerns Pham Van Bach in Mai Van Bô, *Luu Huu Phuoc: Con nguoi và su nghiệp* (LHP: The Man and the Work) (Ho Chi Minh City: NXB Tuoi tre, 1989).

34. The cruel caricature by Mai Van Bô reminds one of C. M., the old unworthy headmaster at the high school Buoi in Hanoi, portrayed by Hoàng Ngoc Phach. Nevertheless, whereas Bô focuses his attention on the *physical aspects* of the fat colonialists, H. N. Phach turns his attention to his moral qualities, the scandalous behavior of an educator yearning for Don Juanism.

35. Apart from the tone, the account of the college years of Mai Van Bô reminds one of vicissitudes of the history of Buoi (Chuyên Truong Buoi, promotion 1914–18) by the writer Hoàng Ngoc Phach, apart from one detail: in twenty years, the average age from one cohort to another has declined, the sensitivity also. Mai Van Bô and his colleagues were twenty years old when they neared the period of university. Hoàng Ngoc Phach and his schoolmates were much older. They were obliged to reconvert to French-indigenous studies late in life. Some were already married and fathers of families, although they had not yet passed the certificate examinations. Furthermore, since the 1930s the baccalaureat has been necessary to enter university, whereas it was the exception in the beginning of the university's history (1918–24).

36. "To befriend" is quite a euphemism because one knows the fate that Mai Van Bô and his friends will reserve "for those people" during the struggles for power a few years later (1945–46). What can be said about nationalist and non-Marxist leaders like Hô Van Ngà and Le Ba Cang or religious chiefs like Huynh Phu Sô, who met the same fate as the Trotskyists Ta Thu Thâu, Phan Van Hùm, Trân Van Thach, Huynh Van Phuong, and Phan Van Chanh?

37. In fact, this accident, which cost Valençot his life, happened a few years before.

38. See statements confirming Hoàng Ngoc Phach on the state of mind of Vietnamese students of the three "countries" during the 1920s.

39. Such as Duong Duc Hiên (law), Nguyên Ngoc Minh (law), Nguyên Si Du (pharmacy), and Le Thiêu Huy and Le Ba Hoan (sciences).

40. Among the "radicals" that M. V. Bô calls, curiously, a "group of positives," we remember: Duong Duc Hiên, Vu Van Cân (future minister), Nguyên Duong Hong, Nguyên Ngoc Minh, Pham Thanh Vinh, and Nguyên Cong Thuyêt in the north; Pham Biêu Tâm (future professor of medicine),

Nguyên Si Du, Le Khac Thiên (doctor), Le Ba Hoan, Lê Ba Toai, Cao Van Khanh (future general of an army corps of the VPA and furthermore younger brother of the last commander-in-chief of the southern army, Gen. Cao Van Viên), and Nguyên Kèn in the center; and Dong Van Chung, Trân Nam Hung, Huynh Ba Nhung, Dang Ngoc Tôt, Lam Chanh Binh, Tran Cuu Kiên, Tran Buu Kiêm (future minister), Nguyên Viêt-Nam, Diêp Minh Châu, Bui Van Hai (Bui Si Hung), Vo Van Tham, Nguyên Dang, Ta Ba Tong, Le Van Nhàn, Quach Vinh Chuong, Truong Công Nhon, and the "sisters" Tô Huê My, Bui Thi Câm (jurist, wife of Pham Ngoc Thuân), Nguyên Thi Thuong, and Nguyên Thi Thiêu.

41. It concerns the new version of the Vietnamese Kuomintang (Hoang Ngoc Phach, 1996).

42. He represents, with the Vietnamese Section of the International Socialist or Vietnamese Socialist Party (Xa Hôi Dang) of which Nguyên Xiên was the secretary general, the other ally of the VCP within the Viet Minh front.

43. One refers to the book published in English by David Marr, *Viet Nam, 1945: The Quest for Power* (Berkeley: University of California Press), which often uses unpublished Vietnamese sources.

44. As proof that all radicals did not follow the boycott instructions in 1945: Drs. Hô Van Huê, Pham Biêu Tâm, and Trân Ngoc Ninh defended their doctoral theses in 1947 and 1948 in Hanoi and Saigon.

45. Led by Nguyên Van To, Nguyên Huu Dang, and Hoang Xuân Han, this association represents an ideal place of meeting and intellectual action as well as one of the communications channels between the Communist Party and the intellectuals.

46. For example, Nguyên Van Vy (director of the French-Chinese Bank), Luu Van Lang (civil engineer), Pham Huu Hanh, Trân Kim Quan, Ho Lai Van, Nguyên Van Duc, Lê Tho Xuân, Khuông Viet, Thuong Cong Thuân, and Vo Hà Tri.

47. About this episode, refer to Marr, *Viet Nam, 1945*.

48. It led to the creation, with acclamations of the crowd gathered at a meeting in Saigon, of a Temporary Administrative Committee of Nam Bo composed of (persons whose names are followed by an asterisk belong in the corpus): Trân Van Giau* (former student of the University of Toulouse and of the université des travailleurs d'Orient [UTO], University of the Workers of the Orient, of Moscow), president; Pham Ngoc Thach* (parti communiste vietnamien [VCP] Faculty of Medicine of Paris), commissioner in charge of foreign affairs; Nguyên Van Tao (parti communiste français [FCP]-VCP, secondary teaching in France), commissioner in charge of the interior; Hoang Dôn Van (confédération générale des travailleurs vietnamiens [CGT VN]), commissioner for employment; Nguyên Van Tây (VCP), commissioner in charge of the inspection of western Nam Bo; Duong Bach Mai* (FCP-VCP, law, University of Aix-Marseille), commissioner for defense; Ngo Tân Nhon (université Indochinoise [IU]), commissioner for the economy; Huynh Van Tiêng* (IU, PCV), commissioner for information and youth; and Nguyên Phi Hoanh, commissioner for finance.

49. This is an interesting document despite a publication once again botched and full of errors, notably concerning the motions voted in Aix! This is how a motion voted in 1927 condemns the Yen Bai repression in 1930!

50. He was the father of the Vietnamist of the College of France, Paul Mus.

51. The presence of jurists on these platforms must not be underestimated, and notably of the publicists Nguyên An Ninh, Duong Van Giao, and Trinh Dinh Thao.

52. He represented the legal opposition to the colonial order, the liberal intelligentsia of Saigon during the government of Trân Trong Kim, and, during the war, the intellectual lobby of the south that was won over to the cause of the government of Ho Chi Minh. After the offensive of Têt in 1968, he went underground and, appointed president of the Democratic Alliance, launched a propaganda campaign abroad on behalf of the National Liberation Front.

53. Hoàng Ngoc Phach, *Duong doi va duong van* (Biographical and Bibliographical Itinerary) (Hanoi: NXB Vien van hoc, 1996).

54. He was a mandarin of the Song dynasty in China and a figure symbolic of the honesty of scholars in the face of adversity.

55. One learns also from archival sources how much the dismissal of Thanh Thai in favor of his son Duy Tân by the superior resident of Annam, Charles, met with strong opposition from high mandarins reputed to be malleable like Hoàng Cao Khai, Nguyen Huu Bai, and Nguyen Huu Dô.

56. The conclusion of Vu Ngoc Phan, *Nhà van hiên dai* (Contemporary Writers) (Hanoi: nha xuat ban Van Hoc, 1989 [1942]), is part of the same problematic of the emergence of a modern literature through contact with French culture and urban society. Between the colonial period, when he taught in the secondary schools of Lang Son and Vat Ninh, and his retirement, we can observe his commitment to the political life of the country: the association for the spread of *quoc ngu,* the presidency of the executive committee of the province of Bac Ninh, the return to teaching in higher education, and an old age, happy on the whole, among children who acceded to the new ruling class. His daughter, Hoàng Thi Thuc, is a professor of orthodontics and a member of Parliament.

57. This is true even when they denounce feudal aspects (most notably arranged marriages imposed by the family), as Hoàng Ngoc Phach does in his novel *Tô Tâm* (1925).

58. The critical inclinations against bureaucratic communism and Maoism only appear late, through contact with the new phase of the class struggle introduced and imposed by China via the political office of the VCP and its leader. Effectively, a number of early companions left zones controlled by the Viet Minh at that time.

59. Even in the most passive form, the *expectation* (designated negatively in Vietnamese by the expression *trùm chan*, "to cover the head"!) adopted by a number of them can be considered to be a form of alignment with the government of Ho Chi Minh. In fact, this expectation jeopardizes the strategy of compromise recommended by France via the Bao Dai solution. It is part of the tradition of avoidance (You Tai) of the scholar.

9   Tran Thi Liên

Henriette Bui: The Narrative of Vietnam's First Woman Doctor

Introduction

The life of Vietnam's first woman doctor, Henriette Bui, is to this day not well known, although her family name is very famous. Her father was Bui Quang Chieu, founder of the Constitutionalist Party and advocate of a reformist path to independence. While his life has been the focus of many studies, the one of Henriette Bui, his daughter, who was a pioneer in her own right, deserves further inquiry. She was Vietnam's first woman to become a doctor of medicine when she was only twenty-eight years old and to be appointed chief physician of a department at a French colonial hospital in Saigon. She was a woman of determination and strength. Always ahead of her time, she went to Japan in the 1950s to study acupuncture.

Until now, French historians studying Vietnam have shown little interest in the role and position of Vietnamese women in their own history. The native peoples of the colonies and Vietnamese women in particular have been studied in very simplistic ways. Observed from a "colonial" perspective, women are perceived in terms of sexual objectification, with all the lasciviousness this implies (Ruscio 1996). Only the historian Nguyên Van Ky, whose work focuses on the condition of Vietnamese women during the interwar years, offers a new and innovative perspective on the question of women in Vietnam. In his book *La société Vietnamienne face à la modernite: Le Tonkin de la fin du XIXe siècle à la Seconde Guerre Mondiale* (Nguyên Van Ky 1995), he discusses Vietnamese women's attempts to achieve emancipation and women in terms of intracouple relations and intrafamily links.

In this chapter, I would like to use the biography of Henriette Bui to examine social changes, including the role of women, that occurred in

Vietnamese society during these interwar years. Henriette Bui Quang Chieu is not representative of the majority of her contemporaries, neither in her career nor in her personal life. Moreover, she does not appear to fall into the categories suggested by David Marr in his book *Vietnamese Tradition on Trial, 1920–1945* (1984). He argued that, in contrast to traditional Vietnamese women, women engaged in politics in Vietnam were also involved in women's organizations and/or worked as writers for Vietnamese newspapers. He suggested that as a result they often joined the Vietnamese anticolonial resistance movements, becoming members of Vietnamese political parties such as the Indochinese Communist Party. On the other hand, Henriette Bui was a woman doctor who wanted to excel in her career and improve her own life as a woman in Vietnamese society. She challenged women's status quo by asserting herself and showing a great deal of independence, which was at that time unacceptable in the social milieu in which she lived.

This essay represents the first step toward a more extensive biographical work on Dr. Henriette Bui. My research is based mostly on interviews I have conducted with her over the years.[1] Other than a few rare photographs, her private archives (letters, diaries, and pictures) were destroyed or lost. Oral sources are particularly important in light of the quasi absence of references to women in the colonial archives and because of the destruction of countless sources during almost thirty years of uninterrupted war in Vietnam (1945–75). The gathering of female memoirs seems to be an urgent task if we want to write the contemporary history of Vietnamese women.

I have also consulted a number of newspapers of this crucial period, such as *La Tribune Indochinoise* (Indochinese Tribune), *Dan Ba Moi* (Modern Woman), and *Phu Nu Tan Van* (Modern Woman's News). But to write a more complete biography, this work will have to be complemented with a more systematic consultation of the press, with further research in the Archives d'Outre-Mer (Archives of the Overseas Colonies) in Aix-en-Provence,[2] and with additional interviews with other personalities who knew Henriette Bui.[3]

1. A Daughter of the Cochinchinese Bourgeoisie

Henriette Bui Quang Chieu was born in Hanoi on 8 September 1906. Her mother, Vuong Thi Y, was a Chinese métis. Her mother's father was a Chinese merchant from Cholon, who managed an opium refinery. Very close to her Chinese relatives, her mother enjoyed ample private means, which she invested in real estate (particularly in Phu Nhuan in the suburbs of Saigon) and the clothing business. With her income, Henriette's mother financed an important part of the medical studies in Paris of her oldest son, Louis. However, she died prematurely of tuberculosis in 1916. Henriette Bui remembers her mother as an independent woman, willful and ambitious, far from the image of the traditional woman of the Confucian society that still dominated Vietnam in the early twentieth century. Henriette Bui gives credit to her mother for sending her children to pursue their university studies in France. On the other hand, her father, Bui Quang Chieu, was from a scholarly gentry family in Hue. He was one of the first Vietnamese students to receive a scholarship to study in France. Having acquired the equivalent of his high school diploma (*baccalaureat*) in Algiers (French Algeria), he continued his university studies in Paris. In 1887, he graduated from the Institut National d'Agronomie (Agronomic National College). Bui Quang Chieu returned to his country with his diploma in hand and French citizenship to boot. He subsequently became a civil servant by taking an agronomic engineering position in the Agricultural Department of the Indochinese Union. He worked all over Indochina: in Tonkin, Annam, Cochinchina, and Cambodia.

Although Bui Quang Chieu was active in business enterprises and various associations and clubs, he was best known for his political activities as the leader of the Constitutionalist Party and as the chief of the newspaper *La Tribune Indochinoise*. He was a well-known political figure in Cochinchina during the interwar period. He claimed to be a follower of Phan Châu Trinh, a reformist who was against resorting to violence to achieve political ends. As Pierre Brocheux wrote:

> Bui Quang Chieu was a determined supporter of Franco-Annamese *association*, not of *assimilation*. . . . Chieu counted on Republican France to develop her colonies. . . . France had the obligation to associate the local elite with public affairs. . . . Modernization would gradually lead Vietnam to autonomy, if not independence, within a framework comparable to that of the British Commonwealth. (1994, 156)

Moreover, Bui Quang Chieu always remained in close touch with the former emperor in exile, Ham Nghi, who had been his reporter in Algiers since his high school days. While the communists considered Bui Quang Chieu to be a fervent French collaborator, the French colonial civil service considered him as "the worst kind of anti-French Vietnamese activist, who pursued the same goals as the other Vietnamese nationalists and the revolutionaries" (Brocheux 1994: 157).

2. Growing Up in Viet Nam (1906–20)

The childhood of Henriette Bui was colored by her family moving from place to place following her father's career as an engineer of agronomy in the colonial civil service, Services Agricoles de l'Union Indochinoise. The birthplaces of her brothers and sisters tell the story. The three oldest were born in Hue: Henri in 1901, Louis in 1903, and Hélène in 1904. Henriette was born in Hanoi in 1906, her sister Madeleine (Bui Thi Long) in Tan Chau (Chau Doc) in 1909, and her brother Camille in Lyon in 1912. From 1909 to 1913, Bui Quang Chieu worked at Tan Chau (Chau Doc) to develop a silk factory there, which then took him and his family to Lyon in France for three years.[4] Young Henriette had her first experience living in France between the ages of four and seven.

Moreover, Henriette Bui was raised in a multicultural environment, Chinese, Vietnamese, and French. She received a Franco-Vietnamese education as well as the basics of Chinese culture taught by her maternal great-uncle. In addition, Henriette owed her great religious tolerance to her social milieu. In the Cochinchinese bourgeoisie of the time, many people were Catholics, but religious affiliation was not a divisive factor among people. Family members were very close regardless of their religion. For instance, Henriette Bui's mother was Buddhist, her second husband and distant cousin, Nguyên Ngoc Bich, was Caodaist, the family of Pham Ngoc Thuan was Catholic, and Bui Quang Chieu was a Freemason (Dalloz 1998).

Henriette Bui remembers her father as an open-minded man, attentive to his children, and extremely liberal. She always used the familiar *tu* when speaking French with her father, while she used the more formal and respectful term of *Bam Ba* when she spoke to him in

Vietnamese. She recalls speaking to him very freely, even when she was in disagreement with him. She also evokes how important it was for her father to transmit Vietnamese culture to them, in addition to their French education. In an interview, she recalled:

> At home, my father never talked to us about politics. On the other hand, he spoke to us often about the history of Viet Nam, since we didn't study it at all at school. He considered it important to also keep Vietnamese traditions alive, all the while studying Western sciences. (8 September 1993)

After studying at the Catholic elementary school of the Sisters of Saint Paul de Chartres (known to its students in Saigon as the Maison Blanche), in 1915 she continued her studies at the École Primaire Supérieure for young ladies and later at the Lycée Marie Curie. As a young pupil, Henriette was quick-witted, with a sharp intellect, but she was also rebellious and undisciplined. She was at the top of her class in all subjects and had a remarkable memory. She studied Latin and Greek. Given her passion for history and geography, she could have chosen a career in academia and taken the Agrégation d'Histoire (the French national exam in history).

In 1920, having not yet completed her first year of *cours moyen* (elementary school), she had already successfully passed the *certificat d'études*, which was a diploma taken at the end of elementary school. She was already more advanced than her classmates. She had dreams of following in the footsteps of her oldest brother, who had left Saigon to study medicine in Paris.

> I was obsessed with the idea of studying medicine in France. As I was a very unruly pupil, I succeeded in getting myself expelled from high school: I would get the best grades for work but always a zero for behavior, and I never got an award because of my conduct. My father asked me all the time: "What are we going to do with you?" And I would answer him: "Send me to France." My father was desperate, asking me what would I do all alone in France. I told him that I wanted to get my high school diploma there and then study medicine. My father thought I was crazy. But every day, I

persisted and annoyed him with this. He ended up giving in. That was in 1921. (8 September 1993)

Many members of the Vietnamese elite sent their children abroad to undertake scientific or technical studies (*dong du* and *tay du*) in order to serve and modernize their country. Bui Quang Chieu also sent his children to France. In Paris, Louis studied medicine, whereas Camille succeeded in the Haute École de Commerce, HEC (Superior Commercial Studies). Moreover, like the majority of his colleagues who were the first to study in France, Bui Quang Chieu was keenly aware of the need to perfectly master the French language and culture in order to claim equal status to the French in Indochina. His motivation was to have his children educated in French high schools.

But sending his fifteen-year-old daughter to study in France was an audacious action in Vietnamese society at that time. Bui Quang Chieu's decision was a testament to his remarkably open-minded character and also showed the independent, particularly obstinate character of his daughter Henriette. The very fact that she was able to go to France to study also suggested the liberal and egalitarian family environment, which had allowed her to realize her dream. However, her father did not expect all of his daughters to go to the university. In fact, her sisters were not motivated to undertake university studies and certainly not to study in France. Her older sister, Hélène, married at a very early age and had the more traditional life expected of a young woman of that time. Her younger sister, Madeleine, married a doctor but also managed a successful beauty salon in Saigon (whose advertisement can be found in the newspapers of the time, *La Tribune Indochinoise* and *Dan Ba Moi*).

Bui Quang Chieu refused all the French colonial government scholarships awarded to his daughter Henriette. He (and also his wife) preferred financing the education of their children themselves. Such an attitude was uncommon among Vietnamese people of his status. Indeed, according to Trinh Van Thao, "a lot of notables' children (southern landowners, Hue court ministers) often received scholarships because of the active support of political personalities of the colony" (1995, 283). Henriette Bui left Saigon Harbor for France in the summer of 1921. She was accompanied by her school friend Georgette Le Thi Yen (future wife of Trân Van Don). A teacher escorted Henriette from

Marie Curie High School and would also be her guardian during her first year in Agen. Henriette was not yet fourteen years old.

3. A Student in France (1922–34)

High School Years in "the Provinces" (1922–26)

After a first year of secondary school at Agen, Henriette continued her studies in Bordeaux. She had no problems adapting to the French way of life. Henriette Bui evokes her daily life at the *lycée*.

> I was well received in France, since there were not many other Asians. . . . As I came from a tropical country, I enjoyed some favors. When the weather was too cold, I had the right to stay in the study room and the right to drink tea in the kitchen. From a culinary point of view, I quickly got used to drinking red Bordeaux wine in the dining hall! The life of a high school student was very disciplined: we were dressed in uniforms, and on Thursdays we had to take a walk in the streets in a group of twenty, whether it was raining, blowing, or snowing. It was very military. We washed up as soldiers, showering in lines. We could have a bath only once a month. (11 February 1993)

During her holidays, from time to time Henriette Bui visited her oldest brother, Louis, in Paris. She spent her summer vacations with her guardian in the region of Lot et Garonne. She also got together with Mrs. Dumas, the aunt of the métis children of the superior resident of Laos (the Laperonnie family), who had taken her under her protection. And she made friends with Rose Lalanne, a student at the *lycée* at Bordeaux, whose brother was a pilot in Indochina. She was invited on several occasions to spend summer vacations with Rose's parents in the South of France in Prades. They lived close to the house of the former resident in Hue, Mr. Charles. There she met the very young Vietnamese prince, Bao Dai. For several years, she also went to England to live with a British family in Bedford in order to practice her English.

Between 1922 and 1924, Henriette Bui was a studious and model student at a *lycée* in the city of Bordeaux. In Saigon, Henriette had never studied English, and her Latin and Greek were not very good. But by working hard she caught up with other French students in those three subjects. She was so well adjusted that she lost the use of her Vietnamese language.

> When my father visited me in 1925, I was so well adapted to French society that I could no longer speak Vietnamese. And my father said to me: "It's unthinkable that you can't write in Vietnamese and speak fluently!" (11 February 1993)

After having studied English and Spanish, her father forced her to choose Vietnamese as her second language for the high school diploma.

She passed the first part of her high school diploma test in Bordeaux, but because of trachoma, an ocular disease, the following year (1924–25) she dropped out of school and stayed at the hospital. She passed the second part of her high school exam (Latin/languages) two years later in Paris in the Fenelon Lycée in 1926. As one of the best students, she was taken under the protection of her philosophy teacher, Mrs. Meyerson, who introduced her into prestigious university circles. There she had the opportunity to meet, through her teacher, Marie Curie (who had family links to the Meyersons) and the famous French historian Charles Seignobos. During her first year of medical studies in 1927, Henriette Bui returned to Saigon for a few months. Meanwhile, her older sister Hélène, to whom she was very close, died following an illness.

Medical Studies in Paris (1926–34)

When Henriette Bui began her medical studies in Paris in 1926, there were still very few women attending French universities. After forty years of political controversy, French women were finally allowed to take the intern examination. The registrarship (*clinicat*) was opened to women in 1911 and the medical *agrégation* (required for teaching in the university) in 1923. The first French woman to pass the *agrégation* exam in medicine in Paris in 1934 was Henriette Bui's contemporary, Jeanne Levy. It was only in 1931 that the medical degree of registrarship (*médicat*) became accessible to women, thanks to the efforts of

Dr. Bertrand-Fontaine. Because of their strong will, this small number of women doctors managed by the early twentieth century to gain social and professional recognition. As Dr. Constance Joel wrote:

> Sustained by their passion to work and by a proud will that made them just as imperturbable before the operating tables as other young males, female students stood out by their sheer desire to succeed. (1988, 159)

Henriette Bui recalls:

> There were very few females: ten women for every one hundred men in medical school. The professors didn't appreciate female students too much, and they rarely missed an opportunity to criticize us. For example, when we didn't know how to answer a question, they told us: "You would do better to return to the kitchen!" In fact, many women students gave up their studies midway through or didn't work after obtaining their diploma because they were married. The rare woman who worked, chose general medicine. . . . As for me, at the end of my fifth year in medical school I chose several specialities: pathological anatomy, obstetrics, gynecology, podiatry, and infant care. I had two exceptional professors: Professor Devraigne (professor of obstetrics and department chief at the hospital of Lariboisière, whose brother was a fellow classmate of my father's during their studies at the INA [Institut Nationale d'Agronomie]) and Professor Lemière. Professor Devraigne liked the Vietnamese very much and always took a Vietnamese intern. (8 September 1993)

Like the majority of women graduates of her epoch, Henriette Bui specialized in children's and women's diseases (Joel 1988, 173). Henriette Bui still remembers the autopsies she conducted when she was a medical student.

> I would go near Censier Daubenton for anatomy courses. For the autopsies, since I was small, the professor invited me to come to the first row. The table was so high that I had the corpse right under my nose! During the autopsies, we were

allowed to smoke. It was at that time that I began to smoke, like all medical students, because the smell was bad, especially when there were lung gangrenes. . . . In the dissecting room, there were fifty half-corpses for every one hundred students, with two students for each half-cadaver that we had to dissect over the entire year. We even had to pass our final exam with the same cadaver. The cadavers were preserved in formic acid. . . . There were some who fainted at the sight of blood. But for me it was nothing. (8 September 1993)

In other instances, Henriette Bui accomplished many internships in the main hospitals of Paris (la Charité, Beaujon, Cochin, Bichat). She still remembered in 1993 her duties in the hospital.

We worked hard at that time, and from the first year the students measured blood pressure and dispensed injections. . . . While working night shifts in the delivery section, we were a dozen or so interns. They gave us mattresses that we threw down on the ground in a room, and we all slept there. . . . In the morning, we went out by the back door by way of Barbès Rochechouard. We went in a cafe to wash up and have a coffee. Whenever I presented myself in the hospitals, they would ask me: "What's she doing here, that Chinese girl?" And they were surprised to see that I spoke French fluently. It was so rare to see a woman doctor, let alone an Asian one! (8 September 1993)

For her thesis, Henriette Bui wanted to choose, to say the least, an innovative subject. She had completed an internship in one department, participating in some of the first experiments on artificial fertilization for sterile couples. Very interested by these clinical trials, she wanted to use this topic for her thesis, but her professor dissuaded her. Following his advice, she wrote on a more "traditional topic" on the phlebitis of gestation. In 1934, Henriette Bui defended her thesis, entitled "The Phlebitis of Gestation," which she dedicated to all her family.

To my grand-parents; to my mother (1878–1916); to my sister, Hélène Nguyên Quac Ve (1904–27) in memoriam; to my father, whose life will always be for me an example of devotion and integrity, that this thesis may be a small demonstration of filial piety, admiration, and respectful affection; To my brother, Dr. Louis Bui, physician in the tubercular hospital of Saigon (Cochinchina) as a sign of affection; to my sister, to my brothers.

Never having failed an exam, she won the medal for her class. That year, only 6 percent of the medical graduates in France were females (Joel 1988, 190).

As Vietnam's first woman doctor, Henriette Bui was an exception, even though she was not the only Vietnamese woman who had pursued a university degree in France. Henriette Bui knew Princess Nhu Mai (the daughter of the exiled ex-emperor Ham Nghi in Algeria), who had graduated head of her class at the INA in the year 1927. Henriette Bui used to meet Nguyên Thi Binh, who was the first Vietnamese woman to graduate in pharmaceutical studies and also was the wife of Hoang Xuan Han, a well-known student from the École Polytechnique. Henriette Bui was very close to Bui Thi Cam, her cousin, the first Vietnamese woman law graduate. Bui Thi Cam married a close friend of Bui Quang Chieu's, Gaston Pham Ngoc Thuan, who was also a law graduate. In 1945, he joined the Viet Minh resistance and was named vice president of the Nam Bo Committee of Administration and Resistance. Henriette Bui was also a colleague of Le Thi Hoang, who defended her thesis in medicine in 1937, and a contemporary of Hoang Thi Nga, the first Vietnamese woman to obtain a *doctorat ès sciences*, in 1935.

During all her years of medical studies, Henriette Bui lived independently but not alone. The first years, she lived on Bonaparte Street (in the Sixth District of Paris) with her brother Louis, later joined by their youngest brother, Camille, who successfully completed his studies at the Haute École de Commerce. When the Maison d'Indochine,[5] a student dormitory for the Indochinese students, opened in the late 1920s, women were not yet allowed to live there. And when her oldest brother married and returned to Vietnam in 1929 she also left the apartment she had shared with him. She then went to live at the Foyer International de Jeunes Filles,[6] a private boardinghouse for international woman students, during the years 1930–31. Afterward, she returned to live on Bonaparte Street with her youngest brother,

Camille, until she finished her studies. Henriette Bui would later evoke her life as a student.

> I got along well with my brothers. When I lived with them, we shared all the daily house chores. One week I would cook, the next week was my brother's turn. . . . Later I rented a room at the international house for female students, Boulevard Saint Michel, just in front of the École des Mines. There were forty-two other nationalities living there, and I made many good friends. (11 February 1993)

From 1931 on, Henriette went regularly to visit her father on Boulevard Raspail. He had been elected to the Superior Council of the Colonies in Paris.

Concerning her material life, Henriette remembers her student years as follows.

> At that time, the university dormitory complex was under construction and the students lived in small, cheap hostels. The students lived under very bad conditions. Some did not eat lunch. They were cold during winter, and many ended up with tuberculosis. If they were ill, they were sent to the hospital for the poor. Student life was very hard. As for me, I lived with my brother in a very small two room flat. We did not have a lot of money, and we did not go out often. (11 February 1993)

Henriette Bui devoted most of her time to her studies and her training at the various hospitals. Most of her friends were French colleagues from medical school such as Dr. Henriette Ferrieu, to whom Dr. Bui dedicated her thesis, as well as young foreign woman students living at the international house. At the time, there were a few Vietnamese students in France.

> There were not a lot of Vietnamese and even fewer Vietnamese females. From the 1930s on, I went to the ball organized for the Têt (Vietnamese New Year) at the Indochina House. I used to meet also the daughter of Hoang Trong Phu, who lived in a hostel on Vignon Street. . . . From time to time, she would come over to take me out. (1 July 1993)

During more than ten years of studies and internships in French hospitals, Henriette Bui acquired a professional status, rare for a woman of that time. She also asserted exceptional independence and adaptability. From her adolescence, she learned not only to live alone but to live as a member of a minority group: being a Vietnamese student in France and a woman in medical school. During the period of her studies, she did not get involved in the political debates and discussions that arose within the Vietnamese student community in France. Henriette Bui preferred to devote her student days to her studies and medical career.

In June 1935, accompanied by her father, she returned to Saigon. Although she would have preferred to stay in France, she respected her father's wish that she return to Vietnam. She also obeyed him when he chose for her a husband, the lawyer Vuong Quang Nhuong. Like Henriette's father, he was a member of the Constitutionalist Party and was her father's close friend. She still recalls the stormy talk she had with her father concerning her marriage. When she told him that she did not want an arranged marriage, he replied: "Though you may be doctor, you remain my daughter. You will marry him!" (1 July 1993).

4. Henriette Bui the Gynecologist (1935–55)

A Woman Doctor

Back in Vietnam, Henriette Bui dedicated herself to her career. Much energy was needed just to work in the interwar years. Without ever getting involved in political or feminist causes, Henriette Bui fought daily battles to assert herself in colonial and Vietnamese society. Dealing every day with prejudices brought on by the very fact that she was a woman and a doctor of Vietnamese origin was a constant struggle. But overall her work as a doctor allowed her some personal freedom and independence.

Soon after her return, when she was only twenty-eight years old, she was appointed chief physician at a clinic in the regional maternity hospital in Cholon. Like many Vietnamese doctors working in the colonial medical system, Dr. Henriette Bui had to face French racial discrimination. It was difficult for her to endure this since in France she had never encountered racial discrimination from her fellow students or her professors. In addition, as a woman in the 1930s in Saigon she was also confronted with sexual discrimination.

To illustrate the social environment of that time and the nature of the relationships between French and Vietnamese, I would like to recount some anecdotes. These anecdotes are all the more significant given that the power relationships between colonizer and colonized do not appear in official sources. In reading the colonial press, one can get a certain idea of discrimination, but interviews with the people who were witnesses are more convincing arguments. They are also able to recall the exact occurrences of the events and to talk about the kinds of discrimination that took place, in particular in the work environment. And, as in French colonial society, the medical profession in Vietnam was divided along the "color line": the French (white) and the Vietnamese professionals (colored people, regardless of whether they were naturalized French). As Henriette Bui recalled later:

> The two worlds remained very separate. Most of the French had a very colonialist way of thinking, if not racist, in their relationships with the sick as well as with their Vietnamese colleagues. Each year, the director general of the Health Department would invite all the doctors working in the hospitals, French and Vietnamese, but we were always separated. I had no friends among the French! This made an even greater impression on me since I felt very French in France, where I had always felt well received! (1 July 1993)

Henriette Bui remembers the double discrimination she suffered every day.

> When I was named chief physician in 1934, I was the very first woman to hold that position. All of the French newspapers (including *L'Opinion*) criticized me a lot. At all levels, my work at the hospital was a perpetual battle [8 September 1993]. From my very first conversation with the hospital department chief, the tone was clear: When I was named, the department chief told me right away: "You will dress in the French fashion." I asked him why: "To be respected!" Then I

answered: "No, I will dress in fact in the Vietnamese fashion so that the people will know how to respect me." Then he told me: "But they will take you for a midwife!" I told him: "I don't care what one takes me for." If I had dressed in a French manner before, at that moment I decided to dress Vietnamese at work. (1 July 1993)

The fact that she worked in the same department as another French woman doctor did not change anything in terms of this discrimination. This woman doctor behaved like the majority of the other French colonial administrators. In hospitals, in their daily communications with Vietnamese people, employees, and patients, the French people's attitude was one of superiority. As Henriette Bui recalls:

I was the only woman doctor of Vietnamese origin, and the French woman doctor whom I replaced, and who subsequently returned, never missed an opportunity to show her disdain for the Vietnamese. Mrs. Eliche had very colonialist behavior. One day she said in front of me: "The Annamites are as dirty as pigs! Everywhere, they spit betel!" So I retorted: "You are right, Doctor, they spit everywhere. It's that we are forced to live with pigs here. What do you expect?!" When she was not satisfied with the work of the nurses or the midwives, she didn't mind beating or giving them a slap in the face. She was very angry at me for defending the midwives and for advising them to lodge a complaint. When she made her rounds and the husband of a sick woman failed to take off his hat, she took it off for him and threw it on the ground! That's how bad it was. (1 July 1993)

This discrimination made itself felt in terms of the exorbitant differences in salaries between the French and the Vietnamese. Officially, the salaries were calculated in terms of racial categories, even for those Vietnamese who were naturalized French citizens. The gap between the salaries of the highest ranked French naturalized and least-qualified French remained enormous. The gap was even greater given the special colonial allowance allocated to French civil servants. This discrimination was hard for Dr. Bui to swallow.

> I earned one hundred piasters while my French colleague earned one thousand piasters, and I had more education than she. In addition, I had to give lessons to the midwives, without any additional income. When I questioned the director of the Health Department on this issue, he answered me: "But you do not have the same expenses as the French. You don't need to eat butter and cheese and drink wine!" So I told him: "And why don't we sleep on the ground!" "But Ms. Bui, you are communist!" he said. . . . Obviously, I was poorly treated. (1 July 1993)

In other instances, Henriette Bui deplored the fact that indigenous hospitals had less financial and material support than the hospitals reserved for the French.

> We did not have the same financial resources as those of the French hospitals such as the military hospital Grall or the French private clinic of Angier. We lacked medicines. For pharmaceutical needs, the maternity hospital depended on the Cho Ray hospital, whereas in the pharmacy of the Health Department there were only French druggists. When I ordered medicines, they always answered that my requests were excessive, and when we were short and I had to borrow from the indigenous hospital I was criticized for not ordering enough. (1 July 1993)

Dr. Henriette Bui recalls another significant anecdote that occurred during a visit to the sanitarium establishments in Saigon-Cholon by the governor's wife, Mrs. Pagès.

> In the maternity hospital, the people slept on bamboo mats and one placed newspapers on the ground to catch the blood stemming from the deliveries. It was very dirty. . . . But the worst was that they had built toilets that looked out directly over the delivery room! It was an incredible house of germs! So, when the wife of the governor came to visit the maternity hospital, I took advantage of the occasion to ask that one seal off the toilets and that tiled walls be installed in the delivery rooms, for blood was splattered everywhere. . . . Afterward

> my department chief criticized me for having made such a direct request. I was scolded. (1 July 1993)

Added to this colonial hierarchy within the hospital was the strong hierarchy between doctors and subordinate employees. In this colonial context, French doctors displayed their superiority by portraying themselves as the agents of knowledge and the architects of Vietnamese medical institutions. Such arrogance only created misunderstandings and conflicts in the hospitals between the French and Vietnamese employees. Dr. Henriette Bui initiated new ways to deal with these cultural issues in the hospital.

> Traditionally, when Vietnamese women give birth they only eat vinegar and pepper, very salty things, but no vegetables or fruits. . . . Seeing that there was beef sautéed with vegetables and bananas on the menu, I told the cook not to sauté it and to give them some cakes instead of the bananas. I thought it was important to take Vietnamese traditions into consideration so that they would eat. I was sharply criticized for having changed the menu. This incident reached as high as the governor's desk. The governor agreed with me. They then said that I had slept with him in order to get him to agree! (1 July 1993)

Henriette Bui's account provides another understanding of colonial medical institutions, the French civilizing mission, and French biases toward Vietnamese people. Without denying some indisputable French medical achievements in Vietnam, we can nevertheless question French doctors' representations of the Vietnamese health system. I will choose two examples to illustrate my point, although further investigation is required. In her doctoral thesis, Laurence Monnais-Rousselot uses the reports of French colonial doctors who described the terrible sanitary conditions in which Vietnamese women gave birth before the implementation of a French colonial health care system. According to Dr. Henriette Bui, the description was excessively biased because in the past Vietnamese midwives generally used scissors from traditional Chinese medicine and not, as the reports described, "a simple fragment of broken bottle or anything sharp . . . , picked up on the ground!" (Monnais-Rousselot 1997, 279).

The French medical experts argued that the high mortality rate in Indochina was due to the environment in Vietnam, such as the lack of hygiene that caused umbilical tetanus and the lack of a public health system. At the Congress on Infancy, which was held in Saigon in July 1934, there was a big difference of opinion between the French and Vietnamese doctors on the cause of the high mortality rate. In their presentations, French colonial doctors argued that the infantile mortality rate was high due to very bad sanitary conditions and practices of the Vietnamese people, such as hereditary syphilis, a total absence of hygiene, ignorance of good delivery practices, and very bad feeding practices for the babies. They then praised the French medical institutions and their work in Indochina, without which the Annamite race would have inevitably suffered. The paper of Dr. Fabry, chief physician at the indigenous hospital of Cholon, on whom depended the maternity hospital where Henriette Bui would work the following year, represented the general attitude of the French medical personnel at that time.

> From the moment he comes into this world, the [Annamese] infant is very old. Product of a long ancestry, he collects directly or indirectly the racial heredity, familial and individual, and whose combinations will fix his moral and physical personality. This is a banal observation, but never sufficiently said, where medicine and morals once again meet and unite. One heritage here dominates all the others: hereditary syphilis, fearsome both for its extreme diffusion and because it kills the infant or makes him a diminished human being. (*L'Impartial*, 2 July 1934)

In contrast, the presentation of Dr. Louis Bui (brother of Henriette), tuberculosis specialist, suggested a different approach to the high instance of tuberculosis and infant mortality in Vietnam. From the outset, he considered tuberculosis to be a "worldwide scourge." Using a comparative method, he argued that tuberculosis "was as frequent in Indochina as in Europe." Using statistical analysis, he compared the spread of the disease in France and Indochina. Pointing out the contagious rather than the genetic aspect of the disease, Dr. Louis Bui showed that there was a difference in health care in France and Indochina. Whereas young French children were sent to the countryside (a treatment recommended by Dr. Granter), such care was not available in Vietnam and often not appropriate in the Vietnamese cultural context. Dr. Louis Bui instead suggested that Vietnamese children ought to be sent collectively to sanatoriums. His sister, Dr. Henriette Bui, added that the disease was caused by poverty, malnutrition, and lack of hygiene in the cities because there were no sewers.

At first, Dr. Henriette Bui worked in the Outpatient Department of pediatrics and then in the Infectious Diseases Department, one of the most difficult places to work. When her French colleague returned to France, Henriette was promoted to chief of the entire department. She worked with about twenty midwives, two auxiliary doctors, and more than fifty midwifery students.

> From 1934 to 1955, I worked almost all the time, and I had almost no time to rest. I worked because I liked it, not for the one hundred piasters. . . . Every morning at eight o'clock I was at work in the hospital. The midwives did their work well, and they had a lot of work: about fifty deliveries every day. As for me, I only dealt with the problematic deliveries, day and night. Besides delivering babies, private maternity practices would send us their most difficult cases. I conducted many caesarians, and also with forceps, but without any anesthesia or antibiotics. For surgical operations, we used chloroform. It was very toxic, and there were nauseated patients. It attacked the liver. It was a very hard job. Every day, I had to sign at least seven, eight death certificates, mostly caused by puerperal infections. (1 July 1993)

Soon thereafter, in October 1935, Dr. Henriette Bui opened a private practice in the center of Saigon on Testard Street. One can see its advertisements in different newspapers of the time (*La Tribune Indochinoise, Dan Ba Moi*). Later, in the years 1938–39, she opened a private office in Cholon, where she treated mothers and their children (gynecology/obstetrics and pediatrics). It was also during these private consultations that she discovered traditional Chinese medicine. She became interested in acupuncture and traditional medicine when her patients suggested she use them when she was unable to help them with Western medicine. In addition, at that time Western medicine was expensive, while traditional medicine was more affordable to many of her patients.

Dr. Henriette Bui developed an important medical practice serving equally the French, Vietnamese, and Chinese (she also spoke Chinese). Some Vietnamese doctors were jealous of her success. In the 1930s doctors in private practice claimed that the doctors working in public institutions and having a private practice was unfair competition. They argued that those who worked in hospitals were able to recruit patients for their own private practices. And in the fall of 1935 Governor-General Robin passed a law forbidding general practitioners working in public institutions to open private practices. Only doctors who had an underrepresented medical specialty in the private sector were allowed to have a private practice. Dr. Henriette Bui was one of the few who were allowed to keep a private practice.

A Modern Woman

With her medical career, Henriette Bui was able to be financially independent and have a certain social status. But as a professional and independent woman she was also the target of much criticism in Saigon, from the Vietnamese and the French alike. Her métis bicultural identity, Vietnamese-Chinese, her Vietnamese-French education, and her university degrees helped her to be confident and assertive in both her professional and personal lives. However, she refused to challenge the hostile environment in medical circles of both the traditional Vietnamese and French colonial societies. Instead she ignored the criticism. She kept on doing her work and living outside the boundaries of traditional norms. It was a personal choice rather than a political stand on feminism.

Her return to Vietnam in June 1935 with her father was nevertheless an event. A crowd welcomed them at the harbor of Saigon. Although the main attraction was her father, she was a personality in her own right, Vietnam's first woman doctor. She represented an achieving and successful Vietnamese woman who had a Western education with university degrees. She was also a role model for women because she represented gender equality in intellectual endowment. A committee of Annamese young women welcomed her and the president of this committee, Pham Thi My, a teacher at a local young ladies high school, told her during a tea party given in her honor:

The glory of your success rebounded on all of us, and without being an unrepentant feminist let me say that your success will help us to fight this prejudice of the intellectual inferiority of women. (*La Tribune Indochinoise,* 21 June 1935)

At the same time, an article on the first page of the women's newspaper *Dan Ba Moi* glorified her accomplishments as a role model for all Vietnamese women (17 June 1935).

Her marriage to lawyer Vuong Quang Nhuong, one of the first Vietnamese law graduates, was also an event. Her father's newspaper, *La Tribune Indochinoise,* devoted the front page to their wedding on 31 July 1935 ("A Great Wedding"), while the women's newspaper *Dan Ba Moi* dedicated its entire first page to this domestic event (5 August 1935).

Two years later, in 1937, people were talking about her again, when she asked for a divorce at the end of that year.

The husband my father had chosen for me was a good man, competent, very nice, and full of attention for me. I had nothing really against him. . . . We were well known, my husband a lawyer, I a doctor. . . . But he complained he never saw me and could not stand that I worked all the time, even in the night because of emergencies. He should have married a traditional woman because as a descendant of the royal family on his mother's side he remained very traditional on that point. But, for me, I was absolutely determined to work. I had not endured all these long years of study just to twiddle my thumbs or play cards! We were simply divorced, and we have remained good friends. But I really created a scandal for the epoch! (1 July 1993)

From then on, Dr. Henriette Bui was an independent woman, financially and socially. This independence for a woman was exceptional as much in Vietnamese society as in French colonial circles. The idea of a woman living alone, working, and having a career in a prestigious field was rare in Saigon in the 1930s. In fact, her lifestyle was constantly the subject of scandal. She wore high-heeled shoes, played sports, went to the swimming pool, and drove a car.

In 1935, the customs were still very traditional. It was only after 1945 that Vietnamese society began to open itself to women. Everything was the subject of scandal. I used to go regularly to the pool and wore a bathing suit, and someone said that I was going naked. And then I would drive my own car in 1935, and it was a real scandal, the idea that a woman drove. In 1938–39, I wanted to learn how to pilot a plane. I thought this would be useful in a time of war in order to go and look for the wounded on the battlefields. But it was such a scandal that I had to stop my lessons. I was too much in advance for my time, and everybody looked at me in the wrong way. (1 July 1993)

In Vietnam, her family, especially the ones who never traveled abroad, did not approve of her lifestyle or career choice. Although she disagreed with her father and brothers on a number of issues, such as divorce, she was very close to them. When the Viet Minh assassinated her father and brothers in September 1945, Henriette Bui suffered a great deal. She lost the members of her family to whom she had felt the closest. She had shared with them the most important part of her life in France. They were the only ones who could understand her.

In 1946, soon after the death of her father and brothers, Dr. Henriette Bui went to France in the company of Nguyên Ngoc Bich. She had known him in Paris in the 1920s–30s, when he was a student at the famous École Polytechnique. Having returned to Vietnam just before the outbreak of World War II, he worked as a civil engineer. In 1945, he decided to join the resistance, like his friend Gaston Pham Ngoc Thuan, although he always refused to join the Communist Party. Held prisoner by the French and tortured in 1946, he escaped death because his fellow students of the École Polytechnique who worked as staff for General Leclerc saved him. Refusing to collaborate with the French, he was sent in exile to France. Henriette Bui and Nguyên Ngoc Bich never officially married, but to this day she refers to him as "my second husband." While Nguyên Ngoc Bich had to stay in France, Henriette Bui went back to Saigon in 1949 and continued to work there during the French-Indochina War.

5. A Medical Career out of the Ordinary (1955–73)

Acupuncture (1957–65)

After the end of the French-Indochina War, Dr. Henriette Bui fulfilled one of her dreams, to study Chinese traditional medicine. She had been fascinated by acupuncture since the time when she had worked in Cholon. Moreover, at that time doctors were exclusively trained in Western medicine and had little knowledge or competence in traditional medicine. During the colonial period, these two schools of medicine remained separate. Western medicine was considered the only official medicine, whereas traditional medicine was considered less scientific and was merely tolerated. At the age of fifty, Dr. Henriette Bui went to study acupuncture in Tokyo and Odawara, Japan, for two years. She then went back to France, where she opened a private practice on the Boulevard Raspail. She resumed her studies of rheumatology and offered consultations in acupuncture.

> In 1961, acupuncture was unrecognized and medical circles had absolutely no belief in it. And yet there were congresses on acupuncture. . . . Chinese, Japanese, and Koreans conducted diagnostic tests with only the pulse. The professors of medical physics, colleagues and friends of my husband [Nguyên Ngoc Bich], began to be interested. . . . Then I worked at the Pitié Salpétrière, in the department of Professor Haaz (radiology) for treatment against pain. I convinced him after curing him of a sciatic crisis with an acupuncture treatment. (22 November 1997)

Meanwhile, Nguyên Ngoc Bich studied medicine to become a professor of medical physics at the University of Paris. But both Henriette Bui and Nguyên Ngoc Bich left Paris in 1964, to find a cure for his advanced cancer. They went to Japan for treatments but then returned to Vietnam, where he died in 1965.

Doctor to the Front (1966–71)

In 1966, a year after the death of Nguyên Ngoc Bich, Henriette Bui stayed in Vietnam and worked with an international team of about twelve volunteers under the aegis of the World Council of Churches from 1966 to 1970. It was an organization similar to Médecins sans Frontières, Doctors without Borders. She was a chief physician of a medical team that cared for the wounded during the American war. During these four years, she worked in a war zone.

> On both sides, there were the same arms, the same methods. . . . It was war. . . . We helped people as best we could. The conditions were very difficult. I remember that during the offensive of 1968 I had to come back with great urgency from Saigon to Cai Be, where the team worked. On the road just outside My Tho, our convoy was attacked and the jeep ahead of us was blown up. There were serious casualties and a lot of dead. . . . I had to step over corpses, and I went into the hospital, which was being bombed. They were operating, and one bomb fell on the operating room. The person they were operating on died. (22 November 1997)

Subscribing to the Red Cross organization's principle of giving equal medical attention to wounded soldiers during a war, Dr. Henriette Bui treated anyone who was injured, even if they were considered "enemies."

> I never spoke about politics. There were some injured communists who came for consultations. I examined them, and I gave them prescriptions for medicine. When we went into the villages, all the chief nurses were communist. I knew it. They were very nice. . . . I was just doing my job, that's all. I saved quite a few who were communist. (22 November 1997)

In 1970, she volunteered for another year and a half in the Hai Ba Trung Hospital in Phu Tho (in the suburbs of Saigon) to work in the gynecology and pediatric department. In 1971, she went to France and retired there in 1978.

6. The Significance of Henriette Bui's Narrative

The personal account of Dr. Henriette Bui gives a new perspective on the cultural and political milieu of the Vietnamese intellectual elite during the interwar period in Vietnam.

Henriette Bui as the Daughter of Bui Quang Chieu

First of all, her life history offers a new approach to the *retours de France* milieu and the social environment in which Henriette Bui lived. Obviously, Henriette Bui was profoundly influenced by her social milieu, the Cochinchinese bourgeoisie of Saigon. And, although she left Vietnam when she was still young, in France she maintained her social network of both the Vietnamese and French milieux of her own social class.

Back in Saigon, her career as a doctor in the hospital and in private practice was her "professional milieu par excellence." But for many of her contemporaries, she had an exceptional life because she did not adopt the lifestyle of a woman of her own social class and was in fact "out of her own social milieu." In France, Henriette Bui knew most of the leading figures of the Vietnamese intellectual elite educated in France, such as Hoang Xuan Han, Nguyên Ngoc Bich, Pham Ngoc Thuan, and Ngô Dinh Nhu. But, as mentioned earlier, she belonged to the minority of Vietnamese women who had a multicultural background. For many of the Vietnamese intellectuals, returning to Indochina was a cultural shock. In Vietnam, relationships between French and Vietnamese were still based on the line of colonizers and colonized people. In contrast, in France the Vietnamese experienced an equal relationship with the French people.

Henriette Bui's life history also provides a new and more intimate glimpse into the private life of her father, Bui Quang Chieu, which is not very well known. Henriette Bui Quang Chieu was the product of two traditions: a Vietnamese tradition with her deep attachment to her Vietnamese identity and culture and her French adopted culture. Like her father, she spent her youth in France, and her personality was molded by two distinct cultures. She represented both the richness of this *métissage* and the burden encompassed by this hybrid culture. Her experience in France was not only unforgettable but allowed her to understand the roots of racial discrimination in colonized Vietnam. Under the French Republic, all French were treated equally under the law. Like her father, Henriette seldom experienced racism and injustice while living in France. But when she returned to Vietnam social injustice and inequality toward the natives was the status quo of the French colonies.

The portrait that Henriette paints of her father is not of the public man but the family man. What is striking in the relationship between father and daughter is the singular mixture of a traditional Vietnamese and modern Western education. The education Bui Quang Chieu gave to his children speaks to both. If one considers the traditional, subservient status of a woman raised according to the Confucian doctrine and in the rigid French society of the interwar years, the path of Henriette Bui is exceptional. Her father played a great part in her unusual itinerary, since he encouraged and supported her during all of these years. In that respect, Bui Quang Chieu was surprisingly "avant-garde" for his time.

Moreover, there was a certain degree of modernity in their relationship, with father and daughter straddling these two cultures: the Vietnamese father who tried to pass on to his children a French education he appreciated and a daughter increasingly independent and Gallic. Although her correspondence with her father during her long studies in France has been lost, his personality had greatly influenced her. Throughout her life, she maintained a privileged relationship with her father, showing for him a deep affection and respect. They did not always agree, and their relationship was sometimes in conflict between "traditions and modernity." Unlike traditional Vietnamese families, in which the filial bond between the father and his children remains rigid, the relationship between Henriette and her father was fluid and changing. And during all of her life Henriette kept a privileged relationship with her father. The picture of herself that she gave to him in 1931 with a dedication illustrates the love and affection that she had for him. She wrote "Toute mon affection, au meilleur des papas." (All my love to the best of fathers). This deep filial respect was a feature of a Confucian education, as testified to the dedication to her father in her thesis of 1934. Henriette Bui acted sometimes with incredible daring and yet observed filial obedience. She was aware of the open-mindedness of her father, and she was able to submit to his paternal authority, as when she accepted the marriage he had arranged for her.

In addition, Bui Quang Chieu was ahead of his time regarding the question of women, and undoubtfully his daughter played a role in his stand. Since 1911, he had fought for the education of girls, and he wrote an article in *Le Temps* (The Times) asking the government to open schools for girls. But at the same time in the newspaper *Phu Nu Tan Van* he argued that the Vietnamese elite (men) had enough to do addressing the issue of colonialism and social classes before they could also make the woman question a priority in their political agenda. Furthermore, he argued that, considering the urgency of social problems in Vietnam, the woman question should not become an additional divisive factor for Vietnamese vis-à-vis the French (*Phu Nhu Tan Van*, 20 June 1929). But by 1935, when his daughter returned to Saigon, he had reconsidered women's position in Vietnamese society. His newspaper, *La Tribune Indochinoise*, celebrated the success of the women graduates returning from France, including his daughter and Hoang Thi Nga, the first *docteur ès sciences*. Furthermore, in an opinion column, he wrote in "The Women's Forum," which appeared in his paper in November 1935: "Our French-educated fellow women citizens of modern ideas have begun to be aware of their social and political role. It's a sign of the times. Many of them have opinions to discuss in public" (*La Tribune Indochinoise*, 4 November 1935).

Both Henriette Bui and her father, however, still disagreed on many issues such as the priority of work in her life and her divorce. The affection and the respect she paid to her father were as important as her desire for freedom and independence. Often criticized by the colonial French and the traditional Vietnamese societies, she found few people who could understand her. If her father failed to grasp her lifestyle, he always remained her Vietnamese reference point. Therefore, I will argue that the relationship between Henriette Bui and her father illustrates a new type of relationship, one rooted in both Western and Asian cultures. Such a relationship, however, did not create a new hybrid type of relationship among Vietnamese people. I suggest instead that it represented a particular situation at a particular time for a particular group of people.

Henriette Bui's Testimony concerning the French Colonial Health Care System in Indochina

In her thesis on the history of colonial medicine in Indochina, Laurence Monnais-Rousselot relies heavily on French colonial and private archives and the memoirs of former Indochinese medical personnel. Dr. Henriette Bui's testimony concerning the colonial medical world in the interwar years offers a new perspective, different from the official discourses of the colonial doctors. She presents the "ambiguity of colonization" (to take up again the term used by P. Brocheux and D. Hémery).

And the use of oral sources on medical questions (patients and medical employees) allows us to better understand the relations between doctors and patients, French and Vietnamese doctors, and French and Vietnamese employees during the colonial period.

In spite of the more unselfish and philanthropic character of the medical function, the doctors strongly believed in Western scientific knowledge and never doubted their superiority over the natives. Above all, they were supportive of the colonial civilizing mission. On that point, Laurence Monnais-Rousselot rightly insists on the importance of the doctor's political function but fails to investigate the ambiguous position of the Indochinese doctors.

> The practitioner educates the masses by demonstrating to them the benefits of Western medicine and thus of the Mère Patrie. . . . The practitioner becomes, as the *métropole* so desired, the best intermediary between the administration and the populations, even the best at getting the local populations to accept "the benefits" of colonization. . . . Helped by the Vietnamese personnel to cover up her absences, he [the practitioner] incontestably played a role in the installation of French imperialism in Indochina. . . . In varying degrees, the medical personnel put its knowledge in the service of colonization. (1996, 257)

The gap remained considerable between the two groups. The French doctors were cut off from Vietnamese society by the colonial reality. Confident in their Western knowledge, these doctors were often ignorant of local traditions. Their own realities were far from the ones of the Indochinese doctors and employees. Laurence Monnais-Rousselot writes:

> The twenties conferred upon him [the Indochinese doctor] equality of status—in the texts—with the metropolitan practitioner. He finally entered into the great family of the "colonial doctors," not without having some difficulties within this microcosm, lacking in unity and little respected. (1996, 258–59)

And I want to use here the term *discrimination* rather than *difficulties*. In addition, Monnais-Rousselot asserts that:

Between European and the Vietnamese doctors, the relationship of power between colonized and colonizers remained strongly present. One would have to wait for the period of decolonization for the French doctors to consider the Vietnamese doctor as partner and to respect different Vietnamese approaches to medical practice. (Monnais-Rousselot 1996: 259)

She argues that: "Paradoxically, the most important hiatus is not to be found between these two protagonists [European and Vietnamese doctors] but between military and civil." Such an assertion shows how the written materials in the archives are biased and that internal disputes among French doctors had to do with their concerns over the interests of their group, such as military versus civil. I suggest that this issue has to do with personal opinion and the French debate over the interests of the military-civil personnel was to the "Vietnamese and Indochinese doctors" certainly not "the most important hiatus."

Henriette Bui as a Vietnamese Woman

The history of Dr. Henriette Bui portrays the life of a Vietnamese woman quite differently from the simplistic popular representation of the "yellow Eves of the white colonizers." Henriette Bui defied this negative stereotype because she was gifted, brilliant, intelligent, and audacious. Raised in both the Vietnamese and French cultures, her life was original and somehow "avant-garde" with respect to both Vietnamese and French criteria on a woman's place in society at that time.

The itinerary of Henriette Bui seems quite unique within the Cochinchinese bourgeoisie. While only boys were expected to go to universities, girls were supposed to marry and those who studied were exceptions. But, paradoxically, it was precisely her francophone environment (and above all her father) that made it possible for her to have a career. Her long stay in France during her youth and her independent life as a medical student played a determining role in the construction of her own unique identity. In France, she developed self-confidence and a strong will to succeed and overcome any difficult situation.

Whereas some Vietnamese women concerned with women's issues joined political organizations and subscribed to the Marxist ideology in social change, Henriette Bui never joined any political party.

She said that she was not interested in politics and as a doctor she was committed to her work.

Thus, her life is interesting not because of what it represents but because of its singularity. Raised in two cultures, Henriette Bui created her own identity from both her Vietnamese cultural heritage and Western culture. She always remained aware of the importance of her Vietnamese cultural identity, and in her view modernity never meant rejection of all that was Vietnamese. Being the daughter of a half-Chinese woman, she also considered herself a métis, or mixed-blood woman. Henriette Bui's life history is also a testimony to race relationships, not only between French and Vietnamese but also between Vietnamese and Chinese in Saigon. She chose for herself the life she wanted, although it was not acceptable in the society in which she lived. Living the life of a "liberated woman," she never joined other women in the struggle for gender equality in the feminist movements in Vietnam and France.

Conclusion

Dr. Henriette Bui was an exceptional woman with avant-garde ideas for her time. As the daughter of a prominent politician, she was the focus of much criticism and many polemics in Saigonese society. But as the first Vietnamese woman doctor, who devoted her life to medicine, she is an important figure in the history of the interwar period. Like her father, she believed that it was important to work within the system and after achieving a certain status to work toward change. As a doctor, she gained recognition for her work and the values for which she stood. Although she never got involved in politics or joined the feminist movement, her life stands as a model for women who try to assert themselves and gain equality in Vietnamese society. Henriette Bui's achievements reveal her true nature as a reformist rather than a revolutionary.

NOTES

Groupe d'Etudes sur le Vietnam Contemporain, GEVC, Paris.

1. I interviewed Henriette Bui her in Paris over a period of six years. Quotations from these interviews are cited by date.

2. Files on the family of Bui Quang Chieu, files on the Vietnamese students in France, and the personal file on Henriette Bui during her time as a medical civil servant.

3. On that note, I would like to express my deepest thanks to Dr. Henriette Bui for the numerous interviews she accorded me, for her kindness in welcoming me, and for her patience in responding to my endless questions. I would also like to express my gratitude to Professor Pierre Brocheux and Professor Gisele Bousquet for their remarks and suggestions in the preparation of this chapter. Christopher Goscha deserves my special gratitude for his valuable comments and editorial work.

4. Lyon's silk industry has depended for its production on the importation of silk from Asia for many years.

5. In the 1920s, the French government decided to build student dormitories in Paris (La Cité Universitaire) in the then suburbs of the city because students, especially foreign students, could not find housing. The dormitories of the Cité Universitaire were divided into different *maisons* (houses). Among them were the Maison du Canada, Maison des États Unis, and the Maison d'Indochine. The Maison d'Indochine was built for the students of Indochina, who were not then allowed to find housing elsewhere. The Maison d'Indochine was also used by the French Sûreté to control the political activities of Vietnamese students. But women were not allowed to live in the Maison d'Indochine.

6. The Foyer International de Jeunes Filles was a private boardinghouse owned by an American woman, which housed foreign woman students. It was in Paris opposite the Jardin du Luxembourg.

SELECTED BIBLIOGRAPHY

On Bui Quang Chieu

Brocheux, Pierre. 1994. "Portrait en blanc et noir d'un bourgeois mal aimé: Bui Quang Chieu." In *Saigon, 1925–1945: De la "Belle Colonie" à l'éclosion révolutionnaire ou la fin des dieux blancs*. Paris: Autrement, 153–58.

Carter, Jay. 1994. "A Subject Elite: The First Decade of the Constitutionalist Party in Cochinchina, 1917–1927," *Viet Nam Forum* 14:211–43.

Cook, Megan. 1977. *The Constitutionalist Party in Cochinchina: The Years of Decline, 1930–1942*. Monash Papers on Southeast Asia, no. 6. Center of Southeast Asia Studies, Monash University. Melbourne, Australia.

Smith, Ralph B. 1969. "Bui Quang Chieu and the Constitutionalist Party in French Cochinchina, 1917–1930." *Modern Asian Studies* 3, no. 2: 131–50.

On the Vietnamese Elite during the Interwar Period

Brocheux, Pierre. 1994. "Elite, bourgeoisie, ou la difficulté d'être." In *Saigon, 1925–1945: De la "Belle Colonie" à l'éclosion révolutionnaire ou la fin des dieux blancs*. Paris: Autrement, 135–52.
Dalloz, Jacques. 1988. "Les Vietnamiens dans la franc-maçonnerie coloniale." *Revue Française d'Historie d'Outre-Mer* 85, no. 320: 103–18.
Monnais-Rousselot, L. 1997. *Medecine coloniale, pratiques de sante et societies en Indochine francaise, 1860–1939*, These de doctorat en histoire "nouveau regime," Universite Paris 7—Denis Diderot.
Trinh Van Thao. 1991. *Viet Nam: Du confucianisme au communisme*. Paris: L'Harmattan.
———. 1995. *L'école française en Indochine*. Paris: Karthala.

On the History of Women Doctors and Colonial Medicine in General

Joel, Constance. 1988. *Les filles d'Esculape. Les femmes à la conquête du pouvoir médical*. Paris: Laffont.
Marr, David G. 1981. *Vietnamese tradition on trial, 1920–1945*. Berkeley: University of California Press.
Nguyên Van Ký. 1995. *La société vietnamienne face à la modernité: le Tonkin de la fin du XIXe siècle à la Seconde Guerre mondiale*. [Paris]: L'Harmattan.
Ruscio, Alain. 1996. *Amours coloniales: aventures et fantasmes exotiques de Claire de Duras à Georges Simenon: romans et nouvelles*. Bruxelles: Editions Complexe.

Part III

Postcolonial Vietnam:
From a Welfare State to a
Market-Oriented Economy

10   Pierre Brocheux

The Economy of War as a Prelude to a "Socialist Economy": The Case of the Vietnamese Resistance against the French, 1945–1954

Introduction

This essay focuses on the economy of the Vietnamese resistance during the first Indochina war and examines to what extent and how it formed the matrix of the economy of the 1955 Democratic Republic of Vietnam (DRV). Ho Chi Minh solemnly founded the DRV on 2 September 1945 in Hanoi, right after the great famine that struck North Vietnam, killing from 1 to 2 million people.[1] The DRV inherited a colonial economy, much destroyed by World War II. As soon as it was created, the DRV was engaged in the war against France in order to gain its independence. By then, the DRV had few resources, particularly in land, since the French and their nationalist allies occupied a large part of the country. Only other strategies made it possible for the Vietnamese leaders to manage the country during the war against the French. What were the mechanisms that allowed the Vietnamese resistance to cope with that situation? In this essay I will show how the Vietnamese organized their economy and what kind of policies they had to adopt and for what purpose. In addition, I suggest that it is important to take into account social practices during the war, as people were forced to change their behaviors to deal with the difficulties.[2]

1. The Legacy of the Colonial Economy

After the proclamation of independence, the new Vietnamese government had to manage its economy. Up until World War II, French capitalists controlled the Vietnamese economy. The largest private French investments were in Vietnamese rubber plantations, mines, and commercial activities.[3] The three main Vietnamese commodities, rice, rubber and coal, were exported, and colonial tariffs gave priority to French industrial products imported to Vietnam. Even the Vietnamese currency system at the time was organized to benefit French capitalists. Vietnamese currency, the piaster, had no value outside Vietnam and had to be exchanged for the franc.[4]

The French refused to industrialize Indochina, and it remained an agricultural producer-exporter as well as an outlet for French imported industrial goods. In the Red River delta and the adjacent provinces of Thanh Hoa, Nghê An, and Hà Tinh, food production did not match demographic growth in spite of the sophisticated traditional rice-growing industry and the hydraulic system built in the 1930s.

Another aspect of the Indochinese economy, in particular in Vietnam, was a local economy that later was to lay the foundation for the economy of the Vietnamese resistance. Based on agrarian production, part of it was used for local consumption and the rest supplied the market for other provinces and regions. It consisted of a wide range of handicrafts both traditional and modern (using metal, textile, and mechanical workshops).[5]

An important characteristic of the Vietnamese economy was its centuries old participation in the Eastern commercial mainstream, as shown by the resilient land and sea communications with China and the rest of Southeast Asia.[6] The French did not force the Vietnamese out of the Chinese or other Asian networks.

During the Great Depression and the following years, 1931–38, France became the principal outlet for Indochinese exports, in particular rice, but due to the relationship between Vietnam and its Asian business partners, China and Hong Kong, its exports were not severely affected by the Depression, and resumed just before World War II.[7]

Indochina was not itself a battlefield during World War II, but most of its infrastructure and machinery were destroyed by Allied bombings. After the war, France drew up an industrial blueprint for reconstruction called the Plan d'Industrialisation de l'Indochine.[8] While many Vietnamese understood the concept of independence in terms of political sovereignty, the Vietnamese Leninists argued that political independence could not exist without controlling the economy. The Leninists formulated a plan for the reconstruction of the Vietnamese economy using the two models available at the time, the Japanese Meiji and Soviet socialism. Walt Rostow had not yet published his theory of development, which suggested that former colonies ought to modernize, industrialize, urbanize, and revolutionize their agriculture. The Vietnamese reconstruction plan was delayed because of the new postwar situation. The French refused to give up Indochina, and the Vietnamese, who had already claimed their independence, refused to give it up. Confrontation was inevitable and was aggravated by the escalation of the cold war conflict.

The economy, then, became an issue, a battlefield, and a weapon. The vocabulary and military tactics of scorched earth, blockade, and *guerre économique*, expressed and materialized those three aspects. What, then, became of these ideal and theoretical premises and purposes under the necessities of war?

2. Theory and Realities

The DRV wanted to create a modern state with a constitution, a national congress elected by universal franchise, distinct ministries, an army, and a currency. For example, the ministries of finance and the economy had their specific agencies for customs and taxation.[9] As the conflict intensified, the war spread to all regions in Vietnam and also to other countries in Indochina. It was a time of chaos, and the whole of Vietnam never came under the jurisdiction of Ho Chi Minh's government. In December 1953, the Vietnamese resistance claimed an estimated population under each sector's control (table 1).[10]

According to the table, the majority of the population was under either total or partial control of the resistance except in South Vietnam, Nam Bo. It is important to mention that such data may not be reliable since the Vietnamese government often used them for propaganda purposes. On the other hand, we know that the French army occupied principal towns, ports, and areas with a high economic value such as coal mines, plantations, and sometimes rice paddies.

The so-called free zones were vulnerable to French "search and destroy" operations.

As a result, the Vietnamese government decentralized its operations and production, including issuing currency to central and southern Vietnam, and then authorized the provincial authorities to do the same. In southern Vietnam, the Committee of Resistance and Administration (Uy Ban Khang Chiên Hanh Chinh Nam Bo, hereafter UBKCHCNB) was assisted by a Committee of Economic Resistance (Uy Ban Khang Chiên Kinh Tê) with subcommittees for finances, production, commerce, and industry. There were also two special subcommittees, one for trading with the occupied zone using Chinese intermediaries called *binh phong* (screen) and the other to control price and taxes.[11]

Currency as the tangible sign of sovereignty was a matter of great political importance. In August 1946, the Vietnamese government issued the national currency, the dong (referred to as Ho Chi Minh's piaster by the French), officially titered 0.375 grams of gold in July 1948. Banknotes were printed in Lien Khu 4, later (1950) in Czechoslovakia.[12] Because there were not enough dong for trade and taxation, the currency was either printed in South Vietnam or replaced with government bonds then used as payment. The dong was not convertible and thus competed against the French piaster, issued by La Banque de l'Indochine (BIC). The resistance authorities did not allow anyone in the free zones to have or use the BIC piaster because the government wanted to use it for its own transactions.[13]

Vietnamese policy favored bottom-up initiatives in decision making. It is not surprising that a French analyst wrote on the "Viet Minh economic policy": "The policies of the government are so few and so

TABLE 1

	Whole Country (estimations)	Free Area	Occupied Area	Shared Control Area[a]
Vietnamese population	21,231,672	12,928,246	6,085,102	2,218,324
North, Bac Bo	10,298,237	7,191,284	1,657,470	1,449,583
Central, Trung Bo	6,463,905	5,195,680	1,035,473	242,762
South, Nam Bo	4,469,430	541,282	3,402,169	525,979

[a]This means that the French controlled the area during the day and the resistance during the night.

simplistic that we can say that the central authorities are free and easy and even almost nonexistent."[14] This comment was made earlier during the war when the Vietnamese had not yet revised their own internal organization. According to some captured documents, the central Vietnamese government was attempting to progressively control the economy and adopted new policies such the one on land reform.

In an article published in *Su Thât* (Truth), Bui Cong Trung, a member of the central committee of the Indochinese Communist Party (ICP), which focused on economic policy, outlined the DRV economy during the war of resistance. He wrote that the war offered a unique opportunity to lay down the economic foundations for the "new democracy" (a communist concept that had been theorized by Mao Zedong in 1940). By roughly presenting the blueprint of the war economy, Trung promoted the embryo of the "socialist" economy. He explained the policy as the following: (1) the Vietnamese had to control the economy in order to reach self-sufficiency while developing state-run and collective sectors; (2) given the importance and influence of the private sector, the state needed to support and subsidize experienced individual entrepreneurs, who, in turn, would train the managers of the new economy; (3) in the immediate future and in every strategic zone (*khu*, or interzone, Lien Khu), the resistance should expand its cultivated areas, develop handicrafts, and encourage barter to substitute for the shortage of money; and (4) finally the policy on land reform should be implemented, the lands owned by "French colonialists and traitors" should be confiscated and redistributed to the poor and landless peasants, and all enemy property and means of production had to be destroyed.[15]

3. The Three Main Aspects of the Resistance Economy

The Relationship between the Free and Occupied Zones

The economies of the free and occupied zones and that of the neighboring foreign countries were interlinked. The zones under the control of the DRV government were not the richest in Vietnam because, as mentioned earlier, the French had regained control of the plantations, the export-producing rice areas, the coal mines, and the towns with the largest factories and mills. While controlling Lien Khu 4 and the plains of Central Vietnam, the resistance government and its troops retreated into the mountains, the forests, and the marshes, where they relied on local resources for foodstuffs, textiles, and raw materials. Food production, weaponry, and management were the top priority in the economic agenda of the DRV. By 1949, the resistance leaders, concerned with the cost of the war imposed on the people, requested that the resistance army become self-sufficient. The *bo doi* (soldiers) and *cân bô* (cadres) had to grow their own food by tilling the land, raising chickens and pigs, and catching fish. In addition, importation of goods from the zone occupied by the French was to decrease drastically. The concept of self-sufficiency was a means to resist the French embargo and at the same time to relieve the population from the burden of supporting the troops who would have otherwise relied on requisitions.[16]

At the beginning of the war, the resistance authorities could get their supplies in the zones; they controlled mainly the Mekong Delta (rice, salt, pepper, and dried fish) and also North and Central Vietnam. In 1948, for instance, the French estimated that the Vietnamese disposed of 150,000 tons of salt from Bac Lieu Province and Kampot (in nearby Cambodia), while salt marshes in northern Ha Tinh and Nghê An provided 12,000 tons.[17]

The DRV's revenue was used to maintain its troops and government staff, to purchase military materials and foodstuffs, and finally to assert the state's existence and authority. The government implemented a new fiscal system to cut ties with the past and erase the bad memories of the colonial regime. For instance, it abolished the poll tax and the three monopolies of opium, alcohol, and salt. It kept the land tax and levies on agricultural production, forest products, salt marshes, and handicrafts. In August 1948, the resistance authorities of Quang Nam Province stated: "We must fight against the erroneous idea that the population should not pay taxes." On this issue, assessments of the situation are contradictory. Some reported people's enthusiasm, while others, undoubtedly more realistic, thought the contrary. Nguyên Thanh Vinh, head of the Economic Committee of South Vietnam, wrote in September 1947, "The population tried by any means to avoid paying taxes." The March–April 1952 report to the UBKCHCNB pointed out that "The Chinese are reluctant to pay agricultural taxes." And in September of that year Pham Van Bach, chairman of the UBKCHCNB, delivered a critical speech in which he denounced the use of coercive measures to levy taxes and fix prices; he also condemned the illegal seizures of commodities and arbitrary arrests. Bach then exposed Vietnamese cadres who had cheated on their incomes and protected their kin and friends who had done the same. In fact, tax evasion was a big problem, for which Bach argued: "We need a minimum of 5 million *gia* [1 *gia* equals 40 liters or 8.8 gallons] of paddy, but we get only 1 million . . . the agricultural tax must provide 60 percent of the budget of southern Vietnam, Nam Bo." The resistance authorities wanted to reduce the burden of direct taxes because Vietnamese were not after all as supportive as the political propaganda claimed. Instead they increased the taxes on exports and imports between the free and occupied zones.[18]

The tax on rice paddy depended on soil classification. In South Vietnam, it was fixed at 10 dong per *mâu* (3,600 *mâu*), in Central Vietnam it was at 50 dong, and in Thai Binh Province in North Vietnam it was at 27 dong. The regional difference in the price was due to decisions of the Uy Ban, local committees, which acted independently. From November 1947 to March 1948, in South Vietnam, Nam Bo, the provinces of Soc Trang, Bac Lieu, and Can Tho provided the bulk of land and production taxes. The total was estimated at 21,300,000 piasters BIC. Taxes on transport were calculated according to the price of rice in Cholon: one picul (60 kg). For instance, in Ben Tre province, the price was 40 piasters, but when it was delivered in Cholon it was at 110 piasters. The owners of boats that sailed from Chau Doc to Saigon-Cholon had to pay 4,000 piasters for every round trip.[19] In North Vietnam, Ho Dac Vy reported that the same rule applied: "The trade between the two zones was heavily taxed."[20] Two-thirds of the revenue of the resistance came from these taxes, mostly on transport. The trade between the free and the occupied zones was very intense.

In addition to the trade taxes, the Vietnamese government imposed taxes on production. It was the same strategy that Admiral Decoux's administration had used during World War II. In Saigon-Cholon, the so-called Viet Minh Bureau of Economic Control decided which villages in the delta would provide rice, and after issuing export licenses it forced rice millers in Cholon to pay two or three piasters per bag (60 kg) of white rice. The rice millers also had to pay a tax proportionate to its energy-machinery power needs (fifty piasters per horsepower). Owners who refused to pay had their mills sabotaged and in some cases burned. In 1949, sixteen rice mills were destroyed by fire.[21] The same control was exerted on the production of fish sauce (*nuoc mam*).[22] In addition to tax revenues, the resistance authorities requisitioned what they needed. They also distributed loans in the form of bonds, which could be used as currency but were never redeemed.[23]

The Escalation of the Economic War

The longer the war lasted, the tougher it became. From the beginning of the hostilities, the French wanted to destroy the Vietnamese economy. The Vietnamese, who believed that the French capitalists were financing the war, wanted to destroy all French properties in Vietnam, such as factories and plantations. In January 1947, the coal mine of Campha was sabotaged, leaving only one site still working, producing only 2,000 tons. In another instance, a telegram from the resistance authority gave the order to "burn all rubber stocks (150,000 tons) in the occupied zone in order to stop its exportation."[24] In the free zone, the Vietnamese resistance authority exploited the mines to a maximum, using the former colonial machinery. The chemicals and metals extracted from these mines were used to make weapons. Ho Dac Vy classified the factories in Lien Khu 4 as in table 2.[25]

On the other hand, the French did everything to disable production by destroying Vietnamese industries. In 1952, most Vietnamese factories and mines were demolished by French air strikes. The work had to be resumed in smaller facilities scattered throughout the countryside. But during that year, while Vietnamese production suffered a great deal, the increase in aid from the Chinese Communists compensated for that loss.

The French not only bombed military targets but also hit civilian industries such as the salt marshes and livestock. In Central Vietnam, between Hôi An and Cape Varella, the salt marshes abandoned for twenty years and reused by the resistance were demolished in June and July 1949. French commandos destroyed 2,500 tons of salt. In October, 8,000 tons were ruined in Ho Do and Phu Nghia.[26] In 1949, between 112 and 88 hectares of salt marshes were ruined in the southern provinces of Tra Vinh and Bac Lieu. And in Central Vietnam 8,000 and 2,500 tons of salt were ruined.[27]

In 1951, the dam of Do Luong, constructed under Governor-General Brévié in 1937, and the dams of Nam Dan and Bai Thuong, all built during the colonial period to prevent drought, were destroyed. As a result, the Vietnamese could get only one harvest instead of two, as they used to in the past.[28]

Throughout the country, during harvest time a "battle for rice" was waged by both sides. In Central Vietnam, Trung Bo, the French protected the harvest in the zones they controlled and destroyed the

TABLE 2

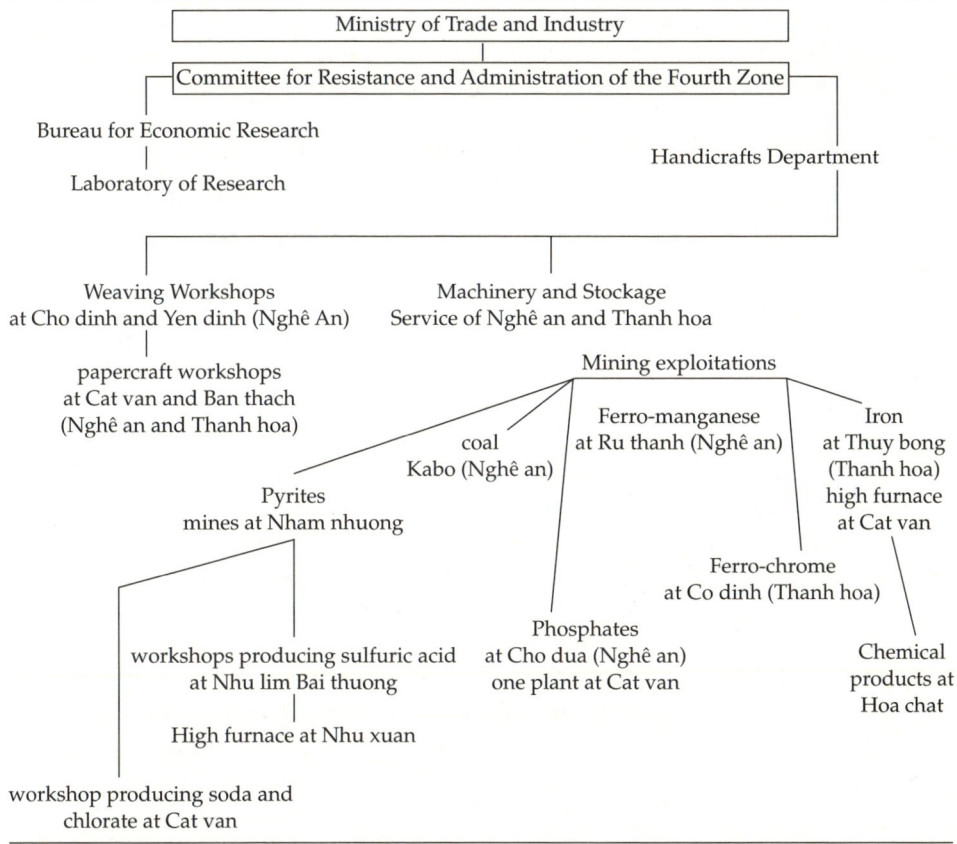

Note: In 1952, most of those sites and workshops were destroyed by the French Airforce and after reconstruction, they were scattered in the forested mountains.

one in the free zone: "We must annihilate their expectations of harvest in the rebel villages by sabotaging the irrigation network" (a directive of the French commander dated 6 July 1950).[29] The nationalist governor of Central Vietnam overestimated the number of French troops needed to protect the harvest of Lê Thuy District and the rice granary of Quang Binh from the resistance (letter dated 19 May 1953).[30]

In Quang Nam Province, the French acknowledged that it was impossible to protect the harvest. They attempted to force farmers to stock their surplus production in guarded barns, but this method never worked. There were many ways to take rice out of the occupied zone. Quotas were granted for free trade (15 percent of the harvest) with special compensations. In order to stop rice evasions, the French would have had to supervise not only the landowners but the sharecroppers, who were paid in kind, and the hydraulic pump owners, who rented out their services. There were also many Buddhist sanctuaries, which had rice paddies, whose production was not controlled by the French.[31]

From 1949 to 1953, the war entered a new phase when the French tried to block the free zone, mostly in the southern part of the Mekong Delta called Transbassac (Viet: Hâu Giang). That area was considered a rice basket. By doing so, the French wanted to stop the export of rice, pepper, charcoal, and other forest products. In fact, through direct sales and taxation the area provided a major source of revenue for the UBKCHCNB. The payments were in piasters BIC, which were used to buy weapons and medicines. The French also prohibited the export of gasoline, electrical supplies, chemical and metal materials, and textiles to the free zone. Ho Dac Vy wrote that it was best not to be ill there since there were no medicines in Lien Khu 4 except in the fifty pharmacy shops in Thanh Hoa and Vinh, which sold expensive medicines imported from the occupied zone.[32]

The Vietnamese resistance's blockade against the enemy zones (Bao Ve Kinh Dich) affected the free more than the occupied zone.[33] At the local level, that situation resulted in temporary deals between French-allied Vietnamese and the local resistance groups. The Hoa Hao military chiefs, allied with the French, who controlled the traffic from the delta to other parts of South Vietnam and even to southern Central Vietnam, turned a blind eye to smuggling in return for bribes or partnerships.[34]

In the end, the French had to lift the blockade at the request of

Bao Dai's government. Trân Van Huu, the prime minister, complained to the French high commissioner that the blockade, which had already imposed losses on the Viet Minh, was also affecting ordinary Vietnamese people, including the nationalist authority's employees, whose salaries were low. Because of inflation, they could barely survive. In fact, black markets and smuggling were common and were controlled mostly by Chinese traders and sects such as the Hoa Hao, Binh Xuyen, and Cao Dai.[35] In the end, the blockade had no impact, since traders and political groups enjoyed much freedom on both sides.

As the French army suffered its greatest defeats on the Chinese border, the economy of North Vietnam, run by both state and private enterprises, and with the help of Soviet and Chinese aid, was slowly growing. According to the report of a former clerk of the colonial bureaucracy, who joined the resistance as a *cân bô* of the ministry of finance and returned to the French and nationalist zone, the Chinese aid provided first necessity commodities and small wares so that the town of Tuyen Quang had a well-stocked market with cotton goods, clothes, sheets, and housekeeping tools. In return, Viet Bac exported building and furniture wood, coffee, cinnamon, and anise seeds to China. Trade with the occupied zone was also officially authorized, and every market had a currency exchange office.[36]

Economically, the resistance in the south was not doing well, however. According to a report: "Self-sufficiency is progressing, but our economy relies on the economy of the enemy. We are unable to control foreign trade, and our blockade against the enemy is inefficient. On the other hand, the enemy's blockade is very effective and has already damaged our economy because of the infiltration of 150,000 counterfeit dong. Consequently, the exchange value of our currency against the piaster BIC has decreased. Living costs are 200 percent more than in the occupied zone. The decision to fix prices is also a failure and has had the contrary effect. It has encouraged smuggling and black markets."[37]

In March 1950, the president of the UBKCHCNB stated: "The French still have the advantage on the economic front.[38] One year after the military conference of Khu Mien Tay K.9, the situation has not really changed, as it was assessed in the proceedings. Although we have won on the battlefield [meaning Viet Bac], we still have many problems with our economy, which is the enemy's primary target. For instance, the infiltration of the counterfeit currency has depreciated the dong, and smuggling has increased. As a result, inflation has taken place. In addition, the enemy has destroyed sugar and textile mills and disrupted communications and transport between Khu 9 and Khu 8."[39]

The lifting of the blockade in May 1953 demonstrates that both the free and the occupied zones were so intertwined that it was impossible to separate them.[40] General Salan, commander of the French army, who accurately pointed out the symbiosis of the antagonists, protested the lifting, which he said was "the only method with which to win an economic war. . . . Because of the agrarian and agricultural reforms, the enemies have drastically improved their food production, mainly in Viet Bac. But the enemy is living at our expense by organizing trading between their zone and ours. . . . Using strict customs controls and a sophisticated fiscal system . . . it is not an overstatement to claim that French military expenditures in Indochina have been used by the enemy to favor its own economy and have also contributed to the enemy military's revenues."[41]

The Resistance and Its Vital Relationship with
Neighboring Countries

The relationship among the three areas of North, Central, and South Vietnam and their respective foreign neighbors was crucial in the independence war against the French. Often those relationships were even closer than the ones among the three Vietnamese regions. Even at the beginning of the conflict Asian countries became involved in the Vietnamese war. While the Indochinese countries, Vietnam, Laos, and Cambodia, were part of one war zone, South China and Thailand were strategic locations for recruitment, military camps, and safe havens for troops. In fact, beginning in 1950 the Thai anticommunist dictator General Phibun Songkhram made no effort to get rid of Vietnamese resistance troops going into Thailand. And when the Chinese Communists took over China they established safe haven zones for their Vietnamese comrades, providing them with military camps.

Cambodia and South Vietnam established an unofficial common border. The UBKCHCNB created a special Committee for Foreign Relations with Cambodia, led by Nguyên Thanh Son. The committee stated that both Cambodia and the Khmer community living in South Vietnam were of importance to the Vietnamese resistance. Nguyên Binh, a military commander of the resistance, planned safe havens for Vietnamese resistance troops in Cambodia.[42] In 1950, the Uy Ban Khang Chiên Kinh Tê was expected to collect seven million piasters by taxing the twelve thousand tons of salt produced in the southeastern Cambodian province of Kampot.[43]

Relations with Thailand were maintained through Cambodia. In northeastern Thailand, the Vietnamese community supported the resistance, and volunteers went to Vietnam via a trail that crossed northern Cambodia. On the coast of the Gulf of Siam, steamers, junks, and a host of sampans were involved in smuggling goods into Vietnam, thus avoiding the French navy's control. The main transit point was at Mai Ruot at the edges of Thai and Cambodian territorial waters,[44] but many islands were also used for transit and shelter. Further north on the peninsula, Laos served as a transit point, providing direct access to Lien Khu 4 and Viet Bac. Prior to the arrival of the Chinese communist troops on the border of Bac Bo, the southern Chinese provinces, principally Guangxi and the island of Hai Nan, were already key meeting points for the two countries. The main road from Guangxi to Vietnam via Long Zhou and Cao Bang had already been established.[45] Chang Fakuei, the former warlord of Guangxi, who sympathized with the DRV, let the Vietnamese operate in his province.

When the Chinese Communist army reached the Vietnamese border, Vietnam was integrated into the Asian strategy of the People's Republic of China.[46] The newly established Chinese government was to supply the DRV with massive aid. It grew considerably in 1952 and in 1953 and culminated in 1954. The aid consisted essentially of military equipment, including large artillery and trucks, and it also supplied the DRV army with training, uniforms, weapons, and emergency medical kits. Finally, China provided the DRV with military advisers and technical experts.[47] In the 1950s, Chinese support of the DRV was crucial in the Vietnamese struggle for independence. With Chinese military assistance, the Vietnamese resistance troops no longer relied on guerrilla warfare, which in the long term was not effective, but instead launched massive military attacks against the French army. In 1950, the French army suffered its first great defeat against the Vietnamese at Cao Bang.

Conclusion

The Vietnamese resistance won the war for two reasons. The first was its economy, and the second was the support of neighboring countries. The economy of the Vietnamese resistance was based on local self-sufficiency in agriculture and handicrafts, short- and medium-range trade, and active regional Asian commercial networks. The resistance troops were able to retreat to neighboring countries, particularly in 1950 when China officially offered the DRV southern Chinese provinces as sanctuaries.

After its victory, or half-victory, in 1954, the DRV, now limited to the north, inherited an economy crippled by war whose new workers were peasants and craftsmen. The Vietnamese government created state-run workshops and factories and encouraged peasants, to whom the confiscated land was given, to enter cooperatives. But, as chapter 11, on collectivization, by Florence Yvon-Tran, demonstrates, the government's attempts to force the peasants to create cooperatives failed.

The communist government of the DRV fortunately did not create a central economy as the Russian revolutionaries did. During the war, with some exceptions, the leaders of the DRV, who were pragmatic concerning the safeguarding of the national united front, avoided dictatorial methods, although in practice local resistance authorities may have used them.

Nevertheless, the "communist war" was responsible for the movement toward rural collectivization and the militarization of industry. State-owned enterprises and agricultural collectivization were the two pillars of the economy of North Vietnam. The Vietnamese communist leaders wanted to build an inward-looking economy subordinated to central planning with priority given to heavy industries. However, the Vietnamese government followed Bui Cong Trung's recommendations and did not eliminate household production, allowing peasants in cooperatives to have private plots. Thus, the household economy was never abolished in Vietnam, although it was contrary to the principle of neo-Stalinist socialism. The anti-French resistance's economy clearly demonstrated the limits of an inward-looking economy and the pipe dream of an independent economy. Today Vietnamese reformers, the architects of Doi Moi, have used as a point of reference that period of resistance, the immediate postwar era, and Bui Cong Trung's economic theories. Like their predecessors, they realize that private enterprise, industries, and business, as well as the agricultural household economy, are not only an important aspect of Vietnamese economy but also vital.

NOTES

Universite Denis Diderot, Paris.

1. Van Tao and Furuta Moto, *Nan doi nam 1945 o Viet Nam: Nhung chung tich lich su* (Testimonies on the 1945 Famine in Vietnam). Hanoi: Viên su hoc Viet nam, 1955. The best discussion is Bui Minh Zung, "Japan's Role in the Vietnam Starvation of 1944–1945," *Modern Asian Studies* 29 (3) (1995): 573–618.

2. For this essay, I draw heavily on the French military archives (Service Historique de l'Armée de Terre, hereafter SHAT). These contain many documents on the zone occupied by the French and their anticommunist allies, but they are also rich in captured documents, many written in *quoc ngu* and duplicated with French translations. 10H. is the serial number of the archives relative to Indochina. SHAT owns more data on Nam Bo (the south) than Bac Bo (the north) and Trung Bo (the center). Hence my essay has more references and illustrative cases from the south than from the other two *bô*. CAOM stands for Centre des Archives d'Outre-Mer in Aix-en-Provence.

3. C. Robequain, *The Economic Development of French Indochina* (London: Oxford University Press, 1944); M. Murray, *The Development of Capitalism in Colonial Indochina, 1870–1940* (Berkeley: University of California Press, 1980); J. Marseille, *Empire colonial et capitalisme français: Histoire d'un divorce* (Paris: Albin Michel, 1984).

4. Yasuo Gonjo, *Banque coloniale ou banque d'affaires: La Banque de l'Indochine sous la IIIe République.* (Paris: Imprimerie nationale, 1993); M. Meuleau, *Des pionniers en Extrême-Orient: Histoire de la Banque de l'Indochine (1875–1975).* (Paris: Fayard, 1991).

5. P. Gourou, *The Peasants of the Tonkin Delta* (New Haven, Human Relations Area Files, 1955). Vu Huy Phuc, *Tiêu thu công nghiêp Viêt Nam (1858–1945)* (Handicrafts in Vietnam) (Hanoi: Nhà Xuât ban KHXH, 1996).

6. P. Y. Manguin, *Les Portugais sur les côtes du Vietnam et du Campa: Études sur les routes maritimes et les relations commerciales d'après les sources portugaises (XVIe, XVIIe, XVIIIe S.)* (Paris: Publications de l'EFEO, 1984). A. Reid, *South East Asia in the Age of Commerce*, vols. 1 and 2, (New Haven: Yale University Press, 1988, 1993).

7. Robequain, *Economic Development*.

8. A. Hardy, "La politique économique française en Indochine de 1944 à 1948," master's thesis, Université Denis Diderot, Paris, 1991.

9. B. Fall, *The Viet Minh Regime* (Ithaca: Cornell University Press, 1956). On the war, see Lt Gal Davidson, Phillip B., *Vietnam at War: The History, 1946–1975* (Novato, Calif.: Presidio Press, 1988); Gal C. Gras, *La guerre d'Indochine* (Paris:

Denoël, 1992); and collected and selected documents edited in G. Bodinier, *1945–1946: Le retour de la France en Indochine, Indochine 1947, Réglement politique ou solution militaire* (Vincennes: SHAT, 1987, 1989).

10. SHAT 10H 282.

11. "Etude sur l'économie Vietminh, 1948" (French document); and "Chanh sach kinh tê tài chanh cua chanh phu hiên nay 1953" (document captured in Rach Gia Province), 10H 3990. Regarding the "screen" or "undercover" operations, the government of the resistance employed Chinese transports, used their shops, and had joint ventures with them. Sometimes it had its own enterprises like the trading company Dan Hoa Thuong Hoi (*Intelligence Bulletin*, September 1950, 10H 3995).

12. Testimony of Ho Dac Vy. A chemist graduated from the University of Bordeaux, Vy worked in the laboratory of the colonial Agricultural Agency in Hanoi. From December 1946 to September 1952, he stayed and worked in Lien Khu 4 in the same laboratory for the DRV. Then he went to the occupied zone with his family and made a detailed statement (fifty-four typewritten pages) on life in the free zone (10H 3990). An important file on DRV currency problems is contained in 10H 3992.

13. 10H 3994. File 234 of 10H 639 contains loan bonds issued by the UBKCHCNB.

14. "Etude sur léconomie Vietminh 1948," 10H 3990.

15. *Su Thât*, 19 August and 2 September 1948. During a secret meeting of the Politburo in Hanoi on 9 November 1946, Trinh Van Binh, state secretary of finance in Ho Chi Minh's government, stated that autarchy would be based on cooperatives and Viet Nam would limit its relationships with foreign countries (CAOM, Conseiller Politique, carton 6).

16. Reports from the resistance captured in Long Chau Sa (provinces of Longxuyen, Chaudoc, and Sadec), 10H 4840. 10H 641 contains a pamphlet, dated 1949, that ordered the local and regional forces of Viet Bac to be made self-sufficient (*Tu cung tu cap*). Ho Dac Vy gave one more reason for raising poultry and cultivating a garden: his salary was just enough to live on for two weeks with his wife and his daughter, so it had to be supplemented with their own production.

17. "Bilan économique et financier du Vietminh en mai 1950," 10H 3991.

18. 10H 13990–98 contain a number of documents on taxes, customs, currency, loans, and so on. On the fiscal documents in Bac Bo and Binh Thuân, province of Trung bô, see 10H 630 and 640.

19. "Etude sur l'économie Vietminh en 1948."

20. Ho Dac Vy, 10H 1037.

21. 10H 3990.

22. In May 1949, importers of *nuoc mam* from Phan Thiet (Trung Bo) had to pay 0.45 piasters per jar at departure and 1.55 on arrival in Saigon. Every junk owner paid 5 piasters per ton (10H 3990).

23. The decrees that launched these public loans are contained in 10H 4695. See also Pham Van Bach's report on public loans in Khu 9 in 1951–52 (10H 3994).

24. 10H 1032, 10H 164.

25. Ho Dac Vy. On the industry of armaments in Nam Bo, see *Lich su quân gioi Nam bô (1945–1954)* (Hanoi: Nhà xuât ban Quân dôi nhân zân, 1991).

26. 10H 1033.

28. *Testimony of Ho Dac Vy*, Ho Dac Vy.

29. 10H 3359.

30. 10H 3166.

31. Ibid.

32. *Testimony of Ho Dac Vy*, Ho Dac Vy.

33. When the French began their blockade, Nguyên Thanh Son, head of Ban Ngoai Vu (foreign affairs) of the UBKCHCNB estimated that 100,000 tons of rice were blocked in the free area. Since rice rapidly deteriorates if it is not safeguarded against rats, moisture, and pests, the resistance was in a bad situation (10H 3990).

34. 10H 3995.

35. Trân Van Huu's arguments were expounded in his letter to the Haut Commissaire de France, dated 17 March 1952 (File 511, 10H 1034).

36. Trân Luu Dzu's (or Du's) testimony (10H 640).

37. Report to the meeting of the Executive Committee of the Communist Party of Nam Bo in February 1950 (10H 4827).

38. Pham Van Bach's address (fifty-four mimeographed pages), 10H 4826.

39. Military conference of Khu 9, 2d semestre, 1951, 10H 4827. Khu 9 was western Nam Bo (Hau Giang), and Khu 8 was central Nam Bô.

40. That stalemate had been foreseen by a French officer whose survey (Intelligence Report No. 3) on "Attaque du potentiel Vietminh" was circulated in the French command in November 1948 (10H 1033).

41. Lettre au ministre des Etats associés, July 1952. 10H 638.

42. On his way to Hanoi in October 1951, Nguyên Binh, alias Nguyên Phuong Thao, military commander of the resistance in South Vietnam, Nam Bo, was killed in a Cambodian village. His diary and many documents were seized and transmitted to the French. In his "Report on the Cambodian Front," Binh wrote that the area around Stung Treng could be made an ideal rear base for the Vietnamese by developing agriculture, husbandry, and textile handicrafts as well as by taxing the Chinese, who exploited forests and produced iron cast (10H 366).

43. "Bilan économique et financier du Vietminh en Mai 1950."

44. *Thailand and the Southeast Asian Network of the Vietnamese Revolution, 1885–1954*, by C. Goscha (London: Curzon Press, 1999), is highly recommended for recognizing the utmost importance of Thailand in the strategic vision and field of operations of the Vietnamese resistance.

45. Captured documents from the Ministry of National Economy, CAOM, Conseiller politique, carton 6, supplement, 1946–1947. In July and August 1948, the French navy captured or sunk two hundred motor or sail junks in the Gulf of Tonkin (Bulletin 12 du Deuxième Bureau, 10H 3997).

46. Chen Jian, "China and the Indochina War, 1950–1954," *China Quarterly* 133 (March 1993): 85–110.

47. Ibid. See also "L'aide chinoise au Vietminh, 1952, 1953, 1954," CAOM, HCI 77. We gained a concrete example of Chinese aid when Nguyen Sy Hien, an officer of the Vietnam People's Army (regiment 52, division 320), who joined the nationalist zone in September 1954, states "The Chinese provided shoes, uniforms, underwear, towels, caps, mosquitoe nets, beakers, flasks, tents, K50 carbines, heavy Russian machine guns, grenades, [and] radio sets," and nearest the border "we got canned meat and cigarettes" (10H 1038). An intelligence report (February 1953) assumed that the Chinese aid provided antibiotics, sulfamids, and antimalarial chemical drugs as well (ibid.).

11

Florence Yvon-Tran

The Chronicle of a Failure: Collectivization in Northern Vietnam, 1958–1988

Introduction

Changes in the reform strategy in 1988 brought to light the growing disparity between the rhetoric of socialism and collectivism and reality. The period of collectivism lasted officially from April 1959 to April 1988, with the closure of the work points and the collective distribution. Up to this day, the period of collectivism still exerts its influence in Vietnam, since it coincides with the political isolation adopted by the government back then. At the time, the few foreigners allowed to visit Vietnam were systematically led to model cooperatives, escorted by official guides and translators. Many were seduced by the propaganda of the official discourse. Those who did not have the privilege of being invited by the government had to rely on official sources. The press, though, was merely an instrument of political propaganda of the Vietnamese government. Only since the mid-1990s have anthropologists, economists, and especially agronomists had access to published data and been able to conduct field research, thereby collecting data on production rates, growth, revenue changes, and the relationships of power in villages. Given this framework, it is difficult to develop a solid overview for this period. In this chapter, I will try to partially determine not whether collectivization failed in North Vietnam but how vast its failure was. In my analysis, I will take five different perspectives into account: (1) the support of the people for the projects of agricultural collectivization; (2) the increase in the size of the collectives based on the government's policies; (3) the internal workings of the cooperatives (especially regarding the organization and distribution of work, the management of collective resources, and the agricultural supplies distributed by the government); (4) income levels, measured mostly as rationed food distributed by the collectives; and (5) the "tax"/share of production output due to the government for rice production coming from the cooperatives.

1. From Experimentation to a State Policy

The Vietnamese leadership decided as early as 1951 to implement agricultural collectivization, even before the agricultural reforms of 1953–56. However, the party officials were asked not to say a word to the peasants in order to ensure rapid growth in agricultural production, which indeed followed.[1] The collectivization policy introduced by Ho Chi Minh in 1955 was slow and carefully managed. In the beginning, based on voluntary support from the peasants, it was supposed to be derived from the notion of work exchange/mutual aid groups from which the cooperatives of semisocialist leanings would be implemented. These in turn were to be gradually replaced with more socialist types of cooperatives, leading to the total elimination of all remaining private property.

As early as the end of 1955, when the agricultural reform was not yet completed, a few experimental cooperatives were established in the districts of Thai Nguyên, Phu Tho, and Thanh Hoa. But by 1957 there were only forty-two such units, not because the authorities were trying to put a cap on the expansion of cooperatives but because of their poor productivity. Their production output was lower than that of the mutual aid teams (not to mention that of the individual peasants), revenue generated by the farming cooperatives was down, production costs were up, and accounting visibility was lacking.[2] In this environment, many of the farming cooperatives (some of which members of the party had joined)[3] asked to leave the experimental cooperatives "not feeling motivated and having little confidence in their management." In all, out of the forty-two experimental cooperatives, nine of them had to be canceled.[4]

The attempt to bring about socialism through the mutual aid groups was not much more successful than the experimental cooperatives. The rate of participation among households fell from 50.1 percent in 1956, to 21.9 percent in 1957. Even if the numbers recorded in

1956 were artificially inflated, this step back matched the withdrawal of party members from the cooperatives in 1957.[5] In other words, without any external pressure Vietnamese did not join these precollective organizations, and when they did many abandoned them. One reason was that "the forced mutual aid groups"[6] were unable to rely on the traditional and spontaneous relationships of mutual aid common among families, village clans, and neighborhoods. Furthermore, mutual aid groups allowed only for relationships based on monetary principles, which ran contrary to the traditional village structures, thus making it difficult to adopt for the peasants. Starting in the middle of 1958, the first signs of a hardening of rural policies appeared, with the establishment of "a policy to fight off the spontaneous development of capitalistic trends." This included several types of measures, some of which were aimed at the most dynamic levels of the rural population and implemented rules such as abolishing loans to peasants, ending the "big four liberties," loans, work for hire, commerce, and the sale of land. In practice, however, these rules don't seem to have been applied very rigorously, and some peasants were still able to lobby local party officials for special permission to hire temporary labor. Other measures focused on lower- and middle-class peasants and tried to push collectivization forward. Thus, from June to December the number of cooperatives grew from 134 to 4,721 and the joining rate of peasant households to the mutual aid teams increased from 41 to 65 percent.[7] Because the majority of districts were hostile to the collectivization and peasants who had only just begun to have access to property rights were not in favor of these measures, the promotion of such a policy must have been imposed by the party's upper management.

In November 1958, during the fourteenth session, the Central Committee officially announced for the first time that the socialist agricultural transformation was to be the central theme of the Vietnamese socialist revolution. That policy was based on Engels's theory on collectivization: "collectivization was easier to implement when social differences were lesser." The theory stressed the importance of implementing collectivization in the countryside as soon as possible. If it were delayed, capitalism would flourish in the countryside, exploiting landless peasants and shrinking the peasantry.[8] In Vietnam, the party wanted to avoid the rapid erosion of its political image and strengthen its power in villages using the economic model of cooperatives. However, even with the official inauguration of the socialist transformation, not only did the rate of new cooperatives not increase but, worse, it decreased. Indeed, by the end of 1958 and in April 1959, only 2,279 new cooperatives were established,[9] that is, at a rate of 569 cooperatives per month versus 764 per month between June and December of 1958. In April 1959, 7,000 cooperatives were registered, representing only 8 percent of peasant households,[10] which meant that "collectivization was not popular."[11]

The Central Committee proclaimed in its April 1959 resolution "that an important majority of the workers in the north had decided to follow agricultural collectivization" and "that the movement was popular."[12] The document, however, did not mention the length of the implementation. Many regional officials did not support it because in their own districts collectivization was unpopular. At the beginning of the 1990s, the agricultural experts of the Vietnamese Central Committee acknowledged that in April 1959 the committee had requested its officials to complete collectivization by the end of the summer–fall campaign, that is, by August–September 1960.[13] This speeding-up process can be explained in part by the impatience of top officials to implement the five-year plan, which had already been delayed, and, second, by the poor agricultural performance. In 1955, the state had managed to commercialize only 13 percent of the rice production, and farming families preferred to cater first to their own subsistence needs.

Thus, Vietnamese officials were ordered to complete collectivization within a short period of time (roughly fifteen months). It is obvious that the freedom of choice clause was not respected. To succeed they needed to forcefully coerce participation and/or falsify the numbers, and to make things worse, contrary to what took place in China, the forced collectivization in Vietnam was done without preparation. The majority of party officials didn't support the project, and the party cells were either weak or did not exist (we should recall the fact that, as E. Moise illustrated, during the agrarian reform the base of the party was in a self-destructive mode). And the indoctrination propaganda of the peasants was particularly ineffective. Yet, during the fall of 1960, official communiqués claimed that collectivization (*hop tac ha*) was for the most part complete;[14] 84.8 percent of peasant households (i.e., 2.4 million people) had joined the cooperatives (41,000 in total), and 76 percent of the rice fields had been collectivized.

Given the strong opposition to collectivization from the end of

1955 to April 1959 (let us recall that at that time barely 8 percent of households chose to participate in collectives), it is difficult to believe that this massive and rapid wave of people joining could have occurred without force. In fact, in the early 1990s the party experts[15] acknowledged the common practice of coercion of that particular period, when local party officials forced the peasants to join the cooperatives.[16]

Instead of using repressive means, Vietnamese leaders implemented clever and flexible coercion methods adapted to the degree of resistance displayed by each group, ranging from simple psychological manipulation to fiscal pressures. For instance, when farm workers were forced to sell off part or all of their land and "work for hire" in order to survive, the party propaganda lured them into believing that the cooperatives would improve their standard of living.[17] On the other hand, toward the small and independent landowners, the party officials claimed that the party "gave them their land," which had contributed to their standard of living, and like the others they should thank the party by joining the cooperatives.[18] While some people were tricked by these arguments, many were not. The party therefore had to rely on stronger and more efficient methods of persuasion. One such means was to make children's admission to schools contingent on their parents joining the cooperative.[19] Furthermore, peasants who refused encountered difficulties with local officials in obtaining documents or administrative authorizations. In villages where the party was strong, those resisting were made to understand that not joining the cooperatives would lead them to being labeled as counter-revolutionaries.[20] The memory, still fresh, of the *"terreur sanglante"* of 1956 also contributed to peasants' decision to do as they were told. The state also decided to impose a higher tax, roughly 37 percent, on independent peasants, who also were not given a leniency term when/if crops were lost. Targeting the "rich" peasants, who were the last to join the cooperatives, the party had to impose economic pressure: work for hire was completely banned, leading to an increase in the cost of labor. Then the state monopoly on the trade of rice paddies was strictly enforced, thus leading as early as that year to important variations between the state pricing and the prices traded on the "free market."[21] Finally, many of the better-off peasants were forced to join the cooperatives. In some areas, the establishment of cooperatives resulted in violent acts:[22] livestock was killed and trees were cut down (because the land for gardens was in the best of cases limited to 5 percent of the total land cultivated and was often taken over by party officials). Their livestock and heavy agricultural equipment were taken over by the cooperatives with little compensation. The peasants joining the cooperatives were expected to keep only light agricultural tools.

In the 1960s, there were also financial incentives provided by the state, such as the right to obtain ration tickets for pork purchase and the ability to purchase sugar, tobacco, cloth, and gasoline at much reduced prices.[23] Did those who joined the cooperatives really benefit according to the promises lavished by the state propaganda? Whatever may be the case, the incentives must have had at minimum a mere secondary influence on their decision to join the cooperatives.

2. Collectivization in the Village: A Slow Process

Based on the resolution of April 1959, the cooperatives were supposed to include thirty to fifty households.[24] The official statistics from that period confirm that the cooperatives included on average fifty-seven households and cultivated thirty-two hectares, which seems to show that the resolution had been diligently implemented.[25] However, this average was slanted since Le Duan, the party secretary, himself recognized that the real size of the cooperatives was closer to thirty households.[26] This illustrates that many cooperatives were even smaller, such as those of Xom Tiên (eleven households), Công Hoa (seven households), and Quôc tri (sixteen households), all in the district of Hung Yên.

During the Third Congress, held in Hanoi from 5 to 10 September 1960, the socialist industrial reform was launched and the role of the socialist agricultural reform was clearly stated: agriculture was to be the foundation for industrial development and later would create markets for the flow of industrial products. Several months later, under the framework of the party resolution of 27 January 1961, a new directive was enacted pushing for the evolution of the semisocialist cooperatives into fully socialist cooperatives and more importantly for the number of collectives to increase over the two following years (1961–62) from 30 to 150 to 200 households. But the new policy met further resistance. By then the size of the semisocialist cooperatives hadn't yet reached the ideal goals, and the "agricultural collectivization movement" had not yet met the expectations of the Central Committee during its fifth session in July 1961. In fact, in many areas peasants opposed the increase in the number of cooperatives and in certain towns, such as Phu Xuyen (district of Ha Dông), some of them even went to the district headquarters to complain. As a result, the growth rate of the cooperatives remained moderate. After an initial push in 1961, their numbers began to shrink, and there was a noticeable decrease by 1963. This failure was most definitely due to the party top officials' inability to control and win support from lower levels of the party.

By 1965 with the escalation of the conflict with the United States, the cooperatives rapidly grew from small clusters to whole villages. This spontaneous change shows that traditionally villages were vital to the defense of the country in the face of foreign aggression. And during the American economic war villages became the pillars of Vietnamese government by providing food supplies.

For about ten years, from 1965 to 1975, most of the cooperatives were based on the village's structure. However in 1976, during the Fourth Party Congress, a new strategy was launched to promote "the rapid and unrelenting progress toward socialism." That strategy was to lead to many changes in agriculture as well as the regrouping of villages' cooperatives into larger regional cooperatives. Yet once again the party's success was limited because more than half of the cooperatives were still small in size, less than 100 hectares.[27] Even for those cooperatives that had doubled in size, the average size was still relatively small, 250 hectares and 486 households (though these were larger in the region of the Red River delta: 350 hectares and 898 households).[28] In reality, the number of regional cooperatives represented roughly a third of the total. This was a far cry from what some "observers" depicted: "giant model cooperatives with 4,000 to 5,000 people and 500 to 700 hectares" (which in fact represented no more than 7 percent of all cooperatives). It may even be that these new large-scale cooperatives were nothing but a facade because in the following year fragmentation began to occur. This fragmentation or breakdown process was most visible within the large-scale cooperatives, in which production was at its worst. By 1983, average cultivated land per cooperative dropped from 202 hectares to 135. And even in the delta it fell from 340 hectares to 250. Here and there, the fragmentation process was accompanied by corrupt practices. For example, in the village of Lang Nho (district of Thanh Hoa), "goods, housing, and village capital found their way into the pockets of ambitious party officials." In many places, the breakdown of the larger cooperatives led to financial conflicts between villages. But the spontaneous breakdown process was vigorously repressed after 1983.

3. Local and Central Authority in the Organization of the Cooperatives

Once collectivization was established at the village level, it became necessary to organize within each cooperative smaller production teams, with each one comprising roughly thirty families. Based on an official agenda, the scope of these teams was to be limited and was to simply provide teams to manage the agricultural work. The cooperatives were still supposed to encompass many other functions such as accounting, planning (for both production teams and individuals and families),[29] and management (financial and inclusive of all resources, land, livestock, and equipment).[30] The party's egalitarian objective led to the introduction of a system of work points (with accounting units to quantify the work), and thus each work team could earn exactly the same work points as all other teams. But to counteract the lack of motivation usually associated with the work points local party officials introduced a system of three contracts, *khoan*, which were to determine how much each team had to produce for the cooperative, what the team produced, and how many work points the team was to be awarded in order to meet its production goals set by the contract. In theory, the contract terms were well defined, but the question of implementation was unclear. The constant reminders sent to the local official committees not to collect capital and private property demonstrate that in fact many teams might already have been working independently.

These "three contracts" were also to be used for the family economic unit, although the party's agricultural experts claim that they were only for a few cooperatives. In the district of Hai Phong,[31] Duong Quoc Cam, a former member of the Agricultural Committee of the Central Committee, admitted that in 1963 the three *khoan* were more widespread at the family economic level than merely a few cooperatives.[32] This practice contradicted the policy of the National Committee for Rural Affairs of 1961, which specifically stated that the three *khoan* should not be used for household labor. But at the local level officials acted independently from the central authority by implementing state policies as they pleased, such as the three *khoan*. It is important to emphasize that the use of the three *khoan* for households was a widespread practice. It not only happened in the district of Vinh Phu, which was then considered a special case, but elsewhere. In the district of Vinh Phu, the local party committee, and especially its secretary, Ngô Kim, encouraged experimentation and after getting positive results with the three *khoan* asked the cooperatives of the district to apply the three *khoan* system, under Directive 68, on 6 September 1966. Nowhere else did local party officials take such a public stance on this issue, most likely fearing retribution by central party officials. In fact, a few years later Ngô Kim was summoned and forced to publish his self-criticism in the journal *Hoc Tap*.

During the war, the autonomy of the work teams was more common. Work distribution was decided at the team level (*an chia o doi*), but party officials continued to remain vital in the relationship between the state and the teams. Party officials handled the delivery of agricultural products (sometimes highly challenged) and the distribution of supplies among teams. The increasing autonomy of the teams can be best explained by the cooperative leaders' inability to control and manage successfully such large-sized cooperatives.

The illegal work performed at the cooperatives, tolerated by local party officials, continued until 1976. At that point, the old teams were abolished and new work units were established: teams responsible for replanting, maintenance, and harvesting as well as specialized teams (irrigation, hydraulics, seeding, plant protection) responsible for the more technical agricultural activities. Thus, many new teams were created such as teams of herdsmen, artisans, fishermen, transport workers, and fruit tree growers. All under the authority of the Management Committee, these new teams or brigades were supposed to conduct agricultural work based on the new system of norms established by the technical services. These norms were established to increase agricultural productivity, but in reality they had a negative impact because they brought about a severe fragmentation of labor. For instance, for rice cultivation there were four hundred norms, which included the preparation of the soil and the harvest. This model created at the Central Committee level failed to meet expectations because the norms were not applied throughout. The system also failed because of the incompetence of the party officials and because agricultural production is not an activity that lends itself to "rural tailoring." At the local level, the work teams, in effect the households, often retained their own work habits, which otherwise would hinder production.

Because of the collapse of rice production in 1984 (reaching only 214 kg per year), some local party officials agreed to include production quotas for families, which was unofficial (*khoan chui*).[33] In the Central Committee, leaders began to experiment with this new practice in October 1980, and the following years it was officially accepted.

Faced with an agrarian crisis, the party leadership resigned itself to passing the famous decree of 13 January 1981, Decree 100, regarding "the production contracts with the teams and workers." This contractual formula was supposed to be merely temporary.[34] The contracts, which allowed for the redistribution of the land, were designed to increase production while protecting the harvests, strengthening the cooperatives, guaranteeing control over the peasants, and leading to "the progress of socialism in the countryside." In reality, the land was divided up among the teams and individual workers (the peasant families), in exchange for which they agreed to stable production quotas for the cooperatives for five years. They agreed to be given production quotas, to be rewarded with work points, and seeding plans matching those of the cooperatives. All surpluses in production (beyond the contractual obligation) were now the peasants', thus motivating them to surpass the quotas. The other aspects of production, such as irrigation, plowing, protection of plants, and the supply of fertilizers, were still the responsibility of the cooperatives and the existing specialized teams. Even though the central leadership requested that local officials allow no more than three aspects of the rice production chain to be controlled by the peasant families, the rule was rarely followed. Instead, the "Decree 100 contracts" were replaced with "white contracts" (*khoan trang*), wherein the peasants themselves remained in control of almost the entire chain of production. This resulted in the party secretary general's decree of June 1985, recognizing that "in many places, control and management of the cooperatives has been allowed to drift aimlessly, and this especially with technical affairs."[35]

During the period of intense forced collectivization, in particular in 1961, many of the small parcels of land belonging to families were taken over by the collectives.[36] Party leaders feared that small family plots would encourage the spirit of private property and individualism among peasants. To counter such illegal activities, party leaders made an official statement to allow the household economy to cultivate 5 percent of the land in order to supply the communities with basic necessities such 25 meat, eggs, and vegetables.[37] Local officials, during the war, often redistributed to peasant families more than the official 5 percent of the attributed land. The number of illegal private household plots varied from region to region.[38] The most private lands were in the highlands, because the cooperatives were concerned with the production of rice, and families essentially used the gardens and the forest. In six years, between 1964 and 1970, private ownership of cultivated areas grew more than 1.5 times because of the clearing of new land. In middle regions, the cooperatives managed to a lesser extent to free up land for family ownership. In the lowlands, it was more difficult to transfer land to private ownership beyond the legal limit because there was no land to clear and household ownership was already high, 8 to 10 percent, although in some areas, such as the district of Nam Dinh, 15 to 20 percent of collectivized land was converted to family ownership.[39]

From 1973 to 1975, the movement toward allowing collective lands to be given to private owners continued. These plots, known as "15 percent," were being sold, mortgaged, and rented. These practices became so widespread that the party had to remind its members in 1974 that this was illegal.[40] During the great leap of socialism in agriculture, 1976–80, Vietnamese leaders started to impose restrictions on private plots, either decreasing their size or even getting rid of them. With the expansion of private property, supplies and work for hire were also an issue.

From 1959 to 1972, agricultural cooperatives received limited aid from the state. From 1958 to 1960, only 50 percent of the aid was distributed to a few model cooperatives.[41] Distribution of fertilizers and equipment was even more limited. In the first part of the five-year plan, the cooperatives received only half of the aid, while the remainder went to state-owned farms. As a result, food supplies dropped from 318 to 288 kg per head between 1961 and 1963,[42] and the state was forced to increase its aid to the cooperatives. Seventy percent of the aid was granted to the cooperatives in 1964 and 84 percent in 1965, although supplies of fertilizer still remained low. But during the war the government's aid dropped again, by 14 percent in 1967 (from the prior year) and 18 percent in 1968. In other words, even though the state was asking the cooperatives to carry much of the burden of the war, it provided little aid in exchange. The cooperatives had to rely on their own resources, including nonofficial measures such as autonomous work teams and private household plots.

In 1972 and 1973, when China reestablished diplomatic relations with the United States, the Vietnamese party leadership brought resources to the cooperatives, such as greater investments (a 39 percent increase),[43] distribution of new varieties of rice, and increased supplies of fertilizer. However, an investigation conducted in 1973 in more than 21,516 cooperatives, and another conducted in 1975 in 1,054 cooperatives, showed that many of the resources were not being used for the collective lands but were being distributed to the small family plots, the "15 percent plots."[44] In fact, it was during that time of "great progress toward a socialist agriculture" that the state diverted industrial investments to meet agricultural needs. Between 1976 and 1978, agricultural investments rose by 40 percent.[45] Short-term loans to purchase fertilizers grew from 408.2 million dong in 1976 to 609.2 million in 1980. Supplies of chemical fertilizers were stable during that period, 1975 to 1978, that is, 761 and 809 thousand tons.[46] But how many of these resources were really being used in the rice collectives is still vague, though probably less than what the state suggests. In 1976, the regional companies were not delivering all that they were supposed to deliver, and new intermediary enterprises, the district companies of agricultural equipment, appeared. Furthermore, the cooperatives probably didn't use much fertilizer because there was not enough water for irrigation. Finally, it seems that the officials responsible for the collectives were simply following in the footsteps of their predecessors, who illegally resold supplies on the free market.

To better understand the extent of the problem, it will be useful to briefly explain how the accounting system for the collectives worked. First, during each campaign, the cooperatives had to keep two sets of books (journals of entry). The first set was used to calculate net revenues (subtracting the costs of production from gross revenues) and various other funds, and to compute the exact value of the "work points" (by dividing net revenues by days of work). Then rations or monetary compensation were to be shared among all members of the cooperative after deducting the state's share and the cooperative's share and/or eventual losses. With a well-managed cooperative, the net revenues usually covered the rations and/or the monetary amount paid back to its members. However, in North Vietnamese cooperatives profits were paid out in goods[47] rather than rations or money. And, worse yet, during the 1970s, when the budgets were typically in the red, the cooperative members were asked to "buy back" their rations.

During the period of forced collectivization, local officials often found themselves unable to apply the official system of norms (which was supposed to compensate the members for the work provided) and instead implemented egalitarian norms,[48] resulting in a widespread lack of motivation. Based on the studies conducted by the National Statistics Committee at the time, the rations per household were on average 750 kgs' worth of food for the year, or 14 kg per head per month.[49] In less productive cooperatives, the rations were lower. However, each member only worked seventy days per year for the collective.[50] The weak rations were due to many factors: lower rice production (down 15 percent between 1958 and 1960), increased demands by the state, and diverted resources or profits. When the peasants realized that the cooperatives were compensating them less than in the days when they cultivated their own parcels of land, many asked to leave the cooperatives.[51] Some cooperatives were dissolved, but in most areas a complete clampdown took place. The party leadership did what it could to prevent the peasants from leaving the collectives.[52]

Statistics for these five years show that the monthly rations paid out per head decreased from 16.2 to 14 kg, even though that year there was a record harvest (5,562,000 tons of food versus 5,201,100 tons in 1961) and work days per member per year practically doubled (jumping from 90–100 days in 1961 to 170–200 days in 1965).[53] The decrease in rations was due to several reasons: first, the reduced supply of food available per head (down from 318 to 304 kg from 1961 to 1965), second, the increase in the state's share (by 1965 the state was draining 26.7 percent of food production), and, third, the rise of the cooperatives' share (also reaching 26.7 percent that year). This left only 46.7 percent of the food to be distributed to the cooperative members.

During the years 1966–72, rations distributed to the peasants were relatively the same as in previous years (roughly 14 kg). It was wartime, and the North Vietnamese peasants were working and producing food mostly for themselves and the cooperatives. Food supplies distributed to the collectives represented 70 percent of the entire production (compared to only 46.8 percent back in 1965). This was in part due to the fact that the officials for the collectives prioritized the village's interests before those of the state and that of their personal, family, or clan interests in a way that did not conflict with those of the collective members. From 1973 to 1975, rations remained flat compared to wartime levels (13.9 and 14.4 kg, respectively). In parallel, days worked on behalf of the cooperatives by their members grew to 322 days per year from 268.[54] Peasants were now working practically each day of the year on the collective lands while being compensated less! While the state's share of production remained flat, around 1 million tons, the cooperatives' share increased by almost 50 percent from 1966–72 to 1973–75 (from 516,000 to 763,000 tons).[55] The data show that the cooperatives used grain to feed livestock (47.9 percent), to plant seeds (40.2 percent), for household consumption (7.2 percent), and for miscellaneous storage (4.7 percent).[56] But studies conducted by the Central Committee found that only two-thirds of the grain destined for livestock ever went to livestock[57] and that 18 percent of the grain intended for seeds for the collective lands was diverted to other uses. Similarly, roughly 175,000 tons of rice per year were being diverted for "miscellaneous" purposes, that is, 16 percent of the volume of rice production that the state was forced to import in 1975. The extent to which production was being diverted leads me to wonder whether the leaders of the cooperatives were not already illegally trading food supplies for industrial goods with the state-owned industries. Whatever may be the case, the increase in illegal activities led cooperative members in some areas to ask again for permission to leave the collectives. These demands stemmed in part from the appeal of the free market but also from a deep discontentment with the immoral behavior displayed by local party officials. Local officials were held responsible for the lack of rations. In 1974 alone, 1,098 cooperatives collapsed due to members' discontent, mostly in the highlands. The fact that some peasants chose to stay in the cooperatives can be explained by the implementation of more liberal rules (implementation of the three contracts).

But during the years of 1976 and 1980, the rations for the cooperative members collapsed. The period of great socialist agriculture was the hardest for the peasants/cooperative members. During these black years, rations were as low as ten to eleven kg per month[58] and even lower in worse off areas (five to six kg per month).[59] The state had raised its quota, and the cooperatives were diverting greater volumes for their own "miscellaneous" funds (now up to 40 percent). By this time, 10 to 15 percent of the grain was destined for livestock and 11 percent for "other purposes."[60] Given the faminelike rewards (low rations) allotted to the cooperative members, it is more than understandable that production slowed considerably. Peasants began to reduce their work-day contributions to the cooperatives, some down to two hundred days per year or four or five hours per day. Others simply abandoned the rice fields. In the district of Ha Nam Ninh, cultivated land decreased by 19 percent between 1976 and 1980.[61]

Rations increased for a short time with the implementation of Contract No. 100 before they collapsed again. After the implementation of Decree 100, rations increased to 20 percent in 1982[62] and 1983. Unfortunately, as the dong began to lose more of its value (in 1986 the inflation rate reached 400 percent), local officials decided to raise the required output in the contracts. Thus, whatever meager production surplus was available for the cooperative members, it was rapidly disappearing. By the end, the only compensation given to the cooperative members was the rations distributed within the collective framework. By 1987, 14.8 percent of production output went toward rations, 27 percent to the state, and 57.5 percent to the cooperatives. Thus, just before the rations and work point system were abandoned, roughly 60 percent of production output was not under the state's control. Part of it was being diverted by local officials via these "other funds," which then amounted to 25 percent of all goods (versus 5 percent in 1973–75) and were used as compensation for services performed by the special teams/brigades (services often fictitious or poorly performed). The inefficiency of the cooperatives, and later the end of the ration system, pushed forward the development of the household economy or what was also referred to as the "free market" (*thi truong tu do*).[63] The development of that household economy was crucial to the survival of the peasants. Household production was consumed directly by the families and/or sold through distribution networks (state or private, depending on pricing).[64]

4. The Collapse of Collectivization

In the fall of 1955, the state instituted a system of compulsory taxes or portions of agricultural production to be paid back to the state. Each peasant was forced to sell to the state at a fixed price a certain amount of rice. This was before broad collectivization was in effect. In contrast to what occurred in China, in Vietnam the state's fixed price remained close to the prices in the free market. The foresight shown with this policy enabled the state to increase the total volume of paddy sold and distributed by the state (from 439,000 tons in 1955 to 738,000 in 1958)[65] and thus to provide a stable and regular food supply to its citizens. North Vietnam, which in the past had had to import rice from the south, was able to export some of its own rice until 1960.[66]

Pressure from the state to collect more rice increased again during the years of agrarian collectivization. At this time, rice collected and supplied to the state increased from 783,446 tons in 1958 to 833,949 in 1960.[67] As mentioned earlier, rice production per person actually decreased, down from 305 to 261 kg.

Decreasing Commercialization of Rice Production
with the Five-Year Plan of 1961

From the time the first five-year plan was implemented in 1951, the government began to encounter difficulties in commercializing the output of the collective economy. Rice commercialization never reached more than 17 percent (with an exception in 1965, when the commercialization rate peaked at 20 percent).[68] In other words, whereas during the period of forced collectivization the government was able to sell and distribute high volumes of rice, later it was no longer able to access surplus production. Official statistics estimated the state's commercialization rate to be 39 percent.[69] That drop can be associated with both the price disparity between state and free market pricing and the lack of discipline among local officials. The state monopoly was gradually eroding as special police units responsible for watching the market were either unable or unwilling to perform their duties.[70] However, the government's difficulties in collecting rice led to a shortage of food in the cities, and city dwellers started to buy rice and meat on the free market at higher prices. As the official channel became inefficient in the distribution of food, small local retailers started to fill up the gap in the supply chain.

During the war, supply to the state dropped from 747 kg per hectare in 1964–65 to 617 in 1966–72,[71] forcing the state to import greater volumes of food (388,000 tons in 1966 and 128,800 in 1972).[72] In parallel, an increasing percentage of household-produced output, which the cooperatives were supposed to control, was being sold on the free market. Studies conducted at that time by Central Committee economists concluded that 53 percent of production was being sold on the free market, while the remaining 47 percent was being sold to the state as part of the compulsory supply at much lower prices. For the production controlled by the peasant families, the commercialization rate on the free market was much higher, 88 to 76 percent. In total, more than two-thirds of family-led production was sold and distributed on the free market, versus a third through state channels.[73]

After the war, even with greater financial and material aid, still greater amounts of agricultural production continued to sell outside of the state-controlled channels. Between 1966 and 1975, the state was commercializing no more than 14.8 percent of the food supply versus 17 percent between 1961 and 1965.[74] By 1975, more than two-thirds of the agricultural output was sold illegally on the free market versus 61 percent back in 1965.[75] Obviously the many government resolutions trying to curb illicit activities on the free market were of limited use. For instance, Resolution 171, of 4 September 1972, stipulated "rigorously managing the market and intervening from the production phase all the way to the final consumers using all necessary means, administrative, economic, and educational."[76] To put things into perspective, let us simply remark that the production volumes sent to the state in 1975 were at the same level as those in 1958. In 1975, volumes sent to the state were as low as 766,082 tons (15.7 percent of total production). To the top officials, the failure to gain total control of agricultural production not only raised doubts about issues of management in the agricultural sector and the redistribution of food but, more importantly, raised questions about socialism in the countryside.

During 1976–80, wanting to regain control, the state leadership decided that it could counteract the problem of limited output given to the state by creating new districts. Their sole purpose was, according to To Huu, vice minister of the Department of Districts, "to guarantee the allotment and centralized management of agricultural, forest, and maritime products, in order to secure the proper supply to the state, set by central planning."[77] To this end, new companies were created to do nothing else but collect food supplies from the cooperatives. Between 1977 and 1980, that new tactic worked, and the government was able to maintain a high commercialization rate (even though production was down to 224.5 kg per year per head, of which only 60 percent went back to the peasants),[78] though not necessarily from the areas with the greatest surpluses.[79] In 1978, at Hai Phong, where production per head was as low as 162 kg, the government was able to collect 15.4 percent of production. In contrast, at Hai Hung, where production per head reached 363.5 kg, the supply to the state was only 19.47 percent.[80] In any case, supply to the state was insufficient to meet the needs of the entire population, given that food production had dropped dramatically during that period. As a result, the state had to increase imports of food, which rose to 2 million tons in 1979.[81]

Since the rural reforms enacted in 1981 and the adoption of the "white contracts" (mentioned above), production between 1980 and 1982 rose from 212 kg per head to 260. At the same time, the share of production supplied to the state rose to 19.7 percent in 1983 (though that year production declined to 248 kg). However, this success was short-lived because during the years 1983–87 volumes supplied to the state dropped from 1,469,400 tons to 968,000, that is, a 34.1 percent decline in five years, while at the same time production had remained stable.[82] Clearly, the drop in supplies provided to the state was not tied to production output rates but rather to resistance at the local level in the countryside. Cooperatives with surplus production refused to fulfill quotas for the state, and companies distributing supplies were also diverting part of the grain collected. At the level of the cooperatives, the situation was similar. Local officials, members of the Management Committee, and party members were themselves diverting part of the production for their own benefit, thus not fulfilling the state quotas. As a result, cooperative members began to gradually reduce the share of production supplied to the cooperatives.[83]

Conclusion

The failure of collectivization in North Vietnam was far greater than originally thought and far more dramatic than in China, where production rates managed to keep pace except during the period of the Great Leap Forward. The inefficiency of many Vietnamese cooperatives, the meager rations distributed by the government, the development of household production units, and free market activity all illustrate the failure of the cooperative system in Vietnam. It is clear that the level of chaos reached in the collectives on the eve of decollectivization was the result of years of worsening situations and originated at its inception. More worrisome still was the state's inability to control and deal with the rise of free market activities and more specifically to deal with the parallel and illegal activities of its local officials, cooperative officials, and state companies. In rural areas, local officials took on the role of "oligarchs." From the very beginning, they were willing to bend the rules with regard to the autonomy of the teams and contracts with households, even though the government eventually disciplined them. I have argued in this essay that the weakness of the state under the leadership of the Vietnamese Communist Party resulted in part from the conservatism of the regime, the inefficiency of the implementation of a liberal economy, and the current difficulties in the transition to a socialist market economy, which has been a dream of party leaders.

NOTES

Université Denis Diderot, Paris. I would like to thank Claire Beliard for kindly translating this essay and Gisele Bousquet for having encouraged me to write it. Certain issues are further developed in my doctoral thesis, presented under the direction of Pierre Brocheux in 1994, "Une résistible collectivisation: L'agriculture au Nord vietnam, 1959–1988." The data presented here are based on field research and "special" sources of data (such as the reports submitted by the Agricultural Committee to the Central Committee; ministries exposing investigation results on the distribution of agricultural production and disparities in income levels among cooperatives; and detailed volumes from the Committee for National Statistics with data never published in the official public statistics, including data regarding the growth of agricultural production sold off by the state and increases in the size of the cooperatives).

1. Production output for paddy went from 3,432,000 to 4,583,000 tons from 1955 to 1958. "NGTCTK" Report (1972).
2. Chu Van Lam (1992), 10.
3. In 1957, studies conducted in thirty-seven of the forty-two experimental cooperatives showed that 40 percent of the party members wished to abandon the collectives. Ibid., 11.
4. BNNTU (1991), 6.
5. Fall (1967), 186.
6. Term used in Aubert (1980), 65, to differentiate it from spontaneous mutual aid.

7. BCHTU (1959), 3.
8. Ibid., 11.
9. Ibid., 3.
10. Ibid.
11. BNNTU (1991), 6–7.
12. BCHTU (1959), 4; BNNTU (1991), 7.
13. BNNTU (1991), 8. The agricultural experts of the Central Committee make it clear that the decisions made during these conferences ran against the majority opinions.
14. Numbers presented in ibid., 8.
15. Ibid., 8. Trân Duc (1991), 25, wrote, "The organizational model originated from above." Chu Van Lâm (1990), 7, notes that "the principle of volunteer participation was not respected." See also Nguyên Dinh Nam (1987), 3.
16. BNNTU (1991), 8.
17. BCHTU (1959), 10.
18. Chaliand, (1968).
19. Various sources confirm this, for example, Bousquet and Trân Quang Thông (1992), 21; and Chaliand (1968), 166.
20. This is suggested in a more subtle way in Lê Van Duong (1990), 75, and Bui Huy Dap (1989), 139.
21. NGTCTK (1972), 224. In 1960, the price per paddy in the tenth month on the "free market" was higher by 42 percent than that of the official price, (0.57 dong vs. 0.40 dong per kilogram).
22. BNNTU (1991), 8.
23. Chaliand (1968), 135.
24. BCHTU (1959), 31.
25. TCTK (1989), 15.
26. Lê Duân, speech of 31 August 1962, in Lê Duân (1979), 54. See also Vo Nhân Tri (1967) and Trân Duc (1991).
27. NGTCTK (1982), 78, 96, 100.
28. Ibid., 96, 100.
29. BCTNTTU (1963), 42.
30. Ibid., 49; speech by Lê Duân quoted in the Lê Duân (1979), 67–68.
31. Chu Van Lam and Nguyên Thai Nguyên (1992), 24.
32. Duong Quoc Cam (1963), 30.
33. Chu Van Lam and Nguyên Thai Nguyên (1992), 51.
34. Let us remind ourselves that at the time many of the authors had bought into the practice of these types of production contracts. See Yvon (1989), 74.
35. Lê Trong, a party economic expert in TCCS 9/1987, 66.
36. Chu Van Lam and Nguyên Thai Nguyên (1992), 20.
37. Speech of Lê Duân dated 31 August 1962, quoted in Lê Duân (1979), 47–54; and speech of Nguyên Chi Thanh, dated 31 August 1961, quoted in Trân Duc (1991), 11.
38. BNNTU (1962).
39. Trân Van Ha (1990), 74.

40. Dieu le hop tac xa xa hoi chu nghia, "the new statutes of the socialist cooperative" (1974), 24.
41. BCHTU (1959), 32.
42. NGTCTK (1991), 87.
43. Calculations based on NGTCTK (1993).
44. NGTCTK (1989), 29. Chu Van Lam (1992), 35, also indicated that the illegal appropriation of supplies had reached significant levels. Competition between the collectives and the privately owned family plots was far greater than in China. According to Aubert, in China dung and mud were diverted but industrial supplies were generally distributed according to plan.
45. World Bank (1991), 24.
46. NGTCTK (1982), 346. I will not discuss here the evolution of mechanized agriculture during these five years, given that a large part of the surplus was sent to the pilot districts.
47. NGTCTK (1991); BCHTU (1959), 27.
48. BCTNTTU (1963), 54–55.
49. NGTCTK (1991).
50. BCTNTTU (1963), 5.
51. BNNTU (1991), 6.
52. Ibid., 9.
53. Ibid., 10.
54. NGTCTK (1989), 106, 108–11.
55. Calculations based on ibid., 108–9.
56. These percentages were calculated based on TCTK (1989), 110.
57. Ibid., 29.
58. See, for example, ibid., 139; and Chu Van Lam (1992).
59. Lê Trong (1980), 26.
60. NGTCTK (1989), 110.
61. Ibid., 88.
62. TCCS (1984), 20. The average is based on studies conducted by the Ministry of Agriculture among 2,315 households.
63. This interesting question will be developed in another essay.
64. Tables from the National Committee of Statistics, NGTCTK (1990), are of limited use.
65. NGTCTK (1972), 210.
66. Tables from Food and Agricultural Organization of the United Nations (FAO) referred to in Fforde and Paine (1983), 122.
67. But also much of the volume sold and distributed for other agricultural products during the years 1959 and 1960: corn, 63.5 percent; green beans, 75 percent; other beans, 81.8 percent; peanuts, 70 percent; cotton, 100 percent; tobacco, 67.2 percent.
68. Other industrial agricultural products also suffered drops, forcing the state to raise prices: +10 percent for peanuts in 1964–65, +15 percent for green beans, and +20 percent for corn.
69. Official estimates, also referred to by the economists A. Fforde and S. H. Paine (1987), table 139.

70. A hypothesis confirmed by Adam Fforde (1984), 13, though without explanation.

71. TCTK (1989), 108.

72. NGTCTK (1989), TCTK (1989), 33; Van Luu Dat (1990), 208.

73. NGTCTK (1972).

74. This was roughly only 50 percent of all industrial agriculture, rush, jute, tobacco, tea, coffee, and sugarcane, destined for exportation. See Fforde and Paine (1987), 29.

75. Ibid.

76. Vu Ngoc Khu (1990), 275.

77. Quoted in Nguyên Duc Nhuan (1992), 351.

78. NGTCTK (1989), 108. In 1980, according to Lê Trong (1980), 26; and Chu Van Lam and Nguyên Thai Nguyên (1992), where production had fallen to 214 kilograms; in certain areas rations distributed by the cooperatives were as low as five to six kilograms per month.

79. NGTCTK (1989), 108.

80. Ibid.

81. Ibid., 133.

82. Production per head in 1983 reached 252.2 kg; in 1984, 247.1 kg; in 1985, 247 kg; in 1986, 245 kg; and in 1987, 238 kg. Calculations are based on UNDP (1990), 69.

83. Nhan Dan dated 28 June 1985.

REFERENCES

In Vietnamese

From *Nien Giam Tong Cuc Thong Ke* (NGTCTK) (Yearbook of the General Statistical Office):
  1991. *Niên giam thong ke Nong nghiep, 1956–1990* (Agricultural Statistics, 1956–1990). Hanoi: Nha Xuat Ban Thong Ke.
  1982. *Niên giam thong ke phat trien nong nghiep o trong giai doan, 1975–1980* (Statistics on Agricultural Development from 1975 to 1980). Hanoi, unpublished.
  1972. *Niên giam Phat trien ngành thuong nghiep o trong giai doan, 1955–1970* (Development of the Trade Sector). Hanoi, unpublished.

From Ban chap hanh trung uong (BCHTU) (Executive Committee of Central Committee):

  1959. *Nghi quyêt cua Hôi nghi Trung uong lân thu 16 (thang 4 1959) vè Hop tac xa nông nghiêp* (Resolution of the Sixteenth Plenary Session on the Agricultural Cooperatives). Trung uong Dang Lao dông Viêt Nam xuât ban (Central Committee of the Labor Party), Hanoi.

1974. *Dieu le Hop tac xa Xa hôi chu nghia.* (Regulations of the Socialist Cooperatives). Hà Nôi, Trung uong Dang Lao dông Viêt Nam xuât ban (Central Committee of the Labor Party), Hanoi.

1990. "Thuc trang Kinh tê-xa hôi o trong giai doan, 1986–90" (The Socioeconomic Situation from 1986 to 1990). *Tap Chi Thong Ke* (Journal of Statistics).

From Ban công tac nông thôn trung uong (BCTNTTU) (Collective Agricultural Committee of the Central Committee):

1963. *Cai tao Quan ly Hop tac xa nông nghiêp.* (Reforming the agricultural cooperatives' management). Hanoi: Su Thât.

From BNNTU (*Ban Nong Nghiep Trung Uong Dang Lao Dong*) (Agricultural Reports of the Central Committee):

1992. *Kinh tê-xa hôi nông thôn Viêt Nam Ngay nay* (The Current Socioeconomic Situation in the Countryside). Hanoi: NXB Tu tuong-Van hoa.

1991. "Tông kêt Hop tac hoa o trong giai doan, 1958–1990, và phuong huong sau 1990" (Results on Collectivization from 1958 to 1990 and Its Direction after 1990), Hanoi. Unpublished report.

1987. "Bao cao Nam 1986" (Reports for the year 1986), Hanoi. Unpublished report.

1962. "Cai tao Quan ly Hop tac xa." (Reforming the Cooperatives' Management). In *Bao cao Nam 1961* (*Report for the Year 1961*). Hanoi: Su Thât.

From Tong Cuc Quoc Gia Thong Ke (National General Statistical Office):

1993. "Su phan bô von dâu tu nông nghiep trong giai doan, 1960–1992" (Distribution of Agricultural Investments from 1960 to 1992), Hanoi. Unpublished report.

1989. "Thu Nhàp dân nông thông o trong giai doan khac nhau" (Rural Income at Different periods), Hanoi. Unpublished report.

1974. "Dieu le Hop tac xa Xa hôi chu nghia" (Regulations of the Socialist Cooperatives), Hanoi.

1969. "Dieu le Hop tac xa Xa hôi chu nghia" (Regulations of the Socialist Cooperatives), Hanoi.

Bui Huy Dap. 1980. "Lua và Lon trong nông nghiêp Viêt Nam" (Rice and Pork in Vietnamese Agriculture). *Nghien cuu kinh te* (Economics Research) 4 no. 116: 31–33. Hanoi.

Chu Van Lâm. 1992. *Hop tac hoa nông nghiêp Viêt Nam: Lich su-vân dê-trieng vong* (Vietnamese Agricultural Collectivization: History, Problems, and Perspectives). Hanoi: Su Thât.

———. 1990. "45 nam nông nghiêp Viêt Nam" (Forty-Five Years of Vietnamese Agriculture). In *45 nam Kinh te Viêt-nam (1945–1990)*. (Forty-five years of Economy in Vietnam). Dao Van Tap chu bien, NXB khoa hoc xa hoi, 95–115. Hanoi.

Duong Quoc Cam. 1963. *Kinh tê hop tac và Kinh tê nông hô* (The economy of the cooperatives and the Household Economy). Hanoi: Su Thât.

Lê Duân. 1979. *Vê Hop tac hoa* (On Collectivization). Hanoi: Su Thât.

Lê Van Duong. 1990. "Phat trien và thai dôi nong nghiêp: Vân Dê Khu vuc san xuât và quan hê san xuât" (Agricultural Development and Change: Problems Concerning the Areas of Production and the Relations of Production). In *Quan hê san xuât và suc san xuât* (Relations of Production and Force of Production). Hanoi: Viên Triêt Hoc.

Lê Trong. 1980. "Ve Thu Lao Lao Dong Trong Hop Tac Xa Nong Nghiep" (Work Compensation in the Agricultural Cooperatives). *Nghien cuu kinh te* (Economics Research) no. 115: 34–41. Hanoi.

1987. *Thuc chat cua khoan moi voi cung cô quan hê san xuat xa hôi chu nghia trong nong nghiêp.* (The push forward of the new contract in its relations to the social and cultural production in agriculture). In *Tap chi công san* (Review Committee), no. 9: 62–68.

Luu Van Dat. 1990. "45 Nam phat triên và su mo ngoai thuong" (Forty-Five Years of Development and Opening of Foreign Trade). In *45 nam Kinh te Viêt-nam* (45 years of economy in Vietnam). Dao Van Tap chu bien. NXB Khoa hoc xa hoi, 187–224. Hanoi.

Nguyên Dinh Nam. 1987. "*Ho Chi Minh doi voi van de pha trien nong nghiep trong TKQD xay dung CNXH o nuoc ta*" (President Ho and the problem of agriculture development during the transition period to socialism in our country). In *Nghien cuu kinh te* (Economics Research), 2(156): 1–8. Hanoi.

Nguyên Trân Trong. 1980. "Ho Chi Minh và Hop tac hoa" (Ho Chi Minh and Collectivization). *Nghien cuu kinh te* (Economics Research) no. 115: 22–31. Hanoi.

Trân Duc. 1991. *Hop tac xa và thoi dai hoang kim cua kinh te hô gia dinh* (Cooperatives and the Golden Age of the Household Economy). Hanoi: NXB Tu tuong-Van hoa.

Trân Van Ha. 1990. *Kinh tê hô gia dinh và kinh tê VAC trong 40 nam qua* (Household Economy and the VAC economy during the last forty years) (V.A.C, vuon, ao, chan nuoi) (gardens, ponds, and animal raising) Hanoi.

Truong Chinh. 1976. "Thuc hiên cai cach ruông dât" (Implementing Rural Reforms). In *Cach mang dân tôc dân chu nhân dân Viêt Nam* (The Vietnamese National People's Democratic Revolution), 2:310–402. Hanoi: Su Thât.

Vu Ngoc Khu. 1990. *45 nam hoat dông cua nganh tai chinh Viêt-nam* (Forty-five years of financial activities in Vietnam). In *45 nam Kinh te Viêt-nam* (*Forty Five years of Economy in Vietnam*) 45, Dao Van Tap chu bien, NXB khoa hoc xa hoi, 243–58. Hanoi.

In French and English

Aubert, C. 1980. *L'entraide agricole dans la Chine du Nord pré-communiste.* Paris: Publications Orientalistes de France.

Banque Mondiale. 1989. *Les réformes économiques au Viêt nam.* Washington, DC: Banque Mondiale.

Bousquet, M., and Trân Quang Thong. 1992. *Projet de recherche sur les systèmes agraires du Fleuve rouge, zone de Thanh Hoa.* Unpublished paper.

Chaliand, G. 1968. *Les paysans du nord Viêt-nam dans la guerre.* Paris: François Maspéro.

Fall, B. 1967. *Les deux Viêt-nam.* Paris: Payot.

Fforde, A. 1989. *The Agrarian Question in North Vietnam, 1974–1979.* New York: M. E. Sharpe.

―― 1984. "Specific aspect of the collectivization of wet-rice. Reflections of Vietnamese experience." London: Dept. of Economics, Birkbeck College, University of London. Birkbeck discussion paper; no. 152.

―― 1983. *The Historical Background to Agricultural Collectivisation in North Viêtnam: The Changing Role of "Corporate" Economic Power.* London: Birkbeck College.

Fforde, A., and S. H. Paine. 1987. *The Limits of National Liberation.* London: Croom Helm.

Kerkvliet, Benedict Tria. 1999. "Accelerating cooperatives in rural Vietnam, 1955–1961." In *Vietnamese Villages in Transition,* Bernhard Dahm and Vincent J. Houben, eds., in cooperation with Martin Grossheim, Kirsten W. Endres, and Annette Spitzenpfeil, 53–87. Passau: Dept. of Southeast Asian Studies, Passau University.

Kleinen, John. 1999. *Facing the Future; Reviving the Past: A Study of Social Change in a Northern Vietnamese Village.* Singapore: Institute of Southeast Asian Studies.

Nguyên Duc Nhuân. 1992. "Le district rural vietnamien ou l'Etat en campagne." In *Habitations et habitats d'Asie du Sud-Est continentale: pratiques et représentations de l'espace,* LASEMA-CNRS, ed. par Jacqueline Matras-Guin et Christian Taillard, 343–76. Paris: L'Harmattan.

Nguyên Tiên Hung. 1977. *Economic Development of Socialist Viêt-Nam (1955–1980).* New York: Praeger.

Quang Truong. 1987. *Agricultural Collectivisation and Rural Development in Viêt-Nam: A North-South Study (1955–1985).* Amsterdam: University of Amsterdam.

Vo Nhan Tri. 1990. *Vietnam's Economic Policy since 1975.* Singapore: Institute of Southeast Asian Studies.

―― 1967. *La croissance économique de la Republique démocratique du Viêt Nam 1945–1965.* Hanoi. Editions en Langues étrangères.

World Bank. 1991. Vietnam restructuring public finance and public enterprises, report no. 10334, VN, Washington.

Yvon-Tran, Florence. 1990. "La lente émergence des réformes rurales." In *Approches Asie,* 10, PuF: 73–103. Nice.

12 Xavier Oudin

Labor Restructuring in Vietnam

The State promotes a multicomponent commodity economy functioning in accordance with market mechanisms, under the management of the state and following the socialist orientation.
—Article 15, Constitution of the Socialist Republic of Vietnam, 1992

Introduction

Vietnam is presently in the process of transforming its economy and consequently its labor relations. In a few words, this process can be described as a "desocialization" of labor relations and the rise of community- or family-based labor relations or self-employment. In effect, the alternative to socialist labor relations, which should be market-based labor relations, is presently still marginal in terms of number of workers involved. This change in labor relations corresponds to a change in the economic and social situation, whose main characteristic is the replacement of a centrally planned economy with market mechanisms and the development of private property.

Labor relations are rendered by labor forms or statuses that characterize the different kinds of relations governing the economy. Labor forms are the result of a given organization of labor at the macro and micro (inside enterprises) levels. At the macrolevel, they reflect the functioning of the economic system. They determine labor relations in the whole country (including the strategy of trade unions) as well as at the level of the enterprise; if nonmonetary activities are also taken into account, as they should be, forms of labor cover a wider range of human relations than those confined to the labor market. They govern the distribution of income, since different kinds of income are associated with different forms of labor; in addition, they represent different interests, or social groups, and have unequal influence on the political process of income distribution. They are associated with different forms of remuneration (the whole spectrum of types of remuneration between fixed salary and pure profit of the self-employed) and differences in productivity that are not necessarily well rendered by labor costs.

In industrialized societies (including former socialist countries), the reference in terms of labor is stable wage work, with a fixed salary, guarantees of stability (up to a life career), unity of the employer and the job, social security, and so on. This has been described as the *typical* form of labor, meaning that it is the main reference in all aspects of social relations, starting with the legal framework (Puel 1989). The main laws and regulations pertaining to labor and social security refer to this typical form of labor.

The reemergence of nonwage labor or imperfect forms of wage labor in Western countries in the last few decades has brought about renewed consideration of the forms of labor. The rise of new forms of nonwage labor questions the economic theory of labor that has mainly considered labor as a merchandise exchanged through a wage contract (Freyssinet 1989). However, protected wage labor in these countries remains the reference, as it is the form of labor of around 80 percent of the labor force.

It is worth considering the socialist countries in this respect, too, since they influenced the Vietnamese building of a socialist economy. Although Marx predicted that wage labor would be abolished, socialist countries have achieved a more complete wage labor system than anywhere else. The New Economic Policy (NEP) can be interpreted as a great leap forward to new labor relations based on a generalized system of wage labor. The main difference with Western countries was not in the forms and organization of labor (both Fordist protected wage labor) but in the ownership of the means of production. State ownership has not abolished wage labor. On the contrary, it has contributed to a faster development of this form of labor through harsh political and social pressure. In the Soviet Union, it took not more than two decades to generalize wage labor, while it took more than one century in Western countries, where it also created social trauma (see the works of Marx or Polyani).

Another aspect of socialist wage labor is the ideological background of a scientific organization of labor. Production on a small scale (at that time, one would speak of precapitalist forms of production) is considered to be inefficient and should be eradicated. Moreover, capital in private hands tends to be invested in speculative activities or commerce, where profit is supposed to be higher (socialist thinkers like P. Baran, for instance, often criticize the waste of capital in nonproductive activities in capitalist economies). Only the state can efficiently allocate labor and capital in more productive activities (i.e., for material production) and at a larger scale.

In developing countries, family enterprises are dominant (especially in farm activities) and wage labor is concentrated in some segments of the economy, in the public sector and the private modern sector. Only a minority of the labor force is engaged in wage relations. Moreover, many wage workers in developing countries do not benefit from the social protection and work outside the legal framework of labor laws. They are not concerned with the minimum wage, working hours, illness, or maternity leaves. In Thailand, which is a middle-income economy, less than 15 percent of the labor force can be considered as "protected" wage workers, that is, engaged in a labor relation defined by law (Oudin 1996).

Southeast Asian countries were characterized by a slow pace in the development of wage labor, compared with their high growth rates, especially in the manufacturing sector, up to the crisis of 1997. There is no doubt that wage labor has been expanding in those countries, but it has taken many forms, such as subcontracting, piece rates, or contract labor. Seasonal and temporary labor is dominant, while it is marginal in developed countries. The question to be asked is whether this is a temporary phenomenon, and the Asian countries will follow a Fordist model, or the essence of new labor relations that characterize an original Southeast Asian model.

Vietnam is a low-income country, where two-thirds of the labor force are working in agriculture. It is also a socialist country (since 1954 in the north, 1976 in the south) that has favored wage labor relations, under the auspices of the state and cooperatives. At the end of the 1980s, Vietnam launched important reforms known as Doi Moi ("renovation" in Vietnamese). It has adopted market mechanisms and permitted free enterprise. As a consequence, nonwage forms of labor have increased considerably. In this chapter, I try to interpret the recent evolution of Vietnamese economic policy through the changes in labor forms, with a special focus on nonagricultural activities.

1. Labor Relations in Vietnam

The Building of Socialist Labor Relations in Northern Vietnam

Socialism was implemented in the Democratic Republic of Vietnam (DRV) as a way to develop and industrialize the country rapidly. Private ownership of the means of production was considered an obstacle to an economic takeoff, not only because of inequalities but because it was scattered and inefficient. Apart from a few companies owned by the French (which were nationalized within a few years), nonagricultural production was run by small artisans with very limited capital. By combining these small units, it was expected that a bigger scale of production would result in a boom in output and would allow production of more complex items (Vo Nhan Tri 1967). Another idea was that too much financial capital was wasted in commercial activities and some measures had to be taken in order to reorientate financial and commercial capital toward productive activities. There was a crackdown on traders (big and small) in 1956, which resulted in a scarcity of everyday goods. After two years of struggle and compromise, the traders were definitely kept apart from small street vendors (Vo Nhan Tri 1967). So collectivization was not only a confiscation of capitalist properties with the objective of a more egalitarian distribution. It was also (and above all) a way to make more efficient use of the means of production (capital and labor).

Production was organized along a scale, with state enterprises at the top. State enterprises were the vanguard of the economy (especially centrally owned enterprises as opposed to the provincial ones). Although their share in employment was not important, they benefited most from the credit and resources of the country, and their workers could be considered the new elite. They were also the main tax providers, and it is not an exaggeration to say that the Vietnamese state was living at the expense of its enterprises, as did local powers with locally owned enterprises (it is still true nowadays, and this explains why the state is so reluctant to give up its enterprises).

The rest of the economy was organized into cooperatives or production groups of different levels, according to a hierarchy in which labor forms were the main discriminating factor. In full cooperatives, the members were wage workers of the cooperative, and the cooperative was in charge of their social protection as well as that of their families. In production collectives of different levels, artisans were more or less loosely bound, with each eventually keeping his or her workshop. It was planned that large cooperatives would have the status of enterprises, while small collective enterprises would be the new cooperatives.

As Vietnam is mainly an agricultural country, collectivization was principally a reorganization of petty peasant production ("big" peasants had been physically eliminated) to a bigger scale, at the commune level. Cooperation has always existed in the Red River delta, as management of the irrigation system requires a gathering of individual forces. In nonagricultural activities, there also was a tradition of cooperation through the artisan guilds in villages and cities.

At the end of 1960, collectivization was nearly achieved. Small private enterprises were totally eradicated in 1961 (they had been gathered on a voluntary basis). The number of artisans and traders in cooperatives was respectively 88 and 99 percent (Vo Nhan Tri 1967, 305, 333). By that time it seems that self-employment had nearly disappeared according to Vietnamese sources (ibid.). Street vendors in particular were sent back to farming activities. However, it seems that an individual sector has always remained, more or less legally. It developed later, and statistics of employment for the DRV in 1974 show that self-employment had reached 14 percent of the nonfarm labor force, more than half of them being in the manufacturing sector. The output of this sector, as recorded by official statistics, was marginal, and therefore productivity was very low (GSO 1976; Vo Nhan Tri 1992).[1] So it seems that the goal of a totally collectivized economy could never be reached. Moreover, beyond what statistics reveal, there are numerous reports of an "external economy," with significant activities of production and distribution of goods outside state control (see Le Thanh Khoi 1982; Fforde and Paine 1987; and de Vienne 1994).

However, the collectivization process in the Democratic Republic of Vietnam was successful if one refers to the level of production. Despite a huge war effort, which drained financial, material, and human resources, production increased significantly after collectivization. Emphasis was put on manufacturing, especially heavy industry and products of common use (coal, fertilizers, tractors, bicycles, fabric, etc.). The growth rate of manufacturing was higher than that of the south (de Vienne 1994 estimates the 1975 value of industrial output in the north as four times that of the south). But it relied on foreign aid, especially for food.

The Failure of Socialization in the South

The same story was to be repeated in 1976 in the south, but unlike in the north it led to economic chaos. Socialism was proclaimed in the whole country in 1976, meaning that the model of the DRV would be immediately implemented, despite the opposition of communist leaders of the south. An ambitious plan of collectivization was launched, with the objective of bringing the reunified country to the status of an industrialized country by the year 2000. The same principles that had prevailed in the economic policy of the young Democratic Republic of Vietnam in the late 1950s were applied. Noticeably, the financial capital (this actually meant commercial capital owned by ethnic Chinese) was to be better utilized in productive activities. The southern piaster was demonetized and financial assets suddenly became valueless. There was a crackdown on *"comprador* capitalists," most of them Chinese, who were accused of counterrevolutionary activities such as trafficking, black marketeering, etc. (Vo Nhan Tri 1992).

In 1978, paddy production was down by nearly 20 percent as compared to 1976. Average yields declined dramatically. Gross domestic product (GDP) per capita went down from U.S.$101 in 1976 to $91 in 1980. Only heavy industry improved. Above all, the diplomatic situation worsened after Vietnamese troops entered Cambodia and China retaliated with a brief and costly invasion (January 1979). Chinese and international aid was cut, except from the Eastern European bloc. Most Chinese fled, often under horrible conditions, and abandoned their commercial and industrial assets.

The economic crisis, and especially the decline in staple production following the forced collectivization in the south, as well as bad climatic conditions, led the party to loosen its stance on the march to socialism in 1979. The main reform concerned agriculture. Peasants were allowed to sell their surplus (i.e., the share of their production above the quota sold at fixed prices to the state) on the free market and to own individual plots for gardening. Small private enterprises were tolerated (those with less than ten employees). State enterprises were also allowed to market surplus production. Material incentives were introduced to boost productivity.

Decisions leaving more freedom for individuals and private activities, and those giving more autonomy in the management of state-owned enterprises, resulted from pressure from the bottom levels when the situation had become chaotic. As soon as the central state felt stronger, it revised previous decisions to regain control of the surplus (of rice or foreign currency) (see Vo Nhan Tri 1990 and Andreff 1993). Tolerance toward private activities did not last long. It seems that small entrepreneurs were at the mercy of the arbitrary decisions of local authorities and encountered multiple obstacles to their activities.

Fforde and de Vylder (1996) report that in 1980 in Hanoi, after a decision easing petty trading, there was a sudden crackdown on street vendors in which thousands were caught and fined.[2] Vietnamese families have plenty of stories of that kind, with the police coming to inquire in the house about the origin of small capital used to set up enterprises such as coffee shops. Petty producers had to buy their raw materials on the black market and hide most of their activities (personal interviews). It seems that it was only after 1992, when the dong was stabilized, that private and individual activities were truly accepted, without the arbitrary intervention of the authorities.

Despite better harvests, the economic situation continued to deteriorate in the mid-1980s. Daily life was very hard, not only for peasantry but even for wage workers in state enterprises. In the harsh time of inflation, from 1984 to 1987, the state and its enterprises faced difficulties in paying their employees decently. In order to make ends meet, state employees had to resort to all kinds of activities, taking advantage of their positions when possible to produce items on their own, with the raw materials of the enterprise, or trading materials to which they had access. The state had no choice but to tolerate and later legalize this kind of practice.

At this stage, it appears that (1) even before the liberation of the south the state had lost control of the entire economy and productive forces compared to the situation in the mid-1960s; and (2) the application of the DRV model in the south was too great of a challenge for the state and resulted in economic and social disaster, with a growing part of the population having to rely on its own to survive, not to mention hundreds of thousands of people who chose to flee the country.

The series of political measures from 1979 to 1986–87 can be interpreted as concessions for more economic freedom grabbed from the state at moments when the situation required it, balanced by countermeasures meant to regain control on the activities of enterprises and individuals. This is also the result of fights at the top of the Communist Party that have always marked the history of contemporary Vietnam (see Post 1989 for details). Clearly enough, more liberal measures were taken when the situation was so serious that there was not much choice left. Doi Moi in particular was the reaffirmation of decisions already taken between 1978 and 1982, which had not been applied because a hard line had prevailed.

2. Doi Moi and the Development of Nonstate Labor

The Doi Moi reform came when the country was on the brink of the abyss. In 1986, Gorbachev told the Vietnamese that the USSR would stop subsidizing their country. Significantly, the reform was adopted under the new leadership of former southern leaders, who had unsuccessfully tried to implement reforms in the late 1970s. Although the Communist Party Congress of December 1986 is usually considered to be the starting point of a new era, it took nearly ten years to enact the major laws that would stabilize the macroeconomic situation, dismantle cooperatives and redistribute land to families, set the framework for foreign investment, and so on. The reform is still in progress, and the pace of it is heatedly debated within the Communist Party and between the Vietnamese government and international agencies.

The Aftermath of the War and the Demographic Explosion

The demographic situation of Vietnam has had a strong and generally neglected impact on economic policy. After the war, Vietnam had a very fast growing population (3.2 percent in 1976) and a high fertility rate (6.1 children per woman). As a consequence, the proportion of youth was very high. In the 1979 population census, the share of population under fifteen years old was over 42 percent (Banister 1993). The population of active age had been decimated by the war, and there were many invalids. Moreover, those who fled the country were often of working age. The army also drained hundreds of thousands of young people.

As a consequence, the dependency rate was very high: every 100 workers had to feed 170 people in addition to themselves.[3] At the macrolevel, this means that most of the resources of society had to be spent on education and health, in addition to the reconstruction of the country. Resources were also utilized for the war in Cambodia, something that Vietnam at that time could obviously not afford. Not much was left for more productive investments, and foreign aid was essential to save the country from bankruptcy.

After the liberation of the south, the authorities decided to send back to the villages thousands of peasants who had gathered in cities because of the war. In addition, many former civil servants of the southern regime were sent to reeducation camps in new rural economic zones, where they were employed in clearing forest areas. As a result, the proportion of people working in agriculture increased for several years, contrary to the worldwide trend. According to official statistics, the proportion of the labor force in agriculture rose from 67 percent in 1976 to 73 percent in 1987–93. After this date, it started to decline. Between the years 1976 and 1987, agriculture was by far the main outlet for people entering the labor market. The labor force increased by 9.2 million people, and 83 percent of them went to work in agriculture.

The decline in fertility (down to 3.7 children per woman in 1993) and the entry of new generations into the labor force reversed the situation. The economic dependency rate fell dramatically, meaning that on average more workers became active. At the national level, this means that education and health are relatively less of a burden. Moreover, low dependency rates favor savings, since the share of people having an income, and therefore likely to save part of it, has increased.

Although the demographic situation improved quickly in the mid-1980s, it in turn had an effect on the labor supply. When the generations born at a time of high fertility got to working age, the number of people searching for employment increased dramatically. In addition, the army demobilized hundreds of thousands after it withdrew from Cambodia in 1988. In the same time, many migrant workers were repatriated from Eastern Europe and others returned from refugee camps in the region.

In the mid-1980s, the number of new entrants into the labor market reached one million per year. We have seen that most of them

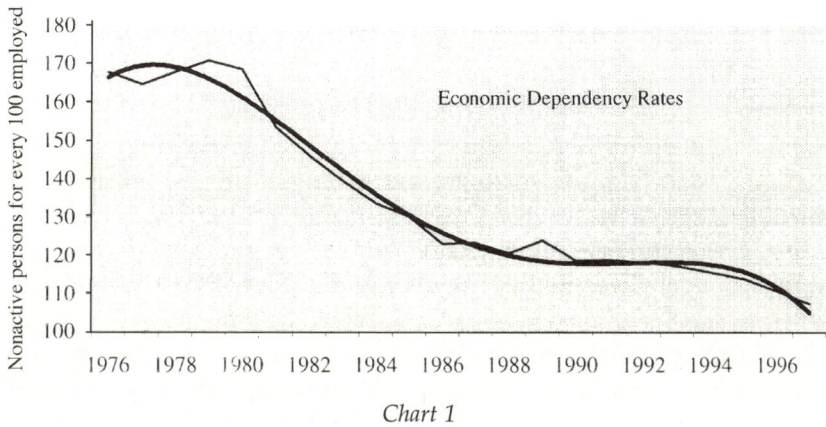

Chart 1

went to work in agriculture. However, it became obvious that this model of development had reached its limit. Developing the economy on an extensive basis was no longer possible in Vietnam because the number of people per hectare of arable land was already very high in the two deltas, and also because new land was more scarce. Moreover, Vietnam needs to increase productivity in the agricultural sector, and this requires more capital and fewer workers.

The labor force turned more and more toward nonagricultural activities. In the late 1970s, there was an average increase of the nonagricultural labor force of 60,000 per year. In the mid-1980s, the average increase was 200,000, and from 1994 to 1997 it reached 700,000. The economic system that had worked since the war was not able to face this challenge.

The Doi Moi Reform and the Evolution
of Employment

With the Doi Moi policy, an important step was taken toward the acceptance of private and individual activities. It coincides with a major change in the demographic situation, resulting in an explosion in the labor supply. In terms of labor relations, it can be interpreted as the renunciation, although temporary, of the goal of a fully collectivized economy. After the end of Soviet aid, the state urgently needed to mobilize financial resources for development. It had to mobilize private savings, foreign aid, and investment as well as capital from overseas Vietnamese. It had to offer the legal framework to attract private and foreign public investments. On the other hand, it had become impossible to continue subsidizing state enterprises and cooperatives. That is why several decrees and laws were adopted in the years following the announcement of the new policy. In 1988, there was the first law on the decollectivization of agriculture. Most cooperatives were dismantled and their assets sold or distributed among members. An investment code was adopted and is regularly amended to attract foreign investment. Private property (except for the land that remains state property) was recognized in the constitution of 1992.

The effect on labor was quite important. First of all, the collective sector has now become marginal. There were 37,000 cooperatives in manufacturing in 1985, and only 1,700 remained by 1995 (GSO 1996). Second, state enterprises and the administration laid off more than one million workers between 1989 and 1992 (World Bank 1993). As a result, nonstate employment doubled from 1986 to 1996. The expansion of nonstate employment came mainly from self-employment, above all in petty trade. Up to 1992, distribution networks were underdeveloped and private trade was severely controlled and limited to local trade. In 1985, the labor force in commercial activities accounted for less than 15 percent of the nonagricultural labor force (it is around 30 percent in Indonesia and in Thailand). There was a great need for traders, and this gap was filled by people laid off from the state sector but more so by newcomers on the labor market.

After a long period, nonagricultural state employment appears to be stable at around three million people. Up to 1985, one can see the growth trend of this sector, reflecting the policy of socialization, especially in the south. But despite a heavy concentration of investment in the state sector, the state was incapable of absorbing the growth of the labor force, and it had to rely on the private and family sector to provide employment to newcomers in the labor market. These sectors have entirely absorbed the growth of the nonagricultural labor force since 1985. It is also significant that Doi Moi was proclaimed at that very moment, showing the relationship between the economic policy and pressure in the labor market.

The reform in state enterprises resulted in the layoff of hundreds of thousands. Soon after, state enterprises started to recruit again. In fact, layoffs in the state sector were selective. Most of the dismissed workers had low levels of education, while at the other end those with

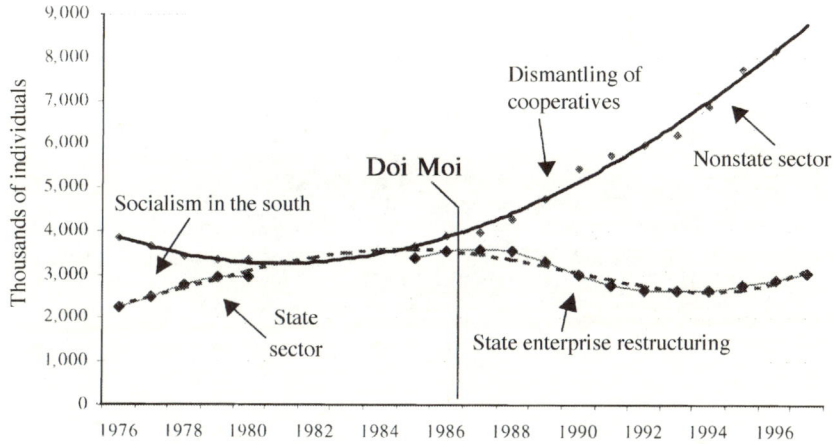

Chart 2. Evolution of nonagricultural employment, 1976–1997. Workers in cooperatives are included in the nonstate sector. (Data from the GSO, various years.)

university degrees were kept. Moreover, the state now continues to attract most of the educated people who enter the labor market (see Oudin 1997). Before Doi Moi, the state sector already absorbed the most qualified part of the labor force. The restructuring of this sector emphasized this human capital concentration, illustrated by the dismissal of the less qualified part of the work force. This concentration of qualifications in a sector is a characteristic of a dualistic labor market. It is emphasized by the tendency of the state sector to recruit people whose parents work in the same sector. Some heads of state enterprises confirmed that they hired new workers through their old workers, asking them to find the people they needed. During the period of massive layoffs, doing so was a way to avoid grievances, since dismissed parents could benefit from redundancy payments and their children would have a chance to be recruited by the enterprise. Half of the workers in state enterprises had their father also working in the state sector (in nonstate activities, the proportion is 26 percent; see Orstom Molisa survey, 1996). Maybe one of the most relevant indicators of the change in the labor situation is entry into the labor market, since it shows in which sector people entered at the start of their working lives. The 1975–95 evolution summarizes the changes that have occurred and gives some indications of the present situation.

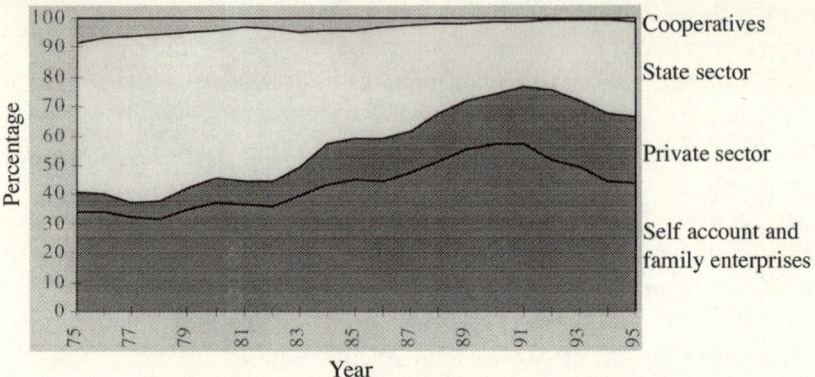

Chart 3. Sector of entry into the nonagricultural "labor market," 1975–1995. (Data from Orstom-Molisa survey, 1996)

These data apply only to people who are still in the labor market. Consequently, as we go back in time we lack information on people who are no longer active. Chart 3 shows the importance of each sector in labor supply absorption (for people who enter the labor market for the first time) through time. The share of the state (the civil service and state enterprises) has been declining steadily since 1977, but there has been a reversal since 1991. It is clear that nowadays the state sector still plays a dynamic role in job creation. Starting from a low point, the private sector is also dynamic insofar as job creation is concerned. It is now the outlet for 25 percent of labor market entrants compared to 5 percent in the years 1977–79. This sector is mainly composed of small and medium-sized enterprises.

The role of self-employment and micro (or family) enterprises in job creation seems to have reached its limits. Although it is still the main sector in which nonagricultural workers start their working lives, its part seems to be declining. It played a main role during the restructuring of the economy, particularly, as we have seen earlier, with the dramatic extension of small trade. But this extension cannot go beyond some limit, and the reversal seen on chart 3 demonstrates it. Self-employment was an efficient buffer when cooperatives and many state enterprises were disbanded.

This picture of the labor force shows the extent of the desocialization of labor relations. Two-thirds of the labor force is in agriculture, where labor is now organized on a family basis. In nonagricultural labor, employment in administration and state enterprises has shrunk to a quarter of the nonagricultural labor force. We are far from the situation of 1965, when virtually all of the labor force was in state or collective units. Moreover, the entire social environment that used to accompany labor positions has disappeared.

This situation has strong implications as far as labor legislation is concerned. Despite quite an advanced labor code and a lot of labor regulations, which are more advanced than in any other Asian country, more than 80 percent of the labor force does not benefit from labor protection, social security,[4] or pensions. Like other developing countries, Vietnam has built its social protection in reference to a dominant wage relation. Unlike other countries, it has gone far in the development of this form of labor, considering that collective forms of labor also offered a similar protection to that of wage workers. Moreover, the area covered by national social schemes was wider than in many countries. It included mother and infant care, preschool, education, family planning, assistance to widows, and so on.[5] The range of action of the trade unions also included all those activities. With the shrinking of wage labor, and the fact that only a part of the private sector abides by labor regulations, it is obvious that social protection has similarly shrunk. As in other developing countries, the new situation requires a new vision of labor regulations, social protection, and trade union action. The wage labor relation is no longer a useful reference, and policymakers should envision more adapted forms of legislation.

Conclusion

The Doi Moi reform, with its acceptance of private enterprise and market mechanisms, and the opening up of the country to foreign capital is by no means a renouncement of socialism. It is a necessary step toward socialism, as was the NEP in the late 1920s in the USSR. Whether or not the Vietnamese government will be able to deal with the consequences of the market economy is difficult to answer. So far, Vietnamese politics shows that the leaders have a clear view of the situation and maintain a firm grasp on society.

Acceptance of a market economy is only a temporary compromise in order to face the disastrous situation to which the former policy led and to attract foreign financial flows to replace Soviet aid. Minimum conditions for getting international aid have been implemented and as much as possible readapted to the view of the government. For instance, subsidies to private enterprises are used for state enterprises (or state-foreign joint ventures). The Doi Moi is a new strategy, with the reinforcement of the state sector through a bigger concentration of capital and qualified human resources. The other side of the coin is that the rest of the population has to rely on its own resources and the state no longer provides education (except primary) and social protection for all.

The socialist model has never been totally implemented because it was beyond the capacity of the state, and forces from the bottom (i.e., the population, local interests, small province-owned enterprises, etc.) have resisted the full collectivization of economic and social activities. The resistance became stronger after reunification. However, this model is still the reference of the Vietnamese government and Communist Party as was restated during the Eighth Congress in June 1996. From 1960 on, it can be seen that the state always oscillated between the march to full socialization of the means of production (including labor) and concessions to individual and local interests. The launching of the Doi Moi policy in December 1986 shows a major concession to the latter, with an adaptation of the strategy of the state to the new internal and external context.

NOTES

Institute of Research for Development (ORSTOM-IRD), Montpellier, France. Oudin worked on microenterprises and the labor market in Thailand (at Chulalongkorn University) and Vietnam (Ministry of Labor, Invalids, and Social Affairs).

1. In 1974, 61 percent of the nonagricultural labor force was in the state sector (enterprises and administration) and 25 percent in cooperatives (GSO 1976). In 1975, the production of the individual sector represented only 2.3 percent of total manufacturing production, against 4.6 percent in 1960 (Vo Nhan Tri 1992, 37).

2. See Fforde and de Vylder 1996, 164, n. 26, after an article in *Nhan Dan*, 6 November 1980.

3. In demography, dependency rates measure the number of individuals outside working age for 100 individuals of working age (usually from fifteen to sixty-four years). I use here the "economy dependency rate" which mea-

sures the number of nonactives and unemployed per 100 employed people. In the United States in 1980, the dependency rate was 106 nonactives for every 100 in the labor force (ILO 1995).

4. According to the government, around 5 million people have a social security card. In fact, this card is useless in hospitals, and individuals must pay full price for medical care. Civil servants continue to get some advantages.

5. Excluding those who had served the government of the south.

REFERENCES

Vietnam Government Publications:

The Constitutions of Vietnam, 1946–1959–1980–1992. 1995. Hanoi: Thê Gioi Publishers.
Documents du VIIIeme Congrès du Parti Communiste de la République Démocratique du Vietnam. Hanoi: Thê Gioi Publishers. Also available in English.

Andreff, Wladimir. 1993. "The Double Transition from Underdevelopment and from Socialism in Vietnam." *Journal of Contemporary Asia* 23, no. 4: 515–31.
Banister, Judith. 1993. Vietnam Population Dynamics and Prospects. Institute of East Asian Studies. Berkeley: University of California.
De Vienne, Marie-Sybille. 1994. *L'économie du Viêt-Nam (1955–1995). Bilan et prospectives, Notes africaines, asiatiques et caraïbes.* Paris: CHEAM.
Fforde, Adam, and Stefan de Vylder. 1997. *From Plan to Market: The Economic Transition in Vietnam.* Boulder: Westview.
Fforde, Adam, and Suzanne Paine. 1987. *The Limits of National Liberation.* London: Croom Helm.
Freyssinet, Jacques. 1989. "Crise, diversification des formes d'emploi, et transformation du rapport salarial." In *Ministère du Travail, de l'Emploi, et de la Formation Professionnelle*, 142–49. Paris: Ministère du Travail, de l'Emploi et de la Formation Professionnelle, Service des Etudes et de la Statistique.
GSO (General Statistical Office). 1976. *Dan so Nuoc Cong Hoa Xa Hoi Chu Nghia Viet Nam* (Population de la République Socialiste du Vietnam). Hanoi: Statistical Publishing House.
———. 1996. *Statistical Yearbook, 1995.* Hanoi: Statistical Publishing House.
ILO. 1995; Economically Active Population, ILO. Geneva (CD-ROM).
Ministère du Travail, de l'Emploi et de la Formation Professionnelle. 1989. *L'évolution des formes d'emploi: Actes du colloque de la revue Travail et Emploi, organisé les 3 et 4 novembre 1988 à l'Assemblée Nationale.* Paris: Service des Etudes et de la Statistique, Ministère du Travail, de l'Emploi et de la Formation Professionnelle.
Ministry of Labor, Invalids, and Social Affairs. 1995. *Labor Code of the Socialist Republic of Vietnam.* Hanoi: Thê Gioi Publishers.

Orstom Molisa. 1997. Report of the 1996 survey (unpublished report). Ministry of Labor, Invalids and Social Affairs. Hanoi.

Oudin, Xavier. 1991. "Development and Changes in the Labor Force in Thailand," *Journal of Social Research* (Bangkok) 14, no. 1: 1–9.

———. 1996. "Le lent développement du salariat en Asie du sud-est." *Mondes en développement* 24, no. 93: 11–21.

———, 1997. "Change in Labor with Doi Moi: New Evidence on Institutional Aspects of Labor in Contemporary Vietnam." Communication au Colloque Euro-Viet, Amsterdam, July.

Post, Ken. 1989. *Revolution, Socialism, and Nationalism in Vietnam*. Worcester: Darmouth Publishing Company, Ltd.

Puel, Hugues. 1989. *Emploi typique et transformation du système d'emploi in Ministère du Travail, de l'Emploi et de la Formation Professionnelle.* Paris: Ministère du Travail, de l'Emploi et de la Formation Professionnelle, Service des Etudes et de la Statistique.

Vo Nhan Tri. 1992. *Vietnam's Economic Policy since 1975.* Singapore: Institute of Southeast Asian Studies.

———. 1967. *Croissance économique de la république démocratique du Vietnam.* Hanoi: Editions en Langues Étrangères.

World Bank. 1995. Vietnam Poverty Assessment and Strategy.

13   Pascal Bergeret

Agro-Commodity Chains in Northern Vietnam: New Mechanisms for Old Stakeholders

Introduction

Since the end of collectivization under the political reforms of "Khoan 10"[1] in 1988, agricultural production in Vietnam has significantly increased. Between 1990 and 1995, the annual per capita production of food crops[2] (expressed in paddy equivalent) jumped from 324.6 to 364.8 kg (a 12.4 percent increase). Similarly, the annual per capita production of pork—by far the main meat product consumed in Vietnam—increased from 11.0 to 13.6 kg (a 23.6 percent increase),[3] taking into consideration a 2.1 percent annual population increase. These increases best illustrate the strong productivity of the agricultural sector. In the Red River delta, food crop production has also increased dramatically. Between 1990 and 1994, the value of total rice production progressed at an annual average rate of 6.04 percent (at 1994 prices). During the same period, the value of pork production grew at an average rate of 6.75 percent per annum.[4] These figures contrast sharply with the food shortages and stagnation of agricultural production during the years preceding the reforms. While rice production still appears dominant, its growth rate is similar to that of other products, like pork. As a result, in northern Vietnam the overall increase of agricultural production seems to be occurring without diversification, unlike other countries that have modernized their agricultural sectors. In China, for example, between 1990 and 1995, while the production of grain remained stable at 445 million tons, the production of pork grew from 22.8 to 32.0 million tons (+40 percent) after a jump of more than 58 percent between 1984 and 1990.[5]

Diversification of agricultural production is often considered a necessary step toward higher income for farmers. The predominantly rice based economy in the Red River delta thus seems to be a cause of the comparatively low growth of its agricultural income. Indeed, research conducted by the Red River Program since 1989 indicates that the regular increase of farmers' living standards in the Red River delta has been brought about essentially by means of nonagricultural activities undertaken by farming households.

This observation is somewhat worrisome because stagnating agricultural incomes can lead to growing dissatisfaction among producers and to the diversion of resources toward other sectors of activity. This would lead to the agricultural sector no longer being in a position to play a leading role in the economy, and rural exodus—so far contained to an acceptable level in Hanoi—could become a major threat.

One of the main factors contributing to the slow rate of agricultural diversification is agro-commodity chains. The rice, pig, and garlic commodity chains of the Red River delta best illustrate how and why producers are reluctant to change from relying on exclusively food security procured by rice production to diversifying their agricultural enterprise. In this chapter, I first describe the main characteristics of these three agro-commodity chains, then for each of them I compare the objectives of the producers, the consequences of the withdrawal of state management in the agricultural production in 1988, the relationships among stakeholders, and, finally, the nature of the risks in such production.

1. Main Characteristics of Rice, Pig, and Garlic Commodity Chains

This essay is based on research on the agro-commodity chains undertaken in the framework of the Red River Project: Pham Hoang Ha 1996, Le Goulven 1996, Vu Trong Binh and François Casabianca 1999, and Le Duc Thinh, Hoang Khanh Phuong, and Dao The Anh 1999. Some complementary interviews were conducted in 1997. Nam Thanh District (Hai Hung Province) was selected for the study of the production part of the commodity chains such as pork production.

The bulk of the rice produced in the Red River delta is locally consumed in rural as well as urban areas. A small part goes to markets in the mountains of the north and northwest regions and beyond, to China. Some years, like in 1994, rice shortages in South China induced very active yet often illegal exchanges with Vietnam. Such transborder flows are difficult to quantify. The rice commodity chain in the Red River delta involves a great number of stakeholders, often of small size: collectors, huskers, wholesalers, transporters, and retailers. Short channels (producers-huskers-consumers) are predominant, as the majority of the population lives in rural areas near the production sites. However, Hanoi and Haiphong cities, as well as the mining province of Quang Ninh (coal mines), are important consumer areas.

Although the Vietnamese government wants to increase the country's pork exports, the bulk of the pork produced in the Red River delta is still essentially consumed in urban areas. In fact, in the pig commodity chain, long marketing channels toward the cities are predominant because pig production is considered a source of cash by the producers and is systematically sold. The diet in rural areas still lacks meat products, whereas in the cities meat consumption is much more frequent. In Hanoi, 40 percent of families eat meat on a daily basis and another 46 percent eat meat every other day (Le Goulven 1996). Research conducted in two communes of Nam Thanh District showed that 40 and 64 percent of people interviewed, respectively, declare eating meat less than three times a month.[6]

Thus, short marketing channels (producers-collectors-rural slaughterers and butchers-rural consumers) play a minimal role in the overall operation of the pig commodity chain. They mainly deal with low-quality meat (high levels of fat), and there is a reverse flow of fat pork pieces from the cities to the countryside (Vu Trong Binh 1996). Long supply chains toward the cities (producers-collectors-transporters-urban slaughterers-urban retailers-urban consumers) play a predominant role in setting the major characteristics of the pig commodity chain, including prices. Moreover, in the cities a dynamic pork-processing sector is developing fast, involving powerful and well-equipped stakeholders.

While all farmers in the Red River delta grow rice and raise pigs, only the most affluent produce garlic. Garlic production only occurs in certain geographical zones of the delta, of which Nam Thanh District is a good example. The garlic commodity chain contains a limited number of operators, among whom wholesalers in the production zones and big buyers near the consumption zones are predominant. Garlic produced in the Red River delta is mainly sold—as dry bulbs or in powder—on export markets, notably in Thailand and Laos. On those markets Vietnamese garlic must compete with Chinese garlic. The production cost of the latter is said to be less than half the production cost of the former (Le Duc Thinh and Hoang Khanh Phuong 1996).

2. Objectives of the Producers

For every farm in the Red River delta, rice and pigs are a necessary, nonsubstitutable product. Rice production is devoted to covering farmers' subsistence needs, and all producers aim at maximizing it. With an average rice area of 600 m^2 per capita and annual paddy production of about 350 kg per capita (General Statistical Office 1996), farmers in the Red River delta seek maximum food security, hence maximum paddy yields, whatever the market conditions may be.

Pig production follows a very different rational pattern. It is a necessity because it provides the source of organic matter to maintain crop yields at an acceptable level within very intensive cropping systems (the land use ratio in the Red River delta is more than two). Pig production largely relies on the use of free resources available on the farm for animal feed (rice bran, small mollusks, and frogs gathered around houses, water taros, water hyacinth, kitchen refuse, etc.) and on low-input winter crops like sweet potatoes. The main expenses related to pig production are the purchase of piglets and sometimes veterinary products. With such feeding practices, farmers can manage to produce two to three pigs a year with a live weight of seventy to ninety kg. Sometimes, if an urgent need of cash arises, pigs can be sold at a smaller weight. Some producers have simply specialized in raising a more important number of animals (sometimes up to ten pigs a year); they often run small agro-businesses and can rely on a steady supply of by-products to feed the pigs (production of rice wine, tofu, or rice husks). Only when market conditions are favorable (i.e., when the ratio of the price of feed to the price of pigs is high) are farmers ready to intensify the production of pigs and to invest more in pig feed. In fact, farmers have significantly increased areas under maize cultivation during recent years, primarily to feed more pigs, thus contributing to greater pig production. Such a double logic combining the use of free feed resources and intensification of pig production when market conditions are favorable explains the fluctuations observed during recent years. For instance, the annual growth rate of pig production in the Red River delta was −4.41 percent in 1991, +12.62 percent in 1992, +16.19 percent in 1993, and +10.99 percent in 1994 (at 1994 prices; General Statistical Office 1996).

Garlic is essentially a cash crop. As a winter crop, garlic can be replaced with other winter crops in the crop rotation (maize, sweet potatoes, potatoes, soybeans, mungbeans, etc.). The magnitude of the area under garlic cultivation in a given year is linked to farm gate prices obtained the year before. Farmers' objective when growing garlic is clearly to earn cash. The total value of inputs necessary to grow garlic is high (seeds, fertilizer, pesticides), which makes this production a risky one, only suited to the most affluent farmers. When market conditions are not favorable, producers prefer to shift to other, less risky productions or to off-farm activities and reduce the acreage under garlic cultivation. This explains the big variations in areas devoted to garlic observed year to year.

3. Consequences of the Withdrawal of State Control

By the end of the 1980s, the state had eliminated price controls and withdrawn from managing the distribution of agricultural goods. Such a brisk withdrawal had immediate and dramatic consequences, as shown in 1989 by the growth of paddy production, which jumped by +7.4 percent (such a result can partly be attributed to the sudden apparition on the market—and in the statistics—of a significant part of rice production previously used to feed the animals because farmers had no incentives to sell it). However, the withdrawal of the state followed different patterns in the three agro-commodity chains considered in this essay.

It can be said that, as far as the rice commodity chain is concerned, state withdrawal occurred in an orderly manner. State enterprises, which before 1988 were in charge of collecting, husking, and distributing rice to urban consumers, organized their own progressive retirement with apparently a great concern for the future of their staffs. For instance, employees of big state rice-processing factories in provincial towns in the Red River delta (like Hai Duong) were offered credit with very favorable terms so that they would be in a position to equip themselves with small rice huskers and start their own individual businesses.

In Hai Duong, an adjacent street to the state-owned processing plant was soon full of dozens of small private husking enterprises. But these new stakeholders were not all old staff of the state factory. A certain number (ten among the twenty husking businesses still operating in this street at present) were individuals who somehow managed to accumulate a small amount of capital during the previous period and wanted to take up such an opportunity to invest in a profitable activity. Other employees of the state factory were less enterprising and preferred staying within the precinct and the payroll of the factory, where they were assigned a small amount of capital to manage in the name of the factory by conducting husking and rice-selling operations. Furthermore, the factory also facilitated the access of its staff to preferential credit by the Agricultural Development Bank in order to develop private microbusinesses of paddy husking and rice selling inside the factory.

A network of private transporters also appeared very quickly. They started by using trucks belonging to state enterprises on a contract basis. But the profits they generated soon enabled them to buy their own transportation. The new transporters became the link between the new private paddy-husking enterprises and new urban wholesalers. In the cities, the withdrawal of the state from distribution channels was the signal for numerous new wholesalers and retailers to establish themselves with the capital they had previously accumulated and which could suddenly be lawfully invested in businesses.

In the countryside, individual husking enterprises were already numerous in 1981.[7] Farmers were allowed to keep for themselves the amount of paddy produced above the quantities requested by their production contract with the cooperatives. Such quantities of paddy retained by individual families had to be locally husked.

As early as 1989, a myriad of farmers established themselves as petty paddy traders. They formed a tight network of paddy collectors in the villages, often transporting on bicycles small quantities of paddy to be processed by the new private husking businesses in nearby provincial or district towns. Thus, at all levels of the rice commodity chain a large number of new private stakeholders, often of modest size, were allowed to conduct business and seize opportunities presented by the withdrawal of the state. However, the state kept control of a regulatory stock of rice called "stock A34" which amounts to 400,000 to 500,000 tons for the whole country. The agents locally in charge of maintaining and renewing this stock remain important stakeholders in the rice commodity chain.

As far as the pig commodity chain is concerned, the withdrawal of the state can be accurately described as a collapse. Big state slaughterhouses suddenly stopped all activities in 1989. But preexisting underground networks involved in illicit pig slaughtering and pork trading were suddenly activated and developed. Unlike rice, a strategic commodity tightly managed by the state sector during the collectivist period, pig production and the trade in pork were more loosely supervised by the cooperatives and state authorities, leaving room for an active black market to flourish (Vu Trong Binh 1996). Such illegal activities were more or less tolerated during the collectivist period. Black market operators seized the opportunity provided by the new economic policy to consolidate their positions, and they soon controlled the whole pig commodity chain. For instance, a good number of rural slaughterers/butchers presently operating were already involved in those activities during the collectivist period, when individual meat businesses were theoretically banned. As a result, in the late 1980s and early 1990s entry by newcomers into the pig commodity chain was very limited. A case in point is provided by pork retailers in the cities: a typical female job, this activity is often reserved for members of old networks long involved in the legal or illegal trade of pork, or to their daughters.[8]

Singularly, decollectivization in 1989 did not immediately affect the garlic commodity chain. State enterprises involved in garlic processing carried on buying garlic from the producers and selling it on export markets in Eastern Europe, the only outlet for Vietnamese garlic at the time. Only in 1991, after the collapse of USSR, were such markets lost and the state enterprises forced to stop their activities. The whole sector was deeply affected and the producers were badly hit, the more so since during the previous period prices had remained high and the sale of garlic was guaranteed by export contracts. In 1992, the area under garlic cultivation in Nam Thanh District dropped dramatically compared to 1991, from 1,000 to 420 hectares (Le Duc

Thinh 1996). Only in the recent years have new markets been found in Thailand and Laos, which provoked a certain revival of activities in this sector. But nowadays the garlic commodity chain is totally controlled by private entrepreneurs.

4. Competition, Negotiation, and Networks

State withdrawal from the rice commodity chain led to the appearance of numerous new stakeholders entering the business without barriers. This state of affairs makes the rice commodity chain an economic system in which competition can play at all levels. For instance, private husking businesses in Hai Duong town are now facing stiff competition from newly established husking businesses located along roads in nearby rural districts on the way to Quang Ninh Province. Transporters from Quang Ninh tend to prefer buying from husking enterprises outside the town because it reduces their costs and allows them to escape police harassment, which is much more frequent in town. As a result, the number of transporters from Quang Ninh buying from husking businesses in Hai Duong town has decreased sharply.

Furthermore, the reduced role of short distribution channels in price setting has given producers easy access to price information. The definition of different rice grades and qualities is objective and clear: it relies on the kind of rice variety considered. Opportunities for fraud are limited. Fraud can only occur when paddy huskers keep for themselves a portion of the rice bran left in the machines and on the floor of the workshop or when a rice retailer mixes different varieties and sells the lot at the price of the most expensive one. But such dubious practices are limited in scope because stakeholders in the commodity chain are free to change partners if necessary.

Thus, the rice commodity chain can be described as a system in which information flows are symmetrical and multidirectional. Price variations at the consumer end at the market are directly conveyed up to the producers along with price differences resulting from the quality of rice. Such a transparent operation makes state control easier even if in certain years the blending of transborder prices results in an active black market with China (principally based on shipments of rice coming from South Vietnam) or if the management of "stock A 34" is sometimes less than orthodox.

The situation in the pig commodity chain appears very different. The distribution channels supplying the cities are predominantly long. In this commodity chain, information flows are asymmetrical and transactions are monopolized by one category of stakeholders: urban slaughterers (Le Goulven 1996). Urban slaughterers were already predominant in the underground channels operating during the collectivist period. They were able to create networks of collectors, which they now totally control. In the absence of any freezing facility, pigs must be slaughtered near the consumption markets and collectors must transport them live to the urban slaughterers as quickly as possible after their purchase from the producers in order to minimize weight losses or mortality risk.

Collectors are totally dependent on the urban slaughterers. Separate networks have emerged in which one urban slaughterer enjoys complete exclusivity with a set of collectors operating in a definite rural area. Urban slaughterers are in fierce competition with each other, not so much over prices but over the share of territory covered by their respective networks of collectors. Such a competition has resulted in concentration, with the emergence of very powerful operators. Down the distribution channels, urban slaughterers have similarly secured a clientele of retailers who come to the slaughtering houses before dawn in order to get their daily supply of pork to sell on the various markets of the cities.

Urban slaughterers thus appear in a crucial position that gives them privileged access to information coming from both rural production zones and urban consumption markets. Moreover, their role is similar to the one of matchmakers between the collectors and the retailers: urban slaughterers generally do not actually buy the animals with which they deal. They only organize the transactions between collectors and retailers, slaughter the pigs, and charge a commission for their service (Le Goulven 1996). The urban slaughterers thus do not bear any of the risks linked to the purchase of the pigs. They arbitrate negotiations between collectors and retailers thanks to their level of information. They manage their networks of retailers by providing credit to them (ibid.). They maintain a very close relationship with their networks of collectors by providing them with accommodations during the nights they spend in the city and by offering them protection against harassment by the police or gangs linked to other urban slaughterers. Transport of live pigs often occurs during the night and can be the occasion for all sorts of dubious, sometimes violent practices: being a pig collector can prove a dangerous job, and good protection by a powerful urban slaughterer is necessary (ibid.). Such asymmetrical flows of information and the predominant role played by urban slaughterers are reinforced by the subjectivity with which the quality of pigs is evaluated.

At the consumer end, the quality of pork is relatively well defined for a given piece of meat on the basis of the rate of fat. For a same cut, differences in the fat content can account for differences of price up to 10 percent (Vu Trong Binh 1996). But as far as live pigs are concerned the appreciation of quality is merely visual or partly based on the knowledge of the pig's history (mainly how it was fed).[9] During the transaction at the slaughterhouse, prices are negotiated when the pigs are still alive. The retailers can only rely on their visual expertise to assess quality, whereas the collectors and the urban slaughterer can rely on information they gathered about the history of the pigs. At the farm level, the probable fat content of the pig only plays a marginal role in price setting. Between a lean and a fat pig (the former being more difficult to sell) price differences rarely reach more than 2 percent (Vu Trong Binh 1996). This state of affairs goes against producers' interests because they are not in a position to benefit from consumers' increased demand for quality pork.

Thus, it appears that the pig commodity chain is still impacted by its history during the collectivist era and the years of state withdrawal. Asymmetrical flows of information resulting from the predominant role of one type of stakeholder and from uncertainties related to quality assessment hinder free competition. Producers are the main victims of this situation. During the week of the traditional Vietnamese New Year (Têt) in February 1997 the retail price of pork jumped by about 50 percent on Hanoi markets and 30 percent in Hai Duong, closer to Nam Thanh District. In Nam Thanh during the same period, pig prices at the farm level only increased 5 percent.

The garlic commodity chain is also monopolized by a limited number of stakeholders, and export markets absorb the major part of the production (about 80 percent in Nam Thanh District; see Le Duc Thinh and Hoang Khanh Phuong 1996). Near Nam Thanh District on the road to Haiphong, there is a small town where about a hundred families are engaged in the trade of garlic, including garlic of Chinese origin reexported to Thailand and Laos. Locally produced Vietnamese garlic represents about 60 percent of the total quantities dealt with by those traders (1995 figures; see ibid.) and is in competition with Chinese garlic.

Although their production cost is double that of Chinese garlic, Vietnamese varieties are appreciated for their strong perfume and their early date of harvest. Furthermore, Chinese garlic is heavily taxed at the border, which increases its price on the final market (the price of garlic increases by U.S.$100 per ton from the Chinese border to Nam Thanh, and the transport costs from Nam Thanh to Ho Chi Minh City in the south represent another $70 increase). Quality is very precisely defined and depends on the size of bulbs and the variety (color, perfume). There are many different categories, and prices seem to fluctuate independently from each other. Price variations on the export markets within a year and between years are high and are linked to the precise and changing nature of the final demand. Moreover, import prices of Chinese garlic are also very unstable. For instance, between January and March 1997 the border price of a particular type of Chinese garlic fell by two-thirds.

Such unpredictable price characteristics make the production and trade of garlic very risky activities for which profits and losses can be high. In fact, price setting takes place largely outside Vietnam, whether in China or on export markets. Such external constraints have imposed a certain degree of solidarity within the Vietnamese portion of the distribution channel. In particular, flows of information about prices are quick and symmetrical.

The profit or loss made by the various stakeholders depends on their own expertise and financial capabilities and on the rapidity with which they react to price changes. For instance, traders must be able to buy big quantities of garlic and send them to the south of the country as soon as prices become favorable. Producers must be able to keep their garlic and store it as long as prices are low. In fact, they have to manage and time the sale of their product to meet the market's sudden demand rather than based on personal or family needs. This kind of logic can only be found among the most affluent sector of the farming population, for which garlic represents an additional income beyond other, more stable sources. One thus understands why garlic production in Nam Thanh remains unstable and limited.

Conclusion

The experience of countries where agriculture has been modernized shows that long-term development of production can only be secured if the producers' risk is not too high. The current situation in the rice, pig, and garlic commodity chains in the Red River delta confirms this fact. The operation of the rice commodity chain shows that producers only have to bear climatic risks, which are inherent to agriculture. The objective for food security, which lies behind rice production, has resulted in strong and stable yield increase.

Symmetrical flows of information and a good level of competition within the distribution channels have reassured the producers that they can leverage the market and sell paddy when they need cash even if that means they will have to buy rice later (Pham Hoang Ha 1996). One can conclude that a certain degree of confidence in the market has established itself among producers. On the other hand, in the garlic commodity chain all stakeholders have to bear a considerable amount of risk and investment in production, since such trade is more speculative. As long as import and export markets remain unstable, outlets are insecure, and mechanisms to regulate the producer's risks are absent, garlic production will not be developed on a sustainable basis.

As far as the pig commodity chain is concerned, the situation is more complex. Because pig production is a necessity on every farm, a minimum supply is guaranteed to the markets. But the somewhat erratic evolution of quantities produced shows that above this minimum level of supply the intensification of pig production faces considerable risk. This is in direct contradiction to the characteristics of urban pork demand, which is regularly growing and requiring higher quality meat to match rising urban incomes. Between urban markets and the producers is wedged a set of stakeholders who are enjoying a predominant position and are able to reap most of the benefits generated by this expanding market.

One understands better from these examples why agricultural diversification out of rice seems to have reached a plateau in the Red River delta, all the more so when urbanization and overall economic growth have multiplied opportunities for nonfarming income. But such a development pattern, if prolonged much longer, will lead to the agricultural sector playing a lesser role in generating household incomes, which can hardly be suited to a country where 70 percent of the labor force is still employed in agriculture.

NOTES

Groupe de Recherches et d'Exchanges Technologiques, Paris.

1. Khoan 10 is a set of policy measures issued by the Communist Party of Vietnam organizing the effective end of collectivization in the agricultural sector. From this date on, agricultural production has been relying on farm households and most marketing operations have been controlled by private stakeholders.

2. These comprise paddy, maize, sweet potatoes, cassava, and potatoes.

3. General Statistical Office 1996.

4. Ibid.

5. Aubert 1996.

6. "Nutritional Status of Mothers and Children under Five Years of Age and Some Affecting Factors in Thai Tan and Quoc Tuan Communes, Nam Thanh District, Hai Hung Province" (Nguyen Chi Tam et al. 1995). This is a report submitted in partial fulfillment of the requirements of field practice for the master of science in community nutrition Program degree, National Institute of Nutrition, Hanoi.

7. Khoan 100, promulgated by the Communist Party in 1981, is considered to have been the first step toward decollectivization of agricultural production in Vietnam. It made provision for individual production contracts to be passed between cooperative members and the cooperative. Once the quantities of agricultural products mentioned in the contract were delivered to the cooperative, the members could keep the surplus for themselves. This policy provided a temporary boost to agricultural production.

8. In the ever changing landscape of trade in the cities of Vietnam, a new trend seems to be appearing, as new itinerant retailers of meat now cruise through the Hanoi streets. They seem to come from suburban districts and compete with the long established fixed retailers (information provided by K. Le Goulven).

9. At present, the pigs marketed in the Red River delta are crossbred between local and western strains. The rate of fat essentially depends on the way the animals are fed.

REFERENCES

Aubert, C. 1996. "Chine Rurale: Le Fossé Villes-Campagnes." *Tiers Monde* 37, no. 147: 535–47.

General Statistical Office. 1996. *Statistical Yearbook, 1995.* Hanoi: Statistical Publishing House.

Le Duc Thinh and Hoang Khanh Phuong. 1996. "Production des Cultures Sèches d'Hiver à Nam Thanh, Hai Hung." Paper presented at the Séminaire Agriculture Familiale et Gestion des Ressources du Milieu dans le Delta du Fleuve Rouge, Hanoi, April.

Le Goulven, K. 1996. "Les Formes de Coordination de la Filière de Viande Porcine dans le Delta du Fleuve Rouge, Vietnam du Nord." Mémoire de Diplome d'Ingénieur en Agronomie Tropicale et de Diplome d'Etudes Approfondies, Economie du Développement Agricole, Agroalimentaire et Rural, Centre National d'Etudes Agronomiques des Régions Chaudes, Ecole Nationale Supérieure d'Agronomie de Montpellier, Université de Montpellier I, France.

Pham Hoang Ha. 1996. "Les Transformations de la Filière Riz au Vietnam: Cas de la Région du Delta du Fleuve Rouge." Master's thesis, Institut Agronomique Méditerranéen, Montpellier, France.

Hoang Khanh Phuong and Eric Le Quéré. 1995. "Description des cultures sèches d'hiver dans quatre communes du delta du Fleuve Rouge." In *L'agriculture du delta du Fleuve Rouge à l'heure des réformes*, 228–54. Hanoi: Maison d'édition de l'agriculture.

Vu Trong Binh. 1996. "La Commercialisation de la Viande Porcine dans le Delta du Fleuve Rouge." Paper presented at the Séminaire Agriculture Familiale et Gestion des Ressources du Milieu dans le Delta du Fleuve Rouge, Hanoi, April.

14 Olivier Tessier

Commuting from the Village to the City: Analyzing the Patterns of Migration of the People of the Northern Village of Hay to Hanoi

Introduction

Since the beginning of the 1990s, the number of Hay village[1] people who work and live outside the village, mostly in Hanoi, has gradually increased even though this movement is not definitive. It seems that nothing can predispose the inhabitants of this enclosed, agricultural village, situated in the Middle Land, more than 130 km from the capital, to migrate. But the increase in economic mobility is not particular to this village, as is illustrated by the development of public transport. At the beginning of the 1990s, there was only one bus per day between the principal town in Thanh Ba District and the capital; now there are from five to seven busses making this trip every day. This is backed up by the results of various recent urban studies, which all reveal the existence of a flux of seasonal or temporary migrants into Ho Chi Minh City in the south (Trân Anh Tuan 1998, 161) and into Hanoi in the north. Estimated at between 20,000 and 30,000 in July 1993 (Li Tana 1996, 11), the population of temporary migrants working in unskilled jobs in Hanoi is currently difficult to assess due to the nature of the phenomenon. In the absence of global figures, it must simply be noted that the capital's population has grown since 1986 at an annual rate of 55,000 people, of which some 22,000 are migrants (Doan Mân Diep, 123).

A policy of economic liberalization and "opening up" began in 1986; Doi Moi, "the revival," is identified by a number of authors as having generated the phenomenon and provided the necessary framework for its expansion. The proposed analyses, whether they be macrostructural or microeconomic, will make the economic dimension the major and at times exclusive cause of the development of the migratory flux. "The controlled opening of the market has led to new possibilities for the work force in terms of mobility" (Henaff 1998, 1), mobility made possible by the combination of two essential factors: the relaxation of restrictions on movement and residence (registration), on the one hand; and on the other the redistribution, in 1988 and 1993, of land to peasants (Li Tana 1996, 4–5). Thus, those migrants questioned in Hanoi suggested that above all their low incomes and underemployment, a result of heavy land taxes, have pushed them to leave (Doan Mau Diep and Trinh Khac Tham 1998, 213; Li Tana 1996, 33), reasons that are similar to those evoked at Ho Chi Minh City (Trân Anh Tuan 1998, 188). It seems realistic to suggest that the relationship between the rural population and the available agricultural land is sufficiently unbalanced that the share of land received by each household in 1993 (on average one *sao*^{2} of paddy field per mouth to feed, which is 0.15 hectares for a family of four) has persuaded some of them to exploit their new autonomy and capacity for decision making away from the village.

An important phenomenon, due to its scale as much as its topicality, which we would like to study not in terms of consequence but in terms of cause, is the village. The fact that there is only one destination tends to define the whole of the phenomenon within its own limits and therefore reduces the complexity of economic mobility to one movement, rural to urban. On the other hand, in light of the village, facts are changed because the question of leaving is no longer obvious, contrary to what the inquiries at the destination say, but is also a choice. "To migrate or not to migrate?" is how P. D. Mahadev and J. L. Racine put it; they note with regard to migration in India, "in one way or another, and whatever their economic status, every family in rural India asks itself this question, and in this way at least one of its members is likely to migrate" (1994, 9). Changing the perspective, taking into account the fundamental fact, which is the decision to migrate, allows us to go beyond this vision of migration as the ultimate stage of the "proletariatization of the peasants," an inescapable consequence of the expansion of capitalism and the market economy (Dupont and Guilmoto 1993, 282), but could on the contrary lead to an overestimation of the capacity of migrants to master and reason out their movements. It is with reference to the field of analysis, which defines the two poles "settling" and "rupture." It is in this framework that the migratory practices of the inhabitants of Hay village will be envisaged and analyzed: are they synonymous with rupture, moving away from the village, or could we consider that the migration is controlled by the peasants, reasoned out as a strategy of diversifying their activities?

The results presented here are based on a series of interviews carried out in Hay village, and to a lesser extent in Hanoi, between 1995 and 1998. The relatively long period, about four years, allowed me to follow, over time, the development of migration and to observe the changes it brought about in the village.

1. Patterns of Migration in the Village of Hay: An Overview

During the period of collectivization (1960–86), the flux leaving the village was principally composed of inhabitants who worked as "civil servants" (teachers, police officers) in the various local organizations (administrative, cooperative, and political), in factories, and on state plantations. Given the restrictions on movement, it was possible to distinguish schematically two movements, the difference being not so much based on the nature of the activities that caused the movement as on the consequences from an accounting point of view and the effect on the village population.

> Permanent or long-lasting migrations, which transformed into a stable and lasting installation near the workplace
>
> Shuttle or pendular migration, that is, all other movements where the common element was the conservation of a principal residence of the village despite, in certain cases, the complete suspension of activity in agricultural production

This situation, which is relatively simple and easy to understand, has undergone two major changes since the beginning of the 1990s.

A significant increase in the number of people leaving, a tendency that has increased since 1992–93

A diversification of methods of migration and destinations, which for the moment is only rarely translated in terms of a lasting change of residence

This last element, the residence,[3] is one of the key indicators frequently used for the analysis of population movements, in that the classic notion of migration is defined by the transfer of the place of residence from the place of departure to the destination. This reference has proved to be insufficient to take into account the possible diversity of movements, as "migration only constitutes the tiny tip of the iceberg where all forms of mobility are overshadowed by too narrow a definition" (Courgeau 1998, 2). The author prefers the spatial notion of mobility, which he defines as "all movements on the physical plane, of individuals or groups of individuals, whatever the length of stay or the distance of the movement" (3). In this definition, the notions of movement and stay seem more apt to translate the reality observed in Hay village, but its general dimension goes beyond the scope of this essay. In effect, the only movements tackled here will be those with an economic purpose, or those that are similar to that, because they leave aside two other population fluxes, conscription and the extravillage matrimonial flux, and because it has had and continues to have, all the more for the latter, a considerable importance as much from a statistical point of view as from a social one. In this patrilineal society, where virilocality dominates, the second flux now represents the principal cause of female emigration, migration of a cultural nature, even if some marriages are motivated by underlying economic interests.

Once this restriction is admitted, it is possible to propose a typology of mobility, based on the periodicity and duration of the movements, criteria that are nonexclusive and whose pertinence is to embrace the diversity of the phenomenon when this is observed in terms of the point of departure, the village. The temporal dimension is, however, dependent on other characteristics proper to each type of movement: for the village studied, the duration of stays away from it, and their regularity are determined in part by the type of activity and the destination of the villagers. The duration, combined and ordered in a function of the two other elements, allows differentiation among five types of movement.

1. Shuttle movements lasting one day or less: the employment of work forces to extract stones in the Ninh Dân Commune or employment in administrative and political structures in the commune. Various opportunities to work near the village (repair work on the road to Phu Tho, for example) drain off more than thirty villagers for six months.
2. Nonperiodic or movements of uncertain duration: villagers working in the construction industry and most often organized into teams (laborers, masons, carpenters), for whom the place of work extends from the village to the northern provinces (Lào Cai); snake hunters, for whom the place of work is similar to that of the construction workers, and who are absent from three days to several weeks, depending on the season.
3. More or less regular short-term movements (from three days to two weeks): pieceworkers (*lam khoan*) working in the factories of Thanh Ba District (tea factories, cementing, arms factories, breweries) and exceptionally (two cases) specialist technical service employees, one in Phu Tho and the other in Bai Bang.
4. Regular medium- (three months) and long-term (six months to a year) movements, which we call intermediary or temporary migration: mostly to Hanoi and to a lesser extent to various places in the ancient province of Vinh Phu and to the south of the country. (T.P. Ho Chi Minh, New Economic Zones of the Central Plateau.) There are also some "professional" jobs occupied by young single people: nurses, teachers, the military.
5. Permanent migration: professional workers (nurses, teachers, the military, skilled workers).

These different sorts of migration and movements can be summarized on an organization chart (chart 1), which will be referred to throughout this essay.

The Network: A Vital Element in Mobility

The vital role played by social and family networks in the recent dynamics of migration in Vietnam has already been examined by

TABLE 1. Different Sorts of Movements, Destinations, and Distances Traveled

Type of Movement	Destination	Distance Traveled
1. Daily shuttles	Ninh Dân and surrounding area	4 to 10 km
2. Nonperiodic of uncertain duration	Village to northern province	4 to 250 km
3. Short-term movement	Thanh Ba District	10 to 30 km
4. Regular (a) medium term (b) long term	(a) Viet Tri, Vinh Yen, Phu Tho, Hanoi (b) Ho Chi Minh City, New Economic Zones	(a) 30 to 150 km (b) over 1,000 km
5. Permanent migration	Thanh Ba and bordering districts, Hanoi	10 to 150 km

several authors (Henaff 1998, 8–10; Dang Nguyên Anh 1998, 183–84; Li Tana 1996, 34–36; Trinh Khac Tham 1998, 214). Hay village confirms the principal aspects already identified but also singles out certain particularities upon which we will dwell.

The first important point is that we cannot talk of an all-encompassing village network but rather a series of small, interconnected networks, occasionally activated when the opportunity arises, which depend on a small number of particularly well informed villagers working for several years outside the village. Individual and circumstantial co-optation leads to a concentration of villagers at the heart of the same company: nine of them are currently working in the same restaurant in Hanoi, five are working in a cushion workshop also in the capital, and six are employed in a specialist military unit making wooden packaging. Take the latter, for example: the barracks on which the specialist unit is based are in the neighboring commune of Vo Lao. Everything began, so to speak, with the recruitment of Mr. Thai as an official worker at the beginning of the 1980s. In three years, from 1993 to 1996, Mr. Thai has taken on five of his cousins as piece-workers. In the same way, Mr. Quang, one of Mr. Thai's cousins, has co-opted two of his nearest neighbors into the same work. There are many examples of such a practice. Suffice it to remember, for the moment, that the links forming this network are above all founded on family and to a lesser extent on neighbors and therefore the framework for these networks preexist the movement of labor for which they are used.

But can we speak systematically of networks as understood from the previous example? The reality is of course far more complicated,

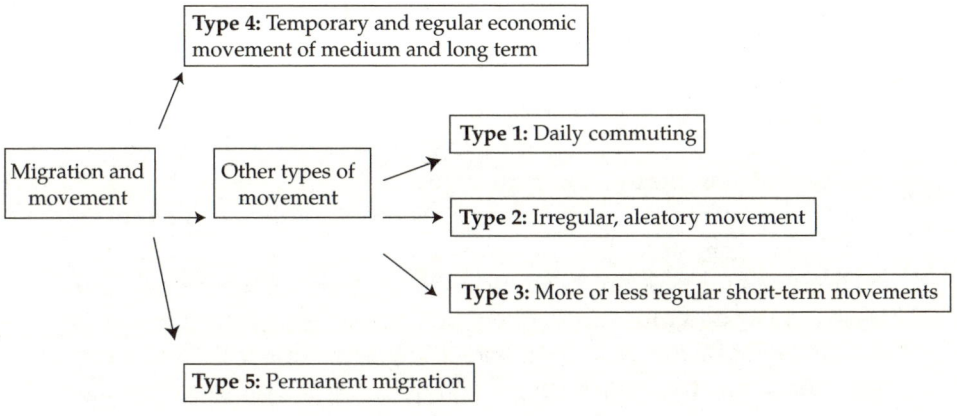

Chart 1. Different types of economic migration

and important variants must be recognized in terms of the nature and form of the network depending on the type of movement. The only constant common to all migrants working outside the village is that a third party has intervened to introduce the employer to the potential employee. This role of "go-between," which sometimes requires payment and creates a relationship of tripolar dependence among the offer, the intermediary, and the demand, is justified by the fact that he or she is the only person with all the information, a position that legitimizes his or her power, function, and prestige. Take the case of Mrs. Anh, who found a job as a pieceworker at a stone extraction site in the commune of Ninh Dân after several years of unemployment, even though the company was going through a critical time. Her employment was made possible through the intervention of her father, former deputy director of the company and now retired. According to Mrs. Anh, another way to obtain a job of this sort is to offer "presents" to one of the heads of department so that he comes down in your favor in front of the head of personnel.

This smallest form of network, created by and around an intermediary, does not always develop further and can remain in its most punctual state. The division into several small networks operating punctually to create a job is a characteristic of low-travel labor movements, especially daily movement, due to the close proximity of the place of work to the village. The person wishing to leave has the benefit of a wide range of possible intermediaries, whether they be parents, neighbors, or friends, and if this network should fail he or she can go and look for another intermediary. That does not mean, however, that it is easy to find a job nearby, notably due to the lack of job offers, but on the other hand it does explain the diversity of methods used and intermediaries having worked for those villagers who occupied or occupy this type of job.

The increased distance between the point of departure and the destination, physical distance as well as social, has provoked two changes. On the one hand, it appears to be a solution to the nebula of small networks, a direct consequence of the decrease in the number of possible intermediaries and the increasing difficulty of finding an intermediary that faces the person wishing to leave. On the other hand, the decrease in the number of networks is compensated for by an increase in their size, competence, and role. A migrant's dependence on these networks is no longer only schematically limited to obtaining a job but will endure in a more or less intense way throughout his or her time away from the village. As for average length and long-lasting migrations, it is possible to identify two types of network.

The first type relies on the existence of a relative legally established outside the village on a long-term basis: due to their function, size, and limited scope, from the point of view of the number of villagers able to benefit from them, they are similar to those characteristic of movements near the village. As an illustration, we can take the case of Miss Ngo, a worker in Ho Chi Minh City, whose job was found by an aunt who had been living there for thirty years, or the case of a young man, Mr. Huy, whose uncle is deputy manager in a factory producing industrial tiles in Yên Bai. Thanks to his uncle's intervention, he was taken on as an office worker.

The second type of network is alternatively based on an internal dynamic: a place where one or more temporary migrants act as the intermediary. The first job found is the result of an offer made by an inhabitant, relative, or friend, who has temporarily returned to the village. The constitution of different networks corresponds to a process of specialization according to the type of activity or the destination and is characterized by the appearance of specific fluxes, which tend, as time goes on, to feed themselves. This internal dynamic and tendency toward specialization is particularly well illustrated by the high number of young, single girls from the village who work as domestic staff or waitresses in Hanoi. Out of twenty-one young, single villagers aged fifteen to twenty-nine now working in the capital, and nine married villagers, thirteen found their first jobs thanks to Mrs. Nhiên, who herself found her job thanks to Mrs. Hop, and seven through one of the young women who had earlier been co-opted by one of the villagers.

If we emphasize this last example, it is because it shows that on a limited scale, in this case a village, a network begun by one or two people will be sufficient to lead to a professional specialization in movements. What is more, unlike the first type of network, the movements have an undeniable cumulative effect, that is to say, the flux is maintained by a chain reaction: considering all age groups together, twenty-five of the thirty villagers currently working in the capital found their first job through this network. The network thus tends to create vocations, in some ways to "create migration," even if the idea of leaving already vaguely existed: the speed with which opportunities are grasped is a good indicator. Back in the village for two days, Mrs. Hop told of the existence of five jobs available in the capital in a restaurant where her younger brother was working. The next day she returned to the capital accompanied by two young, single girls, two married women, and a young man. This speed of departure can be explained by the sense of security that the network has created.

The regrouping of several villagers at the heart of the same firm, as well as their group departure from the village, are two perspectives that help the future migrant and his or her family to take the first step: the network is therefore like a safety net that minimizes risks and disappointments. Another element also affects the decision process: accommodation. Almost all of the villagers stay with their employers (servants, waiters) or at their place of work (factories, construction sites). Mr. Biên,[4] whose twenty-two-year-old daughter works in a restaurant that employs eight other villagers, explains.

> I am not worried about my daughter because according to my nephew, Sang, she is living with others [from the village] and they do not have the time to go out in the evening; they work all the time. She is not exposed to social problems (*ten nan xa hoi*). . . . She earns 350,000 dong per month, and since Têt [about six months ago] she has sent more than 1 million dong.

Two other aspects of the primordial role played by the villager networks merit discussion. First, there are strong links between the members of the household who have left and those who have stayed behind. This link is all the more important when the destination is far away and the period of time spent there is long. Carrying letters, delivering money, or even just simple family visits are the shared tasks of those who return to the village. Information also circulates in the opposite direction: the latest news from the village, requests to send money, somebody getting married, somebody else building a house, and so on. If on an individual scale the frequency of home visits varies and can be as low as one or two per year, on a scale including all of the villagers present in the same place visits are logically more frequent: it is rare that more than a fortnight will pass without one of the villagers working in Hanoi returning to the village. Second, for temporary migrants, and notably for the young among them who do not have the good fortune to share work and accommodations with other villagers, keeping up links with other migrants from the village is often a primordial condition of prolonging their stay in a strange place, far removed from their family and social environment. Moral support and points of reference being indispensable, all the same there is only a small amount of contact with other migrants compared to the contact in places where there are several villagers.

With this in mind, we do not entirely share the analysis proposed by Li Tana, that "traditional, rural values have moved into the city with the migrants and are retained through the spontaneous clustering of their habitat. Indeed, in many ways it is the blurring of distinctions between living at home and living in Hanoi that has served to encourage migration because there is not such drastic change of lifestyle involved" (1996, 45). We should not delude ourselves, though; working conditions are hard, relations with the employer are often difficult and sometimes conflicting, and the more or less regular contact with other villagers does not compensate for the feeling of isolation. The experiences of this young villager,[5] then aged nineteen, serve to remind us of this.

> I left to work in Hanoi with two other young people from my village, aged sixteen and twenty-three. We worked in a factory. The salary was 100,000 dong per month [about U.S.$9].[6] A woman from my village who works as a cleaner found me

the job. . . . In the morning, I would have some instant noodles, then we would work from 6 A.M. till 1 P.M., when we would have lunch. In the evenings, we would go to the factory owner's house to wash, eat, and sleep. I was hungry all the time and could not stand living like that. So after ten days the three of us returned to Hanoi. . . . I think you can only work like that for a certain time, two months perhaps, so as to have some money to come home with. I will have to wait this year. Next time I will probably work in a factory making chair covers in Hanoi. If I go, I will come back to help my widowed mother collect the rice and work.

2. Why Do the People of Hay Migrate to the Cities and Who Migrates?

The analysis of a problem understood on a small scale, here a village, poses the question of its representativeness or "how to put these facts and lack of statistics in a more general context?" (Sagant 1978, 14). If the analysis can only be quantitatively pertinent on the same scale, it allows a clear illustration of country logic, which studies about places of emigration do not always illustrate, or, more or less, to give them coherence in a context in which the phenomenon studied only represents part of a complex whole. It is for this purpose that we have tried to establish the most exhaustive census possible of economic mobility on the scale of the village. The figures presented in table 2 illustrate spontaneous movements at a given moment: it is a picture of the phenomenon that concerns 149 households out of the 165 that make up the village. The table allows us to measure economic mobility. Quantitively, the flux is important: over 130 villagers occasionally or regularly work outside the village. The majority of them (70 percent) are temporary migrants for whom the major destination is Hanoi. This attraction of the capital (44 percent for all types of movement) has already been revealed in other studies (Li Tana 1996, 9; Doan Mau Diep et al. 1998, 212) and is accentuated here by the weak proportion of movements to nearby medium-sized cities (Viet Tri, Vinh Yan, Phu Tho).

Envisaged at a domestic level (the household unit), the movements affect 56 percent of the 149 households questioned. This proportion needs to be explained, 84 households being below the number obtained by a simple accumulation of the figures from the different authorities. The explanation can be found in the multiplicity of possible combinations between the number of members of a household who work outside the village, on the one hand, and the type of movement adopted on the other. An example will explain this better: the Nhieu family is made up of a married couple and their five children—the two youngest are still at school. Of the five remaining active members, three make regular movements. Mr. Nhieu and his third daughter work in Hanoi in a family-run confectioner's owned by their cousins, while the second daughter is a pieceworker in the stone industry in Ninh Dân. This household is classed in the "temporary migration" as well as in the "daily commuting" category. This situation is not unique; in February 1998, 22 households had two members working outside the village, 11 had three people, and 2 had four and five people, respectively.

This diversity makes an exhaustive presentation of the different combinations rather tiresome, but it highlights an aspect that is important in the analysis of the problem: temporary migrations and other types of movement cannot only be explained on an individual scale. The decision to migrate and the option of different types of movement are choices that require social and economic considerations, combining the individual dimension with that of the domestic unit. In table 3, the analysis of certain characteristics of a migrant's profile allows us to

TABLE 2. Movements on 1 February 1998

Type of Movement	Number of Villagers	(% of total of movements)	Number of Households Concerned
Temporary migration			
Hanoi	57	43.5	39
Vinh Phu	17	13.0	16
Other northern provinces	11	8.3	9
South of the country	7	5.2	5
Subtotal	92	70.0	69
Shuttles	10	8	9
Irregular and nonperiodic			
Construction teams	16	12.0	16
Snake hunters	4	3.0	4
Subtotal	20	15.0	20
Short duration	9	7.0	8
Total	131	100.0	84

interpret these choices in terms of family strategy. Whether the classification is according to age or marital status, the profile of temporary migrants is different from that of other villagers working regularly outside the village.

Temporary migrations principally concern young singles (78 percent), between the ages of sixteen and twenty-nine, with an almost equal ratio of men to women. The other forms of migration, however, are dominated by men, 80 percent of whom are married and heads of families. This difference can generally be put down to the strategy of the families at a household level, even if the extent to which it is rationally planned must be qualified.

All of the movements are based on the same logic of complementarity. The development of economic mobility is conditioned by the conservation of agricultural activity in the village. Except in two cases, only one of the couple commutes and/or one or more children are of working age. Temporary migrations are mostly made up of domestic units of more than two workers, that is, households in which the temporary or longer term absence of several of the single

TABLE 3. Age and Marital Status of Migrants

	19 or Less	19–24	25–29	30–34	35–39	40–44	45–49	50 or More	Total Women	Total Men
Temporary migration										
Married men	—	1	3	5	1	—	1	1	—	12
Single men	5	21	7	4	—	—	—	—	—	37
Married women	—	1	1	—	3	1	2	1	9	—
Single women	11	19	3	1	—	—	—	—	34	
Subtotal	16	42	14	10	4	1	3	2	43	49
Shuttles										
Married men	—	—	1	—	1	3	—	—		5
Single men	—	—	—	—	—	—	—	—		0
Married women	—	1	2	1	—	—	—	—	4	
Single women	—	1	—	—	—	—	—	—	1	
Irregular (men only)										
Married	—	—	2	4	2	6	3	—		17
Single	—	2	1	—	—	—	—	—		3
Short-term (men only)										
Married	—	—	1	1	2	1	1	—		6
Single	—	3	1	—	—	—	—	—		4
Subtotal		7	8	6	5	10	4		5	35
Total	16	49	22	16	9	11	7	2	48	84

children over sixteen years of age, or indeed one of the parents, is not detrimental to agricultural production. This logic of complementary activities is generally associated to the idea of "seasonal" migration, that is, departures and absences in accordance with periods of lesser agricultural activity. This idea deserves further discussion.

Nearby or far away, irregular movements are undeniably of a seasonal character in that, with the exception of official workers and a few administrative and political employees for the commune, these movements are broken up according to the key agricultural periods: preparation of the land, planting the rice, and then harvesting, a series of tasks that are repeated biannually since there are two rice seasons per year. The piecework system is compatible with these regular interruptions, but there is no guarantee of returning to the same job after the agricultural season, as Mr. Vuong[7] (thirty-three years old) underlines.

> Before the harvest, I worked as a laborer on the Vâ Lao road, and I hope to work there afterward, but it is not a certainty since I gave my place to one of my friends. . . . My wife is alone for the harvesting, and so I must help her to transport the rice and thresh the paddy fields.

The seasonal dimension of the movements can therefore only be determined by their duration and periodicity, yet they must be defined with reference to the priority given by the migrant to his or her participation in agricultural work.

It is in this sense that temporary migration (regular, medium-, and long-term movements) can only be classed as "seasonal." The appreciation by the individual of the nature of his or her presence depends on each individual's considerations (obligations, distance, job security) and position in the household: composition and alternative solutions in case of absence.

In the few cases in which one of the couple migrates in the medium or long term, priority is given to job preservation outside the village even if this means a loss of manpower at the household level. This deficit of labor can be linked to the amount of work to be done but also to the nature of the work. Mr. Truong[8] (thirty-four years old), father of two, explains that there exists a division of labor according to one's sex.

> My wife has been working in Hanoi since last year. She returns every two or three months. . . . She sometimes comes back for the harvest or reseeding, but if she is too busy she sends me the money and I take on some workers.

The impossibility of frequent returns to the village for diverse reasons, including the risk of losing one's job, is thus compensated for in alternative ways: the paid agricultural laborer and a return to the system of helping each other.[9] Even if a return to the village is possible, economics sometimes prevents it: the cost of a hired hand is less than the sum of the cost of a return ticket to Hanoi plus the lost revenue during the absence. This financial reality explains the absence of Mr. Giao's son.[10]

> For my son, who is in Hanoi, it's his wife who looks after the fields and the house. She has four *sao* of rice, and if the harvest is good she grows four hundred kg of paddy, which is worth what my son earns in over a month. It's better that my son stays in Hanoi because he sends money to his wife with which she hires laborers instead of him coming home to help his wife.

However, more than the obligations and economics that can prevent a return to the village, it is the nature of the population of temporary migrants that means we cannot consider them to be "seasonal." The movement of young and single people from families with over two people who are part of the active population is more likely to be in order to feed one of the mouths of the household than to generate additional revenue. Here the limiting factor is almost never the work force belonging to the household but the small rice-growing area allotted to each household in 1993. Mr. Häc (sixty-three years old), father of eight, four of whom are still single, thus "encouraged" two of his sons (twenty and twenty-three years old) to leave the village, one going to Hanoi, the other to Vinh Yên, while insisting that at the end of the day "it was their decision." This "choice" is perhaps better understood if we consider the following discussion with Mrs. Bao.[11]

My daughter left on the sixth of January with Mrs. Nhiên, who had found her a job as a cleaner. She is housed and fed and earns 200,000 dong per month plus 60,000 dong for rice in the morning. . . . With the arrival of my son's wife [they were recently married and have moved in with his parents], there is not enough work for three women, so she had to leave.

In terms of this economic strategy based on the preservation of agricultural activity in the village, the decision to work outside the village is intrinsically linked to the sort of movement that the person leaving wants to adopt. The decision depends on the position of the person in the household and the composition of the household. The head of the family or his equal prefers short-term migration, which can be seen from the high numbers of married men in table 3. This is also why there are so few married women working outside the village: only four out of the thirteen women questioned made daily trips, and they returned home to the family every evening. In other words, once the men are married they retain a certain mobility to nearby destinations while the women tend to remain in the village.

But, such a distribution of economic mobility is not a foregone conclusion. It is the product of a dynamism of movement that has come about at the cost of an evolution in mentalities.

3. Commuting to the City: A New Way of Life for the People of Hay

The current structure of economic mobility, as is presented in table 2, is the product of a recent evolution. In the first half of the decade, the majority of villagers working outside the village were concentrated in the surrounding dozen or so kilometers and commuted daily between their places of work and the village. The successive and brutal loss of available jobs nearby, the result of a decrease in the activities of some of the district's companies, and a decline in road building in the area, has not dried up emigration. On the contrary a number of villagers have converted or reoriented themselves and therefore their destinations and movements. The number one destination is now Hanoi, which is the principal center of temporary emigration. Temporary emigration has thus become the major flux, creating a phenomenon that we might consider as arising from certain economic conditions in the long term. The opportunities near the village are in decline, and so the villagers leave for further destinations. But the major change that occurred in the middle of the 1990s did not have the same effects on all migrants. Among nineteen to twenty-nine year olds, most of whom were single at the time, 80 percent converted to medium- to long-term migration. For those villagers over the age of thirty, this figure drops by at least 40 percent, with those over thirty preferring to adopt temporary migration or irregular short-term movements. Thus, the attitudes toward conversion vary and illustrate the correlation between the type of movement on the one hand and the age and marital status on the other. This also allows us to better understand the current physiognomy of the economic mobility.

However, this evolution in the dynamics of migration and the inversion of polarity, to the benefit of urban centers, especially Hanoi, is not without its problems. When in 1995 we started to look at the phenomenon, the villagers we met had a negative opinion of the movement to the capital and the other major cities. Some villagers did not hesitate to question the nature of the "work" carried out by the migrants, as Mrs. Nga[12] explains.

> Young girls, often only thirteen years old, and married women, leave to work in Hanoi as servants, but in fact they are employed in private hotels for work that is not proper. Working as a household maid or servant only earns enough money to live on, so how come some of these women come back to the village so rich? They buy buffalo and have houses built.

As can be seen from this extract of an interview, the hostile and denunciatory attitude of some villagers toward the migrants was aimed at that time at the female population. The image associated with a move to the city and the thinly disguised worries about the sort of lives being led by the migrants were deduced from and reinforced by the sums of money acquired by what were believed to be immoral means. The talk was all ambivalent, and the women were at the same time victims and accomplices.

Mrs. Nga's position takes on another dimension, however, when we find out that her daughters, aged sixteen and eighteen, left the village a year and a half later, one to work in a restaurant, the other as a servant. This is not a unique case, far from it. Only six months before her nineteen-year-old daughter left the village for the city, Mrs. Minh[13] had this to say.

> The daughter of Mr. Bien has gone to Hanoi. . . . I wouldn't let my daughters go to Hanoi because of the way of life there. I'm afraid they would have relationships with boys that cannot be controlled by the family. . . . Here the work is never finished. . . . I allowed my daughter to work in Ho Da [a career in stone work in the Ninh Dân commune] because she came home every lunchtime and evening. . . . As for my son, I would be afraid that he would become an alcoholic.

How can such a turnaround in attitude occur in a matter of months? Obviously, there is the fact that the interview was with an external observer who was also a foreigner. But more likely is the fact that in only a few years the perception of moving to the cities has evolved, or at least it has had to be accepted as a reality of the new lifestyle of the village and each peasant household. The evolution at the moment corresponds to a phase in which the status given to migration is changing. To use the words of anthropologist M. A. Kalam with regard to rural-urban movement in India, which was at first seen as a deviation: "the action of an individual choosing to migrate when the majority remain in the village or are against this idea," gradually progressed to "a common practice, socially established, [for] to migrate is no longer a way of reacting but a mere variation on staying put" (Kalam 1994, 65).

The progressive acceptance of migration, which for some villagers is more under duress than assimilated, seems inevitable given the growing number of departures. The villagers, especially the older ones, are now resigned to this fact, as is illustrated by this interview with Mr. Gam[14] (seventy-two years old).

> Many of the villagers leave to work in Hanoi. Everything has changed. Before, the peasants earned a better living than the factory workers and the well read, but now it's the opposite. That's why the peasants must leave to work elsewhere.

However, this evolution does not mean that everyone is ready to leave or be left. For those villagers who remain hostile to the idea of migration, or who hesitate to take the first step, the suspicions that were held before, regarding the nature of the jobs taken by the first migrants, have gradually given way to an argumentation of which the point is no longer the doubtful integrity of the individual who migrates but the harshness of living conditions, safety problems in urban areas, and the small chance of success. The village group,[15] as a group in which everyone knows each other, has influenced and continues to influence the development of migratory practices. At first playing an inhibiting role, letting mystery and doubts hang over the supposed nature of the migrations and also tainting the reputations of the families involved, the village environment has progressively evolved toward a permissive attitude in which, if migrations are not favored, at least they are no longer hindered or denounced. In this sense, the migratory flux is no longer fed by marginalized individuals but is becoming a practice that embraces the whole group.

This evolution of mentalities is all the more rapid and generalized because average and long-lasting migrations have quickly been incorporated into the logic of diversification of activities and/or the reduction of the number of people depending exclusively on family agricultural production. But if these movements are principally reasoned and decided on a household scale, the individual reasons are not necessarily or uniquely economic. In other words, if the economic factor is determinant in the logic of movements, it is not always enough to bring about the decision to migrate. As J. L. Racine notes in relation to migration in India, "the legitimate lure of money (this formula is too strong in many cases where only survival strategies are concerned) is certainly an essential factor in mobility, but besides the fact it does not necessarily imply movement to the towns, it is no more a sufficient condition of mobility" (1994, 314). In the case of the village studied, what are the other possible reasons that could have led some of the villagers to take the first step or more or less could have influenced their decision?

The existence of a logic that is not exclusively economic seems to be a particularly pregnant reality for the population of young, single people who make up the majority of temporary migrants. In order to support this, we will give two examples. Mr. Phuong,[16] the father of a young, single girl who left a few months earlier to work in the capital, explains the departure of his daughter, Miss Hoa (twenty-four years old).

> She met Mrs. Hop one evening, and the next day she left without declaring anything to the commune authorities. It's what she decided. It is not because our family is poor and we pushed her to leave. No . . . it was she who wanted to go and work in Hanoi because a lot of people her age had already gone and she wanted to do the same. Here if she wants to buy clothes or anything else she has to wait for the rice or manioc harvest. Young people do not like to wait. . . . That's the reason she left. At first, of course, we were worried, but as there are other people from the village working with her in the restaurant we are reassured. Also, young Toàn returned yesterday [from Hanoi], and he had a letter from her. . . . I would have preferred her to work in a factory as an official worker.

The second example is that of Miss Huong (twenty years old), who left for the capital in August 1997 with another girl from the village to work in a restaurant, as she says, in order to "buy clothes and have a little bit of money for my wedding." A fortnight later the two of them returned to the village, and Miss Huong told her mother she "would prefer to eat manioc than to leave again."

These two cases are interesting in that the parents affirm that they did not want their children to leave and tried to dissuade them from doing so. It is true that it is possible to analyze the taking of this stance as a defensive attitude aimed at hiding from others (relatives, neighbors) the economic interest that they have in the departure of their children, by adopting a respectable position that does not support migratory practice that will be condemned. These two families are, however, among the most affluent in the village, and temporary migrations no longer have the doubtful connotations that they had a few years before. On the other hand, a categorical refusal on their part would, without doubt, have put a stop to the vague desire of the young girls to leave.

Also, we can propose diverse interpretations of the reasons, combined with the economic factor, that led them to leave the village and profit from their parents' conciliatory attitude. More than necessary and specific conditions, these reasons seem to us to correspond to the general aspirations that we can consider as being shared by the whole of the population of young, single people on the move.

The first is the attraction, or more or less undeniable curiosity, that is aroused by "elsewhere," more particularly towns, including Hanoi, in comparison with a village that the young people often describe as poor, sad, and without leisure activities: the desire to travel, to see something else. This attraction, although it can be considered a condition for departure, is exacerbated by two other motivating factors, which are intrinsically linked. On the one hand, for many migrants leaving the village is a good experience, a source of prestige among their peers; the effect of training is important and cumulative, "because lots of people her age had already left and she wanted to do the same," as Mr. Phuong said about his daughter. On the other hand, departure is a way of escaping, for a while, the family environment, the shackles of social and behavioral constraints that structure and organize home and village life. Temporary migration is seen as a way of satisfying individual aspirations, the thirst for liberty and independence, that village life refuses to recognize or has a tendency to constrain. These motivations attributed to young, single, temporary migrants are not, however, exclusive to them. For example, there is the case of the two villagers, aged thirty-three and thirty-nine years old, one an unmarried mother, the other abandoned by her husband, whom she has not heard from for over ten years. For them, working in the capital represents not only a source of income that allows them to bring up their children, who are still in the village, but also an escape from family pressures and all their other obligations.

As for these unspoken and shameful aspirations, those surrounding the migrants, notably the parents of the youngest among them, are surprisingly conciliatory without being duped. This permissive and often ambiguous attitude held by many of them toward migration is explained by the fact that they see this period, at best, as being economically interesting, and at worst as being a necessary evil that will end with marriage and installation in the village. As for his son, who has worked in Hanoi for two years, Mr. Chiêm[17] explains.

> He should be married next year, for we have just organized the engagement ceremony (*an hoi*). . . . He is going to come

back here because he is the youngest child. He will no longer work in Hanoi.

Here we can see the essential factor that makes the departures acceptable and has allowed migrations of medium and long duration to soar: the movements are in no way perceived as irreversible by those remaining in the village. The whole of the system is based on the willingness of migrants to reintegrate after a relatively long period of time. The abandonment of jobs cannot be seen as failure because it makes other departures possible. The periodic return of migrants for special occasions (Têt, worship, weddings, funerals, and so on) and sometimes, for certain migrants, at key points in the agricultural calendar, reminds us of and reinforces the temporary aspect of the absence. The decision to migrate is therefore all the more easy to take because it is not definitive and only concerns the person leaving, without putting in question the maintenance of the household in the village and the legitimacy of the migrant's roots. It is this that shows the increased number of people who abandon migration (nearly one hundred cases in five years for one village) followed in 30 percent of cases by a new departure after at least a year to be a current practice of young, single people aged nineteen to twenty-nine, which multiplies comings and goings. Their married elders usually limit themselves to one trip.

4. The Migrant: Identity and Representations

From the description presented so far, we can see that the mobility of the villager is based on complementary activities and is driven by economic and social considerations: to preserve the domestic unit of the village and assure its reproduction. This proposition is in line with the conclusions of a number of recent studies on migratory practices, which are based on the articulation of two concepts *living space/invested space* (Rosental 1990, 1408), *place of resource/invested space* (Racine 1994, 356), or even *living space/identity space* (Cadène 1993, 460–61). Our aim here is not to offer an epistemological analysis of the subject but simply to note that all these conceptual approaches place the emphasis on the primordial importance of the links uniting the migrant to his or her place of origin and the preservation of the links, or, as the case may be, the weakening and eventual rupture of them. Taking into account the nature and density of these links allows us to draw up an unlimited plan of analysis on two axes: "preservation migration" (wherein close links are maintained with the village) and "rupture migration" (wherein links between the migrant and his or her village are broken) in which the intensity and nature of the relationships of origin are conditioned by the evolution of the migrants' projects, given their destinations and objectives.

The notion of preservation migration is particularly apt for movements in which the aim is to satisfy concrete needs that were clearly set out at his or her place of origin. This sort of movement can be called "targeted migration" (Landy 1994, 119), where the acquisition of the means with which to satisfy the needs of the village is the aim, often for a village project: the construction of a house, repaying debt, preparation for a special occasion such as a marriage, and so on. The path of Mrs. Huyen[18] is a good example of this strategy of emigration centered on the village, where the only reason for the move to the capital was to earn the necessary money with which to fund the buying of a wooden house (total cost: 3.7 million dong).

> I worked at an elderly couple's house for 150,000 dong per month plus 30,000 dong for food. I was treated well, but I suffered from being away from my husband and children [aged nine and eleven]. I couldn't sleep, and I worked all day. . . . I never went out in all the time I was in Hanoi, and I met no one from the village. . . . I could have stayed on in Hanoi, but as soon as I had enough money I came home and the house owner gave me a 200,000 dong present. At first, I thought about staying for a year, but eight months was enough. When I got back to the village, I slept for four days and four nights without even eating. I couldn't cope with Hanoi because I was not free.

It is highly probable that if Mrs. Huyen's move to Hanoi had not been for a specific and attainable objective, which gave her stay a real sense of meaning, she would not have stayed there for eight months. If, in the same way as this migrant, those villagers who have already established a household in the village migrate above all to improve their families' living conditions, such an affirmation cannot generalize about all of those people wanting to leave. The analysis of the dynamics of these movements has shown that the increase in temporary migration principally affects the young, single population, migrations that are by their very nature the most likely to cause an evolution in the aspirations of migrants and migratory behavior.

The majority of young, single migrants that we met, who tend to have a critical and disenchanted view of their place of origin, do not envisage starting a family and staying for any length of time anywhere other than in Hay or its surrounding areas. This display of willingness coincides with the stability of the marriage area, which has evolved little since the start of the 1990s and remains essentially limited to an area composed of the Ninh Bân Commune and surrounding communes. This localization is reinforced by the weak attraction of nearby medium-sized towns. The second revealing element is the importance of money transfers to the village. Interviewed at her place of work, Mrs. Kim,[19] one of the villagers employed in a restaurant in the capital, explains this.

> I hardly spend anything, and sometimes I don't ask for my monthly salary. I earn 300,000 to 400,000 dong per month, and I send everything to my parents. I don't keep anything here. . . . For Loan and Hang [two girls from the village working in the same restaurant], it's the same. For all the other villagers working here, it's the same; we send our money back to the village. . . . I don't think I'll stay here for good, but while the restaurant needs me I'll stay. . . . In the village, there is work, but we don't earn any money. Here we have no days off, but we are paid.

As for the products of migration thus transferred, if they allow for the acquisition of luxury products (TVs, radios), the purchase of a buffalo or piglets, or the construction of a solid home, they remain a privileged investment, a symbol of putting down roots. The increased number of new constructions of this type over the last five years is undeniably linked to the development of migration. Thus, for example, the savings accumulated by Mr. To after three years in the capital have allowed him to afford a brick house. Miss Hoa provided the money necessary for the construction of a kitchen and stable at the family home. This priority given to prestige spending, which has no direct influence on productivity, aims to maintain or reinforce status in the village and can change the social and economic hierarchy that was imposed during collectivization.

Until now, the upkeep of the village and economic mobility have been on two sides of an apparently insoluble equation, which the villagers seem to have reconciled with success. The plans and motivations of the majority of migrants are inspired by a strategy based on domestic units in the village environment: the village of Hay remains for them the principal place for social and economic investment. On the other hand, the "living areas," the various destinations of emigration, have above all an economic dimension and function: they are "areas of resources" where the potential benefits are only rarely exploited by migrants (education, health, and so on).

Based on similar facts in India, a certain number of authors have analyzed migratory practice as paradoxically being relevant to a process of putting down roots, "leaving in order to stay," in some ways (Kalam 1994, 319). The comparison with India is all the more interesting because in the absence of administrative hindrances or political restrictions permanent migrations and the abandonment of the village only represent a minor phenomenon. It is reasonable to think in the context of North Vietnam, where the available work force for each peasant household is often overabundant, that the noncompetitive combination of temporary migrations and agricultural activity reveals a logic of putting down roots.

The principal problem posed by such an interpretation is the absence of historical depth to the phenomenon. If the migratory practices that we have described have existed for several decades, it would be possible to conclude, without too much doubt, that they stigmatize a strong tendency toward putting down roots. But that is not the case: spontaneous migrations of average and long duration have developed over the last five years. Also it is necessary to place two limits or reservations on a supposedly global and pertinent interpretation in the long term.

The first limit is linked to the apparition of migratory behavior where the place of emigration is not, or is no longer, uniquely seen as a place of resources but also as a place where one hopes to establish oneself in the long term. The maintaining of a strong and predominant link between the migrant and the village must not overshadow one of the inherent consequences of the logic of the movement: the inevitable influence of the place of emigration and migratory practice on the migrants. In fact, if the reality of migrating is often a source of disillusionment, the young migrant, although conscious of his or her belonging to the village unit, also becomes conscious of his or her individual identity (Chaussin 1978, 91). The risks are those of emancipation from a fixed framework for the preservation and reproduction of the domestic unity of the village. Mr. San's story is a good example. When we met him in September 1997, he had decided a few days earlier to settle down definitively in the village after having spent five years in Hanoi, where he had various jobs: cushion maker, looking after motorbikes, waiter in a restaurant. Married for two years and the father of a young son, he had moved in with his parents. He explained the reasons that led him to make this decision.[20]

> I'd had enough of working in Hanoi. I was earning 300,000 dong per month and could not afford to save. Leaving my wife and son in the village was hard. If I work outside the village, I can earn some money but I leave my land fallow.... I am nostalgic about Hanoi, the money and my friends, but I must return to the village.

In November of the same year, Mr. San left once more to work in the capital. He is one of the thirty or so villagers who, after having decided to return to the village definitively, have taken up regular movement. Some of these have again abandoned the idea.

The versatile dimension of the movements, the successive abandonment and rejoining of migration, while revealing a process of putting down roots in the village, also underlines the contradictory character of migration, the opposition between attraction and repulsion, as much from the point of view of their place of departure as from that of the destination (Morice 1993, 367). Are the inevitable changes that imprint migration on the lifestyle of the migrant and the impression he or she has, on returning, of his or her place of origin, susceptible to bringing about change in initial plans from the point of view of compromising reinsertion into the village? To this fundamental question, we will be tempted to respond in the negative, because out of the five cases of temporary migration that evolved into long-term migration, associated with a change of residence, four are the result of a wedding of a young village man to someone from the place of emigration (one in Ho Chi Minh City, two in Hanoi, one in Viet

Tri). Only one person has made the step, an insignificant marginal case, but the migratory logic of it and the strategy adopted at the point of arrival merit a mention. Mrs. Hop,[21] accompanied by her son, was the first villager to migrate spontaneously to the capital in 1991. She is now in the process of buying a small house (eight square meters) in Hanoi, where she has obtained authorization for temporary residence (*dang ky tam tru*) while at the same time keeping her registration (*ho khau*) in the Ninh Dân Commune.

> I want to settle in Hanoi. For me, it is possible because my daughter is married and I am here with my son, who also works: between us we earn a good living. For the others in the village, it is necessary to bring the whole family and buy a house. Of course, I would prefer to be in the village because of my sentimental attachment to it, but it really is very poor and life there is hard. . . . I sold my house, garden (three *sao* and ten *thuoc*), my land on the hill (three *sao*), and my paddy fields (four *sao*) to my brother Thich for 6 million dong. It is a transfer and not an official sale, so I remain officially registered in the commune [Ninh Dân]. If I want to return to live there, it will be easier. . . . I would like my son to marry here [Hanoi] and for him to settle here because life is easier. Otherwise, I will go back, but not to the village, to Dong Xa (a nearby village) near the road so I can do business. In any case, at the end of my life I will return to the village.

Mrs. Hop sums up in a few phrases the complexity and contradictory aspects that some migratory practices can take on: a double strategy concerned at the same time with Hanoi and the place of departure. If her projects come about, she will detach herself from the village but without breaking the connection with it, so putting down residential roots is substituted for putting down psycho-cultural roots, according to the expression of Dupont and Lelièvre (1993, 481). Her logic, which she presents as being exclusively economic, must, however, incorporate other factors: being divorced, her life in the village could only be harder, and this situation without a doubt must have influenced her decision to move to the capital, even if it does not prevent her from hoping to return to the village to live out her days.

Between "resource" and "investment" places, there is a whole range of possible intermediary situations wherein the distance from the place of origin is not inevitably synonymous with rupture, the village taking on little by little the appearance of the mythical *quê huong*, "country of birth," that is so vivid in the imagination of *kinh,* whether they be urban or rural. But what also sheds light on Mrs. Hop's situation are the practical constraints met by villagers at the place of emigration, constraints that represent the second limit to their insertion into the urban zone.

This second limit can come in the form of a question: does not the opposition between "preservation" and "rupture" migration lead to an overestimation of the capacity of peasant households to reason and master their movements, minimizing at the same time the role of control and regulation played by the state and/or the town in the migratory flux? In other words, is the interpretation of putting down roots not erroneous, even fallacious, simply because the majority of migrants do not have any other choice but to return to the village?

This is an essential question because, despite the relaxation of political restrictions on population movements,[22] it is currently legally prohibited to live in a place without being officially registered there. Definitive migration associated with family regrouping and the transfer of residence can therefore only come about in a framework fixed by the state, which tries to limit as much as possible the installation of rural migrants in urban areas. The reality is different: 1993 figures indicate that in the whole country 930,000 people were living in a place different from where they were officially registered, 350,000 of them in Ho Chi Minh City and 140,000 in Hanoi (Li Tana 1996, 9). The author specifies, however, that the figures were probably an underestimation.

Also, if the system of residential registration "probably continues to play a filtering role" (Henaff 1998, 8), it does not constitute an insurmountable barrier to definitive migration. According to an inquiry carried out in 1997 in Hanoi, only 17 percent of migrants interviewed were officially registered, 83 percent of them not having declared permanent residence in the capital (Trinh Khac Tham et al. 1998, 130); and the same authors specify that "any intervention by the authorities to encourage or block migration will be ineffective because migrants are capable of making their own decisions and counting on these links [their networks]" (132). The case of Mrs. Hop is a good illustration.

But two other, much more effective barriers oppose the insertion of people from rural areas into urban areas. The first is of a financial nature. For a migrant earning 300,000 to 500,000 dong per month, whose job is not guaranteed by a work contract or any firm agreement, a lasting establishment in the urban zone, along with family regroupment, seems impossible, notably in view of the impressive disparity between salary and the cost of accommodations that Henaff analyzes as being a factor that explains low geographic mobility (1999, 10). This principal charge, accumulated through daily spending on the family, discourages most migrants who have a vague idea of long-term change, as Mr. Thanh,[23] father of two (three and seven years), explained on his return to the village for a few days.

> Life in the village and at home is sad. I prefer Hanoi; it's more fun, and there are more people and distractions. At night I go watch videos. . . . I would like to live here with my family, but I could never afford it. [In front of his wife, who has just entered the room in which we are interviewing] But it would not be easy, and then again we are used to living here.

Also some of the young single migrants regard marrying a resident of the city as the only way of guaranteeing a long and stable emigration. This method, however, appears to them to be unrealistic and is illustrated by the comments of Miss Hang[24] (nineteen years old), who was asked if she would marry in Hanoi: "No, the city's the city, and the countryside's the countryside; it's very different. Even in my dreams I dare not think of marrying a man from Hanoi. But I would like to."

Going beyond the financial aspect, Miss Hang revealed a second barrier to long-term migration to urban areas: the discrimination suffered by villagers, the suspicious and wary attitude of the urban society toward the migrants. Urban society in general (public authorities, administrators, the police, and so on) sees the migrants as an inexhaustible source of problems, as Li Tana illustrated in the study to which we frequently refer (see, in particular, the last chapter [1996, 59–66]). The image of the migrants conjured up is that they have a supposedly bad lifestyle (instability, homelessness), that they are the cause of problems such as theft, drugs, and prostitution, and that they are a drain on public services (education, transport, welfare).

The depreciation of migrants, which ranges from denouncing their incapacities or their unwillingness to work to pure ostracism, can be seen in this extract from an article in the *Courrier du Viêt Nam* (29 March 1998): "Quatro, these workers [the rural migrants] don't care about basic personal hygiene and are sometimes uncivilized. However, most of them respect each other and remain attached to their laborious nature and their peasant moral values." Other than the intolerable nature of the article ("peasant = dirty, uncivilized"), which leads us straight to the definition "wild," this short extract reflects one of the major contradictions of this discriminatory attitude. From a historical point of view, on the one hand, the cities of North Vietnam are products of the recent and increasing influx of people from agricultural villages.[25] There are few current city dwellers who can claim to have "urban" ancestors going back more than two or three generations. From a cultural perspective, the "moral values" of the peasants, which the governing powers, the press, and the scientific world never cease to reify, are considered by them to be the substream of Vietnamese culture and the foundation of a hard-fought-for national unity.

This social discrimination, which is maintained through words in the absence of distinctive ostentatious signs, is greatly resented by the migrants, often makes their stay in the city difficult, and increases their desire to return to the village. One young girl, Miss Hong (aged twenty-one), having returned to the village, assessed the discrimination in this succinct manner: "The people of Hanoi do not want us." In reaction to this discrimination, many migrants have a negative image of the capital: the majority of migrants we met said they did not like Hanoi.

Without contradicting the intrinsically rural causes of this sense of belonging to the village, this brief overview of the lack of resources and alienation that affect the migrants shows that if fidelity to the village is real it is in part imposed by the surrounding society, in particular the hostility of the urban environment.

Conclusion

It is necessary to remember that throughout this essay, since our research was in only one village, we did not want to generalize a phenomenon on a large scale, to be applied to all North Vietnamese villages. It was done to shed light on the migratory practices lived and viewed at the place of departure, in this case, Hay village.

Throughout the last ten years, 71 percent of the 149 households questioned had one or more of its members holding a nonagricultural job outside the village. The diversity and versatility of the movement, the variation in length and destination, as well as the complementary activity strategy that this implies, and from which putting down roots transpires, are just some of the elements that go to show that economic mobility (geographical and sectoral) is not synonymous with a rural exodus. In putting first the capacity for self-control and the margin of maneuver that the peasants have, however weak they may be, our aim has been to go beyond the mechanical analysis of the inescapable "rural exodus," a consequence of the generalization of the market economy, wherein the peasantry is reduced to a state of resigned passiveness.

However, one cannot get away from the fact that since 1993 temporary migration has represented 70 percent of movements and only one household in three has seen at least one of its members try their luck in the capital. The dynamics of the movements clearly indicate that this predominance has been established and reinforced over the last three years, to the detriment of migrations to nearby places—the volume of which is not extensible and even tends to decrease each year.

The general tendency is then toward preservation movements and migrations, but it is difficult to evaluate the stability of their basis and durability. The increase in average and long-duration migrations, and in a more general way the recent nature of the phenomenon, are sources of uncertainty as to the undeniable nature of putting down roots in the village. Does this exclusively reveal a peasant logic in which migration is conceived as an element of a global strategy of diversification of activities? Or must we envisage strong constraints (material constraints but also the marked hostility of the urban environment toward them) that oppose the lasting installation of migrants in the city as causes that explain this putting down of roots? In other words, must we interpret the current practice, which places the village at the center of migratory behavior, in terms of peasant self-control, reasoned strategy, or the rejection of the urban environment—acceptance by default? This is an essential question in North Vietnam, where more than 80 percent of the population is agricultural. The balance is fragile: the redistribution of land in 1993 allowed peasant families to ensure their own subsistence and leaves the authorities little room for maneuver to succeed in keeping future candidates for installation in the village. Also, at the risk of being construed as too Malthusian, it seems to us that from preservation to rupture there is in the current context only one step, which can easily be overcome.

NOTES

Institute de Recherche sur le Sud-Est Asiatique (IRSEA), Aix-en-Provence; and l'École Française d'Extrême-Orient (EFEO), Hanoi. I would like to thank Robert Carradice for translating this essay.

1. Hay village is one of the four villages of the Ninh Dân Commune.

2. In northern Vietnam (Bac Ba), the surface area is measured in the following way: 1 *thuoc* = 23 m^2; 1 *sao* = 360 m^2 = 15 *thuoc*; and 1 *mau* = 3,600 m^2 = 10 *sao*.

3. "Residence is to be understood as the place where the individual is used to living. . . . This definition must be clear so that we are able to attribute each individual to one place of residence only" (Courgeau 1998, 11).

4. Interview 28/06/1997.

5. Interview 11/08/1995.

6. In 1995, the rate of exchange was around 11,000 dong to U.S.$1. Today it is more than 14,000 dong to U.S.$1.

7. Interview 07/01/1996.

8. Interview 14/12/1995.

9. For more information on this subject, see Oliver Tessier, "Aide et entraide dans un village du nord Viêt Nam: Modalités pratique et motivation." In *Aseanie* 4 (December 1999): 125–59.

10. Interview 28/11/1996.

11. Interview 19/03/1997.

12. Interview 13/06/1995.

13. Interview 06/02/1996.

14. Interview 01/12/1997.

15. "In antithesis with the group dispersed in the urban agglomeration, the village group can also be said to be dispersing (with careful reference to the physics-chemistry notion of the relation between two liquids, one of which in a dispersing phase contains particles of the other, the dispersed phase)" (Maget 1995, 379).

16. Interview 19/07/1997.

17. Interview 25/01/1997.

18. Interview 02/12/1997.

19. Interview 23/02/1998.

20. Interview 30/10/1997.
21. Interview 26/02/1998.
22. Resolution 4 of the Council of Ministers, July 1988 (Li Tana 1996, 4).
23. Interview 09/08/1997.
24. Interview 26/02/1998.
25. For Hanoi, see Papin 1997.

REFERENCES

Bardem, I. 1993. "L'émancipation des jeunes: Un facteur négligé des migrations interafricaines." In *Mobilités spatiales et urbanisation Asie, Afrique, Amérique*. Paris: CSH ORSTOM, vol. 29, no. 2–3: 375–93.

Cadène, P. 1993. "Réseaux économiques et territoire de l'identité: Migration de travail et migration de mariage des membres d'une communauté marchande dans un petite ville de L'Inde." In *Cahier des Sciences Humaines* 29, no. 2–3: 443–63.

Chaussin, E. 1978. "Aspects de la migration des Saora de l'Orissa en Assam." In *Les migrations dans l'Asie du Sud*, Paris, Gabalda, L'Ethnographie, no. 2: 73–92.

Courgeau, D. 1988. *Methodes de mesure de la mobilité spatiale: Migrations internes, mobilité temporaire, navette*. Paris: Institut National d'Etudes Démographiques.

Dang Nguyên Anh. 1998. "The Role of Social Networks in the Process of Migration." In *International Seminar on Internal Migration: Implications for Migration Policy in Vietnam (May 6, 7, 8)*. Hanoi: UNDP Population Council and MARD. Pp. 182–91.

Dao The Tuan. 1997. "Les transformations rurales récentes au Viêt-nam." (Recent rural transformations in Vietnam). Numéro commun Cahier Agriculture, no. 6, Agriculture et développement, pp. 13–18.

Doan Mâu Diep and Trinh Khac Thâm. 1998. "Characteristics of Rural-Urban Migration in Vietnam and Policies to Control It." In *International Seminar on Internal Migration: Implications for Migration Policy in Vietnam (May 6, 7, 8)*. Hanoi: UNDP Population Council and MARD. Pp. 182–91.

Doan Mâu Diep, Trinh Khac Thâm, and N. Henaff. 1997. *Report on the Spontaneous Migration Survey in Hanoi*. Hanoi: Centre for Population and Human Resources Studies.

Du Peng. 1998. "Floating Population in Large Cities: Problems and Countermeasures." In *International Seminar on Internal Migration: Implications for Migration Policy in Vietnam (May 6, 7, 8)*. Hanoi: UNDP Population Council and MARD. Pp. 67–72.

Dupont, V., and C. Z. Guilmoto. 1993. "Mobilité spatiales et urbanisation: Théories, pratiques, et représentations." In *Mobilités spatiales et urbanisation Asie, Afrique, Amérique*, Paris, CSH ORSTOM, vol. 29 no. 2–3, pp. 279–94.

Dupont, V., and E. Lelièvre. 1993. "De la navette à la migration en ville, stratégie et mobilité dans l'ouest de l'Inde." In *Cahier des Sciences Humaines.* Paris: 29, no. 2–3: 465–83.

Fontaine, L. 1990. "Solidarités familiales et logiques migratoire en pays de montagne à l'époque moderne." In *Annales Economie, Societes et Civilisation* (ESC) 6: 1433–50.

Henaff, N. 1998. "Mobilité de la main-d'oeuvre, transition et développement" (International Conference on Vietnamese Studies) Colloque internationale "Etudes Vietnamiennes," juillet 1998, Hanoi, 9 p.

———. 1999. "Rénovation et mobilité de la main-d'oeuvre." In *Population et développement.* 14 p.

Kalam, M. A. 1994. "Ancrage et mobilité dans un contexte Indien: Une perspective anthropologique." In *Les attaches de l'homme: Enracinement paysan et logiques migratoires en Inde du Sud.* Paris: Maison des Sciences de L'Homme. Pp. 61–76.

Landy, F. 1994. "Migration et enracinement dans la Maidan." In *Les attaches de l'homme: Enracinement paysan et logiques migratoires en Inde du Sud.* Paris: Maison des Sciences de L'Homme. Pp. 79–141.

Li Tana. 1996. *Peasants on the Move: Rural-Urban Migration in the Hanoi Region.* Occasional papers, no. 91. Singapore: Institute of Southeast Asia Studies.

Maget, M. 1955. "Remarques sur le village comme cadre de recherches ethnologiques." In *Bulletin de Psychologie* VIII, no. 78: 375–82.

Mahadev, P. D., and J. L. Racine, eds. 1994. "Migrer ou pas?" In *Les attaches de l'homme: Enracinement paysan et logiques migratoire en Inde du Sud,* Jean-Luc Racine, ed. Paris: Maison des Sciences de L'Homme. Pp. 3–29.

Morice, A. 1993. "Un légende à revoir: L'ouvrier du bâtiment brésilien sans feu ni lieu." In *Mobilités spatiales et urbanisation Asie, Afrique, Amérique,* Paris, CSH ORSTOM, vol. 29 no. 2–3, pp. 349–71.

Nguyên Van Dang. 1998. "Allocution du vice-ministre du MARD." In *International Seminar on Internal Migration: Implications for Migration Policy in Vietnam (May 6, 7, 8).* Hanoi: UNDP Population Council and MARD. Pp. 2–4.

Papin, P. 1997. "Des 'villages dans la ville' aux 'villages urbains': L'espace et les formes de pouvoir à Hanoi de 1805 à 1940." Ph.D. Thesis, Université de Paris VII. 2 vols.

Racine, J. L. 1994. "Les attaches de l'homme." In *Les attaches de l'homme: Enracinement paysan et logiques migratoires en Inde du Sud.* Paris: Maison des Sciences de L'Homme. Pp. 313–73.

Rosental, P. A. 1990. "Maintient/rupture: Un nouveau couple pour l'analyse des migrations." Paris: Annales ESC, no. 6, pp. 1403–31.

Sagant, P. 1978. "Du village vers la ville et la plantation." In *Les migrations dans l'Asie du Sud.* Paris, Gabalda, L'Ethnographie, no. 2, pp. 12–33.

Trân Anh Tuan. 1998. "Spontaneous Migration and Resettlement in Ho Chi Minh City: Problems and Solutions." In *International Seminar on Internal Migration: Implications for Migration Policy in Vietnam (May 6, 7, 8).* Hanoi: UNDP Population Council and MARD. Pp. 182–91.

15   Gisele Bousquet

Facing Globalization: Vietnam and the Francophone Community

Vietnam hosted the Seventh Francophone Summit in November 1997. This two-day international conference included forty-nine chiefs of state from countries that, as the constitution of the organization stated, have "French in common." The goal of the conference was to advance economic and cultural ties among members of the Francophone Community, in particular between industrial and developing countries.

The summit was significant for both Vietnam and France. France is currently Vietnam's most competitive European economic partner. Despite an American economic embargo, which prohibited the free flow of capital between Vietnam and American allies and lasted until 1995, Vietnam officially joined the Francophone Community in 1986 in Paris. In that year, the Vietnamese government implemented Doi Moi, the new guidelines for economic reforms, in order to revitalize its economy by encouraging the development of local and foreign investments and international trading partnerships.[1] The Francophone Community was Vietnam's first membership in a nonsocialist international organization. Since then, Vietnam has established ties with many countries and joined other international communities—notably, the Association of Southeast Asian Nations (ASEAN) in 1995, but the Francophone Community remains Vietnam's most important link to the West.

For its part, France views Vietnam as an anchor of French economic expansion in Asia. In a recent political statement, the French president, Mr. Jacques Chirac, stressed Vietnam's importance to

French political and economic interests: "It is through Vietnam that France has the stronger position in Asia."[2]

In the official language of the summit, the francophone conference was held to promote linguistic and cultural continuity among member nations. Building on the history of cultural and educational associations established in the 1960s in postcolonial French countries, the summit planners sought to use linguistic commonality to invigorate political allegiances within the Francophone Community and foster allegiance to France. Indeed, French leaders wished to use the conference to reclaim France's importance to its former colonies and to affirm French centrality in the Francophone Community. As I demonstrate in this chapter, this was not a matter of colonial nostalgia on the part of France. Rather the French sought to use historical, linguistic, and cultural ties as a way to challenge the expansion of anglophone global culture, which France sees as a threat to its own international power and influence.

Thus, in this post–cold war era, Vietnam is negotiating its affiliations with international organizations on the basis of reciprocal economic interests, while France is attempting to use language and culture to improve its standing in the new world order. Using the literature and interviews conducted in Hanoi in the spring and summer of 1997, I will show how the Francophone Summit was a political forum used by both parties in these struggles for global economic and political status.

1. The Francophone Summit

The Seventh Summit and the Franco-Vietnamese Relationship

Decades after the French defeat at Dien Bien Phu, the legacy of French colonialism is still visible in the cosmopolitan city of Hanoi, where the 1997 Francophone Summit was planned and orchestrated. In the contemporary tourist industry, Hanoi has been represented as a "pristine" colonial city. In travel agencies in Paris, the city and its historical sites are often used as the icon of an "imaginary Indochina." Indeed, between 1954 and the late 1980s, Hanoi experienced little urban development, and in the early 1990s, the city seemed little changed since colonial days. Even during the recent growth in urbanization, the city extended its boundaries without destroying either the French quarters, where imposing colonial buildings still stand,[3] or the old houses of the ancient city quarter of Lake Hoan Kiem.

This juxtaposition of colonial relics and Vietnamese historical landmarks symbolizes the complexity of the Franco-Vietnamese relationship. After the end of French colonial rule in 1954, and despite the division of Vietnam and the escalation of the American war, France established a new set of relationships with Vietnam based on mutual economic and political interests. The most important and lasting of these was between the French and the Vietnamese communist parties. The alliance actually began during the French anticolonial war, when the French Communist Party gave political support and guidance to Ho Chi Minh's Indochinese Communist Party.[4] During the American war, the French Communist Party maintained its political commitment to the Democratic Republic of Vietnam, and after 1975, during the postwar reconstruction, the French Communist Party established economic cooperation with Vietnam while the country was still under the American economic embargo.

Although some French tourists go to Vietnam on a nostalgic quest for a French colonial past, the contemporary French expatriate community bears no similarity to the former French colonial society. In 1940, there were about 34,000 French citizens living in Vietnam.[5] In 1997, there were only approximately 2,000 French expatriates, most of them living in Hanoi and Ho Chi Minh City.[6] These expatriates are members of the foreign community working in Vietnam for international businesses and nongovernmental organizations. Like expatriates from elsewhere, they are not putting down roots in Vietnam. Many of them leave after finishing a two- or three-year contract. The few who have married Vietnamese also tend to leave after six to ten years.

In postcolonial Vietnam, the French expatriates are no longer Fanon's Machiavellian "settlers"[7] or Memmi's rude colonialists disfigured by colonization.[8] Few of the French working in Vietnam today ever experienced life under colonial rule in "l'Indochine francaise." In fact, the members of the younger French generation want to disengage themselves from that colonial past, in which they argue they played no role. It is only members of the older generation, former French expatriates, who return to Vietnam as nostalgic tourists.[9]

Membership in the Francophone Community

The members of the Francophone Community are supposed to be countries who "partage le Français en commun," have French in common. Although a shared language, French, is the official criterion, the increasing number of non-French-speaking countries joining the community suggests a different agenda. In fact, few of the member countries have French as their official language. The latter include France, Canada, Belgium, Switzerland, Haiti, the Congo Democratic Republic, Senegal, and Congo. Others list French as their most frequently spoken second language. This is the case for Morocco, Egypt, Madagascar, Romania, Mauritius, and Luxembourg. Many francophone countries were former French colonies or protectorates, such as Senegal, the Ivory Coast, Djibouti, Central Africa, Vietnam, and Cambodia. Algeria, a former French colony and the one with the highest French-speaking population after France, refuses to join the Francophone Community. By contrast, some Eastern European countries, including Bulgaria, Albania, Poland, and Moldavia, have joined the community, although French is not even a second language within their borders.[10]

The Building of the Francophone Community

In order to understand the prevailing debates at the 1997 Hanoi Summit and France's domination in the association, it is necessary to examine the history of the Francophone Community. The community was not a French initiative. Leaders of some newly independent African countries just after decolonization in the 1960s wanted to create a number of cultural and educational associations as supportive networks among themselves.[11] They broached the idea of an international community based on the French language to other African chiefs of state in 1968 at the annual meeting of L'Organisation Commune Africaine et Malgache (OCAM). There the francophone chiefs of state decided to meet once a year to discuss cultural and technical exchanges among their countries. In 1970, twenty-one countries participated in the First Francophone Conference in Niamey, Niger, at which they created the "Agence de Cooperation Culturelle et Technique," or ACCT. Leopold-Sedar Senghor, president of Senegal, who with Habib Bourguiba of Tunisia and Hamani Diori of Niger initiated the concept of a francophone community, best illustrated the spirit of this First Francophone Conference in his speech.

> We want to create everywhere a francophone community that is specifically and broadly a cultural community whose goal is to educate and communicate. . . . This building of a French-speaking community is the first [attempt] of its kind in modern history. It represents the need of our time, [a time] when man, threatened by his own scientific discoveries and progress, wants to build a new humanism that will simultaneously be a measure of man and the cosmos.[12]

But it was not until 1986 that the first official francophone summit was held in Paris.[13] The summit, held every two years, had as its theme bilateral education and economic aid and represented a gathering of all the chiefs of state of the Francophone Community. At the Chaillot summit in 1991, two additional political institutions were established: La Conference Ministerielle de la Francophonie (CMF), a yearly gathering of ministers of foreign affairs, which provided continuity between summits; and Le Conseil Permanent de la Francophonie (CPF), which became the political institution of the community. The CPF is composed of eighteen chiefs of state chosen from among the forty-nine countries in the community.

One of the most enduring organizations established under the auspices of the newly formed Francophone Community was the Agence de Cooperation Culturelle et Technique, or ACCT. This agency provided cultural and technical aid to member countries, particularly developing countries. ACCT's programs included alphabetization, training, assisting in the implementation of projects, and promoting human rights and democracy. Other projects have specifically fostered "francophone culture," that is, francophone arts and humanities and the teaching of the French language. But, as I will show, as the Francophone Community has taken a more visible role in international matters, these programs have generated heated political debates.

Besides its headquarters in Paris, ACCT also established three regional offices: in Lome, Togo, in 1983; Libreville, Gabon, in 1992; and an Asian office in Hanoi, Vietnam, in 1994. These peripheral offices were of strategic importance in the promotion of a global linguistic network and in the strengthening of allegiance to the

Francophone Community in developing countries. In Hanoi, for instance, the ACCT office provided French-speaking Vietnamese people with institutional and educational support in addition to promoting French cultural and educational activities. In the 1990s, in order to increase the community's political visibility, the ACCT created liaison offices in Geneva, Brussels, and New York to "observe" and consult with the United Nations, the International Monetary Fund, the World Bank, and the European Union. In 1996, the ACCT changed its name to reflect its claims to a linguistic alliance. It is now called the Agence de la Francophonie (AF).

Hanoi: A New Direction for the
Francophone Community

The seventh summit in Hanoi symbolized a critical shift in direction of the Francophone Community. While in the past the community had held little political interest for France, over the last several years France has aspired more openly to leadership of the organization by, among other things, pushing for the appointment of a new general secretary to head the Francophone Community. At the 1997 summit, the French president, Mr. Chirac, argued that a general secretary would give the Francophone Community "a face and a voice" (desormais, la francophonie aura une voix et un visage).[14] Chirac proposed the former UN general secretary, Mr. Boutros Boutros-Ghali.

France had in fact begun envisioning the Francophone Community as a way to gain credibility in the international political arena. The French support of the candidacy of Mr. Boutros Boutros-Ghali was a deliberate political maneuver. It clearly indicated that the French political agenda included using the Francophone Community to challenge the new world order led by the United States. France had supported the candidacy of Mr. Boutros Boutros-Ghali for his second mandate as the UN general secretary in 1996, while the United States strongly rejected him because of his open criticism of American foreign policies.[15]

Controversy over the General Secretary Selection

It was in Congo in 1996 that Mr. Chirac called for reorganizing the Francophone Community into a more political entity with a general secretary at its head.¹⁶ It was agreed that an election for the general secretary would be held in Hanoi the following year. But the French appointed the former UN general secretary Mr. Boutros Boutros-Ghali as the interim general secretary, provoking outrage among African leaders,¹⁷ who already disapproved of the new direction of the organization and contested the process by which Boutros Boutros-Ghali was nominated.¹⁸ In the meantime, the African committee had already selected its own candidate, Mr. Emile Zinsou, the former president of Benin. A few months before the summit, in a secret deal, Zinsou was forced by the French delegation to withdraw his candidacy.¹⁹ "L'affaire etait pourtant entendue, M. Zinsou ayant effectivement accepte de declarer forfait sous l'amicale pression de la France" (The deal was indeed done since Mr. Zinsou agreed to give up his candidacy under friendly French pressure).²⁰ The French planned to announce the nomination of Boutros Boutros-Ghali as a fait accompli during the summit. But the Vietnamese delegation disclosed the information to all members of the community upon their arrival in Hanoi. The French government blames the Vietnamese for the discontent: "The French delegation had to face many difficulties, and one of them was a sort of African revolt."²¹

To many African leaders, the lack of democratic process in this election explicitly uncovered a French domination of the Francophone Community reminiscent of former French colonial practice. In protest, the president of the Democratic Republic of Congo (formerly Zaire), Mr. Lauren Desire Kabila, withdrew his country from membership in the Francophone Community, claiming that "he did not want to participate in a neo-colonial organization."²²

The French selection of the new general secretary also provoked negative reactions from industrial francophone countries, including Canada and Belgium, which viewed the action as a threat to their own political influence in the organization. They requested that the general secretary's mandate be shortened to two instead of four years and challenged his role in the ACCT, one of the most powerful agencies in the organization and one in which both countries were influential. Mr. Rene Dehaybe of Belgium had succeeded the Québecois Mr. Jean-Louis Roy,²³ whom the French had accused of promoting his own domestic political career by using his position as ACCT head to promote Canadian trade in Africa.²⁴ Canada and Belgium strongly opposed the French proposal to rename l'Agence de Cooperation Culturelle et

Technique as l'Agence de la Francophonie and the placing of that agency under the authority of the new general secretary.²⁵

Political Divergence in the Francophone Community

Under the new guidelines proposed by Mr. Chirac, the Francophone Community's priority would be projects directly related to the promotion of "francophone culture" and French language. In the name of cultural diversity and linguistic pluralism, the Francophone Community, as redefined by the French, would challenge the expansion of an "Anglophone global culture." As Jean Baudrillard said: "The idea of a French exception, a French difference, is absurd, but a certain American triumphalism and our own relative decline has turned the idea into an obsession."²⁶ France's political rivalry with the United States has been particularly evident in the 1997 political incident regarding the $2 billion joint venture signed between the French oil company, Total, and Iran. The contract, which defies the American Iran-Libya Sanctions Act, was strongly supported by the French government. French prime minister Lionel Jospin argued that American laws apply in the United States and nowhere else and referred to American global domination as the "ultracapitalism."²⁷ The controversy over American commercial spying in Europe is another example of French distrust of American business practices in this new global economy. In fact, at the meeting of the European Parliament in Brussels in February 2000, Europeans brought allegations against the English-speaking countries, led by the United States and England, to use an old military cold war espionage system, called Echelon,²⁸ to eavesdrop on European businesses. Although the American government denies such practices, the French justice minister, Elisabeth Guigou, argues that "Today it appears that the network has been diverted to the purposes of economic espionage and for keeping a watch on competitors."²⁹

In a 1997 newspaper interview, Ms. Margie Sudre, state secretary of the French Ministry of Foreign Affairs and responsible for the organization of the Francophone Summit in Hanoi, argued:

> There is a linguistic competition between France and the United States. Why not understand that we want to maintain our linguistic presence in a world where more than 200 million people speak French? Should the world be controlled

only by the United States? Absolutely not. With other European and African nations, we refuse the cultural hegemony imposed by the English-speaking countries. We will fight to promote the teaching of the French language in order to preserve our cultural heritage.[30]

In another publication, an unsigned article published by Ecole Nationale de l'Administration-Mensuel,[31] the author appropriated a minority discourse by emphasizing the power relation between the francophone and anglophone countries,[32] suggesting that "the Francophone Community, which includes forty-nine very different and for the most part poor nations, is young, fragile, and endangered."[33] And then the author blamed the United States for trying to take over the world.[34]

The ongoing debate about linguistic and cultural claims conceals the real French agenda: the economic expansion and political influence of France in Asia. Although the French propose not to wish to reclaim their colonial role in the former "Union Indochinoise," they are nonetheless asserting a claim to political influence and economic power in both the region and the world as a challenge to the present global order. In her speech during an official visit to Hanoi in 1996, Ms. Sudre reaffirmed the French commercial and political agenda by suggesting that the summit would benefit French business enterprises and commercial ventures in Vietnam and would strengthen bilateral cooperation between the two countries.[35]

However, for other francophone partners, French language and cultural projects are of less concern than explicit issues of economics, international conflicts, and human rights. One function proposed for the new general secretary of the Francophone Community is that of representing the community internationally, but no consensus on his political mandate has been made.[36] The prime minister of Lebanon, Mr. Rafik Hariri, suggested using the Francophone Community "as a platform to promote democracy and encourage development" (L'ambition de faire de l'espace francophone un espace de democratie et de developement) and mediate in regional conflicts. Hariri proposed that the Francophone Community begin by negotiating with Israel to liberate South Lebanon from its occupation.[37] But, although the Cambodian delegation also privately consulted with Mr. Chirac regarding regional problems, no official statement was issued at the summit regarding the future role of the Francophone Community in international conflicts.

Most Canadian francophone projects sponsor aid and development programs in nonindustrialized countries such as Vietnam, and the Canadians also have a strong interest in human rights. The Canadian delegation at the Seventh Summit in Hanoi asked the Francophone Community to take a stand on democracy and act against countries that violate human rights. Mr. Jean Chretien, the prime minister of Canada, blamed the Francophone Community for not doing enough to promote democracy and protect life during such civil wars as the conflict in Rwanda.[38] In response, Mr. Chirac argued that "sanctions did not have a place in the traditions of the Francophone Community" (Les sanctions ne sont pas dans la tradition de l'espace francophone). Chirac's view was supported by Ms. Binh, the Vietnamese assistant minister of foreign affairs, who reminded the delegations that the written constitution of the community specifically states that no country should intervene in the internal political affairs of others.[39] At the press conferences held during the summit in Hanoi, Mr. Chirac avoided questions by foreign journalists, many of them French, on the issues of human rights in Vietnam. The French government, however, maintained that a list of forty Vietnamese political prisoners had been given to Mr. Nguyên Manh Cam, the Vietnamese minister of foreign affairs.[40] He argued that issues of human rights violations could not be resolved within the community but instead should be relegated to the UN. The silence of the Francophone Community over the genocide in Rwanda[41] and over human rights violations in Vietnam illustrates an egregious lack of commitment toward human rights, especially given the fact that these violations concern its own member states.

Moreover, French claims about building a global francophone community based on equality is contradicted by the recent politics of exclusion in France. Over the last few years, France has made it very difficult for people from developing countries to migrate there. Although France has not had an immigration policy since 1974, migration remains an important social and political issue. New repatriation laws and regulations concerning border and population control were recently implemented to stop the flow of illegal migration, in particular people coming from francophone North African and African countries. Recently, many francophone students have been refused scholarships to study in France and others have had their tourist or student visas denied.[42] Students are often accused of staying in France and refusing to return to their homelands after graduation. In Vietnam, while the French government claims to be actively trying to recruit Vietnamese students to study in France, only a few are able to get French scholarships.

Currently, the French government is sponsoring training schools and universities outside of France. Under a new French aid program, the Military Mission and Cooperation (MMC) has opened four military schools on the continent of Africa, one each in the Ivory Coast, Togo, Senegal, and Mauritania in 1998. The goal is to train Africans while avoiding the expense of bringing students to French military schools in France. The French government is hoping to save money by cutting down on its own troops in Africa from the current number of 8,000 soldiers. The promotion of such programs in developing countries reinforces the boundaries between the French and citizens of its former colonies, who will preferably stay in their own countries while accepting French tutelage.

Franco-Vietnamese Collaboration for the Preparation of the Summit

Among the francophone countries, France was the largest financial contributor to the summit at 75 million francs (U.S.$15 million). In Hanoi, the French embassy and French organizations not only supervised the allocation of funding for the summit but also managed most of the preparatory projects, although such preparation was supposedly a collaborative effort between Vietnam and France. These projects included building a new International Conference Hall in Hanoi and renovating both the Opera House, built by the French in 1908,[43] and the Friendship Building, built by the former Soviet Union in the 1980s.

One of the projects was the staging of a "francophone environment." For the first time in the history of the francophone summit, the organizers had to create a citywide illusion that the Vietnamese people were French speakers living in a francophone environment. The past summits had taken place in francophone countries that did not require special attention to the linguistic environment. In an article entitled "The French are Back, and Vietnam Loves It," the American journalist David Lamb described the event as a "collage" of images of French stereotypes pasted onto a background of a nostalgic postcolonial society. "Suddenly everyone seems to be speaking French and eating croissants, again. Old men are wearing berets. Colonial French villas have been repainted. Banners draped over cafes and restaurants proclaim, 'bienvenue' [Welcome].´ The French are back and Hanoi is all smiles."[44]

The staging of this performance involved putting new signs in French and Vietnamese in front of historical buildings, adding French to many English road signs, remodelling parks, and repainting the facades of buildings to improve the look of the city.[45] This joint initiative was intended to improve the look of the city for the Vietnamese tourist industry.

But most importantly the staging required the training of a number of Vietnamese professionals able to perform their work in French during the summit. For this purpose, French crash courses were given to two thousand Vietnamese people who would be in contact with the various francophone delegations and would work for the summit in different capacities.[46] All the candidates for this special language-training program were appointed by the Vietnamese government and were required to be full-time students. During the period of the training, they were able to receive their monthly salaries. Twenty-one groups and sessions were organized according to various professions, such as the journalists, medical doctors, government officials, police officers, receptionists, waitresses, drivers, and electricians. The French Ministry of Education supervised the training and provided ten additional French teachers to the Francophone Language Program at the Alliance Française in Hanoi. A small Belgium delegation of six French teachers was to join the training sessions for a period of three months. Some of them complained that they were not well integrated into the program and were often discriminated against by the Vietnamese students, who did not consider them "French speakers" because they did not come from France.[47]

There were also some controversies regarding the decision to hold the summit in Vietnam. In their political discourse, the French officials argued that the Vietnamese government had requested that Hanoi be the site for the summit. All members of the Francophone Community then voted upon the decision. A French governmental official, Mr. Christian Tannin,[48] member of a visiting francophone delegation, insisted that the Vietnamese government had initiated the Hanoi summit. "We had no control over their decision," he added. A French medical doctor working for a French nongovernmental organization who has lived in the region for the last ten years explained that the decision was made ten years ago when Vietnam was looking for foreign investments and economic partnerships. "The summit," she said, "was then looked upon very positively for Vietnam because at the time their future was very grim under the American embargo." But, she added bitterly, since the lifting of the embargo and Vietnam's new membership in ASEAN, the Vietnamese attitude toward the summit and the Francophone Community had changed. "Now," she said, "the Vietnamese don't care about the summit." Her view was shared by many French expatriates, who expressed their anger at the Vietnamese lack of commitment to the Francophone Community and their lack of gratitude toward France.

Mr. Delalande, the director of the ACCT in Hanoi, explicitly denied a French leadership role in decisions regarding the summit. "The summit," he said, "was one of three goals of Vietnam in its 1986 congress. The first was to gain membership in ASEAN, the second was to host the Francophone Summit, and the third was to negotiate the lifting of the American embargo." He added that the Vietnamese government had since achieved all those goals. The summit, according to Mr. Delalande, was of great importance to Vietnam because it was an introduction to the world community. He argued that Vietnam was using the Francophone Summit as leverage for leadership in the ASEAN community. He said that no other ASEAN country had been able to gather forty-nine heads of state for a summit. He suggested that it was a calculated decision for Vietnam: "c'est pour montrer leur petits copains qu'eux aussi peuvent recevoir 49 chef d'etats" (it would show to their dear friends that they can organize a summit with forty-nine heads of state). Mr. Delalande then explained that it took the Vietnamese delegation many attempts to get the necessary votes to have the summit held in Hanoi. He recalls that "in 1993, they were turned down because they did not know 'how to do it.' " But the second time around, he explained, they had learned the democratic process and started to campaign in francophone African countries to become the host of the 1997 summit.

Official Vietnamese discourse, however, contradicts Mr. Delalande's claim and all the rumors in the French community. According to Mrs. Ton Nu Thi Ninh, the assistant minister of foreign affairs, who was a member of the Vietnamese delegation to the Francophone Community, having the summit in Hanoi was not a Vietnamese initiative but rather part of an agenda proposed by the French, whom she referred to as "nos amis francais" (our French friends). In 1993, she said, the French pushed the Vietnamese delegation to present Vietnam's candidacy to the summit committee, but the Vietnamese government was against it because it was not ready to hold such a summit. According to Mrs. Ton Nu Thi Ninh, the Vietnamese government realized that the summit could be used to promote multilateral relations with all francophone countries, in particular African nations, and prepare Vietnam to host future international conferences. In the following year, 1998, Vietnam hosted the ASEAN summit in Hanoi.

2. Vietnam and the Francophone Community

In spite of the obvious French desire to exert control over the organization, Vietnam was able to use the francophone project to achieve its own political and economic goals. According to Mr. Nguyên Manh Cam,[49] minister of foreign affairs, Vietnam's foreign policies are intended "to promote peace with all countries and to help the rebuilding of Vietnam." Indeed the Vietnamese have welcomed the support of the international community in rebuilding their economy but must constantly negotiate with foreign powers, including France, to maintain their own political boundaries and cultural mores. This is particularly evident in the case of foreign nongovernmental organizations. In an evaluation report on a bilateral project with a Finnish development organization, Vietnamese scholars argued that, although Vietnam badly needed foreign economic assistance, foreign experts should not try to impose their own way of doing business. Using recent history as a point of reference, they wrote:

> During the war, Vietnam always promoted independence and self-reliance to achieve the final victory. Many countries sent huge amounts of material support and advisers to help Vietnam. In practice, Vietnam persisted in a policy of independence and self-reliance; foreign assistance, especially in strategy and tactics, was rarely implemented. Indeed, the battlefields showed that if they had followed the advice of foreign advisers the Vietnamese generals would have lost such important battles as Dien Bien Phu in 1954.[50]

Mr. Nguyên Manh Cam, however, argued that the francophone project had helped Vietnam to strengthen its economic trade with other francophone countries, in particular, Canada, France, and Belgium, and that it had eased Vietnamese relations with members of the European Union. In an interview, Mrs. Ton Nu Thi Ninh, the assistant minister of foreign affairs, emphasized the need for Vietnam to develop political and economic ties with all countries to ensure its future in the global economy. She described the Vietnamese policy as one of "diversifying, increasing various network ties to economic, political, and cultural entities, regionally, interregionally, and globally, in order to have the most possible choices and to assert its own national political and cultural identity in a world marked by an inexorable intensification and globalization of markets."[51]

Vietnamese Economic Ambitions and the Summit

Not anticipating a heated political debate, the Vietnamese had expected the Francophone Summit to focus essentially on issues related to foreign aid and economic development. To some extent, that goal was accomplished with the signing of a new agreement with the francophone countries.

The 1997 Francophone Summit has particularly favored Franco-Vietnamese bilateral cooperation.[52] As France is Vietnam's largest Western European trading partner, so is Vietnam essential to French business: it gives France more Asian visibility. A French business consultant[53] working at the French embassy in Hanoi argues that the summit demonstrated that Vietnam is "for the French the only card to play in the Asian market" or the only way to assure French commercial ventures in the region. He pointed out that French companies had the most licensed projects of any non-Asian country in Vietnam, among them ventures by France Telecom, Societe Generale, Alcatel, Rhone Poulenc, La Vie (Vittel), and Campenon Bernard SGE.[54] He also noted that, although American companies had submitted more and very costly projects, many of them were as yet unlicensed.

During the first day of his visit to Hanoi, Jacques Chirac, the French president, signed business contracts worth more than 4 million francs. France Telecom, for instance, obtained a five-year contract for a joint venture with a Vietnamese company, VNPT, to install 540,000 telephone lines for 2.7 million francs. FivesLille Cement (FCB) signed a contract to build a cement factory at Hoang Mai, which will produce 1.4 million tons of cement per year for 755 million francs. Suez-Lyonnaise des Eaux, a water company, signed a contract for 640 million francs to build a water factory. And, finally, the Tresor Français, a French financial company, will lend 310 million francs to Hanoi.[55] Additionally, France imports about U.S.$400 million worth of clothing, leather shoes, and coffee, which accounts for 6 percent of Vietnam's export revenues.[56]

The Seventh Summit in Hanoi also strengthened the Canadian-Vietnamese relationship. Like France, Canada maintained its diplomatic relationship with the Socialist Republic of Vietnam in spite of the American economic embargo. In 1990, the Canadian International Development Agency, CIDA, established a development cooperation program in Vietnam, and by 1994 the new Canadian embassy had been inaugurated in Hanoi. Since then, Canada has developed numerous educational cooperation programs with Vietnam. Among them is the International Development Research Center, which has spent over C$5.5 million for joint research projects with Vietnamese institutions.[57] In addition to educational exchanges and development projects, Canadian trade with Vietnam reached C$58 million in 1994. Canada exports pharmaceutical, machine, and food products to Vietnam, while Vietnam exports to Canada mostly fish, shellfish, coffee, and tea. Canadian telecommunications has prospered in Vietnam, and in the next few years its contracts could reach C$100 million a year.

But one of the most valuable aspects of the Canadian-Vietnamese relationship may be Canada's strengthened position with ASEAN. Canada is already an economic partner with ASEAN, currently working on construction projects in Indonesia and Malaysia. The Canadians are helping the Vietnamese to better integrate themselves into ASEAN by helping to build a library and training Vietnamese officials and managers in the English language to facilitate their communication with other ASEAN members.[58] Although Canada fully supports all programs of the Francophone Community, it does not share the ambitious French linguistic project, as I noted above. According to the Canadian cultural attaché in Hanoi, Canada contributed U.S.$4 million to the summit but has not contributed to the promotion of the French language in Vietnam. The attaché argued that such projects were of concern essentially to the Canadian French-speaking community of Quebec, not to Canada as a whole.

The Francophone Community has also helped to give Vietnam a presence in Europe. Through its relationship with the European members of the Francophone Community, Vietnam has developed ties to the European Union. Since 1996, the EU has agreed to a five-year plan of cooperation with Vietnam. The projects include one on the elimination of rural poverty and another on controlling the spread of malaria. In addition, the EU has increased its trade with Vietnam. The Vietnamese hope that the Francophone Summit would advance its visibility in Europe appears to have been successful.

Finally, according to Mrs. Ton Nu Thi Ninh, the summit was meant to facilitate "south-south" cooperation, especially between Vietnam and African countries. She pointed out that Vietnam has not yet developed strong ties with other developing countries, particularly in Africa, because of distance and lack of financial resources. In an interview in August 1997, she said that the visit of African heads of states at the summit in Hanoi would help bridge cultural differences. She also said she was very pleased to have read a long article on Vietnam in the magazine *Jeune Afrique,* which she saw as a step forward in making Vietnam more visible in the international community.

The Francophone Project

The current francophone project under the umbrella of the l'Agence de la Francophonie[59] clearly reveals French ambitions to consolidate a political and economic network able to challenge the post–cold war new world order set by the United States. The francophone project includes linguistic and cultural programs that promote educational exchanges among francophone countries. The French newspaper *Le Figaro*[60] notes that "almost 50 million foreigners speak our language, and 155 million have some understanding of French. Every year, 600,000 more people learn it in 414 high schools and 1,056 Alliances Françaises. All of them read our authors and watch our TV programs." The francophone project has been essentially developed in the field of education, which includes teaching French and training Vietnamese students in scientific and technical fields. But the project has also indirectly promoted the French-Vietnamese collaboration in fields such as academic research, technical assistance, and cultural exchanges.

The Francophone Educational Project

Among the francophone programs most important to Vietnam are the university educational and vocational exchanges, AUPELF[61] (Association des Universites Partiellement ou Entierement de Langue Française) and UREF (Universite des Reseaux d'Expression Française).[62] These educational programs promote the development of francophone classes at major Vietnamese universities, including the Superior School of Foreign Trade, the National Polytechnic Institute, Hanoi University, and other universities in Ho Chi Minh City and Can Tho.[63]

In addition to the academic programs, the project includes a media and communications network, including a radio station, RFI,[64] a francophone television channel TV5, and French language newspapers; a "cultural" program promoting francophone arts and literature,[65] and coordination with other cultural institutions, such as l'Alliance Francaise. As a language-teaching institution, l'Alliance Francaise has been a key player in the francophone project, particularly in such countries as Vietnam. Established as a nongovernmental organization in 1883, today it has centers in 134 countries. Over 350,000 persons take French lessons worldwide at l'Alliance Française. In Hanoi, 1,000 Vietnamese students are enrolled in French classes, most of them high school or university students.

Although the Alliance Francaise is one of the most visible French cultural institutions in Vietnam, other educational programs exist in conjunction with Vietnamese educational programs. The recently opened École Supérieure des Technologies Informatiques, the school of computer sciences of Hanoi (ESTIH), is training 120 Vietnamese students in computer science engineering. The Lycée Chu Van An of Hanoi, a high school, was remodeled in 1997 to welcome a new French bilingual program, which required a special audio classroom for bilingual education in French and Vietnamese.[66] The *lycée* is among sixty-seven institutions in seventeen provinces to have received funding and equipment for French bilingual programs. Finally, the French Bilingual International School offers classes from kindergarten to high school.[67]

French Cooperative Projects in Vietnam

Cooperation in scientific research between Vietnam and France falls into four categories.[68] The first research area is science and engineering sciences, hosted at the Centre National de Recherches Scientifiques (CNRS) and the Vietnamese National Center of the Natural Sciences and Technologies. The latter also comprises natural resources and such studies as tropical agronomy and environmental studies, including research on Vietnamese forests, national parks, oceanography, coastal management, and land tenure. The third area of research cooperation includes the social sciences and humanities. Academic research and other activities are hosted at various institutions, such as the École Française d'Extrême-Orient (EFEO),[69] some agencies of the CNRS, the National Library, and the Museum of Natural History. Joint research projects are diverse. They include such projects as the Vietnamese ethnography museum in Hanoi, village studies at the EFEO, the protection of the cultural heritage of Vietnamese ethnic minorities, archaeological studies of the Mekong Delta, and the EFEO's publications series.[70] The last research area is that of economics and law, where work is conducted by agencies of the CNRS, l'Institut Français de Recherche Scientifique pour le Développement en Coopération (ORSTOM), renamed in 1998 as the Institut de Recherche pour le Développement (IRD), and the two bilateral cooperation institutions: la Maison Franco-Vietnamienne du Droit in Hanoi and the Centre Vietnamien d'Enseignement a la Gestion (CFVG).

In the area of technical cooperation, projects of technical assistance are designed to update old systems by bringing new equipment into Vietnam and training Vietnamese experts in new technologies. These projects are in medicine and health care (including the renovation of Vietnamese hospitals) and water management, energy, communications, and infrastructure. Cultural cooperation includes cultural exchanges in art, music, theater, and dance. In both Hanoi and Ho Chi Minh City, French artists are often invited to perform or exhibit their work, while Vietnamese artists are invited to tour French cities to exhibit and perform. All the Franco-Vietnamese projects have been contingent on the support of French educational institutions in Vietnam, which have been very active in teaching French and training Vietnamese experts.[71]

French Research Projects in Vietnam
One of the most significant areas of French-Vietnamese exchange is the bilateral exchange between Vietnamese and French scholars. In this new framework, both French and Vietnamese scholars participate and benefit equally from a collaboration in terms of funding, training,

access to data, and the sharing of methodologies. While the French scholars have access to financial resources, Vietnamese scholars provide the necessary official permission for field research, which, considering the difficulties of carrying out research in Vietnam, is of great importance. These joint projects provide an anchor for Vietnamese and French graduate students as well as established scholars. For example, French graduate students have been allowed to carry out fieldwork in villages to which they would not have had access otherwise, and Vietnamese students have received some training in new research methodologies.

One such joint research project was carried out by the Laboratoire Asie du Sud-Est et Monde Austronesien (LASEMA) and the Centre National des Sciences Sociales et Humaines du Vietnam (CNSSH). It was sponsored by the CNRS and the French minister of foreign affairs and included five Vietnamese scholars of CNSSH, and three scholars of LASEMA-CNRS, among them two anthropologists, Nguyên Tung and Nelly Krowolski. It took place between 1990 and 1992 in the northern village of Mong Phu and documented that village's relationships with seven other villages in the commune of Duong Lam. The project resulted in a 1999 French publication entitled *Mong Phu: Un village du delta du Fleuve Rouge.*[72]

In 1994, following a seminar sponsored by the French Ministry of Foreign Affairs, it was decided to create another village project to coordinate all current research in the delta of the Red River. This particular project was to be multidisciplinary. It included anthropology, sociology, geography, agronomy, and history, and it incorporated studies on many northern villages. Hosted at the EFEO, the team of researchers included seven Vietnamese and four French scholars. The outcome of this collaborative effort will be the publication of an edited volume presenting the results of the "village project" research. Among the participants in that village project was Olivier Tessier, an anthropologist. Tessier's essay "Commuting from the Village to the City: Analyzing the Patterns of Migration of the People of the Northern Village of Hay to Hanoi," included in this volume, is an example of the kind of work that has resulted from such joint and multidisciplinary Franco-Vietnamese research efforts.

The essay in the present volume by Xavier Oudin, an economist at ORSTOM-IRD, who resided for five years in Hanoi, illustrates another kind of joint research project. Entitled "Labor Restructuring in

Vietnam," this essay is one result of a project of cooperative economic research between the French and Vietnamese governments, the purpose of which was to study the patterns of employment and human resources at a time of major change in Vietnamese labor practices. This project was inaugurated in 1996. The agreement for this cooperative project included the long-term residence in Hanoi of French scholars from ORSTOM-IRD, who worked at the Center for the Study of Population and Human Resources at the Vietnamese Ministry of Labor and the Ministry of Social Affairs.

Also in this volume, the essay "Agro-Commodity Chains in Northern Vietnam: New Mechanisms for Old Stakeholders," by Pascal Bergeret, a French engineer in agronomy who has lived in Hanoi for six years, presents one aspect of the social and economic transformation in rural Vietnam. This is a study in applied environmental research, part of the program of cooperation on the natural environment. Pascal Bergeret was the program coordinator of Le Programme Fleuve Rouge, the project Fleuve Rouge, which was created in 1989 to assist Vietnam in dealing with new challenges after Doi Moi and rural decollectivization. The bilateral agreement for the project was signed between the Vietnamese National Institute of the Agronomic Sciences and the Groupe de Recherches et d'Exchanges Technologiques (GRET). Le Programme Fleuve Rouge operated at the local level to evaluate the current rural situation. It was to introduce new technologies in agriculture, taking into account the rural organization adapted for new needs. The program also sponsored Vietnamese engineers in agronomy to be trained at French universities in Paris, Orleans, and Montpellier. Taken collectively, the essays in this book illustrate how this new cooperation between the two countries has advanced French scholarship in Vietnamese studies.

Vietnam and the "Francophone Project"

Vietnam's interests in joining the Francophone Community in 1970 were not only economic and political. The Vietnamese also wished to maintain a cultural and intellectual dialogue with their French counterparts. Mrs. Ton Nu Thi Ninh, for instance, suggested that one reason why Vietnam joined the Francophone Community was because it shared the community's goal of promoting national cultural identity via the French language. She argued that, although French represented the language of a colonial past, its linguistic and cultural legacy is still a part of the Vietnamese national identity.[73]

Many Vietnamese intellectuals and revolutionaries, now the old guard of the leadership of the Vietnamese Communist Party, were themselves educated in French colonial institutions. Although they rejected and fought against colonial domination, they are well versed in French literature and the arts.[74] Over the years, they have kept their political affiliations with French political parties and maintained their relationships with the French intellectual community. General Vo Nguyên Giap, eighty-five years old, is one such Francophile[75] who still converses with foreigners in French.

From 1930 through 1940, the work of many Vietnamese francophone intellectuals, now considered to be "modern Vietnamese literature," was colored by French culture.[76] In their writing, the francophone writers "tried to reconcile the two cultures without repudiating their own, while maintaining a sensitivity to French literary influence and the social and political events of that country."[77] Xuan Dieu, a Vietnamese poet who is said to have introduced a different form of romanticism in Vietnam, says that "the contact with French literature, especially French poetry, injected a flow of new blood into our society" and that Baudelaire, for instance, brought out "this bud of modernity that I had discovered in myself."[78] Not all Vietnamese intellectuals agree. Tao Mat, a playwright for the traditional Vietnamese theater (Cheo), argues that there has been a little French influence on the language and "conversation," but that, overall, French and Vietnamese playwrights are very different.[79]

Unlike Algerians and other people colonized by the French, including those for whom French is the official language, the Vietnamese do not have an advocacy relationship with France and the Francophone Community. Mrs. Ton Nu Thi Ninh argued that the Algerians' ambivalent relationship with the French derives from their continued linguistic subordination to France because French is still used as the official language. She said that in conferences many intellectuals from developing countries sadly reported to her having to rely on French to make philosophical or scientific arguments because they lacked the proper vocabulary in their own language. In contrast, in Vietnam after the liberation in 1945 President Ho Chi Minh proclaimed Vietnamese as the official language of Vietnam. Vietnamese intellectuals have retrained themselves to express their ideas in Vietnamese instead of relying on the French language. As a result, Mrs. Ton Nu Thi

Ninh said, the Vietnamese people have no resentment toward the French and no negative attitudes toward the French language because French colonialism is already part of the Vietnamese past.

In Vietnam, the promotion of the French language serves Vietnam's political purposes. The Vietnamese people, in particular those associated with the Vietnamese Communist Party and the generation of Vietnamese who fought the Americans, are more concerned with American imperialism than French neocolonialism. The Vietnamese share with other countries of the Francophone Community a fear of Anglo-American cultural hegemony promoted through globalization. Mr. Cu Huy Can, delegate to the Francophone Community, suggested that the francophone project was in danger due to the spread of the anglophone language and culture.[80] Mrs. Ton Nu Thi Ninh called the United States the unchallenged superpower. "While the definition of imperialism remains the same," she said, "the new form of imperialism avoids open confrontations but uses economic power to subjugate countries and language as the channel to introduce people to its culture of consumption."

Mr. Nguyên Tuong, the chief editor of the *Courrier du Viêt Nam*, argued that languages were not only the channel of communication but also tools to shape one's mind to a particular cultural mode. Vietnamese people, in particular the youths who were learning English, he said, should not be exposed to the single way of thinking fostered by the anglophone culture. Instead, he suggested, Vietnamese students should learn from other cultures. French culture, he argued, is based on a different thought pattern and offers a different kind of knowledge. Finally, he argued that, although Vietnamese students want to learn from American culture because the United States is today a key player in the world economy, they should not forget their loyalties to countries that helped Vietnam and supported the peace effort during the war. France and Sweden are the two countries that stood by Vietnam, he said, and the Vietnamese people should remember and return the favor.

The Francophone Project in Vietnam:
Reality or Fiction?

While the staging of the summit gave the illusion of the Vietnamese capital as a francophone city, the reality is otherwise. In a French article entitled "Hanoi: The Fiction of the Francophone Project" (Hanoi: la fiction de la francophonie), the journalist Marc Epstein questions the validity of the project in Vietnam, where only a handful of Vietnamese people speak French. Only two out of every one hundred high school students are learning French,[81] and most French-speaking Vietnamese are the elderly, formerly educated under the French colonial educational system. Although Vietnamese officials argue that Vietnamese students should learn both French and Vietnamese, since 1997 English has been the official second language in Vietnam. Before his death in May 1997, Nguyên Khac Vien criticized the ambitious French francophone project in Vietnam, stating: "It is pure illusion to think that a large part of the Vietnamese population will learn the French language."[82] He also strongly responded to the French ambassador's comments, made at an official event in Hanoi, on the necessity for Vietnamese to read French authors in the original language in order to truly appreciate their work. Nguyen Khac Vien rightly pointed out that most French intellectuals themselves were unable to read foreign texts in the original languages, in particular Russian, Chinese, and Japanese. Thus, why should one insist that the Vietnamese learn French in order to read French work? He suggested that the French government should focus instead on promoting and supporting good Vietnamese translations of French works, which are, as he noted, still lacking in Vietnam.

In Ho Chi Minh City, many francophone Vietnamese are Catholics educated in French Catholic institutions, which were closed only in 1975. While during the war North Vietnamese students were learning Russian, southern Vietnamese students were learning English. In 1991, among the older generation of bilingual Vietnamese, as many spoke French as English. In Ho Chi Minh City, many francophones kept their fluency in French. Over the years, the Vietnamese Catholic community in Ho Chi Minh City was able to maintain its ties to the francophone world. But over the last few years, while French is still spoken in Catholic institutions such as convents and churches, English has replaced French in language courses. In 1991, many Catholic schools still offered French in their evening classes. By 1994, French was no longer in the curriculum, and English became the only language taught in evening classes. Hoa, a fifty-year-old former high school teacher and a Catholic, argued that there was a greater demand for English classes because it was easier to get a job if one had some basic skill in English. Although bilingual in French, he complained that in spite of his age he, like everyone else, was forced to learn English in order to survive in the new Vietnamese job market.

As mentioned earlier, Vietnamese became the official language of the Democratic Republic of Vietnam after 1954. Francophone Vietnamese in Hanoi often complained to me that since Vietnamese became the official language they have had no chance to practice their French. Although French was still taught at universities after 1954, only a handful of Vietnamese students learned it. Russian became the most popular language for students, especially those who wanted to pursue advanced degrees in the former Soviet Union. There were very few books in French available and no French newspapers. Many older people complained that they had lost their fluency in French and often lack the necessary vocabulary to read French books despite having maintained ties with relatives who established themselves in France in 1954.

Many of the French overseas Vietnamese, the Viet Kieu, who could not return to Vietnam either during the war or in the postwar period, still helped and communicated with family members back home. Children of these Vietnamese emigrants, many of whom do not speak Vietnamese, are now returning to Vietnam. Their visits often force that generation of francophone Vietnamese to relearn their French. At the l'Alliance Française, elderly men are regular visitors at its library, spending hours reading French newspapers, magazines, and journals.

More recently, because of the coming summit in the fall of 1997, the ACCT, the French embassy, the Canadian embassy and the Alliance Française began organizing many social and cultural activities to present the French language and culture to the Vietnamese public. For instance, in the summer of 1997 the French embassy sponsored a French song contest, inviting amateur Vietnamese singers to perform on Vietnamese television. The embassy also sponsored a series of art exhibits in Hanoi and Ho Chi Minh City of francophone painters, and the Alliance Francaise sponsored music and movie festivals during the year. But most of these programs were geared toward the Vietnamese francophone community, a small segment of the educated Vietnamese elite.

Members of the generation of Vietnamese francophones born after 1954, unlike their parents, learned French as a second language at the university. Manh, a forty-year-old man, said that he learned

French because his grandfather wanted him to do so, even though twenty years ago at the university most students studied Russian. When he finished his studies, he was unable to find employment that would allow him to use his French. Today he has found a job as a receptionist in a French company, but he feels that he has very little opportunity in the current job market, in which English rather than French is required. Hung, a forty-five-year-old French professor at the university who is fluent in French, commented that twenty years ago another issue facing students who wanted to major in French was the shortage of professors of French. Many French teachers had either left the country or died. Vietnamese high school students faced similar problems. There were very few French classes and limited teaching materials, which made learning difficult. Tang, a twenty-eight-year-old, works as a librarian at l'École Française d'Extrême-Orient. She studied French at the university because, as she said, she liked the language. But she said that her skill in French was very technical. She was trained as a translator in economics and business, and that was the extent of her knowledge in French and about France. She does not read French novels or watch the French channel on television. Instead she is taking evening English classes. She said that knowing English would enable her to find a job in a foreign company.

The issue of employment is a very sensitive one for the francophone Vietnamese, who feel that they have learned a language that does not help them find a job. Even French businesses that have settled in Vietnam prefer hiring Vietnamese employees who can speak both French and English. The need for Vietnamese French speakers remains essentially only in the tourist industry. Most of the tourists visiting Vietnam every year are in fact French. Even before the Seventh Francophone Summit, Vietnam had been a very popular country for French tourists to visit. In many travel agencies in France, for instance, organized tours to Vietnam advertised the country as the new frontier of travel adventure. The popular movies *Indochine, L'Amant,* and *Scent of Green Papaya* have also contributed to the promotion of Vietnamese culture and tourism in France.

In Hanoi, francophones agreed that the summit brought a renewal of interest in French among a new generation of Vietnamese but argued that the momentum would drop after the summit. The French government has begun offering over one hundred scholarships a year to Vietnamese students, in particular in the medical fields. These scholarships are usually less competitive, since many Vietnamese medical students apply to medical schools in Australia and the United States. For several years before the summit, ACCT began providing high schools with French teachers and audio-visual equipment. Many of the younger generation of Vietnamese taking French classes at the Alliance Française belong to educated middle-class families. The fee of $20 per session is not affordable for most Vietnamese families living in Hanoi, where the average income is $30 a month.

Mrs. Ninh warned that France needs to maintain all of these educational structures. Vietnam, she said, does not have the resources to keep up the new language training programs alone. French businesses in Vietnam also needed to make a commitment to hire French-speaking Vietnamese in order to create an incentive for Vietnamese students to learn French. "This is not the case today," she said. Furthermore, France also must maintain support for francophone Vietnamese students who have already received degrees in France. Mrs. Ninh strongly criticized the ACCT French officials' obsession with quantitative data on the francophone Vietnamese community and with inducing more Vietnamese students to learn French. She complained that many doctors who went to France to receive medical training felt that when they returned there was inadequate support to maintain their professional skills. Why, she argued, try to recruit more students when those already trained cannot find work and receive little support?

Conclusion

The 1997 Francophone Summit in Hanoi best illustrates how in the post–cold war era Vietnam, a socialist country, is using international organizations such as the Francophone Community to bolster its economic and political status in the global community. In the past, Vietnam traded essentially with other socialist countries, which shared a common political ideology, but its present membership in the Francophone Community is based more on economic interests than political considerations. Although many other francophone countries, in particular the ones in Africa, experienced struggles and turmoil under French colonialism similar to that of Vietnam, unlike Vietnam they did not become socialist states. The Vietnamese delegation at the summit resisted the new political agenda of the organization that would mandate an active role in international political conflicts. Instead the Vietnamese set an agenda for the summit that focused on regional economic development in their own interest. Indeed, their initiative resulted in a number of business deals and bilateral aid agreements between Vietnam and other francophone countries, in particular France and Canada.

In addition to the obvious economic opportunities associated with membership in the Francophone Community, Vietnam's attempt to join other international organizations also indicates its concern over the threat of foreign domination. The new economic reforms of Doi Moi, which resulted in the increase of foreign trade and investments in Vietnam, has also prompted international organizations to attempt to intervene in Vietnamese domestic affairs. For instance, the World Bank and other organizations have been pushing the Vietnamese government to further its economic reforms. Vietnam's membership in many international and regional organizations, such as the Francophone Community and ASEAN, is a way of allowing the Vietnamese government to maintain better relationships with all nations while avoiding control by more powerful countries.

Regarding French interests and initiatives at the summit, the French government's appointment of the former UN secretary general, Mr. Boutros Boutros-Ghali, as the interim general secretary at the 1997 summit in Hanoi, without a democratic election and despite opposition, openly exposes a relationship of dependency between France and other francophone countries. Although France has not actively sought control over its former colonies, it has so far maintained close political and economic ties with many African francophone countries. Using linguistic claims as a political platform, France hopes to challenge the role of the United States as a superpower. As Margie Sudre explained, "Pregnant with dialogue and cooperation today, francophony will be tomorrow a full-fledged player in the international arena."[83] The French claim for the francophone project is well stated in the French newspaper *Le Figaro*: "49 states or governments, 500 million people, a GNP of 13,000 billion francs (10 percent of the world), a trade of 17 percent of the international market, francophony is one of the most important associations among countries in the world."[84]

But beyond the glamorous political propaganda of the francophone project and the display of French interests in Vietnam at the 1997 Francophone Summit lies another fundamental question: is French academia as committed to Vietnamese studies as France is committed to the francophone project? This book represents French scholarship on Vietnam at its best. Many of the contributors were trained at French universities by a generation of accomplished French and Vietnamese scholars, among them Pierre Brocheux, Daniel Hémery, Georges Boudarel, and Nguyên Thê Anh. But the old guard has now retired or is retiring. Some of their positions at academic institutions have not been secured for Vietnamese studies, and some have already been lost to other area studies. As mentioned earlier, a generation of talented young scholars, who in Vietnam took advantage of the francophone frenzy to get scholarships and pursue their research back in France, are facing a grim future in French academia. Without academic positions, their contributions to Vietnamese scholarship may be at risk and the training in France of future generations of scholars in Vietnamese studies may also be at stake. In this respect, France's long-term commitment to Vietnamese studies, and consequently to Vietnam, may be jeopardized.

French is not the official second language of Vietnam, but the francophone project in Vietnam is greatly significant to France, primarily because Vietnam is the anchor for French business opportunities in Asia. For Vietnamese, however, francophony holds little interest. French culture and language are fading away as the older generation of francophone Vietnamese, who themselves fought against French cultural hegemony in colonial French Indochina, die off. Some, like Huu Ngoc,[85] a francophone Vietnamese intellectual, hope that the francophone legacy will not be lost and will continue to have an influence in Vietnamese arts and literature. And even three years after the francophone summit in Hanoi, there were still many French and francophone cultural events presented in both Hanoi and Ho Chi Minh City,[86] which are constant reminders of Vietnam's commitment to the francophone project.

But, as I show in this essay, there is little indication that this torch is being passed to future generations. Every year more Vietnamese students go abroad to study in American, Australian, and British universities, and the popular culture of English-speaking countries is already influencing Vietnamese youth culture in its choice of entertainment and lifestyle. Only a few of the young learn French as their primary second language, and the ones who do are more concerned about job issues than the intellectual endowment of French culture. Most Vietnamese university students in Hanoi learn English as a second language. Only privileged Vietnamese students at l'Alliance Française can afford to learn French as a third language. Regardless of the Vietnamese government's future economic policies and its relations with other countries, the Vietnamese people are active participants in the global economy, the matrix of which is English speaking.

NOTES

Center for Southeast Asian Studies, University of Hawaii. I would like to thank Elizabeth Colson at the University of California, Berkeley, as well as my two colleagues Lyn Lowry and Kathryn Forbes, for reading the first draft of this essay and for making useful suggestions. The data were first presented in two different essays. The first one, entitled "The 1997 Francophone Summit in Hanoi: Analyzing Viet Nam's Ambiguous Relationship with World Powers," was presented at the Southeast Asia Studies Program, Cornell University, in April 1998. The second, entitled "Imagining Indochine: French Discourse on Colonial Boundaries in a Postcolonial Vietnam," was presented at the American Anthropological Association Meetings in Washington, D.C., in November 1997.

1. "La Francophonie contribue a la mise en valeur des ressources humaines: Nguyên Manh Cam, Minister of Foreign Affairs," *Lettre de la Francophonie,* supplement to *L'Annee Du Vietnam,* March 1997 (published by Agence de Cooperation Culturelle et Technique).

2. "C'est au Vietnam que la France occupe la plus forte position en Asie: Les faits sont la," quoted in Jean-Claude Pomonti and Trean Claire, "Jacques Chirac a appele de ses voeux un 'partnariat privilegie' avec Hanoi," *Le Monde,* 14 November 1997.

3. The former French quarter has kept its large avenues shaded by trees and bordered with French-style houses, once homes for the colonial bourgeoisie and now the headquarters for many embassies. And the buildings of the former "administration coloniale francaise," which once symbolized the Indochinese colonial power, are now Vietnamese government offices.

4. Nguyên Khac Vien, *Vietnam: Patrie Retrouvee* (Paris: Editions Sociales), 1977.

5. Pierre Brocheux and Daniel Hémery, *Indochine: la colonization ambigue* (Paris: Editions de la Decouverte), 1994.

6. The largest foreign groups are from Asian countries, in particular Japan and South Korea.

7. Frantz Fanon, *The Wretched of the Earth* (New York: Grove Weidenfeld), [1963] 1991.

8. Albert Memmi, *The Colonizer and the Colonized* (Boston: Beacon Press), [1965] 1967.

9. Besides the large number of Vietnamese living overseas returning to Vietnam as tourists, the French tourists are the most important group among westerners to visit the country.

10. Marc Epstein, "Hanoi: La Fiction de la Francophonie," *L'Express*, 13 November 1997.

11. "Le Royaume de la Francophonie," *Le Figaro*, 10 November 1997.

12. "Partout, la communaute francophone que nous voulons creer sera essentiellement culturelle au sens le plus large du terme: elle aura pour mission de former et d'informer . . . la creation d'une communaute de langue francaise sera, peut-être la premiere du genre dans l'histoire moderne. Elle exprime un besoin de notre epoque, ou l'homme menace par le progress scientifique dont il est l'auteur veut construire un nouvel humanisme que soit en meme temps a sa proper measure et a celle du cosmos," quoted in *Introduction à la Francophonie: Recueil de Textes*, edited by Cyrille Sagbo (Cotonou, Benin: Les Editions du Flamboyant), 1993.

13. *Le Canada et la Francophonie* (Department of Foreign Affairs and International Trade), Hanoi: 1997.

14. Paul Guilbert, "Hanoi celebre l'universalite du Francais," *Le Figaro*, 15 and 16 November 1997.

15. Frederic Fritscher, "Un intellectuel brillant et francophile," *Le Monde*. 18 November 1997.

16. Claire Trean, "Le Role du nouveau 'secretaire general' a la francophonie reste vivement conteste," *Le Monde*, 18 November 1997.

17. Ibid.

18. Stephane Dupont, "La Francophonie veut se doter d'une force de frappe politique et economique," *Les Echos*, 13 November 1997.

19. Claire Trean, "La Francophonie cherche a sortir de ses combats d'arriere-garde," *Le Monde*, 14 November 1997.

20. Claire Trean, "Les travaux preparatoires ont tourne a la foire d'empoigne," *Le Monde*, 14 November 1997.

21. "La delegation francaise a du faire face a une serie de difficultes, dont les unes s'apparentent a une espece de fronde africaine," quoted in "La Francophonie est mal partie," *Le Monde*, 18 November 1997.

22. Claire Trean, "Le Role du nouveau 'secretaire general' a la francophonie reste vivement conteste," *Le Monde*, 18 November 1997.

23. Claire Trean, "Les travaux preparatoires ont tourne a la foire d'empoigne," *Le Monde*, 14 November 1997.

24. Stephane Dupont, "La Francophonie veut se doter d'une force de frappe politique et economique," *Les Echos*, 13 November 1997.

25. Jacques Amalric, "Do You Speak Francais? *Liberation*, 14 November 1997.

26. Roger Cohen, "France vs. U.S.: Warring Views of Capitalism," *New York Times*, 20 October 1997.

27. Ibid.

28. "Echelon is a network of surveillance stations stitched together in the 1970's by the United States National Security Agency with Australia, Britain, Canada and New Zealand to intercept select satellite communications," quoted in Suzanne Daley, "An Electronic Spy Scare is Alarming Europe," *New York Times*, 24 February 2000.

29. Ibid.

30. "Il y a une certaine competition linguistique entre la France et les Etats Unis. Pourquoi ne pas comprendre que nous voulons marquer notre presence, celle de la langue francaise parlee par plus de 200 millions de personnes dans le monde?" "Voudriez-vous d'un monde gere par les seules Etats Unis? Nous, nous le refusons, mais pas seulement la France: l'Europe aussi, l'Afrique, c'est defendre aussi une maniere de penser, de faire, differente: notre langue s'appuie sur un passe, une culture!"

31. "La Francophonie: Pourquoi, et pourquoi faire?" Reprinted in *Le Courrier du Viêt Nam*. 21 July 1997.

32. "Beaucoup de peuples qui ont eu d'etroits contacts avec les cultures dites occidentales notamment francaise, centres sur l'homme et les valeurs humanistes, le respect du droit des peuples et de leur diversite linguistique et culturelle, ressentent de plus en plus fortement le besoin d'echapper tant aux integrismes etouffants qu'a la civilisation et la langue 'mondialisantes' parcequ'ils leur paraissent constitues le plus grand risque d'uniformatisation, et d'abolition dans un nouvel ordre mondial, de ce qui leur reste d'independance."

33. "La Francophonie communaute tres informelle de 49 pays differents, en grande majorite pauvres, est jeune, fragile, menacee."

34. "Mondialisation, Union Europeene, effacement des nations et Etats dans les reseaux du village planetaire. Omnipotence apparente de la civilization etatsunienne, qui accapare et renforce la mondialization . . . La reaction de refus est d'abord instinctive, venue du fond de notre histoire, de la France contre les empires."

35. "Le Septieme Sommet des Chefs d'Etats et de Gouvernement des pays ayant le Francais en partage." Paper distributed by the Ambassade de France en Republique Socialiste du Vietnam. 1997.

36. Claire Trean, "Le Role du nouveau 'secretaire general' a la francophonie reste vivement conteste," *Le Monde*, 18 November 1997.

37. Paul Guilbert, "Hanoi celebre l'universalite du Francais," *Le Figaro*, 15 and 16 November 1997.

38. Claire Trean, "Le Role du nouveau 'secretaire general' a la francophonie reste vivement conteste," *Le Monde*, 18 November 1997.

39. Ibid.

40. Jacques Amalric, "Hanoi: Chirac VRP timide des droits de l'homme," *Liberation*, 13 November 1997.

41. Remy Ourdan, "Au pays des Ames Mortes," *Le Monde,* 31 March 1998.

42. Marc Epstein, "Hanoi: La fiction de la francophonie," *L'Express,* 13 November 1997.

43. The Opera House in Hanoi was modeled after the Grand Opera in Paris. The total cost of renovation has been estimated at $17 million. ("Le Septieme Sommet des Chefs d'Etats et de Gouvernement des pays ayant le Francais en partage," paper distributed by the Ambassade de France en Republique Socialiste du Vietnam, 1997).

44. David Lamb, "The French are Back, and Vietnam Loves It: Francophone Summit Set this Weekend in Hanoi," *San Jose Mercury News,* 15 November 1997.

45. "La signaletique de l'ensemble des sites, de l'aeroport au centre-ville, sera refaite, avec l'aide du Canada. Des projects d'embellissement de la ville, de panneaux indicateurs devant les monuments historiques ainsi qu'un guide du Hanoi francophone sont actuellement a l'etude," quoted in "Le Septieme Sommet des Chefs d'Etats et de Gouvernement des pays ayant le Francais en partage," paper distributed by the Ambassade de France en Republique Socialiste du Vietnam, 1997.

46. "The Alliance Francaise in Hanoi," *Vietnamese Studies* number 124 (1997): 177–86.

47. Interviews with the Belgian teachers at l'Alliance Francaise, May 1997.

48. Charge de Mission a la direction des Affaires Internationales du Conseil Regional de l'Ile de France.

49. "L'Annee du Vietnam," supplement to *Lettre de la Francophonie* 99 (March 1997): 1–4.

50. "Cultural Dimensions in Finnish Development Co-operation in Vietnam," Asian Institute of Technology Center in Vietnam, Hanoi, April 1997.

51. "Diversifier, multiplier les appartenances aux differentes entites economiques, politiques ou culturelles regionales, inter-regionales et mondiales, pour se donner le plus possible d'options et de points d'appui et pour afirmer son identite nationale politico-cuturelle dans le monde marque par l'inexorable intensification et globalisation des exchanges," quoted in "L'Annee du Vietnam," supplement to *Lettre de la Francophonie,* 99 (March 1997): 1–4.

52. "Le Septieme Sommet des Chefs d'Etats et de Gouvernement des pays ayant le Francais en partage," paper distributed by the Ambassade de France en Republique Socialiste du Vietnam, 1997.

53. Interview in Hanoi, May 1997.

54. *Thoi Bao Kinh Te Viet Nam,* 16 July 1997.

55. Stephane Dupont, "La Francophonie veut se doter d'une force de frappe politique et economique," *Les Echos,* 13 November 1997.

56. *Vietnam News,* 26 May 1997.

57. *Canada and Vietnam: A History of Cooperation,* film produced by the Canada-ASEAN Center in cooperation with the Canadian Embassy, Hanoi, 1997.

58. Ibid.

59. The budget of the francophone project cost about 1 billion francs, and the French government has provided two-thirds of it. See "Le Royaume de la Francophonie," *Le Figaro,* 10 November 1997.

60. "Pres de 50 millions d'etrangers pratiquent notre langue et 155 millions la connaissent. Chaque annee, 600,000 autres l'apprennent dans 414 lycees et 1056 Alliances francaises. Tous lisent nos auteurs, ecoutent et regardent nos programmes," quoted in "Le Royaume de la Francophonie," *Le Figaro,* 10 November 1997.

61. Created in 1961 at the University of Montreal.

62. In the field of higher education, the Vietnamese have actively participated in the development of educational francophone projects. For instance, in February 2000, the vice president, Ms. Nguyen Thi Binh, and Ms. Michele Gendreau-Massaloux, the president of AUPELF, met in Hanoi to set up new Franco-Vietnamese educational projects ("Pho Chu tich nuoc tiep hieu truong to chuc tac dai hoc co su dung tieng phap," *Nhan Dan,* 17 February 2000).

63. Margie Sudre, "Hanoi: Capital of Francophony," *Vietnamese Studies* 124 (1997): 145–48.

64. Radio France International.

65. In February 2000, the French government donated thirty French films to Vietnam, which will be shown in the cities during the month of March ("Phap tang Viet Nam 30 bo phim," *Nhan Dan,* 16 February 2000).

66. The *Lycée* was founded in 1907 as the Protectorate High School of Tonkin.

67. In the school, 35 percent are French children, 25 percent Vietnamese, and 45 percent foreigners from other countries.

68. "Cooperation France-Vietnam: Repertoire de la Cooperation Technique et de la Recherche," paper distributed by the Ambassade de France en Republique Socialiste du Vietnam, November 1997.

69. The Franco-Vietnamese agreement for the opening of the EFEO-Vietnam in Hanoi was signed in 1991 under President François Mitterand, by Catherine Tasca, French minister of communications (in the year 2000 she was the French minister of culture).

70. The EFEO has accepted a number of Vietnamese works, but because of financial constraints they have not been published yet. In addition to the posthumous work, every year the EFEO publishes a new dissertation to encourage young Vietnamese scholars.

71. Further details regarding French educational programs in Hanoi appear later in the present essay.

72. Nguyên Tung, ed., *Mong Phu: Un village du delta du Fleuve Rouge* (Paris: L'Harmattan, 1999). Among the contributors are Bê Viêt Dang, Diêp Dình Hoa, Nguyên Duong Bình, Nelly Krowolski, Nguyên Xuân Linh, Trân Van Hà, Vo Thi Thuong, and Nguyên Tung.

73. "Donner un gage vivant de son engagement dans la Francophonie, partie prenante de sa politique etrangere mais egalement de sa politique culturelle qui prone la mise en value de l'identite culturelle nationale et son enrichissement par la fleur d'autres langues et cultures, plus particulierement

la langue francaise—un des legs du passe dans l'histoire de notre pays, dont nous voulons tirer parti—et les cultures des pays francophones."

74. Nguyên Khac Vien, *Reves, Souvenirs, Commentaires* (Hanoi: Thê Gioi Publications, 1997).

75. "Trouvez-leur du travail et ils appredront le Francais," *Le Monde,* 14 November 1997.

76. Huu Ngoc, "Ferment of French Culture in Vietnam," *Vietnamese Studies* 124 (1997): 5–40.

77. Thanh Tam Langlet and Thu Trang Gaspard, "Francophone Vietnamese Authors: An Example of Cultural Exchange," *Vietnamese Studies* 128 (1998): 96–113.

78. Xuan Dieu, "Influence of French Poetry on Modern Vietnamese Poetry," *Vietnamese Studies* 124 (1997): 41–74.

79. "The language in French drama is similar to that of painting. The language of our *cheo* and *tuong* is similar to sculpture, focusing on music, gesture, and conventional choreography in order to create some strong impressions. . . . French theater in general is realistic, while ours is more conventional and symbolic," interview by Huu Ngoc with Tao Mat, in "Ferment of French Culture in Vietnam," *Vietnamese Studies* 124 (1997): 22.

80. *Les Cahiers de la Francophonie* 1 (March 1994).

81. Marc Epstein, "Hanoi: La fiction de la francophonie," *L'express,* 13 November 1997.

82. Nguyên Khac Vien, "Francophony in Vietnam: Illusions-Prospects," *Vietnamese Studies,* n.s. 54 (1997): 149–54.

83. Margie Sudre, "Hanoi: Capital of Francophony," *Vietnamese Studies* 124 (1997): 124.

84. "49 Etats ou gouvernments, 500 millions d'habitants, un PNB cumile de 13,000 milliards de francs (10% du total mondial), des echanges representant 17% du commerce international: la francophonie est l'une des plus imposantes associations de pays de la planete," quoted in Stephane Dupont, "La Francophonie veut se doter d'une force de frappe politique et economique," *Les Echos,* 13 November 1997.

85. Huu Ngoc, "Ferment of French Culture in Vietnam," *Vietnamese Studies* 124 (1997): 22.

86. Among many French cultural events presented in Vietnam, on 25 January 2000 the Ballet of the Opera of Paris gave a show in the opera house of Ho Chi Minh City ("Doan mua ballet Na Hat Opera Paris bieu dien tai TP Ho Chi Minh," *Nhan Dan,* 23 January 2000).

Contributors

Pascal Bergeret, Groupe de Recherches et d'Exchanges Technologiques, Paris.
Gisele Bousquet, Center for Southeast Asian Studies, University of California, Berkeley.
Pierre Brocheux, Université Denis Diderot, Paris.
Agathe Larcher-Goscha, Groupe d'Etudes sur le Viet Nam Contemporain a Sciences Politiques and Associe du laboratoire Peninsule Indochinoise, EPHE-EFEO Paris.
Philippe Le Failler, Institut de Recherche sur le Sud-Est Asiatique (IRSEA), Aix-en-Provence; and l'École Française d'Extrême-Orient (EFEO), Hanoi.
Laurence Monnais-Rousselot, Department of History and Centre d'Etudes de l'Asie du Sud Est, University of Montréal.
Nguyên Van Ky, Independent scholar, Paris.
Xavier Oudin, ORSTOM-IRD, Montpellier, France.
Philippe Papin, l'École Française d'Extrême-Orient, Hanoi.
Phan Thi Minh Le, Université Denis Diderot, Paris.
Emmanuel Poisson, École Française d'Extrême-Orient, Hanoi.
Olivier Tessier, Institut de Recherche sur le Sud-Est Asiatique, Aix-en-Provence; and l'École Française d'Extrême-Orient (EFEO), Hanoi.
Tran Thi Liên, Groupe d'Etudes sur le Vietnam Contemporain, Paris.
Trinh Van Thao, Université Aix-en-Provence.
John K. Whitmore, University of Michigan.
Florence Yvon-Tran, Université Denis Diderot, Paris.

Index

acupuncture, 300
administrative practices, 8
Africa, 142, 427, 430, 433–34
Afrique Occidentale Française (AOF), French West Africa, 143
Agence de Cooperation Culturelle et Technique (ACCT), 424–27, 433, 445, 447
Agence de la Francophonie (AF), 426, 437
agrégation, 282, 285
Agricultural Department of the Indochinese Union, 280
agriculture: agricultural investments, 342; diversification of, 384, 399–400, 411, 417; harvest, 321–22, 362; production of food crops, 373; socialist, 344, 364, 365, 368, 385. *See also* farmers; garlic; livestock; maize; pigs; rice; rubber
agro-commodity chains, 13, 373–74, 377
aid. *See* foreign aid; mutual aid; work exchange
Aix-en-Provence, 266–67, 279
alcohol, 64, 72, 76, 318
Algeria, 424
Algiers, 280–81
Alliance Française, 432, 437, 438, 445, 447, 450
Amant, L' (film), 446
âm sinh. *See* "shade students" Am Vo, 191
Andreff, Wladimir, 362
Ang Duong, 165
Angier, Dr., 149, 173–74

Anh Duê, 202
Anh Nhu, Prince, 188, 201, 202
Annam, 169, 172, 175, 280
anticolonial movements, Vietnamese. *See* rebellions; resistance
anticommunism, 228
apprentices (*hành tâu*) and apprenticeship, 111–19, 121, 126–27
Archives d'Outre-Mer, 279
Assistance Médical Indigène (AMI). *See* Indigenous Medical Assistance Program
Association des Universites Partiellement ou Entierement de Langue Française (AUPELF), 438
Association of Southeast Asian Nations (ASEAN), 14, 421, 433–34, 436, 448
Association of the Annamite Students of France, 267
asylum of Te Truong, mental, 157, 164
Au Co, 90–92
Autonomous Republic of Cochinchina, 236
auxiliary doctors (*médecins auxiliaires*), 142, 150, 157

Bac Bo (province), 325
Bac Giang (province), 118
bach dinh, 35
Bach Mai (hospital), 157–58, 164
Bac Lieu (province), 318–19, 321
Bac Ninh, 112
Bac Son (uprising), 263
Bac Thành, 117

459

Index

Bai Thuong, dam of, 321
Balandier, G., 253
Balazs, Etienne, 114
bamboo hedge, destruction of, 74, 76, 80
Ba Mu, 169
Bangkok, 195
Banister, Judith, 363
Banque de l'Indochine (BIC), 316, 322, 323
Ban Tham, 195
Bao Dai, King, 220, 224, 231–32, 284, 322–23
Bao Ve Kinh Dich, 322
Baran, P., 358
Battambang, 157
Baudelaire, Charles-Pierre, 270, 442
Baudrillard, Jean, 428
Beau, Paul, Governor-General, 143, 201
Bedford (England), 284
Belgium, 267, 424, 427, 432, 435
Ben Tre, 155
beriberi, 175, 178
Bertrand-Fontaine, Dr., 286
Bien Hoa, 145
Binh, Ms. (Vietnamese assistant minister of foreign affairs), 430
Binh Dinh, 217, 237
binh phong ("undercover" subcommittee of UBKCHCNB), 316
Binh Thuan (province), 218
Binh Xuyen, 323
Black Flags, 61
Bloch, Marc, 39
blockade, lifting, 324
bo doi (soldiers), 318
Boëz, Louis, 171
Bordeaux, 266, 284, 285
Boudarel, Georges, 2, 3, 449
Bourguiba, Habib, 424
Boutros-Ghali, Boutros, 426–27, 448
Brévié, Jules, General, 169, 321
Brière (*résident supérieur*), 113
Brocheux, Pierre, 2–3, 251, 280, 304, 449

Bromberger, Merry, 266
bronchitis, 173
Buddha, 90
Buddhism, 281, 322
Bui, Henriette, 10, 179, 278–79, 281, 282–305, 306
Bui, Louis, 288, 295, 296
Bui Chi Nhuan, 193, 196
Bui Cong Trung, 317, 326
Bui Quang Chieu, 278, 280–83, 288–89, 302–3
Bui Thi Cam, 288
Bui Thi Long, 281
Bureau of Hygiene, 165
Bureau of Social Assistance, 159, 172

Cadène, P., 408
Cai Be, 301
Cambodia, 157, 159, 168, 172, 207, 280, 318, 324, 325, 361, 364, 424
Câm Khê (district), 111
Campha, 320
Canada, 424, 427, 435–36, 448
cân bô (cadres), 318, 323
cancer, 173, 175, 178
Canh Anh Duê, Prince, 189, 192, 204, 206
Can Tho (college), 260–61, 319, 438
Canton, 190, 195
Cân Vuong (movement), 190, 218–19, 255–58, 268, 269
Cao Bang, 325
Cao Dai, 264, 281, 323
Cao Xuân Huy, 270
Cape Varella, 320
capital, 358–59, 369, 378; human, 367; symbolic, 252
capitalists, French, 314, 320, 361
Casabianca, François, 374
Catholicism, 206, 281, 444
Cau Do (province), 81
câu dôi, 91
censorship, 225, 229, 230, 269
Central Africa, 424
Central Committee, 333–34, 336–40, 344, 347

Central Vietnam (Trung Bo), 318, 320–21, 324. *See also* Trong Ky
Centre National de Recherches Scientifiques (CNRS), 438, 439
Centre National des Sciences Sociales et Humaines d'Hanoi (CNSSH), 440
Centre Vietnamien d'Enseignement a la Gestion (CFVG), 439
Chaillot summit, 425
Chamber of the People's Representatives, 220–22, 224, 227, 240
Chang Fakuei, 325
Chanh hê (dynastic branch), 192
Charles, Mr., 284
Chateaubriand, François-Auguste-Renê, 270
Chau Doc, 150, 155
Chaussin, E., 412
Chesneaux, Jean, 2, 251
Chieu, Gilbert, 193
China: Communist, aid to Vietnam, 320, 323, 325; Communist revolution, 197–98, 228; domination of Vietnam, 89; ethnic Chinese in Vietnam, 361; trade with Vietnam, 314, 319
China, South, 12, 188, 191, 227–28, 256, 314, 323, 346, 361, 373, 375, 380
Chirac, Jacques, 421, 426, 428, 429, 430, 435
cholera epidemic, 175, 220
Cholon, 180, 290–300, 319
Cho Ray hospital, 293
Chretien, Jean, 430
Chrui Changar palace, 165
chuc sac, 35
citizenship, French, 280, 292
Civil Health Services, 161
civil service, 110, 111, 114, 117, 280, 292, 364, 389; examinations, 108, 119
Clarac, Albert, 161
class, social. *See* social class
class consciousness, 252–53, 259

class struggle, 10, 37, 49, 51, 92
coal mining, 314–15, 318, 320, 321, 322, 375
Cochinchina, 154, 190, 193, 236, 280
Cognacq, Governor, 266
Col des Nuages, 189
collectives. *See* cooperatives
collectivization, agricultural (*hop tac ha*), 12, 331–49, 359–61, 369, 370, 373, 381, 389, 411. *See also* decollectivization
collectors, pork, 381
Colonial Health Advisory Council, 142
colonialism, French, 2, 7, 291, 304, 442–43, 447; colonial authorities, 142, 147, 221; colonial context, 7; colonial economy, 313–15; colonial hierarchy, 294; colonial medical policy, 140–41, 304; colonial myths, 200–201; colonial reforms, 200; colonial repression, 228; colonial school system, 229; mission of, 244, 305; resistance to (*see* rebellions; resistance). *See also* decolonization; neocolonialism
Committee of Economic Resistance (Uy Ban Khang Chien Kinh Te), 316, 318
Committee of Resistance and Administration (Uy Ban Khang Chien Hanh Chinh Nam Bo, UBKCHCNB), 316, 319, 322–24
Communism, 228–29, 259, 260, 262–63, 269, 271, 281, 301
Communist Party, 259, 268; congresses, 336, 363, 370. *See also* French Communist Party; Indochinese Communist Party; Vietnamese Communist Party
Condominas, Georges, 2
Conference Ministerielle de la Francophonie (CMF), 425
Conference of Oriental Countries on Rural Hygiene, 168

462 • Index

Confucianism, 8, 10, 90, 93–94, 97, 102, 104, 226, 228, 230, 240, 252, 254, 256, 258–59, 269–71, 280, 303
Công Hoa (cooperative), 336
Congo, 424
Congo, Democratic Republic of, 424, 427
Congress on Infancy, 295
conjuncturalistic intentionality, 254
Conseil Permanent de la Francophonie (CPF), 425
Constitution (Annam), 223, 229
Constitutionalist Party, 280, 290
contraband, 66, 72
contracts (*khoan*), 10, 338–40, 373; "Decree 100," 340, 345; three, 338–39; unofficial (*chui*), 340; white (*trang*), 340, 348
cooperation, cultural, 360, 435, 437, 438, 439. *See also* exchange programs cooperatives, agricultural, 12, 331–39, 341–45, 347–49, 359–60, 366, 369, 378
corvée, 80
Council of Notables (*hôi dông ky muc*), 23–24, 74, 77
Council of Regents of the Royal Family, 189, 193, 207
Courgeau, D., 390
Courrier du Viêt Nam, 416, 443
Co-Xa, 46
Crayssac, Renê (Director of Customs), 68–69
crops. *See* agriculture
Cudenet (director of Poulo Condore), 219
Cu Huy Can, 443
cung dinh (paupers), 46
cu nhân (top regional graduates), 112, 114–15, 118, 269
cuoi vo, 95
Cuong Dê, Prince, 9, 10, 187–204, 207–8, 230
currency, national (*dong*), 316
customary of the village (*huong chinh*), 117

Customs and Monopolies Department, 66–68, 75, 77, 79, 83
Czechoslovakia, 316

Dai Loc, 218
Dalat, 235, 236
Dam, Prince, 204
Da Nang, 145. *See also* Tourane
Dan Ba Moi (Modern Woman), 101, 279, 283, 296, 298
Dang Nguyên Anh, 392
Dang Thai Mai, 257, 270
Dang Tu Kinh, 191
Dan Phuong (district), 112, 118
Dao Duy Anh, 220, 225
Dao Quang Tich, 122
Dao The Anh, 374
Dao Trong Ky, 119
Dao Trong Tê, 115
David (*résident* of Son Tay province), 67
decollectivization, 349, 366, 379, 441. *See also* collectivization decolonization, 258, 306, 424
Decoux, Admiral, Governor, 230, 319
de Gaulle, Charles, General, 233
Dehaybe, Renê, 427
de Lagrée, Doudart, Dr., 146
Delalande (director of ACCT in Hanoi), 433
D'Elloy (*résident supêrieur*), 223
democracy, new, 229, 317
Democratic party (Dân Chu Dang), 264
Democratic Republic of Vietnam (DRV), 4, 11–12, 160, 233, 313, 315, 317–18, 325–26, 359–62, 423, 445
de Musset, Alfred, 270
denunciations, 70–71
developing vs. developed countries, 358, 369
de Vienne, Marie-Sybille, 360
Devillers, Philippe, 2
Devraigne, Professor, 286

Index ■ 463

de Vylder, Stefan, 362
Di An, 262
Dien Bien Phu, 422, 434
Dinh Du (village), 29
Dinh Ky Than, 110
dinh miên sai, 35
Diori, Hamani, 424
discrimination (racial, sexual, social), 290–93, 305, 416
diseases, social, 158, 171
dispensaries, 151, 155, 160, 165, 170, 178
district magistrates, 109–10
divorce, 298–99, 304
Djibouti, 424
Doan Mân Diep, 387–88
Doan Quan, 116
Doan Tuyet (The Break), 102
Do Chieu, 256
doctors, colonial (*médecins coloniaux*) and indigenous, 142, 145, 150, 157, 294–95, 305
Doi Moi, 3, 4, 11, 12, 13, 326, 358, 363, 365–66, 369–70, 388, 421, 441
Do Luong, dam of, 321
domination (French, American, colonial), 427, 428, 442
don bâu, 35
Dông Cung (Eastern Palace), temple, 189, 192
Dông Du. *See* East movement
Dông Khanh, 111, 117, 191, 201
Dông-Ngac, 24
Dông Thai, 268
Dông Thành (prefecture), 115
dông tri phu, 116
Doumer, Paul, Governor-General, 142
dragon (*rong*), 90, 91, 92
Drouhet Hospital, 164
Dumas, Mrs., 284
Duong Bach Mai, 266–67
Duong Dinh Huy, 38
Duong Duc Hiên, 263–64
Duong Lam (commune), 440
Duong Quoc Cam, 338

Duong Van Gia, 267
Duong Van Tao, 38
Duong Van Viên, 38
Dupont, V., 389, 413
Durkheim, Emile, 253
Duy Tân Hôi (Reformation Society), 190, 192, 194, 197, 203, 255–58

Eastern European bloc, 361, 364
East movement (Dông Du), 191, 193, 195
Ecole des Mines, 289
Ecole Française d'Extrême-Orient (EFEO), 5, 270, 439, 440
Ecole Nationale de l'Administration-Mensuel, 429
Ecole Polytechnique, 288, 299
Ecole Superieure des Technologies Informatiques d'Hanoi (ESTIH), 438
Economic Committee of South Vietnam, 318
economy, Vietnamese: as global economy, 428, 450; as market economy, 369, 389, 417; as socialist economy, 313–30, 342, 345, 349, 356–57, 359, 365
education, 27, 115, 364, 369. *See also* apprentices; colonialism, colonial school system; exchange programs; scholars; students
Egypt, 424
Eliche, Mrs., 292
elite, Vietnamese, 9, 283
embargo: American, 4, 14, 423, 433; French, 318
emigrés, Vietnamese, 197, 445
Engels, F., 254
England, 199, 227, 284
enterprises: private, 368–70, 378–79; state-owned, 326, 366–68, 378, 379 (*see also* collectivization)
epidemics, spread of, 167
Epstein, Marc, 444
Ethnography Museum of Hanoi, 439
European Parliament, Brussels, 428

European Union, 435, 437
exchange programs, 437–39, 446–47, 449–50

Fabry, Dr., 295
Faifoo, 217
Famine, Great, 313
Fanon, F., 423
farmers, 13, 335, 374–78
Fascism, 228, 232, 262
females. *See* women
Ferrieu, Henriette, 289
fertility, 364
Fforde, Adam, 360, 362
Figaro, Le, 437, 448
filial bond, 303
fines, administrative, collection of, 80–81
first-aid posts, stations, 151, 169
folk songs (*ca dao*), 88, 94–97
foreign aid, 320, 323, 325, 332–33, 365
Fourniau, Charles, 2
Foyer International de Jeunes Filles, 288
France, 15, 227, 267, 421–23, 426, 431, 434–35, 436, 443, 448
Franco-Annamese association, 280
Francophone Community, 421–31, 437, 441–43
francophone culture, 306, 431–32, 437–39, 442
Francophone Language Program, 432
francophone project, 437–47
Francophone Summit (1997), 421–22, 431–34, 435–37, 445–50
Freemason, 281
French Communist Party (FCP), 259, 423
French Revolution, 228, 253, 254, 260
French School, in Indochina, 251
French-speaking community, 424–26
Freyssinet, Jacques, 357
Frézouls (Director of Customs), 66

Fries (*haût résident*), 223, 224
Front of the Homeland, 252

Gabon, 425
Gariod (*résident* at Phu Lo), 73
garlic, 374–75, 377, 379–80, 382–84
gender relations, 88, 228, 307. *See also* women
General Inspection of Health Services, 157–59
Geneva agreements, 265
Germany, 199
Gia Dinh, 166
Giai Phong, 238
Gia Lam (district), 69, 118, 126
Gia Long, 9, 76, 188–90, 193, 196, 201–2, 204–5, 207–8
giao thu, 118
giap, 41
Gia Thanh, 192
globalization, 421, 428, 443, 450
Godard, Justin, 165, 260
Goffman, Erving, 253
government, Vietnamese, 319
graduates, top regional (*cu nhân*), 114–15, 118
Grall, Charles, 143
Grall hospital, 151, 163, 293
Gramsci, Antonio, 257
grandes ecoles, 257
Grand Secretariat (Nôi Cac), 119
Granter, Dr., 296
Great Depression, 314
Great Leap Forward, 348
Groleau, Elie, 202–3
Groupe de Recherches et d'Exchanges Technologiques (GRET), 441
Guangxi, 325
Guigou, Elisabeth, 428
Guilmoto, C. Z., 389

Ha Dông (province), 47, 116–17, 146, 167, 337
Ha Huy Tap, 271
Hai Ba Trung Hospital, 301

Hai Duong (province), 111, 377, 380
Hai Hung, 374
Hai Nan, 325
Hai Phong (city and province), 79, 109, 146, 151, 165, 227, 338, 348, 375,
Haiti, 424
Halbwachs, Maurice, 253
Ham Nghi, Emperor, 281, 288
Han (dynasty), 113
Hà Nam (province), 82, 109, 118, 126
Ha Nam Ninh (district), 345
Hành Huong, 263
Hanoi (city and province), 15, 30, 33, 34, 102, 111–12, 313, 375, 387, 389, 392, 394, 396, 397, 401, 403, 404, 406–9, 412–16, 422–23, 426, 429, 431, 449
Hariri, Rafik, 429
Ha Tinh, 269, 314, 318
hâu bô, 8, 109, 111–21, 123, 125, 127, 128
hâu phai, 111–12
Haute École de Commerce (HEC), 283, 288
Hay (village), 14, 387, 389, 392, 402, 411, 417
health care, 9, 11, 140–42, 144, 146, 155, 157–60, 162–63 165, 168–69, 178, 294, 364, 439. *See also* first-aid posts; hospitals and infirmaries; medical training; medicine; *and specific diseases*
Health Corps (Corps de Santé Colonial), 142
heirs, 257, 259, 270
Hémery, Daniel, 1–3, 251, 260, 304, 449
Henaff, N., 388, 392, 414–15
Hennecart, Dr., 146
hereditary rights, 201–3
Hermant, Dr., 161
Hoa Hao, 264, 322–23
Hoàng Cao Khai, 119–20, 256, 268–69
Hoàng Khanh Phuong, 374, 376, 382
Hoàng Mai, 33, 42, 436

Hoàng Mông Can, 269
Hoàng Ngoc Phach, 102, 261, 268–70
Hoàng Quoc Viet, 271
Hoàng Thi Nga, 100, 288, 304
Hoàng Trong Mau, 197, 198
Hoàng Trong Phu, 47, 117, 289
Hoàng Van Hoan, 271
Hoàng Xuan Han, 232, 236, 288, 302
Hoan Kiem (lake), 423
Hoàn Long (district), 24, 38, 117
Ho Chi Minh, 10, 11, 233–35, 237–39, 259, 265, 271, 313, 315–16
Ho Chi Minh City, 383, 387–88, 391, 394, 412, 414, 423, 438–39, 442, 444–45, 449
Hoc Tap, 339
Hô Dàc Di, 260, 266
Ho Dac Vy, 320, 322
Ho Do, 320
Ho Huu Tuong, 267
Hôi An, 320
hôi dông ky muc (Council of Notables), 23–24, 74, 77
Hôi Truyên Ba Quoc Ngu, 264
Hô-Khâu, 36
Hong Kong, 195, 197, 199, 314
Hong Luc (aka Tu Dich), 198
Hop Thuong Quang Nam, 218
hospitals and infirmaries, 9, 142, 145–66, 168–71, 178, 439. *See also* health care; Indigenous Hospitals
Ho Ta Khanh, 233
Hô Van Lai, 263
Hô Van Ngà, 264
huân dao (district educational officer), 112, 117–18
Hue, 165–66, 174, 188–89, 192, 193, 198, 201, 216, 220, 223, 232, 234, 263, 283
Hugo, Victor, 270
human rights violations, 229, 260, 430
Hùng (dynasty), 89, 103, 105
Hung Hoa (province), 111–18
Hung Lac, 89
Hung Yên (province), 109–10, 112, 115, 336

huong chinh (customary of the village), 117
huong su, 44
huong truong, 24, 26, 31
husking. *See* rice
Huynh Thuc Khang, 9–10, 216–39
Huynh Van Tieng, 264

identity, Vietnamese national, 229–30, 412
Imperial Academy (Quôc Tu Giam), 114–15, 117, 189
incest (*loan luan*), 98, 99
income distribution, 356, 388
independence, Vietnamese, 9, 10, 233–34, 271, 314, 315
India, 388, 405
Indigenous Hospitals, 145, 148, 150, 158, 164, 168, 173, 295
Indigenous Medical Assistance Program (Assistance Médical Indigène, AMI), 142–44, 147, 150–51, 154–55, 158–59, 162, 164, 167, 178
Indochina, 154, 324
Indochine (film), 446
Indochinese Communist Party (ICP), 279, 317
Indochinese Congress, 260, 262
Indochinese Tribune. See Tribune Indochinoise, La
Indochinese Union (IU), 144, 263, 264
Indonesia, 366, 436
Infectious Disease Department, 296
infirmaries. *See* hospitals and infirmaries
inspector, imperial (*kinh luoc*), 109, 111
Institut de Recherche pour le Développement (IRD), 439
Institute of Classics and Ancient Civilizations, French, 221
Institut Français de Recherche Scientifique pour le Développement en Coopération (ORSTOM), 367, 439
Institut Nationale d'Agronomie (INA) (Agronomic National College), 280
intellectuals, Vietnamese, 6, 7, 9, 10, 251–52, 255, 257, 258–59, 261, 264, 268–69, 271, 442, 449
International Conference Hall (Hanoi), 431
International Development Research, 436
internships, in French hospitals, 114, 290
investments, industrial and agricultural, 342
Italy, 227
Ivory Coast, 424

Jabouille (*résident supêrieur*), 223
Japan, 188, 192, 194, 227–28, 230–31, 235, 256, 278, 300
Jeune Afrique, 437
Joel, Constance, Dr., 286
Jospin, Lionel, 428

Kabila, Lauren Desire, 427
Kalam, M. A., 404
Kampot, 146, 157, 318
Kaufman, P., 253
Khai Dinh, King, 193, 203, 206, 207
khao vong (banquet of honor), 36
khoan. See contracts
khu (zone), 317
Khu Mien Tay K.9 (military conference), 323
Khuong Thuong, 31, 34, 43–44
Kiên Phuc, 115
Kim Anh (district), 110
Kim Bang, 118
Kim Son, 125
Kim Vân Kiêu, 261
kinh lich (registrars), 113
kinh triêu, 113
Klobukowski, Antony, Governor-General, 143–44, 157

Kobe, 195
Kompong Cham, 167
Kompong Long, 146
Koung Tchéou Wan, 151
Kratié, 146
Krowolski, Nelly, 440
Kuomintang, Chinese, 197, 236
ky muc (notables), 24–36
Ky Ngoai Hau, 189

labor, 13, 356–59, 364, 366–69
Laboratoire Asie du Sud-Est et Monde Austronesien (LASEMA), 440
Lac Long, 90, 92
Lac-Trung (village), 31
Lai Cua, 104
Lalanne, Rose, 284
Lalhuyeaux d'Ormay, Dr., 145
Lamb, David, 431
Lam Ho, 168, 170
Lam Vien, 227
Landy, F., 409
Lanelongue dispensary, 165
Lanessan Hospital, 151
Langlet, Philippe, 2
Lang Nho, 337
Lao Cai, 391
lao nhiêu (old people), 36
Laos, 157, 159, 167–68, 324, 380, 383
Laperonnie family, 284
Larcher-Goscha, Agathe, 9, 187
Lariboisière, hospital of, 286
Laure, Dr., 145
lay, 94
layoffs, 367
leaders and leadership, 257, 313, 318, 340–44, 349, 363
Lê (dynasty), 89
Lê Ba Doàn, 48
Lê Ba Ngu, 48
Lebon, André, Dr., 142
Lebrun, Albert, 199
Leclerc, General, 299
Leduc, Gaston, 266
Lê Duc Thinh, 374, 376, 379–80, 382

Lê Du Tông, King, 28
legend(s), 88–91. *See also* myths, colonial
Le Goulven, K., 374, 375, 381
Lê Hoan, 121, 126
Lê Hong Phong, 271
Lê Ky, 121
Lelièvre, E., 413
Lê Loi, King, 28
Lê Manh Trinh, 121
Lemière, Professor, 286
Lê Ngu, 111
Leopold-Sedar, Senghor, 424
leprosy, 144, 151, 158, 171–72
Lê Thanh Khoi, 2, 360
Lê Thanh Tông, King, 28
Lê Thi Hoang, 288
Lê Thuy (district), 322
Lê Van Kim, 266
Lévecque, Fernand, 201
levies. *See* taxation
liberalization, economic. *See* Doi Moi
liberal-progressive culture, 265
Libreville, Gabon, 425
Lien Khu, 316–18, 320, 322, 325
Lieu Hanh, cult of, 104
Lieurade, Dr., 168
linh co (soldiers of the Native Guard), 69, 71, 79
Li Tana, 387, 388, 392, 414–15
livestock, 320, 335–36
Local Health Bureau, 169
Lome, Togo, 425
Long Xuyen, 155
Long Zhou, 325
Lot et Garonne, region, 284
Luang Prabang, 150
Luc Ngan, 118
Lutte, La (The Struggle), 258, 266, 267
Luu Huu Phuoc, 260–64
Luxembourg, 424
Lycée Albert Sarraut, 266
Lycée Buoi, 261
Lycée Chu Van An, 438
Lycée Marie Curie, 282, 284, 285

Lycêe Paul Bert, 266
Lycée Pétrus Ky, 261, 263
ly dich, 23, 25–26, 35, 38
Ly-Toét, 29, 30
ly truong (village mayor), 7, 23–50, 78–79, 82

Macao, 195
Madagascar, 424
Mahadev, P. D., 388
Mai Dông (village), 37
Mai Ruot, 325
Maison Franco-Vietnamienne du Droit, 439
Mai Van Bô, 260–64
maize, 376
malaria, spread of, 145, 168, 171, 175, 178, 437
Malaysia, 436
male ritual, 97
Management Committee, 339
Manchu dynasty, 197
Mandarin Route, 169
Mandarins, 111, 113–16, 119, 120, 128, 254, 258
Maoism, 253, 264
Mao Zedong, 317
Marcel, Henri, Dr., 167
Marr, David, 251, 279
marriage, 95–97, 290
Marseilles, 266
Marty, Louis, 199, 203
Marx, Karl, 254, 271, 357
Marxism, 260, 267, 270–71
maternity wards, 154, 158–59, 162, 167, 172, 293
matrilineal society, 90
Mat Tran Hoi Lien Hiep Quoc Dan Viet Nam (league of the Popular Resistance of Vietnamese National Front), 235
Mâu, 33, 42, 44, 48
Mauritius, 424
Mâu Ty, 117
meat consumption, 375, 382

medical centers. *See* hospitals and infirmaries
medical training, 285–88, 295, 300
medicine, 158, 220, 296, 300, 304, 322, 439. *See also* health care; hospitals and infirmaries; *and specific diseases*
Médecins sans Frontières (Doctors without Borders), 301
Meiji Restoration, Japanese, 217, 228
mekhums, 167
Mekong Delta, 151, 260, 322, 439
Memmi, Albert, 423
memory, collective, 8, 335
Menaut, Dr., 167
métis children, 279, 284, 302, 307
Meyerson, Mrs., 285
Mi Duong, 202
Miêu-Nha, 33
migration, 11, 14, 387–91, 394–96, 398–401, 403, 405–7, 408–12, 414–17
Military Mission and Cooperation (MMC), 431
Ming dynasty, 89, 102
Minh Mang, Emperor, 29, 33, 113–15, 117, 196, 201–2, 206, 207
Minh Tân, 193
Ministry of Colonies, 144
mobile medicine, 167
mobility. *See* migration
modernity, 217, 229, 256, 303
modernization, 280
Moï, 169
Monnais-Rousselot, Laurence, 294, 304–6
Montel, Dr., 172
Montpellier, 266
Morocco, 424
mortality rate, in Indochina, 229, 295
Moutet, Marius (French minister of the colonies), 222
Movement for National Independence, 225
Movement for Peace, 252

Muong, 90
Mus, Cyprien, 266
Mus, Paul, 2, 251
Museum of Natural History, 439
mutual aid, 332–33. See also foreign aid
My An, 218
My Duong, 204
My Lôc, 126
My Tho, 145, 155, 193
myths, colonial, 200–201. See also legends

Na, 104
Nam Dan, dam of, 321
Nam Dinh (province), 115, 117–19, 126, 341
Nam Dông, 25, 35, 46
Nam Phong, 256–58
Nam Thanh (district), 374–75, 379, 383
Nam Truc, 117
Nam Xang, 118
National Assembly, 235
National Center of the Natural Sciences and Technologies, 439
national government, Vietnamese, in exile, 197
National Institute of the Agronomic Sciences, 441
nationalism, Vietnamese, 187, 191, 197, 236, 281, 313
National Liberation Front of the South, 260
National Marxism, 260
National Polytechnic Institute, 438
National Statistics Committee, 343
Native Guard, 68–69
neocolonialism, French, 443
New Economic Policy (NEP), 357
New Economic Zones, of the Central Plateau, 391
Ngay Nay, 257
Nghê An, 115, 314, 318
Nghi-Tàm, 41

ngoai tich, 46
Ngoan, 42
Ngoc-Xuyên, 42
Ngô Dinh Diem, 232
Ngô Dinh Nhu, 302
Ngô Duc Ke, 229
Ngô Kim, 339
Ngô Kim Liên, 117
Ngô Si Lien, 89, 103
Nguyên (dynasties), 8, 113, 127, 189–90, 205, 206, 207
Nguyên Ai Quoc, 225
Nguyên An Ninh, 257, 260, 266
Nguyên Bach, 32, 38
Nguyên Ba Trac, 220
Nguyên Binh, 325
Nguyên Cam Giang, 197
Nguyên Công Tiêp, 114
Nguyên Dinh Hien, 238
Nguyên Du, 229–30
Nguyên Duc Chiêu, 126
Nguyên Duc Nghinh, 33
Nguyên Duc Tu, 127
Nguyên Duy Hàn, 36–37
Nguyên Duy Thiên, 33
Nguyên Hai Than, 197–98, 235
Nguyên Ham, 190–91
Nguyên Huê Chi, 268, 270
Nguyên Huu Bai, 269
Nguyên Huu Dô, 117
Nguyên Huu Tho, Maître, 268
Nguyên Huu Tô, 115
Nguyên Huu Tuong, 117
Nguyên Khac Truong, 39
Nguyên Khac Vien, 2–3, 444
Nguyên Lân, 270
Nguyên Liêm, 115
Nguyên Lo Trach, 231
Nguyên Manh Cam (Vietnamese minister of foreign affairs), 430, 434–35
Nguyên Manh Tuong, Maître, 265
Nguyên My Ca, 261
Nguyên Ngoc Bich, 281, 299–300, 302

Nguyên Nhu Duy, 126
Nguyên Phuc Anh, 204–5
Nguyên Q. Thang, 233–34
Nguyên Quac Ve, Hélène, 287
Nguyên Quang Bich, 256
Nguyên San, 33
Nguyên Thân, 269
Nguyên Thành Nguyên, 261
Nguyên Thanh Son, 324
Nguyên Thanh Vinh, 318
Nguyên Thê Anh, 449
Nguyên Thi Binh, 288
Nguyên Thi Khang, 102
Nguyên Thi Kiem, 101–2
Nguyên Thuong Hien, 197
Nguyên Trai, 89
Nguyên Truong Tô, 114, 231
Nguyên Tu Chi, 89–90
Nguyên Tung, 440
Nguyên Tuong, 443
Nguyên Tuong Tam (Nhat Linh), 102
Nguyên Van, 39
Nguyên Van Binh, 112
Nguyên Van Châu, 32
Nguyên Van Chi, 33
Nguyên Van Chinh, 39
Nguyên Van De, 208
Nguyên Van Doàn, 30
Nguyên Van Duc, 38, 39, 263
Nguyên Van Huy, 48
Nguyên Van Kiêm, 32
Nguyên Van Ky, 278
Nguyên Van Nghênh, 36
Nguyên Van Ngoc, 8, 88, 234
Nguyên Van Oanh, 36
Nguyên Van Si, 36
Nguyên Van Tao, 267
Nguyên Van Thinh, 236
Nguyên Van Thuc, 39
Nguyên Van Vinh, 38, 230
Nguyên Viêt Tuân, 46
Nguyên Xuong Thai, 221, 235
Nguy Nhu Kontum, 266
Nhat Linh (Nguyên Tuong Tam), 102

Nha Trang, 153, 218
Nhât-Tân, 41
Nhu Mai, 288
Nhuoc-Công, 33
Ninh Binh, 125
Ninh Dân (commune), 393, 398, 404, 410, 413
nôi tich, 46
Nom (language), 227
North African countries, 430
notables. *See* villages

O'Connell (director of Poulo Condore), 219
Office of Strategic Services (U.S.), 233
Office of the State Secretary of the Colonies, 142
Opera House (Hanoi), 431
ophthalmology, 151, 164, 173
Opinion, L', 291
opium, 64, 70, 76, 280, 318
Organisation Commune Africaine et Malgache (OCAM), 424
ORSTOM. *See* Institut Français de Recherche Scientifique pour le Développement en Coopêration
Oudin, Xavier, 358, 440

pacification, 70, 110
paddy collectors, huskers. *See* rice
Pagès, Mrs., 293
Paine, Suzanne, 360
Paris, 285, 425
Parliament, Vietnamese, 229
Parti Progressiste Annamite, 220
Pasquier, Pierre, 206, 220–21, 223
Pasteur Institute, 163, 166
patriarchy, 102
peasants, 8, 13, 23, 25, 259, 333–35, 340, 344–45, 361, 364, 388–89, 404, 414, 416, 418
People's Republic of China, 325
Pham Biêu Tâm, 263
Pham Chu Trinh, 117
Pham Hoang Ha, 374, 384

Pham Huu Uyên, 111
Pham Huy Bich, 111
Pham Khac Hoe, 232
Pham Ngoc Thuân, Gaston, 260, 281, 288, 302
Pham Quynh, 229, 232
Pham Thi My, 297
Pham Van Bach (chairman of UBKCHCNB), 319
Pham Van Dong, 259
Pham Van Triêu, 125, 126
Phan Ba Ngoc, 198–99, 203
Phan Bôi Châu, 9, 187–95, 197–200, 202–3, 207, 219–23, 240, 257
Phan Châu Trinh, 195, 199–200, 217–22, 227, 240, 257, 280
Phan Dinh Phùng, 256, 268–69
Phan Huu Thanh, 118
Phan Huu Tri, 111
Phan Huu Tu, 115
Phan Huy Chu, 29
Phan Kê Tiên, 112
Phan Khôi, 88, 102
Phan Rang, 169
Phan Thiet, 218, 221
Phan Trong Dich, 117
Phan Van Bach, Professor, 260
Phan Van Truong, 257
Phiên Hê, 192
Phnom Penh, 150–51, 153, 165, 173
pho ly, 24–26, 29, 36, 39, 42, 47, 78–79, 82
pho tông, 47
phô truong, 47
Phô Yên, 116
Phuc Xa, 42
Phu Lô (province), 116
Phu Nghia, 320
Phu Nhuan, 280
Phu Nu Tan Van (Modern Woman's News), 279, 303, 304
Phu Tho, 332, 391
Phu Xuyên (district), 110, 337
Phu Yen, 237

Pigneau de Bêhaine, Bishop, 204–6
pigs and pork production, 373–77, 379, 381–82, 384
plague, 175
Plan D'Industrialization de l'Indochine, 315
Polyani, Karl, 357
Popular Front, 100, 161, 257
pork. *See* pigs and pork production
Post, Ken, 363
Poulo Condore (prison), 219, 227, 240
power: balance of, 258–59; political, in villages, 6–7, 21–24, 26, 28, 34, 40, 42, 47, 52, 77; symbolic, 252, 254
prefect (*tri phu*), 109
priests, Vietnamese, 219
Privy Council, 220
production, modes of, 319–20, 332, 338, 340, 343–45, 347–48, 357–60, 373–74, 377, 389
productivity, 365, 373
Programme Fleuve Rouge, 441
propaganda, 197, 207, 331, 334, 336, 449
proverbs, 98, 99
punishment, 80–82

Quang Binh, 234, 322
Quang Nam (province), 115, 218, 237, 318, 322
Quang Ngai, 239
Quang Nghia, 237
Quang Ninh, 375, 380
Quang Phuc Hôi, 197–99
Quang Tri (province), 168
Quang Yen, 146
quan ho, 104
quê huong, 414
Que Son, 238
Quôc Gia Dôc Lâp, 264
quôc ngu, 10, 119–20, 217–18, 227, 229, 230–31
Quôc tri (cooperative), 336
Quynh Lôi, 32, 35–36, 38–39, 51

Racine, J. L., 388, 405, 408
radical left, Vietnamese, 154
Radium Institute, 164
Rangê, Dr., 160
rebellions, 7, 8, 61–62, 69, 89; De Tham in Yen The, 219; tax, 72–74, 75, 83, 218
Red Cross organization, 301
Red River delta, provinces of, 111, 314, 337, 360, 373–76, 384, 440
reeducation camps, 364
Reformation Society. *See* Duy Tân Hôi
refugees, Vietnamese, 3
residence, 390, 412, 413
résident supérieur, of Tonkin, 68–69, 73–74, 77, 79, 122
resistance, 83, 279, 313–15, 317–18, 320, 322, 324, 326, 336. *See also* rebellions
Restoration Association. *See* Viet Nam Quang Phuc Hôi
Retours de France, 302
Rheinart, Pierre, 201
rheumatology, 300
rice, 314–15, 318–22, 334, 339–40, 343, 346, 374–80, 384
Richaud, Etienne, Governor-General, 201
Robin, Renê, Governor-General, 164, 297
Romania, 424
Rosental, P. A., 408
Rostow, Walt, 315
Roy, Jean-Louis, 427
rubber, 314, 320
Ruscio, Alain, 2, 278
Rwanda, 430

Sa Dec, 155
Sagant, P., 397
Saigon, 102, 148, 153, 220, 232, 260, 278, 301
Sainteny, Jean, 233, 235
Saint Paul de Chartres, Sisters of, 148, 282

Saint Simon of Vietnam, 260
sai phai, 111
Sai Van Vu, 38
Salan, General, 324
Salles, Andrê, 206
salt (as commodity), 64, 318, 320
Sarraut, Albert, Governor-General, 144, 159, 171, 199, 206, 207, 257
Sarraut Institute, 173
Scent of Green Papaya (film), 446
scholars (*nho si*), 2, 3, 5, 10, 14, 252, 439, 440, 446–47, 449–50. *See also* exchange programs
School for Mandarins (*si hoan truong*), 109
School of Medicine (Hanoi), 142
School of Practical Medicine (Choquan), 150, 157–58
secretary (*lai muc*), 110
Sêcuritê Nationale, 219
Seignobos, Charles, 285
Senegal, 424
"shade students" (*âm sinh*), 115, 119, 121–22, 127
Siam, Gulf of, 195, 325
si bô, 111
Si Hoan, 126
Silk Threads Office (Ty Luân So), 119
Sister Benjamine (director of Indigenous Hospital of Choquan), 148–49
skin diseases, 172, 175–76
smallpox, 175, 204
smuggling, 322–23
social class, 253, 256, 260, 271, 302, 304. *See also* elite, Vietnamese
socialism, 331, 337, 340–41, 361, 369
socialist revolution, Vietnamese, 271, 333
socialist transformation, 12
socialization, failure of, 259, 264, 271, 361
Socrates, 90
Soc Trang, 319
Sogny, Lêon, 189, 193, 202

Sogny, Louis, 219, 222–23
Son Duong (district), 117
Sonoda (Japanese officer), 230–31
Southeast Asian countries, 231, 314, 358
Southern Republic (1954–75), 258
South Vietnam (Nam Bo), 315–16, 319, 324, 361
Soviet Union. *See* U.S.S.R.
stakeholders, private, 374–75, 378, 379, 382, 384
Stalinism, 260
structuralism, genetic, 253
Student Association, Vietnamese, of Hanoi, 257, 263
students, Vietnamese, in France, 290, 431, 438, 440, 444–46. *See also* exchange programs
Students Committee of Paris, 267
succession, rules of, 202
Sudre, Margie, 428–29, 448
Sun Yat Sen, 197, 228
Superior Council of the Colonies, 289
Superior School of Foreign Trade, 438
Su Thât (The Truth), 235, 317
Sweden, 443
Switzerland, 424,
syphilis, 144, 172, 175–76

Ta Chi Dai Truong, 89
Takêo, 146
Tam Duong (district), 117
Tam Nông, 112, 126
tam tong, 97
Tân Hàm Ninh, 266
Tannin, Christian, 432
Tan Thuat, 197
Tao Mat, 442
Ta Thu Thâu, 266
taxation and taxes, 7, 8, 63–65, 67, 82, 120, 219, 224, 231, 267, 315–16, 318–19, 322, 332, 334, 345, 388. *See also* rebellions, tax
Tây Son, 189, 196, 204

tê, 97
Temps, Le, 303
Terrisse, Dr., 169
Tessier, Olivier, 440
Thach Thât (district), 110
Thai Binh (province), 109, 115, 117, 319
Thai-Hà, 43, 48
Thai Hâ'Âp, 269
Thailand, 12, 325, 358, 380, 383
Thai Nguyên (district), 332
Thanh Ba (district), 118, 387
Thanh Hoa (district), 314, 322, 332, 337
Thanh Nghi, 257
Thanh-Nhàn, 42
Thanh Niên Tien Phong (avant-garde youth), 263, 264, 265
Thanh Nien Xung Phong (Committed Youth), 87
Thành Thai, King, 114, 115, 117, 119, 191, 192, 201, 202, 218, 269
The Van Thu, 267
Thiêu Tri, reign of, 114–15, 207
Thinh-Hào, 37, 42, 47
Thompson, Edward P., 252, 253
thông phan (administrative assistants), 113
Thua Thiên, 117
Thua Thiên Cao, 204
thu chi (second notable), 23
Thuong, 40
Thu Tri, 117
Thuy An, 102
Thuy Anh (district), 117
Tibet, 104
tich cuc, 264
tiên chi (first notable), 23, 38
Tiên Du (district), 121
Tieng Dan (People's Voice), 10, 216–17, 221, 225–28, 230–31, 240
Tiên Hung (district), 115
Tiên Lu (district), 110
tien si, 217, 256
Tien Tsin, 233
Togo, 425

To Huu (vice minister of the Department of Districts), 347
Tokyo, 300
Tông Dôc Trân Ba Lôc, 269
Tonkin, 108, 158, 172, 219, 221–22, 226, 233, 269, 280
Tonkin Institute (Dong Kinh Nghia Thuc), 256
Tonlé Sap, 146
Ton Nhan Phu (Council of the Royal Family), 208
Ton Nu Thi Ninh (assistant minister of foreign affairs), 433–34, 437, 442–43, 447
Ton Quang Phiet, 232
Tôn Tho Tuong, 256
Tô Tâm, 102, 270
Toulouse, 266
Tourane, 145, 189, 221
trachoma, 285
trade unions, 369
traditions, Vietnamese, 282, 294
Trân Anh Tuan, 387, 388
Trân Dinh Nam, 227, 233
Trân Dinh Phien, 221
trang dinh, 35
Trân Hoanh, 221
Trân Huu Luc, 198
Trân Kim Quan, 263
Trân Nhu Niên, 110
Trân Phu, 271
Trân Qui Cap, 217–18, 220, 240
Transbassac (Hâu Giang), 322
Trân Trong Kim, 232–33, 235–36
Trân Van Chuc, 46
Trân Van Don, 283
Trân Van Giau, 260
Trân Van Huu, prime minister, 323
Trân Van Ky, 116–17
Trân Van Thach, 267
Trân Xuân (clan), 38–39
Trân Xuân Chung, 32, 38
Trân Xuân Dinh, 36
Trân Xuân Son, 115, 118
Trân Xuân Tich, 38, 39

Trân Xuân Truoc, 38
Tra Vinh, 321
Treaty of Versailles, 205
Tribune Indochinoise, La (Indochinese Tribune), 279–80, 283, 296, 298, 304
tri huyên, 39, 47–48
Trinh Ba, 39
Trinh Dinh Khai, 265
Trinh Dinh Thao, 265–67
Trinh Khac Tham, 388, 414
Trinh Van Thao, 283
Trong Ky (Annam), 216–17, 221, 222, 229. *See also* Central Vietnam
Trotskyists, 262, 264
Trung Bo. *See* Central Vietnam
Trung sisters, 89, 102–3
Truong Chinh, 259
Truong Phien, 238
Truong Suong, 113
Truong Vinh Ky, Petrus, 256, 262
tuân (village guard), 41
tuberculosis, 151, 172–73, 175–76, 178, 280, 289, 295–96
Tu Dich (aka Hong Luc), 198
Tu Duc, 109, 112, 114–15, 117, 119, 127, 207
Tu Liêm (district), 33
Tu Luc Van Doan (Autonomous Literary Group), 258
tung phai, 111
Tung Thiên, 112, 125
Tu Son, 118
tu tài, 111, 114
Tuyen Quang, 323
tuy phai, 111

Union Indochinoise, 429
United Front, 265
United Nations Conference on Trade and Development (UNCTAD), 14–15
United States, 227, 426, 428–29, 443
Universites des Resaux d'Expression Française, 438
University of Hanoi, 257, 260, 265

Index   475

U.S.S.R., 357, 379, 431; aid to Vietnam, 365; Bolshevist revolution, 254
Uy Ban Khang Chien Hanh Chinh Nam Bo (UBKCHCNB) (Committee of Resistance and Administration), 316, 319, 322–24
Uy Ban Khang Chien Kinh Te (Committee of Economic Resistance), 316, 318

vaccinations, 141
Valençot (headmaster of Lycée Petrus Ky), 261
Valluy, General, 237
Van Thiên Tuong, 269
Varenne, Alexandre (consul), 222–23
Vayrac (Superior Resident), 265
venereal diseases, 151, 164, 173. *See also* syphilis
Vientiane, 165, 166
Viet (people), 90
Viet Bac, 323, 324, 325
Viet Kieu (French overseas Vietnamese), 445
Viet Minh, 233–34, 236–37, 257, 264, 288, 316
Viet Minh Bureau of Economic Control, 319, 323
Vietnamese Communist Party (VCP), 251–52, 254–55, 257, 259, 263–64, 363, 370, 423, 442, 443
Vietnamese Nationalist Party, headquarters in Hanoi, 236
Viet Nam Phuc Quôc Dông Minh Hôi, 264
Viet Nam Quang Phuc Hôi (Restoration Association), 195, 197, 199
Viet Nam Quoc Dan Dang (VNQDD), 263–64
Vietnam War. *See* war, American
Viet Tri, 412–13
villages: customary, 117; customs and traditions, 8, 87–88, 103; economy of, 12, 43–46, 63–65, 72–73, 81–82, 333–35; health care in 168–69; mayor (*ly truong*), role of , 23–52, 78–79; migration from, 14, 387–418; notables, 7, 21–22, 23–26, 28, 29, 30, 31, 34, 39, 40, 48–50, 74, 76, 77–79, 155 (*see also* Council of Notables); political power in, 6–7, 21–52, 335; rebellions in, 7–8, 61–84
Vinh, 150, 322
Vinh Phu (district), 339, 391
Vinh Tuong, 117
Vinh Yên, 117, 401
vo chong (wife-husband), 94
Vo Lao (commune), 392
Vo Nguyên Giap, General, 234–37, 442
Vo Nhan Tri, 360–61
Vo Van Thien, 193
Vu Ban (district), 117
Vu Dinh, 39
Vu Khac Hiêu, 119
Vu Ngoc Phan, 8, 88
Vuong Dinh Quang, 220
Vuong Quang Nhuong, 290
Vuong Thi Y, 279
Vu Trong Binh, 374–75, 379

war, 1, 2; American, 1–2, 301, 346–47, 423; French-Indochina, 313–27; *guerre economique*, 315–27. *See also* World War I, II
Weber, M., 258
women, Vietnamese, 91, 94–95, 97, 100–105, 172, 229, 278, 285–86, 288, 290–91, 297, 302–3, 306, 399; activism of, 100, 101; jobs for, 91, 379; as students, 286, 289. *See also* gender relations workers, 358–59, 364, 366, 369, 391, 400, 416
work exchange, 332. *See also* mutual aid
work points, 338, 340, 345
work teams, 339, 342, 349
World Bank, 366, 448

World War I, 159, 167, 187, 188, 195, 207, 257
World War II, 225–26, 230, 262, 299, 313–14, 319

xa quan, 28
xa truong, 28–29, 33
Xêp But Nghiên, 263
Xom Tiên (cooperative), 336
Xuan Dieu, 442
Xuan Lai, 72
Xu Uy, 264–65

Yên Bai, 268, 394
Yên Dung, 118
Yên-Lang, 32, 36, 38, 42, 44, 116
Yên Lang Ha, 42
Yên Phu, 72–74
Yên-So, 24
Yunnan, 104

Zinsou, Emile, 427
zones (occupied, free), 319, 320, 322–24